SOCIAL
STRUCTURE
AND
PERSONALITY
A Casebook

SOCIAL STRUCTURE AND PERSONALITY

A Casebook

Yehudi A. Cohen

Holt, Rinehart and Winston   New York

7.50

TO SHELLY

WHO MORE THAN HELPED ME FINISH IT

AND

DR. JAN FRANK

WHO HELPED IN HIS OWN UNIQUE WAY

PREFACE

The present volume is a casebook which attempts to provide the student with a theoretical structure in one subbranch of social science. Starting out with a quest for certain kinds of principles underlying the relationships of personality to the social-structural arrangements of society, case illustrations have been selected for those theoretical points and issues which appear to require case illustration; these have been selected from the anthropological, sociological, and psychological literatures. Like most casebooks, especially legal ones, this one attempts to begin with theoretical tools and case illustrations of basic concepts. On this foundation we shall attempt to develop a consistent theoretical approach, starting with relatively simple principles and then working toward more complex and more inclusive principles. The cases form a little more than half of the volume; a considerable number of these are reprinted almost in their entirety; a relatively small number, however, are selections taken from books of considerable magnitude. It will be for the specialized reader to judge whether the latter selections have been taken "out of context" and have changed the intended meanings of the original authors. Naturally, the attempt was made to retain the original meanings intended. In most instances, footnotes and bibliographical references have been omitted from the case selections. Where there are footnotes, they appear at the bottom of the page and refer to materials listed in the Bibliography and Suggested Readings; the latter are located at the end of each chapter.

Around these case illustrations are woven textual and theoretical commentaries. Usually, the case selections from the literatures speak for themselves; however, in almost all instances, they have been introduced, summarized, and related to each other; at other times, they have been elaborated upon at length. In a few instances, the flow of the book has been shifted and short cases from the literatures have been used to illustrate a hypothesis offered in the theoretical discussion. In four or five cases, the role of commentator and editor has been set aside for that of primary source. In the overwhelming majority of instances, only the case selections have been referred to and mentioned in the table of contents and not the textual and theoretical commentaries.

This casebook is not trying to do anyone else's job for him by interlacing commentaries through the case materials. The reader will notice early in the book that the chapter summaries are quite bare; they have been left so deliberately. While there is no equivocation in the theoretical commentaries, even these can be related to the case materials in alternative ways. The case and theoretical materials will speak for themselves; their final significance and their meaningfulness for the development of other ideas and investigations must be left to the reader.

Chapters 11 and 12 are two of my own studies which have not been published elsewhere. Here, too, I have equivocated somewhat in that I have been less than explicit in relating these two studies to the preceding materials. Naturally, I have my own ideas about the theoretical positions of these two studies within the total framework of the rest of the book; other people have theirs. But there is a dangerous trap for anyone who strives to be a theoretician—he must be on constant guard lest he take himself and his ideas so seriously that he leaves no room for either himself or others to search constantly for and entertain alternative ways of thinking about that segment of the universe under particular scrutiny.

There is a custom in American society that the first words in a scientific book are written last. These last, but first, words usually follow a form, as does any culturally patterned custom. But behind the formality is a highly personal process of taking stock—of reliving the many and diverse experiences met with in the course of writing the book which follows, and of thinking about the many people who, in one way or another, knowingly and unknowingly, mentioned or anonymous, were involved in its creation.

This book grew out of a course which I have been teaching for several years in the Department of Sociology of the School of General Studies at Columbia University. And as every teacher-writer knows, no stimulation is more meaningful than that received from one's students. I have often had the feeling while teaching that my students have quietly taken me by the hand and led me through a maze of facts, myths, questions, and ideas—for this I am grateful to them, especially as I recall the quality of the very first lectures, several years ago, which finally resulted in this book.

To my good friend and colleague at the School of General Studies at Columbia, William J. Goode, I owe a special debt of gratitude. It was he who first provided an opportunity to teach the course in the Department of Sociology which led to this book, and the freedom which he gave in developing the course as I wished was absolute. Despite his own tremendous load of research, writing, teaching, and administration, he was never too busy to help me wrestle with a problem and generously provide his energy and insights. He knew when encouragement was needed, without ever being asked for it, and his editorship, during a summer vacation, of the first half of this book was magnificent.

Professor Theodore Newcomb, of the Department of Psychology of the University of Michigan, read the entire manuscript twice. His detailed and general critiques were of the kind that every author hopes for but is fortunate enough to get only once in a great while. He not only read the manuscript, but also listened to the theme which I had tried to set. So keenly did he thus go over the manuscript that he was often able to put into the sharpest language ideas which I had been trying to formulate for several years. My only regret is that I was often unable to make maximum use of his suggestions and insights.

My debt of gratitude to the men and women whose works make up a large part of this volume should be more than obvious. If I have, at times, taken liberties with their hypotheses and theories, it has been in an attempt to increase our understanding of people. I hope that they will accept these alterations in the spirit in which they were made. A few of the authors whose works are quoted extensively made stylistic and editorial changes by deleting materials which I would not have deleted.

Those to whom we are closest are always involved, in many different ways, in a major work. Thus, my greatest and deepest sense of gratitude is to my wife, Rochelle Wexler Cohen. I found in her an inexhaustible source of support, encouragement, and assistance. She listened patiently and critically while I thought through problems aloud. She read the manuscript with a meticulousness that even I found difficult to give to it, and in several instances—especially in the theoretical introduction to Chapter 7—she was responsible for many of my ideas on a subject. Without her, the manuscript would still be lying in a heap in one of my desk drawers.

Y. A. C.

New York City
February, 1961

CONTENTS

SECTION III

IF THE SHOE FITS: THE DEPENDENCE OF INSTITUTIONS ON PERSONALITY PROCESSES

SECTION IV

EFFECTS OF COMMUNITY SYSTEMS ON PERSONALITY   285

SECTION V

SOCIAL CHANGE, ACCULTURATION, AND PERSONALITY   387

SECTION VI

THE SOCIOLOGICAL CONDITIONS OF
PERSONAL DISORGANIZATION

Section I

SOME CONCEPTS AND DEFINITIONS

Chapter 1

A QUESTION OF
APPROACH: I. THEORETICAL

The choice of title for this book is deliberate, and it is meant to refer to a particular area of study. The investigation of any topic requires a definition—an arbitrary statement—delimiting the areas of study. Inquiry into the relationships between personality on one side and society, social structure, or culture on the other is especially nebulous and difficult because of the frequent lack of consistency in deciding what exactly is being studied. There are many controversial issues which confront this branch of social science, such as goals, problems demanding investigation, methods of research, instruments of research, theoretical biases, and the like. Each of these, and others, will be discussed in the course of the chapters to follow.

Before we go on to define the social-structural approach to personality, we must distinguish it from its progenitor, "culture and personality." The latter area of study has tended to concentrate its energies on the meanings which a culture has to the individual as well as on the relationships between personality and different facets of culture, such as culture patterns, ethos, themes, world view, and the like. Within these broad categories of interest, culture-and-personality studies have attempted to learn whether there are any personality processes which are universal (as in the attempt to discover whether the "oedipal conflict" is found in all societies) and how particular cultures mold and shape original "human nature" (as in the attempts to discover the ways in which different biological and acquired drives are satisfied or frustrated in different cultural settings).

In distinguishing the social-structural approach to personality from the culture-and-personality approach, we have no intention of disregarding everything in the latter. The main distinction, as we shall observe in a moment, is in the theoretical approach and in the frame of reference being employed. Thus, we shall discuss the ways in which aggression is molded; the ways in which fantasy behavior is affected by different sociocultural climates; the effects of ethos and world view on personality; and so forth. But in each case, our focus and our approach—as well as our guiding problems—will differ in considerable degree from the culture-and-personality approach.

In defining the field of social structure and personality we shall also be stating its goals. These are three in number. First, we shall inquire into the effects of societal institutions on the socialization of children and on the course of growing up in general. Secondly, we shall look into those dimensions or aspects of personality which are required for the successful functioning of particular institutions. Our third major area of inquiry will be the extremely broad problem of the effects of institutions on the personality processes of adults.

Many of these questions imply cause. We can never know cause fully in the social sciences. But we can *think in terms of* cause, we can proceed as if we were looking for causes, and we can always work toward the unattainable goal of finding causes in human behavior. We can—and, as a matter of fact, we shall throughout this book—attempt to specify the particular social-structural conditions which seem to produce particular effects. The belief that there is "cause" in human behavior—and this is accepted here as an article of faith—is one of the major differences between the culture-and-personality and the social-structure-and-personality approaches. The former does not proceed on the assumption of "as if there were cause." The latter does.

If we had to make a choice, it could probably be said that the social-structural approach to personality draws *philosophically* more on sociology than on anthropology. The emphasis is on the ways of viewing man as well as on data and goals. Throughout our factual and theoretical analyses in this book we shall be concerned almost entirely with the consequences of institutional or social-structural arrangements for the development and functioning of particular aspects or dimensions of personality. We shall inquire into the consequences for the developing personality of social status, of family isolation, of political changes, of populational movements, of caste, of kinship organization, of acculturation, of culture change, and so forth. But we shall also inquire into the consequences of particular personality constellations for the social structure of a society, as in occupations, military and legal institutions, economic organization, and the like.

II

What is meant here by the term *social structure,* which has frequently been used quite loosely? Different sociologists and anthropologists have so many and such diverse ways in which they employ this concept that it would be almost impossible to include all of them within one definition or conceptualization. What is more, it is doubtful that there is any value even in attempting to do so.

More often than not in sociology and anthropology, social structure refers to the institutions of society and to the particular ways in which these institutions are arranged into patterned wholes. Institutions, too, can be conceptualized in a variety of ways. But if we think of an institution as a systematization of human relationships around specific needs and goals, with specific rules and personnel and clearly defined reciprocities, then we can think of a social structure as constituting a totality of institutions—that is, a series of interlocking systems within one total system.

Anthropologists and sociologists are constantly dealing with institutions and with social structure, so much so that it is difficult to imagine many anthropological or sociological analyses which can dispense with these concepts. *But depending on the type of analysis being conducted, social structure must be conceptualized in different ways*. Thus, the notion of social structure as constituting a series of systems within a total system is an almost indispensable one for the complete analysis of any *one* society or community. One of the reasons for this is that in the investigation of individual societies or communities the goal is almost always to determine the principles according to which the systems-within-a-system "keep each other going" in ways which are meaningful to the members of each society and in ways which are compatible with their values, motivations, beliefs, and attitudes.

By social structure we shall usually mean in this book the *positions* in which individuals, families and other groups stand in relation to each other. Essentially, these positions are of two sorts. One type of position with which we shall be concerned is *physical position,* in terms of proximity and distance. In the application of this criterion, the question of whether individuals and family groups are in physical proximity or physical distance will concern us, and specifically, the effects of such positions on socialization practices and on various modes of personality functioning. Also in the application of this criterion, we shall be concerned with the question of whether individuals and family groups are physically stable or move about and engage in concomitant physical disruption of ties and settlement patterns. There are other criteria of physical position which will be examined in turn, especially in terms of their consequences for socialization and adult personality.

The second type of position to be explored is *social position*. Here, too, we shall examine some of the psychological consequences of social proximity and social distance, as, for example, the influences of various kinds of kinship relationships and systems. We shall try to learn the effects of status positions, such as caste and class, on socialization and personality processes in the United States as well as in other societies—and, also, the effects of other kinds of social position. Important here is the fact that social and physical positions more often than not affect and flow into one another. As far as possible, we shall attempt to keep each type of variable separate for analytic purposes, but shall also examine certain problems in which there are several different social and physical positions within the same problem. However, instead of attempting a series of rigid and rigorous definitions at this point we will allow this conceptualization of social structure to come through more clearly in the discussions of the problems which make up this book.

In turning to an attempted delimitation of "personality," we are going to have to hedge somewhat and not be as forthright as in the preceding paragraphs. But there is a reason for this, and the reason is instructive in itself. One of the goals of this book is to maintain as much of a balance as possible between sociological and psychological theory. However, the book is from the pen of a social scientist whose primary commitment is to anthropological and sociological theory, especially in the field of social structure. Thus, it should come as no surprise that elections have been made in *sociological* theory and an attempt has been made to adopt what appears to be a consistent *sociological* frame of reference.

But the matter is quite different for a sociologist turning toward the wide expanse of psychological theory. There are tomes written about perception, achievement, the psychology of projective tests, unconscious motivation, personality struc-

ture, child development, social psychology, and so forth. It would be presumptuous
for a sociologist or anthropologist to say that one theoretical system *vis-à-vis* another
is the more valid or valuable. Such presumption would stem from the fact that there
is no single psychological theory today which would meet the needs of sociology and
anthropology. Perhaps, someday, we shall have a sociological psychology, or an anthropological one. But as matters now stand, any attempt to probe or answer a set
of sociological questions with psychological tools demands foraging through the
many fields and branches of psychology.

This is less than eclecticism. It is an approach of theoretical expediency based
on demands and needs of the moment—that is, depending on the sociological and
anthropological problems which are being faced at any one time. Thus, no one
theory of personality or of motivation or of perception shall be subscribed to. At this
point, only the major avenues which will be followed in examining personality within
a sociological or social-structural context will be outlined. We have to keep in mind,
before anything else, that there is a great difference between personality and behavior. Behavior is an observable phenomenon, or a series of phenomena, whereas
personality consists of processes and mechanisms which are essentially inferences
from observable behavior. We will investigate personality, in this book, in a twofold
way; both avenues, as they shall be applied, will cut across each other.

First, we shall inquire into the *motivations* which underlie and give rise to behavior in the contexts of social institutions. Sometimes, as we shall see, people are
aware of the motivations to their behavior, but there are also many instances in
which they are not. Our task, in this connection, will be to try to learn what conditions of social structure produce similar motivations among members of particular
groups, such as parents, immigrants, participants in different kinds of social institutions, members of a community living together and getting along with each other,
sufferers from emotional disturbances, and so on. The notion of motivation covers
a very wide territory which, as we proceed, will be narrowed down to a series of
working concepts and definitions. It should be emphasized that behavior—and,
therefore, the motivation to behavior—either within individuals or within groups, is
not haphazard, random, or fortuitous. People, whether as discrete individuals or as
members of functioning social systems, do things and behave as they do for reasons.
These reasons (or motivations) constitute the bridges between the social-structural
conditions under which people live and the behavior which they manifest and which
is observable.

Secondly, we shall investigate the ways in which the individual sees or perceives
himself as standing in particular relationships to other persons. This aspect of personality will parallel closely our conceptualization of social structure as being made
up of a system of positional standings within a group. That is, while there is a formalized system of sociological positions in which people are grouped and arranged,
there is also a subjective side to this picture, namely, the ways in which people *see*
or *perceive* their positions—often unconsciously—*vis-à-vis* each other. Thus, as we
shall observe, there is a constant interplay between the structure or system of posi-

tions within a society and the individual's motivations regarding the roles he plays within that structure or system.

There are, in brief, processes *within* individuals and processess *between* individuals. While these can often be studied separately, it soon becomes quite apparent that processes within individuals lead to behavior between individuals, and that behavior between individuals leads to specific consequences within individuals. This, of course, implies a circular or chicken-and-egg proposition. One of our tasks in this book will be to break the circle and attempt to ascertain the points at which one or the other of these two processes is set into motion at any one time.

III

A constant focus will be maintained on the *conditions* in which people function, behave, and grow up, and on the *consequences* of these conditions. The theory of the relationship between different dimensions of behavior and sociological conditions is excellently stated by Inkeles. Writing specifically about industrial societies (though, as we shall see, this theoretical approach has much more general applicability), he observes that ". . . the distinctive roles of the industrial system also foster typical patterns of perception, opinions, beliefs, and values which are not institutionally prescribed but arise spontaneously as new subcultures in response to the institutional conditions provided by the typically differentiated role-structure of modern industrial society. . . .

"The underlying theory is very simple. It is assumed that people have experiences, develop attitudes, and form values in response to the forces or pressures which their environment creates. By 'environment' we mean, particularly, networks of interpersonal relations and the patterns of reward and punishment one normally experiences in them. They include not only access to facilities and items of consumption, necessary and conspicuous, but also such intangibles as prestige, the comforts of security, respectful treatment, calculability in the actions of significant others, and so on. The theory holds that, within broad limits, the same situational pressures, the same framework for living, will be experienced as similar and will generate the same or similar response by people from different countries. This is, of course, not a denial of individual variation, of personality as a determinant of perception, cognition, or affect. Neither is it meant to deny the effect of traditional cultural ways on behavior. These will mute the independent effect of the industrial institutional environment, but it is assumed that they cannot eliminate it. Rather, its force is sufficiently great to assert itself clearly despite the countervailing influence of personal idiosyncrasy and traditional cultural ways of thinking and feeling. Insofar as industrialization, urbanization, and the development of large-scale bureaucratic structures and their usual accompaniments create a standard environment with standard institutional pressures for particular groups, to that degree should they produce relatively standard patterns of experience, attitude, and value—standard, not uniform, pressures. The situation of worker and manager may be relatively standard in the factory, wherever it is located, but relative to each other these positions are by no means uniform. . . .

"To discern this influence of the environment is, of course, not the same as determining either its extent or its intensity. The pressure generated by the institutional setting of industrialism may affect only a narrow range of experience and attitude—possibly only that relating to work experience. It may exert only a moderate influence, producing only a small part of the variance, the main part being accounted for by other factors, such as traditional cultural orientations. These are important problems for further elucidation. For now, we restrict ourselves to a statement of the main proposition—*that men's environment, as expressed in the institutional patterns they adopt or have introduced to them, shapes their experience, and through this their perceptions, attitudes and values, in standardized ways which are manifest from country to country, despite the countervailing randomizing influence of traditional cultural patterns.*" [1]

IV

This book is not committed to any one or two psychological "schools" of thought or theory. Limitations of space prevent a presentation or review of personality theory—in psychology, sociology, or anthropology—upon which we might draw. The attempt has been made, instead, to select or innovate an effective handling for each particular problem. The following is a brief, and by no means inclusive, bibliography which the student can consult in order to acquaint himself with the historical background to this field of inquiry.

BIBLIOGRAPHY AND SUGGESTED READINGS

Four of the articles in the following annotated bibliography are from that excellent compendium of readings, *Personality in Nature, Society and Culture,* edited by Clyde Kluckhohn, Henry A. Murray, and David Schneider (rev. ed.). New York: Knopf, 1955. This is a volume which every student of personality should consult and to which we shall refer from time to time in the course of the chapters to follow.

Erikson, Erik H. "Growth and Crises of the 'Healthy Personality,' " in Kluckhohn *et al.,* 1955, pp. 185-225. After reading this paper, the student should go on to consult Erikson's *Childhood and Society.* (New York: Norton, 1950), a book which has had considerable influence on sociologists and anthropologists who have been interested in the relationships among culture, social structure, and personality. The more advanced student can also consult *Identity and the Life Cycle (Psychological Issues,* Volume 1, 1959), a collection of three of Erikson's papers which are

---

[1] From "Industrial Man: The Relation of Status to Experience, Perception, and Value," by Alex Inkeles, *American Journal of Sociology,* Vol. *66,* No. *1,* July 1960, pp. 1-2. Reprinted by permission of The University of Chicago Press.

relevant to anthropological and sociological interests. This volume also contains the first paper referred to above.

Hallowell, A. I. *Culture and Experience.* Philadelphia: University of Pennsylvania Press, 1955. Contains most of the papers of this distinguished leader in culture-and-personality studies.

Honigmann, John J. *Culture and Personality.* New York: Harper, 1954. The only available textbook, presenting the traditional culture-and-personality approach.

Inkeles, Alex. "Industrial Man: The Relation of Status to Experience, Perception, and Value," *American Journal of Sociology,* Volume 66, pp. 1-31, 1960.

Inkeles, Alex. "Some Sociological Observations on Culture and Personality Studies," in Kluckhohn *et al.,* 1955, pp. 577-592.

Inkeles, Alex and Daniel J. Levinson. "National Character: The Study of Modal Personality and Sociocultural Systems," in *Handbook of Social Psychology,* edited by Gardner Lindzey. Cambridge, Mass.: Addison-Wesley, 1954, pp. 977-1020. This paper, and the previous one by Inkeles, should be read as a unit *vis-à-vis* the articles by Mead and other representatives of the culture-and-personality approach.

Kluckhohn, Clyde. "The Influence of Psychiatry on Anthropology in America during the Past One Hundred Years," reprinted in *Personal Character and Cultural Milieu* (3rd ed.), edited by Douglas Haring, Syracuse, N.Y.: Syracuse University Press, 1956, pp. 485-512.

Kluckhohn, Clyde. "Culture and Behavior," in *Handbook of Social Psychology,* edited by Gardner Lindzey, Cambridge, Mass.: Addison-Wesley, 1954, pp. 921-976. Both of these articles by Kluckhohn are erudite and thorough analyses, and both contain superb bibliographies.

Kluckhohn, Clyde and Henry A. Murray. "Personality Formation: The Determinants," in Kluckhohn *et al.,* pp. 53-67. This article, and the one by Murray and Kluckhohn (see below), must be read as a unit. They are not only lengthy and difficult, but quite technical—yet well worth the effort to understand an important and influential point of view.

Mead, Margaret. "The Cross-Cultural Approach to the Study of Personality," in *Psychology of Personality: Six Modern Approaches,* edited by J. L. McCary. New York: Logos, 1956, pp. 201-252. One of the pioneers of culture-and-personality studies presents her own important approach and viewpoint.

Mead, Margaret. "National Character," in *Anthropology Today: An Encyclopedic Inventory,* edited by A. L. Kroeber. Chicago: University of Chicago Press, 1952, pp. 642-667. A significant statement by one of the leading anthropological authorities in the field.

Munroe, Ruth. *Schools of Psychoanalytic Thought: An Exposition, Critique, and Attempt at Integration,* New York: Holt, Rinehart and Winston, 1955. A rare summary and fairly good clarification of what could otherwise be a tangle of confusing ideas.

Murray, Henry A. and Clyde Kluckhohn. "Outline of a Conception of Personality," in Kluckhohn *et al.,* 1955, pp. 3-49.

Sapir, Edward. *Selected Writings of Edward Sapir in Language, Culture, and Personality,* edited by David G. Mandelbaum. Berkeley: University of California Press, 1949. Containing the papers which can be considered to have "founded" the subdiscipline of culture and personality; of more than historical interest, many of Sapir's ideas are as valid today as they were when first published in the 20's and 30's.

Chapter 2

A QUESTION OF
APPROACH: II. APPLIED

In commencing the study of social structure and personality with inquiries into socialization patterns, we must first provide ourselves with certain conceptual or theoretical tools to analyze our various bodies of data. We shall employ concrete case material as one of our aids in this direction. Our reasoning in the analyses to follow in this chapter may, at times, appear to be somewhat *ad hoc*. To an extent, this is not only inevitable, but it is necessary as well. We must often analyze available cases as though the analyses pertain to these cases only, as though our reasoning were completely circular, and as though there were no predictive value in the hypothesized relationships derived from the analyses. Later on we shall discover whether we can apply the principles and generalizations derived from these cases to other instances which require analysis.

The first principle which we will attempt to illustrate can be stated by paraphrasing the opening statement of the first paper in this chapter, "The Personality of the Kaingang Indians" by Jules Henry; this statement can be taken as a general rule applicable to all social situations: The modal personality of a people or a society cannot be understood apart from the social structure in which it has its being, for the development and functioning of that personality is so correlated with the peculiar structure of a society that one without the other would produce a confusing picture.

After we have read this paper by Henry on the Kaingang Indians of Brazil, we shall attempt two things. First, we shall illustrate this introductory statement by an intensive analysis of the data in order to make explicit some of the ways in which Kaingang social structure and personality are so interwoven with each other, and so effectively "keep each other going," that it is extremely difficult, if not impossible, to understand one without the other. Secondly, we shall use one of the major theoretical dimensions in this book—the determinative effects of physical and social distance— to illustrate a way to break the circle of chicken-and-egg propositions which so often hinder analyses of the relationship of personality and society, or personality and culture, or personality and social structure. Our focus will be on the ways in which we ask our questions and the resulting answers arrived at.

The second principle to be illustrated in this chapter—a principle which is indispensable to any full understanding of why people bring up their children as they do —is the axiom that people's location in a social structure determines which facets of "the culture of their society" they will have access to, and that they will transmit to their children only that part of "the culture of their society" to which they do have access.

Let us put this another way around. In line with the anthropologists' conceptualization of culture as a *range* of behavior which is manifest by members of a society or community, we can think of a culture as a broad spectrum; the status or positional locations of people in a society or community can be thought of as a set of filtering lenses which provide access to one band, or one part, of the cultural spectrum to the *relative* exclusion of others. This principle will be clarified by reading and discussing part of the classic paper by Hsiao-Tung Fei, entitled "Peasantry and Gentry: An Interpretation of Chinese Social Structure and its Changes."

There are, of course, other principles indispensable to the understanding of social structure and personality, but these two will provide our initial focus.

One note of caution should be sounded before reading "The Personality of the Kaingang Indians." In this article Henry does not always clearly differentiate between his data and his interpretations of these data. For the most part, the data appear to be clear of subjective interpretations, but at the point at which he states, towards the end of the paper, that "an important trait of the Kaingang personality is projection," he is presenting his own interpretations of the facts. These explications, however correct and valid they may be, are not facts; their presence or the presence of any interpretive statement in an article does not detract from or negate the facts themselves. We need only bear in mind that both elements are present, and keep them separate in our own minds.

THE PERSONALITY OF THE KAINGANG INDIANS*
By Jules Henry

The personality of the Kaingang Indians cannot be understood apart from the social structure in which it had its being, for the development and functioning of that personality is so correlated with the peculiar structure of Kaingang society that any attempt to describe the one without the other would produce a confusing picture. In order to show, therefore, how the personality of these Indians integrates with the processes of their society it will be necessary to give first a short sketch of the social structure.

The Kaingang are divided into ex-tended family groups of from fifty to three hundred individuals which live by themselves, coming together principally for fiestas, invitations to which may not be refused, though they were often pretexts for mass murder of the invited guests. These groups are endogamous, and their small size makes the degree of inbreeding within them extremely high. The incest taboos are so reduced that the only relationships within which marriages do not take place are between parents and real children and between full siblings.

Although the Kaingang extended

---

* Reprinted with omission of footnotes from (*Character and Personality*), *Journal of Personality*, Vol. 5, pp. 113-123, 1936, with permission.

families are endogamous, they are so not by virtue of specific regulations that make marriages between the groups taboo, but because of the annihilating feuds that have existed among them for at least three hundred years. Correlated with these feuds is the sharp distinction in behavior towards members of one's own group and those of other, or, as the Kaingang call them, "different," groups. Within each group a high degree of positive affect is developed on the basis of libidinal ties that are extended to include a large number of people, but between the groups no such ties are developed. Between the feud groups there is nothing but fear and rage; murder, pursuit, and flight. It is true that some marriages do occur between the groups, but they are few and never prevent the relentless prosecution of the vendettas. Thus, the first point to be considered in a description of Kaingang personality is *the nature of the libidinal ties within the extended families and the manner of their development.*

The attachments of Kaingang children are not confined to their immediate family but are diffused throughout the extended family group through a number of processes. When their mothers leave camp on some errand, the babies are taken care of by some woman who happens to be around, and if the child grows hungry or cries while its mother is away the woman taking care of it will give it the breast. The Kaingang are very fond of children, and even childless individuals of all ages caress them constantly and take them to bed. The children themselves love all this attention: they are at the beck and call of anyone who wants a warm little body to caress and they lie like cats absorbing the stroking of adults. They are impossible to keep track of around the campfire: by choice and from necessity they literally "sleep all over the place." They like to cuddle next to the adults, and in the winter when there may

be only one blanket to shelter a family, the little ones are driven to crawl under the cover of someone else, who welcomes the additional warmth of the little bundle.

When the children are very young they are the objects of adult affection, but when they are about fourteen or fifteen they turn their attention to one another. At this point a striking difference is noticeable between the behavior of the adolescent boys and that of the adolescent girls, for the young men participate in certain warm relationships which are not duplicated by the young women. The young men love to sleep together. At night they call to one another, "Come and lie down here with me, with *me!*" Then there is a shifting and a wriggling so that Nggugn or Waipo or Kanyahé can lie down where he is bidden. In camp one sees the young men caressing. Married and unmarried young men lie cheek by jowl, arms around one another, legs slung across bodies like lovers in our own culture. Sometimes they lie caressing in little knots of three and four. However, I have never seen any signs of complete homosexual relations among the men or the women. I have sat talking night after night to knots of young men, and I have seen them caressing one another in absolutely open fashion in the broad light of day, but I never saw them make a more definitely homosexual gesture. In the whole mass of Kaingang folklore there are only two very short tales of homosexuality. One is about a homosexual relationship between two men; the other tells of a male supernatural that was killed by a man because it sodomized him by trickery. Outside of this I never heard the Kaingang allude in any way to homosexuality.

Like the indiscriminate playing of children these caressings and sleeping parties do not follow kinship lines. Whatever may be the specific obligations of cousins or brothers-in-law they are completely lost sight of in these ephemeral, wholly casual and whimsical masculine contacts. The basis of man's loyalty to man within the extended family has roots in the many warm bodily contacts among them. The violent, annihilating conflicts among men in Kaingang society are all among those who never shared the languid exchange of caresses on a hot afternoon under the green arched shelter of a house nor lain together night after night under a blanket against the cold. The very transient, unfixated nature of these contacts leaves no grounds for jealousy. The relationships built upon these hours of warm affectionate lying together with anyone at all bear rich fruit in the softening of conflicts that spring up among the men.

Positive affective ties are multiplied within the extended family, not only through the widening of the babies' circle of affection and through the caressing among the young men, but also through relationships among the men and women. Although affairs both before and after marriage are numerous, their significance is quite different in character from the majority of similar relationships in our own society. Even though these affairs are characterized by a peculiar absence of jealousy except on the part of the betrayed spouses, once a Kaingang man and woman have been lovers a tie is established between them that is never forgotten, and in times of emergency or great conflict they may come to each other's aid. But love affairs have an even wider implication. People whose mothers have had the same lover look upon one another as siblings, and men frequently view other men's children as their own because the mothers have been their mistresses. In this way the concepts of fatherhood and siblinghood become extremely broad within each extended family so that this group which lives and hunts together and which is already closely in-bred, becomes further united through a strong sense of being one family of parents and children.

The stimulus toward active sexual life which makes this type of feeling possible is provided at a very early age, for not only do the children hear the constant jocular sexual chatter of their elders, but they are directed to intercourse by their own parents. The sexuality of little boys is stimulated by their mothers' manipulation of their genitals before they can walk. Although little children of two and three are told jocularly to copulate with one another, their attention is directed particularly toward adults. Babies are told jocularly to copulate with people anywhere from ten to twenty times their age, and a toddler of three has already learnt to say, "With Waikome," (who may be his grandfather's sister) in answer to the question, "With whom do you copulate?" Children of all ages are pressed into service to remove ticks, and it is not all uncommon to see a little girl of five or six hovering over a supine man picking the ticks off his genitals. A child soon learns to repeat the jokes that go around the campfire, and at an early age becomes the butt of certain kinds of sexual jokes himself. A boy of nine is jokingly taunted with masturbation, told that he has deflowered his fifteen-year-old cousin, or is accused of wishing to copulate with a dog. As two dogs copulate, the entire hunting party roars with laughter and a little girl of six cries delightedly, "They are copulating!" The children may see the boisterous open foreplay of the adults and glimpse the sexual act in the dim light of the early morning. Yet with all this there is no intercourse among children. Jokes about love affairs of children among themselves are never made by adults or by the children. In this society in which gossip about affairs is constant, where jokes about every aspect of sexual relations are forever being made, where children are directed to copulate, where the foreplay of adults is easily visible, there is never a joke about actual intercourse between two children, and they are never seen engaged in sexual foreplay. They receive a great deal of satisfaction from adults and do not bother with one another. But this adult attention often culminates in the sexual experience to which the grown-ups are eager to introduce the child, who is generally enjoyed first by a person much older than he. This is his introduction to a life of sexual philandering that does not end even with marriage. By the time he is fifty the average Kaingang will have had an affair with most of the adults around him.

The extension of the libidinal ties that are developed through the numerous heterosexual relationships is facilitated through the sexual aggressiveness of both men and women. In our society where men are conventionally the aggressors in sex the whole sexual process from courtship to consummation is delayed because the advances must always be made by one person. In Kaingang society, however, where no emphasis is laid upon such a temperamental difference between the sexes, where the same jocular and often violent sexual aggressiveness is permitted to boys and girls, to men and to women, affairs can be begun and consummated much more rapidly and often. Sexual approaches range all the way from the unobstrusive contact of bare legs beside the evening fires, to the open, ribald and aggressive onslaughts of both men and women. Although I never put it to the test, I have a strong feeling that widowed Kundidn, like many of her sex, was stronger than I. Her amorous pinches, punches, and pushes were a trial to me once they had become archived in my scientific consciousness. One day she said to me, "Don't you ever have coitus?" "No," said I, "I have no penis." "That's a lie. I saw it. If I sent someone to you would

you copulate with her? Go along through the bushes and I will send someone after you!" Kundidn's aggressiveness stopped only at direct snatches at the sexual organs.

Angglό, a married woman who was having a passionate affair with Kanyahé, was not averse to pressing another suit on the side. While she was much sweeter and did not square off in the boxer-like manner of Kundidn, she was aggressive enough in her own mild way. She did not pinch so hard nor call so loudly, but if there was no one around, her quiet "I should like to talk to you and see the inside your house" would set me thinking of how I could best avoid her without hurting her feelings. But I might have spared myself much worry on that score, for in this society, which lays no stress upon man's aggressiveness as over against woman's passivity, a woman who makes advances feels no vindictive anger at a repulse. In our society a woman who temporarily steps out of her culturally decreed role of the attacked to become the attacker feels shame that quickly becomes resentment against the desired object if she is rebuffed. The shame that she feels at reversing her part in the drama of the sexes is forgotten if she obtains her desire, and turns to anger if she does not. But the Kaingang women are able to make the same jocular approaches day after day without a change of attitude.

This, then, is the character of the libidinal ties among the Kaingang and the manner of their development. From his earliest days the growing child is passed from one caressing adult to the other. From the moment he understands what is said to him the terms for sexual intercourse are forced upon his mind, drenched always in laughter. His own mother jocularly directs him to intercourse while she nurses him and plays with his little body, and day after day he listens to tales of intrigues in which he knows that he himself will someday share. In this way the foundation is laid for an active, cheerful, and diffuse sexual life.

In our society, where tradition has placed a limit on sexual activity by condemning aggressiveness in women, the sexual process is delayed. In our society, again, but particularly in some primitive societies, whole categories of relatives are excluded as sexual objects by rigorous laws of incest, so that even an enterprising person does not think sexually of close relatives. But the Kaingang know nothing of the sexual dichotomy of the aggressive male and the passive female, and laws of incest bear little weight with them. They view all people except children as spontaneously, vigorously and diffusely sexual, and act accordingly.

The result of the multiplication of libidinal ties of every kind is to draw together all the members of each extended family into a closely knit, sheltering unit within which murder never occurs. Quarrels arise over unfulfilled obligations and the endless adultery, but no blood is ever shed within the extended families. All conflicts within them are resolved on the basis of the warm relationships that have been built up since infancy.

The most striking thing about the

Kaingang is the complete difference in feeling between members of the same extended family and members of "different" groups. Members of different groups do not fondle one another's children; the men of the different groups do not caress one another; and the numerous love affairs that are so important in the welding together of each extended family simply do not exist between them. Thus the processes through which warm bonds are established do not operate between the groups. Coextensive with this difference in the affective picture are the relentless feuds, so that it may be said that there is a correlation between the break in positive affective ties and the existence of vendetta.

An important trait of the Kaingang personality is projection. Within the groups this projection takes the form of attributing to others resentment against oneself for offenses one has committed. The offenses that serve most generally as the basis of this projection are adultery and failures to assist others in hunting. This projection is not only experienced but is acted upon and produces constant quarrels, yet it never results in murder. Diagrammatically it may be expressed as follows:

What I think

(1) I have failed in my obligations to him and have meddled with his wife
(2) and I feel guilty
(5) If you are angry with me I'll be angry with you too.

What I think the other fellow thinks

(3) You have failed in your obligations to me and have meddled with my wife
(4) so I am angry with you.

Feeling angry, the Kaingang precipitates a quarrel, particularly if he is drunk. Thus, on the basis of the resentment that *A* thinks that *B* feels, *A* picks a quarrel with *B*.

The mechanism of projection which produces bloodless brawls *within* the extended families precipitates murder *be-*

tween them. To the Kaingang everything, human or nonhuman, that lies outside the limits of his extended family is a threat, and those threats that loom largest are other extended families and the supernatural. The Kaingang sleep fitfully at night for fear of attacks by vendetta enemies, and the man who enjoys the greatest prestige among them is the one who can do with the least amount of sleep at night. Whenever two extended families, or a few men from two different families, meet by chance in their wanderings through the forests they are in acute terror of an attack from one another. They may wander around together for weeks or even months, but sooner or later there is a murderous outbreak, and always the one who strikes first wins. It is evident from the many feud stories that in such situations the Kaingang go through a definite projection cycle, which may be diagrammed as follows:

My own extended family

(1) My extended family gives security.
(3) I am in constant danger of destruction
(5) Contemplating action, I

Outside of my extended family

(2) Everything outside threatens.
(4) and I must take action against the threat.
(6) project: "The other person fears me because he knows what is in my mind."
(7) He fears and therefore wishes to destroy me.

The Vicious Circle

(8) I must take action to prevent it.

The meaning of (5) is simply that since *A* feels himself in danger of attack he wishes to attack first. Wishing to attack, he imagines that his victim knows his thoughts and may try to murder him at any moment. This situation has an obsessive character, the dramatic intensity of which it is difficult to overestimate.

This projection cycle has, of course, a certain basis in the realities of the actual conditions. The families *are* mutual enemies, who for many generations have lived in fear and hatred of one another. "When will the blow come?" they ask. "Who will be first to strike?"

When the terror-driven Kaingang at last take action against the threat by attacking their vendetta enemies, they are left with a feeling of guilt. It is no abstract sense of inherent wrong in killing that gives rise to the feeling of guilt which the Kaingang experience after slaughtering their vendetta enemies. The inter-marriages, few as they are which take place among the extended families, make the members actually relatives to one another, so that it is impossible to wipe out a family without killing off a number of one's relatives by marriage and even blood kin. Thus the members of the victorious families frequently fall to quarreling after the slaughter, accusing one another of having been responsible for these killings of relatives, which they had all planned together and in which they had all participated. The annihilation of the family of a certain old man called Patklé produced such strong feelings of guilt among the members of the victorious family that a general quarrel ensued. Patklé had been related to Kanyahé, the principal old man of the victorious group, and this relationship formed the central issue of the quarrel. After some of the assassins returned from their unsuccessful pursuit of one of their victims who had been lucky enough to escape the holocaust, Kanyahé burst out, "Let him die alone. You killed my affinal relatives and so stop your slaughter." To which one of the pursuers replied, "It was you yourself who ordered me to kill them; and now you are angry with me!"

It is not enough that the Kaingang should feel guilt about the people they have killed, but they must feel guilt because their own close relatives, members of their own extended families, have been killed by others. They sometimes feel that their relatives have died because they were not there to protect them. Kuthúgn and Kovi went hunting together and separated, and when Kuthúgn returned he found Kovi dead; for while Kuthúgn was away, Kovi had been overwhelmed by vendetta enemies and killed. On the following day Kuthúgn met one of his relatives and asked him, "Well, what happened?" "The enemy killed him." Kuthúgn became angry when he heard this and said, "Now! I said to him, 'Stay here,' but he went on and the ("different") things killed him." What had actually happened was that Kuthúgn had told Kovi to chop out a beehive and had gone on, leaving Kovi alone, so that his complaint that Kovi had not done what he was told is nothing more than an excuse to conceal his own sense of responsibility for Kovi's death.

The sense of guilt that oppresses the Kaingang is sometimes, as in the quarrel of Kanyahé and his relatives, absorbed into the extended families and digested in undercurrents of resentment, but in other cases it finds expression in outbursts of anger, such as that of Kuthúgn in the last instance, which are rooted in a sense of personal guilt.

Now vendetta is a common enough feature of human society, but in many places where it exists there is some social device for stopping the killings at least temporarily. One of the common ways is the *lex talionis,* whereby for every man killed one man from the murderer's group must also be killed. But in Kaingang society there is no way at all of bringing the vendettas to a halt except through extermination of the men of the enemy group. A number of factors contributed to the existence of this condition. The first is the obsessive personality structure just described which makes impossible the acceptance of the *lex talionis.* From time to time men have arisen in Kaingang society who were willing to accept the law of an eye for an eye and tooth for a tooth, but such a socially salutary attitude was incompatible with the obsessive drive toward mass murder that characterized their fellows, so that in the end the ones who had their way were those to whom total destruction of the enemy families was the only solution of the conflict. Pepó, one of the men in a Kaingang feud, was satisfied to live in peace after having killed his brother's murderer. His nature was completely satisfied by the death of one man. But Wainló, the foster son of Pepó's brother, could never forget the murder of his foster father. For years he nourished his hate until with the help of allies he killed all the men of the original murderer's group. Thus the *lex talionis* could not function in this instance because it was repugnant to the obsessive personality of Wainló. But the peculiar character of Kaingang society was given it by its scores of Wainlós, not by its Pepós, and these obsessive individuals worked not only for the destruction of others, but also for the destruction of themselves, for their very obsession with murder made them disregard all odds and plunge themselves into a fight in which the numbers were so overwhelmingly against them that they had no chance of coming out alive. Pandjumbúgn is an excellent example of such an individual. He was alone in an enemy camp, and although his hosts were perfectly willing to accept him, he became so bent upon their destruction that, although they were un-willing to do so, he literally forced them to kill him.

A second factor in the perpetuation of the Kaingang feuds is their feeling that once a feud is started it can never be stopped. In the realm of the supernatural this finds expression in their ideas about the souls of the deceased and in their terror when one of their number dies. The Kaingang fear that the soul of the deceased desires to carry off its relatives is in part an expression of the feeling that when death has struck once it will keep on striking. Paralleling this on the human level is the belief that a feud enemy will never cease his murders, that he can never be trusted and hence can never become a friend.

One more important factor in the perpetuation of the Kaingang feuds is their function as a drain to the tre-mendous aggressiveness of the Kaingang, which manifests itself not only in at-tacks on the Brazilian colonists and in the slaughtering of one another, but even in the utterly wanton gashing of trees and the killing of the tiniest bird that happens to perch on a limb where stick or stone might reach it. The feuds also act as a drain to the resentments that arise from the desertion of hunting companions, from adultery, and from the guilty ac-cusations following feud massacres. In this latter instance, however, the Kain-gang are really moving in a vicious circle, for this hostility needs to be released in new slaughters, which in turn cause new feelings of guilt and produce new quar-rels.

One of the most outstanding characteristics of the Kaingang is the "emotional inbreeding" which appears to characterize personal relationships within the group (this concept will be defined in a moment). Everyone outside the immediate group is "different," the notion of difference here having a decidedly negative, even dan-gerous, connotation. Correlatively, everyone outside the immediate group is seen as a threat and as a potential attacker and destroyer. There is an intense concen-tration of emotions within the immediate group, most clearly manifest in the "sleep-ing parties" of the young men. At the same time, however, feelings of proximity and closeness appear to be quite brittle and there seems to be a constant alternation be-tween approach and withdrawal among people. Lastly, at least in terms of their out-standing personality characteristics, the Kaingang have been described by their ethnographer as being predominantly "obsessive" in their character structure.

"Emotional inbreeding," a term which we are borrowing from Kluckhohn,[1] refers to a tendency in some groups—usually small ones—for individuals to concen-trate all their emotional energies on the members of the group to the exclusion of anyone else. The forces involved in emotional inbreeding are centripetal ones. Psy-chologically, this can be thought of as "putting all of one's emotional eggs in one basket." It is a tendency—which can be found in a family, in a community, in a caste, in an ethnic group, and so forth—to glorify one's own group above all others, to see one's own group as the only possible source of emotional and social satisfac-tion, and to see other groups as threatening or unsatisfying.

Parenthetically, there is a slight similarity between emotional inbreeding and ethnocentrism. Ethnocentrism is the tendency of a group to think of its own ways of

---

[1] Kluckhohn, 1944, p. 53.

behaving as "natural" or as stemming from "human nature"; it is the attempt to evaluate all other cultures from the standpoint of its own. Alien groups, or strange beliefs and practices, are viewed with suspicion and hostility simply because they are different. But ethnocentrism differs from emotional inbreeding in one important respect. Whereas emotional inbreeding is based essentially on an isolationism which stems from the solidity of boundaries, ethnocentrism can and does occur under any and all circumstances. Emotional inbreeding is a rejection of *people* who are of the out-group; ethnocentrism is a rejection of *values* and *behavior,* but not necessarily of the people who practice them. To be sure, ethnocentrism increases when emotional inbreeding increases; but there can be ethnocentrism even when emotional inbreeding is minimal.

Emotional inbreeding is a characteristic or a process which can be observed in a wide variety of social structures; and while it plays a large role in Kaingang personality, it cannot explain very much if it is taken alone, as a single-cause interpretation. It can be seen in many areas of China, where the "inbreeding" of the family seems largely to stem from the intense concentration of emotional relationships between mother and son. This emotional inbreeding also occurs in certain areas of China when families are physically close to each other and live a sedentary life under a system of localized patrilineal clans. Emotional inbreeding can be seen in families of the Navaho Indians, where it largely results from the geographical isolation of the household group. Among the Navaho, too, there is a system of clans (in this case, matrilineal) and there is a very peculiar interplay or dialectic between clanship—a force making for social proximity—and geographical isolation—a force making for social distance. There are some resemblances between the Chinese and the Navaho on the level of personality, but they are minor ones; and much more, in addition to emotional inbreeding, is needed in order to explain differences and similarities between these two peoples. Thus, as these limited comparisons would seem to indicate, emotional inbreeding can occur under a wide variety of social-structural conditions, and it would be very difficult to predict from this process to personality, except within very narrow limits. What these limits are we shall see in a moment.

Nor can we do very much with the Kaingang proclivity to see other people as "different," if we take this factor alone and without relating it to other forces in their social system. Most peoples seem to perceive nonmembers of the in-group as "different." And as soon as this concept is called into play in social life, some negative connotation—varying in different degrees of intensity and significance, of course—attaches itself to this feeling of "difference." We can observe this in our own society, as in caste, ethnic, religious, or class distinctions (although economic, political, and other factors enter into most cases).

Henry has characterized the Kaingang as being "obsessive" in their character structure, but this, too, does not explain very much if it is taken alone. Obsessiveness is a characteristic of thought or of ways of thinking; the *action* which is based on obsessive thinking is generally referred to as compulsive behavior. Since Henry has described Kaingang thought as well as Kaingang action based upon such thinking, we are going to follow modern usage which links the two together; [2] thus, we are going to add to Henry's conceptualization of the Kaingang as obsessive and think of them here as being characterized by an obsessive-compulsive pattern.

What are the features and dynamics of "obsessive-compulsiveness"? Maslow and Mittelmann,[3] employing this concept as a clinical one, describe it as follows: "The most important aspect of the obsessive-compulsive personality is his great need for safety and security. This he attempts to achieve by arranging his world in an orderly, regular way that he can count on, and in which nothing unexpected can happen. He attempts to live by rules and regulations rather than by spontaneous decisions." This need for safety and security does not make the obsessive-compulsive person unique; all people have such needs, but not all people cope with or meet these needs in similar fashion. But people who meet these needs in *these* particular ways, as described by Maslow and Mittelmann, are designated as obsessive-compulsive; this person feels especially helpless, and in his needs for safety and security lives a life of rigid inflexibility.

In attempting to tie together the threads which have been laid out in the foregoing discussion, we have to bear in mind that all human beings need the warmth and affection which is provided by membership in a group—family, kindred, community, sodality, and the like—and from a sense of belongingness within such a group. Furthermore, there inheres in every isolated or bounded small group a tendency to become emotionally inbred.

If a group exists and functions amid other groups, the needs which the members of the group possess—especially the needs for warmth and affection—can be gratified in a multitude of directions, among and through a variety of persons, and in a variety of ways. On the other hand, if a group is isolated from all others—as a family, in a ghetto, as a self-contained nomadic band, and so forth—there is a strong and decided tendency to concentrate all emotions, feelings, and needs within this relatively small group of persons. The isolation of the group isolates the individual from contacts outside his group, and the longer this isolation continues the more the individual loses his ability to form ties outside his group, be this group a family, a community, or a professional society. The isolation of the group forces the individual —in the sense that he has no alternative available to him—to invest all his emotional energies within a very constricted circle.

There are several reasons for this relationship between the isolation of the group and emotional over-investment within it. The first, as has already been noted, is the physical-social factor of the unavailability of other persons and other groups. But there is a second reason, one which is even more fundamental in terms of socio-psychological functioning. We know from many studies conducted by experimental social psychologists that the greater the ambiguity in the environment the easier it is for the individual to form his own judgments about what is going on in that environment. Some investigators may prefer to call this the "projection" of unacceptable wishes, tendencies, impulses, or even fantasied wish-fulfillments, and the like, onto

---

[2] See English and English, 1958, pp. 104, 353.
[3] Maslow and Mittelmann, 1941, p. 389.

other persons and groups. Be that as it may, people almost always tend to form opinions (or hypotheses) about groups of which they have little or minimal knowledge. These opinions, which often become stereotypes, are usually negative and they are easily removed from the realm of fancy to that of "fact." Speaking of such group-stereotypes *cum* hypotheses, Postman notes: "We shall provisionally define the *strength of an hypothesis* in terms of the amount of appropriate information necessary to confirm it or infirm it. The stronger the hypothesis, the less of appropriate stimulus information is required to confirm it or infirm it. This is tantamount to saying that a very strong hypothesis will tend to be confirmed even when most of the available information is inappropriate or that a weak hypothesis will not be confirmed even when a considerable amount of appropriate information is available. It might be interesting to note here that what is generally described as an 'ambiguous' situation would . . . be a situation in which there is little appropriate information for the trial and check of hypotheses." [4]

Each small Kaingang group lives in just such an ambiguous situation. The distance between groups is marked and wide; the boundaries setting off one group from another exist in the mind of each individual and become an integral part of each one's self-image. Very few human groups can either tolerate or permit hatred, rage, and aggression to be directed within the group. And one of the most characteristically provided displacements in many societies is an alien or strange group with which the former comes in contact.

Here is the point at which the vicious circle in Kaingang thinking is set into motion. There are so many sources of anxiety in Kaingang life that a very high level of aggression is understandable. Given the ambiguity of the world around him, the Kaingang individual does not need too many accurate data to substantiate his hypothesis about the evil and cruelty of surrounding groups. Since he starts out seeing all those outside his group as "different"—and therefore treacherous—he feels perfectly justified in directing his aggression and rage at them. (The same progession of events can be observed in race-riots, pogroms, international relations, management-labor conflict, and the like.) Furthermore, just as aggression can be a result of distance and anxiety it also serves to isolate people *further* from each other; that is, aggression can and often does serve the function of keeping people at a distance and from getting close to each other—and no one really wishes to get close to someone who is perceived to be evil and dangerous.

Thus, the hatred which a Kaingang feels for outsiders also reinforces the physical *and* emotional isolation of the small group. And where a group is physically, socially, and emotionally isolated from all other groups the individual tends to magnify and glorify the values of his own group. (Much the same processes appear to operate in the course of "romantic love" in our society.) Such glorification of one's own group and magnification of its value can be expressed in a variety of ways, and one of the forms which it takes among the Kainang is the caressing and almost compulsive bodily contact among men accompanied by bitterness and distrust experi-

---

[4] Postman, 1951, pp. 251-252.

enced toward all those who are "different." And the isolation of the group is not only reinforced on the emotional level by the hatred felt toward all other groups but it is also reinforced by glorifying the value of the in-group. It is, indeed, a vicious and closed circle.

Within this circle, and not necessarily a part of the circle, are two "givens" in Kaingang culture. We have to refer to these processes as "givens" for we have no way of uncovering their origin. The first of these are the destructive and self-destructive feuds and vendettas. There is no way of telling where, why, and how these started. But once they *were* set into motion their place within the vicious circle is easily understood, especially in relation to the second "given" of Kaingang society: their "obsessive" (or obsessive-compulsive) personality structure. The origin of this, too, is something which we cannot explain. But recalling the definition of "obsessive-compulsiveness" offered earlier in this section by Maslow and Mittelmann, we can appreciate the Kaingang's inability to accept the limits of the principle of an-eye-for-an-eye, a-life-for-a-life. For the obsessive-compulsive personality, life is a series of all-or-nothing propositions, and once a feud has been started it cannot be stopped, especially in view of the "fact" that there may be *one* person left in the enemy group who is bent on vengeance. And since this, together with the ambiguity of the environment, makes the world such an uncertain place, *all* uncertainties and potential evil must be destroyed. This in turn helps to breed and reinforce distrust and hatred, and it further isolates the group—socially, emotionally, and physically. And the isolation of the group perpetuates the conditions under which "emotional inbreeding" can continue from generation to generation and which, in turn, allows for the perpetuation of feuds and vendettas. . . .

Now let us turn to an illustration of our second principle, that people's location in the social structure of a society determines which elements or patterns or values in the culture of that society they will have access to. This is a slightly different way of saying something which we all know. For example, one of the dominant values in American society is the worthwhileness of education, either as an end in itself or as a means to a higher social and occupational status. However, we all know also that the son of a longshoreman and the son of a highly successful surgeon or banker *have different access to this value*. There are a wide variety of reasons for this besides the more obvious financial one; we will get to these in Chapter 3, but at the moment we only want to establish certain principles.

The operation of these propositions will be spelled out clearly by the material in the following paper, and they will serve as one of the central sets of ideas throughout this book. In this paper by Hsiao-tung Fei, one of the specific values to which people have different degrees of access is clanship. Putting this another way, clanship (in the China of Fei's 1946 description) is a predisposing value which affects people differently, depending on where they are located in the social structure of their society. Clanship is a way of looking at people from the inside of a group, and a way of living in a society. Fei's article shows that the lower one went in Chinese social structure the less meaning clanship had. If we think of clanship as, among other things, a way of looking at people, we can see how even a basic philosophy of life can be affected by social-structural positions.

The social structure of the society which Fei describes is probably no longer in existence. This, of course, does not invalidate what he has to say; it was a society whose social structure survived many centuries.

PEASANTRY AND GENTRY:
AN INTERPRETATION OF CHINESE SOCIAL STRUCTURE AND ITS CHANGES*

By Hsiao-tung Fei

The polarization of the rich and the poor gives birth to a social dichotomy common in many advanced communities. Benjamin Disraeli used "The Two Nations" as the alternative title for his *Sybil,* a story describing the social life in nineteenth-century England. That describes our traditional China equally well. Probably more than 80 percent of the Chinese are peasants. They are poor but they are economically productive. In a country in which industry and commerce are not yet fully developed, the peasants are the sole producers. Those who stay at the peak of the social pyramid are the leisure class— the gentry—a minority who live on rent collected from the peasants. Wealth and poverty create not only an economic difference which separates the rich from the poor but a social gulf between the two classes as well. The people thus separated carry on their lives differently. The upper class live in a more elaborate structure of social relations and are more sophisticated and more articulate. They are usually considered as the cultured group, while the majority of the population, engaged in the hard work of production, leaves little impression on observers and little trace in historical documents. When the historians exalt or condemn the

Greeks or the Romans, they have in mind only the warriors and the philosophers. Is it not also true that China has been praised and criticized according to that China which is found in Western museums, exhibited in art galleries, and described by writers of bestsellers? The China so represented comprises only the minority, the leisured gentry. A fair view of China, however, should include both the poor and the rich and the relation between them.

Peasantry, the key toward understanding China, is a way of living, a complex of formal organization, individual behavior, and social attitudes, closely knit together for the purpose of husbanding land with simple tools and human labor. Peasants are settled and sedentary. Growth of population on limited resources puts the law of diminishing returns in effective operation. Cultivation of land tends to be intensified. Minute care of the soil and delicate application of human labor hinder the utilization of improved tools. Standard of living lowers as population increases. Animal labor becomes uneconomical. Highly developed application of human skill in handling soil and crops yields a return only sufficient for a bare existence. When work is

* Reprinted with considerable abridgment from *American Journal of Sociology,* Vol. *52,* pp. 1-17, 1946, by permission of The University of Chicago Press. Copyright 1946 by The University of Chicago.

mainly done by hands and feet, the advantage of division of work is reduced. Extensive organization in such enterprises gives no appreciable profit but rather complicates human relations. This accounts for the fact that among the peasant society the basic group is usually small.

The smallness of the cooperative group is characteristic of peasantry. Peasants, unlike nomads, live in settled communities. They are nonaggressive because, on the one hand, extension of land beyond the ability of cultivation means little to them, and, on the other, living in a rural environment, they face no immediate threat of innovation or invasion. Security is a matter of course. There seems to be no necessity for any militant organization on a large scale.

This is perhaps one reason why the family is so predominant in the structure of social organization in a peasant community. The family in a peasant community is a sufficient unit to provide the necessary and minimum social cooperation in everyday economic pursuits. Such cooperation is maintained by, or rather an extension of, another main task of the human race, that of reproduction. The mutual reinforcement of the related functions of life achieves a strong solidarity.

The small size of the basic social unit seems quite contrary to the popular conception of the Chinese social structure. It is often believed that in China the family unit is large. There are big houses in which a large number of kin live together, but this is found only in the gentry. Among Chinese peasants, the basic social unit is numerically small and is mainly composed of parents and children. Evidences from various studies in rural China show no exception. The average varies from four to six persons. However, from the point of view of structure, the basic group among the Chinese peasants is more than a family, as defined by anthropologists. It sometimes includes children who have grown up and married. I have called it the "expanded family." If the principle of expansion carries far, the result will be a clanlike big house, as seen among the gentry; but among peasants such expansion is limited. As a rule, lateral expansion—brothers continuing to live together after marriage—is rare and unstable. The usual practice is that the aged parents stay with one of the married sons. Without any social provision for the old, it seems very natural that the parents should be taken care of by their son.

In a mobile community, nomadic or industrial, an individual has his own locus. He moves about by himself and acquires his social status on his own behalf. But for a settled peasant, it seems that all his activities are bound to the group. The family is a self-sufficient and self-supporting group, in which he maintains his existence and perpetuates his kind. It is the center from which his relations, kinship, local, and professional, ramify. The singularism in extension of social relations differs in principle from the pluralism in modern society. Individuals in such a structure are counted only as members of a certain family.

The traditional ideology in China suppresses individualism in favor of familism. The meaning, or value, of the individual's existence is defined by its being a link in the chain of social continuity which is concretely conceived in terms of descent. The most important task of a man is to continue the family line. Of the three traditional charges against an undutiful son, the failure in giving offspring comes first. The interest of the group is paramount even in such affairs as in modern society are strictly private. The collective responsibility of family members in social contributions or offenses has only recently been abolished by law, though it still persists in practice. Fathers will be held responsible for the crime committed by their children. Wives and sons are often killed solely because their husbands and fathers are revolutionists. Even now district (county) jails are full of prisoners who have committed no crime other than the fact that some of their family members happen to be deserters from the army. I am not certain whether such imprisonment is lawful, but this is the practice and no legitimate protests have been made. For the present purpose, I am taking it as a living evidence of the collectiveness of the family group and the nonrecognition of the individual as such in social responsibility.

The same principle is found in the part played by the family in wider organizations. In community organization the family, not the individual, is the unit. In practice the basic constituents of a local government are families. Local assemblies are represented by family heads; local taxes are collected from families. The family thus is a civic unit. Few have questioned the validity of the family basis of civic society, although democracy in the modern sense is essentially a recognition of equal rights among individuals. Thus in Western democracies individuals enter the civic society directly and the family has no place in the political structure. It is interesting to note that, when modern civic structure is introduced to China, the traditional form persists. The family still supersedes the individual.

The family is thus the basic unit in the social structure of rural China. From this basis larger organizations are formed, but on the whole these are not strong. The peasants recognize kinship. They gather on ceremonial occasions and help each other when they are in need. But it is rare to find wider kinship organizations of a permanent nature among the peasants, and even mutual obligations among the relatives are not pronounced. In local organizations, neighborhood is universal. But as I have seen in the villages near Lake Tai, each house counts five families on either side of it as its neighbors. In Yunnan, however, neighborhood forms a permanent group and possesses a common temple. The function of the neighborhood is limited to ceremonial assistance and recreation. When we come to the village organization, we find that it is not organized by the peasants alone but by the gentry as well. It is, in fact, a rule of the gentry over the peasants. As far as the peasants are concerned, social organization stops at the loosely organized neighborhood. In the traditional structure, peasants live in small cells, which are the families, without strong ties between the cells. They carry on productive work in this kind of small cooperative group. They maintain their own subsistence and at the same time support the living of those who occupy higher positions in the social structure.

The chief occupation of the Chinese people as a nation is agriculture, and they depend on land for their living. As population increases, less fertile land can be utilized. Gradually there emerges a class of landowners who can afford to live without working on the land while they still enjoy the benefits of the land on account of their privileges as owners. This can be done either by employing farm laborers to work for them or by renting the land to tenants. The rise of a nonlaboring rentier class is an important step in the evolution of an agrarian community.

Farm work under primitive technique is drudgery. It is quite conceivable that those who can afford to live without being engaged in hard work will do so even at the expense of their standard of living. It seems that there are two ways of reducing the painful experience in productive pursuits: either to improve tools and utilize animal and natural power or to shift the burden to others. The first is exploitation of nature and the second is exploitation of man. In an agrarian community, when the population has increased to such a huge size as in China, the cost of human labor becomes even lower than animal labor. Under such circumstances, the first way is blockaded. It is small surprise to see that the tools used by the Chinese peasants of today are very much similar to those excavated from ancient archeological sites. Wooden wheels, an old invention, can be seen in their most primitive form on village roads, and even these are not extensively used. Loads are carried on human shoulders with the assistance of a pole. Exploitation of man is the only choice that one can make to avoid physical toil in getting a living.

I venture to think that the indulgence in physical comfort in the form of avoiding any sort of labor, which finds its highest expression in opium-smoking, is a reaction of the peasantry against hardship. Sharp contrasts of this kind are often observed in all cultures. Among the starving mass, the value of food is always exalted; the most extravagant cookery and exotic recipes are always found in poverty-stricken nations; the reckless and lavish maharajas vie with each other in gastronomical display in a famished India. Under the most strict code of sexual relations, periodic license is customary. When a long-suppressed desire becomes realizable, it drives the fortunate few to be unscrupulous. An unduly heightened value usually arises from the negation of the popular practice and normal discipline. The elevation from the common order becomes the goal of the common people. The hardworking Chinese peasant looks toward leisure and comfort with unusual eagerness. The denial by the laboring class of its own importance is expressed in the generally accepted popular saying, as first epigrammatically pronounced by Mencius: "Those who earn their living by labor are destined to be ruled." The self-abdication of the laboring class as the master of their own destiny is the foundation of a social dichotomy—a leisure class on top of hardworking peasants.

There is a social necessity for the gentry to develop a more elaborate social structure for themselves. The economic basis for their class is rent. It is a privilege which has to be protected by political power. Mencius' dictum has to be read in the sense that, in a community essentially agrarian, unless those who do not earn their living by labor can rule the peasants, their position is not secure. It is because an economically unproductive class living upon privileges is politically vulnerable. For the sake of security, the gentry has to be better organized. Better organization spells power. Gentry as a class differs from peasantry both in kinship and in local organizations.

I have said that among the peasants the basic social cooperative group is small. Among the gentry it is different. Big kinship groups are found. Peasants earn their living mainly by their own efforts. They work and they live. The sense of independence is strong. Although the Chinese peasants usually live with their parents who are too old to work and depend on the younger generation for support, the rule of the old is not deeprooted. An adult son who tills the land and brings back necessities for the household is not living under the thumb of his father. But when a person does not earn his living by his own labor but depends on rent, the situation is different. An absentee landowner needs political power for his protection. In holding their privilege, the gentry are militant, as they must be. To be politically powerful and influential, the organization of the gentry has to be big and strong. Division of the household and independence of the young, as very frequently seen among the peasants, are definitely disintegrative forces and will weaken the group solidarity. In the town where I was reared, I was familiar with a number of big houses, each a colony of a number of dependent families, under the rule of a powerful and centralized authority. The head of the house holds the power in financial and social matters, maintaining the discipline of the members and enforcing the family laws. Some of them even have their own law courts. Patriarchy works out in its full strength. The son refers to his father before others as "the terrible old one," which he literally is. He enjoys no intimacy with his father, who seldom laughs in front of his children. A good description of the patriarchical relation is found in the novel *The Dream of the Red Chamber*.

A big house is an empire by itself. The members, like subjects, live under the rule and whim of the patriarch. They know no independence until they themselves are promoted to the position of a ruler. They depend upon their house for their living; their career is determined by the house; for whatever they are worth the house is solely responsible. By such a strong kinship organization, the political power of the house in the larger community is secured. The members, even the servants, of the house enter the power structure of the nation with facility. The position they hold in the government in turn supports the privilege of the house, and their economic basis is thus guaranteed.

As the size of the house grows, generation after generation (the idea being that five generations should live under the same roof), the tension within the organization grows, too. Once an emperor questioned a patriarch by what means he ruled his house successfully. The latter answered by writing three characters: forbearance, forbearance, and forbearance. Yet forbearance has its limits. Houses disperse. But to maintain close relationship among the kin is necessary for the gentry. Then clan appears. A clan is a disinte-

grated house; the individual family in the clan gains a certain amount of independence, while kinship unity is preserved for the common interest.

I think that both the big-family (or the house) system and the clan are the gentry's organizations. Sometimes among the peasants, the clan is found, but it is of another kind. In Yunnan, for instance, I have seen that in villages local organization is formed in terms of clan which includes even members of different surnames. Functionally these are not strictly kinship groups. I shall leave the question open as to the nature of the so-called clan-village. I rather suspect that such an organization among the peasants is a local organization, not a kinship organization. But I am sure that the clan is not universal in China, and the most effective and elaborate clans are found in the gentry. A clan organization among the landless or even petty owners is superfluous. Take my own clan, for instance. When the need for protecting our joint interest in land-holding disappeared, our clan faded away. What is left now is only a name.

For a clan to be effective, it must possess some common property—invariably land. A piece of land is usually contributed to the organization by a member who is a government official, the ostensible pretext being that the products of the land may cover the expenses necessary in the keeping-up of the ancestors' tombs and regular sacrifices. But, in fact, this common property is a common security with which the position of the clan may be maintained in the wider power structure of the community. It finances the education of the young members so that they may be able to enter the scholar class and attain high official positions and protect the interests of their kinsmen. Members of the same clan are under obligation to help each other when help is called for. The clan organization, furthermore, has the authority to set up sanctions against any alienation of land. As is widely observed, individual contract in land transaction is not valid unless it is signed by clan members of the seller. This shows how closely the clan organization is linked up with land rights.

Clan organization, which defines the propinquity among unilateral kin, regulates the inheritance of land in order to prevent any disruption caused by a confusion in the line of descent and to enforce the solidarity of the group. This is known as the *tsung fa* in China, the system of descent. It is of little account when no problem of inheriting large estates is involved. In the villages of petty owners, as I have seen in Yunnan, the spirit of the *tsung fa* is weak. In other words, the people there do not observe strictly the rule of inheritance according to patrilineal descent. What the peasants in general care for most is the maintenance of the working efficiency of the basic group. It has been the custom that, when a married son dies, a substitute will be found to take the place of the deceased, and, when the substitute becomes a widower, he will take another wife. As a result the family unit is bound by no biological relations at all. However, the basic working group achieves its continuity, and life carries on. This will not happen among the sophisticated gentry. The gentry who live on land rights have reasons to adhere to orderliness and discipline in order to hold the property.

The solidarity of the big house and the clan is only one aspect of the strategy of the propertied class. To be powerful and to achieve security, big houses have to be aligned. This is done through an extension of affinal relations. Marriage has been regarded as a family affair and has been customarily defined as an alliance of houses. Choice of mate is made on the ground of family status. Through marriage a number of big houses are confederated into a powerful group. But if we turn to the peasants, we shall see that the main consideration in matchmaking is the working ability of the girl.

It is true that in China kinship is the key to social organization, but it would be wrong to think that kinship is itself so dear to the people. Kinship is only a means by which social groups are organized for different purposes. I do not think that kinship possesses any force of extension by itself and is valued as such. Procreation can be carried on without extensive recognition of kinship ties. It is so recognized because such ties can be used to organize social groups for definite purposes. In China it is the gentry who find it necessary, in order to be powerfully organized, to employ the principle of kinship extensively.

The peasantry and the gentry can further be contrasted by showing their ecological positions. To understand the rural economy of China, one has to bear in mind the fact that, with a very small farm under cultivation, land is closed to ambition. The average farm in China is only a few acres. (In Yunnan a good-sized farm is only about one acre.) Small farming makes accumulation of capital impossible. Villagers put it neatly: "Land breeds no land." In a community in which industry and commerce are not developed, in which land has already done its best, and in which the pressure of increasing population is felt, ambitious people have to seek their fortune not through ordinary economic enterprises but through acquiring power legally or illegally. Just the same they must leave their village for good. When they obtain wealth, they may come back to their village to acquire land, but if they retire to live in the village, the pressure of population will be borne upon them and soon wear them out—and after a few generations the big house will break

down into a number of petty owners
again. Therefore, it is essential for the
rich to keep away from the village.
The place where they can maintain their
power and wealth is the town.

Towns in traditional China are not
founded on manufacturing or commerce.
In China the chief industries, such as
textiles, are mainly peasant occupations.
Owing to the smallness of the farm, the
peasants cannot live entirely upon the
land. It is a matter of necessity to have
some additional income. Moreover, since
agriculture cannot give full employment
to the peasants, they have plenty of time
to carry on industrial jobs in their homestead. Peasants live largely in a self-sufficient economy. The amount they buy and
sell is small. If their commercial activities
are centralized in a fixed locality, say a
town, it will take a big area to support it.
It is feasible only in those areas where
communication is easy and inexpensive,
such as in the Lower Yangtze Valley. In
most parts of China the periodical market
takes the place of the town. It gathers
only once in several days. Its size and
frequency of gathering can be adjusted to
the temporary need from time to time. It
seems clear that the permanent town has
no place in the traditional rural economy.

The traditional town is the seat of
the gentry. The gentry class symbolizes
political and financial power. The town in
which I was born, and which I know
very well, mainly consists of residences of
the gentry, rice stores, pawnshops, tea
houses, and private gardens. There are
also a number of tailors, carpenters,
blacksmiths, and goldsmiths and other
craftsmen. The rice stores and the pawnshops are financial establishments. The
peasants, when pressed by rent or tax or
other crises, have to sell their rice to the
stores at a low price. At the time when
their reserves are eaten up, they come to
the stores to buy at a high price. The rice
stores are therefore similar in nature to

the pawnshops. Tea houses, big gardens,
and magnificent residences are also the
paraphernalia of the gentry. From morning until nightfall, the leisured gentlemen
gather in the tea houses to amuse themselves in sipping tea, in listening to the
story-tellers, in talking nonsense, in gambling, and in smoking opium. It would
appear to a New Englander that such a
town is no better than a concentration
camp of voluntary deserters from life.
But, to them, leisure means prestige as
well as privilege. By displaying the leisure
at their disposal, they stand high in the
eyes of the lower classes. The professionals who live in the town are dependent on the gentry for their employment.
Few of them keep their own shops. They
are called to work in the employers'
houses. This reminds us of medieval
feudalism in western Europe.

Such towns do not lack their charm.
If one is prepared to amuse one's self in
an artistic expression of life, there are
hundreds of small attractions here that
win his admiration. I myself have often
missed much of the delicious food of my
native town and the specialties of all the
towns which I used to visit in my boy-
hood. I will not hesitate to advise a visi-
tor to Soochow to spend at least one day
in a tea house, where he will be aston-
ished at finding the cultured eloquence
with which the average customer talks
and the mellowed and humorous outlook
on life he has achieved. But one will be
grossly mistaken if one thinks that this
represents the ways and manners of the
Chinese mass.

The mass of peasants do not live in
the town. They look at the seat of the
gentry with a mixed feeling of repulsion
and admiration. They support the living
of the minority by paying taxes, rent, and
interests. The annual tribute is their burden. In the Yangtze Valley, with the
social conditions of which I am most
familiar, I believe, it will not be exag-

gerating to say that half of the yield of peasants goes to the town. If the economic reason is still not sufficient to arouse the ill will of the peasant toward the town, he will no longer remain undisturbed in the village when he finds his unsatisfied wife run away from home to work as a maid in a gentleman's big house which he dare not enter. However, the town remains the ideal, the dream, and the incentive of the peasants. It seems that they are not antagonistic toward the town, nor the gentry, as such. What they are against is their own inability to become one of those who exploit them. As long as they believe that paradise is not closed to them, they have no desire to deny that that is where their own hopes and wishes lie.

It would be unfair to the gentry if my analysis stops here. So far we have seen that the gentry is a class which is pre-eminently parasitic. The question then will be raised as to how such a system of exploitation could persist for a long period. Is the cultural achievement of the gentry, with which the peasants have little to do, sufficient to justify their existence? The rich in the town must make more tangible and concrete contributions before they can win respect and gratitude from the peasants. In the eyes of the peasants the gentry do give them political protection. But am I contradicting myself when, on the one hand, I have said that the gentry hold political power for their own interest which means the protection of their own rights of collecting rent from the peasants, and, on the other, I now state that the gentry are protectors of the peasants? It is true that the peasants are the exploited class in the traditional structure and the gentry are their immediate exploiters, but this is true only from our point of view. For the peasants themselves the situation is not so defined. As long as the right of private ownership is recognized, rent payment is an approved

obligation of the tenants. Usurers are hated, but the rate of interest is agreed upon when the loans are made. If the gentry are exploiting the peasants, they do so through institutional means and within institutional limits. Rent and interest are fixed. Abuse of power is found only when the peasants fail to fulfil the contract. There is, however, another form of exploitation which is beyond the control of the peasants, and that is the absolute monarchical power unchecked by popular will and unbounded as the whims of the monarch are unbounded. Against this power, the peasants have to seek protection from the gentry. To make this point clear, I have to go further into the power structure of traditional China.

The center of the power structure is the absolute monarch. From the monarch, power is intrusted to the hierarchy of officials. On the vast continent, with bad communication systems, power is centralized only in name but not in fact. Officials of every rank enjoy such an amount of authority as their immediate superiors will tolerate. "The monarch is as remote as the heaven itself." That which rules the people is the hierarchy of officials. Since the officials are responsible only to their superiors, with the monarch far at the top, there is no legalized mechanism of popular check upon the power. The rights of the people are not protected by law. The welfare of the people is hung by a thread on the good conscience of the power hierarchy. Good conscience rarely appears in those who personify power. Therefore political power becomes sometimes even "more fearful than tigers." Protection from the encroachment of the power upon one's own rights is thus essential. This is achieved not by organized popular action, which results in Western democracy, but by personal approach to the power hierarchy. Since the low official receives power from the one of a higher rank, he has to yield to the will of his superior. If one can influence the superior through personal means, the lower official has to behave amiably toward one, lest he should get into trouble. The direct way of access to the power hierarchy is to enter officialdom one's self. If a man is himself an official, he can protect his and his relatives' private interests not only by the power intrusted in his hands but also by his relation with his fellow-officials. This kind of political maneuver, traditionally known as face-saving, rises from the absence of the rule of law. When a community is ruled by sheer personal will, court politics is inevitable.

It should now be clear why the gentry, being a class of people living on privileges, are anxious to enter into officialdom. If they are not in alliance with the power hierarchy, their position as landowners is threatened. The wrongs done them can never be redressed. Alienation of land by powerful persons is not infrequent. It is a recognized necessity for the rich to hold a position in the hierarchy. Clan organization and affinal confederation are sufficient because they are systems of security through the establishment of a relation to the power hierarchy by kinship.

The gentry mediates between the ruler and the ruled. In the history of China the central power is usually in the hands of alien invaders or social outcasts who seize the political power by unscrupulous means. As soon as the monarch is dethroned, the gentry will join hands with him by filling the rank and file of the officialdom. In their official capacity, they are agents of the ruler, but in their private capacity they are closely related to, and share common interests with, the ruled. Herein lies the popular though not thorough check on the absolute and often alien monarch.

In the traditional system of government the tentacles of the central power stop at the *hsien* (county). Each *hsien*

consists of a number of villages which are usually organized locally by the villagers. The local organization possesses common property and regulates common enterprises such as religious ceremonies and irrigation. The executives of such an organization are elected not by all the representatives of the families but by the respected elders of the village. The respected elders are those who possess land and "face," i.e., connection with the officialdom or with the gentry in town. They are the lower rank of the gentry who are not rich enough to leave the village and live in town.

The central power operates on the people in the following way: When the central government orders the magistrate of the *hsien* to collect taxes or conscribe services, the latter will send agents to the village to carry out the order. The agents themselves are conscripts from the villages. They enjoy no prestige in their own community. In practice, they are only messengers of the magistrate. The government order passes unofficially from the hand of the agent to the local headmen who occupy no official position in the government constitution. The order then will be announced and discussed in the village teashops. All those present may participate. No vote will be taken, but the headman will decide according to the public opinion as well as to his own sense of appropriateness whether the order should be followed. If the decision is in the negative, the agent will be sent back to the magistrate without achieving anything. The responsibility of the failure in executing the order is his. He will be beaten or otherwise punished for the failure. However, court politics follows on the other hand. The elders of the village will call on the magistrate or ask someone among the town gentry to call on the magistrate for negotiation. Since the gentry have connections with the power hierarchy, the magistrate has to consider their suggestions and modify his order in a way he thinks fit. The actual practice is complicated indeed. The maneuver on both sides may involve the mobilization of a big sphere of the power structure. Sometimes the issue may gradually move up to the monarch himself. Very often the monarch, to grant some personal favor, intervenes in local affairs in a way contrary to his own decrees. For a local government official, the gentry are his opposition, although the opposition is usually not frontal and finally appears in the order from his own superior. Although an official, he is in his private capacity one of the gentry. He will write letters to his fellow-officials asking favor for his own kin, relatives, or local people. The gentry-official is the pivot in the traditional Chinese power structure.

Whatever one may say for or against the traditional pattern, it is clear that, as long as the peasants live in the structure, they have to rely on the gentry for protection against the encroachment of the absolute ruler and his officials. . . .

In discussing the ecological differentiation of the peasants and the gentry, I have shown that those who like to hold their privilege as a leisure class have to stay outside the village. This is because in agriculture there is little hope for the accumulation of wealth. It seems that a peasant who works on the land is bound to the land as a peasant. Therefore, we may ask how the gentry emerges. Of course, we must admit that, since there is no social barrier preventing a peasant from entering into the gentry if he can afford to lead a leisurely life, there will be those hard-working peasants who strive to rise from the bottom. But it will take them several generations to climb up the social ladder, each generation promoting itself a little. Despite thrift and endurance, this is not only a long but also a haphazard way, because in the rural community misfortunes of all kinds are not

uncommon. Drought and flood may cause famine. Epidemics may ruin a family. In a period of political disturbance bandits are as bad as locusts in the dry years. It will be most rare for a family to keep up its morale for several generations and to have no misfortune strike at them in the meantime.

Another factor which prevents a hard-working and well-to-do peasant family from rising is the high pressure of population. Upon these the pressure of population is particularly strong. For among the leisure class the birth rate is low because of their degenerated physical conditions, and among the poor peasants infantile mortality is high because of the lack of good care. But among hard-working, well-to-do peasants, the birth rate is as high as that of the poor peasants and the death rate is comparatively low owing to their better living standard. Such a family grows fast. If it cannot expand its estate at the same rate, its standard of living will sink in the next generation. It already required fairly strenuous efforts for a peasant family to maintain its footing, but the hope of rising into the leisure class is slight.

It is quite natural that the common tendency among the peasants is not to rise on the social ladder but rather to sink toward the bottom. A petty owner may become a tenant when he sells his land as misfortune befalls him. He may further sink from a tenant to a landless farm laborer. He may in the end die disgracefully or disappear from the village. These outcasts are desperate. They have nothing to lose but their life of drudgery. They leave the village and plunge themselves into banditry or smuggling, or join the army, or seek employment as servants in big gentry houses. These are economically nonproductive jobs, but it is only by taking up such jobs, in addition to good luck, that the outcasts from the rural society can hope to obtain wealth quickly. Of course, hundreds and thousands of such fortune-seekers die in despair and are forgotten by the world. But, once loosened from the soil, they have freed themselves from the bond of the land. They are the dissatisfied class and thus revolutionary in nature. When the ruling class is strong, they are suppressed. Only a few reach their aim through various kinds of more or less unlawful ways. But if the ruling class is degenerate and weak, they are the uprising group aiming at power. In Chinese history there are several instances where new dynasties were inaugurated by such desperate outcasts.

In peacetime the few successful upstarts when they have obtained wealth will buy land and insinuate themselves into the leisure class. They are looked down upon and looked at with a prejudiced eye by the gentry. Only gradually and especially by means of affinal alliance, are they admitted into the upper layer of the social structure. Not until one of the family members enters into the scholar group and into officialdom is their position in the gentry consolidated.

The gentry are maintained economically by owning land and politically by occupying a position in officialdom. As a landowning class they have the leisure to learn classical literature which is the professional requirement of an official. For nearly a thousand years the monarch has offered regular examinations to recruit officials from the literati. Only a few low classes are excluded from the right to take part in such examinations. Theoretically men from the peasantry are free to enter into the competition. And there are notable cases in which the son of a poor peasant learned the classics on the back of his buffalo while he was working in the field and attained high honor in the examination. But, after all, these are exceptions, for otherwise such stories would not be circulated like legends. It is true that in China there is no such social class

system as the caste system, but it is another question as to whether the Chinese class system possesses high mobility. I have no statistical information to prove the case, but from studies on existing rural communities it is clear that a child from a peasant family engaged in farm work has little chance of receiving a high-school education. I cannot help being cautious in accepting the popular belief that in the good old days everyone had a chance to become an official through equitable examination. The mobility between peasantry and gentry has been rather limited. It is needless to add that the existence of the belief among the peasant in the possibility of promotion to the gentry is important because it gives an incentive and eventually stabilizes the structure at large.

Conversely we may ask how frequently the members of the gentry return to peasantry. As far as my own knowledge goes, I cannot find a single case where a good-for-nothing gentleman picks up farming work again. It seems impossible that the gentry should return to the farm. Manual labor is highly deplored in the current ideology in China, even today. The gentry are especially conscious of it. A long gown that signifies leisure is the emblem of honor and prestige and is the last thing a gentleman will cast away. It is worth more than one's life. I had an uncle who became destitute by his fortieth year. He lived in a bare room and was penniless. But he carried on his life as usual in the tearooms and wore his long gowns until his death. The scene of his death was most pathetic. He lingered on at his last moment and was unwilling to close his eyes, as a cousin of my clan put it who visited him on his deathbed. He was worrying that he would not die as a gentleman, dressed in silk and buried in a coffin of good quality. My cousin comforted him by showing him all that he was going to have when he ceased to breathe. He smiled and then passed away in satisfaction. This incident presents in full the inner psychology of the gentry. The question will then arise as to how he could afford to live up to the standard of a gentleman. The answer is that he was helped by his clan members. The clan is a system of mutual security. When I was young, I frequently witnessed the visits of my clan uncles to my home. They were poor, but they talked and laughed without mentioning any financial need. When they left us, my grandmother used to give them a handsome amount of money as a present. My grandmother was not rich then. I knew very well that she had sent a maid to the pawnshop from our back door in order to get enough money to aid our clan members who were in distress. The same spirit leads an official to offer jobs to his clan members regardless of their ability. The sense of responsibility for mutual aid and collective security among the clan members is stronger than the sense of duty as an official of the government.

The system of clan social security which prevails among the gentry encourages dependence especially when the class has kept away from participating in productive work. A child reared in such an environment is detached from the life of the people. He lives in a big house devoid of sunshine; he grows up in the reverence of the past, in the shadow of his ances-

tors, from whom his privileges are inherited. From the petty court politics among the family members he learns to put on a feigned obedience, is imbued with a sense of futility of all efforts, and is trivial, resigned, conservative, and cowardly. Physically he is weak, slender, and sometimes sterile. Of the six of my clan uncles, three have no children of their own. A similar state of affairs is found among many of my relatives. It seems that the lack of initiative and aggressiveness lead eventually to physical sterility. The gentry in China, like the city dwellers in the West, are the dying population, by which I mean that they cannot replace themselves. They have to rely upon recruits from the countryside.

Posed on the peak of the social pyramid, the gentry possess prestige and privilege. Prestige and privilege attract the daring and the aggressive individuals from the classes below. The new recruits revitalize the gentry, but, when they are assimilated, they become pacified and neutralized. The energy that may cause upheavals is channeled into the petty mobility in the social structure and is finally eliminated in the pattern of leisurely life. The gentry class is in fact a safety valve in social changes. Conservatism becomes the rule of Chinese society, and China as a culture is singular in the history of human kind in its stability and perpetuation.

It is, from one point of view, accurate and correct to say that Chinese social structure has been characterized by clans, among other institutions. But as we have learned in the preceding selection, not all Chinese had equal access to clanship, not all had equal opportunity to participate in clans. And if we recognize that clans and clanship are more than formal sociological principles—that they imply and convey an underlying set of values and a basic philosophy of life—we can see that there are highly specific forces which give gentry access to these values and inhibit the peasantry's access to them.

The idea that people have different degrees of access to the values of their culture not only applies to the positive and desirable ends of social living, but it also has reference to deviant and criminal behavior. As Merton has pointed out, *". . . socially deviant behavior* [is] just as much a product of a given social structure as *conformist behavior."* [5] One way of stating the problem of the differential access to culture as influenced by social-structural position is the problem of *". . . how some social structures exert a definite pressure upon certain persons in the society to engage in nonconforming rather than conforming conduct.* If we can locate groups peculiarly subject to such pressures, we should expect to find fairly high rates of deviant behavior in these groups, not because the human beings comprising them are compounded of distinctive biological tendencies but because they are responding normally to the social situation in which they find themselves." [6] Carrying through logically on this basic tenet, Merton suggests the *". . . central hypothesis that aberrant behavior may be regarded sociologically as a symptom of dissociation between culturally prescribed aspirations and socially structured avenues for realizing these aspirations."* [7] There are many uses and tests to which such a theoretical frame of reference can be put, and we will have the opportunity on many different occasions to refer to this philosophy of sociology. One of the conclusions which Professor Merton has drawn by applying his hypothesis to certain data, in his classic essay on "Social Structure and Anomie," can be excerpted in the following fashion:

> But whatever the differential rates of deviant behavior in the several social strata, and we know from many sources that the official crime statistics uniformly showing higher rates in the lower strata are far from complete or reliable, it appears from our analysis that the greatest pressures toward deviation are exerted upon the lower strata . . . Given the American stigmatization of manual labor *which has been found to hold uniformly in all social classes,* and the absence of realistic opportunities for advancement beyond this level, the result is a marked tendency toward deviant behavior . . . The avenues available for moving toward this goal are largely limited by the class structure to those of deviant behavior. . . . Despite our persisting open-class-ideology, advance toward the success-goal is relatively rare and notably difficult for those armed with little formal education and few economic resources. The dominant pressure leads toward the gradual attenuation of legitimate, but by and large ineffectual, strivings and the increasing use of illegitimate, but more or less effective, expedients.
>
> Of those located in the lower reaches of the social structure, the culture makes incompatible demands. On the one hand, they are asked to orient their conduct toward the prospect of large wealth—'Every man a king,' said Marden and Carnegie and Long—and on the other, they are largely denied effective opportunities to do so institutionally. The consequence of this structural inconsistency is a high rate of deviant behavior. . . . Within this context, Al Capone represents the triumph of amoral allegiance over morally prescribed 'failure,' when the channels of vertical mobility are closed or narrowed *in a society which places a high premium on economic affluence and social ascent for all its members.* . . . A comparatively rigidified class structure, a caste order, may limit

---

[5] Merton, 1957, p. 121.
[6] *Ibid.,* p. 132.
[7] *Ibid.,* p. 134.

opportunities far beyond the point which obtains in American society today. It is only when a system of cultural values extols, virtually above all else, certain *common* success-goals, *for the population at large* while the social structure rigorously restricts or completely closes access to approved modes of reaching these goals *for a considerable part of the same population,* that deviant behavior ensues on a large scale. . . . Goals are held to transcend class lines, not to be bounded by them, yet the actual social organization is such that there exist class differentials in accessibility to the goals.[8]

The last sentence in the selection from Professor Merton's "Social Structure and Anomie" also applies to the situation in China, about which we have just read. Although this over-all problem of the social-structural sources of deviant behavior obtains in this Chinese case, it is important to bear in mind that deviant or criminal behavior is as "cultural"—in the sense of being "natural" or "expectable"—as is conformist or noncriminal behavior. Either one derives from surrounding and impinging social-structural forces, and the "special case" of deviant behavior, if we wish to consider it "special," only illustrates in highly accentuated and kaleidoscopic fashion the general principle that people will have access only to a limited range in the cultural spectrum; therefore, they will be able to transmit to their children only an equally limited range of the cultural spectrum, *depending on where they are located in the social structure of their society.*

In any discussion of social structure and personality, especially one which refers to deviant behavior, the question of "normalcy" or "health" or "sickness" in the psychological sense is often raised. This is a question which we will consider in greater detail in the final two chapters of this book. In the meantime, however, it is important to remember that it is usually persons in the higher social strata who apply these labels. By lower-class standards, for example, the conformist patterns of the upper-middle class and upper classes could be considered deviant.

As Professor Merton has pointed out, deviance is a normal response to social-structural pressures—even in the middle and upper classes, as a complete reading of his paper clearly indicates. At the same time, however, such deviance is often called "sick," "psychopathic," "acting out," "disturbed," and the like. Does the answer or the truth of the matter lie somewhere in between both extremes, or are both conceptualizations valid?

Professor Merton ". . . abandons the position, held by various individualistic theories, that different rates of deviant behavior in diverse groups and social strata are the accidental result of different proportions of pathological personalities found in these groups and strata." [9] If we omit the word "accidental" from the last statement, then we have a description of a theoretical position which does not necessarily have to be adandoned in its entirety. Instead, the proposition can be stated as follows:

People who manifest the kinds of deviant behavior often found in the lower social strata are almost always confronted with an unusual conflict. On one hand,

---

[8] *Ibid.,* pp. 144-146.
[9] *Ibid.,* p. 121.

they have incorporated into their "selves" the values and goals and aspirations which are also provided for members of the higher social strata—the desirables of wealth, comfort, health, adequate shelter and fine food, entertainment, modish clothing, education, and the like. On the other hand, members of the lower social strata are largely denied access to these values and goals by the blocking-off of the avenues and means for reaching these goals. But since these goals have been incorporated into individual self-systems, these goals also become motivations. The denial of access to the realization of these motivations is essentially a conflict of ends and means, and conflicts of this nature always produce high levels of *anxiety*. Anxiety is always discomforting, if not painful.

Now the presence of anxiety is not necessarily indicative of psychological pathology, but if the source of the anxiety is constant enough, and produces a sufficiently *high* level of anxiety, pathological-type behavior results. The conflict of ends and means is much stronger and more intense among members of the lower socio-economic strata. Thus, the various manifestations of the resulting anxiety, especially the deviant or "pathological" ones, would be found with a much greater frequency in the lower social strata. Hence, the proportions of "pathological" personalities in different groups or strata are neither accidental, random, nor fortuitous. Rather, they are the results of particular kinds of social-structural pressures. (It should, of course, be emphasized that we are speaking here of deviant behavior which is sociologically or institutionally relevant, not of personal or idiosyncratic neurosis.)

As in the Chinese situation, in which these principles clearly apply, it must also be borne in mind that the *types* of deviant behavior which people in Western society manifest are also functions of class status. For example, the *types* of deviant behavior found in the higher social strata are almost always more impersonal and less directed against property than is the deviant behavior of the lower social strata. Income-tax evasion and chicanery, stock-market fraud, bribery involving high government officials, and the like, are types of behavior which are *available* to members of the higher social strata but which are not to members of the lower. Thus, while learning modes of deviance in the course of growing up—and this is probably part of almost everyone's upbringing—children in the higher social strata can more easily be taught taboos against "acting out" against persons and property; by similar token, we cannot assume that children in the lower social strata grow up with values which predispose them to deviance by the impersonal means of complex financial transactions and dealings.

SUMMARY

We have attempted in this chapter to lay down and illustrate two working principles. Through the case of the Kaingang Indians, we illustrated the principle that the modal personality of a group cannot be understood apart from the social structure in which it has its being. We saw in this connection how the social system of the Kaingang and their emotional inbreeding help to "keep each other going," and how these tie in with what Henry has called their "obsessive character structure."

With these sets of relationships in mind, we then went on to sharpen our theoretical lenses by endeavoring to illumine the proposition that although personality must be understood within a context of social structure, people's *location* in the social structure of a society determines to which elements, patterns, or values in the culture of that society they will have access. We noted the importance of this principle in the Chinese case illustration as well as in connection with deviant behavior in American society. This theoretical tool will reappear constantly in the chapters to follow—from the discussions of social structure and socialization through the final two chapters, which will deal with social structure and psychosis.

BIBLIOGRAPHY AND SUGGESTED READINGS

Cloward, Richard A. "Illegitimate Means, Anomie, and Deviant Behavior," *American Sociological Review,* Vol. *24,* pp. 164-176, 1959. A paper of exceptional significance which also has an excellent bibliography.

English, Horace B. and Ava Champney English. *A Comprehensive Dictionary of Psychological and Psychoanalytical Terms.* New York: Longmans, Green, 1958.

Holmberg, Alan. *Nomads of the Long Bow: The Siriono of Eastern Bolivia.* Smithsonian Institution, Institute of Social Anthropology, Publication No. *10,* 1950. An unusually striking description of a people constantly on the verge of starvation who roam the jungle in small isolated bands.

Kluckhohn, Clyde. *Navaho Witchcraft.* Papers of the Peabody Museum of American Archaeology and Ethnology, Harvard University, Vol. *22,* No. 2, 1944.

Landes, Ruth. "The Personality of the Ojibwa," *Character and Personality,* Vol. *6,* pp. 51-60, 1937. The personality characteristics of a people who live in isolated family units for most of the year and who congregate during the summer months.

Lipset, Seymour M. "Democracy and Working Class Authoritarianism," *American Sociological Review,* Vol. *24,* pp. 482-501, 1959. The emphasis in this superb research is on values, but it is very much to the point of our discussion in pages 35-38. Its bibliography, too, is worth following up.

Maslow, A. H. and Bela Mittelmann. *Principles of Abnormal Psychology: The Dynamics of Psychic Illness.* New York: Harper, 1941.

Merton, Robert K. *Social Theory and Social Structure* (revised and enlarged edition). Glencoe, Ill.: The Free Press, 1957.

Postman, Leo. "Toward a General Theory of Cognition," in *Social Psychology at the Crossroads,* edited by John Rohrer and Muzafer Sherif. New York: Harper, 1951, pp. 242-272.

Turner, Ralph. "Value Conflict in Social Disorganization," *Sociology and Social Research,* Vol. *38,* pp. 301-308, 1954. An admirable presentation of the distinction between cultural goals and institutional norms.

Section II

SOCIAL STRUCTURE
AND SOCIALIZATION

Chapter 3

FAMILY STATUS
AND SOCIALIZATION

Aberle's statement of the social-structural approach to the problem of socialization is an excellent one:

> At times the relationship of socialization practice to personality is presented as a narrow circle: people who grow up in a particular type of socialization orbit reproduce the same orbit because the personalities they developed make it congenial for them to do so, or impossible for them to do otherwise. "Culture" and "personality," in this view, are in a chicken and egg relationship, and nothing more need, or can be said. If, however, socialization practices can be shown to result from social factors which have their roots in political, economic, environmental, etc., facts, then we can broaden our circle a little: factors which are not *results* of socialization practices can perhaps be seen to affect socialization practices and through them the personalities of constituent members of the society. Hence changes external to the previously mentioned "circle" would be seen as producing changes in constituent personalities.[1]

In order to break any conceptual or theoretical circle, such as the one just pointed to by Aberle, it is necessary to select arbitrarily certain specific variables which are taken as points of departure. The points at which we shall attempt to break the circle are not the only possible ones. But a beginning has to be made somewhere, and it is only by an empirical application of these points of departure that we can go on to determine other possible points in the future. Aberle suggests such points as political, economic, and environmental facts. We will use these in the discussions to follow, but as aspects of somewhat broader processes. Thus, our first sets of analyses in this chapter, beginning with the socialization of the Negro child in the border and southern states, take as their point of departure the social position of the family in the total society. In Chapter 5 we will concern ourselves with an analysis of changes in socialization practices over time, namely, changes in American and Russian socialization practices. Within these processes we shall be able to observe some of the ways in which economic and political factors can influence the content of socialization practices, and we will also have the opportunity to explore further some of the issues raised in the present chapter. In Chapter 6 we will slightly shift the focus of our analysis; that is, in Chapters 3, 4 and 5 we will center our at-

---

[1] Aberle, 1955, p. 1.

tention on the ways in which parents bring up their children and the ways in which these practices are affected by social-structural processes outside the family. We shall still be concerned with these issues in Chapter 6, but there we will look at some of the fundamental problems which people in all societies must solve, namely, problems dealing with the treatment of aggression in the course of socialization, the fantasies of young children, and the transition from childhood to adolescence.

There are two axioms which are central to the social-structural approach to socialization. The first is that *even if* there is a unitary pansocietal culture which is apparently also characteristic of a particular group within it, not all people in that group have equal access to it; or, restated, the sociocultural environment does not affect all persons in a society in the same way. In any social system different people occupy different social positions, and it is these positions which not only determine the aspects of a culture to which people have access but *they determine which aspects of a culture will be transmitted to a person in the course of growing up.* For example, American culture, as a unitary, pansocietal phenomenon, places great value on education. Theoretically, formal education is available to everyone who is capable of benefiting from it. In reality, however, this element of American culture is largely *unavailable* to the child of an unskilled menial laborer who does not earn sufficient money with which to support his family and who requires the financial assistance of his grown children. However, not only is this aspect of American culture unavailable to such a growing person, but by virtue of his parents' placement in the social structure of the United States, it is hardly likely that they would transmit to their child a compelling need or motivation to acquire such an education. Thus, for all intents and purposes, this general American culture value has very little strength for a person coming from this stratum in the social structure.

Let us take another example of this process from a culturally more homogeneous society. The island of Tikopia lies in Polynesia. This is an extremely egalitarian society divided into four clans, each of which is headed by a chief. The culture of Tikopia decrees that it is a crime to strike a chief; if a person should commit such a heinous act, his punishment is to take a canoe out to sea and never return. This is certain death. Every Tikopian learns this in the course of growing up as thoroughly as an American child learns that murder is punishable by death. The same rule, of course, is taught to a commoner-child as well as to a child who will some day become a chief by heredity. Being the son of a commoner or the son of a chief implies different placement in the social structure of Tikopia. Also, this one cultural value or law will have very different meanings and will be transmitted differently to each.

The second axiom of the social-structural approach to socialization is that *socialization is always future oriented.* Parents in any society invariably bring up their children on the assumption that they are anticipating the future for these children. As a matter of fact, this can be considered a universal parental obligation. Parents bring up their children so that the latter *will be able* to fit into a particular kind of social system when they become adults, and they invariably attempt to anticipate the particular kind of world in which these children *are going to live* and train them to live in *that* world, not necessarily the world for which they themselves were trained or the one in which they have actually lived. This is one of the principal reasons for the *persistence* of socialization practices and also one of the principal reasons for *changes* in these practices. As we shall observe in this chapter and in Chapters 4 and 5, when parents assume (often without awareness) that the world in which their children will live will be that for which they (the parents) were reared, they tend to rear their children as they themselves were brought up. When on the contrary, parents assume (often without being aware of it) that their children will live in a different kind of world they will raise them to live successfully in *that* world, even though this means that they will bring up these children differently from the ways in which they (the parents) were reared.

For example, people of the American middle class who were reared in the period between 1915 and 1929 were, in quite a few instances, brought up by their parents to be politically active and outspoken in support of unpopular causes. This was an attitude adaptive to the world in which the parents of those years lived; they had no way of anticipating that this attitude or value would become maladaptive in the late 1940's and 1950's. The parents of the latter generation appear to be bringing up their children differently with respect to outspokenness and affiliations, in almost direct contradiction to the ways in which they had been brought up. Let us take one other example, also from the United States. Those people who were brought up around 1920 were in many instances taught to abhor the idea of a standing peacetime army in America. These very same people now prepare their children to serve in this type of army, with a minimum of emotional and intellectual conflict. We very often say, "Times change." So they do, and parents usually bring up their children to live in "changing times."

THE SOCIALIZATION OF THE NEGRO CHILD IN THE BORDER AND SOUTHERN STATES*

Perhaps the best illustration of the effects of family status on the content of the socialization process is to be found in the development of the Negro child in the United States. This is an excellent starting point, because in popular everyday thinking we generally assume two alternative, though not mutually exclusive, points of view in connection with the problem of the process of a Negro child's growing up. First, it is often assumed that most American Negroes respond in much the same way to the frustrations, humilia-

tions, and objective deprivations which characterize a subordinate position in the caste structure of American society.

The second alternative is to think of variations in response to the caste structure as strictly a function of socialization experiences, that is, idiosyncratic experiences in parent-child interaction. While there is undoubtedly an element of truth in each of these points of view, it is possible to observe uniform variations within the Negro caste according to class membership. That is, not only do adult Ne-

---

* The data presented in this section are taken from E. Franklin Frazier, *Negro Youth at the Crossways: Their Personality Development in the Middle States,* Washington, D.C.: American Council on Education, 1940.

groes behave differently as a result of their class-memberships, but the process of socialization varies by class.

In line with our assertion that status positions define which aspects of a culture will be transmitted to a person in the course of growing up, let us examine the effects of class position or status on the ways in which Negro youths become aware of their racial identity. It is with this process that we shall be primarily concerned. American caste structure as a whole operates in such a fashion that Negroes must at some points in their lives learn that they have an identity different from that of the majority White population. This is a phenomenon which stems from a pansocietal American culture. However, as we shall see, the variety of ways in which this racial identity is taught in the socialization process and the meaning it has to different individuals depend in large part *on the class positions of their parents.*

The material presented here concerning the socialization of the Negro child "to be a Negro" was gathered before the second World War, before many of the social upheavals which were to change the conditions under which Negroes live in the border states, this being the area in which this study was conducted.

Let us examine some of the commonalities which cut across class lines but which are then affected differently by class status. First and foremost, a Negro's consciousness of his racial identity palls or casts a shadow over his hopes and ambitions which he has learned in common with almost all American children, Negro or White. The sharp edge to the all-American maxim that "every man can reach the top as long as he does not quit" is dulled and blunted for Negro youths by definition of their racial identity.

A second major value acquired by

2 Frazier, 1940, p. 39.

Negro youths in the course of growing up is a distrust, wariness, and suspicion of White people. A Negro youth must learn to guard against expressing his more personal feelings, especially those pertaining to relationships between the races. Most emphatically, he is taught never to say anything to Whites which might reinforce the latter's stereotypes of the Negro group. He learns never to trust White people, and even friendly Whites are suspect.

The third major value acquired in the course of socialization is that relationships between the races are governed more by local custom and opinion than by law. The Negro learns while he is growing up that although his relationships with Whites are also governed more by local custom and folkways than by legal forms, there is an entirely separate body of custom and belief applicable to Negroes alone. Thus, especially in the border and southern states, it is an unwritten rule that Negroes are confined to unskilled and menial work; only Whites may fill responsible positions requiring training, education, and skill. What is important to remember in this connection is that American culture is thoroughly imbued with values and attitudes deprecating and ascribing low status to menial and unskilled work. Furthermore, and intimately related to this, a large part of a person's self-valuation in American society is directly dependent on the *type* of work he does, in addition to the monetary returns from the work performed.

"At what age he will become aware of his racial identity and how he will be affected by this awareness are determined in part by the manner in which patterns of discrimination are transmitted to the child." [2] Let us see how this over-all process is affected by the class status of a Negro child's parents.

By lower class is meant here people

who derive their incomes from unskilled and menial labor requiring almost no responsibility, training, or education. Negro youths from such families exhibit, at least on the surface, an "acceptance" or "accommodation" to the Negro's inferior status in the society. However, they give strong indications of a concealed inner conflict over the violent contradiction between their aspirations and self-portraitures as human beings and the inferior status imposed on them by the Whites of the community. "These conflicts were revealed in their expressions of resentment toward subordination to whites, in their sporadic outbursts of aggression, and in their sullen and 'mean' dispositions, which reflected their humiliations and frustrations." [3]

Such a conflict is, to a large extent, both transmitted and reinforced by their parents who, in the daily life of the community, "accept" or are "accommodated" to the inferior social status imposed on them but who give vent to their resentments, hatreds, and rebelliousness only within the guarded security of family and home. No child of any society, or of any ethnic or racial group, can help noticing the contradictions, where they exist, between the ways in which his parents act and feel or believe. Every child looks to his parents as ego-ideals, as positive figures embodying worthwhile goals with whom he can identify and whose image he accepts or incorporates as his own. As a result of the contradictions between the ways in which his parents behave outside and within the home, the lower-class Negro child suddenly finds that he has presented to him an extremely ambivalent or inconsistent ego-ideal.

At the same time that lower-class Negro children hear their parents express resentment against the treatment they receive from Whites, these children are also frequently disillusioned with their parents. For example, if a child reports to his father a clash with a White person he will often be told "that it was his own fault and he 'should have known better.' " [4] Such an occurrence not only destroys a child's confidence in his father's power to protect and shield him against a hostile White world but it generally infuriates him. Incidents such as this are not isolated events but are repetitive and are part of a pattern. If the child is not blamed and chastised by his parents, he is at least admonished to "avoid trouble," since infuriating and humiliating incidents are inevitable. While this attitude tends to foster "accommodation" and "acceptance" it does not lessen the conflict within the child since he still observes his parents' expressions of resentment within the home against these very same incidents.

There is another conflict which is particularly relevant to the lower-class Negro. In the White lower class "fighting is closely tied up with the idea of manhood." [5] Among lower-class Negroes, boys are constantly admonished not only to "avoid trouble" but to "stand up and fight like a man" when threatened by Whites. While such a conflict of values can be observed in other groups, as in the White upper-middle class, the resolution of the conflict is much more difficult for the lower-class Negro boy—or, to state it more accurately, it is much more difficult for the parents of a lower-class Negro child to teach him how to resolve the conflict.

Lower-class Negroes, more so than any other group of Negroes in the border and southern states, are directly dependent upon Whites for their economic and material survival. Hence, lower-class Negroes must often turn to their White

---

[3] *Ibid.,* p. 41.
[4] *Ibid.,* p. 42.
[5] *Ibid.,* p. 47.

employers for financial assistance, since unskilled and menial work is the least remunerative. Often, any assertions of independence or aggression will threaten whatever economic security the lower-class Negro has. Thus, he is not only blocked by the White group from discharging his hostility, but as a parent, who is quite aware of the economic importance of suppressing hostility, he cannot present his children with a consistent set of defenses.

This psychological insecurity and inconsistency in the lower-class Negro is intensified even more by the family organization frequently found in the group. During slavery, the practices of the owners of splitting up families and selling individuals regardless of their family and kin ties prevented the establishment of a tradition of stable monogamous unions. Generally, children were kept with their mothers at least until the age of ten years, but fathers were sold regardless of the ages of their children. Together with many other forces, this helped to establish a tradition among New World Negroes of the mother-centered family (sometimes erroneously referred to as a matriarchy). The effects of this tradition are still to be observed, especially in the Negro lower class, for when a man who is unskilled and uneducated begins to feel that he cannot provide adequately for his family, he has a tendency to desert it. In large part, this desertion helps him avoid the anxieties which would be more pronounced and accentuated if he were to remain with his family and be constantly reminded of his shortcomings as a breadwinner. Such a situation frequently contributes to an unstable family situation for the lower-class Negro child. Herein we can observe one illustration of the ways in which social structure can effect, if not determine, the most fundamental facets of human life, namely, a man's re-

lationships to his wife and children. "Because of the large amount of family disorganization among lower-class Negroes, the child fails to enjoy the security, affectional as well as economic, which children in the middle and upper class enjoy." [6] Thus, economic conditions form a complete circle; they not only create a disproportionate amount of resentment, but they also block expression of these resentments; the circle is completed by the impact of the economic situation on family organization which, as we have just attempted to show, inhibits the transmission of consistent defenses necessary to cope with such anxieties and problems.

Equally important to the lower-class Negro child is the fact that he is physically more exposed to the White group— and to its hostility—than are children of either the middle or upper classes. There are several reasons for this. First, lower-class Negro women who work as domestic servants must often take their children with them to the homes of their employers since they cannot afford to hire someone to care for their children. Secondly, lower-class Negro neighborhoods are, not unlike many other lower-class neighborhoods, crowded, unpleasant, and deficient in recreational facilities. Because of this, lower-class children are often tempted to explore other areas of the cities in which they live and here, too, they have an added opportunity to come into contact with Whites. Finally, lower-class neighborhoods are often racially mixed or border on the lower-class neighborhoods of other races. As children grow older, the normal quarreling which occurs between all children takes on the racial overtones learned from parents. Hence, there are more frequent violent encounters between lower-class Negro children and Whites. Not only does this generate more bitterness in the lower-class child but it is also the earliest situation which brings

[6] *Ibid.*, p. 52.

into focus almost all of the problems discussed above regarding conflicts transmitted to children by parents.

Even in segregated schools these problems are accentuated, or at least reinforced. Not knowing how to cope with the hostile White world around him, the lower-class Negro child almost always develops a low self-esteem, sometimes consciously, and often unconsciously, feeling that he is incapable of handling the daily problems of living with which he must come to grip. In segregated schools, to say nothing of desegregated schools, teachers and administrators are invariably chosen from the upper class. These often discriminate against darker students and lower-class students, and they rarely bother to be subtle in their attempts to instill an identification with upper-class Negro values. "The effect has been to increase the sense of inferiority and insecurity, particularly among pupils from the lower class." [7]

Now let us see how the concepts and values of caste are transmitted to middle-class Negro children. Middle-class families are those which derive their incomes from semiskilled and skilled occupations. Middle-class youths are not as "accommodated" or "adjusted" to caste discriminations as are the parents and children of the lower class. There is a more highly developed and integrated self-portraiture in the Negro middle class, and ". . . middle-class youth are differentiated, on the whole, from those in lower-class families by the fact that they show more sophistication toward their racial status, that they show more consciousness of their social status, and that they are likely to exhibit a greater degree of race consciousness. Their greater self-consciousness and awareness of their status are closely tied

up with the fact that these children show more ambition and a greater determination to rise in the world than lower-class children. The nascent race consciousness of this class is accompanied by a critical attitude toward the deficiencies of the Negro and a deeper resentment of the discriminations practiced by whites." [8]

Middle-class parents also warn their children not to engage in physical fighting with Whites, but such a value is also transmitted as a warning that they should not behave in a manner which would identify them with the lower class. Such training, in part, helps to instill in middle-class youths "a desire to maintain a certain respectability in the eyes of Negroes as well as whites." [9]

Negro middle-class parents are far less inclined to teach their children attitudes of servility to Whites. This is accomplished in a number of ways. The first, as we have just seen, is by verbal teaching. Secondly, since middle-class adults are more skilled and better trained than lower-class persons, their income is more directly dependent on skill and industriousness than on servility. Hence, Negro middle-class youths are less liable to observe their parents "accommodating" themselves to the caste structure on the one hand while giving vent to their hostilities only within the safety of home and family on the other. Thirdly, middle-class parents ". . . think that a self-respecting attitude should prevent people from going where they will be embarrassed. This is not mere rationalization on their part, since they have a sense of personal dignity which they attempt to instill in their children." [10]

But there is much more to this than simple verbal instruction. Negro middle-class parents can accomplish this because

[7] *Ibid.*, p. 111.
[8] *Ibid.*, p. 55.
[9] *Ibid.*, p. 57.
[10] *Ibid.*, p. 60.

their children rarely have contact with the children of their parents' White employers; furthermore, they generally attempt to remain aloof from contact with White children. "Partly because of the conflicts often ensuing from contacts with whites and partly because of the implications of an inferior status when associations with whites occur, middle-class children often remain aloof from white children. . . . The policy of remaining aloof from white children is due also to the fact that when white children reach the age of puberty they are likely to break off their associations." [11] Thus, the pattern of physical and social avoidance, reinforced by a series of fundamental and deep values, is begun quite early in life.

The school situation, especially the segregated one, places almost the same pressures on Negro middle-class children as on lower-class children. However, since the middle class more closely approximates the values of the upper class than does the lower class, Negro middle-class youths experience considerably less pressure and discrimination from their upper-class teachers.

The Negro upper class is composed of families who derive their incomes from professional services, as proprietors and managers and as clerical workers in governmental agencies and industry. Negro upper-class parents exhibit more strongly many of the values which have their earliest expressions in the middle class. First, upper-class parents assiduously avoid inculcating their children with attitudes of subordination to White people. While explaining to their children that they must avoid conflict with Whites, these explanations are always accompanied with the value that fighting is unbecoming to upper-class Negroes. A new slant is placed on caste relationships in the upper class by parental explanations

that only "poor whites" use derisive and derogatory epithets to Negroes. "This is all part of the efforts of upper-class families to protect as far as possible their children not only from the cruder expressions of race prejudice but also from the more subtle forms of racial discrimination. As a rule neither the parents nor their children are engaged in menial occupations where they would be forced to assume, at least, an attitude of subordination toward whites. Generally, the parents studiously avoid taking their children places where they will be subjected to rebuffs because of race or color. Despite such precautions, parents in upper-class families find it extremely difficult at times to explain, without introducing the fact of their racial status to their children, why they cannot go to various places or eat and drink at certain places." [12]

This protection can often go to great extremes, as in forbidding any reference in the home to race or racial problems. In part, this is an attempt by the parents to shield the child from an awareness of racial identity. As a result, since such denial must eventually conflict with social reality, the upper-class Negro is forced to develop a whole series of synthetic rationalizations and "ideal" ego defenses, such as an excessive pride in being a Negro, a preference for being Negro rather than White, and the like.

Negro upper-class parents can undertake such a socialization of their children by virtue, primarily, of their secure economic status. The upper-class Negro community is a relatively isolated one, socially as well as geographically. Upper-class adult Negroes are rarely dependent directly on Whites for their incomes; they live in fashionable, well-kept neighborhoods where play is pleasant and which create little or no desire to explore or have contact with the White world. Upper-

---

[11] *Ibid.,* p. 82.
[12] *Ibid.,* pp. 61-62.

class children do not feel as deprived as lower-class children and many middle-class youths, and they are extremely conscious of their superior social rank, on which they place greater emphasis than they do on their low racial rank. Thus, the insulation with which their parents protect them comes not only from the family, but has its ultimate origins in the world around them. For example, the values with respect to social rank, which they receive at home, are strongly reinforced in the school situation, where they are favorably contrasted with Negro children of the other classes and where their values are almost always held up as the superior ones.

Although all Negro children in the United States must learn a racial identification which is different from that of the dominant White population, the content of this learning differs considerably from one class to another within the Negro caste. In an abstract way, the values of American culture relegate Negroes to a lower status. But we have seen that these values do not affect all Negroes in the same way in the same geographical area. Instead, they have entirely different effects on individuals living under different socioeconomic conditions. Putting this the other way around, Negro parents in different social classes have different access to different segments of the broad spectrum of American culture as it pertains to the status of the Negro. Because of their geographical (neighborhood) and economic positions, the values leading to the status inferiority of the Negro are most clearly transmitted in the course of socialization within the lower-class Negro family. As geographical (neighborhood) position improves, and as we move from the middle class to the upper class, these values lose their strength progressively. Here the traditional pansocietal values of maintaining self-respect and acquiring the desirable ends of American culture are able to find more and more expression in the course of socialization at the expense of values emphasizing the lower socioeconomic status of the Negro. To repeat the hypothesis stated at the outset of this discussion, in any social system different people occupy different social positions, and it is these positions which not only determine the aspects of a culture to which people have access but *they determine which aspects of the culture will be transmitted to a person in the course of growing up.*

The data which we have just considered illustrate some of the influences of class status on the ways in which individuals learn the emotional implications of caste status. However, they also contain many implications for a further problem, namely, the relationship of social structure to the basic biological areas of socialization. That is, individual groups have fairly uniform ways in the handling of breast-feeding, bottle-feeding, weaning, sphincter control, aggression, sexuality, and the like. These consistencies within groups are accented by variations in such practices, which can be seen as we move from society to society and from status group to status group in America.

In their study of "Social Class and Color Differences in Child-Rearing," conducted in Chicago, Allison Davis and Robert J. Havighurst compared four groups of parents with respect to the ways in which they reared their children. These were:

Negro lower class, Negro middle class, White lower class, and White middle class. They found that ". . . middle-class children are subjected earlier and more consistently to the influences which make a child an orderly, conscientious, responsible and tame person. In the course of this training, middle-class children probably suffer more frustration of their impulses." [13] This can be stated somewhat more positively: lower-class children in both races generally enjoy a greater freedom in indulging their instinctual impulses than do children in the respective middle classes.

There is, according to Davis and Havighurst, more breast-feeding, longer breast-feeding, and more demand-feeding among the White and Negro lower classes than among the White and Negro middle classes. Furthermore, there is more oral indulgence among the Negro group as a whole than among the White group as a whole. Similarly, toilet training is begun much earlier in the middle class than in the lower class in both races, although, if we compare both races as wholes, such training is begun earlier in the Negro group than in the White. Unfortunately, however, Davis and Havighurst do not report whether the earlier toilet training in the Negro group is imposed with as much strictness and stringency as the age of imposition would indicate. That is, while it is often assumed that toilet training at six or eight months is traumatic or unpleasant for an infant, the fact is often overlooked that it is possible to impose toilet training at fourteen months with such severity and anxiety that the situation would emerge as far more traumatic than it would at six or eight months. Again, middle-class children are more restricted to the home and are permitted much less freedom of movement than are lower-class children. Translating these physical experiences into psychological terms, we could say that middle-class children are overprotected more than are lower-class children.

It would appear, then, according to Davis and Havighurst, that as we move up the social ladder we tend to find more and greater frustration of basic instinctual processes. It seems clear that such lesser degrees of indulgence in middle-class children are "somehow" related to the orderliness, conscientiousness, responsibility, and the like, of adult middle-class life, although it is difficult to say exactly what such a relationship signifies. "Impulse control," established earlier and much more strictly in the middle class, "somehow" seems related to the quality of middle-class life. These are the qualities which middle-class persons value most highly, especially when they compare themselves to members of the lower class. On the other hand, we must bear in mind that the investigators who carry out such comparative studies of class differences in child-rearing behavior are themselves middle-class persons, that is, people who were *brought up* to value such qualities and to make such (unconscious?) comparisons between their own class and the lower class. Most middle-class social scientists (the present writer included) have no first-hand knowledge of lower-class life. We often write of the lower class as though we knew what a lower-class person thinks, feels, experiences, believes, worries about, longs for, and so forth, whereas we actually do not know. Hence, we do not know the relationship of lower-class adult life to these lower-class socialization practices and, furthermore,

---

[13] Davis and Havighurst, 1952, p. 317.

we have little knowledge of the relationships between middle-class adult life and these child-rearing practices in the middle class. That is, we do not know what there is in the subculture of each class which *produces* greater indulgence or greater frustration in socialization practices. Is there, really, that much less orderliness, conscientiousness, responsibility, and tameness in the lower class than in the middle class? Such a question, of course, does not deny the truth and reality of the differences in socialization practices which such investigators as Davis and Havighurst have found in the different classes. But knowing that there are differences of this sort is but a fraction of the job; we must then proceed to determine what *produces* such differences.

In a more recent study of child-rearing customs in different social classes, Sears, Maccoby, and Levin found that there were few significant differences between middle-class and lower-class mothers in a Boston suburb in the ways in which they brought up their children. Furthermore, their findings were in some respects considerably different from those of Davis and Havighurst.[14]

There are many ways of viewing such contradictory findings. One point of view could be that the facts in one or both of the studies are in error. Another would be to say that the sampling techniques of one or the other were faulty. Still another view could be that both studies are accurate, but that the differences could be attributed to regional and geographical (subcultural) variations.

Bronfenbrenner has taken yet another stand about these different findings. He compared the results of Davis and Havighurst with those of Maccoby, Sears, and Levin, and found that the discrepancies between the two sets of data could be explained, in large part, by changing American values and child-rearing customs over a long period of time.

SOCIALIZATION AND SOCIAL CLASS
THROUGH TIME AND SPACE*
By Urie Bronfenbrenner

A comparative analysis of the results of studies of social-class differences in child rearing over a 25-year period points to the following conclusions:

1. Over the past quarter of a century, American mothers at all social-class levels have become more flexible with respect to infant feeding and weaning. Although fewer infants may be breast fed, especially over long periods of time, mothers are increasingly more likely to feed their children on demand and to wean them later from the bottle.

2. Class differences in feeding, weaning, and toilet training show a clear and consistent trend. From about 1930 till the end of World War II, working-class mothers were uniformly more permissive than those of the middle class. They were more likely to breast feed, to follow a

---

[14] Sears, Maccoby, and Levin, 1957.
* Reprinted from *Readings in Social Psychology* (3rd ed.), edited by E. E. Maccoby, T. M. Newcomb, and E. L. Hartley. New York: Holt, Rinehart and Winston, Inc. 1958, pp. 424-425.

self-demand schedule, to wean the child later from breast and bottle, and to begin and complete both bowel and bladder training at a later age. After World War II, however, there has been a definite reversal in direction; now it is the middle-class mother who is the more permissive in each of the above areas.

3. Shifts in the pattern of infant care —especially on the part of middle-class mothers—show a striking correspondence to the changes in practices advocated in successive editions of U.S. Children's Bureau bulletins and similar sources of expert opinion.

4. In addition to varying with social-class level, methods of infant care appear to differ as a function of cultural background, urban *vs.* rural upbringing, and exposure to particular ideologies of child rearing.

5. Taken together, the findings on changes in infant care lead to the generalization that socialization practices are most likely to be altered in those segments of society which have most ready access to the agencies or agents of change (e.g., books, pamphlets, physicians, and counselors).

6. The data on the training of the young child show middle-class mothers, especially in the postwar period, to be consistently more permissive toward the child's expressed needs and wishes. The generalization applies in such diverse areas as oral behavior, toilet accidents, dependency, sex, aggressiveness, and freedom of movement outside the home.

7. Though more tolerant of expressed impulses and desires, the middle-class parent, throughout the period covered by this survey, has higher expectations for the child. The middle-class youngster is expected to learn to take care of himself earlier, to accept more responsibility about the home, and—above all—to progress further in school.

8. In matters of discipline, working-class parents are consistently more likely to employ physical punishment, while middle-class families rely more on reasoning, isolation, appeals to guilt, and other methods involving the threat of loss of love. At least two independent lines of evidence suggest that the techniques preferred by middle-class parents are more likely to bring about the development of internalized values and controls. Moreover, the effectiveness of such methods should, at least on theoretical grounds, be enhanced by the more acceptant atmosphere experienced by middle-class children in their early years.

9. Over the entire 25-year period studied, parent-child relationships in the middle class are consistently reported as more acceptant and equalitarian, while those in the working class are oriented toward maintaining order and obedience. Within this context, the middle class has shown a shift away from emotional control toward freer expression of affection and greater tolerance of the child's impulses and desires.

In the past few years, there have been indications that the gap between the social classes may be narrowing. Whatever trend the future holds in store, let us hope that the social scientist will no longer be content to look at them piecemeal but will utilize all the technical resources now at his command to obtain a systematic picture of the changes, through still more extended space and time, in the way in which humanity brings up its children.

In Chapter 5, we are going to return to the problem of changes in socialization practices in a much more intensive way. There, we shall look into the over-all political, economic, populational, and general factors in the total society which might produce such changes. And, indirectly, we shall take marked exception to the generalization proffered by Bronfenbrenner in the fifth paragraph of his preceding résumé.

We noted previously that there is a tendency for hostility to be more suppressed or more severely curbed in the Negro middle and upper classes than in the lower class. It is probably true that hostility is also more and more restricted in children as we go up the social scale of the White group. However, we seem to be putting the cart before the horse when we equate greater frustration of hostile impulses with the greater frustration of oral and anal drives in the middle and upper classes. It is true that there is more frustration of hostility in the higher social strata; but does this mean that this greater frustration is part and parcel of the same over-all process under which we include oral and sphincter training? If this conclusion is eventually borne out, as we shall attempt to show later on (in Chapter 6), we would expect that hostility *must* be more severely restricted in the middle class, for example, *because more hostility is aroused and generated in middle-class children.*

This hypothesis is akin to and consonant with the findings of Davis and Havighurst that there is from two to three times as much masturbation among middle-class children of both races as there is among the children of the respective lower classes. As with hostility, we cannot assume that infants and children of the lower classes start out with weaker sexual tensions than their peers in the middle classes. This, they say, ". . . might be explained in terms of the hypothesis that masturbation is in part a palliative to frustration. Children who are frustrated more would masturbate more, according to this hypothesis." [15] In other words, Davis and Havighurst feel that "something" is happening to the child which is impelling him to behave in a certain way. We are carrying this hypothesis even further, insisting that we must look outside the parents to find out why they impose different oral and sphincter disciplines on their children in different classes. Similarly, we insist that we must look to the over-all environment in order to determine what there is in that environment which would produce a greater amount of or greater predisposition to hostility which in turn must be the object of greater control and frustration.

We shall return to the problems involved in the molding of instinctual strivings during socialization in Chapters 5 and 6, where we will spell out some of the lines along which future research might proceed to uncover some solutions to the problems which have just been raised. At this point, however, let us turn our attention to another illustration of the proposition that the status position of the family within the society is one of the principal factors determining which aspects of a culture will be transmitted to a child in the course of his upbringing.

In the case of the socialization of the Negro child, we saw that the same cultural value—that Negroes must learn while growing up that they have a social identity different from Whites—is transmitted differently and with entirely different meanings in the three Negro social classes. By virtue of their racial (that is, biological) identity, Negro parents cannot avoid transmitting this aspect of American culture to their

---

[15] Davis and Havighurst, 1952, p. 318.

children. But they do so in different ways in different classes. In the case which we shall consider in a moment, we are going to study some of the ways in which *occupational* roles of White middle-class fathers determine ways in which these fathers rear their children.

Aberle and Naegele, in the next paper, point out very clearly that the ways in which children of a particular group are brought up, and the goals which fathers have in bringing them up, are greatly dependent on the anticipations fathers have for their future. That is, to repeat the second axiom of the social-structural approach to socialization, parents everywhere have certain ideas about how their children will have to function as mature adults participating in a particular social system. What clearly stands out in the analysis to be presented by Aberle and Naegele is that *a parent's own experiences,* as a result of his participation in the middle-class social system, dictate "what attitudes, skills and qualities his child must have to fit into the adult role system. And the parent is likely to consider his child's *present* behavior as a prognostication of his probable adult behavior." It is through these prognostications that parents attempt to mold and direct their children, and it is through these indicators for future participation in the adult-role system that parents exert various kinds of pressures on their sons. These findings are clearly consonant with the statement by Inkeles, in his paper on changes in Russian socialization practices (which we will read in Chapter 5), that ". . . parents need not be . . . unimaginative and passive agents of their culture, raising their children by rote. . . . Although parents are adults, they may nevertheless still *learn,* and learn what they feel to be major 'lessons,' from their experiences under conditions of social change. This learning, furthermore, may influence the parents to seek purposefully to bring their children up in a way different from that in which they were raised, and in a manner intended better to suit the children for life in the changed social situation."

MIDDLE-CLASS FATHERS' OCCUPATIONAL ROLE AND ATTITUDES TOWARD CHILDREN*

By David F. Aberle and Kaspar D. Naegele

This paper will consider the relationship between the occupational role of the middle-class male and his aims and concerns in the socialization of his children. The approach is deliberately one-sided. We will deal almost entirely with fathers, and scarcely at all with mothers, and we will high-light other aspects of the socialization process at the expense of such matters as feeding practices, toilet training and sexual training. There is no intention of denying the worth of approaches other than that exemplified here. We wish only to stress what seem to be neglected, though obvious and common-sense aspects of the question of socialization.

We will define socialization for the purpose at hand as the process of inculcating in individuals the skills, traits and

* Reprinted with abridgment from *American Journal of Orthopsychiatry,* Vol. 22, pp. 366-378, 1952, with permission.

value attitudes associated with the performance of present or anticipated roles. There are a number of ways of stating problems concerning socialization. One approach is to ask what are the *effects* of certain types of socialization experience? Considerable strides have been made along these lines, in analyzing, for example, the effects of "basic disciplines" such as weaning, toilet training and sexual training. The effects of aggression and dependency training are also receiving attention. Some work has been undertaken regarding the effects of particular kinds of parent-child relationships on the socialization process. When attention is turned to the *causes* of certain types of treatment of the child, there is a tendency in psychiatric and mental health work to investigate the causes of *pathological* parental behavior, and to find its sources in the childhood experiences of the parents: to see that in various complex and unconscious ways parents are repeating, or undoing, or working out problems derived from their own childhood. There is no desire to eliminate either of these approaches. But the focus here will be on an aspect of socialization so obvious that it is sometimes forgotten: the relationship between the adult role of the individual and his orientation to his children.

In every society parents aim to raise their children to become adults capable of assuming the typical adult roles and of being integrated into the social system. Consequently we can expect that within any given social group there will be similarities in the goals and practices of socialization. Similarity of goals depends partly upon the relative uniformity of the parents' long-range expectations as to what sorts of positions the children will ultimately occupy and what consequent skills, attitudes and qualities they must ultimately possess, and partly on the relative uniformity of the definition of the

succession of roles intermediate between infancy and adulthood. Similarities in means depend partly on the fact that they "make sense" to the parents in terms of the goals hoped for, and partly on the effects of having one's efforts inspected by one's neighbors. (In addition to these conscious and semiconscious expectations, parents are influenced by a variety of unconscious factors, derived from both idiosyncratic and general experience. Furthermore, any particular socialization regime has consequences for personality unanticipated by the socializing agents. These unanticipated consequences sometimes take the form of particular types of deviations common in the society, sometimes of "quirks" commonly found in "normal" members of the group.) All in all, child rearing is future-oriented to an important extent. The picture of the desired end product is importantly influenced by the parents' experiences in the adult world, as well as by their childhood experiences. When adult experience changes under the impact of major social change, there is reason to believe that there will ultimately, though not necessarily immediately, be shifts in the socialization pattern as well. The adult's experiences tell him what attitudes, skills and qualities his child must have to fit into the adult role system. And the parent is likely to consider his child's *present* behavior as a prognostication of his probable adult behavior. The parent's evaluation of the child's behavior, however, proceeds not only by direct extrapolation, but also by vaguer, and less conscious processes, in which the connection between present and future behavior is more indirectly and symbolically reckoned.

These rather obvious matters are sometimes forgotten by the psychiatrically oriented—or rather, fall far into the background—in the interests of analyzing more complex and interesting problems of psychopathological behavior. But it is with these things in mind that we shall approach the question of the middle-class father. And perhaps it should be said that one reason we are stressing the father is that he, too, is forgotten or recedes into the background in the face of the overwhelming focus on the mother in recent work.

This presentation is based on data collected in the course of research carried out in a suburb of Boston. The authors of this paper, respectively a social anthropologist and a sociologist, completed interviews with both parents in a series of more than twenty families. Each family had at least one child in a particular nursery school in the community. The parents were selected for our research because after meetings of their group they expressed willingness to serve as subjects. The group is middle-class by our subjective impressions, and by rating according to Warner's Index of Status Characteristics. The members range from upper middle class to lower middle class. Incomes run from about $20,000 per annum to about $3700. One family lives in a two-family house, and the remainder in single-family dwellings, all in "good" neighborhoods. For the most part the fathers are professional men, major and minor executives of medium to large business concerns, owners of businesses, and salesmen (not including house-to-house sales). Only one man is on an hourly wage rate, and the group includes no skilled, semiskilled, or unskilled laborers. Most of the men are college-educated, and the remainder have technical training beyond the high school level. Most of the wives are college-educated. The school itself is "progressive." *All of the men have risen in status in the course of their careers, and almost all feel that they have not yet reached their ceilings* [italics supplied].

Since the families are middle-class,

what is said here is restricted in its implications to the middle class, with no necessary assumption that the remarks that follow have wider application, and some reason to believe that they do not. Most of the families are "normal," in the sense that few parents have sought or appear to need psychiatric advice, few children have appeared in psychiatric facilities, and there are no startling deviations from the norm in the patterning of adult roles.

That part of the project which was concerned with the fathers had as its aim the investigation of the relationship between the father's occupational role and his behavior in the home. More specifically, it was hoped that a connection could be established between the particular satisfactions and strains of each father's occupational setting and his behavior toward his wife and children. While minor relationships of this kind seem to exist, the data appear to illuminate somewhat more general questions.

It became clear in the course of research that the relationship which some fathers could see between their job situation and their behavior in the home was trivial, that some fathers could find no connection, and that still others flatly rejected the idea that there could be any connection. There is good reason for this. In the first place, many features of our social system stress the *separation* of the occupational and the domestic role. In urban middle-class America, there is a deliberate boundary between home and job. This only seems obvious because we all participate in this sort of setup. In the majority of the world's societies, production and consumption units overlap greatly, and the extended or nuclear family is likely to be a basic organized unit of production and consumption. In our middle-class society, universalistic standards ideally govern the selection of individuals for occupational positions:

competence—what you can do—rather than who you are, is, or ideally should be crucial for occupational recruitment, advancement or firing. Family connections are theoretically irrelevant to the allocation of occupational role in the majority of middle-class occupations. There are institutional barriers against nepotism in many organizations, personal fortune and company funds are kept distinct, and of course place of employment and home are ordinarily separate. One's home life may actually affect job performance, positively or negatively. But the effects of home life are treated as irrelevant in many organizations, or as intrusive: something to be recognized only in order to dispel it—such is the role of the psychological consultant in many firms. For many reasons, modern complex industrial bureaucratic society requires this separation, institutionalizes it, makes of it a virtue— and the fathers in our group respond in terms of this norm.

Second, a man is bewildered when he is asked to consider the relationship of his behavior and attitudes on the job to those in the home. For him the two worlds are incommensurable. The occupational world is one of clearly delimited responsibility and authority, of judgment of individuals on the basis of what they can do, rather than who they are, of initiative and persistence, usually of competition, and a world where aggressiveness—in the layman's sense—pays off. In the domestic world, however, there are no such clearcut limits on authority and responsibility; children are to be loved and cared for because they are one's children, and not because of their accomplishments or deserts; competition and aggressiveness are considered inappropriate techniques for gaining one's ends; and ideally emotional warmth, relaxation and the like are to be maximized. Thus the techniques required for dealing with other individuals and making a success in the occupa-

tional world differ point by point from the techniques for dealing with wife and children and making a success of family life and the raising of sons and daughters. It is true that the standards of the occupational world "infect" behavior in the family in many ways, not all of which can be mentioned here. But in terms of ideal patterns, the two spheres are far apart. Hence the unwillingness or inability of fathers to see a relationship need not surprise us. But neither need it deter us from seeking a connection. When we consider the investment of time and affect in the occupational sphere, we are entitled to assume that the eight or more hours a day spent on the job may affect behavior during the other hours of the day. We shall see that while the father attempts to leave the office behind him at home, he *represents* the occupational world to his family (this is particularly clear in the interviews with mothers) and evaluates his children in terms of his occupational role.

We would assume that fathers in this group would be oriented toward their sons in terms of an expectation that they will ultimately occupy positions in the middle-class occupational structure, and toward their daughters with the expectation that they will not. The data confirm this assumption. Without exception fathers desire college training for their boys. One father says that one of his sons may not be college material, and that in this case he should not take up space in college—but he considers this a shocking statement. For girls, the majority of fathers plan a college education, but there is considerably more willingness to admit that the child may not go, either because she does not want to, or because she may get married first.

As for the sons' future occupations, fathers always say initially that they have "no plans" for their children. Further questioning always shows that "no plans" means that any occupation is all right, *if* it is a middle-class occupation. It means that either a professional or a business career is all right. (In the same way, "no plans" with regard to college means, any *good* college, usually with certain limitations as to what constitutes a good college.) Skilled wagework is never mentioned. This drastic limitation is completely unconscious for the fathers. From their point of view this restriction is identical with "no plans." It might be mentioned that if fathers were asked whether academic work represented a possible career for the boy, they tended to reject it. One accepted it as a possibility; one said that it would be fine for his oldest son, since he was shy, irresponsible, bookish, and needed a woman to look after him. Three rejected it contemptuously. It is evident from the rejections, as well as from one of the acceptances, that it is not just a matter of meager financial reward: many a middle-class father does not consider the academic role to exemplify appropriate masculine behavior.

As for the daughters, over half of the fathers who discussed the point would accept the possibility of a career for their daughters, but only as a possibility. Most of these men would prefer that their daughters marry, or expect them to, and the remainder of the group reject a career out of hand. Only two fathers wanted their daughters to know how to earn a livelihood, and both of them have wives who are working or did work during married life.

These findings are "normal" and "obvious" only because we are so deeply imbedded in the life which these fathers represent. Note that no father envisages downward mobility for his son. Also, though many of our fathers come from social and occupational backgrounds quite different from those they now occupy, it is their own present status, de-

rived from adult experience, which they project into the future for their children. So far, then, our assumptions are supported by the data.

One complication is introduced. Fathers do expect their sons to move in the same general occupational world that they do. But in our society occupational choice is theoretically free, and particular occupational positions are achieved, not inherited. Fathers *should* not, and in most cases *cannot* if they would, plan their children's precise future—since almost no one can guarantee a particular niche to his son. That means that fathers cannot foresee *exactly* what skills, values and personality traits are going to be useful for their sons—something that is possible in many other societies. Nor can they plan precisely what steps their sons should take to reach this unknown future. Consequently, in evaluating their sons' present behavior they can only focus on general character traits conducive to success, on symbolic manifestations of those traits, and on a modicum of success in school as an almost essential step toward middle-class occupational status. A different future, marriage, is envisaged for girls, and we can expect a different evaluation of present behavior.

In the light of fathers' expectations for the future, let us examine some typical concerns that fathers express about the present behavior of their children. It must be stated at once that when we say that a child's behavior is a matter of concern to the father, this does not mean that the child is, or will become a problem by psychiatric standards. It means only that the child's behavior is disvalued, is a matter of worry and mild anxiety, is something that the parent would like to change, for the sake of the child (though his own convenience may also be involved). It should also be mentioned that it is possible for a father to become seriously concerned over behavior which a clinician might consider normal, to overlook behavior which might be considered portentous by a clinician, and to pass off some troubling behavior on the assumption that it is "just a stage."

Fifty-six children are involved: 29 boys and 27 girls. The age range is from 13 years to a few months for boys, and from 10 years to a few months for girls. Fathers may not subject very young infants to evaluative comment of the sort we are about to discuss, but this begins early in the child's life. There are many more statements of concern involving boys, and the emotional strength of these concerns is considerably greater with respect to boys than with respect to girls.

The question of securing obedience, and of annoyance at disobedience runs through virtually all the interviews and will not be discussed. The recurrent concerns expressed involve lack of responsibility and initiative, inadequate performance in school, insufficiently aggressive or excessively passive behavior, athletic inadequacies, overconformity, excitability, excessive tearfulness, and the like, and "childish" behavior. In all of these categories more boys were objects of concern than girls; in some, many more boys, and in some no girls were mentioned. Of course no parent expressed concern about all these things in any one child, or even in any one family. But the total tendency clearly indicates that such behaviors as have been mentioned are negatively evaluated when they appear in male children. Similarly, satisfactory performance in these areas of behavior was more often mentioned for boys than for girls. Fathers are pleased if their boys display responsibility and initiative, perform well in school, stand up for themselves, show athletic ability, emotional stability, and so on. Only one father does not want his boys to be particularly athletic. Far less concerns, we have said, are expressed regarding girls. Satisfactions

with girls, though they do include school performance, moral sexual behavior, and the like, seem to focus strongly on the girls' being "nice," "sweet," pretty, affectionate and well liked. For both boys and girls, of course, fathers hope for normal personalities, good adjustment, likeability and popularity.

But all of the traits we have mentioned as matters of concern are—from the father's point of view—prognosticators, direct or indirect, of adult traits which will interfere with success in middle-class occupational life. The ideal-typical successful adult male in the middle-class occupational role should be responsible, show initiative, be competent, be aggressive, be capable of meeting competition. He should be emotionally stable and capable of self-restraint. These qualities are part of the value structure of the occupational world, they are involved in the role definitions of that world, and fathers' discussions of their own jobs show that these qualities have great significance for them. This does a great deal to explain the difference between the father's concern with his son's behavior and with his daughter's. He worries about failures in these areas and is happy over successes, because of his future expectations for his sons. He does not worry so much about his daughters because they will occupy different roles, toward which he has a somewhat vaguer orientation. Occupational career is not taken seriously, marriage is the primary hope and expectation, the same sorts of demands are not made, and the father does not seem to fuss too much as to whether his young daughter will ultimately be a good mate. If she is a sweet little girl, this is enough. We do find that there is some concern with these matters in girls, and that one father is disturbed by his daughter's lack of aggressiveness. But by and large, though the girls are undoubtedly *less* athletic, *less* aggressive, and *more* tearful and emotional, than the boys, this does not bother the father. These qualities do not predict failure in the adult feminine role —quite the reverse. In fact some fathers are troubled if their daughters are bossy —a term not used for any of the boys. Though we know that some of the boys are holy terrors in their play groups, no father shows any concern lest his son be a bully, and some proudly mention that they guess the boy is a bit of a devil. (It might be noted that though the "bad boy" is a stereotype of American life, ambivalently but never wholly negatively regarded, there is no corresponding stereotype for a girl, the phrase "bad girl" having quite different connotations.) We will not deal here with mothers' concerns, but it can be said that mothers do react to what they consider excessive aggression in boys, and that mothers show more concern with girls than do fathers.

Fathers' concern with athletic ability requires a little further discussion. This is a case of indirect and symbolic meaning of present behavior. Fathers are not concerned with athletics because they want their boys to grow up to be professional athletes, but because failure along these lines seems to symbolize for the father inability to be properly aggressive and competitive, now and in the future.

Projection into the future is not intended as a total explanation of the father's concerns. A son's present failures reflect on the father as a father, and this is important. In addition, we see conscious and half-conscious identification with sons in several fathers, and it is undoubtedly present in many more. Some of our most critical or most concerned fathers remark that the boy is "like me," or "reminds me of myself when I was his age." In a sense, we might say that whereas the father's present situation represents to him his son's probable future situation (broadly speaking), the son's present behavior may represent to the father his own past. This identification may produce nurturant behavior. But the identification may result in a highly ambivalent reaction: perhaps difficulties now observed in the son were once successfully overcome by the father, sometimes after a struggle, and these may now be unconsciously reactivated. The identification may thus intensify the degree to which the father attempts to counteract the disturbing behaviors in his son, attempting at the same time to stifle the same tendencies in himself.

It might be mentioned that our sample indicates that fathers become more concerned with male first-born children than with female first-born children, and that subsequent male children, whether they follow boys or girls, are less likely to be foci of concern for fathers. This might be partly connected with the identification phenomenon noted above, since conscious identification is mentioned more often in connection with male first-born children than with other sons. But there are many—too many—other ways to interpret this particular finding, and on the basis of our small sample we are reluctant to choose among them.

We see a good deal of evidence, then, for the belief that fathers' attitudes toward their sons' behavior are different from those toward their daughters'. It is relatively easy to account for a good deal of this difference on the basis of the fact that the father is oriented toward his son as the future occupant of a middle-class occupational role, for which certain behaviors are of great importance—something about which he has direct experience—and toward his daughter as the future occupant of a different middle-class role, that of mother and wife, for which his own standards are less exacting and less well-formed in terms of the girl's present behavior.

This does not mean that because the father uses present behavior as a prognosticator for the future it is a good prognosticator. It has been pointed out that he may well stress the unimportant, disregard fairly severe symptoms, and at times simply reckon present behavior as a "stage." Nor do our findings mean that boys are subject to more strains than girls, or are more likely to be problems in adult life, or the reverse. They only point to a particular relationship: that between father's occupational role, his future expectations for his children, and his evaluation of their conduct. The nature of that relationship has been discussed. What are its broader implications?

On the theoretical level, it is hoped that this paper points to the desirability of much more minute inquiries aimed at relating socialization practices (about which we have said little), aims of socialization, parents' long-range expectations, to parents' adult roles, occupational and other, and to the values connected with those roles. Let us turn our attention not only to the *effects* of socialization practices in a group, but to the *causes* of those patterns. For, far from being fortuitous with respect to the remainder of the social system, many or most of those patterns are somehow integrated with it. The broad outlines of some of these relationships are recognized and have been explored empirically, as in the work of Davis and Havighurst, who have compared certain socialization practices as between class and caste groups and related those practices to the social position of the parents. The present paper works within a class, rather than by comparing two classes, and gives explicit attention to differences of expectations as between boys and girls. A tremendous amount of work, however, remains to be done on these and on more subtle and intricate issues.

Many questions in this general area pressed for our attention in the course of research. Some have been omitted here for lack of space, and some because the data were insufficient for extended discussion. But a few might be mentioned as suggestive of the sorts of problems remaining for analysis. Parents often express a certain ambivalence regarding the use of physical techniques in discipline —an ambivalence probably related to middle-class rejection of force as a means of settling interpersonal tensions or organizational difficulties. This rejection, in turn, has ramifications in the characteristics of role systems in the middle class. The question of means of socialization, largely neglected here, brings to mind the disagreements we sometimes saw between husband and wife as to what means shall be used, and the problem of analyzing to what extent these differences reflect a real difference of opinion regarding goals, and to what extent only a disagreement as to the path to be followed to reach a jointly agreed-upon goal. If the latter is the case, what are the factors which make one technique more congenial to the father, and a different one to the mother? We find a close relationship between these disagreements and another striking phenomenon: faddism in child-rearing techniques. Much of the faddism seems to center about two apparently opposed techniques of child rearing. One (the older) stresses scheduled feeding, early sphincter training, and in general responsibility and self-control. The other (and more recent) emphasizes demand feeding, late sphincter training, and concern for spontaneity and lack of severe inhibitions. Do these two approaches in fact reflect utterly diverse values, or are they simply two aspects of the same general value: individualism, with its responsibility aspect and its freedom aspect, here, as in other areas of life, in tension with each other?

Regardless of the issues about which faddism centers, we must ask how it is possible to have fads in child-training procedures. One factor seems to be the high valuation in our society placed on anti-traditionalism, which is associated with the stress on science, rationalism and progress. This antitraditionalistic attitude opens up the possibility of experimentation, change and faddism in child training, as in other aspects of social life—though there are other social reasons for the existence of faddism as a general phenomenon. A thorough analysis of faddism in child rearing would also involve analysis of the adult feminine role in our society. These examples and partial interpretations only suggest the wealth of problems lying ready to hand. So, finally, this paper represents a very small contribution to a very large potential field: the relating of socialization practices to general American values, to class values, to role orientations, and the like, with due regard for the effects of adult, as well as childhood experiences, in determining parents' attitudes and behavior toward children, and with due attention to unconscious and symbolic connections as well as conscious ones.

SUMMARY

To summarize the main points of this chapter, we began with two axioms. First, that parents' status positions determine which aspects of a culture they will transmit to their children in the course of bringing them up and, secondly, that socialization is always future oriented. In fully understanding these propositions, we must always bear in mind that just as parents do not necessarily transmit a segment of a culture unthinkingly and unimaginatively while rearing their children, so there is no mechanistic relationship between membership in a social class and a particular content of socialization. That is, there is more to class membership than the possession of the material trappings and purchased prestige symbols which are nominally associated with a particular social class. More than anything else, class membership must be understood in terms of filling highly specific roles, of having specific notions of what constitutes masculinity and femininity, of making a living and being a spouse and a parent, of participating in certain institutions and being systematically denied access to others, and the like.

In order for parents to be able to transmit a set of techniques for participating in a specific role system—whether in a caste system or in an industrial bureaucracy —the parents must *themselves* have experienced the role system and the values associated with the role system for which they are preparing their children. What is more, the parents must have achieved some degree of adaptive success in the system or with the values associated with it. These are indispensable requisites in the transmission of patterns from parents to children. For example, Aberle and Naegele note that all the fathers in their sample ". . . have risen in status in the course of their careers, and almost all feel that they have not yet reached their ceilings." In the case of Negro parents bringing up their children in the border and southern states, these parents are transmitting adaptive patterns of behavior which have emerged as the most successful ones possible within the limits set by their economic skills. We can paraphrase this by saying that one can only teach what one knows, and one can only know that which one has experienced personally.

What is especially important in understanding how parental status affects the content of socialization patterns is that the parents are in reality responding to a limited segment of the "culture of their society"—the segment which they have experienced. Once this conception is fully grasped, we are able to see the imprecision —if not the relative meaninglessness—of the platitudes: "culture determines what will be taught to the child," "culture affects personality," "the culture is transmitted through learning in the course of socialization," and so forth. Not only do parents have certain anticipations for the future of their children, and bring them up so that they may fully realize these anticipations, but in the course of socializing their offspring *parents are also transmitting to them the pressures, strivings, and goals which they themselves have found to be the most immediate and demanding in their sphere of the social universe.*

If we confined the construction of our model of social structure and socialization to the analyses of the learning of caste roles in different classes, or solely to the one presented by Aberle and Naegele, we could easily emerge with the erroneous impression that the transmission of a particular segment of a culture through the medium of parental status in the course of socialization is a somewhat mechanical or static affair. That is, we could mistakenly conclude that parents have "tested" the patterns which were taught *them* in the course of *their* socialization and are merely transmitting to their children those habits or social techniques which are the most adaptive to a particular role or occupational structure. To stop at this point would be to miss the main point of this total process. It would be to miss the fact that parents generally respond to the world around them in dynamic fashion; they are not only transmitting techniques, habits, defenses, and instrumental responses, but *they are passing on to their children what they have learned about the world in which they expect these children to participate*—they are transmitting the particular quality or nature of that segment of the social world to which they have been exposed as mature and functioning adults. We shall have the opportunity to observe this again (in Chapter 5) in an historical perspective, where our cases will illustrate how parents sometimes transmit political and sexual values, as well as others, which are quite different from those held by the grandparental generation. These new values are transmitted because the nature of society's pressures and goals have changed.

BIBLIOGRAPHY AND SUGGESTED READINGS

Aberle, David F. "Social System and Socialization," *Conference on Cross-Cultural Research on Personality Development,* Kansas City, May 20-22, 1955, pp. 1-13. Sponsored by the Committee on Personality Development, Social Science Research Council. Mimeographed.

Barber, Bernard. *Social Stratification: A Comparative Analysis of Structure and Process.* New York: Harcourt, Brace, 1957. Especially Chapters 11 and 12 (pp. 264-333). An excellent analysis of some of the issues discussed in this chapter with an emphasis on the dynamics of social stratification, complementing our own emphasis on the dynamics of socialization patterns.

Dai, Bingham. "Some Problems of Personality Development among Negro Children," in *Personality in Nature, Society and Culture,* Edited by Kluckhohn *et al.* New York: Knopf, 1955, pp. 545-566.

Davis, Allison. "American Status Systems and the Socialization of the Child," in *Personality in Nature, Society and Culture,* edited by Kluckhohn *et al.* New York: Knopf, 1955, pp. 567-576.

Davis, Allison and Robert J. Havighurst. "Social Class and Color Differences in Child-Rearing," in *Personality in Nature, Society and Culture,* edited by Kluckhohn *et al.* New York: Knopf, 1955, pp. 308-320.

Frazier, E. Franklin. *Negro Youth at the Crossways: Their Personality Development in the Middle States.* Washington, D. C.: American Council on Education, 1940.

Kohn, Melvin. "Social Class and the Exercise of Parental Authority," *American Sociological Review,* Vol. *24,* pp. 352-366, 1959. An excellent investigation of the conditions under which working- and middle-class parents punish their children.

Lindesmith, Alfred R. and Anselm Strauss. "A Critique of Culture-Personality Writings," *American Sociological Review,* Vol. *15,* pp. 587-600, 1950. This admittedly negative paper has become a classic statement of the dissatisfaction felt by those students who attempt to integrate the concepts of modern sociology with the study of socialization and personality.

Sears, Robert R., Eleanor Maccoby, and Henry Levin. *Patterns of Child Rearing.* Evanston, Ill.: Row-Peterson, 1957.

Chapter 4

FAMILY ISOLATION
AND SOCIALIZATION

In the previous chapter we saw that the content of the socialization process can be affected to a very large degree by the status positions of the family within the total society. In addition to status positions, however, families also occupy physical or spatial positions with respect to each other. That is, families may be physically very close to each other or they may be distant and isolated from each other. In this chapter, we are going to examine some of the consequences of familial isolation for the socialization process. Our general approach here will be similar to that which we used in Chapter 3, namely, to take one sociological condition at a time and attempt to ferret out *its* particular effect on the ways in which parents bring up their children.

We do not wish to imply in any way that these different sociological conditions —caste status, class position, occupational role, isolation—operate independently and exclusively of each other. That is, we do not wish to imply that if one condition is present the others must be absent. All of these, and many others as well, can be present and affect the content of socialization at the same time. What we are trying to do here is to take each one at a time and try to determine what *its* own effects may be.

Again, we are going to study two cases to illustrate the effects of one condition on socialization. In the first instance, we shall read about the consequences of familial isolation on socialization in a Jamaican (West Indian) community. Here, the social isolation of the family is considerably greater than the physical isolation, although the latter in also present. In the second instance, taken from the Teton-Dakota Indians, there are historical factors which have produced the contemporary state of familial isolation: the Teton-Dakota originally lived under conditions in which families were physically proximate to each other; then conditions changed and they now live physically distant and isolated from each other.

We are going to be concerned with one specific effect of family isolation on socialization, the role of the mother in the upbringing of children. We hypothesize for this discussion that *there is an intimate relationship between the isolation of the family and the centrality of the mother in the socialization of children.* That is, we are hypothesizing that where the family is socially or physically isolated, the mother will occupy a significantly more important role in the socialization process than will the father.

There are probably many reasons for the relationship between family isolation and the centrality of the mother in the socialization process, but we will be concerned with only a few of them. First of all, we have to keep in mind the fact that all children need stability and predictability in their interpersonal environments. Without stability and predictability, many different kinds of deleterious effects result.[1] Especially important is the deep-seated need which children seem to have for adults on whom they can depend, or feel that they can depend. Underscoring this phenomenon, Bowlby has pointed out that "the attachment of children to parents who by all ordinary standards are very bad is a never-ceasing source of wonder to those who seek to help them." [2]

Keeping this in mind, let us take the second factor which is important here, that in most societies it is the father who secures a livelihood for his family, and making a living almost always takes a man outside the home. Sometimes he will be gone for the greater part of the day, sometimes for several days, and sometimes for weeks at a time. (We are speaking only of instances where a boy does not accompany his father.) The reason for this is that in most societies in which there are great distances between families and households, such separations are due in large part to the inability of the land to support close concentrations of many households. If the soil is arid, sandy, and rocky, one or two square miles of grazing land may be able to provide only for one household or, at best, two. This seems to be the case among such people as the Navaho of the American southwest. Other kinds of environmental conditions can also force the isolation of the family, as among some hunting and gathering peoples, where many square miles will produce enough small game and fruits, nuts, and berries for only one or two families. But families can be isolated socially and emotionally, as in large cities, even when they are in close physical proximity.

Needing an adult upon whom he can depend, whom he is sure will be at hand when needed, who will give him a sense of safety and security and comfort, who will teach him how to do things, whose admiration he can elicit and on whose shoulder he can cry—if the family is isolated physically, or even only socially—the mother is the only stable and dependable adult with whom the child is constantly in contact. The isolation of the family is a sociological condition which throws the child back on the mother, and she thus becomes the central person in his life and development. The isolated family in this way may become an emotionally inbred group, at the core of which stands the mother.

Two other factors which are extremely important should be pointed to in understanding the relationship between the isolation of the family and the centrality of the mother. The first of these stems from the need of children to identify with the parent of the same sex. The isolated family produces entirely different problems of emotional identification for boys and girls. Given the desire of most boys to identify with their fathers, the latter's absence from the household makes the son-father identification a difficult one to achieve. Since growing up means, in part, emulating adult be-

---

[1] See Spitz, 1945, 1946.
[2] Bowlby, 1952, p. 69.

havior and adopting adult attitudes and motivations, and since a growing boy needs someone after whom to model himself, there will be a decidedly strong tendency on his part to emulate his mother and, thereby, develop a feminine, instead of a masculine, identification. And this is certain to be a confused, unsteady, and uncertain identification, since he knows that he is not female and since, when his father is home, he can observe different modes of behavior which his respective parents manifest. Mere observation, of course, is necessary for the development of an emotional identification, but it is not sufficient. The adult person being emulated has to be a steady one, but he also has to be physically present constantly and consistently. For example, when a boy is learning how to handle his natural store of aggression and a crisis develops, one of his first reactions—consciously or unconsciously—is to follow the example set by the adult whom he knows best and on whom he can rely physically and emotionally.

In almost all societies, men and women have different acceptable ways of expressing and dealing with aggression. If it is the mother who is the stable and dependable adult, the boy will emulate her. Later on, of course, when he assumes adult roles and attempts to meet the demands of those roles, he will find that feminine modes of handling aggression are inappropriate or maladaptive. This inconsistency plus the earlier contradiction of an emotional feminine identification and physical masculinity are major sources of the confusion and uncertainty of his identification. Furthermore, in most societies, aggressiveness and assertiveness are masculine modes of behavior, whereas passivity and mildness are generally feminine modes. (These modes, incidentally, are physiologically and sexually consistent; the fact that they are reversed in an exceptionally small number of societies serves to highlight and point up the constancy of the rule.) When a male who has developed a feminine emotional identification grows up and begins to enter into heterosexual relationships, he finds again—and it is to be expected that this is unconscious—that there is a contradiction between that part of the emotional identification which demands passivity and his physiological constitution which demands assertive intrusion *into* a female partner.

For girls the problem in the isolated family is a somewhat different one. The feminine identification is, of course, consistent on all counts; but it is most meaningful when it is in contrast to masculine identification (these are not absolutes, but they must be made to appear so for heuristic purposes and for brevity). A girl observes how her mother behaves in contrast to her father, just as a boy makes the same observations for himself. In the isolated family, and when the father is not steadily present, the growing girl does not have the opportunity to observe the emotional contrasts which she needs and she does not have the opportunity to test out in relation to her father all that she has learned from her mother—because much of what a girl acquires from her mother in the non-isolated family is through observation of how her mother behaves toward the girl's father. In the isolated family, in brief, she learns how to be a woman but does not have a very good opportunity of learning how to be a woman in relation to a man.

The second factor which has to be pointed out in understanding the relationship between the isolation of the family and the centrality of the mother centers around the natural sexual attachments which children have for their parents of the opposite sex. Here, too, the problem is different for boys and for girls. (It is certainly true that different sociological conditions heighten this attachment and that others minimize them; and it is also possible that the isolation of the family heightens a mother's sexual attraction for her sons.) Where a family is isolated, an important factor to keep in mind is that the growing child does not have playmates from other families with whom to make sexual explorations and discoveries. Since sexual curiosity and interest grow as the body grows and matures, and since sexuality requires object-goals, a growing boy has several alternatives. His mother and sisters are, of course, tabooed for him. He can either repress his sexual strivings and interests—in which case he is certain to develop symptoms of pathology—or he can deflect them to other objects. (These other objects can often be symbolic substitutes or representations for mother and sisters—the unconscious goal still being mother and sisters.) It may be difficult for him to repress his sexual interests in his mother and sisters effectively, since he is in constant contact with them and the contact surely heightens the interests. The difficulty is increased because he does not have other children in whom he can be interested sexually and thereby abate some of the strength of his incestuous inclination. As an alternative to complete repression, he can turn his sexual interests into autoerotic behavior, with a variety of possible accompanying fantasies open to him. He can become interested in animals or inanimate objects, or he can remain in a state of confusion as to the proper outlets and objects of sexual drive.

The major difference in a girl's problem in this situation is that she does not have the same opportunity as a boy does to learn the parental incest taboo. She does, of course, learn it, since the father is physically present on different occasions. But since rules are generally learned in the face of temptation, it is a much more difficult rule for her to learn.

An important point to make here is that we are concerned in these chapters with the consequences of different sociological conditions for the socialization process *per se*. Our concern *here* is *not* with the consequences of these experiences for adult personality. Needless to say, these different experiences in growing up have decidedly crucial consequences for adult personality, but this is an entirely separate area of study and investigation. For example, it can be hypothesized that the emotional identifications of adults who have been reared and who have grown up in isolated families are extremely confused identifications, and that this confusion has profound effects on many areas of adult behavior and activity, from divorce rates to political institutions. But to go into these problems at this point would divert us from looking into the question of why people bring up their children as they do.

Let us now turn to the first illustration for the socialization process of the consequences of the isolation of the family; here the author-editor changes his role from commentator to writer of case material.

STRUCTURE AND FUNCTION:
FAMILY ORGANIZATION AND SOCIALIZATION IN A JAMAICAN COMMUNITY*

By Yehudi A. Cohen

It has long been recognized that the varieties of family organization in contemporary New World Negro cultures represent the end-products of one of the most dramatic acculturative situations in recorded history. Most investigators agree that these family organizations have their primary historical antecedents in the experience of slavery, specifically in the impermanence of family life during slavery. The most striking feature arising from this unique historical process is the fact that "it is undoubtedly the woman who is the linchpin in the organization of the Negro family in the New World in general and in the Caribbean in particular."

The traditional centrality of the mother's position in the New World Negro family is best understood when viewed alongside the loss during slavery of the family institution as the context of procreation; both can be seen as the outgrowths of mutually reinforcing social and economic forces. "No matter how far the moralization of the slave went, his group life, including his most intimate relations with his family, could not resist the fundamental economic forces inherent in the slave system." Slavery in the West Indies was principally an industrial enterprise devoted to the production of sugar. Such an economic system depended primarily on masculine slave labor for its prosperity and survival, and male slaves were shunted from place to place as the need for them arose, regardless of their ties and desires. "Since the Inter-Colonial slave trade was not prohibited till 1825, male slaves were constantly drafted from the more settled colonies to work in the newer, less developed lands."

Family life of the "western" type was an impossibility when the slave's existence had to be devoted primarily to the cultivation and manufacture of sugar and other tropical products. The buying and selling of slaves involved the splitting up of families, whilst the maintenance of discipline on the plantations prevented the husband and father from protecting his wife and children against his white masters and other more favored slaves. The financial value set on slave children and the rewards given to successful motherhood in cash, kind, and promotion from field labor to labor in the house gave a specially high status to the mother, a status which the father could only enjoy if placed in a position akin to that of a stud animal, this leading to a sundering of family ties and the degradation of family life still further.

"Under such circumstances there was no opportunity for permanency in the association between the sexes."

The continuity of economic factors as they affect both the status and role of the male in the West Indian family still operates in the contemporary situation. "There can be no doubt that when a West Indian prospers he tends to marry and live a 'respectable' life." In St. Thomas, for example, "there has been an increasing tendency for upper-class status to become associated with adherence to the monogamic standard," while "legal marriage and monogamic constancy are not

* Reprinted with abridgment, revision, and omission of references from *American Anthropologist*, Vol. 58, pp. 664-686, 1956.

the general rule . . . among the lower class." In Jamaica, where these economic forces can be seen to operate in everyday familial relationships, "those families coming in the category of the 'Christian' family . . . form the better-off group" in the peasant population. Henriques estimates that only about 50 percent of the family groups in Jamaica are stable, monogamous unions, based either on legal marriage or "faithful concubinage." At the same time, "in 1935 nearly half the wage-earning population of Jamaica obtained only intermittent employment. . . ." On the basis of the census of 1943 and of an urban survey in 1946, Cumper estimates that unemployment in Jamaica amounts at least to 25 to 30 percent.

Operating alongside these divisive phenomena were other forces which militated against the survival of African family forms or the establishment of a new tradition of stable conjugal units. Under the conditions of slavery, sexual relations could not possibly have served as the basis of permanent unions; "the impermanence of slave sexual relationship is repeated from Brazil to the United States," especially within the British colonies.

> There were masters who, without any regard for the preferences of their slaves, mated their human chattel as they did their stock. . . . When men of the servile class were ordered to mate, women, who on the whole played a more passive role, had little choice in the selection of mates.

This singular condition of sexuality under slavery was further reinforced by the fact that the slaves could not marry; "slaves were not permitted to form permanent unions on either an African or European model. Family life under these conditions was impermanent." Furthermore, "slavery was inherited in the female line. The child of a slave-woman

was born in servitude, irrespective of the status of the father. . . . Paternity counted for little; the Negroes regarded the children as belonging to the mother rather than the father." The scars of such a history are still to be seen, as in Grenada, where, in 1934, "fully two-thirds of the illegitimate children received no support whatever, or very meagre support, from their fathers."

All these forces, and more, created a social situation in which

> only the bond between the mother and her child continually resisted the disruptive effect of economic interests that were often inimical to family life among the slaves. Consequently, under all conditions of slavery, the Negro mother remained the most dependable and important figure in the family.

One of the outstanding consequences of this peripheral role of the father is the phenomenon of illegitimacy. "The illegitimacy rates common throughout the West Indies vary from 60 to 75 percent of the total number of births," while in Jamaica "approximately 70 percent of all births recorded in 1942 were illegitimate." Since consequences often reinforce their causes, there can be little doubt that West Indian illegitimacy greatly strengthened the mother's structural role in the family as against the father's.

The statistical dominance of mother-centered families in the West Indies in general and in Jamaica in particular indicates the extreme degree to which the mother's centrality in the family is entrenched in the culture. As we shall see, this is true even for those family groups in which an adult male is present by virtue of his sociolegal status as husband and father. "The mother looks after the children whether the father is there or not. She feeds, clothes, and educates them, and it is to her that they turn in times of trouble throughout their lives. . . .

From the point of view of the children, the mother is dependable; the father is not."

The community to be described is relatively prosperous and economically stable, and the frequency of the western "Christian family" is therefore much higher than elsewhere in Jamaica and the West Indies. The data to be presented were gathered in 1950 and 1951.

Contemporary Rocky Roads (a fictitious name) is a community in the central mountains of Jamaica; it is made up of 277 persons comprising 57 households, 15 of which are occupied by single individuals. The Rocky Roaders are descendants of former slaves brought to Jamaica from Africa. Today they are independent farmers, raising mixed crops which they sell for cash at weekly markets. If one looks at Rocky Roads from the air, one sees a winding secondary road, on either side of which households are haphazardly scattered over the mountain and in the valley. Each home appears autonomous and independent of all others, and social relationships correspond in large measure to this physical picture.

Socialization in Rocky Roads is extremely depriving and restrictive in some areas, and equally permissive in others. Infants are not fed whenever they cry but rather at intervals of about four hours, for five to ten minutes at one breast. Temper tantrums are frequent but rarely elicit response. Nor are infants fed when they cry at night. As children grow older they can fetch food for themselves, and their diets improve slightly. This independence, too, is restricted, for the children may only eat food which was not meant for someone else. The difficulty of making the proper discriminations in this sphere is attested by the amount of punishment received on this score alone. Furthermore, children must be content with what they receive at mealtime; after

the age of four or five, children who cry for food after a meal are punished.

Corporal punishment is frequent; until about the age of four, children are slapped. After this age they are switched. In addition to infractions of rules surrounding food, children are punished for fighting, disobedience, breaking things, even accidentally, tarrying too long while on an errand, and the like. This part of the training is carried out almost entirely by the mother; the role of the father in socialization will be discussed presently.

Within a context of severe deprivation and restriction, infants and children of both sexes masturbate frequently and openly. There is never any parental punishment or encouragement of such activity. Toilet training is equally mild and permissive, generally commencing at about the age of two or three years. Control is taught by encouraging the children to imitate their parents and elder siblings; incontinence is punished only when a mother feels that a child has deliberately soiled the house in order to displease her.

For the first seven years a Rocky Roads child does not play with anyone except his own siblings. There are few opportunities for a growing child to establish warm emotional ties with persons outside the nuclear family. The Rocky Roads family is "emotionally inbred," to paraphrase Kluckhohn's description of the Navaho; during infancy, there are almost no influences on the baby from outside the home. An infant never sees any other part of the community, save for one trip to church to be christened and four or five trips to the monthly clinic. His home is his world, and the world's sole representative is his mother or mother surrogate. Rocky Roaders are not given to visiting one another and there are rarely guests or relatives to stimulate the child, or with whom it might establish relationships of one sort or another. Even later, children do not play with anyone except their siblings. A child is confined to his home until the age of about five years, and never ventures beyond it. Friends are not made until seven. The most frequent explanation is that if the children "mix" and play with "strangers," they may be "spoiled" and influenced by them.

Sibling rivalry is often intense, and the quarrels between rival siblings elicit parental punishment. The birth of a child arouses resentment in the one who is now next to youngest, and children thus displaced were often seen attempting to dislodge a nursing child from the mother's breast. This rivalry continues for many years and erupts again over division of the patrimony, but it does not always include all the siblings in the family. Simply, the siblings closest to each other in birth order are most antagonistic, with a proportionate decrease in hostility as the distance between them increases. In very large families it was sometimes possible to observe demonstrations of overt affection between the eldest child and the youngest.

Only the biological mother may nurse the child; informants knew of no violation of this rule. Many parents demand that their unwed daughters seek gainful employment which will enable them to contribute to the support of their illegitimate children. Since many girls must leave the community to find such jobs, they often wean their illegitimate children before 12 months; this is the age until which all children, legitimate and other, are supposed to be nursed. Even if the unmarried mother is able to find employment near her own home, her child receives even more depriving treatment and care than legitimate children of the same age. The illegitimate children are fed even less often than the legitimate, since their working mothers are away during the day; they are not clothed as well, and they receive even fewer of the already

minimal assurances of bodily comfort and care. Their grandmothers frequently complain of the strain of caring for several infants. One female informant summed up the matter concisely: Caring for more than a dozen of her own and her unwed daughters' children, she observed that one of the greatest difficulties confronting a family is that mother and daughters and father and sons are having children simultaneously. This is true, and it adds to the resentment precipitated by economic considerations.

In addition to the greater physical rejection of illegitimate children, they are also subjected to even greater "sibling rivalry" pressures. When there are often legitimate and illegitimate infant cousins within the same nuclear family, children in both categories must cope with the hostility of age-mates as well as that of older and stronger siblings and cousins. This stress, when juxtaposed with rejection in other spheres, is no doubt more trying for illegitimate children. When two cousins are vying for physical attention, a woman will invariably favor her own child as against her illegitimate grandchild.

Parents do have favorites among their children, the most subservient and submissive being favored. These children escape punishment more easily than those considered "meddlesome" or "rude." There are few differences in the training of boys and girls until the age of five, when role training commences. At five years girls begin to learn domestic tasks, beginning with the simplest jobs. Most mothers state that they wish their sons would learn such skills, but the boys adamantly refuse to indulge in domestic labor, except for tending the chickens and hogs and running errands. What the parents fail to report, and only observation discloses, is that girls are just as reluctant to do this sort of work. When a boy refuses to wash floors or dishes, he is not troubled and his refusal is accepted. The girls also begin with the same refusals, but they are switched for them. This accounts, in part, for the fact that girls receive more than twice the amount of whippings than their brothers, and it is also the point at which parents become consistently stricter with their daughters than with their sons. Furthermore, this is the first point at which boys are allowed to assert themselves.

During the first three or four years of a child's life the father is a source of neither gratification nor punishment. After this age, the father begins to administer punishment, but only at the instigation of the mother. It is not until the age of ten, however, that the father establishes any positive and stable relationship with any of his children, and then only with his sons. Yet the father is often physically present. While most of his time is spent in the fields, he does devote some days to the repair of the home; he is often at home during the rainy season, and on Sundays. Even on these occasions, when he is quite relaxed, he tends to avoid the younger members of the household and to keep them at a distance. Only once did we see a father show affection toward a younger child; this was a kiss given to a three-year-old daughter who was admittedly an unwanted child. This man had spent some years in Cuba and the United States, and had many values alien to his own culture.

At seven years, most children begin to attend the school conducted by the local Moravian Church. This appears to be a partial emancipation for the children, for most enjoy going to school. Also at this time, boys are allowed to remain to play cricket on the school green, unless there are chores for them at home; girls must always return home immediately after school.

That children are reared primarily by their mothers for the first ten years is consistent with the history of the Jamaican family. Frazier notes that "in spite of the numerous separations, the slave mother and her children, especially those under ten, were treated as a group." Contemporaneously, a new phase of socialization begins for boys when they reach the age of ten, for a radical change occurs in parent-son relationships. (The relationship between girls and their parents remains unchanged.) At this point, control and domination over the boys is exercised equally by both parents, whereas previously the boys were controlled almost entirely by their mothers. At this time boys begin to spend more time with their fathers. The latter, it should be noted, do not try to alienate their sons from their mothers; nor do the mothers attempt to foster father-son affection or hostility.

At ten years, boys begin helping their fathers in the fields. After learning simple tasks, they proceed to more advanced skills. They stand by and watch their father cultivate and harvest; when he lays down his tools, the boys pick them up and imitate his work. The father corrects his youngsters' work, and as they gain in proficiency the boys take on small agricultural tasks, always under the father's supervision. While learning these skills the boys are never punished for anything they may do wrong. While girls at first refuse to do the work which is demanded of them, and are punished, boys are eager to work in the fields and never require strenuous inducement. Children learn very early that the father will rarely punish except at the mother's instigation. Hence, from the earliest age boys and girls ask to be taken with their fathers to the fields. Girls are never given such permission; boys rarely receive it before they are ten.

True emotional dependence usually arises in contexts of authority in the course of socialization, and in Rocky

Roads it is the mother who is the first and most significant source of authority and object of dependence for the children. The centrality of the mother, structurally as well as functionally, focuses attention on the contrasting peripheral role of the father. The latter's position in the family can be seen through the development of his sons during and after adolescence, in their emergence as fully functioning members of the community.

Adolescence begins at departure from school, usually at fourteen years. As a period of transition, adolescence is characterized by the initiation of heterosexual intercourse and by the assumption of a larger share of adult activities preparatory to full-fledged adulthood. Simultaneously, there is a gradual weaning from dependence on parents; this is seen in the greater degree of free movement now granted the maturing youngsters.

Economic relationships to parents during adolescence can be viewed in part as the medium through which earlier experiences are realized. At about fourteen years, a boy begins to spend all his time cultivating on his father's land. He is given a portion of land, and he is relatively free to grow what he wishes; technically, he enjoys absolute ownership of all that the land yields. But since parents are not obligated to support their sons after adolescence, every son must contribute from one-third to one-half his earnings to his parents for his room and board. The remainder of the money is his to do with as he pleases. The degree of discipline over a boy decreases as his earnings increase. As he grows older, a young man becomes more and more independent of his parents, until he reaches the point in early adulthood where he no longer has to consult his parents about his decisions. Unmarried adult men spend as little time as possible at home, usually coming there only to eat and sleep. They do not consult their parents about anything, and their parents rarely question their activities.

The young men's unfolding social and economic independence of their parents, particularly of their fathers, is the first climactic illustration of the functional implications of the father's structurally peripheral role in the family. The second ramification is in the men's delay of marriage. In this case, the father's peripheral role during socialization is a condition which makes possible the maximization of processes inhering in mother-son relationships.

The mother's role as the primary source of authority and object of emotional dependence is thoroughly established in the adult male's character structure. For example, during the post-adolescent "rebellion," which is quite prevalent, and which we shall describe in Chapter 6, it is the mother, not the father, who brings the sons into line by refusing to cook for them or care for their clothes. This dependency on the mother is manifest in the men's attitudes toward marriage. A man rarely marries while his mother is still alive, for, as informants themselves put it, so long as a man has someone to cook his meals, mend his clothes, and care for his living quarters, he will not think of marrying. When his mother is no longer alive, he will seek to marry a woman who has money so that she "can help him out." In the absence of such a desirable person he will seek a girl who can do something, such as dressmaking, "to help herself," for should he cease to earn money he will be sure of some income for the family. His primary expectations of his wife are to cook for him, clean and mend his clothes, and care for his home. In his own words, he expects of his wife very nearly what he previously expected of his mother.

This dependence on the mother may be related to another factor. Within a context in which children are not permitted to play with others until the age of about seven years, it is curious that the only proscription on sexual choice is the incest taboo. In other words, for the first seven years of his life a Rocky Roader is in a situation in which all persons are sexually taboo. There are no other rules in the culture enabling him to discriminate between permissible and tabooed sexual objects. Given his similarity of perception of wife and mother, it might be possible to further understand, in part, his deferment of marriage. And it is this deferment of marriage which provides the basis for the recurrence of a relatively large population of illegitimate persons within the community.

Proscriptions against incest are probably requisite conditions for all social life. The confinement of sexual restrictions to incest within the nuclear family and the failure to adopt other sexual restrictions are easily understood in the light of the group's history. In Rocky Roads the taboo includes cousins, uncles, and aunts, since they are often members of the same nuclear family because of the structural responses to illegitimacy. It was observed earlier in this paper that the mating of slaves as "chattel" inhibited the formation of stable conjugal units during slavery, and it is easy to see how such practices militated against the adoption of other sexual proscriptions. The confinement of taboos governing sexual choice to members of the nuclear family is reinforced primarily by the confinement of young children to their families of orientation during their formative years. As will be observed shortly, the "emotional inbreeding" of the Rocky Roads family is intimately related to the structural centrality of the mother, a phenomenon which resulted from the economic vicissitudes of slave ownership. Slave owners rationalized their behavior with respect to the reproduction of slaves in economic terms. Similarly, it is curious that the

contemporary Rocky Roaders rationalize their delay of marriage in economic terms. Informants stated that a man should not marry until he is able to support a family; "foolish ones get married even if they can't support a family." Most informants felt that a man is able to support a family when he is thirty-five, but most men do marry before that age.

However, the economic factor alone is insufficient to explain the delay of marriage. First, most men begin to acquire some use of their fathers' lands by the time they reach late adolescence or early adulthood. The amount of land thus acquired generally corresponds roughly to the amount which will be inherited. Secondly, in almost 75 percent of Rocky Roads families the women survive their husbands and rarely remarry. When a man dies he invariably leaves his land to his wife. In practice, this means that the widow has title to the land while her sons work it; the proceeds from this land are the sons', and out of it they must provide for their mothers.

In discussing marriage, the men often cite the economic responsibilities which the formation of a family entails. Generally speaking, a man's foremost goal is the achievement and maintenance of great economic wealth; hence, he will tend to avoid any situation which will tax his economic resources. A Rocky Roads man is able to maintain a state of emotional equilibrium as long as he is capable of meeting his economic obligations, maintaining economic self-sufficiency, and hoarding money in his competitive struggles to outdo everyone else in the community; marriage arouses anxieties about his ability to succeed economically. The avoidance of marriage, generally until his late twenties or early thirties, is in part an avoidance of these anxieties.

These anxieties in the face of marriage can be illustrated by a man's behavior—his extreme tension, nervousness, and generalized anxiety—two or three days before his wedding. The reason for this extreme nervousness, informants mirthfully report, is that "he doesn't know what he is getting into." The groom is tense, they say, because he has no idea of what the economic burdens are going to be like, and he suffers anxiety over meeting his obligations. The symptoms which we treated at our improvised daily clinic were severe and chronic headaches and sleeplessness. These are accompanied by a remarkable rise in pulse rate, generalized irritability, and an incapacity to work. These symptoms seem to disappear within a few days after the wedding. Prospective brides are calm before their weddings, and are never "unsettled" as are their future husbands.

There is a third structural area in which the historically produced centrality of the mother or, by contrast, the father's peripheral position emerges clearly. In a way, the mother's centrality in the Rocky Roads family contributes to its eventual disintegration; this is a process which is repeated generation after generation. The climax of an individual's relationships to his family or orientation occurs in the inheritance of property. Theoretically, a man is supposed to make a will leaving his property to his wife; upon her death the land is to be distributed equally among all her legitimate children. When a man makes a will, he invariably keeps its contents secret lest some members of the family be disappointed and quarrel with him over its terms. Men generally leave their land and money to their wives, but occasionally land is willed directly to the children.

The land is not always divided equally; sons usually get a larger share than do daughters. On occasion, poorer sons will get more than others, and favored sons will get more than less favored children. These inequalities almost always generate feuds and animosities among siblings. Residues of old quarrels emerge; one often catches references to sorcery during quarrels over the patrimony. Such quarrels are not easily forgotten, for there are several factors which militate against the re-establishment of peace. First, there is always the divided land to remind the participants in the quarrel of its source. Secondly, a Rocky Roader who is deprived of land believes strongly that his deprivation is due to some concerted interpersonal effort directed at him which aims at his impoverishment.

With respect to property, the Rocky Roader can think only in terms of individual, private holdings. Competition for land is divisive in the family as well as in the general community. This is particularly important in family relationships, for quarrels over the patrimony often deal a final blow to the already minimal cohesiveness of the family group.

Since almost all significant emotional dependencies are concentrated on the mother, the father is not a primary agent of socialization to whom the children are tied emotionally. But he is the person who distributes the land among his sons. His word possesses some authority; his will is never contested in a court of law, even though the Rocky Roaders know that this can be done. (This may be due in part to fear of the father's ghost.) During the significant years in which patterns of dependence are established, the father has little emotional or symbolic hold on his sons; hence, after his death, his figure does not possess the emotionally charged internalized authority which would be necessary to preserve the family in the face of bitterness between the brothers over the patrimony. Without a common emotional bond to the father established in the early years, it is almost impossible for the Rocky Roads family to continue as a functioning and perpetuate unit from one generation to another.

GIRL

The psychological relationships of women to their families of orientation are different from the men's, but this difference is one of emphasis which covaries with different emphases in structural relationships. The first significant variation is in the rule that, while boys must be supported until they are fourteen, girls must be supported as long as they live at home. The second variation derives from the first, namely, that an unmarried girl must seek permission for everything she wants to do. The third difference is that girls do not have to contribute toward their maintenance while living at home.

When a girl leaves school her first wish is to find remunerative employment. The girls have only been trained for household labor; since there are rarely such jobs for more than half a dozen girls in and around Rocky Roads, many leave the community to seek work in the urban areas. Before accepting such a position, a girl must receive her mother's permission—not her father's—and even while away from home she is subject to her mother's—not her father's—discipline and must return home whenever called. We knew of no refusal to heed such a call. While at home, an adolescent girl must keep her mother informed of all her movements, and she may be punished for remaining away from the house too long or for leaving it without permission. A girl cannot come and go as she pleases until she reaches adulthood, at about twenty years.

While girls attempt to maintain the same independence of parents as do their brothers, they are at home more often and are therefore subject to greater parental scrutiny of their activities. The dependency of women continues after they are married. Specifically, this dependence is on the mother, not the father. Women react with much greater intensity than do men to the mother's criticism. Daughters respond to the death of a mother with greater sorrow than do sons. Like their brothers, married daughters frequently visit their mothers, but they do not visit their parents' homes for the express purpose of visiting their fathers.

The internalization of a greater degree of dependence by the women is largely a function of continuity in relationships to their mothers. While it is principally the juxtaposition of discontinuity of ties during socialization and the peripheral role of the father which provides the basis for the recurrent disruption of ties among brothers in quarrels over the patrimony, the girls' continuity of dependence on the mother precludes certain experiences among them. One of the most significant weakenings in the relationships of men to their families of orientation is their "adolescent rebellion" which emerges when they realize that they do not have to inform their parents of their activities or seek their approval. The girls do not experience such a patterned "rebellion" at any time in their lives. Their continuity of socialization and feelings of belonging in turn contribute immeasurably to their training for the maintenance of a central position within the family. The strength of this continuity is further reflected in the fact that while the division of the patrimony arouses divisive rivalries among brothers, women rarely enter into quarrels over the father's legacy, either among themselves or with the men. These continuities of socialization and structural membership are further reflected in the fact that illegitimate girls continue to reside with their grandparents after adolescence and are rarely forced either to fend for themselves or to leave the community.

The structural-functional processes described thus far emerge thematically in two contrasting pictures which exist side by side. The continuity of culture from generation to generation is one of the prime requisites of any societal grouping. One of the outstanding recurrent characteristics of Rocky Roads is the diffuseness and weakness of ties throughout the community. In large measure, this aspect of social structure has many of its significant roots in the weakness and repetitive disintegration of male sibling ties. The latter, in part, closely parallel both the sociopsychological rejection of a number of men by virtue of their illegitimate status, and the weakness of the father's image in maintaining familial solidarity. An attempt has here been made to show that these are intimately related to the historically determined structural and emotional centrality of the mother.

Synchronic processes often reflect diachronic ones; the thread which runs through the history of Rocky Roads culture is the structural-functional centrality of the mother. This, we have attempted to show, is reinforced by the women's continuity of socialization and belongingness.

When the prime authority—the adult male—of the patripotestal family dies, his authority immediately transfers to the adult female—the mother—of the family, and the group continues to function much as it did before. In no instances in which the father's authority was adopted by the mother were there any indications that her centrality had weakened. Upon the death of a father his widow continues to receive not only the obedience which she had previously gotten but also the obedience which was her husband's due.

In Rocky Roads the inculcation of masculine and feminine values appears to occur primarily through the arousal of different motivations in given areas of behavior during the course of socialization rather than through an emphasis on different patterns of identification. One of the most significant differences between the sexes is in the area of assertiveness

and independence. At no time are girls permitted to assert themselves, while boys are often allowed to assert themselves without fear of punishment. The first point at which this occurs is at about five years, when the boys refuse to do the work which their sisters must do. This differential treatment of assertiveness is reinforced at various stages of the life cycle. Girls must return immediately from their errands, while boys are allowed to tarry. Boys are allowed to remain to play cricket after school, while girls must return home immediately. Adolescence marks the next point at which there is a sex differential in socialization. Girls remain with their mothers within the restricting confines of the home, while boys begin to lead relatively independent lives. The submissiveness of the women is reinforced even in adulthood; until that stage they may do few things without their mothers' permission. Their brothers have long since assumed the roles of independent breadwinners.

While these differences between the men and the women are essentially "personality" differences, they also have their implications for the broader social structure, particularly in the continuity of the community culture from one generation to the next. We have seen that the quarrels among brothers over the division of the patrimony serve as a catalyst in mobilizing the divisive and isolating forces already present within the nuclear family. It was also observed that the women almost never quarrel over shares in the father's legacy, either among themselves or with their brothers. And we have seen the roles played in this process by the centrality of the mother, the peripheral and emotionally weak position of the father in relationship to his sons, the continuity in the girls' socialization and the discontinuity of the boys' ties to the family.

In any given social situation, we must always bear in mind that the people of whom we are speaking have a history. The article which we have just finished reading attempted to show how the centrality of the mother in this Jamaican community had its original roots in an historical condition, namely, slavery. But history is never a cause. It only sets the stage on which many forces can be played out. The history of any group, especially as it affects the ways in which its children are going to be brought up, is a set of preconditions, a set of potentialities, the final effects of which are largely determined by what has happened to the group since that history was set into motion. The conditions under which this community has lived since its emancipation from slavery changed little between 1800 and 1950; thus, we can understand that the forces which originally set the centrality of the mother into motion were little changed during that period of time. If the conditions under which these people live were suddenly to change, we would anticipate that there would be an abrupt discontinuity between historical events and contemporary patterns. What we are attempting to find out is how such patterns are kept going once they have been set into motion.

For example, it is often possible to observe the centrality of the mother in socially isolated American middle-class families living in apartment houses (that is, in close physical proximity to each other) in many different cities. It would be extremely difficult to discuss and analyze this complex without referring to the fact that a large proportion of American families once lived in physical isolation from each other on the frontier. But very few families still live on the frontier. It would be misleading to say that because many families had once lived on the frontier, many families are now socially isolated. Instead, we would have to understand what *new* conditions have arisen to help perpetuate an old pattern which arose under entirely different conditions.

In the foregoing case study, we have seen some of the effects of familial isolation on socialization processes primarily as they are manifest in adult behavior. Compared to the kinds of observations which can be made on children's development by highly trained psychologists, the data on the children themselves in this Jamaican community are most superficial. The reasons for this are twofold, especially as they apply to such investigations. First, it is extremely difficult for social scientists to get at the fine points of personality development in children under varying social conditions. Students of social systems do not have the requisite training which would enable them to accumulate such data. And even if they did possess such skills, the exigencies of the conditions under which they carry out their research rarely leave them the time to gather such information. This is not to say that such materials should not be collected; on the contrary, they are necessary and should be accumulated by individuals who are trained in gathering such information.

Secondly, anthropologists and sociologists, despite the differences between them, are primarily concerned with the dynamics and functioning of working social systems; thus, by contrast, they are relatively uninterested in children *per se*. This is understandable. Children are not culture-bearers and they do not participate actively in institutional processes. They do not inherit—except nominally, if they are minors —they do not marry, they do not produce food, they do not defend the society in times of war, they do not build houses and irrigation systems, and the like. It is in the doers of these things, and in the doings of them, that social scientists are primarily interested. Even the process of socialization, which is recognized by all social scientists as a major function and responsibility of adults, is viewed generally as an adult function, and little attention is devoted to the objects of this process, namely, the children themselves. Whether the lead for such direct observations will come from psychology, anthropology or sociology is irrelevant. What is important is that we sorely need a series of studies making direct observations on children under different social conditions—without, of course, going to the opposite extreme of neglecting the adults.

For these reasons, as well as others, Gordon Macgregor's material on the Teton-Dakota Indians is especially valuable and pertinent. Not only does he give us an excellent picture of the social-structural and cultural changes among the Teton-Dakota, but he also tells us about ten Teton-Dakota children among whom we are able to observe the effects of the new conditions of Teton life on growing individuals. It must be borne in mind that the material on the children which Macgregor presents was not intended to illustrate the issues under discussion in this chapter. As a matter of fact, these data were originally presented in much greater detail to illustrate the disturbing effects of a transitional cultural stage on the children of this society. We have omitted most of these data from the present selection, and have culled only those which appear to bear on the problems we are endeavoring to understand, the centrality of the mother in the isolated family. As we shall see shortly, most of the children in Macgregor's analysis appear to have severe emotional problems focusing upon their mothers.

WARRIORS WITHOUT WEAPONS*

By Gordon Macgregor

Historical records and information gathered from old men on the reservation at the beginning of the twentieth century indicate that the Teton-Dakota society was probably organized somewhat as follows. The fundamental social unit was the biological family, but the family always lived with from ten to twenty related families in a small band or *tiyospaye*.

The band formed an extended bilateral family or group of people related by blood and reckoning descent through both the male and the female lines. The main biological family of the *tiyospaye* was that of the chief, and all other families were related to it. In the old bands the families were usually related through the male line, for men commonly brought

* Selections reprinted from *Warriors Without Weapons: A Study of the Society and Personality of the Pine Ridge Sioux*, pp. 52-136 and 153-181, by permission of The University of Chicago Press. Chicago: University of Chicago, 1946.

their wives from other bands to their family group. Occasionally the band included other families who joined either to escape some unpleasant social pressure or to become the followers of a renowned warrior. There were also larger bands of related and unrelated extended families, which maintained social unity the year round.

The bands customarily camped separately during the wintertime, but late each spring groups of bands joined in a camp circle or encampment for their annual religious ceremonial, the Sun Dance, and for the cooperative buffalo hunts. War parties were made up from men of one or several summer encampments. Each band camped in its assigned section of the circle, the band with the leading chief of the encampment pitching their tepees in the section opposite the camp entrance. The encampments are not always defined in descriptions of Dakota social organization because they were not permanent the year round and were constantly shifting in band membership.

Today there is no tribal organization of the Teton-Dakota, and the subtribes and odd bands settled on the reservations have become new tribes or social groups. For example, the Oglala and Brule and families from other Dakota subtribes who came into the last Red Cloud Agency and were moved to Pine Ridge have now become the Pine Ridge Indians. The *tiyospaye* is the only social unit particularly characteristic of the former Teton-Dakota social structure which has remained important in the reservation society.

The Teton had a governmental organization, which was developed only among the encampments. The political pattern of one Oglala group was organized in the following manner. The main political body was the Chiefs' Society composed of the heads and leaders, forty years of age or older, who elected their own members. This society elected the Seven Chiefs of the Tribe, who held office for life. The position was partially hereditary, as it was the practice to elect a son or younger relative to fill the vacancy of a deceased chief. These seven chiefs appointed the Four Shirt Wearers, the real councilors of the division, who also held office for life but could resign their position.

Four executive officers of the encampment, the *wakicun*, were also appointed by the Seven Chiefs of the Tribe to hold office for a year. It was the particular function of this group to organize and control the camp.

The four *wakicun* selected two messengers, a herald, and two *akicita,* or head police, who in turn selected two others to serve with them. The *akicita* selected a body of police, or designated a group in one of the men's societies to serve as such, to keep order in the camp. These police had much authority and disciplined severely those who upset the camp life, even to killing a murderer. On the buffalo hunt this group kept the hunters in order, so that no greedy or overexcited person would run in and stampede the herd.

In each encampment were men's societies, one group from which the police were selected, a second group to which headmen belonged, and a third group of warriors. New members were elected by each society in a secret meeting, and one man might belong to several. Membership in these societies was one means of rewarding the brave in battle and the cooperative in camp life. A second function of the societies was the distribution of property by which members honored others and helped the aged and unfortunate.

This social organization was democratic in that all heads of family groups participated in the council and in the annual election of camp officers. There is some evidence to show that the four *wakicun* were the original heads of the encampment and that the great war chiefs were a development that came after the first contacts with whites in the eighteenth century. Men like Red Cloud, who achieved a great reputation during the fighting with the whites in the middle of the nineteenth century, were classed as "chiefs," although originally within the encampment organization they were only warriors who became temporary leaders during raids.

Nowadays the old *tiyospaye* no longer exist as organized units, but they are the bases of most of the rural communities. There are also on the reservation communities of related mixed-blood people and villages which have not developed from the native social groups. The difference in origin of full-blood and mixed-blood communities can be found in the desire to cling to either Indian or white lines of descent and ways of living.

The biological family of father, mother, and children merged with the extended family group with which it lived, hunted, and shared its food and social life. It was not the exclusively important group, as it is regarded usually by white people. Today, however, the individual family has risen in importance, largely because it has become the essential economic unit in the livestock, farming, and wage-work economies which the Pine Ridge Indians have successively followed on the reservation. The individual family was also forced into greater importance because of the white man's administration, which dealt directly with these units following the concept of white social organization. Although cattle and land were issued to individuals, it was expected that they would be operated and utilized by the biological family.

The family now lives with greater independence of related families in its own farm home. The father, as head of the family, is usually its chief support, but his work is often irregular and not usually devoted to a single occupation. The circumstances which have made it impossible for the men to work steadily as cattlemen or farm laborers or to produce a regular income have affected their status and respect within their own families. Frequently, it has been necessary for the mothers to earn wages to keep the family fed and clothed. This has increased the importance of the mother in the family, a change which has altered the children's relationships to both parents. The new relationships are particularly apparent in the present training of the children in the home and development of children's personalities which are to be described in detail in following parts of the study.

Formerly the father assumed some of the training and disciplining of the boys, which was the basis of an intimate bond. This most important relationship between father and son—developing from the training of a boy for his economic and social role—has been badly dislocated by cultural changes. Compared to their position in the former nomadic life, the majority of fathers have no career and little social role to which they can introduce a son. A man may have a small herd of cattle or horses which a boy learns to care for early in his life, but there are now few special techniques which the father can pass on to his son. By the time a boy is 14 or 15 he can compete with his father as a common wage-earner. The father's role of teacher has been minimized not only by the disappearance of the men's former occupations and goals in life but also by the introduction of schools among the Dakota. Even the fathers who do not desire the white man's life for themselves appreciate the fact that it will be to their children's advantage to understand this way of living. They want the school to give their children such understanding and send them to school with this expectation.

The boy growing up in a Dakota family today does not appreciate the difference in the relationship that exists between his father and himself and that which existed between his great-grandfather and grandfather. He does, however, become aware of his father's lack of a continuous occupation and of the absence of a real career in which his father and the men of his community might offer him some participation. They have given him social drives, but modern Indian society offers little reward that produces a feeling of achievement. He has been pushed to early adulthood. Arriving at its threshold, he finds himself on an equal footing with the men of his community but, like them, without status or life-purpose.

The mother is the center of the present-day family, because she has assumed greater responsibility for its direction and support. The mother's role has also gained by the present isolation of the individual household. Formerly the family lived in a camp with several other related families, with whom the child associated freely. Now the child living in a farmhouse on an allotment is forced to spend much more time with his own family and especially with his mother. One small full-blood boy described very aptly the mother's position in the family by pointing to an ear of corn which had six small kernels sprouting from one end, "Mother, the ear of corn is like you, and the little things are the children."

The early attachment to the mother often becomes so strong that it is carried through adulthood. One man states, "My son gets lonesome when he is away from his mother." "My wife is that way, too," he adds complainingly; "she does not like to live away from her folks. I have a nice place, but she is like a suckling colt to stay so close to her mother." Mother-daughter relationship is commonly a very lasting one, and, after marriage, the daughter is constantly returning home to visit, to have her babies, or to help her mother in emergencies.

Although the observed mother-child relationships appear in general to be very pleasant and close to the ideal of affection and respect, there are mothers whose relationships to their children are bad according to Dakota standards and those of good mental hygiene as well. Observers in this study heard mothers call their children "dumb," "crazy," or a "crybaby." One mother had to be stopped by the school principal from beating her child with her fists, because she heard that a teacher called the child "Public Enemy No. 1." Enraged little boys were also seen striking their mothers.

There are other mothers who appear indifferent toward their children. Two small children were found who did not know their mother, although they lived at their grandmother's home less than five miles away from her. Some mothers have deserted their husbands and children to live with other men. On the other hand, children who find relationships with their mothers intolerable run away to live with other relatives. Children were permitted to leave their tepees in the old days, but such behavior in the old culture was considered a great affront to the parent's reputation. The frequency with which children are now voluntarily living away from their parents' home without disapproval by the adults may be looked upon as symptomatic of cultural breakdown.

In cases of separation from their wives, fathers often seem particularly indifferent about their children, leaving them for the wife or grandparents to support, without regard for the wife's or grandmother's ability to do so. In leaving the children with the wife, the fathers are following customary practice, but in the past there were the wife's relatives and the families of her band circle to help feed a few more mouths.

The relationship between brothers has been described as the strongest in the Teton-Dakota kinship system. This is still manifest, and brothers are close comrades and playmates. In the former life the older brother undertook the training of the younger in many of the technical skills of men. Brothers today retain their close attachment throughout life, helping one another in the fields, sharing food, and bringing their children to one another's homes. In a crisis brothers join forces as they did in the past. One Indian stockman said, "If I have trouble with somebody, then all my brothers here would come to help me, and there would be big trouble."

The present behavior between brother and sister is one of the most marked changes from the kinship pattern of the former culture. The old avoidance has disappeared, but mutual respect is still observed. Little girls of six or seven, who were formerly taught to avoid their brothers, now may sleep in the same bed with them. They ride to school in the same busses, they play and fight together, and older brothers even accompany younger sisters to dances when their parents cannot act as chaperones. Loyalty to the sister is still strong. This was observed in the behavior of an older man who attempted to avenge his sister's murder. The pattern is approaching that of white children in both the mixed-blood and the full-blood families, but the taboo against intimacy between brother and sister is not lost entirely among the latter. In the modern Rabbit Dance, performed by couples neither full-blood brothers and sisters nor those classes as such in the Sioux kinship system will dance together.

In the old extended family or *tiyos-paye* camp, a man's tepee usually stood next to that of his married brother, and in front might be the tepee of a married son. Family homes are geographically widely separated today in comparison with the band camp, and the associations within an extended group are less frequent and intensive; but the individual usually does have a few members of his extended family close by. Grandparents may be living in a tent beside the house, with brothers or sisters as the nearest neighbors. Frequently a relative not belonging to the biological family may be living in the home. All these relatives in the family circle for the most part continue to maintain the relationships of the kinship system.

The grandparents exemplify the ideal of kindliness and generosity of the old Sioux culture. The grandfather, formerly a counselor to the young, still attempts to continue this function, but his prestige has declined because he can no longer participate in activities formerly carried on by the older men and because he does not understand the changing ways.

It is difficult to ascertain how much of the kinship terminology that embraces the extended family is now used by the present youngest generation, for they have learned English terminology, which they use in the presence of white people. Some children draw a clear distinction by saying to a white person, "That is my father—of course, he is really only my uncle—but we call him 'father' in Indian." Another child will say, "My mother is here for me," if he believes this is the stronger argument for being excused from class, but in another circumstance he will mention the same individual as his aunt. Other children use the English kinship terms at home, calling the "fathers" and "mothers" of the extended family "uncles" and "aunts" and behaving toward them differently than toward their own fathers and mothers. This change is more marked among the mixed-blood people, because of their greater use of

English and the classifications which white relatives make. The adoption of English kinship terminology appears to be a strong factor in breaking down the ties and behavior patterns of the extended family organization.

Among full-blood families which still speak Siouan, the language aids in the preservation of the old terminology and related behavior. When members of the extended family live as neighbors, they continue to act according to the role of their relationships position. Thus a child born into such a group receives treatment as a son, a grandson, or a brother from those he is taught to call "father," "grandfather," or "brother." If the younger people appear lax in this behavior, a grandparent will often reprimand them for not adhering to the Indian way.

The extended family group which formerly erected its lodges together is now stretched in a line of separated homes. When a family increased, an older man might take his children and perhaps the families of his brothers and sisters to some distance below the original band site or to another creek and form another group, which ultimately developed into a separate community. This followed the process by which new bands were created in the former society. Most of the present-day reservation communities are thus derived from original bands.

A few houses have been built near the old sites, but there is no evidence of anything resembling a village or clustering of the homes of the descendants of the band.

This pattern of the extended family living on adjoining lands was created in part by the allotment system, when a man, his wife, and children received adjoining allotments of land. As the children grew up and married, they built their homes on their own allotments, thereby retaining the family grouping and establishing a family neighborhood. Other members of the original band also received allotments along the same creek, so that the descendants of the band have maintained a community grouping. All these families can trace their common relationship to the original large extended family group; but, with each new generation and the growing importance of the individual family, the common relationship becomes weaker and less meaningful. The new family neighborhoods are developing into independent extended family groups.

On the other hand, several factors, such as the geographic separation of families and the development of new extended family groups, have led to the disintegration of original band groupings. The individual and the individual family can, if they desire, support themselves on a farm or by wage work without the assistance of others and can find companionship and social life and work elsewhere. Such separation of the individual from his or her relationship group rarely took place in the old days, except by moving away with one's entire family or joining another band by marriage.

This dispersion of families over and outside the reservation has weakened the cooperation of the extended family and community groups. Frequently the stay-at-homes, the older people and women and children, have been asked to look after the horses or a few cattle of the absentees. Such cooperation is willingly given, but very often there is no return of assistance by the people who have gone away. This is due to changing attitudes. Those who have gone away expect those at home to cooperate by caring for property left behind, according to Indian custom; but, like white men, they have come to regard money earned on the job as belonging exclusively to themselves and their immediate families. Those left behind are at a disadvantage under both customs.

Parents try to use the old control of criticism, since chaperonage has become impossible, but criticism seems to have lost its former weight with the young people. Parents therefore frequently turn to white controls and ask school principals or police to bring back runaway daughters or to punish young men who have seduced them.

The breakdown in family control and the failure of the child-training system are not the only causes for increasing sexual delinquency. From time immemorial this has been a symptom of and sequel to general social disorganization. On the reservation the sex delinquency is to be found among the most disorganized generation—the parents—as often as among the young people. Hence it is probable that the illicit sexual behavior of parents and the amount of gossip about it in the community cause as much delinquency among the younger people as lack of social control.

The modern social structure, with its poverty, lack of adequate roles and cultural objectives, and social conflicts arising out of lost controls and changing attitudes, is strongly conducive to insecurity for the group and for the individual. As each Dakota man or woman now looks back to the past either from experience or through the stories which have been told him, he senses the self-assurance and the ability of his ancestors to cope with life. They were united and secure in the life they followed, and their institutions gave good reinforcement within the group. By comparison, the modern Indian way of life is one of emptiness, one in which family and community are losing their integration. The contemporary life, as compared with the culture that was functioning in the middle nineteenth century, is only a shadow. Attitudes and values of that culture still strongly affect the behavior patterns of the people, but some of its social institu-

tions are gone or are only vestigial. The realization of cultural loss and being neither Indian nor white in any cultural sense adds to the Indian's insecurity and isolation in the modern world.

This insecurity of the adults, which is now so apparent from the material point of view in their meager incomes and from the psychological point of view in their inconsistent behavior and conflicting attitudes, creates an atmosphere which cannot help having repercussions upon the children as they grow up. The young children can only sense the confusion and the uncertainty of their parents without understanding the causes, and so they themselves feel insecure. This insecurity in the environment is one of the most significant aspects to keep in mind as we turn to the children's training and social adjustments.

Once the Indian baby began to enjoy the mother's breast he was nursed whenever he whimpered, day or night, and he also was allowed to play freely with the breast. A small child was not supposed to cry in helpless frustration, although later to cry in rage could "make him strong." It is generally assumed that Indian mothers return to their old "spoiling" customs as soon as they can be sure they will not be bothered by the health authorities.

It is said that the oldest boy was nursed longest and that the average nursing period was three years.

Nor is the Dakota child fed, bathed, and put to sleep by the clock. Today white methods are used increasingly by the more assimilated Indian families, but the stronger discipline characteristic of the training of white children comes chiefly from the schools on the reservations.

Most mothers on the reservation today nurse their babies. Where the mother's milk is insufficient or unsuitable for the baby, Indian Service nurses and doctors advise the substitution of canned milk. The scheduled feeding practiced by white mothers is advocated by reservation nurses and doctors, but this advice is infrequently followed, so strong is the Dakota belief that a child should be fed whenever he frets. Resistance to scheduled feeding is also due to the fact that Indian families do not regulate their daily life by the clock.

Reservation doctors and nurses recommend weaning between the 9th and 12th months, and some women now abruptly wean their babies at this time. But most mothers extend the weaning process over a period of many months, gradually introducing solid foods. The time of weaning reported to interviewers in this study ranged from 9 to 36 months, with the majority falling in the period of 11 to 18 months. In the cases of prolonged nursing, as Erikson puts it, the child weans the mother.

The most effective means for cultural change lay in the education of the young people. Although the school established under the first agent at Pine Ridge got off to a bad start when the matron attempted to cut off the boys' long braids and thus threw the students into flight, the first classes soon had a large number of the children around the agency in attendance. The formal school program was patterned after that of the schools in the East, but half the time was devoted to industrial training, agriculture, and housekeeping.

Children were virtually kidnapped to force them into government schools, their hair was cut, and their Indian clothes thrown away. They were forbidden to speak in their own language. Life in the school was under military discipline, and rules were enforced by corporal punishment. Those who persisted in clinging to their old ways and those who ran away and were recaptured were thrown into jail. Parents who objected were also jailed.

Where possible, children were kept in school year after year to avoid the influence of their families [these data were gathered during the 1930's].

To begin the account of the findings of this study about the personality structure of Dakota children, sketches of ten children are presented. These children vary in amount of Indian blood from full-blood to three-sixteenths, and their ages range from eight to sixteen. They come from the three communities of the study. The personal and social adjustments of these children vary from excellent to very poor. Some of these variations may be partly accounted for by physical conditions or family losses, which may befall the individual in any society; but the influence of their particular cultural position and social climate is apparent in most of these personalities.

Red Bird is an eight-year-old girl whose degree of Indian blood is reckoned in thirty-seconds, a fractionation which signifies that her ancestors intermixed with whites several generations ago. Since then there has been marriage into the full-blood group. Red Bird now lives with her paternal grandmother and grandfather, Amelia and Frank White Horse. Their home is in a full-blood community composed of the grandfather's extended family group.

Red Bird's tests indicate that there may be already some sexual disturbance. Her practice of hanging around the girls' washroom before and during school hours, her interest in older girls, and her attention to her appearance also suggest a possible overdevelopment of sexual interest. This may be stimulated by association with her mother.

Red Bird has become very uncertain of herself from her family situation. Rejection by her mother has been a distinct shock. Although her mother has made clothes for her, visited her in school, and taken her home for a week or two, this brief indulgence without a continued affectionate relationship has been very unsatisfying. Her father once offered her much support, but his departure from the family scene and his responsibility for other little girls have created consternation in Red Bird's mind. Toward her indulgent grandparents, she reveals no deep affection. In one test, she stated that the happiest things she could remember were "when Grandpa and Grandma died" and "when Uncle went to war." This untrue statement about her grandparents shows not only the lack of any close bonds with them but also probably wishful thinking stirred by resentment or anxiety. The best thing that could happen to her, she says, is "go to heaven." This remark epitomizes Red Bird's unhappiness, if not a real wish to be dead. A child with her attitudes and anxiety is indeed in serious difficulty.

The Running Elks, a family of pure Indian descent, live in an attractive, painted farmhouse surrounded by small trees and a low fence. The father built this house through a rehabilitation loan from the government. Later he purchased land adjacent to the house for a garden. The house is superior to most full-blood homes on the reservation.

The father died several years ago when Winona and Robert were five and three years old. For many years the father had been an employee of a neighboring white storekeeper, driving the store truck and working in the white man's field. He spent most of his vacations visiting other reservations to see the Indian fairs and celebrations, particularly the Sun Dances. Winona and Robert remember their father clearly and look upon the summer trips taken with him and the rest of the family as high points in their lives.

The mother remained a widow until recently. A neighboring widower moved into the house to help her with the chores after her oldest boy went into the Ma-

rines. After discussing the matter through the mails with her elder son, the mother decided to marry this man. Whether the younger children were also consulted could not be learned, but doubtless there was some discussion of the event beforehand. The children's relations with him were not reported.

Winona's test scores—an I.Q. of 141 by the Arthur test and 117 by the Goodenough Drawing Test—place her among the most intelligent of the tested group of Dakota children. Although she has good drive toward intellectual achievement, her interests run to practical and commonplace matters, as her school work shows. She is self-contained, but she places no undue restraint on her sense of humor or her ability to act with good understanding and to make decisions. She is, however, outwardly cautious and formal, following the behavior of a well-trained Dakota girl.

She keeps up her contacts with other people but feels little dependence upon them. She also has a tendency to consider relationships and situations for her own benefit. With most adults, and particularly her teachers, Winona is compliant, but with her mother, Winona feels some resentment because she attempts to control Winona's behavior more than she likes. The mother, as a woman frequently ill and upset by the loss of two children and a husband, does not appear to have given Winona the intimate associations that a child needs. The mother's recent marriage and previous ambiguous relationships with a man who has supplanted her beloved father may also cause some of Winona's unfriendliness toward her. The relationship with her mother appears to have directed Winona toward becoming self-contained, and the restrictions which her mother placed upon her have handicapped her in making wider social contacts and developing a better basis for making friends. Otherwise, Winona is an extremely able and well-adjusted young girl who is learning to live in her community without becoming suppressed or losing the best personality qualities of her Indian heritage.

In his personality development Robert appears to be a boy who has been somewhat overprotected at home because, as a small child, he was thought to lack robustness and vigor. This has retarded slightly the development of his social techniques, so that he appears in his social behavior younger than he actually is. However, with his intellectual endowments and continued associations with many other children at school, he should develop rapidly. Like his family, he will probably adapt to white life, but he will also be proud of and content in his Indian heritage.

Charlie is a fourteen-year-old full-blood boy with a round and merry face, who lives in a dilapidated log cabin on the outskirts of a small town. The family consists of father, mother, and older brother and sister. About five years ago Charlie lost a brother a year younger than himself.

Charlie appears to be a young adolescent unsure of his family ties and with no loyal relatives to support him in the community. He tries to build up favor and attention for himself by good performance in school work, but this is only a show that does not win him the satisfaction or security he desires. He appears to be anxious and floating in a social milieu that affords him no moorings.

Melville Le Gasse is a boy of nine, whose black hair, brown eyes, and light-brown skin mark him with stronger Indian characteristics than is expected of persons of less than one-quarter Indian blood. He has the full physical development expected of a boy his age. Until the fall of 1942, Melville and his family were almost the only mixed-bloods in their full-blood community. They moved here about five years before from a white farming district in a neighboring state, leased several allotments of land, and borrowed money to start a cattle herd. In their former home the family associated with whites and near-whites. Melville had no playmates of his own age in the neighborhood; for one year he attended a kindergarten in the near-by town.

In his social relationships in the Indian day school in 1942, Melville sought his teacher's protection and gave her his confidence, particularly about his home life and the difficulties of his parents. Melville admired her and her home, which is superior to any of the other homes he has visited. He played with the boys in class but had difficulty because he demanded to be the center of attention. Occasionally he would pick a fight and then run to his teacher crying or complain later to his mother that he was picked on. He was looked upon as something of a sissy because of his slightly effeminate behavior. This quality was heightened when he accepted the leading feminine part in a class play—a role that no "good" Sioux boy would consider. Occasionally he ran away from school for an afternoon to play with an older boy and a distant relative. Melville showed good interest in his studies, but his teacher felt he was capable of doing better work.

Melville's insecurity and anxiety appear to be derived from the precarious economic and social status of his family. His mother is unsatisfied in her social ambitions and anxious over the family's economic position. She disparages his father before Melville. She also indulges and overprotects her son and keeps him from better social development by restricting his play with age mates. Melville, lacking ties with parents or age mates, puts himself in a submissive position to gain their protection.

Ginny is an eight-year-old girl with light-brown complexion, bright dark eyes, and a round, cherubic face. Outside her Indian community she might be easily taken for a little French girl, and not without reason, for she has more French than Indian heritage, with only three-eighths Indian blood. Ginny is an energetic and competent little girl, quite able to look out for herself and her brother Peter, who is a year younger.

At present only Ginny, Peter, and an older brother, Alexander, aged ten, attend school. Alexander is a rather sullen and effeminate young boy who frequently makes complaints about his teachers. This usually brings his mother to his defense or wins him a temporary absence from school. He quarrels with Ginny and his brother. Fighting among the children now at home appears to be a common occurrence. Contrary to Sioux custom, the younger ones are punished by their mother if they start trouble with the older ones.

Ginny's tests show a well-organized, superior intelligence; she scored an I.Q. of 119 on the Arthur test, although only 99 on the Goodenough. She has a wealth of imagination, which she freely and fully reports. This quality is a great help to her as a release and escape from strong depressive and aggressive feelings. These feelings appear to be derived from a deep-rooted insecurity in her brothers and sister and concern about her relation to her mother, who, she feels, has greater affection for the other children. Their quarrelsome and antagonistic behavior increases this uneasiness.

Mickey is nine years old, the youngest of the nine children of a white man and a woman of three-eighths Indian blood. All the children have white skin and features that reveal none of their Indian heritage.

Some of his responses to the tests show that he has no real love or respect for his father. Instead of the idealized picture that some young children paint of their fathers, Mickey seems to view his father as an aloof, irritable, unaffectionate old man. Mickey's feelings for his mother and his family reflect the constant come-and-go of people. His concept of a family is one of a friendly yet slightly unstable group of people, rather than a loving and cohesive unit that would help to give him a firmer feeling of security. He feels that his mother is a friendly, though not loving, authority from whom he can obtain very little real affection. His relation to his brother Ralph is not so satisfying as Mickey would like, for Ralph is quite inconsistent in his behavior. He appears to like Mickey, yet at times he becomes quarrelsome and domineering. It is possible, although the evidence is scanty, that some of this difficulty arises from Ralph's jealousy over Mickey's greater popularity with all their relatives.

Priscilla is a thin, frail girl of eleven with a dark skin and a sober countenance. She has nine-sixteenths Indian blood. Her birth was normal and her first year of life a healthy one. About the time of her second birthday she began to have convulsions, which appeared occasionally until she was seven. These "spells," as the family called them, frightened and bewildered them. Noticing that when she was made to cry she frequently went into a convulsive state, they treated her with utmost caution and have continued to do so, even though this sickness seems definitely over.

Priscilla's tests show that she has a very superior intelligence (I.Q. 137 on the Arthur test) and is generally quick in her mental approach, with an excellent grasp of ideas and their interrelations. She, no doubt, enjoys this intellectual superiority, for she is making her best adjustment in her intellectual and imaginative life. Her efficiency is somewhat lowered by an overdeveloped habit of daydreaming. She is an impressionable and somewhat immature girl, sensitive to the outer world. She withholds herself from social contacts, which suggests some insecurity. At home this insecurity tends to become confusion over her relationships with parents and adult brothers and sisters. She does not wish to abandon the protection and petting that she is used to, yet she would like to assert her independence and be more mature.

Andre is a handsome ten-year-old boy of three-eighths Indian blood who attends the fourth grade of the local day school. He lives with his three sisters, his father, and his mother in an outlying town of a predominantly white and mixed-blood population. An older sister is a nurse in a hospital on another reservation. The family have an attractive, small frame house. The parents are both employed, attend church regularly with their children, and are looked upon as good citizens in the community.

Andre looks upon his mother as the boss of the family, even asking her permission to go hunting with his father. This, he says, he learned from his good friend, the minister, who is always preaching that women should care for and run their families. Andre, who always attended church with his parents as a little boy, now goes to Sunday school and in summer attends a Bible school.

In his behavioral approach, Andre is realistic and able to get along fairly well with both age mates and adults. He does show a little insecurity, which appears to stem partly from his earlier separation from other children, necessitated by sickness, and partly from the predominance of women around him. But this insecurity has not affected his adjustment deeply. Andre has made a good adjustment to his father and mother. He respects his mother as a competent woman and admires his father.

Carmelita is a sixteen-year-old girl of three-eighths Sioux blood. She also has French and a little Canadian Indian blood from her father. Although her complexion is dark, she looks more French than Indian.

Until Carmelita attended boarding school, she lived at home and went to a day school in the rural area of the reservation. Her family live in a community of mixed-blood families, who are closely interrelated. They are successful cattle operators, running their herds individually. In social matters, however, they are a very cooperative and closely knit social group. Carmelita's father has an allotment in this community. He was very prosperous during World War I but shortly afterward lost all his holdings through a sudden misfortune and became impoverished. The family were forced to move to another community where the father could get a small job. They struggled for many years and have finally built up a good home and cattle herd in the community where they now live.

The father, troubled by extremely poor eyesight, is helped in his work by a son about twenty years old. The mother, an energetic and very able woman, runs the family. She is one of the most capable housewives in her district and is active in the women's club and community social affairs.

The construction of her personality does not seem at first glance to be in keeping with her observed behavior at home and at school. When her activities are examined closely, however, it can be seen that she is really behaving in accordance with her sense of insecurity and her limitations. Aware that she is handicapped in academic work, she puts all her energies into social activities. For this she has learned a routine of behavior, after the pattern of her mother, which gives the appearance of spontaneity and leadership and which wins her praise from family and teachers without straining her beyond her capacities. She manages her schoolmates as the deputy of the teacher and thus has a role of some importance among them which does not require originality on her part and affords a sort of friendly but impersonal relationship with them that satisfies her needs. This type of behavior in a Sioux, and especially a Sioux girl, is unusual enough to merit attention and praise from the teachers, which would compensate to a large extent for her lack of skill in intellectual realms.

Rather than being a genuine leader,

she is a conformer, but it so happens that the pattern to which she conforms is one of leadership as seen in her family. She is still very dependent upon the protection of her mother, and to maintain it she adheres to her mother's conventional standards as well as her pattern of managing those about her. Such behavior on the part of a girl does not sit well with the boys, and her relationships with them may in time cause her difficulty.

SUMMARY

In summarizing this chapter, we can also reiterate the theoretical approach which has been employed thus far and which will continue to be used. We have taken one highly specific sociological variable—here, the isolation of the family— and have striven to discover what effects this particular factor might have on the content of the socialization process. In both cases studied, we have seen that the isolation of the family has similar effects on the agent of socialization as well as on the content of the socialization process. In the Teton-Dakota situation, although the picture is complicated by a radical process of culture change, we were able to see how this social-structural factor also colored the emotional difficulties of the children.

To be sure, the isolation of the family, as a sociological condition, never operates alone and independently of other social-structural factors. The net results of familial isolation vary, for example, in different social classes in contemporary United States society, in divers racial or ethnic groups. There are many kinds of situations in which we can observe familial isolation—in urban apartment houses as well as in rural areas. But the fact that the two situations share this factor in common should yield other commonalities between them. As we proceed in our analyses, we shall learn about the ways in which some of these social-structural factors combine to produce different results, depending on the variables with which we are dealing.

There has been extraordinarily little empirical research into the problem of the effects of familial isolation—social or physical—on the course of growing up. It is an area of inquiry which requires more investigation, and its gleanings promise to be high. In the growing and legitimate interest in applying the findings of social science to problems in education, delinquency, child rearing in general, mental illness, and so forth, much has been missed by neglecting to investigate the degree of a family's isolation or proximity to others. If the family is as important as most students of behavior and motivation seem to think, then the position and location of the family in sociological space is extraordinarily crucial.

BIBLIOGRAPHY AND SUGGESTED READINGS

Bowlby, John. *Maternal Care and Mental Health*. Geneva: World Health Organization, 1952.

Leighton, Dorothea and Clyde Kluckhohn. *Children of the People: The Navaho Individual and his Development*. Cambridge, Mass.: Harvard University Press, 1947. A careful and well documented study describing growing up in a society in which families are often widely separated, but in which the effects of this distance are modified by matrilineal clan organization.

Levy, David M. *Maternal Overprotection*. New York: Columbia University Press, 1943. Although this book does not deal with family organization ("family" does not even appear in the index), it does deal with the peripheral role of the father; indications from the case material which Levy quotes are that these are largely isolated families.

Spitz, Rene A. "Hospitalism: An Inquiry into the Genesis of Psychiatric Conditions in Early Childhood," *Psychoanalytic Study of the Child*, Vol. *1*, 1945, pp. 53-74. New York; International Universities Press.

Spitz, Rene A. "Hospitalism: A Follow-up Report," *Psychoanalytic Study of the Child*, Vol. *2*, 1946, pp. 113-117. New York: International Universities Press.

Chapter 5

CHANGES OVER TIME
IN SOCIALIZATION PRACTICES

CHANGES IN AMERICAN PRACTICES

In our discussion of class differences in American Negro socialization practices, especially the material presented by Davis and Havighurst in Chapter 3, it was pointed out that we do not know why different classes bring up their children differently in the areas of feeding, sphincter training, sexual training, and the like; nor what elements in social classes *produce* differences in these areas of socialization. We rejected the hypothesis that middle-class life is much more "tame" or much more "orderly" than lower-class life. We also reject the hypothesis offered by Bronfenbrenner that diverse media of communication are able to narrow the gap between lower- and middle-class modes of child rearing.

The reason for the latter position can be stated as follows. When it comes to values, emotions, ways of perceiving children, and the like, physicians (let us begin here arbitrarily) are as much a product of their social climate, and are as subject to the effects of social-class membership and other sociological factors, as anyone else. They have certain skills and certain specific knowledge. But they do not initiate customs in the area of values and socialization any more than do bankers or art dealers. When one pediatrician tells a mother to feed her children to their demand, and another tells her to put them on strict schedules, the chances are that neither is speaking from a deductive examination of all the available scientific literature. As scientists—and in this the medical profession is certain to concur—we should not attribute magical power and properties to physicians as is done in many preliterate societies. Medical and clinical theory and practice are often extremely culture-bound, and it should surprise no one that they change and shift in accordance with alterations in the value system of the total society. To cite but one example, in the United States there was a decided shift in psychoanalytic theory after World War II from an emphasis on sexuality to dependency problems. There were probably many reasons for this, but we should not discount the fact that at about the same time American society as a whole was concerned with the care of the individual as a responsibility of government, with the problem of "the welfare state," and the like.

Nor can we accept the notion that the popular "family" magazines are particularly influential in precipitating changes in child-rearing customs in the United

States. These publications depend on the widest possible circulations and on advertising. The attempt to innovate in the area of socialization would automatically antagonize some segment of the reader population, and would threaten, if not actually cut, the volume of circulation and subscription. Hence, these magazines generally publish those ideas which are currently acceptable.

The same skepticism could be applied to the possible role of the government's *Infant Care Bulletins,* published by the Children's Bureau of the United States Government. These bulletins, devoted to the problems of "how to bring up children," generally reflect the consensus of middle-class values and are reflections more often than forerunners of broad events taking place on a large canvas.

An historical analysis can often provide leads and hints which the study of a single functioning system cannot. Specifically, an inquiry into historical changes in American or other patterns of socialization may give us some idea of what there is in different social classes which produces or makes for different ways of bringing up children. The historical cases which we shall consider in this chapter may prove fruitful in this direction.

In stable, slowly changing societies, child-rearing customs persist with amazing tenacity, and even over long periods of time they do not appear to change. Most theorists seem to proceed on the assumption that such practices more or less have a life of their own, and that people tend to bring up their children in more or less the same ways in which they themselves were brought up. We know, however, that such practices in the training of children even within the purely biological spheres of life have changed—sometimes in what appear to be "trends" or "fads"—in American society.

Why have such changes occurred? Is it because individuals become dissatisfied with the ways in which they have been raised and rationally decide that there are "better" ways? This may sometimes be the case, but the view is often held that the unconscious forces instilled in an individual in the course of his socialization are so powerful that they cannot be overcome by sheer rational volition alone. There must, then, be other forces at work which impinge on parents with such power that they can override, to a large extent, the forces which have been set into motion within them by dint of their own infantile and early childhood experiences. Do socialization practices change because individuals are dissatisfied with the "end products" of the socialization processes to which they were subjected and therefore wish *their* children to have quite different personalities? It is probably correct to assume that the overwhelming majority of the population could not formulate the "end products," in personality terms, of one mode of oral training as against another, or one type of sphincter training as against another. As a matter of fact, it is probably safe to say that no social scientist or psychoanalyst can provide such answers without at least stipulating "all other things being equal." Since all other things are never equal, such formulations are only hypotheses and abstract theories. What, then, changes parental behavior in a society and what keeps it stable?

It was posited in Chapter 3 that parents transmit to their children only that segment of the culture to which they have access and that socialization is always future-oriented. This is clear enough when a social system is fairly stable or is not changing too rapidly. That is, if a man wants his son to become an industrial executive, and if he himself has achieved a fair measure of success in a business bureaucracy, we can understand quite readily how he can bring certain kinds of pressures, as against others, to bear on his son so that the latter will be able to meet his father's expectations for him. And on the basis of such a set of predictions, we can also go on to predict which segment of the culture this man has available to him and which he will pass on to his son with respect to education, sexual behavior, aggression, money, places of residence, clothing styles, recreation, and so forth. However rapidly the culture of American society can be said to be changing, there is still a very strong continuity of culture from one generation to the next.

But what happens when not only the political structure of a society has been radically changed but when there has been an almost complete upheaval in the over-all culture of that society? What happens when there is a wide chasm of discontinuity in the quality of experience from one generation to the next? How do parents antic-ipate *this* kind of future for their children?

To study these questions, case material from the United States and from the Soviet Union will be considered. The American material is to an extent, the simpler, so we shall start out with that set of data and then go on to the case of the Soviet Union. The American material will be divided into three parts: (1) A paper by Martha Wolfenstein on changes in American child-rearing practices during the first half of the present century, (2) analysis of the data in her paper, and (3) a short paper by Bruner on an American Indian tribe to illustrate a hypothesis to be prof-fered in the second part of this section. The second half of this chapter will be de-voted to the Russian data, and it will be divided into two parts: (1) A selection describing the nature of the pressures being exerted on the Soviet citizen—as an adult—by his government, and (2) a paper by Inkeles describing the effects of these pressures on Soviet modes of child-rearing over the course of three generations.

In connection with these analyses, too, we should like to restate a note of caution sounded earlier. These studies are based upon and interpret events which have al-ready happened; they are not predictive studies in the sense that they forecast what will happen, as people often do in experimental sciences. But these *ad hoc* analyses are indispensable in order to be able to establish hypotheses about what may happen when given changes occur in Asia, Africa, South America, different parts of the United States, and so forth. Nature provides experimental situations and is doing so with increasing rapidity; we must be prepared with theories and hypotheses derived from *ad hoc* analyses when these new experiments are being "run" by forces occur-ring on a world-wide scale.

The paper to follow, by Martha Wolfenstein, will serve several functions. In addition to its relevance to the questions mentioned, it provides an excellent illustra-tion of some of the differences between the "cultural" approach to personality and socialization processes and the "social-structural" approach. We shall consider these differences in the discussion following her paper.

Dr. Wolfenstein, a psychologist, undertook an analysis of the materials contained in the *Infant Care* bulletins of the Children's Bureau of the United States Government. Her paper is divided into two main parts; the first is an analysis of the *Infant Care Bulletins* over a thirty-five year period, and the second is an attempt to speculate about the reasons for the changes which she found in these bulletins.

THE EMERGENCE OF FUN MORALITY*

By Martha Wolfenstein

A recent development in American culture is the emergence of what we may call "fun morality." Here fun, from having been suspect if not taboo, has tended to become obligatory. Instead of feeling guilty for having too much fun, one is inclined to feel ashamed if one does not have enough. Boundaries formerly maintained between play and work break down. Amusements infiltrate into the sphere of work, while in play self-estimates of achievement become prominent. This development appears to be at marked variance with an older, puritan ethic, although as we shall see the two are related.

As a basis for the discussion of fun morality I shall present an analysis of ideas of child training of the past thirty-five years. In these one can observe a changing conception of human impulses and a related altered evaluation of play and fun which afford clues to the transformation of moral outlook. The changing ideas in child training will be taken as phenomena of American culture, as part of a larger set of adult attitudes. This paper will consist, then, of two parts: first, an analysis of a selected sample of child training literature, and second, some hypotheses about a moral trend which it seems to illustrate.

The ideas on child training which I shall present are taken from the publications of the United States Department of Labor Children's Bureau. These publications probably express at any given time a major body of specialized opinion in the field, though how far they are representative would have to be determined by further study of other publications. In taking these publications as indicative of certain changing attitudes, I leave undetermined to what extent these attitudes are diffused among parents and also to what extent parents' actual behavior with their children conforms to these ideas. Both these topics would require further research.

The innovations in child training ideas of the past few decades may readily be related to developments in psychological research and theory (notably behaviorism, Gesell's norms of motor development, and psychoanalysis). However, the occurrence and particularly the diffusion of certain psychological ideas at certain periods is probably related to the larger cultural context. A careful study of the ways in which psychological theories have been adapted for parent guidance and other pedagogical purposes would show that a decided selection is made from among the range of available theories, some points being overstressed, others omitted, and so on.

The *Infant Care* Bulletin of the Children's Bureau, the changing contents of which I shall analyze, was first issued in

* Reprinted with abridgment from *Journal of Social Issues*, Vol. 7, No. 4, pp. 15-25, 1951, with permission.

1914. The various editions fall into three main groupings: 1914 and 1921, 1929 and 1938, 1942 and 1945 (i.e., the most drastic revisions occurred in 1929 and 1942). For the present purpose I shall mainly contrast the two ends of the series, comparing the 1914 edition with those of 1942 and 1945 (the two latter are practically identical), and skipping over the middle period. Thus I shall attempt to highlight the extent of the change rather than to detail the intermediate stages (which in any case show some complicated discontinuities).

As the infant embodies unmodified impulses, the conception of his nature is a useful index of the way in which the impulsive side of human nature generally is regarded. The conception of the child's basic impulses has undergone an extreme transformation from 1914 to the 1940's. At the earlier date, the infant appeared to be endowed with strong and dangerous impulses. These were notably autoerotic, masturbatory and thumb-sucking. The child is described as "rebelling fiercely" if these impulses are interfered with. The impulses "easily grow beyond control" and are harmful in the extreme: "children are sometimes wrecked for life." The baby may achieve the dangerous pleasures to which his nature disposes him by his own movements or may be seduced into them by being given pacifiers to suck or having his genitals stroked by the nurse. The mother must be ceaselessly vigilant; she must wage a relentless battle against the child's sinful nature. She is told that masturbation "must be eradicated . . . treatment consists in mechanical restraints." The child should have his feet tied to opposite sides of the crib so that he cannot rub his thighs together; his nightgown sleeves should be pinned to the bed so that he cannot touch himself. Similarly for thumb-sucking, "the sleeve may be pinned or sewed down over the fingers of the offending hand for sev-

eral days and nights," or a patent cuff may be used which holds the elbow stiff. The mother's zeal against thumb-sucking is assumed to be so great that she is reminded to allow the child to have his hands free some of the time so that he may develop legitimate manual skills; "but with the approach of sleeping time the hand must be covered." The image of the child at this period is that he is centripetal, tending to get pleasure from his own body. Thus he must be bound down with arms and legs spread out to prevent self-stimulation.

In contrast to this we find in 1942-1945 that the baby has been transformed into almost complete harmlessness. The intense and concentrated impulses of the past have disappeared. Drives towards erotic pleasure (and also towards domination, which was stressed in 1929-1938) have become weak and incidental. Instead we find impulses of a much more diffuse and moderate character. The baby is interested in exploring his world. If he happens to put his thumb in his mouth, or to touch his genitals, these are merely incidents, and unimportant ones at that, in his over-all exploratory progress. The erogenous zones do not have the focal attraction which they did in 1914, and the baby easily passes beyond them to other areas of presumably equal interest. "The baby will not spend much time handling his genitals if he has other interesting things to do." This infant explorer is centrifugal as the earlier erotic infant was centripetal. Everything amuses him, nothing is excessively exciting.

The mother in this recent period is told how to regard autoerotic incidents: "Babies want to handle and investigate everything that they can see and reach. When a baby discovers his genital organs he will play with them. . . . A wise mother will not be concerned about this." As against the older method of tying the child hand and foot, the mother is now told: "See that he has a toy to play with and he will not need to use his body as a plaything." The genitals are merely a resource which the child is thrown back on if he does not have a toy. Similarly with thumb-sucking: "A baby explores everything within his reach. He looks at a new object, feels it, squeezes it, and almost always puts it in his mouth." Thus again what was formerly a "fierce" pleasure has become an unimportant incident in the exploration of the world. Where formerly the mother was to exercise a ceaseless vigilance, removing the thumb from the child's mouth as often as he put it in, now she is told not to make a fuss. "As he grows older other interests will take the place of sucking." (Incidentally this unconcerned attitude towards thumb-sucking is a relatively late development. The 1938 edition still had an illustration of a stiff cuff which could be put on the infant at night to prevent his bending his elbow to get his fingers to his mouth. The attitude towards masturbation relaxed earlier, diversion having been substituted for mechanical restraints already in 1929.)

This changing conception of the nature of impulses bears on the question: is what the baby likes good for him? The opposition between the pleasant and the good is deeply grounded in older American morals (as in many other ascetic moral codes). There are strong doubts as to whether what is enjoyable is not wicked or deleterious. In recent years, however, there has been a marked effort to overcome this dichotomy, to say that what is pleasant is also good for you. The writers on child training reflect the changing ideas on this issue.

In the early period there is a clear-cut distinction between what the baby "needs," his legitimate requirements, whatever is essential to his health and well-being, on the one hand, and what the baby "wants," his illegitimate pleasure strivings, on the other. This is illustrated, for instance, in the question of whether to pick the baby up when he cries. In 1914, it was essential to determine whether he really needs something or whether he only wants something. Crying is listed as a bad habit. This is qualified with the remark that the baby has no other way of expressing his "needs"; if he is expressing a need, the mother should respond. "But when the baby cries simply because he has learned from experience that this brings him what he wants, it is one of the worst habits he can learn." If the baby cries, "the mother may suspect illness, pain, hunger or thirst." These represent needs. If checking on all these shows they are not present, "the baby probably wants to be taken up, walked with, played with," etc. "After the baby's needs have been fully satisfied he should be put down and allowed to cry." (This position remains substantially unchanged up to 1942.)

In 1942-45, wants and needs are explicitly equated. "A baby sometimes cries because he wants a little more attention. He probably needs a little extra attention under some circumstances just as he sometimes needs a little extra food and water. Babies want attention; they probably need plenty of it." What the baby wants for pleasure has thus become as legitimate a demand as what he needs for his physical well-being and is to be treated in the same way. (*Cf.* a recent television advertisement in which Angelo Patri is quoted as saying: "Youngsters today need television for their morale as much as they need fresh air and sunshine for their health." *New York Times,* November 14, 1950.)

The question of whether the baby wants things which are not good for him also occurs in connection with feeding. The baby's appetite was very little relied on to regulate the quantity of food he took in the early period. Overfeeding was regarded as a constant danger; the baby would never know when he had enough. This is in keeping with the general image of the baby at this time as a creature of insatiable impulses. In contrast to this we find in the recent period that "the baby's appetite usually regulates successfully the amount of food he takes." Thus again impulses appear as benevolent rather than dangerous.

Formerly, giving in to impulse was the way to encourage its growing beyond control. The baby who was picked up when he cried, held and rocked when he wanted it, soon grew into a tyrant. This has now been strikingly reversed. Adequate early indulgence is seen as the way to make the baby less demanding as he grows older. Thus we get the opposite of the old maxim, "Give the devil the little finger and he'll take the whole hand." It is now: "Give him the whole hand and he'll take only the little finger."

The attitude towards play is related to the conception of impulses and the belief about the good and the pleasant. Where impulses are dangerous and the good and pleasant are opposed, play is suspect. Thus in 1914, playing with the baby was regarded as dangerous; it produced unwholesome pleasure and ruined the baby's nerves. Any playful handling of the baby was titillating, excessively exciting, deleterious. Play carried the overtones of feared erotic excitement. As we noted, this was the period of an intensive masturbation taboo, and there were explicit apprehensions that the baby might be seduced into masturbation by an immoral nurse who might play with his genitals.

The mother of 1914 was told: "The rule that parents should not play with the baby may seem hard, but it is without doubt a safe one. A young delicate and nervous baby needs rest and quiet, and however robust the child much of the play that is indulged in is more or less

harmful. It is a great pleasure to hear the baby laugh and crow in apparent delight, but often the means used to produce the laughter, such as tickling, punching, or tossing, makes him irritable and restless. It is a regrettable fact that the few minutes' play that the father has when he gets home at night . . . may result in nervous disturbance of the baby and upset his regular habits." It is relevant to note that at this time "playthings . . . such as rocking horses, swings, teeter boards, and the like" are cited in connection with masturbation, as means by which "this habit is learned." The dangerousness of play is related to that of the ever-present sensual impulses which must be constantly guarded against. (In 1929-38, play becomes less taboo, but must be strictly confined to certain times of the day. In this period the impulse to dominate replaces erotic impulses as the main hazard in the child's nature and the corresponding danger is that he may get the mother to play with him whenever he likes.)

In the recent period play becomes associated with harmless and healthful motor and exploratory activities. It assumes the aspect of diffuse innocuousness which the child's impulse life now presents. Play is derived from the baby's developing motor activities which are now increasingly stressed. "A baby needs to be able to move all parts of his body. He needs to exercise . . . At a very early age the baby moves his arms and legs aimlessly . . . As he gets older and stronger and his movements become more vigorous and he is better able to control them he begins to play." Thus play has been successfully dissociated from unhealthy excitement and nervous debilitation and has become associated with muscular development, necessary exercise, strength, and control. This is in keeping with the changed conception of the baby in which motor activities rather than libidinal urges are stressed. For the baby who is concerned with exploring his world rather than with sucking and masturbating, play becomes safe and good.

Play is now to be fused with all the activities of life. "Play and singing make both mother and baby enjoy the routine of life." This mingling of play with necessary routines is consonant with the view that the good and pleasant coincide. Also, as the mother is urged to make play an aspect of every activity, play assumes a new obligatory quality. Mothers are told that "a mother usually enjoys entering into her baby's play. Both of them enjoy the little games that mothers and babies have always played from time immemorial." (This harking back to time immemorial is a way of skipping over the more recent past.) "Daily tasks can be done with a little play and singing thrown in." Thus it is now not adequate for the mother to perform efficiently the necessary routines for her baby; she must also see that these are fun for both of them. It seems difficult here for anything to become permissible without becoming compulsory. Play, having ceased to be wicked, having become harmless and good, now becomes a new duty.

In keeping with the changed evaluation of impulses and play, the conception of parenthood has altered. In the earlier period, the mother's character was one of strong moral devotion. There were frequent references to her "self-control," "wisdom," "strength," "persistence," and "unlimited patience." The mothers who read these bulletins might either take pride in having such virtues or feel called upon to aspire to them. The writers supposed that some mothers might even go to excess in their devoted self-denial. Thus the mothers were told that for their own health and thus for the baby's good they should not stay bound to the cribside without respite, but should have some pleasant, although not too exhaust-

ing recreation. The mother at this time is pictured as denying her own impulses just as severely as she does those of her child. Just as she had to be told to let the baby's hands free occasionally (not to overdo the fight against thumb-sucking), so she must be counseled to allow herself an intermission from duty. (In the 1929-38 period parenthood became predominantly a matter of know-how. The parents had to use the right techniques to impose routines and to keep the child from dominating them.)

In the most recent period, parenthood becomes a major source of enjoyment for both parents (the father having come much more into the picture than he was earlier). The parents are promised that having children will keep them together, keep them young, and give them fun and happiness. As we have seen, enjoyment, fun, and play now permeate all activities with the child. "Babies—and usually their mothers—enjoy breast feeding"; nursing brings "joy and happiness" to the mother. At bath time the baby "delights" his parents, and so on.

The characterization of parenthood in terms of fun and enjoyment may be intended as an inducement to parents in whose scheme of values these are presumed to be priorities. But also it may express a new imperative: you ought to enjoy your child. When a mother is told that most mothers enjoy nursing, she may wonder what is wrong with her in case she does not. Her self-evaluation can no longer be based entirely on whether she is doing the right and necessary things, but becomes involved with nuances of feeling which are not under voluntary control. Fun has become not only permissible but required, and this requirement has a special quality different from the obligation of the older morality.

I should now like to speculate on the connection between the attitudes revealed in this child training literature and a wider range of attitudes in American culture today. The extent of diffusion with respect to class, region, etc. of the attitudes I shall discuss would be a topic for further research.

The changing attitudes towards impulse and restraint, the changing treatment of play, the changing evaluation of fun which we have found in the child training literature would seem to have many counterparts in other areas of adult life. Play, amusement, fun have become increasingly divested of puritanical associations of wickedness. Where formerly there was felt to be the danger that in seeking fun one might be carried away into the depths of wickedness, today there is a recognizable fear that one may not be able to let go sufficiently, that one may not have enough fun. In the recent past there has been an increased tendency to attempt by drinking to reduce constraint sufficiently so that we can have fun. Harold Laswell has defined the super-ego as that part of the personality which is soluble in alcohol. From having dreaded impulses and being worried about whether conscience was adequate to cope with them, we have come round to finding conscience a nuisance and worrying about the adequacy of our impulses.

Not having fun is not merely an occasion for regret but involves a loss of self-esteem. I ask myself: What is wrong with me that I am not having fun? To admit that one did not have fun when one was expected to, arouses feelings of shame. Where formerly it might have been thought that a young woman who went out a great deal might be doing wrong, currently we would wonder what is wrong with a girl who is not going out. Fun and play have assumed a new obligatory aspect. While gratification of forbidden impulses traditionally aroused guilt, failure to have fun currently occasions lowered self-esteem. One is apt to feel inadequate, impotent, and also unwanted. One fears the pity of one's contemporaries rather than, as formerly, possible condemnation by moral authorities. In our book, *Movies, A Psychological Study,* Nathan Leites and I referred to this new obligatoriness of pleasure as "fun morality" as distinguished from the older "goodness morality" which stressed interference with impulses. We noted a particular type of current American film heroine, the masculine-feminine girl, whose major merit consists in making the achievement of fun not too effortful. She initiates the flirtation, keeps it casual, makes it clear that she does not require excessive intensity from the man. At the same time she supports his self-esteem by implying that she never doubts his resources for having fun, however cool or abstracted he may seem. She affords a relief from the pressures of fun morality.

David Riesman, in *The Lonely Crowd: A Study of the Changing American Character,* has observed how extensively in business and professional life work and play have become fused. Activities formerly sharply isolated from work, such as entertainment, have become part of business relations. Aspects of the personality such as pleasingness or likeability, formerly regarded as irrelevant to work efficiency, have been increasingly called into play in working life. Relations with work associates have become less and less sharply distinguishable from relations outside of working hours. Thus there has been a mutual penetration of work and play. Work tends to be permeated with behavior formerly confined to after work hours. Play conversely tends to be measured by standards of achievement previously applicable only to work. One asks oneself not only in personal relations but now also at work: Did they like me? Did I make a good impression? And at play, no less than at work, one asks: Am I doing as well as I should?

In the past when work and play were more sharply isolated, virtue was associated with the one and the danger of sin with the other. Impulse gratification presented possibilities of intense excitement as well as of wickedness. Today we have attained a high degree of tolerance of impulses, which at the same time no longer seem capable of producing such intense excitement as formerly. Is it because we have come to realize that the devil does not exist that we are able to fuse play and fun with business, child care and so on? Or have we developed (without conscious calculation) a new kind of defense against impulses? This defense would consist in diffusion, ceasing to keep gratification deep, intense, and isolated, but allowing it to permeate thinly through all activities, to achieve by a mixture a further mitigation. Thus we would have preserved unacknowledged and unrecognized the tradition of puritanism. We do not pride ourselves on being good and we secretly worry about not having enough fun. But the submerged super-ego works better than we know, interspersing play in small doses with work and applying a norm of achievement to play. Instead of the image of the baby who has fierce pleasures of autoeroticism and the dangerous titillation of rare moments of play, we get the infant who explores his world, every part of whose extent is interesting but none intensely exciting, and who may have a bit of harmless play thrown in with every phase of the day's routine. We get the adult whose work is permeated with personal relations and entertainment requirements, the impact of which is far from intensely pleasurable, and whose playtime is haunted by self-doubts about his capacity for having as much fun as he should.

I should like to add a further instance which epitomizes this tendency to fuse work and fun, manifestly to make work more agreeable, but in effect probably reducing the impact of fun. Recently a ten-year-old boy showed me one of his school books. It had the title "Range Riders" and showed on the cover a cowboy on a galloping horse. The subtitle was "Adventures in Numbers"; it was an arithmetic book. The problems involved cowboys, horses, and so on. The traditional image of the American schoolboy has been that he sits with a large text book propped up in front of him, a book representing the hard and tedious lessons which he wants to evade. And inside the text book he conceals a book of wild west stories, detective stories, or the like, which he is avidly reading. These two books have now been fused into one. I do not know whether this succeeds in making the arithmetic more interesting. But I have a suspicion that it makes the cowboys less exciting.

Since the foregoing was written a new edition of the *Infant Care* bulletin was issued, in the fall of 1951. This perpetuates many of the tendencies of the 1942-45 editions, but also shows some changes. Fun morality remains prominent. The new parents are told that they are making a good start if they can enjoy their baby. The child should learn that mother and father are "two people who enjoy each other." Introducing the baby to solid foods will be "fun" and "amusing" for the mother, and the baby will "enjoy the new experience more if you are having a good time." The mother should arrange the baby's bath so that it will be "the pleasant time it should be. . . . If you feel hurried, bath time won't be the fun for either of you that it should be."

The difficulty of achieving fun, which, as we have observed, tends currently to worry adults, is now ascribed to the infant as well (following the general tendency to see the infant as the model of impulse life). The infant now may suffer from boredom. And this has become the main reason for autoerotic activities. The baby may suck his thumb out of "loneliness or boredom." He may rock or bang his head because of "boredom." In toilet training the baby the mother must take care that it does not become a "hateful bore" for him. Masturbation is mentioned only in the section on toilet training: "sometimes a baby handles his genitals when he is on the toilet, or at other times when he is undressed." While it is not said explicitly that he does this out of boredom, we might infer it on an analogy with thumbsucking, rocking, and head-banging since we are told that the baby may also get bored on the toilet. Thus the autoerotic activities which were first derived from fierce impulses, later from less intense exploratory tendencies, now arise as an escape from boredom. The dwindling of impulsive intensity has proceeded further than before.

The exploratory impulse of the baby continues to be stressed. We have interpreted this as an attempt to conceive the child's impulsive endowment in harmless terms. But the puritanical condemnation of impulses seems to be catching up with this displacement. Bounds must now be set to the baby's exploration. "We know that if we leave him free to creep everywhere he'd get into trouble." Thus we must "set a limit" for the baby "while he explores."

There are still more striking signs that the belief in the dangerousness of impulses is breaking through the defenses that have been erected against it. In 1942-45 the view was advanced that the early gratification of the baby's demands led to the subsequent moderation of demands. There is now a conflict on this point. In some areas the precept is maintained, notably in relation to sucking and food preferences. But in respect to the impulse to dominate it has been reversed. The apprehension of the twenties that the baby may get the upper hand if his parents give in to him reappears. The baby may get the parents "at his mercy by unreasonable demands for attention." Although the baby's need for companionship and for being held when he cries is stressed, the mother is also warned: "If you get in the habit of picking your baby up every time he whimpers, you may do more harm than good." The gratified demand is apt to grow rather than subside. The mother "may find her baby getting more and more demanding."

Thus the conflict about facing and accepting human impulses is far from solved. The attempt to dilute and diffuse impulses seems to lead, on the one hand, to doubts about adequate impulsive intensity, boredom and the difficulty of achieving fun. On the other hand, the anxiety that impulses in one form or another will tend to grow beyond control has not been successfully warded off.

Dr. Wolfenstein, as has just been seen, attempts to relate these changes in ideas of child-rearing practices to other changes in American *culture,* specifically, to changing *ideas* about fun, play, and amusement. Whereas these were originally viewed as wicked and evil, the ideas about them altered so that they have come to be viewed as wholesome. As a matter of fact, she indicates, there has arisen in American society something of a compulsion to have fun, and a person who fails to enjoy himself is almost pressured into feeling somewhat inadequate as a result of his "not having a good time."

While it is true that the American values about "fun" have shifted, to cite a change in values is not to explain such changes. The alteration in values in child-rearing practices may be part of this gross evolution, but it does not provide us with any clues as to *why* any of these changes have taken place. A possible explanation may be uncovered by relating the alterations in socialization practices just described by Dr. Wolfenstein to certain changes in the nature of social-structural relationships in American history, specifically, the changes resulting from the sudden growth of American cities during the first two or three decades of the twentieth century. There are many qualities which are variously attributed to urban life, such as anonymity, social disorganization, loss of social control by primary groups, and the like. It is our contention in this discussion, however, that these changes in socialization prac- tices occurred because, in the city, patterns of instinctual gratification, as well as other patterns of behavior, are often learned *outside the home*. It will be our hy- pothesis that those women who were born around 1910 and after, unlike *their* mothers, began to learn many patterns of behavior outside the home—in school and with playmates and from the media of mass communication—and this change in the *context* of learning of itself produced new variations in the *content* of what was learned. As a result, these women brought with them an entirely different set of values from that held by their mothers when they began to rear their own chil- dren.

In connection with some practices, as we have just seen, there were major shifts from 1914 to 1929 to 1942, while in other areas there were shifts from 1914 to 1942, without any breaks in 1929. We can assume that most women who become mothers, at least for the first time, do so by the age of twenty-three years. Hence, women who became mothers for the first time in 1914, were born around 1891. The new mothers of 1930 were born around 1907. Those who began rearing children in 1942 were born around 1919.

Kinsey and his associates, in their study of the sexual behavior of a sample of American women, discovered that there was a radical revolution in the sexual habits of American women at the turn of the century. "Among females in the sample who were born before 1900, less than half as many had premarital coitus as among the females born in any subsequent decade. . . . Practically all of this increase had occurred in the generation that was born in the first decade of the present century and, therefore, in the generation which had most of its premarital experience in the late teens and in the 1920's following the first World War. The later generations ap- pear to have accepted the new pattern and maintained or extended it." [1] They then go on to point out that changes in educational patterns or in travel had little to do with this fundamental revolution in sexual behavior for women. ". . . The data in- dicate that girls living away from home while attending college have a smaller pro- portion of their premarital coitus in the college town, and a larger proportion of it while they are at home, during vacations. This is no new development, for it seems to have been equally true of all generations for the past forty years, including the

---

[1] Kinsey *et al.,* 1953, pp. 298-299.

generation born before 1900." [2] "In spite of the increased amount of traveling which the present generation does, and the increasing use of facilities like tourist camps, the number of girls who had coitus in rented facilities had, in terms of percentage, remained more or less constant for all the generations included in the sample." [3] Nor did the introduction of the automobile appear to change the sexual behavior of American women, for these data indicate that the horse and buggy had served more or less the same functions, in their day, as does the contemporary automobile.

On the basis of the findings of Kinsey and his associates, it appears safe to generalize and say that more and more women, after 1900, were beginning to accept the idea of instinctual gratification *for themselves* in apparent contradiction to the verbalized morality of their society at that time. Such attitudes toward instinctual gratification *are almost always transmitted in some fashion to children*.

In searching to discover how some of these changes came about, it may be recalled that women who became new mothers in 1914 were born about 1891. These women represented the greater (that is, pre-1900) puritanism and stricter morality of American society with respect to instinctual gratification. Hence, it is not surprising to find that the bulletin issued in 1914 represented the dominant attitudes and majority practices of 1891—the attitudes which were undoubtedly reflected in the ways in which these mothers of 1914 were brought up. The second group of mothers (the 1930 group) were born about 1907. It is in this group that the great post-1900 shift in sexual behavior began to take place. Concomitantly, a shift begins to appear in the view of the baby and his instinctual life. No mention is made of his erotic activities but one must still be careful of junior: beware lest he dominate his mother's schedule. The avoidance of any mention of the baby's erotic activities may be a measure of the uncertainty of the times regarding sexuality. Changes in behavior over time proceed gradually and by stages, and in the emergence of any new pattern there are always admixtures of the old. Those women who were born in 1907 (and became mothers in 1930) could not have entirely escaped the pre-1900 influences of their mothers, even though the urban influences under which they lived may have played a dominant role. Any pattern needs time, among other things, to cement it and this is what appears to have happened. In 1942, Americans were becoming somewhat more certain about their instinctual behavior, it would appear, for the baby is now viewed as completely harmless, and erotic play is seen in a broader behavioral context.

We have seen that the introduction of the automobile and greater frequencies and extents of travel for women did not in themselves provide the necessary and sufficient conditions to trigger changes in expression of instinctual strivings. In other words, mechanical and physical-spatial factors of mobility do not seem to have effected this great change. Therefore other areas must be dissected to learn which conditions could have made such changes possible.

In 1865, there were no American cities with populations of one million. By 1910, New York City had a population of almost three and one-half million. Chi-

---

[2] *Op. cit.,* p. 310.
[3] *Op. cit.,* p. 314.

cago had more than one and a half million, and Philadelphia had more than one and one-fourth million people. Nine other cities had populations of more than 300,000. Despite the growth of cities, however, the majority of Americans lived in rural areas. In 1900, thirty million people lived in cities while the rural population was forty-five million. The majority of Americans, then, still lived a rural existence with relatively stable and persistent traditions, in communities where kinship ties still played some role in daily life, where people who had been school-mates and childhood friends associated with each other. In short, most Americans lived in an environment productive of and conducive to a traditional way of life, where change came relatively slowly.

Although immigration from abroad dropped after 1900, especially after 1918, the growth of cities continued unabated. Industry accounted for an average increase of 20 percent in the populations of New York, New Jersey, Pennsylvania, and Connecticut. The development of the oil industry accounted for the phenomenal growth of urban centers in California, Oklahoma, and Texas. In 1900, the urban population was 40 percent of the total; in 1910, it was 45.8 percent; in 1920, it reached 51.4 percent.

There are many ways of characterizing a rural environment in which the family is both a unit of production as well as of consumption. For our immediate purposes, however, what is most important is that almost everything which children learn in such an environment is learned from parents and other relatives who are attached to the family. In this environment there is little chance to escape the scrutiny of these people for long. (The increasing frequency of sending children to school in rural areas is beginning to produce some of the effects which we shall discuss in a moment in connection with growing up in an urban environment.) The skills, the habits, the attitudes, the values, the sentiments, and the like, which one learns from parents are among the strongest and the most enduring, for they are identified with those persons towards whom one has the most intense emotional relationships possible during the formative years. The strength of the emotional bonds between parents and children underscores the strength of what is learned from them. In a rural area, one has few opportunities to acquire values concerning sexual behavior outside the home. One not only adopts the attitudes and values held by parents but one is more apt to adhere to these attitudes and values because they have been learned in a situation of a particular sort. Before the industrial revolution in the United States, most people born in rural areas tended to remain there. They continued to live their lives, for the most part, with those persons with whom they grew up, with whom some of the most fundamental patterns of emotional behavior were learned in childhood. The guilt, the shame, the need for approval, the desire for belongingness, and the like, which are learned during the earliest years of psychological vulnerability are always the strongest; and the patterns of behavior which they underlie also tend to remain the strongest when the associations with those in whose midst such patterns were learned are retained. Hence, it is not at all surprising that adult patterns of behavior as well as of socialization tended to remain relatively constant before the turn of the twentieth century.

The working of the land, especially in relatively small holdings, usually requires a particular kind of social structure. Where land holdings are family holdings, the family becomes a solidary unit with respect to it. Generally within less than a generation, land becomes a symbol for a small farmer—and a sacred one, at that—of family, of life, of permanency, of stability, all bound up in one. So basic and central is the concept of land as a *symbol* that it is clearly and explicitly recognized as such in the Common Law of property, especially in the law of "adverse possession" of land: For instance, if I own a parcel of land and someone comes and settles on the land and works it and improves it while I fail to eject him or otherwise reassert my claim to it for a given period (anywhere from seven to twenty-one years, depending on the jurisdiction) he owns the land at the expiration of the statute of limitations, and I have lost my claim to it. The law reasons, apparently, that it is in the interests of society to have land in use; it also appears, however, that the law implicitly, but clearly, recognizes the quality of the individual's attachment to the land worked.

The family as a unit of production as well as of consumption involves close ties based on blood, the most inalienable ties imaginable, and in addition to its symbolism of family solidarity it also carries with it the sociological footfall and emotional implications of one's parents, grandparents, and the tradition they represent. In the isolated farming homestead, instinctual impulses, especially sexual ones, were drastically curbed. This became part of the tradition, and it continued even when homesteaders began to acquire neighbors. We are not quite certain why this was so, that is, what there was in the social structure which produced such asceticism. A possible hypothesis, at least as a starting point for future research into this period of American history, would be that the settlers of the vast American farming lands brought with them the puritanism of eighteenth- and nineteenth-century New England, and the isolation of the homestead reinforced and maximized this tradition. Since the members of a family were sexually taboo to each other by the rules of incest and since the isolated homestead was the primary social unit of interaction, it is possible that this isolation necessarily had to lead to an accentuated puritanism. This tradition, however, was not only proscriptive of sexual impulses but of instinctual gratification in general. How the isolation of the homestead entered into the picture to thus affect other areas of behavior in addition to the sexual ones, if it did indeed play a role in these other areas, is something which has not yet been investigated systematically.

Since the social system within which this tradition took root remained relatively stable for several generations, it is understandable that the content of the socialization process remained equally stable and unchanging. But an industrialized city is a different kind of environment, and it leads to and requires a social structure based on considerably different needs and principles. One of the unique characteristics of the city is the machine. A machine does not produce food. A corollary to this is the fact that a man does not work at a machine with his family. He may be friendly with his bench-partners—*but only because they work together, and not because they are relatives or childhood friends.* He works at a machine, draws a paycheck, and buys food. If he can get more money by working at a different machine, he moves to it—

and acquires new bench-partners. Sometimes the machine moves; then he moves with it, often to a new community or to a new neighborhood—ties to people thus become that much weaker. A man working at a machine is not economically dependent upon the values and social opinions of others, except under special circumstances; *skill*—an impersonal commodity—is what matters. Often, it is competitive skill which is offered for sale to an employer. The values of social relations are not acceptance, belongingness, approval, intimate warmth, and the like. Substituted for them are wagework, piecework, guaranteed yearly wage, and the like. And since ties to people are that much weaker and looser, it does not take much imagination to realize that *people behave much more experimentally and nontraditionally and follow their own inclinations when they are away from the scrutiny of people with whom they have been in lifelong association and who are the symbolic reminders of the emotions—guilt, shame, fear, love, approval, reward—associated with things their parents taught them.*

But the implications of these processes are far more profound. How do these affect the children? Father leaves home in the morning and returns in the evening. He brings home the bacon. Actually, however, he does not. He brings home some money, which mother then takes to the supermarket to acquire food. This appears as a logical sequence to American adults. One of the difficulties, however, is that the child has no idea for many years that there is a relationship between his father's going to work in the morning and his mother's going to the supermarket. It is not until much later that he is able to relate all these processes to each other and thereby develop *the sense of family* which his cousin on the farm developed at a much earlier age. The preconditions for a sense of independence and individuation are thus set very early in the city.

The child goes to school; he is not educated at home. By education we mean how a person learns to live in society with his fellow man. Much of his religion, his political values, his abstract concepts are taught to him by strangers. He does not have one teacher, but many. Away from home—at school, on the way home from school, at the playground, at summer camp—he begins to learn something about how one generation begets another. *"Away from home"* is the important variable in this connection. His parents, and the preceding generations, have lost their grip on him; what is more, they have almost lost their claim to him, for he is learning from people—teachers and playmates—to whom his emotional attachments are usually weak. The preceding generation has lost its claim to him, for teachers (to say nothing of his playmates) are *not* "parent images." If they were, or even substitutes for parents, the abrupt break between the generations would not be as marked. But the child is now learning from people to whom he does *not* have parental ties and as a result, and for all intents and purposes, he is "learning on his own."

We know that some things in culture change more quickly than others. There is no systematic theory of culture change which enables us to predict the precise rate and extent of change, but there are a few generalizations which appear to be valid. For example, it can be posited that *those things which are learned outside the home are much more susceptible to change than those which are learned from parents at home.* To illustrate this generalization, let us take a specific sociocultural instance.

The case which we shall consider to illustrate this hypothesis comes from the Mandan-Hidatsa people of Lone Hill. Bruner presents his material on culture change within the context of a hypothesis which focuses on the *age* at which customs and habits are learned. However, as will be seen, it is also possible to apply our hypothesis to the data in Bruner's paper. That is, Bruner demonstrates that what is learned early in life is resistant to change while that which is learned later in life is most susceptible to change. We are simply adding to his hypothesis by emphasizing the social-structural aspects *vis-à-vis* the chronological one, saying that what is learned inside the family is most resistant to change and that which is learned outside the family is most susceptible to change. Bruner, accepts this addition as a valid one [personal communication].

CULTURAL TRANSMISSION AND CULTURAL CHANGE*
By Edward M. Bruner

Students of acculturation agree that in every contact situation some aspects of the native culture change more than others, but they do not agree on why this is so, nor on how to characterize that which has changed and that which has not in categories that have cross-cultural validity. Nor do they understand why a change in one area of culture sometimes precipitates radical change or disorganization throughout the entire culture pattern while other times a very modest or even negligible readjustment occurs.

A rather striking pattern of differential change emerges from a comparison of the contemporary culture, as I observed it in 1951, 1952-53, among the unacculturated segment of the Mandan-Hidatsa population, with the aboriginal culture, of approximately 1850-1860. This division into contemporary and aboriginal periods is convenient and provides a time span of about one century.

Within the social organization the Crow type kinship system is still largely

intact but the entire age-grade society system, which was such a colorful feature of aboriginal life, has completely disappeared. The extended family has given way to the nuclear family, residence is no longer matrilocal, and the clans have diminished in importance.

Far-reaching economic changes have occurred, but there has not been change in the basic roles of male and female. The aboriginal Mandan-Hidatsa had a dual economy adjusted to the fertile river-bottom lands. The women attended to household tasks, and engaged in maize, bean, and squash horticulture in small garden plots, while the men fought hostile nomads and hunted bison, antelope, deer, and small game. Fishing, gathering, and a wide network of trading relationships were important supplements to the economy. In the contemporary period major changes were precipitated by the dependency relationship to the government and by necessary adjustments to the American economy. Nevertheless, sexual

* Reprinted with abridgment from *Southwestern Journal of Anthropology,* Vol. *12,* pp. 191-199, 1956, with permission.

role conceptions have persisted. Women see themselves as housekeepers, mothers, and gardeners, while Indian men derive most satisfaction from the roles of soldier, cowboy, athlete, and hunter. A relatively large noncash income is derived from the woman's labor in small garden plots and in the gathering of wild fruits and berries, and from the man's ability as a hunter of deer and pheasant. Unacculturated Indian men have never taken to large-scale farming for the market nor have any but a few become economically successful cattlemen.

The aboriginal Mandan-Hidatsa had a very complex and highly developed ceremonial system, which no longer exists. Sacred public ceremonies are not performed in contemporary society, and everyone has been converted to the Congregational or Catholic Church. Christianity may not be deeply felt nor fully understood by the Indian people, but it has replaced the native religion. However, particular aspects of the religious system have persisted. Shamans continue to cure the sick with the aid of their medicine bundles, and there is a widely accepted belief in ghosts who are thought to be returning spirits of the dead.

The value system, as I have inferred it from my observations among the Mandan-Hidatsa and from the published ethnologies, shows a remarkable persistence. A good man was, and is, one who respects the old people, is brave and demonstrates fortitude, conforms to the obligations of the kinship system, is devoted to village cooperation and unity, is generous, gives away property in public, gets along well with others, and avoids overt expressions of aggression in interpersonal relationships.

Thus kinship, values, and traditional role conceptions have persisted virtually intact, despite vast change in the larger units of social organization, in the economy, and in most of the religious-

ceremonial system. With the possible exception of values, there has been change and persistence within each aspect of culture.

That which was traditionally learned and internalized in infancy and early childhood tends to be most resistant to change in contact situations. This suggests that we view a culture from the perspective of cultural transmission, the process by which the content of culture is learned by and communicated to members of the society. It says that if we knew the point in the life career of an individual at which every aspect of culture was transmitted, we would find that what changes most readily was learned late in life and what was most resistant to change was learned early.

A re-examination of the Mandan-Hidatsa data from the perspective of cultural transmission and the early learning hypothesis reveals the following: that which persists, i.e., kinship, role conceptions and values, was learned early, and the primary agents of cultural transmission were members of ego's lineage. The age-grade society system and the religious complex, which no longer exist, were learned late, from agents of transmission who were not members of ego's lineage and who were all respect-relatives.

A widely extended kinship system was the basis of aboriginal Mandan-Hidatsa social structure; every interpersonal relationship was determined by kinship. Thus it was absolutely essential that the growing child learn kin terms and behavior early in life, so that he could relate properly to others. The kinship system was learned by a young boy mainly from his mother, older brother, maternal grandfather, and mother's brother who was classified as an older brother; and by a young girl mainly from her mother, older sister, and maternal grandmother. These are all members of the same lineage. The father took little part in routine economic and social training.

The Crow type kinship system is still learned early in contemporary Mandan-Hidatsa society. We studied kinship among children between the ages of six to ten, and found that unacculturated children knew how to behave toward their relatives in terms of the Crow pattern, although no child had any conception of the kinship system as a system. Some children did not know the correct behavior toward relatives with whom they interacted infrequently, as in the case of those who lived in another village, but no child behaved incorrectly toward a close relative with whom he had frequent contact.

Religious knowledge was learned late in life in aboriginal Mandan-Hidatsa society and is in sharp contrast with, for example, the practice among Catholics, where children begin religious training at a relatively early age. With few exceptions a man under the age of thirty did not, and was not, expected to know the traditions, origin myths, or religious rituals of the tribe. In Mandan-Hidatsa thought a man younger than thirty was not mature: he was thought to be reckless and irresponsible. Religious knowledge and lore were slowly revealed to a man after the age of thirty, and this process of religious learning continued throughout his entire life career.

The agents of religious transmission were primarily members of the father's lineage and clan, all of whom were respect-relatives. Religious knowledge was not freely given: it had to be purchased from selected ceremonial fathers. A man spent a considerable portion of his productive time in the acquisition of goods which he gave to ceremonial fathers in return for religious knowledge. An old man who had purchased many ceremonies had attained the cultural objective: he was successful and was respected by all. He subsisted in part on gifts and on the goods he received from the sale of religious knowledge to younger men.

Some evidence has been given that kinship persists and was learned early, and that religion did not persist and was learned late. Additional evidence to support the hypothesis could be offered from other segments of the culture. It is in the context of kinship and at the same point in the life career that role conceptions and the value system are internalized. The age-grade society system was not even entered by an individual until the age of seven to eight, and serious society activity did not begin for a boy until the age of fifteen to seventeen, with the first fasting experience. The graded structure of the societies was such that only an older person, who had passed through the entire system, had full knowledge and understanding of this aspect of aboriginal culture. Parts of religion that do persist, such as fear of ghosts, were learned early in that returning spirits of the dead were and are used in Mandan-Hidatsa society to frighten and discipline young children, and are comparable in function to our bogeyman and the Hopi Soyoko Kachinas.

That religion is learned after the age of thirty in Mandan-Hidatsa society should not be regarded as unique in cultural transmission. All cultures vary not only according to their culture patterns, but also according to the age-grading of the educational process, the age at which each aspect of culture is internalized. The variation in this important dimension of culture is well-known in traditional anthropology, and is amply documented in the life cycle sections of many ethnological reports. For example, in Trukese society such key activities as weaving, canoe building, complex religious techniques, and genealogical knowledge are not acquired until about the age of forty. It is frequently stated that in primitive society the social world of the child coincides with adult reality but the reverse may prove to be the case—that there will always be a discrepancy between childhood and adult learning. This may be universal, since the situation of the child is universally, by the biological nature of the case, different from the adult, and because this situational difference is intensified, universally, by cultural definition.

A final question concerns the applicability of the early learning hypothesis to cases of culture contact other than the Mandan-Hidatsa. If it is applicable it will have relevance to those applied programs in many parts of the world where the question is asked: What are the hard and soft parts of culture; what is most and what is least resistant to change?

As a working assumption, I submit that the early learning hypothesis is universal, as it identifies one variable that may aid in the understanding of differential culture change everywhere, although its explanatory value and importance will vary considerably in different situations. Any principle must always be considered in conjunction with alternate hypotheses as no one principle will ever be sufficient to explain the totality of differential change in any given case. Even within the framework suggested here, resistance to change may be a function of other factors in addition to relative age of learning, such as the degree of affect and ego involvement in the learning situation. The early learning hypothesis will work out differently in different cases as the acculturation process itself is selective. Cases vary according to the availability of alternatives, the extent and direction of pressures for change, and the general

circumstances in which the people find themselves. *The early learning hypothesis simply orders the cultural content in terms of potential resistance to change: the actual sequence of change is dependent upon a multiplicity of factors in the contact situation.* Change in any segment of culture, whether learned early or late, will not occur unless there is a reason for it to change.

Partial support for the universality of the early learning hypothesis is provided by two frequently stated anthropological findings as to which aspects of culture tend to persist longest in contact situations. One group of students has found that core culture, implicit values, cultural orientations, and personality are most resistant to change. Another group of students interested in social structure suggests that family and kinship institutions tend to persist.

These findings are not unrelated. Values and personality on the one hand and family and kinship on the other may well be aspects of life that are generally learned in infancy and early childhood and thus tend to be most resistant to change. Indeed, personality and kinship are usually separated by us as being in different categories, but from the point of view of the individual who internalizes them, both come across early in the socialization process and in the same bundle. Psychoanalysts tell us that the first self-other differentiation is basically, in our lingo, a kinship one, when the child differentiates self from mother and later mother from other objects. This is how a kinship system is built into and internalized by an individual and how it, in turn, provides the context for the further development of personality.

To conclude the discussion of our original problem, namely, changes in socialization patterns and in patterns of instinctual gratification, it appears that there are processes which go on in an industrialized urban setting which allow for greater in-

dividual freedom in the gratification of instinctual strivings and that these are processes which allow for changes in such behavior at a faster and more dramatic rate
than in a rural setting. Where the bonds of primary groupings are greatly weakened,
individuals are more likely to experiment with their own deep biological strivings;
*when they have thus found that such instincts are neither dangerous nor catastrophic
nor "bad," they almost automatically transmit these deep feelings to their children
in one way or another.* Furthermore, when these children live in the same environment or in the same total-learning context, they, too, tend to maintain the pattern
which had been established by previous generations, reinforce the pattern, and transmit it to their children.

CHANGES IN RUSSIAN PRACTICES

Some societies change even more rapidly and drastically than the United States.
If parents were only transmitting the social habits and techniques which they had
learned are the most adaptive, their children, who might be faced with an entirely
different sort of world, would find that what they have been taught in the course of
growing up is highly maladaptive. In Inkeles' study, "Social Change and Social
Character: the Role of Parental Mediation," which we shall consider shortly, he
points out that if parental responses to social change were idiosyncratic, the results
in the next generation would be completely randomized. That this is not the case is
due to the fact that ". . . it is in the nature of social structure, particularly in modern industrial society, that large groups of the population will be exposed to and
perceive on-going change in similar fashion. . . . One very probable reaction to
the experience of social change is to adjust the training of children to better prepare
them for life in the future as the parent now anticipates that life in the light of his
own experience. There is reason to assume, therefore, that the influence of large-
scale change occurring at any one time may be reflected in the character of the *next*
generation because of the mediation by parents living under and experiencing
change."

What *is* the experience of on-going social change in the Soviet Union? Change
is not an abstract or formless phenomenon; all social change is specific, and whenever we speak of it we have to particularize those aspects of the environment to
which we are referring. Thus, when we speak of the effects of social change on socialization processes, we must know to which specific and concrete pressures parents
are responding. The next selection, by Inkeles, Hanfmann, and Beier gives us a concrete and concise picture of some of the changes and pressures which Soviet adults
experience. After viewing these new pressures in the over-all sociocultural environment, we shall go on to read Inkeles' paper on changing modes of Russian socialization patterns.

MODAL PERSONALITY AND ADJUSTMENT TO THE SOVIET SOCIO-POLITICAL SYSTEM*

By Alex Inkeles, Eugenia Hanfmann, and Helen Beier

Two main elements are encompassed in the study of national character. The first step is to determine what modal personality patterns, if any, are to be found in a particular national population or in its major sub-groups. In so far as such modes exist one can go on to the second stage, studying the interrelations between the personality modes and various aspects of the social system. Even if the state of our theory warranted the drafting of an "ideal" research design for studies in this field, they would require staggering sums and would probably be beyond our current methodological resources. We can, however, hope to make progress through more restricted efforts. In the investigation we report on here we studied a highly selected group from the population of the Soviet Union, namely, former citizens of Great Russian nationality who "defected" during or after World War II. We deal, furthermore, mainly with only one aspect of the complex interrelations between system and personality, our subjects' participation in an adjustment to their Communist sociopolitical order. We find that certain personality modes are outstanding in the group, and believe that we can trace their significance for our subjects' adjustment to Soviet society.

SAMPLE AND METHOD

An intensive program of clinical psychological research was conducted as part of the work of the Harvard Project on the Soviet Social System. The Project explored the attitudes and life experiences of former Soviet citizens who were dis-

placed during World War II and its aftermath and then decided not to return to the U.S.S.R. Almost 3,000 completed a long written questionnaire, and 329 undertook a detailed general life history interview. The individuals studied clinically were selected from the latter group. Criteria of selection were that the interviewee seemed a normal, reasonably adjusted individual who was relatively young, had lived most of his life under Soviet conditions, and was willing to undertake further intensive interviewing and psychological testing.

The group studied clinically included 51 cases, forty-one of whom were men. With the exception of a few Ukrainians, all were Great Russians. Almost half were under 30, and only 8 were 40 or older at the time of interview in 1950, which meant that the overwhelming majority grew up mainly under Soviet conditions and were educated in Soviet schools. Eleven had had a minimum education of four years or less, 22 between four and eight years, and 18 advanced secondary or college training. In residence the group was predominantly urban but if those who had moved from the countryside to the city were included with the rural, then approximately half fell in each category. As might be expected from the education data, the group included a rather large proportion of those in high-status occupations, with 11 professionals and members of the intelligentsia, 7 regular army officers, and 9 white-collar workers. Sixteen were rank-and-file industrial and agricultural workers, and five rank-and-file army men.

* Reprinted with omission of footnotes, bibliographical references, and biographical notes from *Human Relations,* Vol. *11,* pp. 3-22, 1958, with permission.

In keeping with the occupational pattern but running counter to popular expectations about Soviet refugees, a rather high proportion were in the Party (6) or the Young Communist League (13). Again running counter to popular expectations about refugees, the group was not characterized by a markedly high incidence of disadvantaged family background as reflected either in material deprivation, the experience of political arrest, or other forms of repression at the hands of the regime. Ten were classified as having been extremely disadvantaged, and 15 as having suffered minor disadvantage.

All of the Soviet refugees have in common their "disaffection" with Soviet society. The clinical group included mainly the more "active" defectors who left Soviet control on their own initiative, rather than the "passive" who were removed by force of circumstance. Thirty-four had deserted from the military or voluntarily departed with the retreating German occupation armies. In general, however, the clinical group was not more vigorously anti-Communist than the other refugees. They overwhelmingly supported the principles of the welfare state, including government ownership and state planning, and credited the regime with great achievements in foreign affairs and economic and cultural development. They refused to return for much the same reasons given by other refugees: fear of reprisal at the hands of the secret police, because of former oppression, opposition to institutions like the collective farm, or resentment of the low standard of living and the absence of political freedom. In psychological adjustment, finally, they seemed to reflect fairly well the tendency toward adequate adjustment which characterized the refugees as a whole.

With regard to the parent refugee population, then, the clinical group was disproportionately male, young, well educated, well placed occupationally and politically, and "active" in defecting. In its internal composition, the sample was also unbalanced in being predominantly male, but otherwise gave about equal weight to those over and under 35, in manual vs. white-collar occupations, from urban or rural backgrounds, with education above or below the advanced secondary level.

Each respondent was interviewed with regard to his childhood experience, some aspects of his adult life, and his adjustment to conditions in a displaced persons' camp. Each took a battery of tests which included the Rorschach, TAT, a sentence-completion test of 60 items, a "projective questions" test including eight of the questions utilized in the authoritarian personality study, and a specially constructed "episodes" or problem-situations test. We regard the use of this battery of tests as a matter of special note, since most attempts to assess modal tendencies in small-scale societies have relied upon a single instrument, particularly the Rorschach. The various tests differ in their sensitivity to particular dimensions or levels of personality, and differentially reflect the impact of the immediate emotional state and environmental situation of the subject. By utilizing a series of tests, therefore, we hope that we have in significant degree reduced the chances that any particular finding mainly peculiar to the special combination of instrument, subject, and situation will have been mistakenly interpreted as distinctively Russian. In addition the use of this battery enables us to test our assumptions in some depth, by checking for consistency on several tests.

Each test was independently analysed according to fairly standard scoring methods, and the results were reported separately. In reporting their results, however, each set of analysts made some observations on the character traits which seemed generally important to the group as a whole. Further, in drawing these conclusions the analysts made use of a criterion group of Americans matched with the Russian sample on age, sex, occupation, and education. The availability of such test results posed a challenge as to whether or not these general observations, when collated and analysed, would yield any consistent patterns for the group as a whole.

To make this assessment we selected the eight major headings used below as an organizing framework. We believe that they permit a fairly full description of the various dimensions and processes of the human personality, and at the same time facilitate making connections with aspects of the social system. These categories were, however, not part of the design of the original clinical research program, and were not used by the analysts of the individual instruments. While this circumstance made for lesser comparability between the tests, it acted to forestall the slanting of conclusions to fit the analytic scheme. The statements in the conclusions drawn by the analysts of each instrument were written on duplicate cards, sorted, and grouped under all the categories to which they seemed relevant. The evidence with regard to each category was then sifted and weighed, and where there were ambiguous findings the original tables were re-examined for clarification. Relevant impressions based on the interviews were also drawn on. Similarities and differences between those in our sample and the matching Americans aided in grasping the distinctive features of the Russian pattern. On this basis a characterization of the group was developed under each heading of the analytic scheme.

It should be clear that the sketch of modal personality characteristics presented below is not a simple and direct translation of particular test scores into personality traits. Rather, it is an evalua-tive, summary statement, following from the collation and interpretation of conclusions drawn from each test, conclusions which were in turn based both on test scores and on supplementary qualitative material. The word modal should not be taken too literally in this context. We have relied on some test scores when only a small proportion of the sample manifested the given response or pattern of responses, if this fits with other evidence in developing a larger picture. In stating our findings we have been freer with the evidence than some would permit, more strict than others would require. We attempted to keep to the canons of the exact method, without neglecting the clinical interpretations and insights. In this way we hoped to arrive at a rich and meaningful picture of the people studied, a picture that would provide an adequate basis for an analysis of their adjustment to the socio-political system.

BRIEF SKETCH OF RUSSIAN MODAL PERSONALITY CHARACTERISTICS

1. *Central Needs*

Since all human beings manifest the same basic needs, we cannot assert that some need is unique to a given national population. Among these universal needs, however, some may achieve greater strength or central importance in the organization of the personality, and in this sense be typical of the majority of a given group.

Probably the strongest and most pervasive quality of the Russian personality that emerged from our data was a need for *affiliation*. By this we mean a need for intensive interaction with other people in immediate, direct, face-to-face relationships, coupled with a great capacity for having this need fulfilled through the establishment of warm and personal contact with others. Our subjects seemed to welcome others into their lives as an indispensable condition of their own existence, and generally felt neither isolated nor estranged from them. In contrast to the American subjects, the Russians were not too anxiously concerned about others' opinion of them and did not feel compelled to cling to a relationship or to defend themselves against it. Rather, they manifest a profound acceptance of group membership and relatedness. These orientations were especially prevalent in test situations dealing with relations between the individual and small face-to-face groups such as the family, the work team, and the friendship circle.

Closely linked with the need for affiliation is a need for *dependence* very much like what Dicks spoke of as the Russians' "strong positive drive for enjoying loving protection and security," care and affection. This need shows not only in orientation towards parents and peers, but also in the relations with formal authority figures. We did not, however, find a strong need for submission linked with the need for dependence, although Dicks asserts it to be present. In addition there is substantial evidence for the relatively greater strength of *oral* needs, reflected in preoccupation with getting and consuming food and drink, in great volubility, and in emphasis on singing. These features are especially conspicuous by contrast with the relative weakness of the more typically compulsive puritanical concern for order, regularity, and self-control. However, our data do not permit us to stress this oral component as heavily as does Dicks, who regards it as "typical" for the culture as a whole.

Several needs rather prominent in the records of the American control group did not appear to be of outstanding importance in the personality structure of the Russians. Most notable, the great emphasis on *achievement* found in the American records was absent from the Russian ones. Within the area of interpersonal relations our data lead us to posit a fairly sharp Russian-American contrast. Whereas the American records indicate great strength of need for *approval* and need for *autonomy,* those needs were rather weakly manifested by the Russians. In approaching interpersonal relations our American subjects seemed to fear too close or intimate association with other individuals and groups. They often perceived such relations as potentially limiting freedom of individual action, and therefore inclined above all to insure their independence from or autonomy within the group. At the same time the Americans revealed a strong desire for recognition and at least formal acceptance or approval from the group. They are very eager to be "liked," to be regarded as an "all right" guy, and greatly fear isolation from the group. Finally we note that certain needs important in other national character studies were apparently not central in either the American or the Russian groups. Neither showed much need for dominance, for securing positions of superordination, or for controlling or manipulating others and enforcing authority over them. Nor did they seem markedly distinguished in the strength of hostile impulses, of desires to hurt, punish, or destroy.

2. *Modes of Impulse Control*

On the whole the Russians have relatively *high awareness* of their impulses or basic dispositions—such as for oral gratification, sex, aggression, or dependence— and, rather, *freely accept* them as something normal or "natural" rather than as bad or offensive. The Russians show evidence, furthermore, of *giving in* to these impulses quite readily and frequently, and of *living them out*. Although they tended afterwards to be penitent and admit that they should not have "lived out" so freely, they were not really punitive towards themselves or others for failure to control impulses. Of course, this does not mean complete absence of impulse control, a condition that would render social life patently impossible. Indeed, the Russians viewed their own impulses and desires as forces that needed watching, and often professed the belief that the control of impulses was necessary and beneficial. The critical point is that the Russians seemed to rely much less than the Americans on impulse control to be generated and handled from within. Rather, they appear to feel a need for aid from without in the form of guidance and pressure exerted by higher authority and by the group to assist them in controlling their impulses. This is what Dicks referred to as the Russians' desire to have a "moral corset" put on his impulses. The Americans, on the other hand, vigorously affirm their ability for *self*-control, and seem to assume that the possession of such ability and its exercise legitimates their desire to be free from the overt control of authority and the group.

In this connection we may note that the review of individual cases revealed a relative lack of well-developed *defensive structures* in many of the Russian subjects. Mechanisms that serve to counteract and to modify threatening feelings and impulses—including isolation, intellectualization, and reaction formation—seem to figure much less prominently among them than among the Americans. The Russians had fewer defenses of this type and those they had were less well established.

3. Typical Polarities and Dilemmas

Within certain areas of feelings and motives individuals may typically display attitudes and behavior that belong to one or the opposite poles of the given vari-

able, or else display a preoccupation with the choice of alternatives posed by these poles. Such preoccupation may be taken to define the areas of typical dilemmas or conflicts, similar to the polarized issues, such as "identity vs. role diffusion" and "intimacy vs. isolation," which Erikson found so important in different stages of psychological maturation.

In our Russian subjects we found a conscious preoccupation with the problem of *trust vs. mistrust* in relation to others. They worried about the intentions of the other, expressing apprehension that people may not really be as they seem on the surface. There was always the danger that someone might entice you into revealing yourself, only then to turn around and punish you for what you have revealed. Another typical polarity of the Russians' behavior is that of *optimism vs. pessimism,* or of faith vs. despair. One of our projective test items posited the situation that tools and materials necessary for doing a job fail to arrive. In responding to this item our Russian subjects tended to focus on whether the outcome of the situation will be good or bad for the actor, while the Americans at once sprang into a plan of action for resolving the situation. Finally, we may include under the typical polarities of the Russians' attitude that of *activity vs. passivity,* although in the case of this variable we found little indication of a sense of a conscious conflict. However, the subjects' choice of alternatives in the projective tests tended to be distributed between the active and the passive ones, while the Americans' preference for the active instrumental response was as clearcut and strong as was their generally optimistic orientation.

The pronounced polarities of the Russians' orientation lend support to Dicks's assertion that "the outstanding trait of the Russian personality is its contradictoriness—its ambivalence." Two qualifications, however, must be kept in mind. First, the strength of our Russian subjects' dilemmas may have been greatly enhanced by the conditions of their lives, both in the Soviet Union and abroad. Second, the American subjects also show some involvement in problematic issues, though they were different from the Russian ones. Thus the problem of "intimacy vs. isolation" or "autonomy vs. belongingness," to which we have already alluded, seemed a major dilemma for Americans whereas it was not such an issue for the Russians.

4. *Achieving and Maintaining Self-Esteem*

In their orientations toward the self, the Russians displayed rather low and *unintense self-awareness* and little painful self-consciousness. They showed rather high and *secure self-esteem,* and were little given to self-examination and doubt of their inner selves. At the same time they were not made anxious by examination of their own motivation or that of others, but rather showed readiness to gain insight into psychological mechanisms. The American pattern reveals some contrasts here, with evidence of acute self-awareness, substantial self-examination, and doubting of one's inner qualities.

We were not able to discern any differences between Americans and Russians in the relative importance of *guilt* versus *shame* as sanctions. There were, however, some suggestive differences in what seemed to induce both guilt and shame. The Americans were more likely to feel guilty or ashamed if they failed to live up to clear-cut "public" norms, as in matters of etiquette. They were also upset by any hint that they were inept, incompetent, or unable to meet production, sports, or similar performance standards. The Russians did not seem to be equally disturbed by such failures, and felt relatively more guilty or ashamed when they

assumed that they had fallen behind with regard to moral or interpersonal behavior norms, as in matters involving personal honesty, sincerity, trust, or loyalty to a friend. These latter qualities they value most highly and they demand them from their friends.

5. *Relation to Authority*

Our clinical instruments presented the subjects with only a limited range of situations involving relations with authority. These did not show pronounced differences in basic attitudes between Russians and Americans, except that Russians appeared to have more fear of and much less optimistic expectations about authority figures. Both of these manifestations might, of course, have been mainly a reflection of their recent experiences rather than of deeper-lying dispositions. Fortunately, we can supplement the clinical materials by the life history interviews which dealt extensively with the individual's relations with authority. A definite picture emerges from these data. Above all else the Russians want their leaders—whether boss, district political hack, or national ruler—to be warm, nurturant, considerate, and interested in the individuals' problems and welfare. The authority is also expected to be the main source of initiative in the inauguration of general plans and programs and in the provision of guidance and organization for their attainment. The Russians do not seem to expect initiative, directedness, and organizedness from an average individual. They therefore expect that the authority will of necessity give detailed orders, demand obedience, keep checking up on performance, and use persuasion and coercion intensively to insure steady performance. A further major expectation with regard to the "legitimate" authority is that it will institute and enforce sanctions designed to curb or control bad impulses in individuals, improper moral practices, heathen religious ideas, perverted political procedures, and extreme personal injustice. It is, then, the government that should provide that "external moral corset" which Dicks says the Russian seeks.

An authority that meets these qualifications is "good" and it does what it does with "right." Such an authority should be loved, honored, respected, and obeyed. Our Russian subjects seemed, however, to expect that authority figures would in fact frequently be stern, demanding, even scolding and nagging. This was not in and of itself viewed as bad or improper. Authority may be, perhaps ought to be, autocratic, so long as it is not harshly authoritarian and not totally demanding. Indeed, it is not a bad thing if such an authority makes one rather strongly afraid, make one "quake" in expectation of punishment for trespassing or wrongdoing. Such an authority should not, however, be arbitrary, aloof, and unjust. It should not be unfeeling in the face of an open acknowledgment of one's guilt and of consequent self-castigation. Indeed, many of our subjects assumed that authority can in fact be manipulated through humbling the self and depicting oneself as a weak, helpless person who needs supportive guidance rather than harsh punishment. They also assumed that authority may be manipulated by praise or fawning, and seduced through the sharing of gratificatory experiences provided by the supplicant— as through the offer of a bottle of liquor and the subsequent sharing of some drinks. Russians also favor meeting the pressure of authority by evasive tactics, including such devices as apparently well-intentioned failure to comprehend and departures from the scene of action.

Throughout their discussions of authority our respondents showed little concern for the preservation of precise forms, rules, regulations, exactly defined rights, regularity of procedure, formal and explicit limitation of powers, or the other aspects of the traditional constitutional Anglo-Saxon approach to law and government. For the Russians a government that has the characteristics of good government listed above justifies its right to rule by virtue of that performance. In that case, one need not fuss too much about the fine points of law. By contrast, if government is harsh, arbitrary, disinterested in public welfare—which it is apparently expected to be more often than not—then it loses its right to govern no matter how legal its position and no matter how close its observance of the letter of the law.

6. *Modes of Affective Functioning*

One of the most salient characteristics of the Russian personality was the high degree of their *expressiveness* and emotional aliveness. On most test items the Russian responses had a stronger emotional coloring, and they covered a wider range of emotions, than did the American responses. Their feelings were easily brought into play, and they showed them openly and freely both in speech and in facial expression, without much suppression or disguise. In particular they showed a noticeably greater *freedom and spontaneity in criticism* and in the expression of hostile feelings than was true for the Americans. There were, further, two emotions which the Russians showed with a frequency far exceeding that found in the Americans—*fear,* and *depression* or despair. Many of the ambiguous situations posited in the tests were viewed by them in terms of danger and threat, on the one hand, and of privation and loss, on the other. Undoubtedly this was in good part a reflection of the tense social situation which they had experienced in the Soviet Union, and of their depressed status as refugees, but we believe that in addition deeper-lying trends were here being tapped. These data provide some evidence in support of the oft-noted prevalence of depressive trends among the Russians.

7. *Modes of Cognitive Functioning*

In this area we include characteristic patterns of perception, memory, thought, and imagination, and the processes involved in forming and manipulating ideas about the world around one. Of all the modes of personality organization it is perhaps the most subtle, and certainly in the present state of theory and testing one of the most difficult to formulate. Our clinical materials do, however, permit a few comments.

In discussing people, the Russians show a keen *awareness of the "other"* as a distinct entity as well as a rich and diversified recognition of his special characteristics. Other people are usually perceived by them not as social types but as concrete individuals with a variety of attributes distinctly their own. The Russians think of people and evaluate them for what they are rather than in terms of how they evaluate ego, the latter being a more typically American approach. The Russians also paid more attention to the "others' " basic underlying attributes and attitudes than to their behavior as such or their performance on standards of achievement and accomplishment in the instrumental realm.

Similar patterns were evident in their perception of interpersonal situations. In reacting to the interpersonal relations "problems" presented by one of the psychological tests they more fully elaborated the situation, cited more relevant incidents from folklore or their own experience, and offered many more illustrations of a point. In contrast, the Americans tended more to describe the formal, external, characteristics of people, apparently being less perceptive of the individual's motivational characteristics.

The Americans also tended to discuss interpersonal problems on a rather generalized and abstract level. With regard to most other types of situation, however, especially problems involving social organization, the pattern was somewhat reversed. Russians tended to take a rather broad, sweeping view of the situation, *generalizing* at the expense of detail, about which they were often extremely vague and poorly informed. They seemed to feel their way through such situations rather than rigorously to think them through, tending to get into a spirit of grandiose planning but without attention to necessary details.

8. *Modes of Conative Functioning*

By conative functioning we mean the patterns, the particular behavioral forms, of the striving for any valued goals, including the rhythm or pace at which these goals are pursued and the way in which that rhythm is regulated. In this area our clinical data are not very rich. Nevertheless, we have the strong impression that the Russians do not match the Americans in the vigor of their striving to master all situations or problems put before them, and to do so primarily through adaptive instrumental orientations. Although by no means listless, they seem much more *passively accommodative* to the apparent hard facts of situations. In addition, they appeared less apt to persevere systematically in the adaptive courses of action they did undertake, tending to backslide into passive accommodation when the going proved rough. At the same time, the Russians do seem capable of great bursts of activity, which suggests the bimodality of an *assertive-passive pattern* of strivings in contrast to the steadier, more even, and consistent pattern of strivings among the Americans.

To sum up, one of the most salient characteristics of the personality of our

Russian subjects was their emotional aliveness and expressiveness. They felt their emotions keenly, and did not tend to disguise or to deny them to themselves, nor to suppress their outward expression to the same extent as the Americans. The Russians criticized themselves and others with greater freedom and spontaneity. Relatively more aware and tolerantly accepting of impulses for gratification in themselves and others, they relied less than the Americans on self-control from within and more on external socially imposed controls applied by the peer group or authority. A second outstanding characteristic of the Russians was their strong need for intensive interaction with others, coupled with a strong and secure feeling of relatedness to them, high positive evaluation of such belongingness, and great capacity to enjoy such relationships. The image of the "good" authority was of a warm, nurturant, supportive figure. Yet our subjects seemed to assume that this paternalism might and indeed should include superordinate planning and firm guidance, as well as control or supervision of public and personal morality, and if necessary, of thought and belief. It is notable, in this connection, that in the realm of conative and cognitive functioning orderliness, precision of planning, and persistence in striving were not outstandingly present. Such qualities were rather overshadowed by tendencies toward over-generalizing, vagueness, imprecision, and passive accommodation. Countering the image of the good authority, there was an expectation that those with power would in fact often be harsh, aloof, and authoritarian. The effect of such behavior by authority is alienation of loyalty. This fits rather well with the finding that the main polarized issues or dilemmas were those of "trust vs. mistrust" in relations with others, "optimism vs. pessimism," and "activity vs. passivity," whereas the more typically Ameri-

can dilemma of "intimacy vs. isolation" was not a problem for many Russians. Though strongly motivated by needs for affiliation and dependence and wishes for oral gratification—in contrast to greater strength of needs for achievement, autonomy, and approval among the Americans —our Russian subjects seemed to have a characteristically sturdy ego. They were rather secure in their self-estimation, and unafraid to face up to their own motivation and that of others. In contrast to the Americans, the Russians seemed to feel shame and guilt for defects of "character" in interpersonal relations rather than for failure to meet formal rules of etiquette or instrumental production norms. Compared with the Americans, however, they seemed relatively lacking in well-developed and stabilized defenses with which to counteract and modify threatening impulses and feelings. The organization of their personality depended for its coherence much more heavily on their intimate relatedness to those around them, their capacity to use others' support and to share with them their emotions.

RELATIONS OF MODAL PERSONALITY AND THE SOCIOPOLITICAL SYSTEM

In the following comments we are interpreting "political participation" rather broadly, to cover the whole range of the individual's role as the citizen of a large-scale national state. We therefore include his major economic and social as well as his specifically political roles. This may extend the concept of political participation too far for most national states, but for the Soviet Union, where all aspects of social life have been politicized, it is the only meaningful approach. Specifically, the questions to which we address ourselves are as follows.

Assuming that the traits cited above

were widespread among the group of Great Russians studied by our project, what implications would this have for their adjustment to the role demands made on them by the social system in which they participated? To what extent can the typical complaints of refugees against the system, and the typical complaints of the regime against its own people, be traced to the elements of non-congruence between these personality modes and Soviet social structure?

A full answer to these questions would involve us in a much more extensive presentation and a more complex analysis than is possible here. We wish to stress that our analysis is limited to the Soviet socio-political system as it typically functioned under Stalin's leadership, since this was the form of the system in which our respondents lived and to which they had to adjust. To avoid any ambiguity on this score we have fairly consistently used the past tense. We sincerely hope that this will not lead to the mistaken assumption that we regard the post-Stalin era as massively discontinuous with the earlier system. However, to specify in any detail the elements of stability and change in post-Stalin Russia, and to indicate the probable effects of such changes on the adjustment of Soviet citizens to the system, is beyond the scope of this paper. As for the personality dimensions, we will discuss each in its relations to system participation separately, rather than in the complex combinations in which they operate in reality. Only those of the personality traits cited above are discussed that clearly have relevance for the individual's participation in the socio-political system.

Need Affiliation. Virtually all aspects of the Soviet regime's pattern of operation seem calculated to interfere with the satisfaction of the Russians' need for affiliation. The regime has placed great strains on friendship relations by its persistent programs of political surveillance, its encouragement and elaboration of the process of denunciation, and its assignment of mutual or "collective" responsibility for the failings of particular individuals. The problem was further aggravated by the regime's insistence that its élite should maintain a substantial social distance between itself and the rank-and-file. In addition, the regime developed an institutional system that affected the individual's relations with others in a way that ran strongly counter to the basic propensities of the Russians as represented in our sample. The desire for involvement in the group, and the insistence on loyalty, sincerity, and general responsiveness from others, received but little opportunity for expression and gratification in the tightly controlled Soviet atmosphere. Many of the primary face-to-face organizations most important to the individual were infiltrated, attacked, or even destroyed by the regime. The break-up of the old village community and its replacement by the more formal, bureaucratic, and impersonal collective farm is perhaps the most outstanding example, but it is only one of many. The disruption and subordination to the state of the traditional family group, the Church, the independent professional associations, and the trade unions are other cases in point. The regime greatly feared the development of local autonomous centers of power. Every small group was seen as a potential conspiracy against the regime or its policies. The system of control required that each and all should constantly watch and report on each other. The top hierarchy conducted a constant war on what it scornfully called "local patriotism," "back-scratching," and "mutual security associations," even though in reality it was attacking little more than the usual personalizing tendencies incidental to effective business and political management. The people strove hard to maintain their small group structures, and the regime persistently fought this trend through its war against "familieness" and associated evils. At the same time it must be recognized that by its emphasis on broad group loyalties, the regime probably captured and harnessed somewhat the propensities of many Russians to give themselves up wholly to a group membership and to group activity and goals. This is most marked in the Young Communist League and in parts of the Party.

Need Orality. The scarcity element that predominated in Soviet society, the strict rationed economy of materials, men, and the physical requirements of daily life seem to have aroused intense anxieties about further oral deprivation that served greatly to increase the impact of the real shortages that have been chronic to the system. Indeed, the image of the system held by most in our sample is very much that of an orally depriving, niggardly, non-nurturant leadership. On the other hand, the regime can hope to find a quick road to better relations with the population by strategic dumping or glutting with goods, which was to some extent attempted during the period of Malenkov's ascendancy, although perhaps more in promise than reality.

Need Dependence. The regime took pride in following Lenin in "pushing" the masses. It demanded that individuals be responsible and carry on "on their own" with whatever resources were at hand, and clamored for will and self-determination. Clearly, this was not very congruent with the felt need for dependent relations. At the same time the regime had certain strengths relative to the need for dependence. The popular image of the regime as one possessed of a strong sense of direction fits in with this need. Similarly it gained support for

its emphasis on a massive formal program of social-welfare measures, even if they were not too fully implemented. This directedness has a bearing also on the problem of submission. Although the regime had the quality of a firm authority able to give needed direction, it did not gain as much as it might because it was viewed as interested in the maximation of power *per se*. This appears to alienate the Russian as he is represented in our sample.

The Trust-Mistrust Dilemma. Everything we know about Soviet society makes it clear that it was extremely difficult for a Soviet citizen to be at all sure about the good intentions of his government leaders and his immediate supervisors. They seemed always to talk support and yet to mete out harsh treatment. This divided behavior pattern of the leadership seemed to aggravate the apparent Russian tendency to see the intentions of others as problematical and to intensify the dilemma of trust-mistrust. On the basis of our interviews one might describe this dilemma of whether or not to grant trust as very nearly *the* central problem in the relations of former Soviet citizens to their regime. The dilemma of optimism vs. pessimism, of whether outcomes will be favorable or unfavorable, presents a very similar situation.

The Handling of Shame. The regime tried exceedingly hard to utilize public shame to force or cajole Soviet citizens into greater production and strict observance of the established rules and regulations. Most of our available public documentary evidence indicates that the regime was not outstandingly successful in this respect. Our clinical findings throw some light on the reason. The regime tried to focus shame on nonperformance, on failures to meet production obligations or to observe formal bureaucratic rules.

To judge by the clinical sample, however, the Russian is little shamed by these kinds of performance failures, and is more likely to feel shame in the case of moral failures. Thus, the Soviet Russian might be expected to be fairly immune to the shaming pressures of the regime. Indeed, the reactions of those in our sample suggest the tables often get turned around, with the citizen concluding that it is the regime which should be ashamed because it has fallen down in these important moral qualities.

Affective Functioning. The general expansiveness of the Russians in our sample, their easily expressed feelings, the giving in to impulse, and the free expression of criticism, were likely to meet only the coldest reception from the regime. It emphasized and rewarded control, formality, and lack of feeling in relations. Discipline, orderliness, and strict observance of rules are what it expects. Thus, our Russian subjects could hope for little official reward in response to their normal modes of expression. In fact, they could be expected to run into trouble with the regime as a result of their proclivities in this regard. Their expansiveness and tendency freely to express their feelings, including hostile feelings, exposed them to retaliation from the punitive police organs of the state. And in so far as they did exercise the necessary control and avoided open expression of hostile feelings, they experienced a sense of uneasiness and resentment because of this unwarranted imposition, which did much to color their attitude to the regime.

Conative Functioning. The non-striving quality of our Russian subjects ties in with the previously mentioned characteristics of dependence and non-instrumentality. The regime, of course, constantly demanded greater effort and insisted on a more instrumental approach to problems. It emphasized long-range planning and deferred gratification. There was a continual call for efforts to "storm bastions," to "breach walls," "to strive mightily." With the Russian as he is represented in our sample, it does not appear likely that the regime could hope to meet too positive a response here; in fact it encountered a substantial amount of rejection for its insistence on modes of striving not particularly congenial to a substantial segment of the population. Indeed, the main influence may have been exerted by the people on the system, rather than by the system on them. Soviet official sources have for many years constantly complained of the uneven pace at which work proceeds, with the usual slack pace making it necessary to have great, often frenzied, bursts of activity to complete some part of the Plan on schedule, followed again by a slack period. It may well be that this pattern results not only from economic factors such as the uneven flow of raw material supplies, but that it also reflects the Russian tendency to work in spurts.

Relations to Authority. In many ways the difficulties of adjustment to the Soviet system experienced by our subjects revolved around the gap between what they *hoped* a "good" government would be and what they *perceived* to be the behavior of the regime. Our respondents freely acknowledged that the Soviet leaders gave the country guidance and firm direction, which in some ways advanced the long-range power and prestige of the nation. They granted that the regime well understood the principles of the welfare state, and cited as evidence its provision of free education and health services. The general necessity of planning was also allowed, indeed often affirmed, and the regime was praised for taking into its own hands the regulation of public morality and the conscious task of "raising the cultural level" through support of the arts and the encouragement of folk culture.

Despite these virtues, however, the whole psychological style of ruling and of administration adopted by the Bolsheviks seems to have had the effect of profoundly estranging our respondents. A great gulf seemed to separate the rulers and the ruled, reflected in our respondents' persistent use of a fundamental "we"-"they" dichotomy. "They" were the ones in power who do bad things to us, and "we" were the poor, ordinary, suffering people who, despite internal differences in status or income, share the misfortune of being oppressed by "them." Most did not know that Stalin had once asserted that the Bolsheviks could not be a "true" ruling party if they limited themselves "to a mere registration of the sufferings and thoughts of the proletarian masses." Yet our respondents sensed this dictum behind the style of Soviet rule. They reacted to it in charging the leaders with being uninterested in individual welfare and with extraordinary callousness about the amount of human suffering they engender in carrying out their plans. Our subjects saw the regime as harsh and arbitrary. The leaders were characterized as cold, aloof, "deaf" and unyielding to popular pleas, impersonal and distant from the people's problems and desires. The regime was seen not as firmly guiding but as coercive, not as paternally stern but as harshly demanding, not as nurturant and supportive but as autocratic and rapaciously demanding, not as chastening and then forgiving but as nagging and unyieldingly punitive.

The rejection of the regime was however by no means total, and the Bolshevik pattern of leadership was in many respects seen not as totally alien but rather as native yet unfortunately exaggerated. This "acceptance" did not extend to the coldness, aloofness, formality, and maintenance of social distance, which were usually rejected. It did, however, apply to the pressures exerted by the regime, which were felt to be proper but excessive. Coercion by government was understandable, but that applied by the regime was not legitimate because it was so harsh. The scolding about backsliding was recognized as necessary, but resented for being naggingly persistent and caustic. And the surveillance was expected, but condemned for being so pervasive, extending as it did even into the privacy of one's friendship and home relations, so that a man could not even hope to live "peacefully" and "quietly." The elements of acceptance within this broader pattern of rejection have important implications for the future of the post-Stalin leadership. They suggest that the regime may win more positive support by changing the mode of application of many of its authoritarian and totalitarian policies without necessarily abandoning these policies and institutions as such. Indeed in watching the public behavior of men like Khrushchev and Bulganin one cannot help but feel that their style of leadership behavior is much more congenial to Russians than was that of Stalin.

The preceding discussion strongly suggests that there was a high degree of incongruence between the central personality modes and dispositions of many Russians and some essential aspects of the structure of Soviet society, in particular the behavior of the regime. Most of the popular grievances were clearly based on real deprivations and frustrations, but the dissatisfactions appear to be even more intensified and given a more emotional tone because they were based also on the poor "fit" between the personality patterns of many Soviet citizens and the "personality" of the leaders as it expressed itself in the institutions they created, in their conduct of those institutions

and the system at large, and in the resultant social climate in the U.S.S.R.

SOCIAL CLASS DIFFERENTIATION

Since personality traits found in the
Russian sample are merely modal rather
than common to the group at large, it
follows that sub-groups can meaningfully
be differentiated by the choice of appropriate cutting points on the relevant continua. As a way of placing the individuals
in our sample on a common scale, three
elements from the total range of characteristics previously described were selected. They were chosen on the grounds
that they were most important in distinguishing the Russians as a group from
the Americans, and also because they
seemed meaningfully related to each
other as elements in a personality syndrome. The three characteristics were:
great strength of the drive for social relatedness, marked emotional aliveness,
and general lack of well-developed, complex, and pervasive defenses. The two
clinicians rated all cases for a combination of these traits on a three-point scale.
Cases judged on the basis of a review of
both interview and test material to have
these characteristics *in a marked degree*
were placed in a group designated as the
"primary set." Individuals in whom these
characteristics were clearly evident, but
less strongly pronounced, were designated as belonging to a "variant" set. The
"primary" and "variant" sets together
constitute a relatively homogeneous group
of cases who clearly revealed the characteristics that we have described as
"modal." All the remaining cases were
placed in a "residual" category, characterized by markedly stronger development of defenses, and in most instances
also by lesser emotional expressiveness
and lesser social relatedness. This group
was relatively the least homogeneous of
the three because its members tended to

make use of rather different combinations
of defenses without any typical pattern
for the set as a whole. Subjects placed in
the "residual" group appeared to differ
more from those in the "variant" set than
the "primary" and the "variant" sets differed from each other. However, even
the "residual" pattern was not separated
from the others by a very sharp break:
emotional aliveness and relatedness to
people were present also in some members of this group. Each of our 51 cases
was assigned to one of four social-status
categories on the basis of occupation and
education. All those in group A were
professionals and higher administrative
personnel most of whom had university
training, and all those in the D group
were either peasants, or unskilled or semiskilled workers with no more than five
years of education. Placement in the two
intermediary categories was also determined by the balance of occupation and
education, group B consisting largely
of white-collar workers and semi-profes-
sional and middle supervisory personnel,
and group C of more skilled workers
with better education.

Table 1 gives the distribution of
cases among the three personality types
within each of the four status groups. It
is evident that the primary pattern has its
greatest strength in the lower classes, becomes relatively less dominant in the
middle layers, and plays virtually no role
at all in the top group. The "residual"
pattern predominates at the top level and
is very rare among peasants and ordinary
workers.

Since the distinctive patterns of adjustment to the Soviet system by the various socio-economic groups will be the
basis of extensive publications now in
progress, we restrict ourselves here to a
few general observations. First, we wish
to stress that, as our interviews indicate,
both the more favored and the rank-and-
file share substantially the same range of

complaints against the regime, find the same broad institutional features such as the political terror and the collective farm objectionable, and view the same welfare features such as the system of education and free medical care as desirable. In spite of these common attitudes our data suggest that personality may play a massive role with regard to some aspects of participation in and adjustment to the socio-political system. The educational-occupational level attained and/or maintained by an individual in an open-class society is one of the major dimensions of such participation. This is particularly the case in the Soviet Union, where profes-

sional and higher administrative personnel are inevitably more deeply implicated in the purposes and plans of the regime, are politically more active and involved, and are subjected to greater control and surveillance. It seems plausible that persons in whom the affiliative need was particularly strong, expressiveness marked and impulse control weak, and the defensive structures not well developed or well organized would be handicapped in competition for professional and administrative posts in any society; they certainly could not be expected to strive for or to hold on to positions of responsibility in the Soviet system.

TABLE 1

Status Distribution of Personality Types Among Former Soviet Citizens

		Personality Type		
Status	Primary	Variant	Residual	Total
A	—	1	12	13
B	2	8	6	16
C	3	4	2	9
D	8	3	2	13
TOTAL	13	16	22	51

The pattern of marked association between certain traits of personality and educational-occupational level clearly invites a question as to whether the personality really affected the level attained and held, or whether the appropriate personality traits were merely acquired along with the status. This question raises complex issues which we cannot enter into here. We do wish to point out, however, that the characteristics on which our psychological grouping was based belong to those that are usually formed at an early age and are relatively long enduring and resistant to change. At first glance this affirmation of the early origins

of the patterns described seems to be inconsistent with their observed association with educational-occupational level. However, the contradiction exists only if one assumes that obtaining a higher education and a superior occupation in Soviet society is a matter either of pure chance or exclusively of ability, unrelated to family background and the person's own attitudes and strivings. The data on stratification and mobility in Soviet society show, however, that persons born into families of higher social and educational level have a much better chance than do others to obtain a higher education and professional training. Consequently, many people of the professional and administrative class grew up in families of similar status, and in those families were apparently reared in a way different from that typical of the peasant and worker families. Presumably this produced enduring effects on their personality formation, which were important prior to exposure to common educational experience.

In addition, mobility out of the lower classes may have been mainly by individuals whose personality was different, for whatever reason, from that of the majority of their class of origin. Such differences can easily express themselves in a stronger drive for education and for a position of status. We must also allow for the role played by the regime's deliberate selection of certain types as candidates for positions of responsibility. Finally, there is the less conscious "natural selection" process based on the affinity between certain personality types and the opportunities offered by membership in the élite and near-élite categories. In this connection we are struck by the relative distinctness of the highest status level in our sample, since only one person with either of the two variants of the modal personality of the rank-and-file shows up among them. These results bear out the impression, reported by Dicks, of radical personality differences and resultant basic incompatibilities between the ruled population and the rulers. The latter, we assume, are still further removed from the "modal pattern" than are our subjects in the élite group.

We have yet to deal with the question of how far our observations concerning a group of refugees can be generalized to the Soviet population and *its* adjustment to the Soviet system? The answer to this question depends in good part on whether personality was an important selective factor in determining propensity to defect among those in the larger group

who had the opportunity to do so. It is our impression that personality was not a prime determinant of the decision not to return to Soviet control after World War II. Rather, accidents of the individual's life history such as past experience with the regime's instruments of political repression, or fear of future repression because of acts which might be interpreted as collaboration with the Germans, seem to have been the prime selective factors. Furthermore, such experiences and fears, though they affected the loyalty of the Soviet citizen, were not prime determinants of his pattern of achievement or adjustment in the Soviet socio-political system. The refugee population is not a collection of misfits or historical "leftovers." It includes representatives from all walks of life and actually seemed to have a disproportionately large number of the mobile and successful.

Though we are acutely aware of the smallness of our sample, we incline to assume that the personality modes found in it would be found within the Soviet Union in groups comparable in nationality and occupation. We are strengthened in this assumption by several considerations. First, the picture of Russian modal personality patterns which emerges from our study is highly congruent with the traditional or classic picture of the Russian character reported in history, literature, and current travellers' accounts. Second, much of the criticism directed by the regime against the failings of the population strongly suggests that some of the traits we found modal to our sample and a source of strain in its adjustment to the system are widespread in the population and pose an obstacle to the attainment of the regime's purposes *within* the U.S.S.R. Third, the differences in personality between occupational levels are consistent with what we know both of the general selective processes in industrial occupational systems and of the deliberate selective procedures adopted by the Soviet regime. Because of the methodological limitations of our study, the generalization of our findings to the Soviet population must be considered as purely conjectural. Unfortunately we will be obliged to remain on this level of conjecture as long as Soviet citizens within the U.S.S.R. are not accessible to study under conditions of relative freedom. We feel, however, that, with all their limitations, the findings we have reported can be of essential aid in furthering our understanding of the adjustment of a large segment of the Soviet citizens to their socio-political system and of the policies adopted by the regime in response to the disposition of the population.

In their volume on *How the Soviet System Works,* Bauer, Inkeles, and Kluckhohn point out that most societies are held together by face-to-face group loyalties. "It is characteristic of the Soviet system, however, that such loyalties are deemed intolerable. Soviet publications are filled with attacks on 'familyness.' " The loyalties represented by "familyness" would be intolerable to any totalitarian system. "So-called 'family groups' . . . develop among persons thrown together by common interests. Thus, the manager, the Party organizer, and the production engineer of a factory, some local Party officials, and certain officials of the Ministry in charge may be bound together by common interest in the attainment of good production records for the factory. Not only do they help each other by legal means, but each inevitably becomes involved with the others in responsibility for illegal or quasi-legal methods that might be used in order to attain the production goal. 'Family groups,' besides aiding each other in a positive fashion, cover up and protect each other." [4]

Traditionally, at least outside urbanized centers, Russian society, too, was held together by face-to-face group loyalties which had their basis in local kinship systems. Blood ties, being the most indestructible of human bonds, can often, and generally do in agricultural societies, give rise to broader loyalties which are almost as difficult to destroy. It is not at all surprising that vestiges of such loyalties should have been retained among the mass of Soviet peoples. And the quality of such ties is to be seen in the very word chosen to describe them: "familyness."

The success of any civil—especially a totalitarian—structure in its vertical entrenchment depends on its success in the subversion of kin ties and kinship structure; one of the ways in which this is done is by "the enforcement of decrees issued by the ruling group for the purpose of attaining its power aims." [5] "The civil power must, in one way or another, subvert kin solidarity and deflect that esprit de corps towards itself, in order to extend its authority throughout the social structure." [6] There is a model or precursor of the Soviet pattern in the history of the Dahomeans of West Africa. Diamond has reconstructed this culture history and he writes of the process as follows: "It appears that the whole region of [Dahomey] from the northern boundary of Whydah to Yoruba country was, up to the beginning of the seventeenth century, divided into tiny local sovereignties. . . . These autonomous sovereignties

---

[4] Bauer, Inkeles, and Kluckhohn, 1956, p. 77.
[5] Diamond, 1951, p. 15.
[6] *Op. cit.,* pp. 3-4.

were probably localized clans, or clusters of clans, each with a paramount chief." In the course of their early history, these autonomous clan-communities were destroyed by warfare. As "the scattered kin societies within the Whydah-Abomey axis were coagulating into civil society . . . the Aladaxonu became the civil authority, building and manipulationg a power structure that was designed to wrest from the subordinated kin groups their customary political, social, economic and religious functions." [7]

This process of subverting the kinship structure for the attainment of power within a civil structure was accomplished in Dahomey by several means, among which one during the seventeenth century was outstanding even though the attempt was short-lived. "The instincts of the Dahomean rulers, as instruments of the State striving-to-be, were sound as stone." Morris reports:

'In Dahomey, children are taken from their mother at an early age, and distributed to places remote from their villages of nativity, where they remain with little chance of being ever seen, or at least recognized, by their parents afterwards. The motive for this is that there may be no family connections or combinations, no associations that might prove injurious to the King's unlimited power. Hence each individual is detached and having no relative for whom he is interested is solicitous only for his own safety which he consults by the most abject submission.' [8]

Thus, one does not have to be a social scientist to know the growing child's relationship to his family, or the role of the family itself, for some of the broader implications of socialization for social and political change. It is quite possible that the ways in which the post-revolutionary rulers of Russia tampered with the traditional bases of the Russian family were geared to the same end. The legalization of ease of divorce, the legalization of abortion, the encouragement of children to inform on their parents, the legalization of free choice of spouse, the abolition of polygamy, and the like, may have served the same functions in Russia as the relocation of children in seventeenth century Dahomey. In this light, it is not unlikely that the subsequent changes in Soviet laws with respect to divorce and abortion were an attempt to set limits to the possible social disorganization which might have resulted. It is quite possible that the Russian leaders felt that their work had been done, and they were now in a position to control the processes transpiring within the new family structure which they had sought to bring into existence.

Objectively, the social and political institutions effected by the new Soviet rulers demanded that individuals renounce their traditional patterns of interpersonal reliance and learn to live as responsible *individuals* rather than as members responsible to tightly-knit groupings. It demanded, in brief, a greater degree of *individualization* and *individuation*. We have seen that the attainment of this goal has not been easy for the ruling Soviet classes; nor have they failed. As Inkeles points out in the paper to follow, whatever success the Russian leaders have achieved has been accomplished through the socialization process. This is not to say that the accomplishment

---

[7] *Op. cit.*, pp. 10, 14.
[8] *Op. cit.*, p. 26.

was made through verbal teaching; rather, parents consciously or unconsciously recognized the new demands which the system would make upon succeeding generations and brought up their children to meet those demands. Voluntarily or involuntarily, consciously or unconsciously, parents always have a duty to their children to rear them in such fashion that they will be able to adapt to the social world in which they are going to live. Thus, there has been a marked decrease in religious upbringing and in the maintenance of strong family ties and traditions *in the socialization process.* There arose an increasing emphasis on "getting along," on staying out of trouble, and on keeping a sharp eye on one's own security and safety. This is an individualistic way of looking at the world. This greater emphasis on values of individuation is also to be seen in the inculcation of highly personalized moral values and in the emphasis on education and knowledge—something one acquires by one's self and as a responsible agent—as ends in themselves. Finally, in the emphasis during socialization on techniques for dealing with the established government, we see another reflection of the post-revolutionary emphasis on "adjustment" as a personal or individualized process.

SOCIAL CHANGE AND SOCIAL CHARACTER: THE ROLE OF PARENTAL MEDIATION*

By Alex Inkeles

In his general essay on national character Gorer provides a clear and succinct formulation of one of the major premises underlying most of the related literature. Gorer indicated that we can deal with the simple but imposing fact that "societies continue, though their personnel changes" only because we can assume that "the present generation of adults will be replaced in due course by the present generation of children *who, as adults, will have habits very similar to their parents.*" Implicit in this general pattern, of course, is the further assumption "that the childhood learning of the contemporary adults was at least very similar to the learning which contemporary children are undergoing."

Gorer recognizes, and indeed states explicitly, that this model is probably not applicable to "societies which are in the process of drastic change." As Margaret Mead points out, however, so few individuals may now hope to grow up under conditions of sociocultural stability that we may regard this situation as almost unusual, and its products as in a sense "deviants." Gorer's model, therefore, requires elaboration, extension, and adjustment to enable it to deal adequately with national character as it develops and emerges under conditions of social change. The question is essentially this: Insofar as rapid social change interrupts the simple recapitulation of child training practices and produces new modal personality patterns, by what means are such changes mediated or effected?

The literature on national character contains several important and interesting efforts to answer this question. Margaret Mead, for example, has explored the sig-

* Reprinted with abridgment from the *Journal of Social Issues,* Vol. *11,* No. *2,* pp. 12-23, 1955, with permission.

nificance for personality development of growing up in a culture that is no longer homogeneous, and posits the development under those circumstances of what she calls a "tentative" personality syndrome. Riesman, developing in full detail a point also made by Mead, has discussed the significance for social character of growing up under the strong influence of peer group pressures and standards. Erikson has stated the implications for personality development that arise from the absence of adequate and valued role models with which to identify, and from the associated lack of roles through which the individual can find socially sanctioned and culturally meaningful outlets for the discharge of his emotions.

Despite the diversity of these studies they seem to have one element in common in their approach to the role of the parent as "child rearer" under conditions of social change. Implicitly, if not explicitly, the parent is conceived as having available a relatively fixed repertory of child training procedures provided by his culture and learned by him in the period of his own childhood. Two main alternatives as to his utilization of those techniques are then generally considered. On the one hand, the parent is seen as acting as the passive agent of his culture, raising his children according to the procedures he had learned earlier in his own childhood, even though these techniques may have lost their appropriateness. It is assumed in that case, that as his children grow up the gulf between parent and child will rapidly grow great, and relations will become strained as the child meets and learns the conflicting behavior patterns and underlying values of his "own" new culture. On the other hand, the parent may know enough not to try to apply the training procedures under which he was raised, and in that case he either surrenders to other cultural surrogates such as peer group, teachers, mass media,

etc., or borrows, and of course generally ineptly applies, some prefabricated set of rules. In the lower classes the borrowing might be from the local baby clinic, and in the upper classes from books and lectures on child rearing. In short the parents will manifest what Mead terms "disturbed and inconsistent images of their children's future."

Without doubt these descriptions are faithful to the facts in many situations. Nevertheless, they seem to have made inadequate allowance for the positive adjustive capacity of human beings and for the process of continuous interaction that goes on between them and their sociocultural environment. Very often the global impact of Western contacts on a nonliterate people may be almost totally disorienting, but parents need not be either unimaginative and passive agents of their culture, raising their children by rote, nor so disorganized and disoriented as is suggested by Mead's discussion. Although parents are adults, they may nevertheless still *learn,* and learn what they feel to be major "lessons," from their experiences under conditions of social change. This learning, furthermore, may influence the parents to seek purposefully to bring their children up in a way different from that in which they were raised, and in a manner intended better to suit the children for life in the changed social situation. This has been clearly recognized by Aberle and Naegele, who in a passage not easily duplicated elsewhere in the literature affirm that:

All in all child rearing is future oriented to an important extent. The picture of the desired end product is importantly influenced by the parents' experiences in the adult world, as well as by their childhood experiences. When adult experience changes under the impact of major social change, there is reason to believe that there will ultimately, although not necessarily immediately, be shifts in the socialization pattern as well.

Of course, if either the parental experience of change or the response to it were purely idiosyncratic, then even where such experiences were widely distributed their effect on the character of the next generation would be essentially randomized. But it is in the nature of social structure, particularly in modern industrial society, that large groups of the population will be exposed to and perceive ongoing change in similar fashion. Furthermore, it follows both from the existence of modal personality patterns and the shared cultural heritage of those in the subgroups of any population that they are very likely to react to this experience in systematically patterned ways. One very probable reaction to the experience of social change is to adjust the training of children to better prepare them for life in the future as the parent now anticipates that life in the light of his own experience. There is reason to assume, therefore, that the influence of large-scale social change occurring at any one time may be reflected in the character of the *next* generation because of mediation by parents living under and experiencing the change.

To test these assumptions one would ideally want a research design permitting the exploration of two distinct although intimately related questions. The first involves the hypothesis that parents who have experienced extreme social change seek to raise their children differently from the way in which they were brought up, purposefully adapting their child rearing practices to train children better suited to meet life in the changed world as the parent now sees it. To test this hypothesis we would need detailed information about the child rearing practices utilized by two consecutive generations of patents in the same culture, the first of which lived and raised its children in a period of relative stability, whereas the second lived and brought up its children under conditions of fairly extreme social change. A different requirement is posed by the question of how effective the parents in the second generation are in developing new traits or combinations of traits in their children. The extension of the ideal research design in this direction would require that we secure data on the modal personality patterns prevalent in the third generation. We would anticipate that as a result of their different socialization experience those in the third generation would manifest modal personality patterns different in important respects from those of their parents in the second generation.

Clearly such a design is extremely difficult to execute. Fortunately, however, we can approximate the ideal, although admittedly very imperfectly, through the utilization of some of the materials collected by the Harvard Project on the Soviet Social System. In that research program detailed life history interviews were conducted with about 330 former Soviet citizens, yielding a well-balanced sample in regard to such factors as age, sex, and occupation. The interview extensively explored the life of the respondent in both his family of orientation and procreation. Particular attention was paid to the values in regard to character development and occupational goals that dominated in child rearing as practiced by the respondent's parents and by the respondent himself in the role of parent. Through an exploration of these data we may hope to see some of the effects of social change in the Soviet Union as the parents who "lived" the change adjusted their child rearing practices in response to their own adult experiences, and thus acted as intermediaries in transmitting the effects of their current change to a future generation.

We may begin by testing the first assumption, namely that a generation experiencing extreme social change in adulthood will adapt the methods whereby it raises its children, and that as a result its children will be reared differently than it had been and yet more in keeping with the changed social realities. For our first generation, which we shall call the "Tsarist" generation, we need a group that raised its children during a period of relative social stability. The most recent period of that sort in Russia unfortunately falls as far back as the time immediately preceding the First World War, roughly from 1890 to 1915. Since we are interested in child rearing practices, and particularly of people who raised their children to adulthood (taken here as age 15) in those years, then eligible respondents would have been at least 33 by 1915 and at least 68 by the time of our interview in 1950. Indeed, most of those who could qualify as parents in our first generation were probably dead by 1950, and in any event only three of those living appear in our sample. We can learn about the child rearing practices utilized by that generation, therefore, only by relying on what their children report to have been true of the parents. The children of the Tsarist generation do, of course, appear in our sample. In this group we include all respondents over 45 in 1950, and we call it the "Revolutionary" generation because its members, born in 1905 or before, were young adults at the time of the Revolution and lived as mature individuals through the subsequent Civil War and the later periods of momentous social change represented by the forced collectivization and industrialization programs. It was this second generation that was raising its children to adulthood during the main period of Soviet development.

It will be recognized, therefore, that, although dealing with the child rearing practices of two different generations of parents, we draw our information from but a single set of respondents, namely those in our sample over 45 years of age in 1950. In telling us how their parents brought them up they provide us with data about the child rearing practices of the Tsarist generation, whereas in describing the training of their own children, they provide our materials on the child rearing practices of the Revolutionary generation. Although limits of space do not permit presentation of the evidence, we have data that indicate that this procedure of ascertaining the child rearing values of an earlier generation by accepting the description given by those who had been the children of the group being studied, is methodologically less suspect than might appear to be the case. The description by the youngest generation in our sample of the manner in which it was reared agrees so closely with the report of how the training was done as related by the middle generation, which actually reared the children, as to yield correlations of .89 and .95 on the two available comparisons.

Relative to the child rearing materials we have a detailed summary code of the dominant values governing child rearing, both as to character and occupational goals, characteristic for each generation acting as parents. In no case, however, is the rating of the parent based on his observed behavior, but only on the values deduced by us to have been operative on the basis of the interview. Furthermore, as already noted, the respondents from the prerevolutionary Tsarist generation could not speak for themselves and we had to rely on the retrospective report of their children.

In the following analysis a larger number of code categories has been grouped into a set of six major dimensions that were prominent value orientations in the child rearing efforts of those in our sample. The value of "tradition" was coded mainly for emphasis on religious upbringing, but it included as well references to maintenance of strong family ties and traditions; "adjustment" reflects emphasis on "getting along," staying out of trouble, keeping an eye on your security and safety, etc.; "achievement" was coded when parents stressed attainment, industriousness, mobility, material rewards, and similar goals; "personalistic" was checked when the parent was concerned with such personal qualities as honesty, sincerity, justice, and mercy; "intellectuality," where the emphasis was on learning and knowledge as ends in themselves; and "political" when the focus was on attitudes, values, and beliefs dealing with government and particularly with *the* government of the land.

When we consider the profound differences, during their years of child rearing, in the life experience of the Revolutionary generation as contrasted with that of its parents in the Tsarist generation, what differences may we expect in their values with regard to child rearing? The revolutionary upheaval of 1917 and the subsequent programs of forced social change struck a great blow at the traditional structure of Russian society and profoundly altered it. Massive programs of expansion were undertaken in industrialization, in urbanization, in formal organization and administration. The pattern of rural life, in which the bulk of the population was involved, was drastically revised through the forced collectivization of agriculture. Centralized political control and political terror were ruthlessly imposed. Opportunities for mobility increased greatly. Under these circumstances we might well expect the traditional values to suffer the greatest loss of emphasis, with a consequent shift to stress on either simple successful adjustment or the more secularized morality represented by the personalistic values

and the pursuit of knowledge as an end in itself. In addition, our knowledge of the growing opportunities for advancement, associated with the generally expanded development of the formal occupational structure, leads us to anticipate that greatly increased weight would be given to achievement. Finally the central role played by the state in Soviet affairs, the existence of the political terror, and the additional fact that our respondents were disaffected from the political system, lead us to anticipate heightened concern with political considerations in child rearing.

In Table 1 we have indicated the distribution of emphasis among the dimensions in our set of dominant value orientations. The relative stability of the gross rank order is testimony to the fact that both generations of parents represented a common cultural tradition which they carried forward through time. Nevertheless, it is clear that there have been very substantial shifts in the relative weight of several value orientations, and they go largely in the expected direction. Perhaps the most striking finding is the sharp decrease in emphasis on the traditional values, accounted for overwhelmingly by the decreased emphasis on religious training and belief. Under the impact of industrialization and urbanization, perhaps abetted by the antireligious and "proscientific" propaganda conducted by the regime, parents in the Revolutionary generation clearly shifted toward an emphasis on more secular values. This shift is reflected in the increased emphasis on learning (intellectuality) and positive personal qualities *as ends in themselves* rather than as *means* to the attainment of the good life lived, as it were, "in the sight of God." Thus, secular morality replaced traditional and religiously based morality.

Perhaps most directly and explicitly related to the intervening experience of the parents under conditions of social change is the increased attention paid to political considerations in the education of one's children. The greater emphasis on political problems arises from the fact that the Soviet regime has progressively "politicized" more and more areas of human activity that in most Western societies fall outside the political realm. A person at all alert to his situation and surroundings could therefore hardly fail to realize that if he wished to prepare his child adequately for life under Soviet conditions he must train him to an awareness concerning the political realities of the system, even though such training had not been important in his own childhood. This interpretation is borne out by the statements made by our interviewers.

TABLE 1

Child Rearing Values of Parents in Russian Pre-Revolutionary and Post-Revolutionary Times

	Distribution * of Emphasis in	
AREAS	Tsarist Period	Post-Revolutionary Period †
Tradition	75%	44%
Achievement	60	52
"Personalistic"	32	44
Adjustment	16	21
Intellectuality	12	22
Politics	12	20
Number of Respondents	77	78

* These percents total more than 100, since respondents were scored for as many themes as cited, but percentaging is on the basis of total respondents.
† The percentages in this column have been adjusted to equalize for the effect created by the larger number of responses given by our informants in describing their own activity as parents, as against the manner in which they had been raised by the Tsarist generation.

Finally, it is necessary to comment on the major instance in which the data fail to confirm expectation, namely in regard to emphasis on achievement values. This failure is, of course, only relative, since achievement was the most emphasized value in the rearing of children by those in the Revolutionary generation. Nevertheless, in absolute weight it declined in importance even though it had been expected to increase. It might be that since our respondents were refugees from the system, and since many of them looked upon too active pursuit of a career as suggesting involvement with the regime, they did not admit fully the importance they actually attributed to inculcating achievement strivings in their children. On the other hand, it may be that the expectation was unrealistic quite apart from specific Soviet conditions. There is some evidence that values such as security, adjustment, and personal attractiveness are becoming ever more important foci in child rearing in the United States and that stress on achievement *as an end in itself,* although still prevalent, has become somewhat old-fashioned. This pattern may be associated with the combination of mass industry, education and communication, and the consumer culture of which the Soviet Union is but one example.

All told, however, the data certainly seem strongly to support the assumption that the experience of extreme social change that the Revolutionary generation underwent did have a marked effect on that generation's approach to the rearing of its children. As compared with the way their parents raised them, they can hardly be assumed to have merely "recapitulated" the earlier pattern of child rearing. On the contrary, having experienced marked social change, they adjusted their child rearing practices, the better to prepare their children for the life they expected those children to lead.

To test the effectiveness of the changed general child rearing orientations of the Revolutionary generation, we would need data on the personality patterns prevalent among their children in the third generation, which we unfortunately do not have. Nevertheless, we can make a very approximate approach to our second question concerning the effectiveness of the changed child rearing emphases if we shift our attention to the realm of occupational choices. In that area we have data not only on the values stressed by parents, but we also have information on the values which the individual held in regard to himself. In treating value orientations relative to the occupational world we are, of course, dealing not with personality patterns in a psychodynamic sense, but rather with something more closely akin to "social character" as it has been defined by Riesman and Inkeles.

The influence of their experience with social change on the child training practices adopted by the Revolutionary generation is perhaps even more strikingly evident in the area of occupational choices. In addition to asking about the specific occupations for which parents wished to prepare their children, we asked the reasons for the selection. The reasons cited provide us with a guide to the values that were dominant in the home atmosphere created by the parent for the child. Considering the nature of the social change experienced by the Revolutionary generation and described above, we might again well expect that as part of the general weakening of the traditional way of life there would have been a decline in the importance of family tradition, as against self-expression or free choice, as values emphasized in orienting the child toward the occupational world. In addition it is reasonable to assume that economic and material rewards would have come to be much more stressed among the goals set before the child, as would the necessity of finding work that permitted an appropriate accommodation to the highly politicized occupational structure in Soviet society.

As a comparison of the first and second columns of Table 2 indicates, three of these four expectations are rather strongly supported by the responses of our interviews. We see, to begin, a sharp decline in the importance of family tradition as a criterion in shaping the child's occupational orientation, along with a marked increase in the role played by self-expression or free job choice. In addition, we may note the much greater emphasis on guiding the child toward a job that is politically desirable, which for our respondents generally meant one safe from danger of political arrest and not too directly involved in the regime's political objectives. Finally, it should be observed that here again the data fail to support our expectation that the material and psychic rewards on the job—roughly equivalent to earlier discussed achievement value—would be more emphasized by the Revolutionary generation than by the Tsarist generation. Indeed, the relative weight of such rewards as values to

be emphasized in orienting children toward the occupational world declined

markedly from the one generation to the
next.

TABLE 2

Changing Values Concerning the Occupational Realm

| | Distribution of Emphasis among Values Stressed | | |
| | In Child Rearing by: | | In Hypothetical Choice by |
VALUE AREAS	"Tsarist" Generation	"Revolutionary" Generation	"Soviet" Generation
Rewards	41%	25%	14%
Tradition	35	14	11
Self-expression	21	38	62
Politics	3	23	13
Number of Responses (equal to 100%)	58	63	931

Now to return to our original research design, do we have any evidence
that the different child rearing patterns
utilized by the middle generation as a
response to their experience of social
change actually were effective? Or did the
parents in that second generation, despite
their apparent intention, act in fact as
passive agents of the culture and, *nolens
volens,* raise their children in their own
image and much as the first generation
would have done the job? For a proper
answer to this question we should have
access to the children of the Revolutionary generation, and to data on their job
choices coded by the same categories
used to describe the child training values
of their parents. Unfortunately we can
only approximate each requirement. Respondents on both our written questionnaire and oral interview remained anonymous, and we therefore have no way of
identifying the actual children of the
Revolutionary generation. But we can
secure a reasonable equivalent of that
third group, which we call the "Soviet"
generation, by taking all respondents

under 35 in 1950. Most of them were
raised and reached adulthood in the same
period in which the Revolutionary generation was acting in the parental role
and could well have been their children.
As for the values that governed their job
choices, we are obliged to draw on our
written questionnaire, which presented
the respondents with a choice of precoded
categories not strictly comparable with
those used in assessing child training
values. For example the check list included the omnibus category "I feel suited
to it," which we have equated here with
"self-expression," but which obviously
could have meant many more things to
the respondents.

Quite apart for such methodological
difficulties, it would be naïve to expect
a near-perfect correlation between the
values that the parents in the Revolutionary generation stressed while they reared
the Soviet generation and the ones which
that generation emphasized in its own
job choices. Such training always produces only an approximation of the parents' desire. More important, those in the

Soviet generation have had their values shaped by many influences other than those exerted by their parents. Nevertheless, our expectation is that on the whole the pattern of value orientations of the Soviet generation will be quite close to those that were stressed in child training by their parents in the Revolutionary generation as contrasted with those inculcated in an earlier era by the Tsarist generation. The relative degree of fit between the two sets of orientations may be taken as a rough measure of how successful the Revolutionary generation was in training the Soviet generation to orient in new directions.

The appropriate comparison may be obtained by examining the third column of Table 2—which contains the distribution of emphasis in the operative values guiding the job choices of the younger generation—in relation to the first and second columns. The over-all comparison strongly suggests that those in the Revolutionary generation were highly successful in their purposive effort to shape the values their children would carry into adulthood. This is most evident in the marked emphasis that the Soviet generation places on self-expression rather than family tradition as a criterion for its job choices, much in keeping with the lesser emphasis that its parents had put on tradition in orienting their children's thoughts about the world of jobs and work. Even if we make allowance for the strong pull of the actual code category, "I feel suited for it," this interpretation would clearly not be materially affected.

It will be noticed, further, that in raising children those in the Tsarist generation gave extremely slight attention to political considerations, whereas those in the Revolutionary generation stressed it very heavily, indeed more heavily than tradition. In their own job choices, those in the Soviet generation again show the apparent influence of their parents' con-

cern for this dimension, although in their own value scheme it does not loom quite so large as it did in their parents' efforts at socialization. Finally, we may note that material and psychic rewards such as income and prestige had roughly similar relative weight, as compared to politics and tradition, in the child rearing practices of the Revolutionary generation and in the actual choices of the Soviet generation.

It seems reasonable to conclude again, therefore, that the Revolutionary generation did not merely act passively as the agent of the old culture, recapitulating in its own parental activities the socialization practices that had earlier been used by *its* parents. On the contrary, it may be said that the middle generation, responding to its experience of social change under the Soviet regime, in large measure turned away from the pattern of child rearing under which it had been raised earlier and in its approach to the new Soviet generation stressed goals and values of a different sort. It appears, furthermore, that this training of the youth in new value orientations was relatively successful.

Because the numbers are small and the sample unusual, the material presented here is perhaps little more than suggestive of the results that might be yielded by research specifically designed to increase our knowledge in this area. Indeed, a stronger case could have been made with the material at hand had not rigorous limits of space precluded the presentation of quotations from our interviews that show graphically the way in which conditions of social change experienced by the parents influenced their approach to raising their children. Nevertheless, the material presented should serve to alert us to the role that the parent plays, through both purposive and unconscious adjustments in his child rearing practices, in mediating the influence

of social change to his children and consequently in better adapting them for the
changed social conditions they may meet
as adults. Furthermore, although the
demonstration presented above dealt only

with the more surface level of attitudes
and value orientations, there is reason
to believe that similar processes operate
with regard to the development of personality at deeper levels.

There are only a few points which we should like to add to Inkeles' clear and
penetrating paper. The fact that large groups of the population will perceive on-
going social change in similar fashion should not be taken to mean that parental
response to changing features of the social system is always so regular and consistent
that succeeding generations are always reared to be in perfect harmony with over-all
changes in the sociocultural environment. On the contrary; social change invariably
produces a degree of disharmony between internalized values of individuals and the
demands of the environment. This is clear from the foregoing selections of this
chapter.

To an extent, such disharmonies and discrepancies are inevitable. Although we
do not know all the reasons for this—and we will be returning to this problem again,
especially in connection with the relationships between personality and total social
systems, in Chapter 9—there are some factors which are readily apparent and which
should at least be mentioned at this point.

First of all, even though it can be posited without reservation that parents train
their children in a manner consonant with the demands of the social environment—
and not necessarily as they themselves were brought up—the parents' responsiveness
to their environment is somewhat limited by two factors. The first such limitation is
derived from the parents' own experiences in the course of growing up. Thus, for
example, a parent who was brought up in a sexually repressive home would not
be able to transmit sexual values consonant with an urban environment *as easily* as would a parent who grew up in a sexually permissive home. The second
limitation derives from the parents' experiences as *adults*. Thus, for example, a
parent who, for one reason or another, failed to achieve any success or satisfaction
in a professional occupation would be less likely to teach his sons the value of learning or education for its own sake than a parent who did achieve considerable success
and satisfaction in a similar occupation. In other words, parents' experiences during
childhood as well as adulthood place some limitations on what they can select out of
the environment to transmit—and with how much pressure they will transmit it—
to the following generation. There has been little, if any, systematic research into this
problem, but it does demand investigation.

The second factor which should be mentioned at this point is that even within
the most consistent and patterned socialization practices within a group, or within
a family for that matter, there are often conflicting values which are transmitted in
the course of socialization. Thus, parents may teach their children that honesty is
the best policy and that marital fidelity is the proper norm of adult behavior. At the
same time, many children learn early in their lives—from their parents as well as
from the general social environment—that honesty is not always the best policy, for

it is not always effective for achieving the goals of individuals in, let us say, a particular social class. Similarly, in the close scrutiny to which parents are subjected by their growing children, the latter often learn that marital fidelity is but an ideal by which only some mortals abide; and it is through parental quarrels and parents' reading matter that children learn the proper conditions and rationalizations which allow for varying degrees of marital infidelity.

Third, and closely related to the material presented above by Inkeles, there are often certain personality predispositions and values which are so deeply and thoroughly ingrained in the personalities of individuals that many generations of external pressure by a new sociocultural environment are required to dislodge them. Thus, despite the tremendous pressures exerted by the post-revolutionary Soviet regime, it has been extremely difficult to dislodge "the Russian's need for affiliation." At the same time, however, many of these pressures have helped to perpetuate this "need for affiliation." Some of these basic and fundamental traditional values—the very depth and tenacity of which are demonstrated by their persistence in the face of governmental pressures—are the ones which interfere most with the attempt of the Soviet rulers to create the "new Soviet man": disciplined, working steadily and consistently, puritanical in conduct and motivation. But no one can completely escape social reality, and Inkeles has been able to demonstrate that there *have* been marked changes in Russian patterns of socialization.

Similarly, ethnic and religious affiliation and participation can often affect the degree to which a person will respond to sociocultural pressures in, for example, the area of sexual behavior. Kinsey and his associates found that "the accumulative and active incidences of premarital coitus have been distinctly higher among those females in the sample who were less actively connected with religious groups, and lower for those who were most devout. . . . This, in general, was true for the Protestant, Catholic, and Jewish groups. In many instances the differences between devout and inactive members of particular groups were very marked. The differences between Protestant, Catholic, and Jewish females of the same degree of devoutness were usually less than the differences between the various levels within any one religion." [9] (These data do not indicate whether religious devoutness and a low incidence of premarital coitus coexist with close family attachments, and whether less active religious connection and high incidences of premarital coitus go hand in hand with loose family attachments. This may well be the case, but Kinsey and his associates did not investigate the quality of family relationships in their samples.) Thus, we can generalize and say that gross changes in the sociocultural environment will produce change in some portions of the population and in the same areas of socialization but, for a variety of reasons, will produce fewer and slower changes in others.

SUMMARY

This chapter began with a rejection of two hypotheses. We set aside the contention of Davis and Havighurst that many middle-class socialization customs could be

---

[9] Kinsey *et al.*, 1953, p. 304.

explained by the "tameness," and the like, of middle-class life. And exception was taken to Bronfenbrenner's generalization that the changes which have occurred in middle-class child-rearing practices took place in those groups which are most exposed to the media of mass communication. While his generalization is undoubtedly correct as a correlation, the implied explanation in his generalization is open to serious question.

In order to illustrate our point that the sources of change in modes of child rearing are to be sought in events and forces in the total society, we examined two historical cases. The first was from American society, specifically, through Wolfenstein's analysis of the *Infant Care Bulletins* of the Children's Bureau, and the second was from Russian changes. In both instances, we saw that there were no simple cause-and-effect explanations. Rather, the material which was presented tended to underscore the proposition that socialization is adaptive and future-oriented and the hypothesis that that which is learned outside the home will tend to change more rapidly than that which is learned inside the home. Furthermore, to reiterate the point made at the conclusion of Chapter 4, any analysis of the socializing functions of the family must consider actively the position and location of the family in sociological space. Thus, as we learned from the investigation of the social-structural factors proceeding alongside changes in American socialization customs as reflected in the *Infant Care Bulletins,* populational shifts and concentrations in urban areas allowed for greater experimentations with biological impulses—but *not* as a result of anonymity—which, in turn, were reflected in the ways in which parents treated their own children.

BIBLIOGRAPHY AND SUGGESTED READINGS

Bauer, Raymond A. "The Psychology of the Soviet Elite: Two Case Histories," in *Personality in Nature, Society and Culture,* edited by Kluckhohn *et al.,* pp. 633-650. New York: Knopf, 1955. A worthwhile description of the reflection of governmental pressures in the lives of two former Soviet citizens.

Bauer, Raymond A., Alex Inkeles, and Clyde Kluckhohn. *How the Soviet System Works: Cultural, Psychological, and Social Themes.* Cambridge, Massachusetts: Harvard University Press, 1956.

Bruner, Edward M. "Primary Group Experience and the Process of Acculturation," *American Anthropologist,* Vol. 58, pp. 605-623, 1956. An important systematic study of the mechanisms involved in different patterns of socialization among the acculturated and unacculturated people of Lone Hill.

Diamond, Stanley. *Dahomey: A Proto-State in West Africa.* 1951, Doctoral Dissertation, Columbia University. University Microfilms, No. *2808,* Ann Arbor.

Gorer, Geoffrey. "The Concept of National Character," in *Personality in Nature, Society and Culture,* edited by Kluckhohn *et al.,* pp. 243-245. New York: Knopf, 1955.

Kinsey, Alfred C., Wardell B. Pomeroy, Clyde E. Martin and Paul H. Gebhard. *Sexual Behavior in the Human Female.* Philadelphia: Saunders, 1953

Mead, Margaret. "Social Change and Cultural Surrogates," in *Personality in Nature, Society and Culture,* edited by Kluckhohn *et al.,* pp. 651-662. New York: Knopf, 1955. This, and the paper by Gorer, provide an interesting contrast to the theoretical approach employed by Inkeles in his paper on changes in Russian socialization practices.

Miller, Daniel R. and Guy E. Swanson. *The Changing American Parent: A Study in the Detroit Area.* New York: Wiley, 1958. A factual account of some trends.

Chapter 6

AGGRESSION, FANTASY,
AND ADOLESCENCE

In this chapter, we are going to consider three topics: aggression, fantasy, and adolescence. Each of these can be studied independently of the other two, but we have included them under one heading for two reasons. First, they often, in social reality, do go together. This is especially true during adolescence in American society, when the potential for creative fantasy is often highest—but, unfortunately, frequently stifled for one reason or another. We are not referring only to fantasies about aggression—which, also, can be creative and constructive if they are channelized in socially and personally useful directions—but to fantasies in general. These deal with earning a living, sex, winning independence, marriage, raising a family, conquering the polar ice-cap or Mount Everest, discovering a cure for cancer, and so forth. None of these fantasies is necessarily an aggressive one, and each can be highly creative and constructive in one way or another.

The second reason for including these three topics under one heading is in the nature of a proposal. Thus far, in the history of sociology, fantasy has not been considered a legitimate area of research. Our proposal is that the social-structural conditions under which people live are very relevant to fantasy-behavior, and that we have much to learn about social structure *per se* and about the effects of social structure on the growing-up process from an inquiry into fantasy which is sociologically as well as psychologically relevant. Fantasy behavior occupies different amounts of time and energy in different children, adolescents, and adults; we do not know whether these differences are constitutional, psychological, or sociological. Undoubtedly, all three play a role, but we have to know the relative importance of each. People in different societies and subgroups have different kinds of fantasies, but we know very little about the sociological factors involved.

When we read the writings of psychoanalysts, novelists, and clinical psychologists, we find that most people create in the privacies of their own minds certain kinds of fantasies centering about aggressive actions which, if they were acted out overtly and concretely, would incur the unswerving wrath of society. These fantasies accrue to the individual's mind throughout life, beginning in childhood, and they are usually exacerbated and intensified during adolescence. In American society, for example, it may be "acceptable" to fantasy aloud about becoming a hobo or retiring at an early age to a Shangri-la in the South Seas, but not about murdering one's parents. It is probably safe to say that most people in American society would reject such imaginings as inconsistent with consciously held ideals and would probably deny their universality.

But even assuming a universality of such murderous ideas—if only for the sake of argument—would we also expect that (1) such fantasies would be of equal strength and intensity under all sociological conditions, and that (2) such mental images would be equally disturbing for the individual under all sociological conditions? Would we also expect that the nature of adolescence—the period during which these are often very strong—is the same under all social-structural conditions? The answer to these questions is probably in the negative, as will be seen from the three sets of data which we will consider in this chapter. What we shall attempt to do in these discussions is to show how these three areas—aggression, fantasy, and adolescence—are affected by the nature of quality of the growing individual's primary sociological relationships.

FAMILY ORGANIZATION AND AGGRESSION

We hypothesized at the end of our discussion of caste and class differences in socialization (in Chapter 3) that the greater suppression and curbing of aggressive behavior which we find as we move up the social scale from the lower to the upper classes might be a function of the fact that more aggression is *aroused* in children of the higher socioeconomic strata. What little evidence is available indicates that the problem is of far greater concern to the middle class than it is to the lower. It is our hypothesis in the present discussion that this greater concern with aggression in middle-class socialization is a function of the fact that middle-class family organization arouses and generates more aggression in children rather than a function of the greater orderliness and tameness of middle-class life, as was implied by Davis and Havighurst.

To illustrate this hypothesis we are going to make a much wider comparison than the one between urban middle- and lower-class families, and we are going to compare two groups of children from a well-to-do middle-class urban background and from a poor lower-class rural background. These are extremely wide differences, and one could argue, with some justification, that these two groups are not comparable within a framework of social classes. To an extent, this is true; but we are far *more* interested here in different types of family organizations and relationships than in social-class status as a phenomenon in itself. The comparison of urban and rural families is also a much clearer one than a comparsion of different kinds of families in a city, because as soon as we place families in an urban context we have to be extremely careful of the extent to which the *city*—independently of classes or other sociological divisions—affects the arousal and socialization of aggression in children. For our purposes, we shall be more concerned here with the subjective, informal, spontaneous, personally and immediately meaningful aspects of family life than with the place or role of the family within a systematic structure of social stratification.

CHILDREN OF THE CUMBERLAND*

In a charming and simply written volume, entitled *Children of the Cumberland,* Claudia Lewis, a nursery school teacher, presents a systematic and human picture of what it is like to be a child of a poor family in the Cumberlands, Tennessee. She begins her book, however, with a brief description of the children of upper middle-class families who attended the Harriet Johnson Nursery School in New York City.

The children in the New York nursery are highly imaginative children who make excellent, constructive, and creative use of the many toys and paraphernalia provided for them. But they are also easily irritated and upset, and they are easily provoked to screaming and kicking and fighting. These children are familiar to most of us; they vaccilate and alternate between periods of quiet play and contentment on the one hand and unpredictable outbursts of aggression at playmates and teachers and inanimate objects on the other. They are lively and exuberant; they are also provocative and attention-seeking. When their playmates retaliate against provocation, they seek the protection of adults; equally frequently, they are characteristically ready to defy and rebel against adult authority.

By contrast, Miss Lewis writes, "When I think back to that month of July spent out in the meadow with those twelve or fifteen children and try to find a way to characterize the 'atmosphere' of this little Summerville [Tennessee] nursery school, the two words that seem inevitably right are 'inactivity' and 'silence.' " [1] This is not to say that the children of the Cumberlands were completely withdrawn or apathetic. "For a three-week period . . . I kept careful count of all instances of tears, screams

(if any!), hits, or fights among the children that might be called 'disturbances of the peace,' exclusive of conflicts with adults (which were almost never in the picture) and tears due to physical hurt. Seven was the maximum for one morning, among eleven children, ages three to five. On no other day did so many occur. Compare this with twenty in one morning in the four-year-old group of thirteen children at the Harriet Johnson Nursery School, on a day considered by the teacher a comparatively peaceful one." [2]

There are, as this would indicate, some children in the back-woods region of Summerville who are sometimes noisy, pugnacious, and teasing; at times, they can hit and fight each other for the things they want or gang up on one of the group; *occasionally,* they can even rebel against authority. Such predispositions are undoubtedly to be found among children of all societies and groups. The question confronting us here is not why children have these predispositions—to anxiety, hostility, fear, defiance of authority, and the like—but, rather, what social and environmental conditions will maximize them to the point where they become characterological *and set some of the limits within which their parents socialize them;* under what conditions will these remain mere predispositions to the extent

---

* Based on material from *Children of the Cumberland,* by Claudia Lewis. New York: Columbia University Press, 1946.
[1] Lewis, 1946, p. 24.
[2] *Ibid.,* p. 31.

that they appear only sporadically and, thus, not obviate any adjustments in the socialization pattern with respect to them?

Miss Lewis states this problem admirably and points to what appears to be the correct avenue for exploring its solution:

And here we come to the outstanding difference between the two groups. "Rebel on occasion," I say. But why does the occasion arise so seldom among the mountain children, and why, when it does arise, are the manifestations of rebellion so mild in character? Why doesn't J.W. [in Tennessee] ever hit the teacher and call her Dope, and fling himself on the floor in a tantrum? Likewise, why are his conflicts with the other children, and indeed all of his aggressive expressions colored with less emotional intensity than David's [in New York]? And why, whether or not it has any connection with his aggressiveness, is his creative output also lacking in what we might call the "intensity" that characterize Stephen's [in New York]?

Here we see that we cannot meaningfully describe such differences as a matter of "degree." The factors responsible for them are imbedded in the particular kind of home and community conditions, standards, patterns, under which the children grow up.[3]

New York is one of the largest cities in the world in which, to earn a living, people "hold jobs." There are many areas of impersonalization in a metropolis; such an industrialized urban environment has profound implications for practices of child rearing, some of which we shall turn to in a moment. Summerville, on the other hand, is a completely rural area of poor, small landowners, most of whom, at the time Miss Lewis made her

observations, were on relief. There is no electricity and no plumbing; some families do not even have outhouses. Summerville homes are really shacks gone to seed and, by New York standards, are terribly overcrowded and unpleasant.

Very often, one can, as a disinterested observer, ascertain or establish a rough index of the tone of the social and emotional environment in which a person grows up by describing the social and emotional environment into which he is born. In a metropolis like New York, for example, a person is born in a building— a hospital—in which he will not live a week or ten days after his birth. The people who assist his mother in delivering him are invariably strangers to her or are paid functionaries with whom she has limited and formalized contact. It is a biologically sterile environment, and it also contains the potentiality for being socially and emotionally sterile. With few exceptions, the child is brought to the mother at regular intervals to be fed, then to be separated from her again. Relatives and friends may visit the mother, but at prescribed times; they may never handle the baby. In its authoritative, arbitrary, anxiety-ridden rigid rules, the social structure of the hospital, in effect, says: These people are separate and, except for the polite forms, have nothing to do with each other.

In Summerville, a person is born in the very midst of those with whom and in whose company he is going to be brought up, live, and die. Miss Lewis describes some of the dominant themes surrounding a birth in Summerville:

The morning the baby was born, I stopped at this house to pick up the two little boys for nursery school as usual, not knowing the new baby had come. The boys came to the door and just looked out at me. I could see that they were not cleaned up for school. I

---
[3] *Ibid.,* p. 53.

called to them but they couldn't seem to find any words and continued to stand in the doorway just staring at me. I got out of the car to see what was the matter and was met on the porch by a neighbor woman who asked me to come in and see the baby. With a little hesitance I asked, "Does Mrs. Smith want me to?" "Oh yes!" I learned afterwards that it is customary for practically the whole community to file in and see a new baby on the day of its birth. . . .

The porch door burst open suddenly and in came a little girl from across the road, sneezing and blowing and bringing in a blast of cold air with her. Right up to the bed she went, and leaned over and looked at the baby lovingly, all to the satisfaction of the mother. . . .

This is how life begins for most Summerville children. Sometimes the doctor is not needed—the birth is so easy that the call for him is canceled at the last minute. Occasionally a baby is born in the hospital in Oakmont. But whatever these deviations may be, the baby is sure to find himself immediately the loved darling of his own family and of his host of relatives. He will seldom be out of his mother's arms. And when he is, his sisters and even his brothers will grab him up and cuddle him, for these boys never heard it suggested that it might be sissy for them to fondle and care for babies.[4]

This is how life begins for most Summerville children, and an environment based on spontaneous warmth has its effect on the child from the very beginning. Miss Lewis reports that he is fed on demand, toilet training starts at about eighteen months, and weaning from the breast occurs at about two years. But what is even more important, he is constantly surrounded by friends and relatives, people who are integral parts of his environment. The middle-class child in New York generally sees relatives and his parents' friends at irregular intervals. When such visits are made, they are outside the normal course of everyday, hour-by-hour flow of events. In a New York environment, it is not at all improbable that visits to or by friends and relatives are interruptions of spontaneous activity; they constitute very real discontinuities for the child.

But there is a source of even greater and more meaningful discontinuity for the urban middle-class child, one which exists within the family itself. To find this source, let us begin with the fact that the urban family is not a unit of production. In our analysis of Martha Wolfenstein's paper on "The Emergence of Fun Morality" (in Chapter 5), we were able to observe one set of implications of this fact for one aspect of the socialization process; here we will observe other implications of the same phenomenon for still another aspect of socialization. Not only do children need warmth, affection, physical care, and attention when they are growing up, but they seem to need a tremendous amount of physical stability and predictability in their environment. Most urban children have their mothers as a point of social stability and predictability throughout the course of a day. However—and there are very few empirical data to substantiate this hunch—it often appears that children are often beset with a relatively high degree of instability and discontinuity by the fact that the father is in the home in the morning, leaves for most of the day, and

---

4 *Ibid.*, pp. 69-71.

then returns. How disconcerting this is to children—and for how many—it is difficult to tell. But it is probably disturbing for many children to some extent. For example, it is not difficult for an outside observer to notice the increasing demands for attention which a child, especially a boy, makes of his mother, or the sudden outbursts of disobedience and recalcitrance, at around the age of two-and-one-half to four years, when his father returns home from work. This is undoubtedly a demand for attention, as well as resentment at the mother's giving her attention to someone else, but it assumes much broader significance—namely, anxious and provocative behavior in response to discontinuity—when we view it in the context of other comparable instances.

It has often been observed that children from an urban middle-class environment are noisy, provocative, and irritable when there are adult visitors in the home. There are some situations, admittedly unique, in which a child has grown up for the first two, three, or four years of life—for example, on a farm or an extended trip—in *constant* association with *both* parents. When such people return to an urban environment, their children usually are extremely disturbed over the fact that the father goes off to work every morning. It is the discontinuity in relationships and the discontinuity in the fixity of the environment which provokes anxiety and the resultant behavior which is generally interpreted as "aggression." The reasons for this are not too difficult to discern. All children look to parents as protectors; when this relationship is interfered with, either by discontinuity through daily and repetitive separation or by the intrusion of relatively strange people into the environment ("strange" means alien in terms of normal structure and functioning of environment) anxiety and aggressive behavior are "normal" responses.

The child in Summerville, on the other hand, lives in an entirely different world, sociologically speaking. He has no need to lash out and strike at the world because it is an extremely secure and protecting place. The children with whom he plays, his relatives, and the friends of his parents are intimately part of his household scene. People moving in and out of the homes are part of the continuity of life, rather than being occasionally intruding factors who make daily life a series of discontinuities. Children are easily fitted into the activities and functions of their parents. The world is predictable and safe because there are almost always the same people present continuously. There is no need to rebel against and challenge authority, except occasionally and sporadically, because it is stable, consistent, and safe. Let us take one example of some of these processes recorded by Miss Lewis:

Wayne Edward had not been to nursery school for several days. His little sister Virginia was coming as usual, bounding out to the gate as she heard our car approaching, holding her jar of milk in one hand and a bunch of flowers for teacher in the other. Sometimes Wayne Edward would be there at the gate, too, but obviously not cleaned up for school.

"Why aren't you coming, Wayne Edward?" I would ask. "Don't want to. Good by, Virginia!" was the cheery answer. I knew that occasionally Wayne Edward stayed home for something like a hog-killin', but he had never been absent for days, like this. I went around to see his mother one afternoon to find out what the trouble was.

She explained that her husband had been laid off W.P.A., and the boy wanted to stay home too, to be with him.

"I don't want to force him to go to school. He might get a contrary spell and then you'd have a difficult time with him." "Does he often get contrary spells?" I asked. "No, he's a right good boy and never has given me no trouble, and that's why I don't want to start in making him contrary now. And anyway hit wouldn't do no good to force him to go to kindergarten. He wouldn't like it then and there'd be no point in it, just like you can't force a child to go to grammar school. If he ain't willin' to go then he won't learn nothin'."

One morning about a week later the children all rushed to the fence of the play yard at the nursery school to watch a horse and wagon pass on the highway. Who should it be but Wayne Edward and his daddy, the boy in the driver's seat, holding the reins, looking for all the world like a small edition of the man sitting beside him.

When we took Virginia home later that day, we passed them on the road again. They had left the wagon at grandpa's and now were taking the horse to the barn. The little boy was riding, the big jovial man walking. "He'll be back at school when I go back to work," he called out. "I can't get rid of him now! He wants to stick right with me!" [5]

We have in Miss Lewis' description a social system within which there is almost unlimited opportunity for identification with parents. In psychological theories of childhood development—and these stem almost entirely from observations made of urban individuals—much attention is devoted to the need of the child to "incorporate the image" of the parent or surrogate with whom he is identifying. The use of the word "image" in this context is more correct than most people realize. More often than not, the urban child—especially the male child—has little more than an "image" of the father on which to model himself and with whom he is supposed to identify. There is more certainty of the world, and greater predictability of social environment, when there is a real person, who is present most of the time, with whom to identify and after whom to model himself. (Compare this picture, for example, with the one confronting the growing Rocky Roader, described in Chapter 4.)

The "placidity" and "lack of emotional spontaneity" often reported for rural children—in contrast to urban children—is thus often misunderstood. It can be speculated that what is often referred to as a "lack" in rural children is not a "lack" at all. It is more probably a sense of security, a sense of certainty, as well as a feeling of belongingness and immediate involvement in the daily life of the family group. In these terms, it would be highly improbable that a rural child would experience the need for "emotional spontaneity" which has come to be so highly

---

[5] *Ibid.*, pp. 86-87.

valued for middle-class urban children. Nor, it should be added, does this involve solely the question of greater or lesser "punishment" for urban as against rural children, or "frustration," or the imposition of various "disciplines" on the child—though Miss Lewis felt these could not be entirely ignored in explaining the behavior of her particular group of Cumberland children. Children in all societies are punished, frustrated, and subjected to divers disciplines. Where there is a sense of belongingness and of identification with the larger group, as well as a sense of certainty about surrounding adults, the adaptability of children appears almost unlimited.

This may appear to contradict slightly what was said in Chapter 5, in the discussion of Wolfenstein's paper on "The Emergence of Fun Morality." There it was noted that movement from the farm to the city provided a potentiality for greater freedom—and therefore, by implication, greater spontaneity—in many areas of behavior. It must be kept in mind, however, that much of that analysis was based on the findings of Kinsey and his associates that a great increase in premarital coitus coincided with the rise of cities. These data do not, however, tell us anything about the subjective side of this behavior: we do not know the frequency of premarital intercourse for individuals, only for groups or categories; nor do we know how much emotional and physical freedom and spontaneity characterized—or still does characterize—premarital sexual behavior, or how much of this behavior is impelled by experimentation, curiosity, peer-group pressure, or even anxiety or uncertainty over sex-identity. In the previous chapter it was noted that changes in morality were consonant with a change in social structure; similarly, in connection with the problem of "emotional spontaneity" in children, it should be stressed that the "placidity" of rural children is consonant with *their* environment, while the "normal" behavior of urban children is consonant with *their* environment.

FAMILY AND FANTASY

It has been shown that in industrialized societies the family ceases to be a unit of production. While there is considerable romanticism and nostalgia in many discussions of the fact that families living under conditions of industrialization are no longer economically productive, the implications of such a factor are many and objectively real. The loss of material productivity in such families not only has profound effects on relationships between family members—as, for example, in the possibilities or potentialities for greater freedom and independence for individual members—but the consequences for relationships and institutions in the community at large are equally great.

Although children are not participants in the family and community in the same qualitative sense as are adults, the fact that the family in an industrialized society is not a productive unit is as fraught with consequences for growing children as it is for their parents. While it is of the utmost importance to know what is *done* to children by their parents or surrogates, such knowledge avails us little unless we know the over-all sociological *conditions* within which such experiences occur. For example, it is probably true that children in almost all societies grow up with an ambivalent or conflicting opinion of their parents. Parents are unconsciously viewed as simultaneously the embodiment and representation of all that is good—by virtue of the physical and emotional gratification which infants and young children receive from them—and as representations and embodiments of things that are bad—because of the simple fact that in all societies parents must impose limits, frustrations, and punishments if children are to survive physically and socially. Such conflicts and ambivalent emotions, however, are not lost with the passing of childhood; they are engrafted permanently onto the personality and continue into and through adulthood. These unconscious conflicts are very frequently projected into the many ideational systems—such as mythology and folklore, religion, political behavior, drama, and the like—which are found in all societies. These projective systems are essentially elaborations of the fantasies—the unconscious aspects of day-dreams, if we so wish to label them—which all people, children and adults, experience. Like all behavior, fantasies are culturally patterned, that is, they are shared within ranges by most of the members of a group and they are integrated into other aspects of the culture.

Two facts are striking about such fantasies. First, the degree of conflict underlying or constituting them are not of the same intensity in all societies or under all social-structural conditions. In some, the conflict is extremely mild; in others, it is severe. Secondly, even the most severe of these conflicts do not *necessarily* lead to disorganized or aberrant behavior. Such results depend on the conditions under which they occur.

It can be hypothesized that when a child can *share* his fantasies with significant persons, especially with his adult ideals, there is much less likelihood for disorganizing effects from these conflicts than when he cannot share them. To illustrate this hypothesis, we are going to read about children in Bali. Babies and very young children are almost universally teased in Bali to an extreme degree, both physically and emotionally. To defend themselves, they appear to develop an unresponsiveness to the provocations of adults, especially of their parents. But underneath the bland façade, these children seem to lead an active and interesting fantasy-life.

CHILDREN AND RITUAL IN BALI*

By Margaret Mead

In Bali, children are called "small human beings," and the conception of the nature and place of the child is different from that of the West. The whole of life is seen as a circular stage on which human beings, born small, as they grow

* Reprinted with abridgment from *Childhood in Contemporary Cultures*, edited by Margaret Mead and Martha Wolfenstein, pp. 40-51, by permission of The University of Chicago Press. Chicago: University of Chicago Press, 1955.

taller, heavier, and more skilled, play predetermined roles, unchanging in their main outlines, endlessly various and subject to improvisation in detail.

The world of the dead is one part of the circle, from which human souls return, born again into the same family every fourth generation, to stay too briefly—dying before they have shared rice—or for a long time, or even for too long, for it is inappropriate for great-grandparents to be alive at the same time as their great-grandchildren. Such lingerers have to pay a penny to their great-grandchildren, chance-met on the street. The newborn child and the aged great-grandparent are both too close to the other world for easy entrance into the temple. The baby cannot enter until after a special feast at three and a half or seven months, and the very aged enter through a special side gate.

The new born are treated as celestial creatures entering a more humdrum existence and, at the moment of birth, are addressed with high-sounding honorific phrases reserved for gods, the souls of ancestors, princes, and people of a higher caste. Human beings do not increase in stature and importance, as is so often the case in societies where men have only one life to live; rather, they round a half-circle in which middle age, being farthest from the other world, is the most secular. There is little acceptance of any task being difficult or inappropriate for a child, except that an infant at birth is, of course, expected to do nothing for itself. Words are put into the mouth of the infant, spoken on its behalf by an adult; the hands of the seven-month-old baby are cupped to receive holy water, folded in prayer, opened to waft the incense offered to it as a god, and when the ceremony is over the child sits dreamily repeating the gestures which its hands have momentarily experienced.

The Balinese may comment with amusement but without surprise if the leading metallophone player in a noted orchestra is so small that he has to have a stool in order to reach the keys; the same mild amusement may be expressed if someone takes up a different art after his hands have a tremor of age to confuse their precision. But in a continuum within which the distinction between the most gifted and the least gifted is muted by the fact that everyone participates, the distinction between child and adult—as performer, as actor, as musician—is lost except in those cases where the distinction is ritual, as where a special dance form requires a little girl who has not reached puberty.

This treatment of human history as an unending series of rebirths is matched in the treatment of the calendar. The Balinese have a whole series of weeks, of three, four, five, six, up to ten days, which turn on each other, like wheels of different sizes, and there are important occasions when two or three weeks recurrently coincide. These have special names and may be an occasion for festival—like Galoengan, a New Year's feast associated with the souls of the dead, and a postfestival season of special theatricals. But, although there is a way of noting the year in a continuous irreversible sequence, it is seldom used. A man who has labored long to recopy a sacred text on pages of lontar palm will simply note, when his task of intricate elaboration of a beautiful archaic script is over, that this was finished on the such-and-such, a recurrent combination of days—as we might say, on Friday the thirteenth of September. The principal calendrical unit, the ceremonial year, is two hundred and ten days long. The lunar calendar simply marks the pattern of planting and harvest.

Children, then, are smaller and more fragile than adults, as well as closer to the other world. Their essential personality characteristics—gaiety or seriousness, gentleness or harshness—are recognized early, and those around each child combine to set its formal character in an expected mold. The baby of six months with silver bracelets welded on its tiny wrists, waves and bangs its arms; if someone is hurt in the process, there comes the exclamation, "Isama is harsh." It takes only a few such acts to stereotype the judgment which will be echoed and re-echoed through its life, setting and defining its ways, but quite forgotten after death as other events—day of birth, experience in other incarnation—combine to give new personality. So, while the people take ritual pains over a corpse— that the individual may be born again fleeter of foot or more beautiful of face —they cannot describe the character or the looks of someone who died two years ago. Personality characteristics are accidents, held gently constant through any given incarnation, that dissolve at death. But the baby who is identified as "gay and mischievous" has a way of life plotted out for it, which again is independent of age. Old men who have been "gay" all their lives still know who sleeps with whom in the fields at night in the brief, wordless first encounters which for the Balinese represent the height of passion; and men and women, labeled "serious," may bear many children, but people will comment instead on their industriousness in the rice fields or their faithfulness at the temple.

The child is made conscious of its sex very early. People pat the little girl's vulva, repeating an adjective for feminine beauty, and applaud the little boy's phallus with the word for "handsome male." The child is fitted into words appropriate to its caste, gestures appropriate to each ceremony, and before the child can walk, it is taught to dance with its hands. Before he can stand, the little boy, who has sat on his father's knees while his father played the *gamelan,* begins to play himself. Peeking over a house wall, one may see diminutive girls of three, sitting all alone, practicing hand gestures. The child learns to walk around a single walking rail, learning that it is safe as long as it holds to this central support, in danger of falling when it loosens its hold and strays out into the unknown. When it learns to walk, its ventures away from support and parents are controlled by the mother or child nurse mimicking terror and calling it back with threats that are random in content—"Tiger!" "Policeman!" "Snake!" "Feces!"—but constant in theatrical affect, until the child learns that undefined outer space may at any moment be filled with unknown terrors.

In the village, in familiar territory, the child learns the directions—*kadja,* the center of the island, where the high mountain of the gods stands; *kelod,* toward the sea, the point of least sanctity; and *kangin,* to the right, *kaoeh,* to the left, when one faces *kadja.* Every act is likely to be expressed in these terms as babies are bidden to come a little *kadja* or to brush a speck off the *kelod* side of their face, and little boys of different caste play together happily but learn that the boy of higher caste must get into bed first or sit on the *kadja* side of the food tray.

Children learn the vertical hierarchies of life—that the head, even of a casteless peasant child, is something sacred, that a flower which has fallen to the ground from an offering carried on the head may not be replaced in the offering, that those of highest caste or sanctity must be given the highest seats. As they learn to speak, they learn that the words addressed to them by their elders and superiors are never the words in which they may answer, although sometimes the lesson is imperfectly learned, and a low-caste boy will marvel at the fact that "they say Brahman parents are very polite to their children, that they say *tiang* to them," not knowing that the children must reply with an exaggeratedly more polite term *titiang,* in which the pronoun "I" is made more self-deprecating by a stylized stutter.

From birth until long after they can walk, children live most of their waking hours in human arms, carried in a sling or on the hip, even sleeping suspended about the neck of an adult or a child nurse. They learn a plastic adaptation, to take cognizance of the other's movement in limp relaxation, neither resisting nor wholly following the pounding of the rice or the game the child nurse is playing. When there is teaching to be done, the teacher uses this flaccid adaptivity and, holding the hands and body of the learner with vigorous, precise intent, twists and turns them into place or pattern. Verbal directions are meager; children learn from the feel of other people's bodies and from watching, although this watching itself has a kinesthetic quality. An artist who attempts to draw a group of men will draw himself over and over again, feeling the image.

The children are everywhere. Very little babies cannot enter the temple, but the toddler is present in the midst of the most solemn ceremonial, attached to parent or grandparent, watching the blessing of the trance dancer, the throw of coins of the diviner, the killing of the fowl as exorcism. Women attending a theatrical performance carry their babies in their arms, and the front row of every performance is given over to the very small children, who watch and doze and are hastily rescued when the play threatens to break the bounds of the audience square and to involve the crowd in the plot. At the shadow play the children sit in front, and the puppet master increases the number of battles in the plot in proportion to the number of children. As the women kneel in the temple, placing the petals of a flower between their praying fingers, a flower is placed in the hands of the child who is with them. For the temple feast, small children, who at other times may run about stark naked, will appear elaborately dressed, boys in headdress and kris.

They look like dolls, and they are treated like playthings, playthings which are more exciting than fighting cocks—over which the men spend many fascinated hours—or the kites and crickets which amuse little boys. Everyone joins in the mild titillating teasing of little babies, flipping their fingers, their toes, their genitals, threatening them, playfully disregarding the sanctity of their heads, and, when the children respond by heightened excitement and mounting tension, the teaser turns away, breaks the thread of interplay, allows no climax. Children learn not to respond, to resist provocation, to skirt the group of elders who would touch or snatch, to refuse the gambit when their mothers borrow babies to make them jealous. They develop an unresponsiveness to the provocative intent of others at the same time that they remain plastic to music and pattern. It is a childhood training which, if followed here, would seem dangerously certain to bring out schizoid trends in the growing child's character.

But there is one great difference between Bali and the changing Western world as we know it. In the Western world children are traumatized in childhood in ways which are new and strange, for which no ritual healing, no artistic form, exists in the culture. Those who are very gifted may become prophets, or artists, or revolutionaries, using their hurt, their made deviancy, or their innate deviancy exaggerated by adult treatment as the basis for a new religion or a new art form. Those who are not so gifted or who are less fortunate in finding a medium for their gifts go mad or

dwindle away, using little even of what
they have. We are beginning to recognize
how damaging a trauma can be—administered by a parent who is ignorant of the
world the child lives in and lived out by
the child in a still different world later.
The present emphasis in America is
on the application of psychiatric techniques—in childhood itself—to undo the
damage, take out the false stitches, re-
learn the abandoned stance. Our conception of life is a sequential, changing, and
climactic one. So a trauma in childhood
is seen as producing mental damage or
intolerable yearning, which must then be
solved in later life—and solved alone by
the traumatized individuals.

Old Bali is a striking example of a
quite different solution, in which the
child each day meets rituals accurately
matched to the intensities and the in-
satiabilities which are being developed by
the interplay between itself and others.
Little children are not permitted to quarrel, they are not allowed to struggle over
toys, or to pull and claw at each other—
there are always elders there to separate
them, gently, impersonally, and inexor-
ably, and so completely that, in over two
years of living in Balinese villages, I
never saw two children or adolescents
fight. When conflict arises, the elder child
is continually told to give in to the
younger; the younger, responding to the
invitation of the older, is jealous of every
favor and demanding of anything the
elder has.

But day after day, as the child is
prevented from fighting, he sees magnificent battles on the stage, and the children
are part of the crowd that streams down
to the river bank to duck some character
in the play. He sees the elder brother—
who must always be deferred to in real
life—insulted, tricked, defeated, in the
theater. When his mother teases him in
the eerie, disassociated manner of a witch,
the child can also watch the witch in the

play—the masked witch wearing the accentuated symbols of both sexes, with
long protruding tongue, pendulous breasts,
covered with repulsive hair—watch her
recurrent battle with the dragon, who in
his warmer and puppy-like behavior resembles his father. He can see the followers of the dragon attack the witch
and fall down in a trance, as if killed,
only to be brought back to life again by
the magic healing power of the dragon.
These followers of the dragon, like the
younger brother, go further than he will
ever dare to go in showing hostility to his
mother, in open resentment of her laughter. He sees his possible destructive wish
lived out before his eyes, but in the end
no one is slain, no one is destroyed, no
one is hurt. The trancers, who have fallen
into convulsions when they attack the
witch, are revived by holy water and
prayers, the play ends, the masks are
taken off, the actors lay aside their golden
garments for stained workday clothes; the
young men who lay twitching in convulsions half an hour ago go off singing
gaily for a bath. Over and over again,
as babies in their mothers' arms, as tod-
dlers being lifted out of the path of a pair
of dancing warriors, as members of the
solemn row of children who line the audience square, they see it happen—the play
begins, mounts to intensity, ends in ritual
safety. And in the villages, when theatrical troupes under the protection of the
dragon mask, patron of the theater and
enemy of death, parade about a village
in which they have just arrived, people
buy a little of the dragon's hair as bracelets for their children to protect them
from evil dreams.

In this absence of change, the experience of the parent is repeated in that
of the child, and the child, a full participant in ritual and art, is presented
with the last elaborations almost with its
first breath. The people themselves treat
time as a circular process rather than a

progressive one, with the future ever behind one, unrolling beneath one's feet,
an already exposed but undeveloped film.
Here we find a perfect expression of the
historical nature of culture, in which any
separation between cause and effect, any
attempt to turn either childhood experience or adult ritual into the cause, one
or the other, is seen to be a hopeless
endeavor. The two recur together, at
every stage; the teased baby of the witch-
like human mother watches the witch on
the stage, and the teasing mother, even
as she teases her baby, also sees the
witch, attacked, apparently destroying,
but in the end doing no harm. The effect
on child and mother must both be reckoned in a round of simultaneous events,
repeating and repeating until the child in
arms again becomes a parent.

And yet, in spite of their conception
of life as a circle, we may, if we wish,
break the circle—as they are unwilling
to do—and, for purposes of a type of
scientific analysis born of our Western
conceptions of time, space, and causality,
ask the question: What happens as babies
born to Balinese parents, equipped at
birth with the same potentialities as other
human babies, learn to be Balinese? How
do they make the ritual of Balinese life
part of themselves and so become as able
to dance the intricate dances, carve or
play or weave or go into trance, as did
their parents or their grandparents? How
do they learn to be Balinese and so perpetuate Balinese culture? This is no question which treats Balinese culture as a
mere projection from childhood experience. The themes enacted in the Balinese
theater have a long history. On the
shadow-play screen there appear the
heroes and heroines of the *Ramayana,*
the great Indian epic. The witch Rangda
is also the Javanese Tjalonarang, and she
is also Derga, the destroyer. The dragon
is found around the world—in Japan, in
the streets of New York for Chinese New

Year, where he blesses the local mer-
chants whose restaurants may contain a
juke box or a cigarette-vending machine.
It is only in the particular details of the
plots that one can find the distinctive
mark of Balinese culture—in the refusal
to let the witch die, in the permission to
show a violence on the stage which is not
permitted in real life, and in the way in
which artist, actor, and priest participate
in everyday life.

But children in Bali, like human
children everywhere are born helpless,
dependent, and cultureless and must be
bathed and fed and protected, taught to
balance and to walk, to touch and to re-
frain from touching, to relate themselves
to other people, to talk, to work, to become sure members of their own sex, and
finally to marry and produce and rear
children. We cannot find that which is
distinctively Balinese in the mere presence of the witch and the dragon, who
recur in many forms throughout the
world. It is necessary to look at fine details of difference. For example, the Balinese witch has got hold of a dragon's
fiery tongue—and the Balinese dragon
has no tongue at all. This can be seen as
a part of the way in which the witch
combines all the gross, overaccentuated
aspects of secondary sex characters. In
the Balinese ideal physical type, both
men and women are slender; male breasts
are more pronounced than among us;
women's breasts are high and small; hips
of both sexes are closer in dimensions.
Men are almost beardless, and the muscles of their arms are not developed. The
witch's hairy legs and long pendulous
breasts accentuate the frightening aspects
of highly developed sex differences, and
we find, counterpointing her, protecting
the people from the illness and death she
brings, and presiding with her over the
theater, the dragon, a mythical creature,
wearing lovely fluffy, feather-like "hair"
or crow feathers sent especially by the

gods. Only as the Balinese witch is contrasted with her historical predecessors and as the Balinese dragon is seen in a world perspective of other dragons, is it possible to say what is distinctively Balinese. In the same way, by placing Balinese childhood experience in a context of our knowledge of child development, we can see in what particular ways Balinese children, while repeating universal human experiences, also have special ones.

The Balinese infant has preserved a kind of neonatal flexibility, which in the children who have been studied in Western culture tends to disappear very early, so that both the way a baby relaxes in its mother's arms and the way the mother holds it are sharply contrasting to our patterns. The disallowance of infancy, as adults speak in behalf of the child or press its compliant learning hands into ritual gestures, is again distinctive; and the way in which the child is constantly discouraged from walking, taught to use its right hand rather than the left, which is exposed by the carrying posture, left free to drink from its mother's breast when it chooses, as it is carried high above her high breast, but fed in a helpless prone position as a mound of prechewed food is piled on its mouth—all these details go to build the kind of Balinese personality which will be receptive to rituals danced and acted by others who have been treated in the same way. The constant provocative teasing and threatening which never reaches any but a theatrical climax, the denial of all violence and expressed hostility toward siblings, the serial experience of being the pampered baby, the displaced knee baby, and the child nurse, who, as guardian of the baby, stays to see the usurper dethroned in turn, all these form a background for the plots of ritual and theater to which the child is exposed.

But there is something more here than the correspondence between childhood experience and dramatic plot, something different from the sort of cultural situation discussed by Roheim when a terrifying infantile experience—of a male child sleeping beneath the mother—is abreacted by initiation rites in adolescence. In Bali the absence of sequence even in the life-span of the individual and the absence of discontinuity between ritual role and everyday role seem crucial. The artist, the dancer, the priest, is also a husbandman who tills his rice fields. Occasionally an artist becomes so famous that he lets his fingernails grow as he does no other work, and, say the Balinese, he begins to grow fat and careless and lazy, and his artistic skills decrease. The priest may stand robed in white during a ceremony, officiating at the long ritual of inviting the gods down to earth, dressing them, feeding them, bathing them, presenting them with dance and theater, and then sending them back again for another two hundred and ten days in heaven. But the day after the ceremony he is a simple citizen of the village, only owing the land which he cultivates to his work on feast days as guardian of the temple.

Nor is there any gap between professional and amateur. There are virtually no amateurs in Bali, no folk dancing in which people do traditional things without responsibility to an artistic canon. There are enormous differences in skill and grace and beauty of performance, but prince and peasant, very gifted and slightly gifted, all do what they do seriously and become, in turn, critical spectators, laughing with untender laughter at the technical failures of others. Between the audience that gathers to watch the play and the players there is always the bond of professional interest, as the audience criticizes the way the actor or actress who plays the princess postures or sings, rather than identifying with her fate—

however lost she may be in some dense theatrical forest.

Nor is there any gap between rehearsal and performance. From the moment an orchestra begins to practice an old piece of music, there is a ring of spectators, aspiring players, substitute players, small boys, and old men, all equally engrossed in the ever fresh creation of a new way of playing an old piece of music. Where in Java the shadow-play screen divided men from women, the women seeing only the faint shadow on the screen, the men the brightly painted figures, in Bali people can sit on either side, in front to watch the finished play, behind—and this is where little boys prefer to sit—to watch the individual designs on the figures and the deft hands of the puppet master. When a village club decides to learn a new play—a play in which the main serious parts are traditional and the parts of clowns, servants, and incidental characters are all improvised, never set, even in consecutive performances—half the village attends the rehearsals, enjoys the discussions of costume, the sharp words of the visiting virtuoso come to teach a dance step, the discovery of some new talent among the actors. In the rectangular piece of ground which becomes a four-sided stage as the audience gathers around it, isolated pairs of curtains borrowed from a theater with a quite different style of handling surprise may be set up near each end. The actors, their crowns a little askew, sit in almost full view dozing behind these curtains or among the audience, and then, as they make their appearance, part the curtain for a prolonged stylized "entrance," from which they later return to their full visibility offstage. People advance from the audience to pin up a dancer's fallen scarf, and dramatic scenes of chase and conquest will be pursued into the midst of the audience.

Thus in Bali the ritual world of art and theater and temple is not a world of fantasy, an endless recurrent daydream, or a new set of daydreams woven from the desperations of the gifted of each generation. It is rather a real world of skill and application—a world in which members of a dance club scheme to get money for the gold of a new headdress or to buy new instruments for the orchestra; where long hours are spent in the basic work of learning to dance; where disciplined hands and wrists and eyes that click to one side in perfect time to the music, are all the result of continuous, although relaxed, rather dreamy, work. And the temple feasts, where many of these activities combine to make a great spectacle, are called appropriately "the work of the Gods."

Children have not only the precocious postural participation in prayer and offering, dance and music, but also a whole series of parallel participations. A little boy will be given bamboo clappers with which to imitate the clapping of the dragon's tongueless jaws and, covered by his mother's cloth shawl—the same shawl with which the witch will dance in the play and which she will carry in her arms as if it were a baby—goes about clapping in imitation of the dragon. In the non-ceremonial seasons, when life is a little less crowded, secular dance clubs go about with a tinkly orchestra, which has a hurdy-gurdy quality, and a little girl dancer, who dances with the young men of the village and, in between, dances as the witch, combining the beautiful ballet of the witch's disciples with being the witch herself and placing her foot firmly on the neck of a doll, enacting her role of bringing death.

Children stay in a deep resistant sleep during a childbirth in their houses, a sleep from which it is necessary to shake them awake, lest they see the witches which may come to kill the child. But the same children participate with delight in the play in which the witch child, after stealing a doll, born of a man and dressed as a woman, is chased up a tree or into a near-by stream. Children make puppets of banana leaf and parody the puppet master, especially the puppet master who performs with puppets in the daytime, whose screen has shrunk to a single line of thread. They draw in the sand with twigs while master artists work at little shallow wooden tables. And children may form clubs of their own, make their own dragon and witch, and progress about the village, collecting pennies for further finery for the masks.

If one follows these activities carefully, notes the expressions on the children's faces at different kinds of ceremonies, follows the same child on different occasions, and watches the play in which the children think they are reproducing the full theatricals, one begins to get clues to the dynamic mechanisms by which the children, born human like all other human children, become such very different people from other people—as Balinese. The mother who teases her child—who borrows a baby to provoke its jealousy, although preventing any expression of jealousy of a real sibling; who borrows a baby to set on its head, although at the same time protecting its head from real insult—has learned that all this is a safe game. When she watches the witch dance and watches the men and women who have gone into trance and are slow in coming out, she watches with the same relaxed enjoyment or ready criticism for some ritual or technical defect with which she watches the trance dance in which children dance as goddesses. But the child, teased into a violent temper, screaming and clawing to get the borrowed baby away from his mother's breast, has not yet learned that all this is safe. In his intensity and grief, in his fervent acceptance of his mother's theatrical amends for a real hurt, he still shows

a capacity for hurt which will not be manifest later. Even as he withdraws from the recurrently disappointing sequences which have no climax, he learns to trust the arts, and he learns to avoid hurting responsiveness to human stimulation.

The faces of the children who watch the trance dance in which little girls replace dancing wooden puppets—and as child dancers are indulged by the parents and wilful in their demands—are as relaxed as their parents' faces. But during the witch dance the children's faces are strained and anxious. When the witch dances or when some woman worshiper in the temple is possessed by the witch, the fingers are flexed backward in a gesture of fear, spoken of as *kapar*—the gesture made by a baby falling or a man falling from a tree—for the witch is both frightening and afraid, the picture of Fear itself. But when children play the witch, especially when they play her without benefit of costume or music or any of the elements which accompany the finished ritual, their hands are bent like claws, and they threaten an attack in witchlike gestures which can be found in many parts of the world. When the young men, who, as followers of the dragon, fall down before the witch's magic, thrust their daggers against their breasts, they thrust them in response to an intolerable itching feeling in their breasts—a possible reciprocal to the mother's breast during the period when they were so teased, provoked, and given only theatrical climaxes.

When Balinese children are frightened of strangers or strange situations, their elders shout at them, "Don't show fear!" and they learn not to run but to stand stock still, often with their hands pressed over their eyes. In situations of danger or uncertainty—during childbirth in a tiny one-room house, after an accident for which one may be blamed—

children and older people also fall into a deep sleep from which it is hard to rouse them.

The Balinese move easily in a group. A whole village may make a pilgrimage of two or three days to make offerings at the seaside or in the high mountains. A troupe of Balinese went to the Paris Exposition in 1931, and a troupe visited New York in 1952. But one Balinese, isolated from those he knows and taken to a strange place, wilts and sickens; people say it is because he is *paling*— disoriented—the word used for trance, insanity, for being drunk, confused, or lost. And the Balinese are mortally afraid of drunkenness, where the clues to the directions, the calendar, the caste system, the framework of life—which gives safety

as the walking rail gave it to the little child who learned how dangerous it was to venture away from it—are lost or blurred.

Following the children as they grow up reveals that, even within the simultaneity of ritual satisfaction and individual fear, the capacity to enjoy such rituals, to dance the lovely dances and fill the air with music, has been—in the case of the Balinese—developed at certain costs. The culture contains—or did contain until the recent upheavals about which we know little—ritual solutions for the instabilities it created, and the people, on their little island, were safe. But it was the safety of a tightrope dancer, beautiful and precarious.

The ability to share feelings, emotions, fantasies—that is, communicate and express them to significant persons and receive a certain amount of "feedback" as a result of the expression—is one of the prime requisites for the maintenance of psychological equilibrium. The facilitation of such emotional communication is one of the tasks of every social-structural system. At the end of this book, when the relationship of psychosis to social structure is discussed, observation will be made of what happens to adults when they cannot make use of the lines of communication provided by the social structure or when the social structure breaks down and they are no longer provided with effective and consistent lines of communication.

At this point, however, we wish to concern ourselves with the effects of a particular kind of social-structural relationship for the maintenance of emotional stability in children. Dr. Mead pointed out in her paper that the Balinese system of socialization ". . . is a childhood training which, if followed here [in the United States], would seem dangerously certain to bring out schizoid trends in the growing child's character." What seems to militate against the manifestations of such trends in the character of the Balinese child?

There is a set of conditions which appears to prevent the consequences of this socialization in Bali which might be expected in a society such as ours—in Bali there is no *overt* or grossly manifest difference between the child's and the adult's fantasy world. The drama which transpires on the Balinese stage mirrors in a public setting the dramatic conflicts which most probably transpire within the individual Balinese. The mother in Bali is a gratifying and succoring person; she feeds her children, she is a source of warmth and comfort. These experiences arouse positive feelings in the Balinese baby toward her. But, at the same time, she is extremely provocative, teasing, and hostile toward her child, arousing markedly negative feelings in him. Not unlike children in almost all societies, though certainly more extreme in the contrasts, Balinese children would therefore emerge as being noticeably ambivalent in their feelings about their mothers. These conflicts, so transparently portrayed on the Balinese stage, undoubtedly *are* fantasies. But it is an eternal, unresolvable conflict; the witch in the drama, who, as Dr. Mead seems to think, surely represents the mother, cannot be slain permanently, for the loss of the nurturent aspect of the mother would be too painful. Nor can the negative feelings be denied completely, and the witch-like mother is at least temporarily slain.

It is true, as Dr. Mead pointed out, that Balinese drama has very deep areal and historical sources. But what is important here, at least for our purposes, is that Balinese children are able to maintain a fairly stable equilibrium despite the severity of the conflicts which they must experience by virtue of their experiences as they grow up. It is our hypothesis or contention that they are able to do so because of the extent to which they are able to share their fantasies with their peers and significant adults as they observe and experience stylized drama.

Both early childhood and adolescence are periods of great psychological vulnerability, but most people seem to come through these periods rather well. There are surely many reasons for this, just as there are many reasons why a few people fail to come through these periods in healthy fashion. Since we are concerned here with the sharing of emotions in a particular social-structural context, we shall investigate only one parameter of this issue: Although very little has been written about this, clinical psychologists and others who work with adolescents often remark in discussions that they are impressed by the fact that one rarely observes psychosis in an adolescent who has at least one "best friend" with whom to share *and exchange* intimate confidences and feelings. These clinicians admittedly understand little of the processes involved in this, but it is a problem for research which should yield important facts and concepts. Such research would have to determine, among other things, the degree and extent to which the need for emotional sharing is similar in childhood and adolescence and the extent to which it is different. It would also have to ascertain the extent to which children and adolescents who are predisposed to psychosis are unable to form friendships and the extent to which it is the absence of such friendships which sometimes helps to precipitate psychosis. But assuming that there is a continuity from childhood to adolescence, there is much that we can learn about the latter period from work which has already been done with children. For example, Bowlby's review[6] of investigations of emotional disorders in childhood, and the voluminous literature on this problem in the annual *The Psychoanalytic Study of the Child,*[7] would seem to indicate strongly that sociological-emotional isolation, among other factors, plays a prepotent role in the emergence of emotional disorders in childhood. The impressive array of data gathered by clinicians working with children and adolescents in American society, and such data as those presented by Margaret Mead in the foregoing paper, appear to support the hypothesis

6 Bowlby, 1952.
7 *The Psychoanalytic Study of the Child,* 1945 to present.

that when children are able to *share* even the most conflictful fantasies, they can avoid serious psychological malfunctioning.

ADOLESCENCE

While the sharing of fantasies appears to be of great importance in the maintenance of emotional equilibrium, such communication is but one part of a larger and broader whole—a personal sense and inner certainty of belonging, of inclusion within a group, of filiation. However important such awareness is in adulthood, it is doubly so in adolescence. Adolescence is one of the most fascinating stages of life, and it has been the subject of considerable speculation and theorizing. So powerful are its currents, especially in American society, that most people seem to feel a need to attribute the events of these years to the changes which take place in the physiology of the adolescent. Perhaps there is some comfort in this view, but as more and more data are gathered concerning adolescence in different social contexts the more it appears that the physiological changes of this stage of development have only a limited relationship to the emotional patterns of adolescents.

The next paper is a study of adolescence in Rocky Roads, Jamaica. Again, the writer shifts from his role as commentator to the author of an original source. Its final theoretical section, in which adolescence in Jamaica is compared with adolescence in Manus, appeared in the original source and will substitute for a summary comment on this topic.

"ADOLESCENT CONFLICT" IN A JAMAICAN COMMUNITY*
By Yehudi A. Cohen

Since Margaret Mead's reports of adolescence in Samoa, students of behavior have differentiated between adolescence as a biological and physiological stage of maturation—pubescence—and adolescence as a sociological and cultural phenomenon—as an age category. It is now a truism that the *Sturm und Drang* which is so characteristic of adolescence in American society is not so much the automatic result of the physiological changes of puberty but rather of the social and cultural contexts within which the individual learns to cope with these changes.

Before a person can marry—in any society—he and she must pass through a period of adolescence, even if that period lasts only a week. It is true that not all societies have a term for adolescence or give it a definite place in their social structures, but it is probably equally true that no society permits a child to marry and assume the prerogatives and responsibilities of adulthood. Before an individual may exercise such rights, he and she must

* Reprinted with abridgment from *Samiksa: Journal of the Indian Psychoanalytic Institute,* Vol. *9*, pp. 139-172, 1955.

first become an adolescent, no matter how small and temporally insignificant the interval between culturally defined childhood and marriage might be.

The character of adolescence, the presence or absence of storm and stress, does not, however, depend on the length of the period or its elaboration within the social structure of a group. In Polynesia, for example, adolescence is given formal recognition within the social structure to a rather elaborate degree, youths and young girls merely having to provide entertainment for their villages and to cement friendly relations between villages by reciprocal group visits. In the societies of Polynesia adolescence is an enjoyable period of courtship, growth and maturation, with an almost complete absence of conflict with age groups above and below their own. No less lengthy is the adolescence of the Manus of the Admiralty Islands, and this is a period free from storm and stress. But unlike the adolescence of Polynesian societies, that of Manus is one of sexual repression and eternal supervision. *The Sturm und Drang,* the misery, the rebelliousness, the constant bickering which one would anticipate in such an adolescence do not come during adolescence but after marriage, after entrance into sociological adulthood.

In the present paper we propose to discuss adolescence in Rocky Roads, Jamaica, in the West Indies. Adolescence in this community resembles that of the Manus in several respects. It appears in the social structure of the community as a definite and recognized period, though not quite as elaborated as among the Manus. Furthermore, it is almost entirely free from turbulence and strain, although the occupants of this category are considerably freer and less subject to supervision than are Manus adolescents. Finally, what might be termed the "adolescent conflict" comes to the fore at the

end of adolescence and in the early years of adulthood, although the *themes* of rebellion are very different from those of the Manus.

A Rocky Roader is considered to have reached adolescence when he leaves school, usually at fourteen years. Adolescence never lasts more than five or six years, and it is a period of transition. The alterations in parent-child relationships find their expressions in the greater degree of free movement which the maturing youngsters are now granted and begin to experience. As a period of transition it is characterized by the assumption on the part of adolescents of a larger share of adult activities, preparatory to full-fledged adulthood, plus a gradual weaning from dependence on parents, a process which, as we shall see, is never really completed.

The most significant learning which takes place during adolescence is of an economic nature. Through parental urging and guidance the younger members of the community learn the techniques of accumulating money and of exploiting those situations which promise financial gain. It is during this period of life that a Rocky Roader learns that practically everything occupies a position subordinate to food and money. He learns to recognize the economic potentialities of a noneconomic situation and acquires the skills of reacting appropriately. It is during this period that a Rocky Roader begins to learn those patterns of interpersonal relationships which are not of an economic nature, for as he grows older more and more acquaintances are made. The anxieties, inhibitions, and feelings of guilt which surround food and money in Rocky Roads are fully crystallized by the end of adolescence, and the young person is then ready to enter adulthood.

When a boy leaves school he spends all his time cultivating his father's land. He is given a portion of land to cultivate and he is more or less free to raise whatever crops he wishes. A boy does not pay rent for the land which he borrows from his father and technically enjoys absolute ownership of all that the land yields. But Rocky Roads parents, according to the rules of the culture, are not obligated to support their sons after they have reached adolescence. As a result, every son must contribute anywhere from one-third to half his earnings to pay his parents for his room and board. This is one of the incentives for adolescents to keep working. No parent will house and feed an adolescent son who does not contribute to the family coffers. As we shall see below, this is one of the dominant facets of the rebellion which comes, not in adolescence, but in early adulthood.

The remainder of a lad's money is his to do with as he pleases. Again, this is absolutely true as an ideal, but is somewhat qualified in actual practice. At fourteen a boy may no longer expect his parents to buy his clothes. The money which he now earns may be spent only for clothes and for occasional entertainment of which the parents approve. The rest must be saved for future investment in land. A boy who spends his money indiscriminately and in violation of parental direction will receive a flogging.

While working on a portion of his father's land a boy seeks to hire himself out for wage labor whenever possible. There are two aims to the labor of an adolescent, in addition to paying his parents for his room and board. First is the desire to accumulate enough money so that he can purchase or rent land and begin a career of economic self-sufficiency. There is never the stated desire among the lads of the community to be able to acquire land so that they can be completely free of their fathers. No matter how much land a boy can rent or purchase he stills holds on to the land which his father allows him to use; re-

linquishing a parcel of land is tantamount to giving up part of one's income, something no Rocky Roader will ever do; he never feels that he has enough land, and he always attempts to buy and rent more and more land.

The second goal is directly connected to the first. The constant and prepotent aim in life in Rocky Roads is the maintenance of economic independence and self-sufficiency. It is about this time in life that this motivation becomes fully crystalized and assumes the proportions with which it is carried throughout life. That is, this is the first time that a Rocky Roader is capable of verbalizing his strivings and his needs to accumulate money. Whenever a boy of thirteen or younger is asked why he saves whatever pennies he earns, he puts his motivation in terms of parental encouragement in this direction. At fourteen years and older his motivation is in terms of himself: "Me want to be rich, man, me want to be rich." Earlier he would have said: "My daddy flog me if me no save."

For the girls the pattern is slightly different. The first important variation shows up in the cultural rule that, while boys need not be supported after the age of fourteen, girls must be supported as long as they live at home. The second important distinction is that a girl must seek permission for everything she wants to do. The third difference is that girls do not have to contribute toward their maintenance while living at home.

When a girl leaves school her first wish is to find remunerative employment. The only thing for which the girls have been trained since early childhood is household labor. Since there are rarely such jobs for more than a half-dozen or so girls in and around Rocky Roads, they must leave the community and seek work in the urban areas of the island. As a result, it is quite rare to find an adolescent girl or a young adult girl in Rocky

Roads. Only the daughters of the very rich (and there are few of these) can afford to remain at home, tending the house, and doing occasional work in the gardens. In addition to the money which the girls earn from their work as domestic servants, the freedom they enjoy makes such opportunities enticing, indeed.

Before accepting such a position a girl must receive her mother's permission; even while away from home she is subject to her mother's discipline and must return home whenever called. We knew of no instance in which a girl refused to return to Rocky Roads at her mother's behest. Whatever a girl earns is hers, and so long as her parents are not aware how she spends her money she may do with it as she pleases. Girls of this age return home under specified conditions. Pregnancy or illness are the primary causes of their return to their parents' home. But if one of her parents is ill or if her labor is required at home she will be instructed to leave her job. Most return to Rocky Roads to marry, but some find their husbands in the towns or in the capital.

While an adolescent girl is at home she reverts to the absolute control of her mother. She must keep her mother informed of all her movements, and she may be flogged for remaining away from the house for too long a period or for leaving the house without permission. A girl cannot come and go as she pleases until she reaches adulthood. While at home she may learn dressmaking, a skill which will immeasurably increase her chance for marriage, or she may attend some of the 4-H classes which are sponsored by the island's government where she may learn cooking, sewing, and gardening.

While discipline and dependence training remain unchanged for female adolescents, the exercise of discipline over the boys decreases as they grow older. But it never completely disappears during

adolescence. The most important factor in this respect is a youth's earning capacity, for a measure of a man's independence of his parents is the amount of money he earns and contributes to the household. The greater an adolescent's earning capacity the less right does his father have either to chastise or flog him.

The almost complete absence of overt or verbalized aggression on the part of children toward their parents continues during this period as it does throughout most of life. Aside from attempting to run away when threatened with corporal punishment, children make no attempts whatever to defend themselves, and not only do they deny ever entertaining any ideas of aggression toward their parents, but they adamantly refuse even to entertain the hypothetical possibilities of such a thing. Adolescents denied vehemently that they ever entertained the notion of striking their parents, destroying their property, or leaving home. When asked what would happen if they ever did strike at their parents they responded that such a thing could never occur and, hence, they could not even consider the possible consequences. Characteristically, adolescent informants either became heatedly indignant or laughed uncontrollably when asked such questions.

All an adolescent can do after a beating, informants of all ages reported, is content himself with walking away and muttering, "Poppa had no right to hit me." When asked when the last flogging was received, each adolescent, no matter what his or her age, answered, "six years ago." The shame over being flogged is no less during adolescence than it was during childhood. No adolescent will ever directly answer whether the flogging received was justly deserved. "Poppa (or Momma) thought so," was all we could learn.

Most Rocky Roads children first experience heterosexual intercourse at about fifteen years. Some commence their sexual activities as early as ten years and some at a somewhat later date. These childhood sexual unions are usually made after school hours, the couple going off to the bush on the way home "to have connection." Informants of all ages claimed that there are no particular anxieties surrounding first heterosexual experience and all are aware that female sexual activity involves more learning than does male sexual behavior. So far as could be determined from informants of both sexes of all ages and of all statuses, almost all girls reach orgasm by the third time they experience sexual intercourse, although some are able to do so the first time. Boys do not experience any impatience with their girl friends while they learn and never laugh at girls who have difficulty in reaching orgasm. "Man must learn," they say.

In reality, however, and despite nearly universal claims to the contrary, the initiation of heterosexual behavior does arouse considerable anxiety in men and women. These anxieties appear to center around fantasies of one's own inadequacy in performance, fears of detection and punishment, concerns over resulting illness, the possibility of pregnancy (even though most, at this age, lay claims to ignorance of the facts of conception), and the like. In other words, beneath the surface of cultural acceptance and license of premarital sexual behavior is a personality or emotional picture of quite different sorts.

Most girls begin their heterosexual activities prior to menarche which usually begins between sixteen and eighteen years. Parents disapprove of such behavior, they admit, for it is an independent act of which parents have no knowledge and over which they have no control. They do not appear upset when they learn of the sexual activities of their sons, for the boys of the community are at all times allowed slightly more freedom than are their sisters; their minimal assertions of independence are tolerated while similar behavior among girls is punished.

Aside from the motives of sexual gratification there appear to be hardly any positive emotions involved in the formation of sexual friendships. There is no particular affection between premarital sexual partners. The notion of romantic love, either during adolescence or at any other time of life, is wholly absent from Rocky Roads culture and, as a matter of fact, an individual may have an affair while still nurturing a not too superficial dislike of the other person. There are no terms of endearment or characteristic demonstrations of affection between adolescent sexual partners. The only criterion for the maintenance of a sexual relationship is mutual physical gratification; if either fails to satisfy the other sexually, the relationship is immediately dissolved.

Girls generally start bearing illegitimate children about the age of eighteen. There is no taboo covering illegitimacy in Rocky Roads; illegitimate children are not discriminated against in any *formal* way; nor are their mothers or fathers censured for such parentage.

As a result of the proscription against the assumption of the initiative in sexual relationships on the part of the girl, some girls find that they must go for long periods without any heterosexual intercourse, and they turn to homosexual activities as a substitute. Homosexuality never completely supplants heterosexuality, but is indulged in as a temporary substitute. There is no known homosexuality among the men of the community. Masturbation also appears to be completely absent among the adult men, and although there is a slight incidence of such activity among the women, it is known to occur when both homosexual and heterosexual outlets are totally absent. Neither is particularly frowned upon, although it is known by the Rocky Roaders that homosexuality is punishable by law. It is interesting to note, parenthetically, that the inhabitants of Rocky Roads do not know the word masturbation; nor do they have any single word or phrase to denote the activity.

Nonsexual friendships during adolescence are generally of the same sort as those of late childhood. That is, individual boys, for example, might walk to their fields together, but only because they happen to be neighbors. A youth spends his entire day at cultivation, almost always on his father's land, and is rarely permitted to remain out of doors after nightfall. Nor are there any cliques, gangs, or formal groupings among adolescents. Sexual partners are rarely together except on occasions of sexual intercourse. Should they meet on the road they will stop to chat for a moment or two and then proceed on their own ways.

The transition from adolescence to adulthood is more marked for the young men than for their sisters. There are no distinctive symbols by which one can differentiate an adult from an adolescent; nor are there any formal ceremonials or the like which might formally mark one's advent into adulthood. An individual's positional change in the community's age-grading structure is rarely discussed and is usually granted by tacit consensus. The manner of transition from adolescence to adulthood is radically different for each of the sexes.

A man is recognized as an adult at about the age nineteen, sometimes a year earlier or later. A lad is considered an adult by the community when he is permitted to stop and join a group of adults loafing along the main road for as long a period as he pleases, or when he is allowed to join in a game of dominoes at the general store with three or four other adults.

It is rare for Rocky Roads youths to make mistakes in this matter. Should a young chap think of himself as an adult before consensus has granted him that status, he will be sent on his way with considerable laughter and teasing by the men whom he has attempted to join. Such an occurrence is rare, for two reasons. Rocky Roaders prefer to associate with persons of their own ages and statuses; they make no attempts to lay claims to higher age statuses than their culture has granted them. But the second reason is even more important. We do not know how consensus in the community operates, but it was easy to see that it operates in a very uniform and harmonious fashion throughout all layers and facets of community life. When a boy is accorded the privileges and prerogatives of an adult by his parents he can be quite sure that he will receive the same treatment from the other adults of the community.

Rarely does a discrepancy arise. As a result, a boy who is still regarded as an adolescent by his parents will not make any attempts to act like an adult before the other members of the community. Age-grading does not appear to be a source of conflict in Rocky Roads.

The same criterion for adulthood cannot operate in the case of the girls, for one reason. Women never congregate along the main road to loaf and pass the time of day; nor may a woman ever join a group of idling men. Nor may an unmarried woman join the gossiping circles which meet at the dressmaker's shop or at the general store. A girl becomes an adult when she begins to come and go as she pleases; she must still answer to her parents for her actions at their insistence, and they can restrict her if they feel it necessary. Girls attain this status at about twenty-one.

Toward the end of adolescence, or shortly after he becomes an adult, a Rocky Roads man goes through a period of turmoil and rebellion, and, as such, can be described as a young adult experiencing an "adolescent rebellion" or "conflict." During the period of premarital adulthood, a Rocky Roader continues to live in the home of his parents, but once he has reached this age-category *he does not have to seek parental permission for anything. He does what he wants and goes where he pleases.*

His economic responsibilities remain much the same as during adolescence. He continues to work his father's land, plus whatever land he may manage to rent, and to hire himself out for wages to other members of the community. Again, the goals are the same. The young man is constantly striving to maintain a sense of personal equilibrium through economic self-sufficiency and to reinforce this feeling through the accumulation of more money with which he will be able to rent or purchase more land. He must still contribute toward his own support and occasionally help his father in the fields.

The young Rocky Roads adult evidences his conflict and gives expression to it in four separate areas of his interpersonal relationships. These are: (1) his avoidance of his parents; (2) his refusal to work; (3) the formation of close friendships; and (4) his preoccupation with generalized criticisms of almost everyone. To be sure, not all young adult Rocky Roaders exhibit all of these behaviors. Almost all, however, evidence the first, second, and last patterns in varying degrees. We shall discuss each of these in its turn:

(1) The initial emergence of the severe conflict of early adulthood occurs at the point at which the young men become fully aware of the cultural value that an adult is almost completely independent of his parents. When this realization comes, the unmarried young men begin to have almost nothing to do with

their parents. They spend as little time as possible at home, usually coming home only to eat and sleep. They never consult their parents about anything and their parents rarely question their activities. From the one extreme of complete dependence the young men shift to one of complete apparent independence. When they are not in the fields or at some sort of work they are either loafing in groups along the main road or are engaged in their habitual activity of playing dominoes either at the general store or at the tailor's shop. So marked is this aspect of parent-child relationships at this period that parents never know when their sons have left the home to go into the fields and when they have returned. Parents almost never ask their adult sons where they are going and the latter never volunteer the information. The only interest parents seem to have in their sons at this time is that they make their regular contributions of food and money to the home.

(2) Several months after the onset of the avoidance of parents almost all of Rocky Roads young adults begin to manifest the second characteristic mode of rebellion which accompanies this almost compulsive elusion of their parents. This is an equally determined laziness on the part of the young men. Just as no pattern of behavior emerges spontaneously and full blown so does this evolve gradually until it reaches its apparently preconceived goal. Little by little the young men ease up in their work in the fields, until finally they cease working completely. They allow their crops to become overgrown with weeds, they do not plant or plan for new crops, and they do not remove food from the ground for sale at market. They spend most of their days lolling in the sun and gambling at dominoes; there is no noticeable increase in their attentiveness to the young women.

For about a month or so his parents pay no attention to his lethargy. Then the man's mother—for it is she, not his father, who now, as always, deals with a situation involving food—chides him from time to time for his indolence; as time goes on, however, more and more pressure is brought to bear on him. Characteristically, his mother becomes more and more severe in her criticisms. Often, she deliberately seeks him out with his friends and not only upbraids him but also insults him, telling him that he is lazy (a dire insult), a poor man who can get nothing for himself and growing poorer. Rarely does he answer her. Her anger, however, becomes most earnest when she threatens her son that he will soon find himself without a roof over his head, with no one to cook his meals, and no one to care for his clothes. At first, he disregards these threats, or at least appears to, for he makes no effort to return to his work. The threats continue until the day he returns home to find that his mother has not cooked any dinner for him. This is the final episode, for, almost invariably, he returns to work the following day. On the surface, his rebellion is at an end and his mother resumes cooking for him. But his feelings of unhappiness and generalized resentment do not disappear at this point. Not unlike the onset of the pattern, these feelings recede in a gradual process which covers many months.

(3) A rather prevalent technique of expressing the conflict characteristic of this period in Rocky Roads is the formation of very close friendships. The deviant quality of this mode of behavior is not immediately apparent, but it becomes such when it is viewed within the total framework of interpersonal relationship in Rocky Roads. In the first place, these friendships deviate from the norm of social relationships in the community, for there are very few friendships among the adults. Rocky Roads is an economically competitive community; this rivalry

is characterized by the Rocky Roaders themselves with the maxim that "one man's fall is another man's rise," and, conversely, "one man's rise is another man's fall." But the competitiveness of the members of the community is not the only socially divisive factor within the group. The severity of the aggression training is pointedly successful in the almost complete inhibition of aggressiveness, the latter taking its place alongside economic competition as one of the dominant themes governing interpersonal relationships. Specifically, the inhibition of aggressiveness is manifest in the avoidance of situations in which aggressive impulses and behavior are liable to become overt. (Silence is a characteristic response to a stressful situation as well as a form of hostility in the community.) Rocky Roaders conceive of almost everyone as aggressive, and their need to avoid hostility leads them, inevitably, to the avoidance of other people.

Within the context of the cultural situation a somewhat clearer understanding of the formation of friendships and the factors which inhibit them in Rocky Roads can be seen. The friendships which these young men form are elaborations of a pattern in which most adult men of the community participate. This is a system of labor-exchange in which two men reciprocally exchange their labor. In this arrangement, a Rocky Roader who needs help on his land or in repairing his home will ask someone—always of the same economic and social standing—to help him for the day. The recipient of this labor may be called upon at any time to repay the day's work with another. This is an economic, not a social, associational pattern. Among the very young adults of the community, this is elaborated to a level of social (or noneconomic), as well as economic, friendship. Not only do these pairs of friends exchange their labor when they need the

help of another, but they do *all* their
work together. Furthermore, just as they
are inseparable during their hours of
farming, they spend almost all their non-
working hours in each other's company.
They walk to and from their farms together, they join groups of loafing men
together, and they loaf together. What
is more, they generally go through the
period of refusing to work together. It is
interesting to note that just as this pattern of close friendship during early
adulthood is but an elaboration of social
processes already present in the culture
of the community, so are these relationships subject to the same anxieties which
pervade interpersonal relationships in
Rocky Roads in general. Each member
of every pair believes that he is a better
friend than his partner, that he is the
more "loving" of the two, while the other
is participating in the relationship for
purely selfish reasons and will never grant
a favor which he is not forced to. Characteristically, these accusations are not
made one *to* another but rather one
about the other. These friendships continue past the period of *Sturm und Drang*
of early adulthood, but with noticeably
diminished intensity and intimacy. For
some reason, these friendships are dis-
continued after the marriage of one of
the partners.

Before leaving this area of behavior,
it should be pointed out that no Rocky
Roaders in this age-category ever form
or join gangs or cliques of any sort. This
particular behavior is always exhibited
in pairs of men. Furthermore, there were
no evidences which we could discover of
overt homosexual behavior in these relationships.

(4) The final characteristic mode
of rebellion of this period is one which
is familiar to almost all observers of
"adolescent" behavior—generalized and
repetitive criticisms of (apparently)
everyone and everything. But it should

be noted that Rocky Roaders at this
stage of development—not unlike their
peers in other cultures with a comparable
period of storm and stress—do not criti-
cize and reject everything. Their inces-
sant verbal hostility seems to be directed
at those areas of the culture which are
apparently most seriously conflict-ridden.
There are four predominant targets on
which the young men generally concentrate.

(a) The first lies within the economic sphere. Among the strongest of
proscriptions in the culture of Rocky
Roads is the rule that it is grossly improper to inquire of someone how much
money he or she earns. Yet, while this
rule is a very conscious one, almost all
Rocky Roaders are possessed by an insatiable curiosity about the economic
affairs, activities, and standings of their
neighbors, and the lengths to which they
will go to satisfy their curiosity are often
remarkable. It is the young adults of the
community who react most violently to
the violations of secrecy which normally
surround economic activities. They complain constantly and without letup of the
snooping, prying, and surreptitious delv-
ing into the economic affairs of others.
They conclude from these facts that
people are "no good," for they "won't
leave you alone." It appears that one of
the greatest difficulties in this area is not
so much the realization that transgression of the rules is not the exception
but the norm, but that growing Rocky
Roaders are never informed of the prevalence of transgressions and are never
taught the responses adequate to and
effective against violations of secrecy.

(b) The second target is very much
akin to the first, only here the behavior
involved is aggression. As was pointed
out before, one of the characteristics
of interpersonal relationships in Rocky
Roads is the inhibition of aggressiveness;
this inhibition is inculcated in the in-

dividual by the time he reaches adulthood. But at the same time feuds, malicious gossip, sorcery and accusations of sorcery, and bitter references to suspected conspiracies aiming at economic ruination of disliked neighbors are rampant in the community. Rocky Roaders can be said to be quite accustomed to aggression by the time they reach adulthood, if we think of floggings as aggressive. But the very aims of these floggings are the eradication of aggressive responses and demonstrations of self-assertiveness —accomplished long before the individual emerges into the broader world as an adult. His bewilderment in this area of behavior as a young adult is much the same as it is in the area of economic secrecy. Disarmed of all personal weapons of aggression, taught never to react aggressively, yet faced with the demands of the world that aggression be countered with aggression, the young adult in Rocky Roads is a bewildered individual.

(c) The third area which preoccupies these young adults in their constant criticisms of their culture is religious behavior. The organized religion of Rocky Roads is a Moravian church which is revivalistic in nature. Basic to it is the notion that since everyone has been born sinful he must be "saved," or "reborn." When reborn, he accepts Jesus Christ as his personal savior, and thereby is cleansed of his sins. Only those who have been reborn can go to heaven.

Aggression and desires for wealth are deemed "sinful." It was illuminating to listen to adult informants express disbelief of the testimonials (a necessary part of salvation) rendered by their fellow villagers during prayer meetings. But in their accusations of religious hypocrisy, most Rocky Roaders do not issue blanket accusations; instead, their references are to specific individuals and their actions. For the young adults, however, this provides excellent ammunition, for they are able to reinforce their accusations and give them greater potency by incorporating them into the religious sphere. Not only do young adults accuse everyone in the community of religious hypocrisy, but they go even further by stating that the church itself is committing a sin by encouraging people to claim rebirth and salvation when it knows that such claims are false. In this connection it should be pointed out that one hardly ever sees a young adult in church, either on Sunday or at the midweekly prayer meetings.

(d) The last mode of rebellion is not so much one of generalized criticism as of rejection of values. The most outstanding in this respect has to do with the system of social classes in Rocky Roads. The most important criterion of social-class position is wealth, status varying directly with earnings. This factor is absolute, and there are few exceptions to it. There are other criteria, such as occupation and skin color, but they occupy a decidedly secondary position. The members of the community are completely aware of their system of social classes, but they are not particularly preoccupied with it. The smoothness and efficacy of its operation was demonstrated by the ease with which every informant was able to class-type every individual in the community, including himself, and the almost complete unanimity of opinion among informants in doing so.

The most prominent exceptions to this near unanimity were the young adults of the community. Their errors could be attributed to the fact that they were new to the social-class system of the community. A Rocky Roader cannot be said to enjoy class status until he or she has reached adulthood. Nor is an individual's class position determined by his or her parents' social standing. Prior to adulthood a Rocky Roader operates outside the class structure. Upon reaching adulthood he must learn the criteria for class status, the status of all his neighbors, and the manner in which he must function within the system. But his being a newcomer does not entirely explain his deviation from the judgments of the rest of the community. Almost every young adult who was in conflict with the community deviated by class-typing himself one status higher and almost everyone else one status lower, than did others. In doing so, by their own statements, these deviants completely disregarded the criterion of wealth, and the secondary criteria of occupation and skin color. Instead, they applied their own criteria, standards emerging directly from their own conflicts and feelings of unhappiness. Whenever they were asked to explain their consistent downgrading of almost every member of the community, they explained that almost everyone failed to "live lovingly," and that they pried into other people's financial affairs, strove for great wealth, gossiped, indulged in sorcery and feuds, and furthermore, claimed to have been reborn and saved, while in reality they violated the rules of true Christianity. As for themselves, these young adults claimed that they were righteous and upright members of the community, and, accordingly, classed themselves as upper-class.

In a way, this young-adult period may be termed the final stage of socialization in Rocky Roads, for an entirely new set of behaviors must supplant many of the ones inculcated by parents. The confusion of the period is but one indication of the efficacy of the socialization processes to which the individual has been subjected from birth to adulthood. One source of this confusion and bewilderment is the absence of any models from whom to learn. In childhood and adolescence there are parents who serve as standards and whose actions can be emulated in the absence of previously established patterns of response. With the individual's advent into adulthood *he is completely on his own*, primarily because of his total dissociation from his parents after his transition from adolescence to adulthood. In the absence of such authority, the new patterns of adulthood must be learned—and they must be learned quickly—almost entirely by means of trial and error. The process is infinitely more confusing than the mystifying contradictions in parental behavior experienced during childhood. The culture of Rocky Roads does not make any allowance for this period of readjustment and does not recognize it as a transitional stage of development. Nor is any allowance made in actual behavior. A twenty-year-old Rocky Roader is subject to the same pressures and demands of the culture as is a status peer of many more years' experience.

Most cultures strive for the happiness of their members throughout all stages of the life-cycle and in only relatively few do we find age-categories characterized by extreme unhappiness, by what has become so picturesquely known as *Sturm und Drang*. The latter is a form of anxious unhappiness, almost patterned, which is often attributed to the reemergence of biological strivings in conflict with acquired moral strictures, to conflicting and contradictory demands made upon the growing individual, and either to an altered body or to the necessity for revising the body image. These no doubt do play significant roles in the "adolescent conflict" where it does occur. It, therefore, may prove rewarding to look into structural relationships of stressful age-categories in the social organization of another society for more insight into the possible causes of this *Sturm und Drang* period.

In the culture of the Manus of the Admiralty Islands, the years of early adulthood are also characterized by storm and stress, by extreme misery, unhappiness, and emotional disturbance. In contrast to that of Rocky Roads, Manus socialization is characterized by extremely severe and restrictive sexual training. The two cultures differ radically in their emotional training as well, for in Manus "the children are allowed to give their emotions free play; they are taught to bridle neither their tongues nor their tempers." But there are also points at which the two cultures are remarkably similar in the training of children. As in Rocky Roads, Manus children are taught respect for property from their earliest years, and even "before they can walk they are rebuked and chastised for touching anything which does not belong to them." A good baby or a good child "is one who never touches anything and never asks for anything not its own." The length of adolescence in Manus is roughly comparable to that of Rocky Roads, although sexual relationships during this period in Manus are covered by a blanket taboo which is supernaturally enforced. In neither society are there any indications of rebellion or stress during pubescence or culturally defined adolescence.

Manus marriages are arranged, and there are strict taboos prohibiting the couple from seeing each other before the wedding. Their initial sexual experiences after the marriage ceremony are "feared and hated" and produce "only . . . shame and hostility." [8] Both spouses are miserable and unhappy in their relationship, but it is somewhat easier for the groom than for the bride, for marriage in Manus is strictly patrilocal. The girl resents her status, "she frets and scolds," and "she grows more and more sulky

every day." During the first months of her marriage she frequently returns to her parents or she is simply "very likely to run away." [9]

Erikson[10] has pointed out that growth is the achievement, during successive stages of maturation, of a personal identity through the mastery of the "body" in relation to society and its culturally significant demands and goals. This, he indicates, can only come about through the internalization of images of persons whom the individual can "trust," through a juxtaposed simultaneity of "inner certainty as well as outer predictability." [11] Where this balanced polarity is found to be wanting or absent, the many forms which anxiety is known to take occur. Putting this in somewhat atomistic terms, this balance will be upset when the individual, by dint of past or present experiences, is unable to relate himself to his (imaged) meaningful persons or when the group withdraws its (imaged) approval and predictable trustworthiness. There is, then, a constant triadic interplay: the individual, his society, and his sense of identity, the latter varying with the relationships between the organism and the group, and in its turn mediating the balance between the two.

Most observers of human behavior are familiar with the behavioral manifestations of such a balance when it is both delicate and tenuous. Where, in practically any society or social system, the incorporated image of the world which is normally trusted is an uncertain one, the slightest disturbing nudge is often sufficient to alienate the individual from his meaningful interpersonal relationships, to question his own worth, and to further remove himself from supporting individuals. For "as long as there is a

---

8 Mead, 1939, p. 64.
9 *Ibid.*, pp. 65-68.
10 Erikson, 1950.
11 *Ibid.*, p. 219.

sense of blame, there are also irrational attempts at restitution for the damage done—and such guilty restitution often results only in more damage." [12]

While maintaining his own tripartite interplay of person-ego-society, however, Erikson continues to adhere, fundamentally, to the traditional psychoanalytic view of adolescence as the "return of the repressed." "But in puberty and adolescence all sameness and continuities relied on earlier are questioned again, because of a rapidity of body growth which equals that of early childhood and because of the entirely new addition of physical genital maturity." [13] It is during adolescence, writes Erikson, "that the question arises whether or not the future was anticipated in earlier expectations. . . . What the regressing and growing, rebelling and maturing youths are now primarily concerned with is who and what they are in the eyes of a wider circle of significant people as compared with what they themselves have come to feel they are." [14]

According to Erikson's notion of the stability and integrity of a system of ego-identity, however, we should not expect to anticipate a significant questioning of identity during the years following pubescence unless there has been a disruption in relationships between the individual and his meaningful group. The sudden physiological changes of puberty are not in *themselves* sufficient to provoke a re-examination of identity any more than the physiological changes of the menopause, for example, can be assumed to provoke universally a questioning of ego identity. Such physiological changes can and often do trigger such fundamental re-examinations in our own society as well as in others. In Rocky

Roads and Manus, however, the conflicts surrounding the sense of relatedness come long after the transformations of puberty, and, as a result, these bodily changes are not identifiable as themes in the content of their "adolescent conflicts." What has, in fact, occurred in both these groups is that there have been abrupt and sharp breaks between the maturing individual in his new role and those meaningful persons upon whom he has come to rely for a sense of belongingness.

The natives of Rocky Roads and Manus experience several things in common during their stressful early adulthood. In both societies the young adults experience situations—interpersonal stimuli—for which they are not only totally unprepared but for which the appropriate responses were completely and effectively repressed during the course of socialization. In the case of the Rocky Roader, the realization that people violate the rules of economic secrecy and by aggression are disturbing and anxiety-provoking; sexual intercourse at marriage appears to border on the traumatic for the Manus. In both societies the young adults make pronounced efforts to avoid these stressful situations. In Manus the young bride runs away from her husband; in Rocky Roads the young man refuses to work, thereby dissociating himself from those significant aspects of the social context which produce painful experiences.

But are these perceptions of disturbing phenomena sufficient to provoke these distressful storms and misery? "Discontinuity [in socialization] involves a presumption of strain," as Benedict has indicated.[15] But Benedict also goes on to point out that *when individuals are fortified by a "solid phalanx" of either age-mates or other solidary groupings, such*

[12] *Ibid.*, p. 29.
[13] *Ibid.*, p. 227.
[14] *Ibid.*, pp. 265-266.
[15] Benedict, 1952, p. 529.

as kin groupings, they can "often swing between remarkable extremes of opposite behavior without apparent psychic threat." [16] "It is self-evident," writes Rollo May, "that the experience of isolation is first cousin to anxiety; more specifically, psychological isolation beyond a certain point always results in anxiety." [17]

The sharp discontinuity of socialization and the isolation experienced by the young adults in Rocky Roads and Manus are not so much an abrupt shift in the biological and social demands made on the individual but rather a loss of a feeling of identification with the significant group of reference, the group to which the individual had all along felt he belonged. There is no doubt, in Benedict's terms, that the individual in both these societies would be able to behave with a minimum of conflict in areas which are otherwise immediately disturbing if he had some "solid phalanx" behind him: of identification and the approval which had previously protected him against the anxieties of the situation.

In summing up his position on *The Meaning of Anxiety*, Rollo May points out that a common denominator of the conflicts which underlie anxiety "can be found in the dialectical relationship of the individual and his community. . . . Where there is 'freedom from' without corresponding interrelationship, there is the anxiety of the defiant and isolated individual. . . . In the individual who is characterized by independence without corresponding relatedness, there will develop hostility toward those whom he believes to be the occasion of his isolation." [18]

What are these dialectical and social-structural events in the life of the Rocky Roader shortly after he enters adulthood and embarks on his period of rebellion?

Simply put, he does not have to seek parental permission for anything; he does what he wants and goes where he pleases. His complete independence appears to be a ready answer to all he has sought since his early years, beginning with his great needs to explore the world outside his home, his slightly later enjoyment of school as an escape from parental domination and control, up to his complete exploitation of the cultural rule that an adult is almost completely independent of his parents. But as punishing as his parents may have been, they were still the locus of the group to which he *belonged,* the group from which he derived his values, and the group within which he found whatever rewards and warmth his culture allowed. It is this dissociation from his significant group of reference, rather than the anxieties engendered by previously proscribed behavior, or by gross physiological changes, which is the true source of his anxiety and rebellion.

This can be seen in somewhat sharper perspective when we view the experiences of the young women of Rocky Roads who occupy the status of young unmarried adults. The latter are subject to more or less the same training in socialization as are their brothers; they, too, learn, when they become adults, that most people in Rocky Roads violate some of the most fundamental prescriptions of the culture. And yet the young women of the community rarely manifest the stress and rebelliousness which can be observed among the young men of the community. The difference between the sexes in their relationships to the total community is the continuity of the females' belongingness to the family group, specifically to their parents. Girls, the culture says, must be supported by their parents as long as they live at home; even

---

[16] *Loc. cit.,* emphases supplied.
[17] May, 1950, p. 170.
[18] *Ibid.,* pp. 212-213.

when they are not at home they are subject to their parents' control. Never do the young women of the community experience the abrupt isolation which is experienced by the young men.

Similar sociological processes can be seen to operate among the Manus. Among these people, the individual grows up with a definite sense of belonging to a family and to a larger kinship group. The strongest relationship of the individual during the years of socialization is to the father, who always sides with the child against the latter's mother who is the source of discipline and control. Marriage, for a Manus girl, involves going to live with her groom's parents, often in a different village. But that alone does not account for her misery, her bickering and her running away; patrilocal residence in other societies does not always produce such behavior in young brides. Accustomed to very warm and solidary relationships in her parent's home and in her kin group, the Manus bride is transported to a kin group or "village where she must now live but to which she in no sense belongs." [19] There are very real barriers which keep the Manus bride from establishing rapport and intimacy with her new group. She must not pronounce the names of her husband or those of his kinsmen, just as she must avoid her husband in public and eat separately from him.

For the groom, life at this point is far less stressful, for he continues to live with "the people with whom all his ties are closest, from whom he has learned to expect all his rewards since childhood. . . . To them he has a strong sense of belonging." [20]

Were the misery, the *Sturm und Drang,* and constant friction with the world in Rocky Roads and Manus young

adults due solely to the perception and experience of disturbing stimuli, we might anticipate that they would continue for longer periods than they actually do. In reality, however, they abate; they do so according to much the same principles which we have postulated as their original source. Denial and punishment with respect to food becomes, we have seen, one of the most significant mechanisms of socialization in Rocky Roads. Truly unpleasant as such growing up may be, food proves to be the primary means of relating to people, especially to the mother, who almost entirely alone inculcates this training. And it is only when the mother re-establishes this relationship with her son—via food and bodily care—that he is able to resume his activities without manifest anxiety. In the re-establishment of his interpersonal relatedness, and in the resumption of his activities, he is able to admit again to his greatest strivings—especially his desires to amass wealth—and thereby relate himself once again to the broader social world.

Frigid at marriage, the Manus girl appears to remain so most of her life. But her terrible anxieties seem to abate when she is able to relate herself actively to the group which produced her isolation and her unhappiness. This she does by producing children. Not only are the women bound more firmly to their marriages with the advent of children, but the men take a greater interest in their wives, and for the first time husband and wife plan together in economic enterprises, these constituting one of the most important sources of prestige among the Manus.

The notions of blame and the demands for restitution which individuals make when thrust out of their environ-

---

[19] Mead, 1939, p. 65.
[20] *Loc. cit.*

ments of significance and their self-created isolation provide excellent clues to the anxieties which underlie their behavior. The Rocky Roader who refuses to work, in his particular mode of rebellion, is saying, in effect: "You did not produce food (for me) when you were supposed to; now, neither will I." Rejected as an infant by a deprivation of food and by an unfriendly world, he rejects that environment with the very same techniques and weapons. And it is curious that he can only return to his group, via the performance of his new status (food producer), when his mother, too, participates in this tragicomedy by threatening him with deprivation of food and then producing a token meal for him.

Violent rebellion against the significant social order is often symptomatic of a longing for and dependence upon that order; this the Rocky Roader demonstrates in simple fashion.

The Manus girl who flees her new household (it is not yet a home) did not suffer, during her earlier years, the severe deprivation of the Rocky Roader. After marriage she runs away from a cold, hostile, rejecting environment, one made worse by the trauma of sexual intercourse, to her parents' home where her mother's nurturance is always available and where her father not only offers his affection but does so without humiliating her sexually.

SUMMARY

This chapter was begun with the assertion that although fantasy, aggression, and adolescence can be studied independently of each other, they can also be included under one heading. Aggression, to take one starting point, can stem from any number of sources. Especially in children, but almost equally often in adolescents, aggression can be a concretization of fantasies. That is, fantasies during these stages of development can assume qualities of reality for individuals, and they can act on them. Since, as it is generally assumed by psychologists, fantasies most often deal with the wish-fulfillment of frustrated desires or impulses, and since frustrated aggression is often the springboard for childhood and adolescent fantasy, the three topics of this chapter have an almost ineluctable relationship to each other. Sexual fantasies, too, are especially frequent during different periods of childhood and during adolescence. But, as indicated in the first paragraph of this chapter, there are many other kinds of fantasy which are not necessarily aggressive or sexual.

It has been seen how the spatial and temporal relationships of children to their parents help to maximize or minimize the sense of belongingness or isolation which the former have and, in turn, the relationship of these feelings to degrees of aggressiveness and hostility. It also has been hypothesized that when a child can share his fantasies with significant persons, especially adult ideals, there is less likelihood for disorganizing effects from conflictful fantasies than when he cannot share them. Future research will have to determine the extent to which social-structural conditions affect other types of fantasies and the degree to which they help to render fantasies disorganizing or constructive.

BIBLIOGRAPHY AND SUGGESTED READINGS

Belo, Jane. "The Balinese Temper," in *Personal Character and Cultural Milieu* (3rd edition), edited by Douglas Haring, pp. 157-180. Syracuse, New York: Syracuse University Press, 1956.

Bateson, Gregory and Margaret Mead. *Balinese Character: A Photographic Analysis.* New York: Academy of Sciences, 1942.

Benedict, Ruth. "Continuities and Discontinuities in Cultural Conditioning," in *Personality in Nature, Society and Culture,* edited by Kluckhohn *et al.,* pp. 522-531. New York: Knopf, 1955.

Bowlby, John. *Maternal Care and Mental Health.* Geneva: World Health Organization, 1952.

Eggan, Dorothy. "Instruction and Affect in Hopi Cultural Continuity," *Southwestern Journal of Anthropology,* Vol. 12, pp. 347-370, 1956. A very moving and insightful study of what it is like to grow up as a Hopi, and the effects on this experience of the expanding modern era.

Erikson, Erik H. *Childhood and Society.* New York: Norton, 1950.

Hollingshead, August B. *Elmtown's Youth: The Impact of Social Classes on Adolescents.* New York: Wiley, 1949.

Knowles, John. *A Separate Peace.* New York: Macmillan, 1959. One of the finest and most penetrating novels on adolescence.

Lewis, Claudia. *Children of the Cumberland.* New York: Columbia University Press, 1946.

Linton, Ralph. "Age and Sex Categories," *American Sociological Review,* Vol. 7, pp. 589-603, 1942. An excellent introduction to the problem.

May, Rollo. *The Meaning of Anxiety.* New York: Ronald, 1950.

Mead, Margaret Mead. "Administrative Contributions to Democratic Character Formation at the Adolescent Level," in *Personality in Nature, Society and Culture,* edited by Kluckhohn *et al.,* pp. 663-670. New York: Knopf, 1955. A cogent statement which can, and should, arouse interesting debate.

Mead, Margaret. *Coming of Age in Samoa,* in *From the South Seas.* New York: Morrow, 1939.

Parsons, Talcott and Robert F. Bales. *Family, Socialization and Interaction Process.* Glencoe, Illinois: The Free Press, 1955. An attempted integration of a Freudian view with a sociological one, which has immediate relevance to the three topics discussed in this chapter.

The Psychoanalytic Study of the Child. New York: International Universities Press, 1945-present. Psychoanalytic theory and case material dealing with psychological development through adolescence. An indispensable annual publication for anyone concerned with personality development and functioning.

Section III

IF THE SHOE FITS:
THE DEPENDENCE
OF INSTITUTIONS ON
PERSONALITY PROCESSES

Chapter 7

OCCUPATIONS AND PROFESSIONS

As we turn to the relationships of personality to institutional structures, our tasks become somewhat more difficult than they were in the study of the determinants of socialization practices. There are many reasons for this, two of them outstanding. First, it is essential at this point to have a conceptualization of *personality,* as this term will be used in the following analyses. Second, while children growing up can be thought of as passive receptors of the forces emanating from their environment, adults are constantly engaged in on-going relationships with, or in maintaining, the institutions of their society; they are adapting to these institutions as creatively as they can; they shut certain institutional spheres for one reason or another, or they attempt to change the institutions; or, as still another alternative not exclusive of the others, they attempt to study and understand these institutions. This interplay of people and institutions in active fashion makes the study of adult personality in relationship to institutional contexts extremely complex.

In this chapter and the next two, several case studies dealing with the relationships between certain aspects of personality and a limited number of institutions will be examined. In this chapter, two institutional frameworks which include relatively small numbers of people—business executives and academic scientists—will be studied. Chapters 8 and 9 will take up institutional frameworks which include larger segments of society. These cases will be used to formulate some of the over-all principles involved in the relationship of the individual to the total society.

But in order to undertake these tasks we need certain tools, the most important of which, as we noted, is a way of thinking about "personality" for our purposes. We are going to attempt to present a general way of looking at the relationships between personality and institutions; this view—it can more precisely be called a point of view—will center specifically around very limited aspects of personality. We will attempt to spell these out in greater detail later on. But at this point it is important to note that we have no intention of constructing a precise definition or general theory of personality; nor, as we pointed out at the very beginning of this book, do we plan to adhere to any single theory of the psychology of personality.

Personality in this analysis is to be viewed in terms of its moorings in specific and localized time-space contexts; as a result, we shall be concerned with neither "individual differences" nor with the features, processes, structure, and dynamisms of personality in all places and at all times. Just as certain aspects of childhood were discussed from the point of view of the effects of particular environments—depending on the cases being discussed—and not in terms of what happens to children by virtue of their being children, so adult personality can be discussed in the context of individual and highly specific social-structural environments. That is, instead of analyzing in *general* terms the personality factors involved in earning a living, in participating in a military structure, in a sense of responsibility, and so forth, each of these will be studied in detail.

The term "personality" carries three implications upon which we shall focus. It signifies, first, the person who is the point of convergence for our observations. Second, "personality" is the level on which experience is meaningful and immediate. Third, "personality" refers to an individual and systematized style of propensities to behave in certain ways.

No analysis of a social system can be complete unless we remain aware constantly of, and examine, the *person* who participates in and maintains this social system. For purposes of sociological analysis, the person is a hypothetical construct which derives from a statistical mode; he is not the unique individual. We need such a hypothetical person in mind because we are interested in more than statistically average and observable behavior. We have to carry our thinking to the abstraction of *the* person if we are going to be able to borrow some of the theoretical tools of those psychological disciplines which concern themselves almost entirely with the individual and with individual differences.

Each person—again, in a statistically modal sense—carries with him a complete armamentarium of psychological or internal predispositions, susceptibilities, propensities, and inclinations which are elicited by different catalytic sociological conditions. In addition to these psychological characteristics, each person has a *personal* system of integrating experiences and perceptions, a system which is made up of several parts, each of which is interdependent with all the others. This system enables him—and, thereby, makes possible modal responses within the group—to perceive stimuli within himself and within the environment, to organize his perceptions and these stimuli in ways which are meaningful to him, to respond to his perceptions and to the stimuli in a consistent or fairly predictable manner in terms of his relationships to other people. In other words, an individual's actions are not only sociologically relevant and meaningful, but they are direct expressions of, and direct paths of inquiry to, a personal and internalized system of energies, needs, perceptions, aspirations, inclinations, actions, and so forth, *vis-à-vis* different sociological conditions.

But an individual also has a systematized style of propensities to behave in certain ways. An individual does not only participate in social systems and institutions; he is in a constant state of "relationship" or "relatedness" to others and to himself. That is, he is not only close to others or distant from them in a characteristic way; he is not only comfortable and secure with some or anxious, afraid, and guarded in the presence of others; he is not only striving for dominance in relation to others or for equality or for submission; but, he is also in a constant state of attempting to fulfill (fulfilling sometimes means thwarting or frustrating) his own biological and emotional needs in ways which will give meaning to his life, as he sees it through the lenses provided for him by his culture. Especially in relationship to himself, the individual lives in the immediate moment *and* in the future; just as he keeps one eye on the present behavior of his children while bringing them up and another on the future, so does he constantly evaluate his own present experience in terms of aspirations which he has for himself in the future. Thus, people are not only future-oriented in bringing up their children, but they are future-oriented in their own adult existences. While some people often *seem* to be living for the moment only, without any apparent orientation to the future, it can safely be said that such absence of orientation exists only in highly pathological conditions in which the denial-through-fear-of-the-future is still an attempt to cope with the future—if only through an attempt to ward it off. This complex interrelationship among (1) an individual's participation in and maintenance of the institutions in which he participates; (2) the personal system of predispositions, susceptibilities, propensties, and inclinations which he brings to diverse sociological conditions; and (3) his relationship to himself, as well as to others, in terms of present experience and anticipations for his future—this state of being a person in the most highly personal and intimate way imaginable is the third connotation of a person's personality, his sense of being.

If we have focussed entirely on the present and on the future and have studiously avoided any reference to past experience, let us hasten to state that this has been done deliberately. We have not done this because of any denial that the past plays a great role in personality. To the contrary; there is no personality system which has not been molded (this implies past experience), and there is hardly a person who does not, to some extent, live in his own past as though it were part of the present. Past experience does play a very great role in the relationship of personality to social structure, but we do not feel that enough is known about this role at present; a theoretical statement will have to emerge out of many studies such as those which we are going to read.

Since our primary commitment is to the study of the relationship of personality to social structure, we must possess one variable or specific theoretical tool to relate the two in such a way that we can see how they "lock" into each other instead of only existing side by side. We need a conceptual keystone, hinge, or linchpin at which social systems and personality *meet* in a dynamic way and at which they keep each other going in a mode or an orbit which is meaningful to the person and to the society. This approach is meant deliberately as an alternative to the strategy of "correlations"—the method of stating only that witchcraft is an example of covert hostility, or that Latin American Indians are passive because they belong to an inferior caste and consequently have to seek a peaceful relationship between man and the universe, or that social disorganization brings with it a high rate of psychological pathology. Such correlations may be true, but they contribute little to an understanding of the ways in which social systems and personality support each other and keep each other going.

In order to find this conceptual keystone—one which we will be able to use in many different kinds of studies—we will have to select one rather limited aspect or subsystem of "personality." This variable is not intended to be synonymous with all personality or all personality processes, but it does cut across and make contact with the three aspects of personality just discussed: the person as a participant in social institutions; as being characterized by a personal system of predispositions; and as a person in relationship to himself in terms of present experience and anticipations for the future.

We are going to call this limited aspect or subsystem of personality the "self," and we suggest that this is the key which locks the personality into a particular social or role system. The "self" is the facet of personality which enables the person to "fit" into an institutional or role system and which enables him to maintain that system; but the "self" makes up only *one* aspect of the "person" in the triad of person-personal-personality.

"It seems necessary," writes Hallowell, "to assume self-awareness as one of the prerequisite conditions for the functioning of any social order, no matter what linguistic and culture patterns prevail. If such be the case, the phenomenon of self-awareness in our species is as integral a part of a human sociocultural mode of adaptation as it is of a distinctive human level of psychological structuralization." [1] *The "self" is the individual's portraiture and perception of his own person, first, as a discrete and unique entity and, secondly, as one who stands in particular relationship to other persons or "selves."* There are three major parts to the "self."

The first, and perhaps most important, is the constitution of the "self" as the point of consistency for the individual, and, "the urge to consistency can indeed be accepted as a primary mechanism." [2] The consistency which characterizes the "self" underlies the dominant processes of what is often called "character" structure. "The term character stresses the habitual form of a given reaction, its relative constancy." [3] The individual's "self" orients him toward other persons as well as toward his own person; "all orientations are part of the human equipment, and the dominance of any specific orientation depends to a large extent on the peculiarity of the culture in which the individual lives," [4] specifically, on the goals which a society defines as desirable and attainable. The consistency of personality predispositions, of behavior, and of orientation to others makes up the essential unity of the individual, and enables him to function as a bearer and transmitter of his culture and as an effective protagonist on the stage of a society's role systems.

The second parameter of the "self" is its constitution as a standard of comparison for the individual, a point of reference against which he may measure his own actions and the point at which he compares himself to others. Culture is learned through observation and precept. For the growing and maturing individual, those from whom he learns are models whose actions serve as norms. The more clearly his actions approximate those of the model in the prototype situations, the more

1 Hallowell, 1955, p. 75.
2 Murphy, 1947, p. 532.
3 Fenichel, 1945, p. 467.
4 Fromm, 1947, p. 78.

certain he feels of "doing the proper thing." The greater the discrepancy, the more likelihood of his self-censure or of censure from the social group. Here, incidentally, can be seen a source of the dictum found in every society that there are certain (social) things which one is "supposed to do." Whether a model is physically present or not is obviously irrelevant, for every meaningful and significant model is internalized within the individual and becomes the guiding line for action. The closer his behavior is to these guiding lines the more "socially acceptable" and "adequate" does he view himself, and he thus assumes that others will see him in the same light.

Naturally, the internalization of models into the "self" is far more complicated than this, for at certain levels of stratification in some societies, children notice that the actions of these models are at variance with those of the population majority. However, since we are attempting to set some theoretical base-lines for an understanding of the relationship of personality to institutional or role systems, we need not complicate the analysis with these special instances.

When we say that the "self" is a standard of comparison for the individual and a point against which he may measure his own actions we mean that all people "set standards for themselves." These may be moral or ethical standards governing relationships with other persons or they may be "minimum standards." Thus, a scientist may set a standard of "honesty" for himself, however he defines it, below which he will not allow himself to fall; or he may set standards of "perfection," knowing that the can never really meet them. If a businessman, he may set a standard of honest dealings with customers. Or he may set a financial standard of a net profit of $200 weekly. Or, he may set as his minimum a goal that he must earn at least $50 more per week than his closest competitor, or that he must provide his wife with a dress at least half again as expensive as their neighbor. All such base-lines of human life are guides for action which become incorporated into the central system of the personality—the "self." When people are able to meet these goals, to achieve the expectations they have for their own lives, they feel more "adequate" and acceptable to themselves as well as to others; this is what often makes the difference in the ability of people to continue to function adequately, and, psychologically speaking, to "hold together" or remain in "one piece."

The third ingredient of the "self" is its maintenance of the individual in particular positions vis-à-vis other persons. While there is some overlap between this and the second parameter of the "self," there is a vital difference between the individual comparing himself to others and his maintenance of positions vis-à-vis others. A person may compare himself to others in terms of the positions which he and they occupy, but he can also make such comparisons with reference to criteria or according to tests which have nothing to do with relative positional standings. One person, for example, may "see himself" as proximate or close to other people, another as distant and removed from them; a third may view himself as superior. One type of person may "see himself" as functioning best when he is part of a large organization or role system, responsible for those people with whom he is in constant association, while another might "see himself" as being responsible for his own actions only. Illustrations of types of self-perception are endless, but the important point to bear in mind is that people *act* in accordance with the ways in which they "see themselves," with the ways in which they behave, and with the roles which they occupy. *These actions include not only the ways in which they behave toward others, but the particular role systems into which people will "fit," and they include the role systems which are dependent upon particular personality-types.*

There are two reasons for this. First, an individual's actions—for example, the way in which he earns a living—must be in harmony with the ways in which he thinks of himself, for if the two were not in accord the individual would not be able to perform effectively. Second, certain role systems tend to recruit only persons who "see themselves" in particular ways—so that they may rely on these people and depend on them to "feel comfortable" in doing the things the role system demands of them. Thus, certain institutions are dependent on personalities in the sense that these institutions perpetuate themselves through the invariable recruitment of individuals who "fit." (If a man's picture of himself is of a gregarious backslapper whose only desire is to make tremendous amounts of money, no amount of training, native intelligence, or promise of honorary titles would enable him to spend his life in a laboratory mapping the brain of a bee. And the role system into which such a job would be classed would have no interest in recruiting him for the task.)

The title of Section III refers to two separate processes as one. First, reference is made to the question of "fit," second, to the question of the dependence of institutions on personality; this may seem paradoxical because, while we can speak of a shoe fitting a particular foot, we do not ordinarily think of a foot being dependent on size or shape of the shoe. Actually, however, there is a limited—but important—dependence of institutions on personality processes (for example, if we magically reared a generation which could not stand the sight of blood, the nature of our medical institutions would alter dramatically).

The question of the "fit" of personalities into institutions or of the dependence of institutions on personality is not a question of institutions being the outgrowth or the results of personality. Instead, we must view institutions (including occupations) in the sociopolitical and economic environment as *givens;* "they are there" to begin with. How they got "there" is a question of history. To cite one example, while it would be invaluable to know the personality factors which "made for" the institutions of Nazi-German society, it may be impossible to trace them accurately. It would appear that *most* Western countries are capable—or have the potentialities within them—of developing many of the institutions which culminated in Naziism. The British, French, Belgians, Dutch, and the like, have exhibited such tendencies in their treatment of colonials. The Americans exhibited such behavior toward each other during the Puritan period as well as toward American Indians after that period; some institutions in the American South are also not dissimilar. One would be hard put to find much difference between some of the institutions of South Africa of 1960 and those of Germany during the period 1933-1945. Such racist and oppressive institutional organizations, of course, are of an entirely different order than prejudice or bigotry, and it is doubtful whether they are simple, direct outgrowths of personality processes.

Instead—and taking institutions as "givens"—the questions of "fit" deals with the extent to which an individual's self-perception or self-image enables him to participate in an institutional or role system in the light of the imperatives of that system, the limitations it imposes on its members, and the potentialities it affords them. The question of the *dependence* of an institution or role system on personality deals with the extent to which people's perceptions of their own and others' "selves" set limits or produce variations in the contours of the institution or role system. In other words, the "self" has to be viewed as a mechanism from two separate vantages —as a pivot which enables the individual to "fit" into a structure and also as a pivot on which a particular structure rests. These concepts will be clarified in the case studies of this chapter and Chapters 8 and 9.

We have seen, especially in Chapters 3 and 5, that parents must *experience* a social system or changes within a social system in order for them to be able to transmit these to their children while bringing them up. Similarly, before an individual has matured sufficiently to participate fully in a particular role system *he must have experienced that system in the course of growing up.* He does not, of course, experience the actual system of the business executive, or of a scientist, or of a soldier, or of a Negro adult on the labor market, or of a participant in a legal framework. *But he does experience the system into which he will later "fit" in a series of prototype situations into which he is consciously or unconsciously placed by his socializers, and which, in turn, produce a particular self-system within him.* The assumption of responsibility and initiative, performance in school, aggressive and assertive behavior of particular sorts, athletic adequacy and prowess, and the like, of which Aberle and Naegele speak in their study, are prototypes of the situations into which the growing individual is expected to "fit." Similarly, the isolation (or loneliness), the avoidance of and rebellion against parents, and the like, are a few of the prototypes cited by Anne Roe as having been experienced by the individual who later becomes a scientist. We have also observed (in Chapter 3) the nature of the prototype situations experienced by the growing Negro child in different social classes. The Hopi child learning a kinship system and the Balinese child sharing his fantasies with adults are witnessing enactments of the social systems in which they will later participate.

It can be assumed that each prototype situation—or, more accurately, each combination of prototype situations—produces its own system of self-portraiture in the growing and maturing individual. And, it can be assumed further, the self-system produced by such prototype situations enables the individual to "fit" into the role systems for which he is being prepared by his parents, consciously or unconsciously.

In the absence of a scheme of types of self-systems which could be related to participation in role systems, sociologists and anthropologists will have to improvise their own tools. At least to begin with, such a paradigm of self-systems would have to consist of polarities; as the relationships of these self-systems to institutions and role systems are more fully developed and understood, it will be possible to see each pair in a polarity as opposite extremes along a continuum, and then fill in the points along the continuum as the indication for them arises.

The following six-dimensional proposal is not meant to be an inclusive or exclusive one; half a dozen polarities are presented as an arbitrary *number,* not as an arbitrary scheme or paradigm. These emerge out of the conceptualization of "self" and are intended to serve only heuristic and illustrative ends at this time. Future research may help in the formulation of an internally consistent and strategic scheme of self-systems. Perhaps the following six illustrations will help to bring us a little nearer that goal:

(1) A self-system based on impenetrable boundaries *versus* one based on open or fluid boundaries. In the first, the individual functions in his environment primarily on the basis of a core of motivations existing within him, and derives satisfactions from within; he is relatively impervious to external stimuli or suggestions. In the second, the individual has a weakly developed sense of "self," operates within his environment primarily on the basis of cues from outside his own person, derives almost all gratifications from the external world, is easily suggestible and swayed by external stimuli, and can take on any social role as long as there is some measure of prestige or approval from surrounding people.

(2) The field-dependent *versus* the field-independent person. (This polarity is partly based on the experimental work of Witkin.) [5] This set of polarities closely resembles the first and appears to overlap it considerably: the field-dependent individual is constantly looking to his environment for cues to guide his behavior; his sense of values is dependent on those of others whom he considers prestigeful or powerful; he is extremely sensitive to the opinions of others for his self-esteem and sense of worth. The field-independent person, at the opposite extreme of the continuum, takes his directions for his behavior almost entirely from within himself, independently of cues in his environment; his values are fully internalized, and they are impervious to the influences of others' sets of values; he pays little heed to the opinions which others have of him.

(3) The third dimension is based on the individual's perception of the *space* he occupies in his environment. At one extreme is the person who perceives himself as being "in the middle of things." At the other extreme is the person who views himself as being "off to one side," as an onlooker, or as being on the fringe of all significant activities.

(4) The fourth dimension is closely related to the third and, for want of a better term, can be referred to as the security-insecurity polarity of self-portraiture. This dimension is the *stance* which the individual sees himself as taking. One side represents security—the individual sees his person as standing upright, firmly on

---

[5] Witkin *et al.,* 1954, pp. 24-60.

the ground and against his background; on the other, insecurity—the individual sees himself as standing at an angle to the ground, teetering in uncertainty.

(5) The fifth dimension deals with a facet of the individual in interpersonal or social relationships—anxiety. At one extreme of the continuum is the individual who is usually anxious in interpersonal contacts, while at the other is the individual who is generally free from anxiety in such relationships.

(6) A sixth possible dimension—and the final one to be suggested as an illustration—consists of the withdrawn person *versus* the person who can extend himself to others and is consistently interested in them.

It should, of course, be borne in mind that any scheme of self-systems can only be developed and applied by taking the various permutations and combinations of the different dimensions and attempting to learn how such *combinations* help to produce a particular kind of "self" which does or does not "fit" into an institutionalized role system. In other words, it is important to bear in mind that such polarities are *dimensions*; no one can characterize a person in his entirety, because different aspects of each of these dimensions can be interrelated within one person to help make up his "self."

As we shall observe, there is an entirely different self-system which mediates the "fit" between personality and institutional systems in each of the several instances which we shall analyze. Within the sphere of the professions, for example, the business executive's "self" places him in an entirely different kind of relationship to his parents and thus to the world at large than does the "self" of the scientist. The American's ideas of "self" appear to be considerably different from those of the German; correspondingly, these different self-systems have different institutional consequences for American and German military organizations. Similarly, previous case studies showed that the growing Negro individual in the Southern and border states learns a self-system specifically relevant to his caste-status, and that the self-image which emerges varies by class position within the Negro caste in that geographical area. Concomitantly, this image of one's "self" largely determines the manner in which the individual will "fit" into the segment of the caste structure which is most relevant to his station in life. Among the Hopi, to take another example, growing individuals are provided with a self-system which permits for an effective interdependence between the individual and Hopi institutions under normal conditions; under conditions which disrupt the smooth functioning of institutions, individuals are not able to "fit" into the institutional structures of the society and, as a result, considerable social and emotional conflict results. Similar processes will be noted in the instances of participation in a legal framework as well as within total systems under conditions of drastic sociocultural change.

Another tool needed, in addition to psychological ones, is a conceptualization of the various institutions which will be discussed. In the cases which will be studied, *the nature of the institution under consideration* will be outlined as clearly as possible. In dealing with the interrelationships between personality and professional occupation, it is necessary to define the nature of the tasks of executives and scientists and gain some idea of the nature of professionalism in general.

This is not the place to list investigations into personality characteristics of members of different occupations. There have been studies of physicians and student-physicians, lawyers, grocers, clergymen, salesmen, artists, nurses, social workers, executives, mechanically skilled persons, scientists, occupational therapists, librarians, engineers, teachers, airplane pilots, and the like.

Almost all of these studies have been conducted by psychologists or by members of the profession being investigated. As a result, such inquiries frequently exhibit one basic defect so far as the sociologist or anthropologist is concerned. Missing in almost all of them is any awareness of the nature of social institutions in general, or of the role systems—as institutionalized arrangements—whose members are being placed under the psychologist's microscope. "Fitting" into the role system of, let us say, medicine, law, business, or science is more than *being* a physician, lawyer, executive, or scientist. Such a question of "fit" also includes the *structuralization* of medicine, law, business, or science as institutionalized systems—each with its own institutional imperatives, its own status system, its own set of values. In other words, each of these role systems has a structure of its own, and it is this concept of structure which is lacking in most studies of occupation and personality which have been published. What is important to bear in mind, however, is that these lacks are not limitations of these studies *per se* but, rather, lacunae for the needs of sociology and anthropology.

In trying to correct these lacks, there will be one question which will guide us throughout: What is the nature of this role system or institution *into which* the individual must "fit" or which *rests on* certain personality processes in individuals? This question deliberately presupposes that an institution has a structure, boundaries, and contours. Although all the institutions of a society are interrelated within a complex whole, each institution has its own imperatives, its own boundaries *vis-à-vis* those of other institutions, and its own contours: it occupies a particular position and a particular range of sociological space on a societal map.

THE PROFESSIONS

The word "profession" is difficult to define sociologically. Goode, Merton, and Huntington, in a volume devoted to *Professions in American Society,* suggest that we ". . . cannot neatly divide all occupations into the two categories, 'professional' and 'nonprofessional.' Instead, it becomes useful to think of occupations as falling somewhere along a dimension of 'professionalism.' " [6] In the light of this postulated dimension, they go on to suggest the following conceptualization of professions and professionalism:

"It is possible, for example, to set apart all occupations which require state li-

[6] Goode *et al.,* ms., p. 2.

censure, but the definiteness and clarity of this formal criterion creates a class of occupations which share few common social patterns, and which are highly disparate in prestige, power, technical training, group solidarity, and self-controls. Moreover, this criterion, like that of a professional association or a code of ethics, can be seen as a resultant of professionalism. If an occupation becomes more professionalized, it is likely to require licensure of its members, to formulate a code, and to organize an association. However, an occupation cannot achieve professional status by mechanically and directly taking on these particular attributes, any more than it can by simply asserting that it is a profession. The social patterns which are shared by the professions do in fact give rise to similar formal actions, and these are worthy of analysis. If however these formal actions are derivative from more fundamental social patterns which give the professions great structural importance in modern society, then it is these common patterns which justify extended attention.

"The development and application of abstract scientific technical knowledge to the weighty problems of an industrialized society are carried out through fulfillment of professional role obligations. These professional tasks must be discharged by highly trained personnel, and under certain social conditions. Professionals must be relatively free from lay control, since outsiders by definition cannot adequately evaluate their work. Professionals are in fact granted far wider discretion and autonomy than other workers in dealing with problems of great importance to individuals and the community: life and death, the problem of evil, justice, the discovery and dissemination of scientific knowledge, as well as construction and industrial production. Precisely because the community grants professionals a wide area of discretion, but correspondingly demands great responsibility from them, individual practitioners must accept internally a set of norms which regulate their conduct. Against the temptation to exploit the ignorant client, there has developed a strong service orientation in the professions. The society would not grant so much respect and trust if it were generally believed that the individual professional decides each problem with an eye solely to maximum profit. Such a service- or collectivity-orientation is not, of course, simple altruism, but is supported by both colleagues and clients, so that conformity is rewarded and deviation punished. The major professions have been granted both indirect and direct power to control the standards of professional behavior as well as who shall be admitted to training and who shall practice. Most legislation relating to any profession is shaped by the representatives of that profession. Moreover, the legal controls are minimal, and set standards that are less stringent than those of the profession itself." [7]

In any attempt to relate personality to participation in professional, or any, occupations, a question of strategy has to be decided upon at the outset. Only empirical research in the future will be able to determine whether several related occupations must be grouped into one gross category or whether very fine distinctions have to be made between even closely related occupational groups, or even

---

[7] *Ibid.*, pp. 8-9.

within individual occupational categories. For example, is it correct to distinguish between business executives and scientists, or should they both be grouped together and treated as one category *vis-à-vis* nonprofessionals? Should we differentiate between executives in corporations which produce consumer's goods and those employed in service-oriented corporations? Should we follow Anne Roe's differentiation of scientists into discrete categories, or should we assume that all scientists are of one gross category? Although Roe's findings tend to support the former alternative, considerably more information is necessary before any over-all generalization can be offered to cover all occupational groups.

Although any American corporation or business enterprise is basically subject to the needs and pressures of the total economy—which may extend beyond the borders of the United States—we can overlook this in our attempt to understand the processes of "fit" between personality and the performance of roles within the business structure. At the same time, we must have some idea of the *imperatives* or demands of the role of the business executive before we can appreciate how a particular kind of self-system facilitates the individual's "fit" into this role system. In other words, if a person has to "fit" into the role system of the business executive, what *is* this role into which he must "fit?" The following selection provides an excellent picture of the formal role imperatives or requirements of the business executive. It will be followed by a psychological study with the focus on the "self" of the executive.

THE EXECUTIVE FUNCTIONS*

By Chester I. Barnard

The coordination of efforts essential to a system of cooperation requires an organization system of communication. Such a system of communication implies centers or points of interconnection and can only operate as these centers are occupied by persons who are called executives. It might be said, then, that the function of executives is to serve as channels of communication so far as communications must pass through central positions. But since the object of the communication system is coordination of all aspects of organization, it follows that the functions of executives relate to all the work essential to the vitality and endurance of an organization, so far, at least, as it must be accomplished through formal coordination.

It is important to observe, however, that not all work done by persons who occupy executive positions is in connection with the executive functions, the coordination of activities of others. Some of the work of such persons, though *organization* work, is not executive. For example, if the president of a corporation goes out personally to sell products of his company or engages in some of the production work, these are not executive

* Reprinted with abridgment by permission of the publishers from Chester I. Barnard, *The Functions of the Executive,* Cambridge, Mass.: Harvard University Press [pp. 215-234], Copyright, 1938, by The President and Fellows of Harvard College.

services. If the president of a university gives lectures to a class of students, this is not executive work. If the head of a government department spends time on complaints or disputes about services rendered by the department, this is not necessarily executive work. Executive work is not that *of* the organization, but the specialized work of *maintaining* the organization in operation.

If we mean by executive functions the specialized work of maintaining systems of cooperative effort, we may best proceed for general purposes to find out what work has to be done, and then, when desirable, to trace out who are doing that work in a particular organization.

The executive functions serve to maintain a system of cooperative effort. They are impersonal. The functions are not, as so frequently stated, to manage a group of persons. I do not think a correct understanding of executive work can be had if this narrower, convenient, but strictly speaking erroneous, conception obtains. It is not even quite correct to say that the executive functions are to manage the system of cooperative efforts. As a whole it is managed by itself, not by the executive organization, which is a part of it. The functions with which we are concerned are like those of the nervous system, including the brain, in relation to the rest of the body. It exists to maintain the bodily system by directing those actions which are necessary more effectively to adjust to the environment, but it can hardly be said to manage the body, a large part of whose functions are independent of it and upon which it in turn depends.

The essential executive functions, as I shall present them, are first, to provide the system of communication; second, to promote the securing of essential efforts; and third, to formulate and define purpose. Since the elements of organization are interrelated and interdependent, the executive functions are so likewise; nevertheless they are subject to considerable specialization and as functions are to a substantial degree separable in practice. We shall deal with them only as found in complex, though not necessarily large, organizations.

When a complex of more than one unit is in question, centers of communication and corresponding executives are necessary. The need of a definite system of communication creates the first task of the organizer and is the immediate origin of executive organization. Since communication will be accomplished only through the agency of persons, the selection of persons for executive functions is the concrete method of establishing the *means* of communication, though it must be immediately followed by the creation of positions, that is, a *system* of communication; and, especially in established organizations, the positions will exist to be filled in the event of vacancies.

In other words, communication position and the "locating" of the services of a person are complementary phases of the same thing. The center of communication is the organization service of a person at a place. Persons without positions cannot function as executives, they mean nothing but potentiality. Conversely, positions vacant are as defunct as dead nerve centers. This is why executives, when functioning strictly as executives, are unable to appraise men in the abstract, in an organization vacuum, as it were. Men are neither good nor bad, but only good or bad in this or that position. This is why they not infrequently "change the organization," the arrangement of positions, if men suitable to fill them are not available. In fact, "executive organization" in practice cannot be divorced from "executive personnel"; and "executive personnel" is without important meaning except in conjunction with a specific arrangement of positions.

Therefore, the problem of the establishment and maintenance of the system of communication, that is, the primary task of the executive organization, is perpetually that of obtaining the coalescence of the two phases, executive personnel and executive positions. Each phase in turn is the strategic factor of the executive problem—first one, then the other phase, must be adjusted. This is the central problem of the executive functions. Its solution is not in itself sufficient to accomplish the work of all these functions; but no others can be accomplished without it, and none well unless it is well done.

The most important single contribution required of the executive, certainly the most universal qualification, is loyalty, domination by the organization personality. This is the first necessity because the lines of communication cannot function at all unless the personal contributions of executives will be present at the required positions, at the times necessary, without default for ordinary personal reasons. This, as a personal qualification, is known in secular organizations as the quality of "responsibility"; in political organizations as "regularity"; in governmental organizations as fealty or loyalty; in religious organizations as "complete submission" to the faith and to the hierarchy of objective authority.

The contribution of personal loyalty and submission is least susceptible to tangible inducements. It cannot be bought either by material inducements or by other positive incentives, except all other things being equal. This is as true of industrial organizations, I believe, as of any others. It is rather generally understood that although money or other material inducements must usually be paid to responsible persons, responsibility itself does not arise from such inducements.

However, love of prestige is, in general, a much more important inducement in the case of executives than with the rest of the personnel. Interest in work and pride in organization are other incentives that usually must be present. These facts are much obscured as respects commercial organizations, where material inducements appear to be the effective factors partly because such inducements are more readily offered in such organizations and partly because, since the other incentives are often equal as between such organizations, material inducements are the only available differential factor. It also becomes an important secondary factor to individuals in many cases, because prestige and official responsibilities impose heavy material burdens on them.

Following loyalty, responsibility, and capacity to be dominated by organization personality, come the more specific personal abilities. They are roughly divided into two classes: relatively general abilities, involving general alertness, comprehensiveness of interest, flexibility, faculty of adjustment, poise, courage, etc.; and specialized abilities based on particular aptitudes and acquired techniques. The first kind is relatively difficult to appraise because it depends upon innate characteristics developed through general experience. It is not greatly susceptible of immediate inculcation. The second kind may be less rare because the division of labor, that is, organization itself, fosters it automatically, and because it is susceptible to development (at a cost) by training and education. We deliberately and more and more turn out specialists; but we do not develop general executives well by specific efforts, and we know very little about how to do it.

The higher the positions in the line of authority, the more general the abilities required. The scarcity of such abilities, together with the necessity for keeping the lines of authority as short as feasible, controls the organization of executive work.

So far we have considered the first executive function only as it relates to the formal communication system. It has been emphasized several times that informal organization is essential to formal organizations, particularly with reference to communication. This is true not only of the organization as a whole, or of its ultimate subordinate units, but also of that special part which we call the executive organization. The communication function of executives includes the maintenance of informal executive organization as an essential means of communication.

Although I have never heard it stated that this is an executive function or that such a thing as an informal executive organization exists, in all the good organizations I have observed the most careful attention is paid to it. In all of them informal organization operates. This is usually not apparent except to those directly concerned.

The general method of maintaining an informal executive organization is so to operate and to select and promote executives that a general condition of compatibility of personnel is maintained. Perhaps often and certainly occasionally men cannot be promoted or selected, or even must be relieved, because they cannot function, because they "do not fit," where there is no question of formal competence. This question of "fitness" involves such matters as education, experience, age, sex, personal distinctions, prestige, race, nationality, faith, politics, sectional antecedents; and such very specific personal traits as manners, speech, personal appearance, etc. It goes by few if any rules, except those based at least nominally on other, formal, considerations. It represents in its best sense the political aspects of personal relationship in formal organization.

This compatibility is promoted by educational requirements; by requirement of certain background; by conferences and conventions; by specifically social activities; by class distinctions connected with privileges and "authority." A certain conformity is required by unwritten understanding that can sometimes be formally enforced, expressed for its negative aspect by the phrase "conduct unbecoming a gentleman and an officer." There are, however, innumerable other processes, many of which are not consciously employed for this purpose.

The functions of informal executive organizations are the communication of intangible facts, opinions, suggestions, suspicions, that cannot pass through formal channels without raising issues calling for decisions, without dissipating dignity and objective authority and without overloading executive positions; also to minimize excessive cliques of political types arising from too great divergence of interests and views; to promote self-discipline of the group; and to make possible the development of important personal influences in the organization.

To summarize: the first executive function is to develop and maintain a system of communication. This involves jointly a scheme of organization and an executive personnel. The processes by which the latter is accomplished include chiefly the selection of men and the offering of incentives; techniques of control permitting effectiveness in promoting, demoting, and dismissing men; and finally the securing of an informal organization in which the essential property is compatibility of personnel. The chief functions of this informal organization are expansion of the means of communication with reduction in the necessity for formal decisions, the minimizing of undesirable influences, and the promotion of desirable influences concordant with the scheme of formal responsibilities.

Another executive function is the assignment of responsibility—the delegation of objective authority. Thus in one sense this function is that of the scheme of positions, the system of communication, already discussed. That is its potential aspect. Its other aspect is the actual decisions and conduct which make the scheme a working system. Accordingly, the general executive states that "this is the purpose, this the objective, this the direction, in general terms, in which we wish to move, before next year."

I suspect that at least nine-tenths of all organization activity is on the responsibility, the authority, and the specifications of those who make the last contributions, who apply personal energies to the final concrete objectives. There is no meaning to personal specialization, personal experience, personal training, personal location, personal ability, eyes and ears, arms and legs, brains and emotions, if this is not so. What must be added to the indispensable authority, responsibility, and capability of each contributor is the indispensable coordination. This requires a pyramiding of the formulation of purpose that becomes more and more general as the number of units of basic organization becomes larger, and

more and more remote in future time. Responsibility for abstract, generalizing, prospective, long-run decision is delegated *up* the line, responsibility for definition, action, remains always at the base where the authority for effort resides.

The formulation and definition of purpose is then a widely distributed function, only the more general part of which is executive. In this fact lies the most important inherent difficulty in the operation of cooperative systems—the necessity for indoctrinating those at the lower levels with general purposes, the major decisions, so that they remain cohesive and able to make the ultimate detailed decisions coherent; and the necessity, for those at the higher levels, of constantly understanding the concrete conditions and the specific decisions of the "ultimate" contributors from which and from whom executives are often insulated. Without that up-and-down-the-line coordination of purposeful decisions, general decisions and general purposes are mere intellectual processes in an organization vacuum, insulated from realities by layers of misunderstanding. The function of formulating grand purposes and providing for their redefinition is one which needs sensitive systems of communication, experience in interpretation, imagination, and delegation of responsibility.

In bare outline, then, these are some of the imperatives set forth by the role system in which the business executive participates, into which he must "fit." It will be profitable, in examining Henry's paper on "The Business Executive," to bear in mind the picture presented earlier by Aberle and Naegele in their portrayal of the self-system which middle-class fathers attempted to implant within their sons. Henry's analysis is essentially a composite picture of the business executive which affords us an opportunity to see how such a person actually does "fit" into a particular institutional framework.

THE BUSINESS EXECUTIVE:
THE PSYCHODYNAMICS OF A SOCIAL ROLE*

By William E. Henry

The business executive is a central figure in the economic and social life of the United States. His direction of business enterprise and his participation in informal social groupings give him a significant place in community life. In both its economic and its social aspects the role of the business executive is sociologically a highly visible one. It has clearly definable limits and characteristics known to the general public. These characteristics indicate the function of the business executive in the social structure, define the behavior expected of the individual executive, and serve as a guide to the selection of the novice.

Social pressure plus the constant demands of the business organization of which he is a part direct the behavior of the executive into the mold appropriate to the defined role. "Success" is the name applied to the whole-hearted adoption of the role. The individual behaves in the manner dictated by the society, and society rewards the individual with "success" if his behavior conforms to the role. It would punish him with "failure" should he deviate from it.

Participation in this role, however, is not a thing apart from the personality of the individual. It is not a game that the person is playing; it is the way of behaving and thinking that he knows best, that he finds rewarding, and in which he believes. Thus the role as socially defined has its counterpart in personality structure. To some extent, too, the personality structure is reshaped to be in harmony with the social role. The extent to which such reshaping of the adult personality is possible, however, seems limited. An initial selection process occurs which reduces the amount of time involved in teaching the appropriate behavior. Persons whose personality structure is most readily adaptable to this particular role tend to be selected, whereas those whose personality is not already partially akin are rejected.

This paper describes the personality communalities of a group of successful business executives. The research upon which it is based explored the general importance of personality structure in the selection of executive personnel. Many aptitude tests have been employed in industry to decrease the risk involved in the hiring of untried personnel and to assist in their placement. These tests have been far less effective in the selection of high-level executive personnel than in the selection of clerical and other non-administrating persons. Many business executives have found that persons of unquestioned high intelligence often turn out to be ineffective when placed in positions of increased responsibility. The reasons for their failure lie in their social relationships. No really effective means has yet been found to clarify and predict this area of executive functioning. It is to this problem that our research was directed.

From the research it became clear that the "successful" business executives studied had many personality characteristics in common. (It was equally clear that an absence of these characteristics was coincident with "failure" within the organization.) This personality constella-

* Reprinted from *The American Journal of Sociology*, Vol. *54*, pp. 286-291, 1949, by permission of The University of Chicago Press. Copyright 1949 by The University of Chicago.

tion might be thought of as the minimal requirement for "success" within our present business system and as the psychodynamic motivation of persons in this occupation. Individual uniqueness in personality was clearly present; but, despite these unique aspects, all executives had in common this personality pattern.

ACHIEVEMENT DESIRES

Successful executives show high drive and achievement desire. They conceive of themselves as hard-working and achieving persons who must accomplish in order to be happy. The areas in which they do their work are clearly different, but each feels this drive for accomplishment. This should be distinguished from a type of pseudo-achievement drive in which the glory of the end product alone is stressed. The person with this latter type of drive, seldom found in the successful executives, looks to the future in terms of the glory it will provide him and of the projects that he will have completed—as opposed to the achievement drive of the successful executive, which looks more toward the sheer accomplishment of the work itself. The successful business leader gets much satisfaction from doing rather than from merely contemplating the completed product. To some extent this is the difference between the dreamer and the doer. It is not that the successful executives do not have an over-all goal in mind or that they do not derive satisfaction from the contemplation of future ease or that they do not gain pleasure from prestige. Far more real to them, however, is the continual stimulation that derives from the pleasure of immediate accomplishment.

MOBILITY DRIVE

All successful executives have strong mobility drives. They feel the necessity of moving continually upward and of accumulating the rewards of increased accomplishment. For some the sense of successful mobility comes through the achievement of competence on the job. These men struggle for increased responsibility and derive a strong feeling of satisfaction from the completion of a task. Finished work and newly gained competence provide them with their sense of continued mobility.

A second group relies more upon the social prestige of increased status in their home communities or within the organizational hierarchy. Competence in work is of value and at times crucial. But the satisfactions of the second group come from the social reputation, not from the personal feeling that necessary work has been well done. Both types of mobility drive are highly motivating. The zeal and energy put into the job is equal in both instances. The distinction appears in the kinds of work which the men find interesting. For the first group the primary factor is the nature of the work itself—is it challenging, is it necessary, is it interesting? For the second group the crucial factor is its relation to their goals of status mobility—is it a step in the direction of increased prestige, is it appropriate to their present position, what would other people think of them if they did it?

THE IDEA OF AUTHORITY

The successful executive posits authority as a controlling but helpful relationship to superiors. He looks to his superiors as persons of more advanced training and experience, whom he can consult on special problems and who issue to him certain guiding directives. He does not see the authorities in his environment as destructive or prohibiting forces.

Those executives who view authority

as a prohibiting and destructive force have difficulty relating themselves to superiors and resent their authority over them. They are either unable to work smoothly with superiors or indirectly and unconsciously do things to obstruct the work of their bosses or to assert their independence unnecessarily.

It is of interest that to these men the dominant crystallization of attitudes about authority is toward superior and toward subordinates, rather than toward self. This implies that most crucial in their concept of authority is the view of being a part of a wider and more final authority system. In contrast, a few executives of the "self-made," driving-type characteristic of the past of business enterprise maintain a specific concept of authority with regard to self. They are the men who almost always forge their own frontiers, who are unable to operate within anyone else's framework, and to whom cooperation and team work are foreign concepts. To these men the ultimate authority is in themselves, and their image does not include the surrounding area of shared or delegated power.

ORGANIZATION AND
ITS IMPLICATIONS

While executives who are successful vary considerably in their intelligence-test ratings, all of them have a high degree of ability to organize unstructured situations and to see the implications of their organization. This implies that they have the ability to take several seemingly isolated events or facts and to see relationships that exist between them. Further, they are interested in looking into the future and are concerned with predicting the outcome of their decisions and actions.

This ability to organize often results in a forced organization, however. Even though some situations arise with which

they feel unfamiliar and are unable to cope, they still force an organization upon it. Thus they bring it into the sphere of familiarity. This tendency operates partially as a mold, as a pattern into which new or unfamiliar experiences are fit. This means, of course, that there is a strong tendency to rely upon techniques that they know will work and to resist situations which do not readily fit this mold.

DECISIVENESS

Decisiveness is a further trait of this group. This does not imply the popular idea of the executive making quick and final decisions in rapid-fire succession, although this seems to be true of some of the executives. More crucial, however, is an ability to come to a decision among several alternative courses of action— whether it be done on the spot or after detailed consideration. Very seldom does this ability fail. While less competent and well-organized individuals may become flustered and operate inefficiently in certain spots, most of these men force their way to a conclusion. Nothing is too difficult for them to tackle and at least try to solve. When poorly directed and not modified by proper judgment, this attitude may be more a handicap than a help. That is to say, this trait remains in operation and results in decision-making action regardless of the reasonableness of the decision or its reality in terms of related facts. The loss of this trait (usually found only in cases in which some more profound personality change has also occurred) is one of the most disastrous for the executive: his superiors become apprehensive about him. This suggests an interesting relationship to the total executive constellation. The role demands conviction and certainty. Whenever a junior executive loses this quality of decisiveness, he seems to pass out of the socially defined role. The weakening of other aspects of the ideal executive constellation can be readily reintegrated into the total constellation. The questioning of the individual's certainty and decisiveness, however, results in a weakening of the entire constellation and tends to be punished by superiors.

STRONG SELF-STRUCTURE

One way of differentiating between people is in the relative strength or weakness of their notions of self-identity, their self-structure. Some persons lack definiteness and are easily influenced by outside pressures. Some, such as these executives, are firm and well-defined in their sense of self-identity. They know what they are and what they want and have well-developed techniques for getting what they want. The things they want and the techniques for getting them are, of course, quite different for each individual, but this strength and firmness is a common and necessary characteristic. It is, of course, true that too great a sense of self-identity leads to rigidity and inflexibility; and, while some of these executives could genuinely be accused of this, in general they maintain considerable flexibility and adaptability within the framework of their desires and within the often rather narrow possibilities of their own business organization.

ACTIVITY AND AGGRESSION

The executive is essentially an active, striving, aggressive person. His underlying motivations are active and aggressive—not necessarily is he aggressive and hostile overtly in his dealings with other people. This activity and aggressiveness are always well channeled into work or struggles for status and prestige—which implies a constant need to keep moving, to do something, to be active. This does not mean that they are always in bodily movement and moving physically from place to place (though this is often true) but rather that they are mentally and emotionally alert and active. This constant motivator unfortunately cannot be shut off. It may be part of the reason why so many executives find themselves unable to take vacations at leisure or to stop worrying about already solved problems.

APPREHENSION AND THE FEAR OF FAILURE

If one is continually active and always trying to solve problems and arrive at decisions, any inability to do so successfully may well result in feelings of frustration. This seems to be true of the executives. In spite of their firmness of character and their drive to activity, they also harbor a rather pervasive feeling that they may not really succeed and be able to do the things they want to do. It is not implied that this sense of frustration comes only from their immediate business experience. It seems far more likely to be a feeling of long standing within them and to be only accentuated and reinforced by their present business experience.

This sense of the perpetually unattained is an integral part of this constellation and is part of its dilemma. It means that there is always some place to go, but no defined point at which to stop. The executive is "self-propelled" and needs to keep moving always and to see another goal ever ahead, which also suggests that cessation of mobility and of struggling for new achievements will be accompanied by an inversion of this constant energy. The person whose mobility is blocked, either by his own limitations or by those of the social system, finds this energy diverted into other channels. Psychosomatic symptoms, the enlargement of interpersonal dissatisfactions, and the development of rationalized compulsive and/or paranoid-like defenses may reflect the redirection of this potent energy demand.

STRONG REALITY ORIENTATION

Successful executives are strongly oriented to immediate realities and their implications. They are directly interested in the practical, the immediate, and the direct. This is, of course, generally good for the immediate business situation, though the executive with an overdeveloped sense of reality may cease to be a man of vision; for a man of vision must get above reality to plan and even dream about future possibilities. In addition, a too strong sense of reality, when the realities are not in tune with ambitions, may well lead to a conviction that reality is frustrating and unpleasant. This happens to many executives who find progress and promotion too slow for their drives. The result is often a restlessness rather than an activity, a fidgetiness rather than a well-channeled aggression, and a lack of ease that may well disrupt many of their usual interpersonal relations.

THE NATURE OF THEIR INTERPERSONAL RELATIONS

In general the mobile and successful executive looks to his superiors with a feeling of personal attachment and tends to identify himself with them. His superior represents for him a symbol of his own achievement and desires, and he tends to identify himself with these traits in those who have achieved more. He is very responsive to his superiors—the nature of this responsiveness, of course, depends on his other feelings, his idea of authority, and the extent to which he feels frustrated.

On the other hand, he looks to his subordinates in a detached and impersonal way, seeing them as "doers of work" rather than as people. He treats them impersonally, with no real feeling of being akin to them or of having deep interest in them as persons. It is as though he viewed his subordinates as representatives of things he has left behind, both factually and emotionally. Still uncertain of his next forward step, he cannot afford to become personally identified or emotionally involved with the past. The only direction of his emotional energy that is real to him is upward and toward the symbols of that upward interest, his superiors.

This does not mean that he is cold and that he treats all subordinates casually. In fact he tends to be generally sympathetic with many of them. This element of sympathy with subordinates is most apparent when the subordinate shows personality traits that are most like those of the superior. Thus the superior is able to take pride in certain successful young persons without at the same time feeling an equal interest in all subordinates.

THE ATTITUDE TOWARD HIS OWN PARENTS

In a sense the successful executive is a "man who has left home." He feels and acts as though he were on his own, as though his emotional ties and obligations to his parents were severed. It seems to be most crucial that he has not retained resentment of his parents, but has rather simply broken their emotional hold on him and been left psychologically free to make his own decisions. We have found those who have not broken this tie to be either too dependent upon their superiors in the work situation or to be resentful of their supervision (depending, of course, upon whether they are still bound to their parents or are still actively fighting against them).

In general we find the relationship to the mother to have been the most clearly broken tie. The tie to the father remains positive in the sense that he views the father as a helpful but not restraining figure. Those men who still feel a strong emotional tie to the mother have systematically had difficulty in the business situation. This residual emotional tie seems contradictory to the necessary attitude of activity, progress, and channeled aggression. The tie to the father, however, must remain positive—as the emotional counterpart of the admired and more successful male figure. Without this image, struggle for success seems difficult.

THE NATURE OF DEPENDENCY FEELINGS AND CONCENTRATION UPON SELF

A special problem in differentiating the type of generally successful executive is the nature of his dependency feelings. It was pointed out above that the dependency upon the mother-image must be eliminated. For those executives who work within the framework of a large organization in which cooperation and group-and-company loyalty are necessities, there must remain feelings of dependency upon the father-image and a need to operate within an established framework. This does not mean that the activity-aggression need cannot operate or that the individual is not decisive and self-directional. It means only that he is so within the framework of an already established set of over-all goals. For most

executives this over-all framework provides a needed guidance and allows them to concentrate upon their achievement and work demands with only minimal concern for the policy-making of the entire organization. For those executives who prefer complete independence and who are unable to work within a framework established by somebody else, the element of narcissism is much higher and their feelings of loyalty are only to themselves rather than to a father-image or its impersonal counterpart in company policy. These feelings differentiate the executives who can cooperate with others and who can promote the over-all policy of a company from those who must be the whole show themselves. Clearly there are situations in which the person highly concentrated upon self and with little feeling of dependency loyalty is of great value. But he should be distinguished in advance and be placed in only situations in which these traits are useful.

The successful executive represents a crystallization of many of the attitudes and values generally accepted by middle-class American society. The value of accumulation and achievement, of self-directedness and independent thought and their rewards in prestige and status and property, are found in this group. But they also pay the price of holding these values and of profiting from them. Uncertainty, constant activity, the continual fear of losing ground, the inability to be introspectively leisurely, the ever present fear of failure, and the artificial limitations put upon their emotionalized interpersonal relations—these are some of the costs of this role.

One of the limitations in the material which we have just considered concerning the "fit" of the individual into the formal role of the business executive is that we do not have a clear-cut and explicit picture of how these people—those in Henry's composite picture—came to be as they are as particular personality types or as persons with particular self-images. We have seen how they do "fit" as adults, but we lack the historical dimension for a complete understanding of them. It is possible, of course, to formulate some hypotheses concerning the population described by Henry from the material presented by Aberle and Naegele in Chapter 3. But such hypotheses must remain tentative; they only provide leads or directions for future research in this area because the two studies do not deal with the same populations. We can only hypothesize that the children in the Aberle and Naegele study are also the adult subjects of Henry's paper and put this hypothesis to the empirical test. This remains for future inquiry.

At the same time, however, these two papers on the role system of the business executive illustrate admirably the general processes of "fit" and the dependence of an institutional or role system on a personality-type for its effective functioning. Barnard has given us an outline of the contours, boundaries, and imperatives of this system, and paralleling this outline, Henry's statement early in his paper that "in its economic and social aspects the role of the business executive . . . has clearly definable limits and characteristics . . ." implies boundaries and contours into which certain people "fit" and others do not. And Henry's analysis also enables us to see how the "self" mediates the "fit" or "not-fit" of the person into this system. For example, in his statement that "they conceive of themselves as hard-working and achieving persons . . ." we see one aspect of the self-perception of the person who successfully "fits" into this role; in Henry's finding that all "successful executives have strong mobility drives" can be observed the individual's perception of the sociological space which he occupies. Other aspects of the "self" of the successful executive emerge from the description of the particular kinds of relationships which he has—and which he "sees himself" as having—toward authority and, from the portrayal of his attitudes, toward his parents. It is true, for example, that many other kinds of people have strong drives for social mobility (as, for example, certain kinds of scientists), but the important point to keep in mind is the particular *combinations* of "self"-features *in relation to a particular set of institutional or role boundaries.* Thus, as will be seen shortly, certain kinds of scientists have strong mobility drives, but this orients the "self" toward particular role systems in an entirely different way when this factor is juxtaposed with different attitudes toward authority, parents, aggression, and so forth. One of the clearest statements in Henry's paper on the ways in which role boundaries and "self" interact with each other is to be found in his assertion that "whenever a junior executive loses [the] quality of decisiveness, he seems to pass out of the socially defined role."

In turning to the study of American scientists, we will be able to observe in somewhat clearer detail the development of certain personality features of participants in a second occupational system. Like many other role systems in contemporary American society, that of the scientist has become highly differentiated into various categories and subcategories. In the present context, we are going to be dealing almost exclusively with *academic* scientists who, it is our impression as well as others', are by temperament and level of creativity quite different from scientists in the employ of government and industry.[8]

The practice of an academic scientific vocation requires that the individual possess certain qualifications—personalitywise—just as one must possess parallel qualifications to "fit" into the role system of the business executive. To understand this, we must first get a picture of this scientific job. That is, we must find out what are the contours and boundaries of the role system of academic science into which a particular personality-type (or types) must fit; and, concomitantly, what is there in academic science, as a role system, which makes it dependent on particular personality types?

Let us begin by examining the relationship of the individual to his finished product within the boundaries of the scientific role system. Where the business executive may design and conceive of the material product which his company produces (even if it is a service), he does not necessarily have anything to do with the actual construction or fashioning of that product. The scientist, on the other hand, not only conceives of and designs the product which he turns out—his researches and his lectures—but he is in direct physical and concrete contact with that product at all times. At the same time, however, financial rewards accrue differently in both role systems: the executive's goal is usually monetary profit, and this may often vary with the rate and quality of his output; the scientist's goal is usually knowledge and professionally published articles or books, and as long as he maintains a minimum of productivity his income remains relatively constant within the stratum which he occupies in the structured hierarchy. (Income from outside the formal role system is usually disregarded in prestige rankings and evaluations.)

In his activities, the business executive is, by necessity and by definition, part of a "team." While the scientist is also a member of a bureaucratic organization, with its own lines of communication and its own systems of sanction and reward, and while "team" research and coauthored publications are increasing steadily in frequency, the scientist, at least in *theory,* and potentially, is a "lone wolf." If he wants to measure the effects of sixty drops of water on a nine-day-old egg, or if he wants to lecture to his class on the effects of earthquakes on California political organization, it makes little difference whether his colleagues are out playing golf or not. This is true at least as far as the imperatives of the formal role system are concerned.

We saw in Henry's analysis of the successful business executive that he has freed himself of his dependencies upon his parents; those who have not weaned themselves of these ties apparently have most difficulty in executive positions. Most specifically, this refers to dependency on the mother. "The tie to the father, however, must remain positive—as the emotional counterpart of the successful male figure. Without this image, struggle for success seems difficult." The demands of academic science as a formal role system, at least in the United States, imply

---

[8] For an elaboration of this admittedly dogmatic statement, see Whyte, 1956, especially Chapter 16, "The Fight Against Genius."

apparently different prototype relationships to parents. The demands of American academic science are such that a person functioning in such a role system must be ready to come to conclusions which are entirely independent of his feelings for other people or his ties to them—independent, as a matter of fact, of even his own personal beliefs.[9] This is an occupation which requires almost complete individuation; such a role system would, therefore, function most effectively when composed of persons who are predisposed, by virtue of their personalities, for a relatively high degree of individualism. And the prototype of all human ties, of course, are those which transpire in early family relationships.

But there are different kinds of science: the physical or natural sciences, which deal with nonhuman materials; the social sciences, which deal almost exclusively with problems in human behavior, but whose subject matter is no less physical or natural. The observation and analysis of human behavior implies and requires a certain aloofness and detachment from people. To observe and analyze behavior in a detached and disinterested manner equally calls for a relatively high degree of social distance *while* maintaining a high degree of contact with people. (That such a vocation may in turn reinforce and fit into the needs for distance and a subjectively felt sense of superiority is a separate problem, at least as far as the present analysis is concerned.) The subject matter of the physical sciences, on the other hand, does not require *the same kind* of aloofness and detachment from people, for these sciences do not deal with people. Thus, it could be hypothesized that persons who become social scientists would reveal a different kind of—that is, different goals and feelings in—distance and detachment from people in the family-prototype-situation than those who go on to become physical scientists. In other words, this hypothesis would lead us to expect that those who function best in the social sciences are people who have learned techniques of avoiding deep personal interactions *while still interacting with people* to a far greater extent than those who function best in the physical sciences.

It is sometimes said in half jest that one becomes an anthropologist because he cannot stand his culture; that one becomes a sociologist because he cannot stand his society; and that one becomes a psychologist because he cannot stand himself. Whether there is any element of truth in this bit of folklore is probably not for a social scientist to say. But there is another facet to being a scientist which is of far greater importance. The man who becomes a successful business executive undoubtedly has been brought up to place great personal value on financial profit, on material productivity, and on "pride of productivity." Also, he very likely has been taught, though not necessarily deliberately, in the course of his growing up to be far more concerned with *action* than abstract ideas, even though he recognizes the necessity of ideas as a means to an end. The stereotype of the scholarly scientist is clearly embodied in the popular adage that "those who can—do; those who can't—teach." To perform the roles of scientist, by contrast, one must place a high value—in terms of "good" or moral worth—on learning, knowl-

---

[9] For an opposing point of view of the categorical demands of science—that is, what they should be—see Rollo May's statement, 1958, especially pages 10-15.

edge, education, and scholarship. Such values are acquired as maturity is gained and they are part of an individual's self-system, for they express clearly his picture of himself, of his goals, his aspirations, and his sense of identity.

Many people are brought up to hold the values of knowledge very high, and yet only a few become academic scientists. And of those who do become scientists, some are far more creative than others. We do not know the reasons for this, nor do studies such as the one by Anne Roe tell us why some scientists are more adept at and have a greater proclivity for "tapping the resources of their unconscious" in work than do others, nor why a gifted minority of scientists have a flair for rapid and quick-fire insights which tend to transcend the limits and boundaries of their contemporary scientific fields. A full understanding of such processes is probably a long way off, and it undoubtedly falls more within the province of individual psychology than any other discipline. It has been mentioned here only to focus attention on one neglected area in these analyses.

Let us now turn to Anne Roe's study of American scientists to see how individuals "fit" into the role system of science, in terms of their personalities and in terms of the imperatives of the role system itself.

A PSYCHOLOGICAL STUDY OF EMINENT PSYCHOLOGISTS AND ANTHROPOLOGISTS, AND A COMPARISON WITH BIOLOGICAL AND PHYSICAL SCIENTISTS*

By Anne Roe

This is the third in a series of studies designed to investigate the existence of relationships between life history, intellectual functions or personality characteristics, and the selection and pursuit of a particular science as a profession. The subjects of the study are men who were selected for their eminence in research, as judged by their peers. The data comprise verbatim life histories, discussion of the work of the men and results of the Thematic Apperception Test, and the Rorschach. In addition, there were obtained, for comparison with these groups of eminent men, group Rorschachs of members of university faculties in the same fields. The psychologists have an

average age of 46.7, the anthropologists 49.4; for all social scientists the average age is 47.7. The physicists averaged 44.7 years and biologists 51.2.

Half of the psychologists and three of the anthropologists had professional fathers. Only 4 of the 14 psychologists came from families with rather good incomes, but 7 out of the 8 anthropologists came from families that were well-to-do. Incidence of the professional fathers in the other groups was 45 percent for the biologists and 73 percent for the physicists (experimentalists 50 percent; theorists 84 percent).

Number of children in the parental family and birth order of these subjects

* Excerpted from "A Psychological Study of Eminent Psychologists and Anthropologists, and a Comparison with Biological and Physical Scientists," by Anne Roe, *Psychological Monographs*, Vol. 67, No. 2, 1953.

are similar to those for the biologists and physicists. Comparison of the observed number of first-born with the calculated expected number shows the incidence of the first-born in these groups to be reliably greater than chance ($p < .01$). Cattell and Brimhall also remarked on the high incidence of first-born in their sample of 855 scientists. For their group it was possible to check incidence of first-born in each family size from 2 to 7 and in all of them it proved to be greater than chance. Of the 25 scientists in my group who were not first-born, 5 are oldest sons, and 2 of the second-born were effectively the oldest during their childhoods because of the death of older sibs, one at birth, one at age 2. Complete data are not available for 3, but for the others the average number of years between the subject and his next older brother was 5. The possible significance of this will be discussed later.

All of these men are married and most of them have children. Average age at marriage of all three groups of scientists is rather late, which is doubtless in part connected with the long educational histories. The social scientists, however, differ greatly from the others in the permanence of their marriages. Among the biologists there have been three divorces (15 percent); among the physicists, one (5 percent); but five of the psychologists (36 percent) and four of the anthropologists (50 percent) have been divorced, and of these several have been divorced more than once.

One of the striking differences between the social scientists and the others is the amount of material which was spontaneously offered in the interview. In part this may be due to the greater understanding among this group of the general problem and the relevance of details of personal history, but in perhaps larger part it is a reflection of their greater ease of verbalization.

The interviews were very little structured. The subject was asked at the outset for information on general family background, early family and school life, and everything that related to his choice of vocation. I interrupted as little as possible, usually only to clarify a point or to recall him to pertinent material. Later I asked specifically for information on health, religion, and present leisure interests, as well as on use of imagery. Sometimes the projective material suggested questions for later interviews, but under these circumstances deep probing is impossible. The combination of projective material and life histories recorded verbatim offers excellent cross checks.

This group [of psychologists] came from lower to upper-middle-class backgrounds and the economic level varied from quite poor to well-to-do. Many of them had feelings of apartness relative to themselves or their families but it is rare for these to be colored with inferiority feelings. More than half of them had some definite sense of personal or family superiority, and family concern with social status, in one way or another (as striving, as recollection of striving in the parental generation, or as conscious of belonging to the "best people").

Inquiries about health during childhood and later uncovered a number of problems of varying sorts, [but] it would appear that health and constitution have not played any clear role in this group generally. In only one instance does it seem likely that they contributed significantly to difficulties in social integration.

The average economic level of the anthropologists is clearly higher than that of the psychologists, and concern with the social status of the family or a firm conviction of the social superiority of the family is evident in all but one instance. This did not always result in the development of a definitely socially snobbish attitude in the subjects, but there is good evidence that most of them did consider themselves superior in one way or another. All but two went to private schools, either elementary or secondary, and this would certainly tend to foster these attitudes.

Health during childhood and adolescence was apparently good for only 3 of [the anthropologists]. Another had good health until an attack of rheumatic fever during secondary school, with some sequelae, which have not interfered in his field work. There are 5 who apparently had constitutional difficulties. Three were undersized or underweight, and in addition one of these had a number of allergies and the other had a number of serious illnesses, sufficient to have affected his early schooling. One was oversized ("I don't know whether it was pituitary or overeating, because eating was about the only satisfaction I had"). Another was always the tallest in his age group which sometimes gave rise to awkward situations. Another said, "My mother or at least I, had the idea that I was always a sickly child and I was always having to go to bed but there was nothing really wrong with me."

As in the case of the psychologists, the importance of the discovery of the possibility of doing research as a factor in choice of vocation is clear.

Although there is not much difference in the general socioeconomic background of the different group of scientists (except for the subgroup of theoretical physicists, 84 percent of whose fathers were professional men, as contrasted with about 50 percent in each of the other groups), there does seem to be a difference in their social attitudes. Among the biologists and physicists I encountered no direct expression of feelings of personal superiority and there were very few by inference. One of the physicists did say that the family considered themselves extra privileged in spite of their extreme poverty;

there are a few others who probably had some vague feelings of family superiority on one basis or another, and there are some who were conscious of their intellectual superiority, but they seem not to have translated this into social terms. It is, of course, not certain whether this is because these groups don't think in such terms, and hence it would not occur to them to mention it, or because they actually do not have such attitudes. I think it is primarily the latter, although the former may play some part in it—it is an aspect of their rather general indifference to or avoidance of personal interaction. But among the social scientists, in at least half of the psychologists and in most of the anthropologists, a feeling of social superiority has definitely played a role in their development. In some instances this feeling is a product of the family's or particularly the mother's strivings (or a paternal grandmother's).

In the matter of early interests (the term refers to spontaneous activities) this group differs markedly from the physical scientists, almost all of whom displayed early interest in mathematics, chemistry, physics or gadgeteering, and very few of whom were ever interested in literature or the humanities. Two of the psychologists and one anthropologist began in chemistry but quickly shifted. Literature and the classics, and less frequently social welfare interests, were common among both anthropologists and psychologists, as were some natural history interests, particularly among the anthropologists. The biologists included men whose early interests had been in natural history, in literature and in chemistry or physics, although the latter interest seems to have been aroused largely because these were the only sciences available in high school. In the histories of the social scientists and of the biologists the importance of the discovery of the possibility of doing research is highlighted, and this was often the factor that gave the final determination to their choice of vocation, or that fixed them in it once it was chosen. This particular aspect did not appear among the physical scientists, but this may well be because the difference between gadgeteering and experimental work is really a matter of degree and emphasis; the possibility of doing things yourself is obvious, whereas in the other fields it is not. It would seem that this may be an indictment of the pedagogical techniques in general use.

Among the biologists 5 lost father or mother before the age of 10, and the parents of two others were divorced (when the subjects were 9 and 16). Among the physicists, 5 lost a parent by death (at ages 5, 6, 9, 15 and 17) and the parents of one were divorced. There was only one divorce among the parents of the social scientists (and they remarried) but the mother of one of the anthropologists died at his birth and 4 psychologists lost their fathers by death (at 8, 12, 14 and 17) and one also his mother at 17. In the case of the biologists and physicists where the losses occurred very early, it seemed possibly to be a factor in the acceptance of isolation by the subjects, but among the psychologists and at least one of the physicists whose losses were later, the effect seems to have been more one of increasing the problems of adolescent reaction to authority, and this effect seems to have been greater in the case of the psychologists who have been more concerned with personal relations from the start.

A special factor, occurring generally only in the theoretical physicists, was the apparent effect of severe childhood illnesses which contributed to personal isolation. In all of the groups there are a number who had developmental problems related to constitution—abnormalities of size or general weakness. Unfortunately I have been unable to find comparative figures for the general population.

Patterns involving overprotection and firm, if not overt, control are very common in the group [of social scientists]. They are commoner among psychologists than among anthropologists among whom there was more overprotection and more open hostility. Over half of this group reacted with more rebelliousness than is generally usual, and of these a number are still angry or rejecting or disrespectful of one or both parents.

The data on intrafamily relations are more complete than for the other groups, partly because of the fact that these groups are professionally more aware of the possible significance of such relations and are generally freer in such discussions. But there is additional, if inferential, evidence from the TAT protocols, and I think there is no doubt that the groups do differ in these respects. Both the physicists and the biologists early developed ways of life which involved very much less of personal interaction, and neither group shows anything like the extent of rebelliousness and family difficulty that the psychologists and anthropologists show.

There are also many more in the other groups who were isolates as children, or who had only one or two close friends, and the age of beginning heterosexual interests is very different. Among the biologists and physicists it is rare for there to have been any extensive dating in high school or early college. Half of the social scientists began dating in high school and dated happily and extensively from then on. Only four of them did very little or no dating until they were through college. Two of the psychologists apparently never dated any girl but the one each married (rather late in life) and have never had much social life since. These are very atypical for the group. Although a number of the social scientists, particularly those from self-engrossed homes, speak of being shy for a time, shyness was rarely the serious problem that it was with many of the biologists and physicists.

There are two Jewish families in the social scientist group, one devout and the other non-practicing. The others are all Protestant families, with most of the major churches and several of the smaller groups represented. The parents usually attended church, but frequently for social reasons. Only two of the subjects ever go to church now and one does not do so for religious reasons.

About half of the parents of the psychologists were personally uninterested in religious matters (as demonstrated in church attendance), but only two families made a point of not attending church. Nevertheless it was customary to send the children to Sunday School and all of the Protestant children did go for at least a time, even the son of free-thinkers. Seven of the subjects stopped going fairly early, and while two encountered some family opposition in withdrawing there was no personal crisis or conflict over religion. Five others were quite active in various ways, in young peoples' societies, in the YMCA, in teaching Sunday School, and continued their interest through college or beyond. Three of these were professionally interested, one actually serving as a missionary for some time and two studying religious education.

Among the anthropologists the picture is similar. One of them who came from a Jewish family had a little religious schooling, but it was not important to his parents or to him. One was the son of parents who had a family tradition of agnosticism on both sides, and religion never was a concern to him. The other six were all sent to Sunday school, although the parents of two were personally uninterested. Four of these soon dropped out, usually because of boredom, but the other two retained interest for

some time, but have no church affiliations now.

Of the 64 scientists studied altogether, whose religious backgrounds were not known when they were selected, none came from Catholic families. Five came from Jewish homes, and all of the rest had Protestant backgrounds. These include two Mormons and two Quakers. Among all of them the picture is much the same. Most went to Sunday School; very few now have any church connections. Two biologists are very active in church work; another contributes to a church but does not attend. Among the physical scientists none is personally active in any church, although there are five who have maintained some church connections, usually to please their wives. Among the social scientists, one is still personally interested in church, one goes occasionally, but not for religious reasons, and one pays dues but never attends. A few of them are militantly agnostic, but for the most part they are just not interested.

Analysis of content [in the TAT protocols] shows striking differences. Both biologists and physicists are much less interested in interpersonal relations generally, and more inclined to handle them in distance-getting ways than are the social scientists, although many of these are uneasy about them. But the unease is of a different sort and a manifestation of a considerable concern with such relations, rather than a dislike for them. Both biologists and physicists show a considerable independence of parental relations, and without guilt, particularly in the case of the physicists, whereas the social scientists show many dependent attitudes and much rebelliousness, accompanied frequently by guilt feelings. The attitudes of helplessness so noticeable among the social scientists are much less common in the biologists and physicists. The biologists are definitely more restrained than the other two groups in their expression of aggressive attitudes; the social scientists are the freest in this respect.

What is most striking about these results, however, is the fact that the TAT rarely gives any indication that the subject is a man of considerable attainments. Sometimes, some amount of drive is shown, but for the most part this is not very evident in the stories, nor is there any clue in them as to what has made it possible for these men as a group to have achieved as conspicuously as they have.

Knowledge of Rorschach test varies in the group from none to fair acquaintance. . . . There are no major differences between psychologists and anthropologists with respect to their use of locations in the blots, and a particular pattern seems to be characteristic of most of them. They produce an absolutely large, but relatively small, number of whole responses—they can deal with large concepts, can generalize adequately, if sometimes sweepingly, but are usually more interested in smaller, and less often noticed details. They are quite good observers and tend to look at things which are not likely to strike most people. They are, however, quite casual and unsystematic in the way they go about things, sometimes to the extent of considerable disorganization in the approach. They are so productive, and so many responses occur to them so rapidly that they make no attempt to sort them out, nor do they need to rely upon any technique of procedure to stimulate further responses.

All of the social scientists give an adequate number of popular responses. A number of them tend to considerable use of original responses, about which they are likely to be rather uncritical. Anatomy and sex responses are relatively common, and are used by almost half of the group to an amount considered excessive. The range of responses is a rather curious and interesting one, since it is customarily very broad in terms of number of categories, and at the same time may show stereotyping or restrictedness of some sort. This is more often in terms of particular individual perseverations of themes, but the restriction may be in terms of excessive use of animal and human responses. The wide range would be associated with their general productivity and must also indicate a pretty general receptivity. That it does not mean an undesirable diffusion of interests would seem to follow from the fact that they are also restricted, as well as from their actual behavior. The frequent emphasis on human responses may well have vocational significance.

Form responses are those in which the concept is determined entirely by the outline of some blot area. Form quality indicates the general soundness of thinking, and more extensively of the soundness of the subject's contact with reality in general. Half of the group do not rate very high in this respect, since they receive entries for excessive use of poor or vague forms. The point may be the nature of the "reality." Psychologists are generally less concerned with what may be called external reality than they are with inner realities (e.g., motivation) and must often disregard the apparent reality and search further. (Is this rationalization?) This may be less true of anthropologists. Whatever the explanation, the fact is that social scientists are relatively unconcerned with formal qualities.

Shading responses are those in which the tonal quality of the blots is used as texture or vista. Shock is scored when disturbances in the level or time or quality of responses appear on the shaded cards. It is supposed to indicate serious anxiety. It may be a reflection of an insecurity related to early failures, or loss of interpersonal relations which have been accepted or somehow coped with; and that it is not necessarily by itself, a serious indication. It occurs in about 50 percent of this group and is severe in about half of those who show it at all.

Some of the anthropologists start a response with free action and then tone the action down so that it becomes very restricted. This is not characteristic of this subgroup generally, and does also happen among the psychologists although less frequently. It suggests as a possible interpretation a need to repress too direct an interest in persons. Anthropology would be a good vocation for those who feel this way, since the interest in persons can be followed in a somewhat depersonalized way. To some extent, this is also true of experimental psychology. The use of human movement in these subjects would indicate consistent interest in persons, but an interest which has been frequently restricted in some way and which is sometimes carried to extremes. . . . It is not the picture that they are generally self-absorbed, but rather that they have considerable emphatic capacity.

Perhaps the comments most frequently found in the individual analyses refer to the general productiveness of the men in these groups, to their rather uncritical attitudes, and a sort of haphazard use of rational controls—that is, that they can be rational when they wish to be but generally feel no compulsion to make a point of being so. A very great sensitivity is also extremely noticeable in almost all of the records and it usually implies a great awareness of other persons. It may sometimes result in any easy irritability, but I think more often not. In most of the protocols, there is evident fairly free aggression, which is clearer and stronger generally among anthropologists, and more obviously oral among the psychologists. There are a number in which there seems to be a strong consciousness of hidden things, but this is not always accompanied by anxiety. Most of the subjects are fairly warm persons, but this is not always the case. Conflict over dominance and authority is common. There is also evidence, particularly among the psychologists, of needing to hold and to feel nurturant attitudes.

The Rorschachs from these 22 social scientists can now be compared with those obtained from the 20 biologists and the 19 physical scientists previously studied.

It appears that the social scientists are significantly more productive on the Rorschach; that the biologists use relatively fewer responses not dominated by form than the others; and that the biologists are definitely the best adjusted. The two latter differences are certainly related, since the nature of adjustment shown by the biologists is one in which rational control and caution are emphasized.

Some qualitative differences may be indicated also. The biologists are the least freely aggressive; the social scientists, particularly the anthropologists, the most so, and with greater likelihood of oral elements. There are great differences between the biologists and physicists in their handling of anxiety, but the social scientists show no consistency in this respect. In the over-all picture the similarities are greater than the differences. This is to be expected from the fact that there is considerable heterogeneity within the separate groups, and from the fact that these men are all functioning adequately.

The group Rorschach was given to 104 psychologists and 25 anthropologists members of university faculties. Only 9 checklist items show significant differences; these, if they can be accepted at face value, would indicate that the eminent group, in addition to its greater productivity, used fewer whole and more unusual detail responses, including more anatomy and sex responses and more concept-dominated series of responses, and finally, tended to proportionately more color than movement responses. These can be subsumed under a general attitude of greater productivity and reactivity, more originality, and less control.

Comparison of eminent biologists with other biologists produced a different picture—the more eminent men had rather better controlled, if somewhat more restricted, protocols. Here the opposite is true. In the case of physicists no important differences were found. Comparisons on the checklist between all of the eminent men and all of those who took the group Rorschach show a few major differences which are not related to the longer individual protocols. Among these the most marked are the greater use of unusual blot areas by the eminent men, and their freer use of anatomy and sex responses and of perseverating responses.

The direct study of eminent men raises numerous and very difficult problems. One clearly does not have the complete freedom of a biographer writing centuries after the lifetime of the subject. But these difficulties are more than compensated for by the value of direct clinical and test data.

It is evident that the family backgrounds of the 64 scientists studied are by no means randomly selected with respect to the population at large. According to census reports for 1910 only 3 percent of the gainfully employed men in the country were professional men. One-eighth of the group came from farm homes; and the fathers of 31 percent were in business, many of them owning their own. Only two fathers were skilled laborers. None of the scientists came from homes in which the father was an unskilled laborer and none came from families of very great wealth. Cattell and Brimhall in 1921 found 51 percent incidence of professional fathers for the 66 leading scientists they studied.

What seems to be the operative factor here is that in practically all of these homes, whatever the occupation of the father, learning was valued for its own sake. Its concomitants in terms of possible better income or social position were not scorned, but it was rare for these to be the most important factor. This certainly was a major factor in the facilitation of intellectualization of interests. In my opinion this, rather than the possible associated intellectual levels, is the important aspect here. "Over-intellectualization" may be a middle-class characteristic and it may interfere with libidinal development in other spheres, as some psychoanalytic writers have pointed out. Yet it seems to me doubtful whether one can develop the sort of intense personal involvement which is characteristic of these scientists without some degree of this, if a channeling of energy in one direction means a lessening of it in others. There is a serious problem here. Unquestionably overintellectualization is frequently a technique for escaping emotional problems, especially those bound up in interpersonal relationships, but it is not necessarily so. I believe it is possible to concentrate upon intellectual activities without having a relatively sterile life emotionally, but we certainly have not developed educational techniques which foster this.

I have reported a greater than chance incidence of first-born among these eminent men. The problem of birth order is an extremely tricky matter statistically, and I would not be inclined to pay much attention to this finding in a group of 64 were it not that Cattell and Brimhall reported the same finding in a group of 855 scientists. It could be argued that the point here also is that intelligence levels are higher in the first-born, for which there is some evidence, but it seems much more probable that both of these facts are results of the same cause, whatever that is.

Certain aspects of the data offer evidence on the basic importance of the need to achieve or to keep independence which is so well met by a career in research. There are no Catholics in the group. The Protestant church to which all but five of the scientists' families belonged have varying degrees of insistence on the authority of the church over its members' interpretations of life, but all but three of these subjects have dismissed organized religion as a guide and usually had done so by late adolescence. In this respect, also, they have achieved independence. The dearth of Catholics in research science is corroborated in other studies and the Wesleyan survey found that production of scientists from Catholic institutions is uniformly low.

More of these men than not, as boys, pursued rather independent paths, playing with one or a few close friends, instead of with a gang, following their own particular interests (shifting or not) with somewhat more than the usual intensity. There are some to whom this does not apply, but it is fairly characteristic, and such interests were more often intellectual than not, except among the experimental physicists and biochemists. It is, of course, true that their high level of intelligence would, in itself, have some of these effects.

There are no general patterns by which they approached science as a career. The modal age at which the decision was made was during the last two undergraduate years, but in some cases it was made in early childhood or as late as the second year of graduate work. The introduction may have been through natural history interests, through gadgeteering, through interest in laboratory sciences as found in high school courses, or for the social scientists, through dissatisfaction with literature as a means of studying the behavior of people, or through a service motivation. When the decisive point can be determined it was usually the discovery of the possibility of doing research, of

finding out things for oneself. For some this was understood very early—as with those experimental physicists who spent much of their childhood playing with erector sets, radios, and all the other equipment that permit manipulation and construction. For others, it came as a revelation of unique moment. Once it was understood that personal research was possible, once some research had actually been accomplished, there was never any question. This was it. The educational implications are obvious enough. There has been no question since. From then on, absorption in the vocation was so complete as seriously to limit all other activities. In the case of the social scientists, at least for those for whom people themselves provide the data, this did not limit social participation; for the others it intensified an already present disinterest. Although a few of them have cut down somewhat on their hours of work as they have grown older, it is still the common pattern for them to work nights, Sundays, holidays, as they always have.

Most of them are happiest when they are working—some only when they are working. In all of these instances, other aspects—economic return, social and professional status—are of secondary importance.

Being curious plays a major role— a trait which many aspects of our educational practice tend to discourage. It is of crucial importance that these men set their own problems and investigate what interests them. No one tells them what to think about, or when, or how. Here they have almost perfect freedom. Their limitations are only those of equipment and time, and the limitations of their own understanding.

The question also arises as to why one subject chose one field of science and others chose other fields. Apart from the often overlooked matter of necessary contact with the field, there is some further evidence from the study. The problem of coping with early affectional loss has been mentioned. It would also appear that there are some, particularly among the experimental physicists, who seem early to have formed direct relationships with objects rather than people, not compensatorily. In others, a generalized anxiety, of unknown cause, and possibly only an exacerbation of normal anxiety, is alleviated by concentration on a particular field. For example, I know biochemists who seem to me to live in a very dangerous world—they are always conscious of the presence about them of dangerous microorganisms. They tolerate this in part because they are able to manipulate these organisms to some extent professionally. I am sure, however, that to them psychologists live in an equally dangerous world, surrounded by irrational emotional people, a situation which they would find quite intolerable.

The social scientists stand apart as having been more concerned at an earlier age, about personal relations (or as being willing to tolerate this concern as such, without translation). This may reflect an unconscious uncertainty over the consciously felt superiority that characterized half of the psychologists and most of the anthropologists. It is also certainly related to their difficulties in freeing themselves from their parents. The other groups seem to have been able, fairly early, to work out an adaptation not nearly so dependent upon personal relationships, but rather strikingly independent of them.

Certainly psychology to some extent, particularly social psychology, and anthropology to a large extent, particularly cultural anthropology, offer an ideal vocation to the person whose conviction of personal superiority is not accompanied by asocial characteristics; they permit a somewhat Jovian survey of their own society as well as others, and maintain the social scientist in a state of superiority just because he is able to make the survey. (This accounts nicely for the observation that some rather paranoid indications in the test material are not accompanied by forms of paranoid behavior, except perhaps as regards their own colleagues.) The experimental psychologists are generally less concerned with people as people, although this is by no means true of all of them. The further observations that a conflict over dominance and authority is common in the group, and that in a number of their homes the mother was dominant indicate the possibility of difficulties in achieving masculine identification.

In this respect it would seem very probable that the physicists, particularly the experimentalists, were able to identify more easily with their fathers than the other groups and hence to follow comfortably in science which has rather more of a "masculine" tinge in our culture than the others do.

Another finding of considerable importance is the differences of imagery which are associated with the different fields of science, and which accord with and perhaps explain some of the test data. Briefly, the biologists and experimental physicists tend strongly to dependence upon visual imagery in their thinking; the theoretical physicists and the social scientists, to dependence upon verbalization or similar symbolization in theirs. Nothing is known about the development of these modes of thinking, but it seems probable that they were developed early (they are associated with father's occupation) and played a part in the choice of a science. Further, it was shown that those scientists whose preferred mode of thinking differed from that characteristic for their science also differed in some aspects of their early history, and in the things they did or the ways they went about their work. (This is good reason for not using such a factor selectively—their contributions have a special place.) The domination of the formal qualities of the blots in the biologists' Rorschachs, which the others do not show, is in accord with this, as is the generally much more fluid verbalization of the social scientists.

Doubtless, also, some intellectual factors enter. So far as the test used is a measure of these, it is clear that the theoretical physicists surpass all other groups on both verbal and spatial tests. The experimental physicists are high on the spatial and relatively very low on the verbal test. Psychologists are at about the mean for this total group on all three. Anthropologists are high on the verbal and lowest on both spatial and mathematical. These patternings are probably of importance in selection of vocation—particularly the relatively low nonverbal abilities of the anthropologists and the relatively low verbal ability of the experimental physicists.

In the foregoing selection, Dr. Roe has given a startlingly clear portrayal of the personality of the academic scientist and differences between different types of scientists; unfortunately, due to limitations of space, it has been possible to present only a limited amount of her data. But her data support strongly our hypotheses concerning the relationships between the imperatives of academic science and its various subdisciplines, on the one hand, and the "self" of the person who participates in his chosen field, on the other.

Necessary to the role system of academic science are "rugged individualists," and these it tends to recruit, at least as far as the truly creative men of eminence are concerned. And Dr. Roe has also shown how such personalities develop. But independence and individualism can take several forms and have multiple sources; and the structures and origins—in juxtaposition with each other—of these personality characteristics selectively "fit" into one subdiscipline (or role system) or another. Thus, the social scientists develop a sense of apartness and independence largely through their rebellion against their parents, through a sense of social superiority, in their interest in and concern with personal relations, and so forth. From the Rorschach material, it appears that one of the factors directing people toward psychology or anthropology is that psychologists are generally more concerned with internal reality while anthropologists are more concerned with external reality. The physical scientists develop a sense of apartness and independence through a set of factors which tended to encourage early social isolation and they tend to handle people in distance-getting ways. There is, in brief, a very neat interplay here between the ways in which people "fit" into a role system and the ways in which this system depends on particular personality-types, especially through its recruitment of these types.

SUMMARY

To summarize this chapter: an attempt has been made to spell out some of the theoretical tools necessary for an exploration of the relationship between personality and social institutions. For purposes of sociological analysis, this discussion has focussed on the "self" as a subsystem of personality which, it was posited, relates personality and social institutions in such a way that they "lock" into each other. The "self" is the subsystem of the personality which enables the person to "fit" into an institutional or role system and which enables him to maintain that sociological system. It was also emphasized that paralleling a conceptualization of the "self" must be as clear an outline as possible of the nature of the institution under consideration.

To illustrate this approach, the role systems of the business executive and of the academic scientist were examined. In each case, it was shown that persons with particular kinds of self-systems were recruited for the respective role systems and that, reciprocally, these self-systems helped to maintain the institution, in terms of the latter's imperatives. In the case of the business executive, institutional demands necessitate the recruitment of persons who maintain strong masculine identifications, who are able to accept authority and to delegate it. The role system of academic science, on the other hand, seems to recruit and to depend on individuals who have largely rebelled against parental authority, who work as "lone wolves," who value intellectual over financial achievements. Institutional imperatives of the two sociological systems demand quite different self-systems.

BIBLIOGRAPHY AND SUGGESTED READINGS

Caplow, Theodore and Reece J. McGee. *The Academic Marketplace.* New York: Basic Books, 1959. An anatomical-sociological study of the structure of the university, with a clear description of institutional pressures and criteria for success.

Cohen, Yehudi A. "Space, Science, and Society," *Midstream, Vol. 4,* pp. 26-40, Spring 1958. An attempt to place the materials of the second part of this chapter in the perspective of political climates.

Fenichel, Otto. *The Psychoanalytic Theory of Neurosis.* New York: Norton, 1945.

Fisher, Seymour and Sidney E. Cleveland. *Body Image and Personality.* Princeton, New Jersey: Van Nostrand, 1958. A modern approach to the "self."

Fromm, Erich. *Man for Himself.* New York: Holt, Rinehart and Winston, 1947.

Goode, William J., Mary Jean Huntington, and Robert K. Merton. *The Professions in American Society.* Manuscript.

Hallowell, A. Irving. *Culture and Experience.* Philadelphia: University of Pennsylvania Press, 1955.

Hammer, Emanuel F. (editor). *The Clinical Application of Projective Drawings.* Springfield, Illinois: C. C. Thomas, 1958. A comprehensive survey of all types of drawings which can be employed as projective tests.

Hartmann, Heinz. *Ego Psychology and the Problem of Adaptation.* New York: International Universities Press, 1958. A basic introduction to the study of man's relationship to himself and to the world, as important today as it was at its first publication in 1939. Especially Chapter 2, "Adaptation."

Machover, Karen. *Personality Projection in the Drawing of the Human Figure.* Springfield, Ill.: C. C. Thomas, 1958. An empirical projective test which is probably, though not certainly, the least culture-bound of all the tests available, and which may eventually provide social scientists with a basis for a cross-cultural taxonomy of self-systems.

May, Rollo, Ernest Angel, and Henri F. Ellenberger (eds.). *Existence: A New Dimension in Psychiatry and Psychology.* New York: Basic Books, 1958.

Merton, Robert K. "Bureaucratic Structure and Personality," in *Personality in Nature, Society and Culture,* edited by Kluckhohn *et al.,* pp. 376-385. New York: Knopf, 1955. A classic study of the effects of participation in a role system on the personality of the participant.

Murphy, Gardner. *Personality: A Biosocial Approach to Origins and Structure.* New York: Harper, 1947.

Parsons, Talcott. "The Professions and Social Structure," in *Essays in Sociological Theory* (revised edition), by Talcott Parsons, pp. 34-49. Glencoe, Illinois: The Free Press, 1949.

Roe, Anne. *The Psychology of Occupations.* New York: Wiley, 1956. This and the following book by Roe contain broader and more incisive analyses based on the material presented in this chapter.

Roe, Anne. *The Making of a Scientist.* New York: Dodd, 1953.

Schilder, Paul. *The Image and Appearance of the Human Body.* New York: International Universities Press, 1950. One of the original and germinal works on body-image theory and "self"; a difficult but rewarding book to read.

Tagiuri, Renato and Luigi Petrullo. *Person Perception and Interpersonal Behavior.* Stanford, California: Stanford University Press, 1958. A summary by more than twenty-five authors of current knowledge and research in self-perception and social behavior.

Whyte, William H., Jr. *The Organization Man.* New York: Simon & Schuster, 1956.

Witkin, H. A. *et al. Personality through Perception: An Experimental and Clinical Study.* New York: Harper, 1954.

Chapter 8

INSTITUTIONAL INTEGRATIONS

In the previous chapter analysis was made of processes regulating the "fit" of particular self-systems into the role systems of the business executive and the academic scientist and of some of the processes governing the dependence of these institutions on these self-systems for the institutions' effective functioning. The role systems of business executives and academic scientists are rather small systems. But as we move from these relatively restricted areas of social organization into broader areas which encompass larger segments of a society, we find that there are some instances in which the question of "fit" does not arise; rather, the question becomes one of the dependence of an institution on given self-systems for its effective functioning. Similarly, there are instances in which the question of the dependence of the institution on personality does not arise but the issue of "fit" becomes the strategic one.

It should be stated clearly at this point that we are not certain why some institutions involve *both* the questions of "fit" and "dependence"; why some involve *only* the question of "fit"; and why some involve *only* the question of "dependence." It is to be hoped that sufficient research into these problems will someday enable us to formulate some generalizations about them. In the meantime, however, it can be hypothesized tentatively that those institutions and role systems which rely on *universal* recruitment from the total population—for example, the Western army or the legal system—involve only the question of "dependence," not "fit"; those which recruit *selectively* from limited segments of the population—for example, business executives, academic scientists, caste—involve at least the question of "fit," and sometimes "dependence," too.

In this chapter three institutions will be examined: military structure, caste structure, and legal systems. In the first and the third, the principal issue will be the dependence of the institutions on personality; in the case of caste structure, the central problem will be the question of "fit."

MILITARY STRUCTURE

Contemporary military organization, especially in the United States, is so structured—because of perceived social needs—that it relies on almost universal

225

recruitment of late adolescent and young adult males. As such, it draws upon all social strata; all ethnic groups, with minor exceptions; and all regions of the country. In its basic outlines, military organization is roughly similar throughout the Western world. This basic similarity refers to a caste-like division of commissioned officers and enlisted men, horizontal as well as vertical lines of communication, and patterns of authority underlying these vertical lines of communication. As such, it is different from a Masai warrior group, a Plains raiding party, or a Murngin retaliatory party bent on blood-vengeance. Western military structure is based on masses of men dependent on highly complex means of supply; they are subject to distant, anonymous, arbitrary authority which is transmitted through the vertical lines of communication. The goals of Western military structure are roughly the same through the civilized world; the structure's relationship to its respective total society is almost uniquely peculiar to the Western world, and it is relatively uniform in nature from society to society within that geographical area, although some Eastern armies resemble Western ones in many respects. These criteria, then, provide a basis for comparison of military organizations between different Western nations.

With respect to the relationship of the individual to the institutional framework of the military in the United States, for example, the question of "fit" is not of immediate theoretical relevance. The structure has several unique means of disposing of individuals who do not "fit," one of which is through the "Uniform Code of Military Justice," which defines customary and deviant behavior in *penal* terms. This code was subject to drastic revisions after the Second World War, probably due to the shift from the reliance of the American army upon a special class of persons (the pre-war, peacetime soldier) to a dependence on *mass peacetime* recruitment. In other words, given its new raw material, namely, the conscripted "GI," on which it now relies entirely, the military structure redefined its all-encompassing penal code to cover *all* personality types, rather than the special types on which it relied before the Second World War. It did not (because it could not) demand that the mass citizenry "fit" itself into the old and traditional military concepts during peacetime; it was almost as if the rational ideology changed to meet the changing conditions of different kinds of personnel, namely, the reluctant nonprofessional soldier or sailor. To hypothesize—the pre-World War II American army was the kind of institution which involved the question of "fit," the post-World War II army is an institution in which, at least in theory, the question of "fit" is no longer relevant.

Although Spindler's paper on "American Character as Revealed by the Military," which will be read in a moment, was devoted primarily to an attempt at uncovering American personality characteristics through an analysis of relationships within the military structure, it can also be used for the purposes under discussion here. It can be taken as *given* that the American's "high valuation of self makes him reject any competing value" *vis-à-vis* the German's greater emphasis upon and need for group belongingness and identity. Thus, in the dependence of the military on the modal personality structure in either country, *slight variations within a common pattern emerge in the institutional contours.* In the American army, Spindler (an anthropologist) noted a neglect by officers of enlisted men's needs—this being related to American modal attitudes toward status and authority—and weak authority and discipline. The military ideal of tightly knit and solidary groups cannot function with the raw personality material of the American; concomitantly, group solidarity in the American army was comparatively weak. These modal differences between the German and American valuations of "self" appear to have strong historical roots; in a comparison of American and German frontier movements and expansion, Gerhard notes that in the German expanding frontier, "whether the land was distributed in separate strips or whether a contiguous piece of land could be managed from one farm, the form of settlements almost everywhere was the village, not the individual farmstead," [1] while in the American case individual farmsteads were the general rule. Given the German's modal attitudes toward "self," status, and authority—which also appear, from Gerhard's analysis of the expanding frontier, to have historical roots—several things are understandable: (1) that status differentiations in the German army were more clearly demarcated and accepted than in the American army; (2) that authority and discipline remained strong, with a consistent adherence to explicit rules and maintenance of lines of communication; and (3) that strong group solidarity was characteristic of the system. If the American army, at least on a nonformal level, did not make allowances for the institutional consequences of general American personality processes, it would have failed completely in achieving its goals; similarly, the German army had to make its own allowances. Simply put, general American personality processes *set the limits* for the final shape of the small-group nuclei of American military structure; similarly, characteristic German personality processes set comparable limits for the internal organization of the latter's military structure.

AMERICAN CHARACTER AS REVEALED BY THE MILITARY*

By George D. Spindler

Though much has been written about American "character," relatively little has been accomplished in a systematic way because of the complexity of the source of personality—American culture. Social stratification and regional differences blur the picture. Middle-class Americans seem more like their European counterparts than they do their fellow countrymen above and below them in the class structure, and the western rancher and the eastern farmer seem to have little in common other than fresh air.

If any broad but valid generalizations are going to be made about a national character structure, a control situation must be utilized. Lacking a neat laboratory abstraction, the social scientist must use what already exists in social and psychological reality, applying objective methods in systematic analyses.

The ideal control situation is not easy

[1] Gerhard, 1959, pp. 220-221.
* From *Psychiatry*, Vol. *11*, pp. 275-281, 1948. Reprinted by special permission of The William Alanson White Psychiatric Foundation, Inc., by whom the copyright is held.

to find. It must lend itself to accurate definitional analysis; it must be a situation that involves a cross section of the whole cultural population; and if valid cross-comparisons are to be made to provide illumination of the conclusions reached, it must be one which is held in common by several different cultural units.

One of the few situations that meets these criteria is the military. Every Western nation has one; they involve, especially in time of war, an immense sample of the national group; and their structural elements are universally similar.

In the process of human adjustment, personality is revealed. If it is known specifically what is being adjusted to and the aggregate of adjusting units is large enough, it is possible to abstract the essence of group personality. It is in this way that the military can be used, after it has been analyzed and defined.

By setting up the problem in this manner, some of the usual difficulties may be avoided. If individuals from the whole range of class and regional backgrounds show something in common in their adjustment responses to a defined situation, that element may safely be included as part of the national character. It cannot necessarily be stated that it is *the* national character, but at least that element is present in enough cases to make it significant, and several of those elements combined together create a personality type that may have important predictive value in problems dealing with the psychology or sociology of the society under consideration.

In this paper the elements of the military will be summarized, the adjustments of Americans to these elements described as typical attitudinal tendencies, and some hypothetical arguments for their sociocultural origin posited.

A basic premise that many analytic attempts have failed to consider is that different orders of phenomena must be separated: the adjustments of soldiers to the military, and the characteristics of the military itself. An admittedly artificial separation, it is nevertheless vital to clear description and systematic procedure. In the following summary that separation is intended.

The military is a self-contained, vicinally isolated social entity. It provides for all of the primary biological needs excepting the sex drive and all the socio-psychological needs excepting those concerned with family interaction and heterosexual affection. The maternal functions of protection, nurture, welfare, and the paternal functions of authority, discipline, and justice are maintained. Because of these separative characteristics it may be termed a "subculture."

To analyze this subculture the social scientist may use the method of the non-dated and nonlocalized constructed type. Forms of social relationship and organization whose development may be predicted under certain general conditions can be used to provide the structural framework and their characteristics considered under the special impact of the situation being examined.

Two types of social structure are here considered to be especially pertinent to analysis of the military—the group or band and the bureaucracy. The former is the basic social relationship in all militaries, from the warrior band of Comanches to the amazingly complex modern army. The latter is especially characteristic of military organization in the West since the breakdown of feudalism.

Besides these typological concepts there are historical and functional aspects which must be considered. The heritage from feudalism, which is a historical force of major proportions, is common to all contemporary Western military organization. Though in many ways antithetical to the bureaucratization of the military, it has been thoroughly integrated into the system.

The functional forces that are effective are those involved in the ends to be attained, the destruction of the will, lives, and material resources of the enemy as an extension of the power of the state, and the means and instruments, the employment of masses of men and material in an organized, concentrated way to attain those ends.

The process of cultural diffusion has contributed directly to the specific content of the forms derived from these forces and provides one rationale for considering the military as universal in its characteristics throughout the entire West.

Following these methods, the element of significance for the group is found to be "intermindedness" or "social solidarity," as a sustaining force for cooperative action and morale. Men do not, as a rule, fight for abstractions. The drive is simple —"I can't let the other guys down."

Those elements related to the bureaucratic component are: a hierarchy of offices with parallels of status supported by ritual and social distance; the exercise of authority through these offices to maintain discipline; and integration, orderliness and coordination, supported by discipline, resulting in calculability of behavior.

These elements are typical of groups and bureaucracies everywhere. They are applicable to the military situation because the conditions for their formation are ideal. Groups of the primary type form whenever common experience is shared and intimate coexistence produces psychic interaction. The bureaucracy develops in every large-scale enterprise, where organization of authority and calculability of behavior is always necessary. The unusual interpersonal intimacy of life and the anxiety-producing type of experience in the military give group solidarity a special emphasis; and the absolute necessity for calculability in military operations exaggerates the bureaucratic components.

The essence of the heritage from feudalism, considered in its historical perspective, is the tendency of officer ranks to form "castes," supported by a system of special privilege, by certain culture complexes of the "horse and sword" type, and by the concept of differential honor. This heritage, integrated with and corollary to the hierarchical office statuses of the bureaucratic structure emphasizes the presumed superiority, in all areas of interaction, of the officer over the enlisted man.

The employment of masses of men and the machines of war for the ultimate purpose of subjugating the enemy and destroying his human and material resources gives the military the functional characteristic of "power." An accompanying element of individual masculine "virility-hardness" is inevitable if men are going to contribute force to a power organization.

For the sake of ease in handling the material the characteristics of the military may be condensed to: a hierarchy of offices with parallel status and overtones of "caste"; impersonalized authority and rigid discipline—exercised and maintained through these offices; power; orderliness and calculability; hardness-virility; group solidarity in the primary sense. These six elements may be regarded as a set of cultural stimuli to which each individual must respond and make adjustments as he enters and lives in the military. How he does so will depend upon his pre-service personality, molded by his life experience in the socio-psychological milieu provided by his mother culture.

The social psychologist's units of personality are values and attitudes. A value may be defined as "any element, common to a series of situations, which is capable of evoking a covert response in an individual," and an attitude as "the covert response evoked by such an element."

Attitudes vary greatly in specificity, as do the values to which they append. The evidence from clinical data shows that the most generalized value-attitude systems are acquired early in life. The systems acquired in adult life are more likely to be specific habits of response superimposed and integrated with the framework of the generalized system.

The adjustments of servicemen are behavioral responses that are the overt manifestations of value-attitude systems that they brought with them into service. The military subculture presents stimulus elements to them that they have already met in their mother culture and have acquired generalized attitudes towards. These attitudes are particularly emotionally laden because of the parental and ego-threatening aspects of the situation. Since generalized attitudes are capable of extension to any specific set of elements within a genera of elements, they determine the course of adjustment and are revealed by it. The description of American personality will be in these terms.

Generalizations must be based on minutiae. The following descriptions are based on War Department studies of the attitudes of the American troops; a questionnaire and interview study of veterans on the Wisconsin campus; the results of such investigations as the Doolittle committee on officer-enlisted man relationships; the participant-observer experience of the author—with checks provided by the observations of three other individuals; and the descriptive opinions of other social scientists. The material was first brought together by rank, then the attitudes and their value expression that proved to be most characteristic were abstracted into the series of generalizations

following. Allusions are made to the corresponding German type to provide a base-line comparison.

The American tends to place value on status only in relation to the amount his station commands. Senior officers were careful to maintain their status with appropriate ritual and rigidly maintained social distance. Junior officers somewhat guiltily accepted the implications of their role. Enlisted men completely rejected the whole business. The polls show almost unanimous resentment against the implications of the status hierarchy, and the "caste" tendencies of the system were the most violently rejected aspect of the military. It is also noteworthy that the officers, though accepting the system more than the enlisted men, did not value status highly for itself, but utilized it to secure personal benefits—the senior, his villas and private aircraft; the junior, his luxurious clubs, better food, transportation for pleasure, and avoidance of work. This tendency was carried so far that the needs of the enlisted men entrusted to the care of officers were seriously neglected and constituted one of the major weak points in the American military. This is to be contrasted to the willing acceptance of the status system and all its implications of "caste" by the Germans of all ranks, who found security in a definite hierarchical placement, and were somewhat less prone to abuse their position. The generalization to be derived here is that Americans resent status and "caste" when they don't have it but tend to use it, when they are favorably placed in the hierarchy, for self-oriented purposes.

Authority and its corollary—discipline—are given low value by the American. The only people who consistently value it positively are those who are responsible for its execution—mostly higher ranking officers. The adjustment of the majority on the receiving end is one of constant avoidance and negation. The sparse, but emotionally laden GI vocabulary is a good barometer of attitude. There are no terms approving of authority or discipline, and at least twenty-five most foul expressions denoting extreme distaste. One phenomenon, the very widespread looting and black-market activities of enlisted men and junior officers, deserves special mention. Though expressly and repeatedly defined in directives as a crime against military authority, it developed into big business, and openly, involving at least eighty percent of the personnel. Terms denoting "good looter" were terms of approbation. To generalize—the American values authority and discipline negatively. His high valuation of self makes him reject any competing value. Obedience to authority is ego-humbling since superior authority exists on the premise that the organization is more important than the individual, and authority exercises discipline to attain calculability which in itself means the dehumanization of relations and the immersion of the individual in the system. The German's "immediate obedience" trait and the anxiety about possible outbreaks against authority indicate a totally different sort of attitude.

Power is not the emotionally significant value to the American that it is to the German, who regards "Kraft" and "Recht" as synonymous. The mightiness of the military is regarded as a source of self-protection. American troops are extremely reluctant to advance unless the enemy position has been saturated with shells or bombs. Captured German officers frequently criticized the slowness and lack of determination of American attack.

Orderliness and calculability are prized highly by a minority of career officers and noncommissioned officers. But the majority of Americans responded to the military version of these elements negatively. "Efficiency," which was appreciated highly and was an important basis for morale, was considered to be the opposite of army order. There was nothing resembling the compulsive attitude of the German concerning the value of this element, and it seemed to furnish little security for the majority.

Hardness-virility is not regarded as an ideal to be attained by harsh disciplinary measures as it is by the German. Americans seem to discredit the masculine soldier-ideal. Their adjustment to the demands of this element is one of "tough-boy" aggressiveness. The swaggering, cocky, impudent gang-boy adjustment is more typical than the "iron heart in an iron body" one. Related to this characteristic, as one side of a coin is to the other, is the American attitude toward women. Their contempt for them and their somatic function is revealed by extravagant use of the term "fucking," which takes the place of practically every adjective or adverb with a disagreeable connotation.

Group solidarity is valued highly. In fact it is the only feature of the military for which Americans seem to have any nostalgia. They, like Germans, and all other fighting men, find it to be the source of emotional security under the stress of combat, or the exigencies of daily life away from home. In order to receive this security they must give up their ego. Under prolonged stress, however, the group becomes a threat to survival and to the renewal of bonds with loved ones because of the demands it exerts, and finally the men grasp tightly once more their egos and withdraw their "love" from the group. This happens sooner in the case of the American than it does for most other nationalities and is another indication of the egocentricism of the type.

It is obvious that the central orientation of the American character is self-interest, to the point of domination of all other values. It is the dynamic force that binds all the traits together, that gives to type its *Gestalt*.

The abuse of the privileges accorded status by the officers, the widespread blackmarket and looting activities of all lower ranks, the rejection of authoritarian and disciplinary demands that tend to overwhelm and subordinate the self, the reluctance to expose ego to damage until machine power has done all it can, and the relatively speedy withdrawal from the group when under stress, are all very positive indications of this central tendency. The "tough-boy" attitude is less directly integrated with the pattern, but it is related in its genesis. Pride in "efficiency" as against army "orderliness" is not a necessary corollary of the *Gestalt* but it does not detract from it and supports further the pattern of rejection of anything stemming from a superordinate entity.

The value-attitude systems described here are derived from two general sources: the culturally patterned behavior towards the child; and observation and instruction in the patterns of behavior characteristic of the individual's society.

Compared to a primitive, non-Western culture like that of the Alorese the culturally patterned behavior towards the child in the family situation shows some general similarity throughout the entire West. It consists of three main processes: good maternal care; discipline demanding obedience to parental directions; and restriction of the biologically determined drives broadly related to sex. This milieu furnishes Western man, in the broadest sense, with the potentialities for strong superego formation, based on willing introjection of parental demands; an attitudinal idealization of parents which tends to exaggerate their capacity for good and harm; and encouragement of the curiosity and executive capacities. The repressive features of taboo and restriction on pleasure-seeking impulses, particularly those related to genital sexuality, interfere with the difficult integrative tasks of childhood, creating anxieties that may be relieved by strict obedience or object-channelized hostilities.

If this generalization is valid it means that Western man is equipped with values and attitudes broadly capable of adjustment to the military situation and its particular demands, where discipline and order issue from authority that occupies the psychological position of parent. Despite the negation of the military elements by Americans this holds true for them or an effective army could not have been produced.

But because of historical accident, and a process of social evolution that is not completely understood, there exist many variants of this basic psychocultural theme. The modal German family apparently tends to emphasize more the disciplinary phases of paternal behavior towards the child, in a male-dominated society. This process doubtless plays an important role in the development of the German personality type alluded to in the previous section. On the other hand, there is some evidence that the contemporary American family emphasizes relatively less the disciplinary aspects, with the mother the center of both discipline and love, in a female-dominated society.

These "matriarchal" tendencies, to the extent they exist, extend maternal concern and care and tend towards overprotection. The psychodynamics of its results are complex, but among the most important effects is the inflation of the growing child's ego, to the extent that he may always be reluctant to surrender it to any group or interest not for his own direct personal benefit, or be placed in a subordinate position. This is directly pertinent to the characteristic egocentric orientation of the American. It further clarifies the relatively low value placed on status, power, authority, and discipline. They are not only dominated by self-value, but the coercion through love in the mother-dominated family does not prepare the individual for strict obedience or leave him with an attitude of over-exaggeration of authority's power. It also sheds light on the "tough-boy" attitude. It may be regarded as the unconscious attempt to shake off the shackles of dependency on "mother." The low estimation of women in general is probably a reaction against life-long domination by females.

This culturally conditioned behavior towards the child is the source of the most generalized value-attitude systems, capable of extension to any generically similar set of stimuli. Insofar as it exists as a uniform tendency among a modal population it is the source of an American basic personality structure. Beyond this the specific content of the character type and the degree to which the basic tendencies are expressed are defined by observation and instruction in the patterns of behavior characteristic of the individual's society. This latter field is more directly affected by social, economic, military, and political events than is the former. Experience in it will logically either reinforce or inhibit the tendencies established in the first field. The integration of the dynamic results of experience in both fields, the final result, including both form and content, is the social or "national" character.

The egocentric tendencies of the American type are so marked that it is safe to assume that they were formed in a process which involved reinforcement. The two fields are congruent in American culture.

Few Americans grow up without being imbued with the ideals of self-initiative, independence, individual freedom in religious, economic, and political affairs, and success—to be gained through personal endeavor. These egocentric values are fundamentally related to the frontier way of life that only recently passed from the American scene. Though they are today sometimes in direct conflict with the demands of an industrialized, urbanized society, they exist in force. Because of the conflict between ideal and reality Americans are particularly prone to anxieties, some of which find their expression in the high valuation of security-giving group solidarity. They also reinforce the egocentric-creating tendencies of the family milieu.

The impetus given ego-centered individualism by the "free-competition" type of capitalism that is still very active in this country is another important contributing factor. There is probably no attitude that is more typically American than: "I want to make a pile, and make it quick, and I don't care too much just how I do it." This force is so powerful that it alone accounts for much of the flavor of the character that has been described.

Protestant doctrines of salvation through good works, and the work ethic, "God looks after those that help themselves," are likewise functionally related to American egocentricism, acting as reinforcing, channelizing institutions which emphasize and shape the dynamic tendencies derived from early childhood experience.

The negation of authoritarian and disciplinary demands in the military situation finds its precedence in the institutionalized ideal of revolution. One of our hallowed documents, The Declaration of Independence, states ". . . whenever any form of government becomes destructive of these ends (life, liberty, and the pursuit of happiness), it is the right of the people to alter or abolish it . . ." The person who negates authority, who scorns status differentials associated with authority, meets approval. This is immensely different from the German situation where there is no precedence for revolt, there never having been a successful one, so no escape from or defiance of authority can be approved.

These social, political, economical, and religious forces impinge upon the broad outlines of the basic personality of the American child as he leaves his family and passes to maturity through instruction and experience in his culture's patterns and foibles, and so forms his character. The extent to which each person is exposed to all of the influences described in both fields is different in each case, but these tendencies are logically functionally related to the character type revealed and so seem to constitute a valid reconstruction of its genesis.

The military has been analyzed and defined into six major elements, the value-attitude systems of an American type in reference to those elements described, and some hypotheses for its psychocultural origin stated. The analysis of the military and the American characterological tendencies are valid. The hypotheses for their genesis are provisional and suggestive.

The method and its results have academic value because of the material it may reveal for an extension of our knowledge about the inter-relationship between personality and culture. It has practical value insofar as it may enhance prediction. Knowledge of this sort can be useful in the consideration of the development of an effective military force, or psychiatric problems related to the service. It can also be a dangerous weapon in the hands of a ruthless politician. Hitler utilized understanding of this sort in his appeal to the German people.

CASTE STRUCTURE

Thus far, two situations have been observed—the role systems of the business executive and the scientist—in which both the questions of "fit" and "dependence" were strategic and relevant; and one situation—military structure—in which the issue of *dependence,* but not "fit," were germane to an understanding of institutional processes. At this point we shall turn to a fourth, and sociologically more inclusive, institutional area in which the question of dependence of institutional organization on personality is almost entirely absent; instead, the question of "fit" is not only theoretically relevant but is crucial to the survival of many of the participants in the system. This is the institution of American caste.

Participation in the caste system of the United States is defined by biological inheritance; if the biological criteria were suddenly and magically to disappear, it is safe to predict that the caste structure would also disappear. But people's personalities and psychological needs, especially those of the dominant caste, would not change. Thus, caste structure is almost wholly *in*dependent of the personalities of the participants; in addition to its dependence on biological differentiations, it is by far more dependent on socioeconomic conditions which were set into motion by historical processes and which have become, to a large extent, somewhat self-perpetuating.

From the point of view of the relationship of personality to institutional processes, the most relevant and crucial issue is that of the "fit" of individuals into the caste system which, as was emphasized earlier, must be viewed as a "given," at least for sociological analysis. In the discussion of social structure and socialization, it was seen that, at least for the Negro in the United States, there are many facets to the world of caste, these being determined in large measure by geographical area and by social class. The economic opportunities open and available to a lower-class Negro are radically different from those available to an upper-class Negro. Correspondingly, a Negro child born into a lower-class household must and does learn an entirely different self-system from that acquired by a child born into an upper-class Negro family. We also saw that it is the specific image of "self" learned within the respective classes which prepares the individual later to "fit" into the socioeconomic institutions which are available to him.

The question of the "fit" of the Negro into the caste system is not one of helping to maintain the institution but is rather an issue of physical and emotional survival. Given the economic vicissitudes which confront a lower-class Negro in the border and southern states, namely, the availability of menial and unskilled work at extremely low wages, he must learn a self-system which pivots about low self-esteem, ingratiation to Whites, as well as distrust of Whites. If he is to survive physically, he must acquire a complete repertory of defenses which enable him to deny his aggression to Whites; these must be automatic responses because dangerous situations often arise spontaneously and without warning, as well as recurrently. If he fails to deny his aggression the results can often be realistically catastrophic; if his unconscious defenses against the display of aggression towards Whites begin to weaken, he may experience a sense of impending catastrophe to his "self."

In a volume on *The Mark of Oppression: a Psychological Study of the American Negro,* Abram Kardiner and Lionel Ovesey, two psychoanalysts, gathered considerable case material from Negroes of all social strata. Kardiner and Ovesey were concerned with two separate but closely interrelated problems: first, the effects of caste structure on the individual personality and, second, the psychological techniques or mechanisms which these individuals had to employ in order to survive and function within the realistic boundaries of that caste structure. The following selection is a brief résumé by them of their findings and conclusions.

NEGRO ADAPTATION: A PSYCHODYNAMIC ANALYSIS*

By Abram Kardiner and Lionel Ovesey

It is a consistent feature of human personality that it tends to become organized about the main problems of adaptation, and this main problem tends to polarize all other aspects of adaptation toward itself. This central problem of Negro adaptation is oriented toward the discrimination he suffers and the conse-

* From *The Mark of Oppression: A Psychosocial Study of the American Negro,* by Abram Kardiner and Lionel Ovesey, New York: W. W. Norton & Co., 1951, pp. 302-305.

quences of this discrimination for the self-referential aspects of his social orientation. In simple words, it means that his self-esteem suffers (which is self-referential) because he is constantly receiving an unpleasant image of himself from the behavior of others to him. This is the subjective impact of social discrimination, and it sounds as though its effects ought to be localized and limited in influence. This is not the case. It seems to be an ever-present and unrelieved irritant. Its influence is not alone due to the fact that it is painful in its intensity, but also because the individual, in order to maintain internal balance and to protect himself from being overwhelmed by it, must initiate restitutive measures in order to keep functioning —all quite automatic and unconscious. In addition to maintaining an internal balance, the individual must continue to maintain a social façade and some kind of adaptation to the offending stimuli so that he can preserve some social effectiveness. All of this requires a constant preoccupation, notwithstanding the fact that these adaptational processes all take place on a low level of awareness. The following is a diagram of a typical parallelogram of forces:

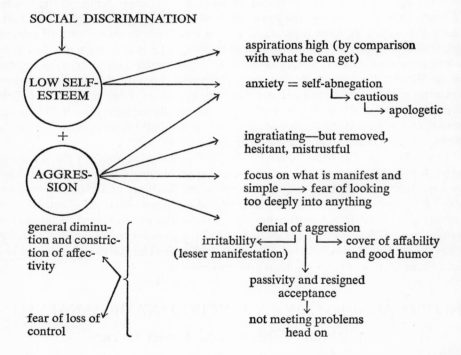

In the center of this adaptational scheme stand the low self-esteem (the self-referential part) and the aggression (the reactive part). The rest are maneuvers with these main constellations, to prevent their manifestations, to deny them and the sources from which they come, to make things look different from what they are, to replace aggressive activity *which would be socially disastrous* with more acceptable ingratiation and passivity. Keeping this system going means, however, being constantly ill at ease, mistrustful, and lacking in confidence. The entire system prevents the affectivity of the individual that might otherwise be available from asserting itself.

This is the adaptational range that is prescribed by the caste situation. This is, however, only a skeletal outline. Many types of elaboration are possible, particularly along projective or compensatory lines. . . .

The disposition of aggression is susceptible to elaboration. The conspicuous feature of rage lies in the fact that it is an emotion that primes the organism for motor expression. Hate is an attenuated form of rage, and is the emotion toward those who inspire fear and rage. The difficult problem for those who are constantly subject to frustration is how to contain this emotion and prevent its motor expression. The chief motive for the latter is to avoid setting in motion retaliatory aggression.

The most immediate effect of rage is, therefore, to set up a fear of its consequences. Fear and rage become almost interchangeable. When the manifesta-tions of rage are continually suppressed, ultimately the individual may cease to be aware of the emotion. In some subjects the *only* manifestation of rage may be fear.

The techniques for disposing of rage are varied. The simplest disposition is to suppress it and replace it with another emotional attitude—submission or compliance. The greater the rage, the more abject the submission. Thus, scraping and bowing, compliance and ingratiation may actually be indicators of suppressed rage and sustained hatred. Rage can be kept under control but replaced with an attenuated but sustained feeling—resentment. It may be kept under control, but ineffectively, and show itself in irritability. It may be kept under sustained control for long periods, and then become explosive. Rage may show itself in subtle forms of ingratiation for purposes of exploitation. It may finally be denied altogether (by an automatic process) and replaced by an entirely different kind of expression, like laughter, gaiety, or flippancy.

One of the characteristics of culture is that it provides the members of a society with a fairly complete range of predictions about the behavior of their fellows. Thus, all other things being equal, an American can predict how individuals are going to behave when they come to his home for dinner; he can predict the behavior of a teacher and students in a classroom, within limits; he can predict much of what a physician will do when visiting a patient; and the like. Such predictions are made generally without any realization that he, himself, is indulging in such behavior. He usually becomes conscious of the extent of his everyday predictions only when people deviate from the norm. Then, the American is likely to say, "Who would have thought he would do such a thing?" One of the very real problems confronting the lower-class Negro is that he *cannot* always predict how Whites are going to behave towards him. He knows that even kind Whites are to be distrusted, although one can occasionally allow oneself a degree of freedom when dealing with Whites who are not bigoted. But one can never generalize; this is a rule of the battlefield of caste. Hence, one of the requirements made on the Negro's personality, if he is to "fit" into the contours of the institution of caste and abide by its imperatives, is to evaluate every single situation on its own merits. White people, the lower-class Negro must know, are unpredictable, especially when they are thinking in economic terms. Hence, one must always be hesitant and wary, and one must approach every situation with a literalness which, in a white man, would be diagnosed psychiatrically as "obsessiveness." By literalness is meant that one must focus on what is manifestly clear and simple and avoid looking too deeply into anything involving people, for one can never know what really exists beneath the surface. If a lower-class Negro is to "fit," and if he is to avoid coming into overt physical conflict with the institutional structures about him, he must not only have a particular kind of self-image, and be ingratiating and passive and seemingly unaggressive, but he must also be an extremely literal individual.

The upper-class Negro, on the other hand, faces a considerably different reality of caste. First, as we have already seen, the upper-class Negro enjoys a degree of social and economic insulation which other Negroes do not possess. This protectiveness stems not only from the geographical self-sufficiency of upper-class Negro communities, but more so from the upper-class Negro's relatively complete independence of Whites in earning a living. The consequences of such insulation have been discussed previously. The upper-class Negro's self-portraiture is built to cope more with his relationships within the Negro caste than with Whites. His concerns, although they do, perforce, involve his identity as a Negro *vis-à-vis* Whites, primarily center about his identity as an *upper-class* Negro rather than just as a Negro. Thus, the question of "fit" which confronts an upper-class Negro pertains more to his relationships to other Negroes as a member of the upper class; the issue of "fit" into the caste system is important to him, for it will often determine the professional avenues which are open to him, but is not as crucial as it is to the lower-class Negro in terms of social and physical survival.

The institutional imperatives which confront an upper-class Negro are the institutional requirements of the Negro upper class. These, as we saw in our discussion of the inhibition of instinctual impulses within the various classes of both castes, involve a greater degree of internalized control over the processes of psychic life, specifically, over sexual and aggressive impulses. The lower-class Negro also is required to exercise an extreme degree of control over his aggressive impulses in general and over his sexual strivings with respect to Whites. But what is important is the fact that the upper-class Negro must develop such controls because of his relationships *within* the Negro caste, that is, because of his relationships to Negroes of other social classes. These controls are not required because of the possibility of *physical* threat, but rather because of *social* threat. They are required of the individual if he is to maintain his status—to "fit" into the position—of a member of the upper class. His self-portraiture, then, is more a function of his class position than it is of the quasi-legal pressures of caste.

LEGAL SYSTEMS

There are many parameters to any legal system; in the present discussion we will concern ourselves with the concepts of responsibility and liability as these are related to patterns of self-perception. One of the difficulties in dealing with legal systems in different societies is the fact that while every society possesses such a logical system which has evolved through time, not all legal codes are written, and this absence of written codes makes any comparative study of legal behavior difficult, to say the least. However, it is possible to compare these systems on certain levels and for particular purposes.

Legal scholars generally view the body of law of any society as a relatively autonomous system, built upon basic—although often changing—premises and building up into a highly symmetrical, internally consistent and logical system. At the same time, however, few, if any, students of comparative law assume that the law develops independently of other aspects of the culture and social structure of which it is a part. For example, almost every society has a set of legal concepts centering about and defining the status of women; these, examination soon discloses, closely reflect general social and cultural values of the status of women. Similarly, the laws of property and inheritance are generally direct outgrowths of, among other factors, the kinship system of a society.

While it is difficult to compare legal systems which are wholly unrelated to each other, there are characteristics which *all* share. First, a legal system is dependent upon and exists inside the totality of the experiences of the members of a society even though it may appear to be a relatively autonomous structure. Thus, all societies have definitions of the status of women and all have kinship systems; these are in turn reflected in their legal systems. Since we know that it is possible to compare societies according to their concepts of the status of women and according to their kinship systems, it follows that we should also be able to compare diverse and unrelated legal structures.

The second characteristic common to all legal systems—and with which we shall be primarily concerned in this section—is the concept of liability and responsibility. This concept states for which action or actions an individual is responsible and for which he must assume liability. Not all societies, of course, hold people liable and responsible for the same acts. For example, willful and deliberate murder is not considered criminal in all societies; concomitantly, such murder in some societies sets into motion different kinds of liability. In some, an individual has to answer to the state or another corporate political body for his act, while in still other societies the state can exact punishment not only from the murderer himself but from his kinsmen as well; in still others the murdered man's kinsmen can seek out the culprit or the latter's kinsmen and, on their own initiative, avenge the death of their fellow group member.

The question of which kinds of social structures have different definitions and conceptions of criminal behavior and responsibility is an extremely important one. But we are concerned here with an entirely different aspect of this problem, namely, the relationship between different conceptualizations of the "self" and notions of legal liability and responsibility.

It has been stressed repeatedly that any institution must be seen as part of meaningful human experiences and that we cannot look at institutions as "things" which can be replaced and substituted for each other like piston rings on an automobile. Thus, it would be "unthinkable," according to the formal legal system, for an American to accept responsibility or liability for a relative's criminal actions. It would be "unthinkable" for an American to be electrocuted for a murder committed by his brother or cousin, and it would be equally "unthinkable" for an American man to assume legal liability for his daughter's adultery, as among the Bantu Kavirondo about whom we shall read shortly. The investigations and discoveries of psychoanalysis leave little room to doubt that what we think is "thinkable" and "unthinkable" is closely related to emotional processes of the deepest order. This refers not only to the formalized systems of such philosophers as Kierkegaard and Nietzsche, but to the most central concepts of a total cultural system. While a society's concepts of liability and responsibility are generally defined in a formal manner, the legal *limits* of responsibility relate directly to the implicit values and feelings about "self" and others held by its members.

The *legal* concept of responsibility cannot exist in contradiction to the *feelings* of responsibility which people hold. These feelings are extensions of the self-systems of the members of a society, that is, the quality and structural positions of the ways in which people stand in relationship to each other and *see* themselves in relationship to each other. In a society in which the individual "selves" are so insulated from each other that the individuality of the person is viewed as paramount—by himself and by others—members could not be expected to extend their feelings of responsibility to include many persons. On the other hand, in a society in which the individual "self" has meaning only as a function of its positional standing *within a group,* it could be expected that feelings of responsibility would extend to many persons. To this extent, then, the concept of responsibility within a legal system—and such a concept is indispensable to any legal system—would be dependent on the processes of personality and self-perception which characterize the members of that group; that is, the self-system characteristic of the members of a society sets the *limits* for the *degree* or *range* of legal responsibility—in much the same fashion as the self-system of a society sets limits for the structure of small groups within a military organization.

It was said a moment ago that under one set of sociopsychological conditions people *extend* their feelings of responsibility to include many persons while under different conditions people do not make such extensions. The use of the term "extension" in this context implies two things. First, it implies a conscious or voluntary process. This implication should not be taken too literally, for we can seriously question the extent to which such processes are conscious and deliberate as well as the degree of control people have over such thought processes and action once certain values and self-systems have been set into motion.

The second implication is considerably more important. "Extension" implies "giving." All societal and human relationships are—or should be—reciprocal. Thus, "giving" implies "receiving." When an individual "extends" his feelings of responsibility and liability to include others he perforce expects—and has the right to expect —several other things in return. Most obviously, he expects the other persons to reciprocate such feelings of responsibility and liability. Such a principle of reciprocity refers, of course, to adults and rarely does it include children. For example, a man may be held liable and responsible for certain actions committed by his minor son. At the same time, however, the son is completely free of any liability or responsibility for his father's actions. In American society, a man's liability for his son's actions ends when the latter becomes an adult and at no time does the son become liable for any of his father's actions. In other societies, as among the Bantu Kavirondo, about whom we shall read, a son does not reciprocate legal liability and responsibility with his father while he is a minor, but he does assume legal liability for some of his father's actions—as well as the actions of some other people—when he becomes an adult.

The "extension" of feelings of responsibility implies a particular kind of emotional relationship among the members of a group. In a society in which an individual is *not* expected to extend his feelings of responsibility beyond himself, a considerable amount of insulation and isolation of the individual "self," a particular kind of emotional separateness, is found. Similarly, where extensions of feelings of responsibility include others the individual not only expects reciprocal feelings of responsibility to include his own actions, but also expects a particular kind of emotional support and acceptance from other members and from the group as a whole. Where an individual assumes responsibility for other members, he throws his emotional lot in with the rest of the group. Where he does not assume such responsibility, he plays a lone emotional game. Before going on to describe these relationships in two preliterate societies, let us attempt to illustrate some of these principles in American society.

One of the central themes in the structure of interpersonal relationships in the contemporary United States is the individual's need for independence and autonomy, a need which often appears to indicate a fear of too close or intimate association with other individuals and groups. Americans often seem to view extremely close and intimate ties with others as limiting their freedom of action, and they therefore take many psychological measures to insure their individual autonomy and independence. One of the greatest pressures placed on growing American children is that they act "independently" and with "autonomy." (This need for autonomy in American children has become so important in recent decades that one leading psychologist has suggested that the development of autonomy is one of the stages of development, and an early one at that. There is little evidence to support the notion that the development of a sense of autonomy is as great or as important in all societies.[2]) These self-perceptions in contemporary American society find their close parallels in the American legal system. Confining our examples to the family, which is the most tightly-knit group in the United States, we have already alluded to the discontinuity in legal relationships as they affect parent and child. A man is not liable or responsible for his wife's criminal actions, nor she for his. As a matter of fact, spouses may now sue each other in many jurisdictions, not only in matters involving

---

[2] See Erikson, 1950, pp. 222-224.

property but in matters involving bodily harm. Siblings have no legal liability or responsibility for each other's actions at any time of their lives. Children of any age have no liability or responsibility for their parent's actions and, as a matter of fact, cannot be held liable for the support of their parents—unless the latter are completely destitute. Curiously, one of the few instances in which Americans enter into a relationship involving joint liability is the corporation. But important to bear in mind in this connection is that a corporation is more often than not a *secondary* institution; in most cases it involves individuals who have never met and who have nothing to do with each other in the maintenance of the institution, except in very indirect ways.

It was pointed out in the discussion of "self" in Chapter 7, that every individual in every society must be permitted to maintain full awareness of the individuality of his "self." How can such self-awareness be maintained where an individual assumes responsibility for others and where others assume responsibility for him? Is there no *individual* responsibility in such societies? There is; and it is in the light of these questions that the notion of joint or shared responsibility and liability assumes its particular shape.

A short while ago it was stated that in a society in which the individual "self" has meaning only as a function of its positional standing *within a group,* feelings of responsibility would extend to many persons. In view of the necessity for the maintenance of individual self-awareness, it would be expected that a balance or "compromise" would be struck between the two. And this is exactly what happens. In societies in which there is joint or shared responsibility and liability there are actions or areas of behavior in which there is joint liability *and* areas in which there is purely personal or individual responsibility ("several liability," to use the technical legal term). In societies in which there is joint liability, the areas or actions covered by this principle are far fewer than those in which individual responsibility obtains. Thus, it would appear that the concept of joint liability is a "token" or "symbolic" one, but the fact that it exists is extremely important for an understanding of the relationship between personality processes and institutional processes.

To illustrate these principles we will take two cases. The first—the Yurok Indians of California—have a legal system quite similar to ours, though with some significant differences. The second—the Bantu Kavirondo of Kenya, in Africa—have a legal system very different from ours, and they will illustrate the concept of joint liability.

The Yurok Indians are hunters, fishermen, and gatherers who live near the Pacific Ocean in extreme northern California. Residence is in permanent villages which generally contain about twenty-five houses; there is a fairly frequent shifting of habitation both within and between villages. Game is sufficiently scarce to make salmon fishing the principal occupation, but famines are extremely rare. Within the village there is "no definite community sense" [3] and, hence, no larger political unity. The Yurok are patrilineal, "yet a group of kinsmen is not a circumscribed group, as a

---

[3] Kroeber, 1925, p. 14.

clan or village community or tribe would be." [4] The Yurok "might easily have had clans by making a rather slight addition to their social concepts. They did not make the addition, and remained without clans." [5]

All ownership is private and individual, "and the Yurok recognizes no public claim and the existence of no community. His world is wholly an aggregation of individuals." [6] All tracts of land are privately owned, as are fishing sites; the individual has rights of permanent alienation of land by sale. Furthermore, the Yurok possess their own currency, composed of dentalium shells and other scarce materials. Yurok finance is not highly elaborated but "the persistence with which the Yurok desire wealth is extraordinary." [7] The Yurok individual concerns himself with little else beside the quest and desire for personally and individually amassed wealth. "When he has leisure, he thinks of money; if in need, he calls upon it. He schemes constantly for opportunity to lodge a claim or to evade an obligation. No resource is too mean or devious for him to essay in this pursuit." [8]

An individual's position within the community is determined almost entirely by his economic position. Persons are enslaved only because of debt, never as the result of warfare. "Debt arose from legal rather than economic vicissitudes, Yurok industry and finance being insufficiently developed for a man to fall gradually into arrears from lack of subsistence or excessive borrowing. The usual cause was an act of physical violence or destruction of property; striking a rich man's son, for instance, or speaking the name of a dead person of wealth." [9]

Yurok social structure can be characterized as an individuated social system; this type of organization revolves around the nonsharing and personal amassment of wealth. (Some of the factors involved in this motivation will be discussed in Chapter 11.) Such economic behavior is the mainspring of *individuated* accumulation of wealth as an end in itself rather than as an intervening step in either cooperative or competitive generosity, sharing, reciprocity, and the like.

Intimately related to the absence of closed groups within an individuated social structure is the fact that wealth does not accrue to individuals who are politically dominant by virtue of inherited status; in such societies, sociological superordination and subordination derive almost directly from economic success and power. These statuses are not inviolate, and systems of ranking in this type of social structure—which, under certain conditions, become "class" systems—appear to be open and fluid. Stemming from the absence of closed groups is a highly individuated legal and moral responsibility; in such a society the group does not assume responsibility for the individual's actions under any circumstances.

With these principles of social structure and self-portraiture among the Yurok in mind—as an example of this kind of social system—let us now look at the prin-

---

[4] *Ibid.*, p. 21.
[5] *Ibid.*, pp. 5-6.
[6] *Ibid.*, p. 3.
[7] *Ibid.*, p. 40.
[8] *Ibid.*, p. 2.
[9] *Ibid.*, p. 32.

ciples of Yurok law. It should be possible, without our going into detail, to make some very realistic comparisons of Yurok and American law, relating these comparisons to common features on the social-structural level.

Professor Walter Goldschmidt writes of Yurok law, and its relationship to Yurok social structure, as follows:

The third feature of the protestant ethic of Northwest California society is the individuation of moral responsibility; that is, the placing of responsibility for the individual's worth and his acts upon the individual himself. He was neither the creature of some unseen power nor the product of circumstance, but the master of his own fate. To this there were exceptions, such as bastards whose circumstances of birth determined their character, and shamans, whose possession of power was viewed as lying beyond their individual will. But the normal citizen was held personally responsible for his acts and so conceived of himself.

We may see this conception in legal philosophy, with its recognition of liability and intent. Indeed, liability laws placed responsibility upon an individual in a more far-reaching manner than our own, perhaps because of a certain underlying magical identification between the individual and his property. With respect to Yurok law, Kroeber has written that "damage must be fully compensated for even though inflicted without a shadow of intent; but if the infringement is willful, or malice is evident, added compensation is due for intent." More impressive, though less direct, are the psychological implications of the recognition that wounding a man is less serious than drawing a bead without shooting. The explanation can only lie in the concept of intent or the philosophical notion of will, where it is assumed that in wounding a man the intent to wound is evident, but in drawing a bead the intent to kill is evident. . . .

Closely associated with this individuated self are the concepts of sin and guilt, which were to be found among the Northwest Californians. Present tribal members regularly use the word "sin" to describe morally disapproved behavior. The White Deerskin Dance is specifically designed to rid the world of the contaminating influence of the cumulative sins of individuals of their commmuty. Descriptions of child-rearing practices indicate the direct, overt introduction of these notions in the constant moralizing and placing of responsibility upon the child for his own conduct. The evidence for the internalization of this pattern of responsibility, and its expression in the form of guilt, is somewhat nebulous, but not entirely wanting. Aside from the conceptualization of sin and the expression of deep moral concern over wrongdoing, it appears in one rather unique situation. In the treatment of certain sick children, the shaman decides that there is no intrusive disease object, but that the immoral act of some ancestor is responsible. . . .

Kroeber says of these stories that "the sin committed is always extremely shameful in native eyes, though to us it may approach the venial. In fact, the nature of the wrongdoing illustrates vividly the Yurok puritanical preoccupation with sin. The guilt is religious: something impure and defiling is involved. But it is also a violation of custom, law, and recognized morals." This is not the place to examine in detail the implications of this remarkable practice (of confession sins which may have caused children's illnesses), with its analogy both to the Catholic confessional and present-day psychoanalytical practice. But it does offer evidence of the personalization of the moral act and the internalization of guilt.

Finally, this pattern of individuation is expressed in the personality characteristics of the people. The Northwest Californian is extremely aggressive in his interpersonal relations; he is hostile to his fellow men and expects hostility toward himself; he never relaxes his barriers of suspicion. The myths demonstrate these components which may be observed in the real world—aggressiveness, bickering and drive toward personal success. They also demonstrate certain reaction patterns—compulsive demand to work, withdrawal in the geographic sense and obedience and submission to the absolute powers of the creator gods.

Other personality traits were also involved. There was a constant theme of loneliness running through the mythology, and loneliness is an expected concomitant of individuation and hostility. More remote, perhaps, is the notion of romantic love, so familiar to us but so rare among primitive peoples. Here again individuation is implicit, for romantic love involves both the individuated self and the individuated other.

In summary, the Northwest Californian ethics placed the focus of moral responsibility upon the individual, a moral responsibility which internalized the command to industriousness, self-denial, and personal aggrandizement; a moral demand which produced a pattern of individuated guilt and the concept of sin.[10]

PRINCIPLES OF YUROK LAW*

By A. L. Kroeber

These are the standards by which the Yurok regulate their conduct toward one another:

1. All rights, claims, possessions, and privileges are individual and personal, and all wrongs are against individuals. There is no offense against the community, no duty owing it, no right or power of any sort inhering in it.

2. There is no punishment, because a political state or social unit that might punish does not exist, and because punishment by an individual would constitute a new offense which might be morally justified but would expose to a new and unweakened liability. An act of revenge therefore causes two liabilities to lie where one lay before.

3. Every possession and privilege, and every injury and offense, can be exactly valued in terms of property.

4. There is no distinction between material and nonmaterial ownership, right, or damage, nor between property rights in persons and in things.

5. Every invasion of privilege or property must be exactly compensated.

6. Intent or ignorance, malice or negligence, are never a factor. The fact and amount of damage are alone considered. The psychological attitude is as if intent were always involved.

---

[10] Quotations from "Ethnics and the Structure of Society: An Ethnological Contribution to the Theory of Knowledge" by Walter Goldschmidt, *American Anthropologist*, Vol. *53*, pp. 515-518, 1951.

* Reprinted from *Handbook of the Indians of California*, by A. L. Kroeber, Bureau of American Ethnology, Bulletin *78*, Washington, 1925, pp. 20-22.

7. Directness or indirectness of cause of damage is not considered, except in so far as a direct cause has precedence over an indirect one. If the agent who is directly responsible cannot satisfactorily be made amenable, liability automatically attaches to the next agent or instrument in the chain of causality, and so on indefinitely.

8. Settlement of compensation due is arrived at by negotiation of the parties interested or their representatives, and by them alone.

9. When compensation has been agreed upon and accepted for a claim, this claim is irrevocably and totally extinguished. Even the harboring of a sentiment of injury is thereafter improper, and if such sentiment can be indirectly connected with the commission of an injury, it establishes a valid counter-liability. The known cherishing of resentment will even be alleged as prima facie evidence of responsibility in case an injury of undeterminable personal agency is suffered.

10. Sex, age, nationality, or record or previous wrongs or damage inflicted or suffered do not in any measure modify or diminish liability.

11. Property either posesses a value fixed by custom, or can be valued by consideration of payments made for it in previous changes of ownership. Persons possess valuations that differ, and the valuation of the same nonmaterial property or privilege varies, according to the rating of the person owning it. The rating of persons depends partly upon the amount of property which they possess, partly upon the values which have previously passed in transfers or compensations concerning themselves or their ancestors.

One doubtful qualification must be admitted to the principle that the Yurok world of humanity recognizes only individuals: the claims of kinship. These are undoubtedly strong, not only as sentiments but in their influence on legal operations. Yet a group of kinsmen is not a circumscribed group, as a clan or village community or tribe would be. It shades out in all directions, and integrates into innumerable others. It is true that when descent in reckoned unilaterally, a body of kinsmen in the lineage of the proper sex tends to maintain identity for long periods and can easily become treated as a group. It is also conceivable that such patrilinear kin units exist in the consciousness of Yurok society, and have merely passed unnoticed because they bear no formal designations. Yet this seems unlikely. A rich man is always spoken of as the prominent person of a town, not of a body of people. In the case of a full and dignified marriage, the bond between brothers-in-law seems to be active as well as close. Women certainly identify themselves with their husbands' interests as heartily as with those of their parents and brothers on most occasions. These facts indicate that relationship through females is also regarded by the Yurok; and such being the case, it is impossible for a kin group not to have been sufficiently connected with other kin groups to prevent either being marked off as an integral unit. Then, a "half-married" man must have acted in common with the father-in-law in whose house he lived; and his children in turn would be linked, socially and probably legally, to the grandfather with whom they grew up as well as with their paternal grandfather and his descendant. So, too, it is clear that a married woman's kin as well as her husband retained an interest in her. If the latter beat her, her father had a claim against him. Were she killed, the father as well as the husband would therefore be injured; and there can be little doubt that something of this community of interest and claim would descend to her children. Kinship, accordingly, operated in at least some measure bilaterally and consequently diffusively;

so that a definite unit of kinsmen acting as a group capable of constituted social action did not exist.

This attitude can also be justified juridically, if we construe every Yurok as having a reciprocal legal and property interest in every one of his kin, proportionate, of course, to the proximity of the relationship. *A* has an interest in his kinsmen, *X, Y,* and *Z* similar to his interest in his own person, and they in him. If *A* is injured, the claim is his. If he is killed, his interest in himself passes to *X, Y, Z*—first, or most largely, to his sons, next to his brothers; in their default to his brothers' sons—much as his property interests pass, on his natural death, to the same individuals. The only difference is that the claim of blood is reciprocal, possession of goods or privilege absolute or nearly so.

It may be added that this interpretation of Yurok law fits very nicely the practices prevailing in regard to wife purchase. Here the interest in a person is at least largely ceded by her kinsmen for compensation received.

It is men that hold and press claims and receive damages for women and minors, but only as their natural guardians. The rights of a woman are in no sense curtailed by her sex, nor those of a child by its years; but both are in the hands of adult male trustees. Old women whose nearer male kin have died often have considerable property in their possession. The weakness of their status is merely that they are unable to press their just claims by the threat of force, not that their claim is less than that of a man.

It may be asked how the Yurok executed their law without political authority being in existence. The question is legitimate; but a profounder one is why we insist on thinking of law only as a function of the state when the example of the Yurok, and of many other nations, proves that there is no inherent connection between legal and political institutions. The Yurok procedure is simplicity itself. Each side to an issue presses and resists vigorously, exacts all it can, yields when it has to, continues the controversy when continuance promises to be profitable or settlement is clearly suicidal, and usually ends in compromising more or less. Power, resolution, and wealth give great advantages; justice is not always done; but what people can say otherwise of its practices? The Yurok, like all of us, accept the conditions of their world, physical and social; the individual lives along as best he may; and the institutions go on.

Among the Yurok, as we have just seen, the individual "self" is isolated from others within a system of constant and repetitive invidious comparisons; concomitantly, we have observed a fundamental parameter of the legal system—the notion of responsibility and liability—in which every individual is liable for his own actions to other individuals. This, in brief, is a social system in which responsibility is wholly individual. What is important to bear in mind in this connection is that a legal system, especially its concepts of responsibility, and the like, are not arbitrarily and capriciously *imposed* on individuals, and to which they must "adjust." The Yurok are an excellent illustration of this principle, for they possess no sanctioned governmental authority which is capable of imposing such a system on the members of the society. Rather, we must view the process from another vantage: in order for such a system to function effectively certain personality processes must exist in the members of the society. Clearly, the Yurok legal system is dependent on the particular personality processes of the Yurok for its effective functioning. Every legal system must contain a clearly defined notion of responsibility and liability; Yurok personality, especially that facet of it which is to be observed in the Yurok self-system, sets very definite limits for the ranges and extent of responsibility.

Although the American legal system is based on the presence and functioning of a strong state organization, roughly similar processes can be observed in the American legal system. The concepts of responsibility and liability, in terms of their individualistic nature, are known to all, and there is no need to enter into them. However, we can observe some of the processes of individualistic relationships in the *evolution* of American law, with which we can bridge the gap from the Yurok to the Bantu. The dependence of Western legal concepts of responsibility and liability and culturally patterned self-systems—and the relationship of these self-systems to kinship organization—can be observed in two areas of legal liability. Until the nineteenth century, for example, husband and wife were legally one person to the extent that a wife, technically known as *feme covert,* was a person "whose legal personality is merged in that of husband and wife . . ."; [11] a married woman's legal status was thus referred to technically as "incapacity of coverture." Socially and culturally, too, until about the nineteenth century, a woman's identity was lost in her legal (marital) relationship to her husband; any other legal concept of the responsibility of woman during that time would not have had any sociocultural bases on which to stand. Similarly, under English common law, all felonies were once punishable by death. "After judgment of conviction was pronounced the felon could not be a witness in court, his chattels were forfeited to the crown, and his real property escheated (that is, passed to the person of whom he held property, which would be the crown, or with us, the state). There was said to be 'corruption of blood,' so that he could not inherit or transmit by inheritance. The United States abolished forfeiture and corruption of blood, in case of conviction in Federal Courts, in 1790. New York abolished them except in case of conviction of treason. Some states by constitution abolished forfeiture and corruption of blood entirely, and they are now substantially done away with. In England, in 1814, they were abolished except in cases of murder, and in 1833-34 were abolished entirely." [12]

It will be seen, in the two brief examples given above, that such changes, which can be viewed as basic and extremely meaningful to the Anglo-American system of law, hinged upon ties of kinship, conjugal in the first, consanguineal (as well as conjugal) in the second. It was mentioned earlier that the experiences of an individual in the course of growing up constitute a series of prototype situations, the experiencing of which allow for future participation in adult role systems. One of these is the positional standing of the "self" in relation to other "selves" in the family; among other things, the family in which one is reared is the prototype for all future kinship relationships. When ties between the generations of parents and children are weakened, it is to be anticipated that the ties among kinsmen in general will be correspondingly weakened. Putting this in other terms, when the "self" becomes more distinct, more insulated, and more distant from the "selves" which make up the

---

[11] Pound, 1939, p. 185.
[12] *Ibid.,* p. 91.

family in which an individual is raised, his "self" will be commensurately removed from those of his kinsmen, as well as from the total community; it will become more highly individualistic in nature. The reflections of these processes on the legal level are to be seen in the greater separateness of the "self" of the woman in the marital relationship, and even more clearly in the growing loss of the concept of communal or kin responsibility in "corruption of blood."

In the example of the Bantu Kavirondo, about whom we shall read next, we can observe some of the consequences in the legal system of a "self" which stands in extremely close proximity to other "selves." Although most of the selection which follows deals with some of the mechanics and values underlying the legal system of the Bantu Kavirondo, these data have a great deal of pertinence for our interests when we view them in the light of a legal system *made possible by* certain kinds of psychological processes, specifically, by a particular system of self-portraiture. In other words, when we read the next selection we should keep this question in mind throughout: What sorts of people must these be who can maintain such a legal system or, to put this in other terms, on what kinds of personality processes does such a legal system depend?

The Bantu of North Kavirondo (the Logoli and Vugusu) live in the westernmost portion of Kenya, in Africa, in a fertile area. The social groupings of these people are the patrilocal extended family, the lineage, and the patrilineal exogamous clan; of these, the clan is the locus of solidarity and feelings of responsibility. Land is owned by the clan, the individual having rights only of use. Subsistence derives from cattle as well as from agriculture.

Speaking of their customary legal system, Wagner writes as follows: "Law and custom which in their totality make up tribal culture are not merely an inventory of rules of conduct, but a coherent system of relationships between individuals and groups. These relationships do not merely entail the observance of certain actions and the avoidance of others, but ideologies and values, mental and emotional attitudes as well. Thus 'family law,' in the fuller sense of the word, comprises the totality of relationships, as expressed in actions and attitudes, that knit the members of the family together into a social unit, while the formulated 'laws'—such as regulate paternal authority, the rights and duties of husband and wife, inheritance and succession, etc.—demarcate the main lines and limits only along and within which these relationships work. The maintenance of law and custom is thus equivalent to the maintenance of effective relationships." [13]

The lines of relationships which we define as the social structure of any group are essentially extensions or demarcations of the sociological placements of the individual "selves" in a group. That the legal system of a society has its very definite effects on the behavior of its members is clear from the above paragraph. But at the same time that the legal system does set limits for the behavior of the members of the group, the particular positional standings of the members of the group in turn set the limits for the *ranges of the legal* concepts of liability and responsibility. This

---

[13] Wagner, 1940, p. 205.

is clearly exemplified in the following statement by Wagner: "Clan solidarity, for instance, comes into operation only when challenged by the murder of a clan member or some similar occasion, but the specific type of relationship between the members of the clan on which this solidarity is based has to be permanently maintained, so that the law of solidarity may come into action whenever the need for its realization arises." [14]

THE RESTORATION OF BREACHES OF THE LAW AMONG THE BANTU KAVIRONDO*

By Gunter Wagner

This legal system takes cognizance of four main categories of legal offenses:

(1) When a person refuses to pay a debt or to fulfill a customary obligation, such as may be demanded by the rules of kinship or that may result from partnership in cattle or some other possession.

(2) The second class denotes a range of offenses that in Europe would be classed as both civil and criminal, such as adultery (by or with a married woman), theft, assault, arson, etc. Another aspect of the second class deals with offenses of a more serious nature, such as rape, murder, or witchcraft. It nowadays has the connotation of a sinful and morally strongly condemnable act, but it is uncertain to what extent this connotation is due to mission or other recent influences.

(3) The third category consists of offenses against property or life which have been committed accidentally or at least without the full intention and responsibility of the offender, such as physical injuries inflicted by carelessness in handling weapons, or the accidental destruction of a neighbor's house by fire or of his crops by cattle.

(4) The final category consists of violations of important taboos or rules of ceremonial conduct, pre-eminently of such rules as the prohibition of incest and the avoidance of one's mother-in-law or the desecration of objects used in the ancestor cult.

In the first type or category of offense, no actual wrong has been done which needs to be undone. The fact that a claim has become overdue does not involve the notion that the creditor is entitled to compensation for the delay suffered in materializing his claim. The dispute merely has to be decided in favor of one of the disputing parties. In the second and third categories, the offense has to be undone by inducing or forcing the accused person to compensate the damage he has caused to the accuser. If the offense was unintentional (class 3), he merely has to restore the damage or pay cattle in equivalent value, while in the case of an intentional offense (class 2) the double amount has to be replaced or a fine in cattle is levied that is considered ample compensation. This double compensation was interpreted by . . . informants as aiming to restore the goodwill of the wronged person towards the offender and not as a fine in the sense

[14] *Loc. cit.*

* Adapted and excerpted from "The Political Organization of the Bantu of Kavirondo," by Gunter Wagner, in *African Political Systems,* edited by Meyer Fortes and E. E. Evans-Pritchard, London: Oxford University Press, 1940, pp. 215-219.

of a penal sanction. This interpretation is corroborated by the fact that after the settlement of a case (either under class 2 or class 3) the plaintiff, if he has won the case, is expected to make a counter-payment, or rather gift, to the defendant as a sign of his satisfaction and reconciliation with him. Breaches of taboo (the final category) . . . are restored by performing the appropriate sacrifice or purification ceremony, after which social relations are resumed with the offender by his fellow beings, who have avoided him in the meantime. If the broken taboo involves another person—as in the case of a violation of the mother-in-law taboo—the purification rite is usually followed by the participation of both persons in a common meal.

It appears from this brief survey of the types of breaches recognized and the methods employed in dealing with them that the restoration of law and order aims at the settlement of claims and the reparation of damages rather than at the punishment of the offender. This fact has two important consequences. The one is that jurisdiction takes place only when solicited by the victim or victims of the offense, as all offenses are conceived as being injurious to the interests of a particular person or group of persons, but not to the tribal society as a whole. It is a logical implication of this conception that, not only every material object, but also every human being has its "owner" or "owners." A typical case which illustrates this principle is that of serious physical harm suffered by a small child owing to the negligence of its father or mother. If the injuries, e.g. burns, are attributed to the carelessness of the mother, the father of the child can claim damages from his wife's father or brothers (as those responsible for her conduct), if to the carelessness of the father, the child's mother's relatives can claim damages from the father of the child or his kinsmen. Compensation for damages is thus claimed by and received from persons who, according to European notions, are not at all or only very indirectly affected by the offense.

The second consequence which follows directly from the first is that there is no tribal judicial authority, but that justice is administered by and between those groups of persons who are affected by the offense in question. . . . Within the clan, the size of the group which will take judicial action is determined in each particular case by the extent and nature of common interests which are affected by the dispute or damage done. It is not a definite type of offense, but the seriousness of the situation, the amount of social disruption that threatens from it, which determines the composition of the judicial body. The creation or a maintenance of common or mutual interests within the clan is therefore of paramount importance to the individual immediately affected by a breach of the law, as he needs support from other persons if he is to realize his claims and reparations for damages. By sharing common interests—economic, social, ritual, etc.—the damage suffered by one member of the group (lineage, subclan, or clan) becomes a concern of all and, moreover, support of a member of the group in one case invites his reciprocal services in another. This identification of a given group within the clan with the rights and duties of each of its members is the second reason why it is impossible to make a distinction between civil and criminal law. Whether the initiative in taking judicial action comes from the wronged individual or from the clan or any of its subgroups of which the individual is a member and the specific interests of which are affected, in both cases that group acts, in a sense, as the accuser and as the judicial authority at the same time.

A distinction, however, must be made

between law administered within a group and between different groups. When a legal dispute or an offense involves two clans, the clan of the wronged person tries to obtain justice by negotiation with the clan of the offender, which, in turn, stands behind the offender and either rejects the claim or assumes responsibility for his action. When, however, a breach of law occurs within a given group and the nature of the offense is such that it affects those interests which are specific to the group and not further divisible, a restoration of the breach by compensation is obviously impossible, as it would necessitate the splitting up of the group into two units, the one which gives and the other which receives the compensation, an action which would destroy the solidarity of the group. Thus, if a person commits adultery with one of his father's or brother's wives, the usual compensation of a heifer is not paid, as a father and his sons form a property-holding unit in which the payment of compensation by one member to another member would be pointless. If a person kills a member of his subclan, no compensation would be paid either (among the Vugusu), as they say that the loss of life affects the whole subclan and not merely the immediate kinsmen. The action taken in such and similar cases furnishes a clear criterion of the nature of the solidarity that prevails within the group in question. Where it is deemed that no legal action (i.e. the imposition of a compensation) can be taken owing to the indivisibility of the common interests of the group, merely a sacrifice is performed to propitiate the spirits and a purification ceremony which frees the offender from his ritual impurity and renders it safe for his relatives and neighbors to resume social relations with him.

In the case of repeated offenses, the only possible procedure is to expel the offender from the group and to withdraw from him the right for protection by the clan as well as the clan's responsibility for his deeds. The attitude towards an habitual offender thus differs fundamentally from that towards an occasional offender. Whereas the latter—no matter how serious the offense committed by him—is considered to have acted within a set of particular conditions and circumstances and against the interests only of the people directly or indirectly affected by the offense, the habitual offender becomes a source of danger to everybody in the tribe. He is, therefore, placed outside legal protection of the clan and maybe killed by anybody when he is caught in the act of committing his next offense. Thus persons who have come to be regarded as dangerous witches or incorrigible thieves are first driven away from their clan and then, at the next provocation, put to death by the method of lynching carried out by as large and mixed a group of persons as possible to avert the possibility of a blood feud from arising. Such group action in the face of threatening danger, taken spontaneously, i.e., without a hearing of the case and often on the spur of the moment, is clearly not the same as institutionalized jurisdiction by the tribal society through recognized judicial authorities. It is rather that in such cases the person of the accuser becomes multiplied and that the tribal group by being accuser and public opinion at the same time cuts short the usual judicial procedure. It will be seen, therefore, that the occurrence of indiscriminate group-action in the face of dangerous witchcraft and habitual crime does not invalidate the basic principle of jurisdiction, viz. that it comes into force only when solicited by the victim or victims of the offense and takes place only within and between those groups of persons whose common interests are affected by the offense.

Traditionally, among the Bantu Kavirondo, a man retained legal responsibility for his married daughters, as did brothers for their married sisters. We have seen one example of this responsibility. In another, a man could be expected to pay damages if his daughter committed adultery, the damages being paid to her husband. The corollary to this liability was a privilege on the daughter's part, namely, that a woman could at any time seek refuge and protection with her father and other patrilineal kinsmen if any serious conflict arose between her and her husband. But clan solidarity is breaking down under modern conditions. One of the consequences of this weakening of solidary group membership is the fact that "the wife's father, formerly responsible for his daughter's marital conduct and liable to pay compensation to the husband in the case of her unfaithfulness, can no longer be taken to court to make such payments. . . . The result of these tendencies is that the married woman remains less firmly bound to her own kin than formerly and correspondingly becomes more dependent upon her husband, who now assumes the sole legal responsibility for her. The less the wife's kin become involved in her marriage relationship, either as guarantors of her good conduct or as protectors against the husband's abuse, the more does the wife depend on her own resources for strengthening her position in the family and the husband's clan. In the present phase of transition this new development may assist in upsetting the stability of the marriage bond, but it furnishes the basis on which marriage may be reintegrated as a more personal relationship and the family as a more evenly balanced and more independent unit. A readjustment along these lines will be necessary if the wider kinship groupings continue to deteriorate." [15]

This brief reference to historical change among the Bantu peoples of North Kavirondo is intended to serve two purposes for us. First, it is a type of comparison *within* a culture which helps to demonstrate that the relationships to which we have pointed are not accidental or fortuitous. That is, it helps to demonstrate that there is, indeed, a meaningful relationship between a sense and feeling of responsibility and sociological relationships, because when one is removed or even altered there is a corresponding change in the other. Secondly, this historical reference is intended to re-emphasize the necessity of using historical materials for the illustration and testing of hypotheses dealing with the relationships between culture and social structure, on one hand, and personality, on the other. Two such attempts were made in Chapter 5, in connection with changes in the social structure and changes in socialization practices. The historical component for adult personality is merely being introduced at this point; there will be opportunities to see its overriding importance, by itself and in conjunction with other kinds of comparisons, in subsequent chapters.

SUMMARY

We have moved alternately between situations in which the strategic questions centered about the problem of dependence of institutions on personality and situations in which the principal issue has been the degree of "fit" of personalities or self-

---

15 Wagner, 1939, pp. 46-47.

systems into the contours of institutional frames. As we move into the area of the relationship of personality to *total* social systems in Chapter 9, we find that our major problem, once more, is the question of the degree of "fit" of individuals into these working systems. As will be observed, the degree of such "fit" is never an absolute value; under given conditions, individuals will "fit" easily and smoothly into the social systems in which they live and for which they were brought up to participate in; under other conditions, within the same societies, these same individuals will appear to "fit" hardly at all.

BIBLIOGRAPHY AND SUGGESTED READINGS

Cohen, Yehudi A. "Some Aspects of Ritualized Behavior in Interpersonal Relationships," *Human Relations,* Vol. *11,* pp. 195-215, 1958. A comparison of military and caste structures with respect to the elicitation of ritualized behavior as a result of the "needs" of institutions.

Erikson, Erik H. *Childhood and Society.* New York: Norton, 1950.

Gerhard, Dietrich. "The Frontier in Comparative View," *Comparative Studies in Society and History,* Vol. *1,* pp. 205-229, 1959.

Goldschmidt, Walter. "Ethics and the Structure of Society: An Ethnological Contribution to the Sociology of Knowledge," *American Anthropologist,* Vol. *53,* pp. 506-524, 1951.

Hoebel, E. Adamson. *The Law of Primitive Man.* Cambridge, Massachusetts: Harvard, 1954. The standard text on law and culture.

Kroeber, A. L. *Handbook of the Indians of California.* Bureau of American Ethnology, Bulletin *78.* Washington, D. C., 1925.

Pound, Roscoe. *The Formative Era of American Law.* Boston: Little, Brown, 1939.

Powdermaker, Hortense. "The Channeling of Negro Aggression by the Cultural Process," in *Personality in Nature, Society and Culture,* edited by Kluckhohn *et al.,* pp. 597-607. New York: Knopf, 1955. An excellent analysis of some of the mechanisms involved in "fitting into" the caste structure.

Schneider, David M. "Social Dynamics of Physical Disability in Army Basic Training," in *Personality in Nature, Society and Culture,* edited by Kluckhohn *et al.,* pp. 386-397. New York: Knopf, 1955. An excellent account of the pressures to mold people to "fit" into the army and the ways in which individuals cope with some of these institutional pressures.

Wagner, Gunter. "The Changing Family among the Bantu Kavirondo," Supplement to *Africa,* Vol. *12,* 1939.

Wagner, Gunter. "The Political Organization of the Bantu of Kavirondo," in *African Political Systems,* edited by M. Fortes and E. E. Evans-Pritchard, pp. 197-236. London: Oxford University Press, 1940.

Chapter 9

TOTAL SOCIAL SYSTEMS

In the introduction to an article dealing with the problem of "The Interpretation of Pueblo Culture," John W. Bennett observes that "it can be taken as a general rule that intensive research upon the same preliterate people by a variety of ethnologists gives rise to considerable controversy and disagreement over the nature of fundamental institutions and expressions."[1] Bennett states the problem of interpreting the several pictures of Pueblo culture (of which the Hopi are a part), but he leaves the issue of whether these peoples are "this" or "that" largely unresolved. Many scholars would agree with the statement by Douglas Haring, who notes that "Dr. Bennett's analysis speaks for itself, and the student will have to make up his own mind—or seek further factual information."[2] As we shall observe in the course of the discussion to follow, there is still another alternative.

The problem of the interpretation of Hopi culture stems from the fact that these Indians of the American Southwest are presented in two contrasting—if not contradictory—lights by different investigators. Aberle puts this state of affairs in the following terms: "Hopi society is often described as peaceful, harmonious, and operating with a minimum of physical coercion. Yet child rearing is said to be repressive and adult life constrained, and the Hopi are often characterized as anxious, mistrustful, and full of suppressed hostility. It is [our] contention . . . that these features of Hopi society are closely related to one another—that the truth does not just lie 'somewhere in between' but lies in understanding how these two aspects are bound together."[3]

Some years ago, Leo W. Simmons, a sociologist, collected and edited the autobiography of Don C. Talayesva, a Hopi Indian called Sun Chief. This document is almost unrivaled in portraying the meaning of a culture to an individual member of a society. As noted in previous discussions, one of the most significant things which any individual in a society has to learn is the ways of resolving the contradictions and discrepancies in the value system of his society. Sun Chief's autobiography is given even greater value and interest by Aberle's careful and systematic analysis of it from the points of view of individual psychology, sociology, and anthropology. His monograph, from which selected portions are reprinted here, goes to the very core of the problem of the supposedly contradictory pictures of Hopi culture and motivation, and it enables us to see how the two extreme portrayals of Hopi society

---

[1] Bennett, 1946, p. 361.
[2] Haring, 1956, p. 202.
[3] Aberle, 1951, p. 1.

are intimately related to each other. From Aberle's analysis of Talayesva's autobiography can be derived several principles of the ways in which individuals do or do not "fit" into their societies—principles which are relevant not only to the Hopi but to almost all other societies as well. Aberle's ethnographic material is taken from the best primary sources on the Hopi.

THE PSYCHOSOCIAL ANALYSIS OF A
HOPI LIFE HISTORY*
By David F. Aberle

The Hopi are a group of Shoshonean-speaking American Indians living in the well-known pueblo type of "primitive apartment-house" towns placed on and at the foot of three mesas—extensions of the larger Black Mesa—in northeastern Arizona. The area has long been inhabited by the Hopi, Oraibi, for example, having been settled about 1200 A.D. The history of the group, though it includes little aggressive warfare, is full of conflict with the Spanish, with non-Pueblo Indians, and with Americans. Farthest from Santa Fe of all the Pueblo groups, the Hopi were influenced by the Spanish less than any other Pueblo Indians were. Oraibi, the westernmost of the Hopi towns, had even less contact with the Spanish than other Hopi towns. Nevertheless, from them its people acquired new crops, stock, and herding practices, and perhaps some religious behavior and witchcraft beliefs. A period of loosened control of the Southwest by the Spanish and Mexican governments was marked by greater and more frequent incursions of marauding non-Pueblo groups. Extensive contact with the American government began in the 1870's. Pro- and anti-American factional sentiments beginning in the 1880's recall similar developments during the period of Spanish contact. Oraibi was particularly hostile to the Americans, resisting schooling, census, and land surveying. Factionalism in this town reached so high a pitch that, in 1906, the anti-American faction, the Hostiles, were forced to leave Oraibi and found a new town, Hotevilla, which itself later gave rise to still a third town, Bakabi. The formerly pro-American, friendly Village chief of Oraibi changed his attitude and expelled Christian converts from the village. They founded New Oraibi. Migration from Oraibi to all these settlements and to Moenkopi reduced the population from 600 (in 1906) to 112 (in 1933). Furthermore, though Hotevilla and Bakabi were able to set up full-scale ceremonial cycles after the split, Oraibi suffered a marked deterioration in its ritual cycle. Oraibi is perhaps more antagonistic to the Americans than are other Hopi towns, and possibly it is more tension-filled.

In considering the Oraibi split of 1906, two aspects of the event must be kept in mind: the structural features of Hopi social organization which make such splits a recurrent possibility, and the tensions which occasion the splits. Hopi social organization is characterized by a weak development of central political control and organized hierarchical office, little executive and legislative power, and the strong orientation of individuals to

* Excerpted from "The Psychosocial Analysis of a Hopi Life History," by David F. Aberle, *Comparative Psychology Monographs*, Vol. *21*, pp. 1-133, 1951.

their clans and religious societies rather than to the village as such. This means that there are comparatively few institutional barriers to prevent fission and the resultant formation and growth of new towns. In addition, in 1906 there was a set of tensions that provided the motor force for the split: a struggle for land rights among groups in the town, and a division among the Hopi on the question whether they should adapt a friendly or a hostile attitude toward the Americans. Leaders of the Hostile faction, which was also the faction whose members considered themselves deprived of their rightful share of land, resorted to a reinterpretation of mythology as a basis for claiming that their actions were legitimate.

Authorities disagree as to whether splits are invariably the product of serious internal tension or are occasionally the result of an amicable decision to handle overcrowding and similar problems by division and resettlement.

The Hopi country is exigent for a farming and herding people, and the life of a Hopi is arduous and filled with uncertainties. Scarce and uncertain rainfall, a short growing season with the posibility of killing frosts at the beginning or the end of the crop cycle, cold winters, and hot summers all make hard work necessary and its products unpredictable. Sources of water include rainfall, springs, intermittent washes, and seepage from springs which collects in dunes. Crops can be grown on these dunes. Men do most of the field work, and women the garden work. Most farming is with hoe and digging stick. Fields and gardens require constant attention, which extends sometimes to the building of individual shelters to protect plants from flying sand, and the digging of small individual ditches to bring water to each plant. Rain, when it comes, may be so violent as to wash out crops in wash-irrigated fields. In spite of the Hopi's use of drought-resistant breeds of corn, hard work, and constant vigilance, famine has always been a threat; even today it is customary to have a year's corn supply stored away as a safeguard. The story of the famine of 1860-1862 is still told.

Hopi society is characterized by a weak development of a central political authority, by the absence of a clear-cut hierarchy among offices and among groups within the society, by the lack of any true techniques of legislation to meet novel situations (reinterpretations of tradition are the bases for decisions), and by the lack of a well-implemented executive arm in the central political unit. The chief groupings of significance are the clan, the religious society, and the household: the "chief's talk," the only central grouping in the society, plays a definitely subordinate part.

The most significant unit of the kinship system is the matrilineal clan. These clans are substantially identical in every village. Kinship relations of some sort can be established with virtually all Hopi and, if it appears desirable, can be extended to other Pueblo Indians and even to the Navaho. Clans are grouped in unnamed phratries. A clan is composed of one or more traceable matrilineal lineages. The senior woman of the senior lineage of a clan is a person of considerable significance; she heads the clan and holds the clan fetish. A clan also possesses a kiva— an underground ceremonial chamber, used as a place of ceremonial retreat and men's lodge. The male clan leader is also an important figure. He is selected from among the brothers or the sons of the senior woman. The clan is also an important landholding unit, as will be seen. There is clan and phratry exogamy. In addition, there is no marrying into the father's clan, and rarely is there marrying into the father's phratry. Thus, the clan unites individuals in a solidary unit, allocates land, and, through the senior woman and the male clan leader, has an important control function in the society.

The religious societies, which are linked to clans in a rather complicated fashion, are responsible for putting on the ceremonials of the annual cycle. Most of them are for men; a few are for women. Sometimes, though not always, the same man is the leading male of the clan, leader of the ceremonial group tied to the clan, and head of the kiva in which the society meets. (The situation, however, is often more complex than that.) The leader of a society picks his own successor from among his sister's sons, usually on the basis of ability, and trains the man he selects. The procedure is the same for the selection of the Village chief from the appropriate clan (the Bear clan). This means that, in general, the positions of Village chief, leader of a religious society, and male leader of a clan descend not only within particular clans but in certain family lines within each clan. That is, while the top offices of Hopi society are not completely ascribed by birth, they are at any rate rigorously circumscribed thereby. They can only be achieved by a man who is born into the "correct" family of a particular clan. Even though there are important exceptions to this rule, especially if a society is in danger of dying out, this limitation on achieved status is a factor of considerable significance, as will be shown.

The membership of a religious society is made up of men from a number of clans, including the clan which provides the leadership. A man joins a ceremonial society by selecting a ceremonial father from that society. Membership in the initiation societies of childhood (Powamu and Katcina) and manhood (Wowochim, Singers, Agave, and Horn), however, is usually determined by the parents' choice of the ceremonial father, a selection in which the child has no voice. The two childhood initiation societies are mutually exclusive, and so are the adult initiation societies. Beyond that, a man may theoretically belong to as many societies as he wishes—at least he may at Oraibi. It is probable, however, that responsibilities in any one society are time-consuming enough to prevent a man from joining many. Initiation into a society may also result from trespass and from disease. Each society is conceived of as causing and curing a disease, the particular disease being termed the "whip" of the society. If a man trespasses on the secret activities of a society he may fall ill with that disease, but he can ward off this danger by initiation into the society. A man who is cured of sickness by a society joins it.

All Hopi, men or women, are members of one of the two childhood initiatory societies, Powamu or Katcina, which have other major responsibilities beyond initiation, as do the adult initiation societies, to which men alone belong. There are three women's societies; a woman may belong to one or more of them. Men hold important ceremonial offices in them, but in spite of the Hopi belief that the presence of women—their "smell"—is disliked by supernaturals, women take the majority of roles in these ceremonies. As in most areas of Hopi life, there is no taboo against menstruating women.

Some of the religious societies are more "important" than others, since their ceremonies are viewed as being more vital to the total ceremonial round.

Thus, crosscutting the groupings and ties based on clanship are those of the religious societies, to which all men and some women belong. The leaders of these societies are figures of authority and prestige. The members of a religious society form a solidary unit and achieve relative prestige according to the station of their particular society.

As has been said, chieftainship in Oraibi resides in the Bear clan. The most important village officials are the headman of the Parrot clan and the headman of the Pikyas clan; the Tobacco chief, normally of the Rabbit clan; the Crier chief, leader of the Greasewood clan; and the War (police) chief, of the Badger or the Coyote clan. Although they assist the Village chief, their principal functions are in their own clans and societies. The Village chief has important functions in the allocation of land, as will be shown later.

For handling recalcitrants there are few sanctions except public opinion. The principal problems which might require adjudication are land disputes, claims of farmers for reparation for destruction of crops by herds, and failure to respond to the pleas for public-work groups. The War chief was a more effective executive in earlier days, when his prestige and power were reinforced by his role as a leader of war parties.

Thus, the factors which make for a certain fragility of the total Hopi social structure are the weakness of the central political organ and the fact that relationships of solidarity and authority are stronger within the clan and the religious society than they are between clan and society members and the central governing body. On the other hand, the crosscutting network of lines of obligations, solidarity, and authority formed by the clan and the society make for general cohesion: every individual is oriented to several types of structures in the total system. Furthermore, the Hopi are bound together by the recognition that the total round of ceremonies is essential for the well-being of the community. Although this factor is integrative in this sense, it must be pointed out that when a split does occur and the ceremonial cycle is disrupted, individuals are likely to experience feelings of loss of religious protection from the calamities of drought, crop failure, and disease.

Further consideration of the clan and the household and their internal differentiation is required to lay bare the skeleton of the social organization.

The kinship system is of the Crow type. An individual is a member of his mother's clan and is a "child" of his father's clan but not a member of it. A number of individuals are classified in the same category of relationship—though this does not imply that they are treated absolutely identically, without any regard for personal feelings or degree of lifelong intimacy. Thus, the same term is used for own mother, mother's sister, mother's mother's sister's daughter, and in fact all members of the clan whom one's mother calls "sister." Within the clan, the children of all women whom one calls "mother" are one's "brother" and "sister." In addition, all persons whose fathers are members of the same clan call one another "brother" and "sister." For a woman, all children of her clan "sisters" are termed "children"; and for a man, all children of his clan "brothers" are "children." All women of the father's clan below the grandparental generation are "paternal aunts." There are many other relationships structured by this system which need not be elaborated here.

A unit of central significance within the clan is the household or group of households. This is composed of a woman, her daughters, sometimes her daughters' daughters, the unmarried sons of these women, and the husbands of all married women. Thus, such a household contains a group of closely related women who have grown up in the same family and have always worked together. The husbands of these women, on the other hand, are drawn from a variety of different groups and retain ties of major significance to their clan of birth and the household in which they grew up. They have no particular ties to one another, except when brothers or clan brothers marry sisters. In fact, a man ordinarily refers to his mother's, rather than his wife's home as his own. To the end of his life he returns to his mother's, and later to his sister's home on feast days. (The sister will ordinarily continue to live in her mother's home after the mother's death.)

Thus, a man is strongly oriented toward his own clan. In addition, his relationship with his sister throughout life is one of warmth and affection, uncomplicated by avoidance or respect patterns. To a degree he is an outsider in his wife's family, and his children are members of her clan, whereas his sister's children belong to his clan. Under these circumstances his disciplinary rights regarding his own children are weak, and those toward his sister's, strong. Toward a sister's son, then, the mother's brother is the chief disciplinarian and source of punishment. As his been pointed out, he may also be the source to which the younger man looks for the inheritance of ceremonial office.

A sister takes a warm interest in her brother's children, in addition to having an affectionate relationship with the brother himself. Paternal aunt and nephew are linked by a very positive bond, which is strongly tinged with sexual joking. The aunt suggests that she would very much appreciate sex relations with her nephew, and her husband makes joking protestations of jealousy. This joking begins very early in the child's life; there may be actual sex contacts later. The aunt's husband, who is called by the same term as the male grandparent, also indulges in harsh practical joking, which the child may reciprocate when he grows old enough to do so. A Hopi's ties to his father's clan members are important and are characterized by warmth, intimacy, and ease.

The child's relationship with grandparents on both sides is a warm one. They are quite indulgent toward him.

The relationship of mother and son is an important one. Toward the child in early life, the mother is quite indulgent, scolding and threatening but seldom punishing, and in general fostering. The male child grows away from the mother through the very early role-patterning of work which occurs in Hopi society: he soon follows his father to the fields. He continues, however, to recognize his mother's key position in the household, a recognition enhanced if she is the senior woman of the clan. As senior woman, she is able to influence her brother's selection of a successor, toward the son she prefers. A mother's advice in the choice of a wife, and her advice in general, carry much weight. Occasionally there is serious strife between mother and son.

The father is the principal preceptor of the male child. From an early age the child accompanies him to the fields and helps him with herding and farming. Nevertheless, the father is not the principal disciplinarian or ceremonial instructor, though he does teach the boy Katcina dancing. With the mother he selects the boy's ceremonial father, in this way determining his son's future society memberships. Thus, there is an important limitation on the possibility of achieving status in accordance with self-set goals.

Between brothers, cooperation is the rule, whether or not they marry into the same clan or household. Even brotherly rivalry over women does not lead to vengeful behavior. Relative seniority is of little moment, except in early life, when the older brother assists in the training of the younger.

There is general agreement that Hopi children, at least during the first two years of life, are indulged and are relatively unrestricted. They are nursed on demand; transition to solid food is gradual; sphincter-control training is mild and is delayed until the second year, and the general attitude is one of indulgence toward these wanted children. A great many relatives participate in indulging the child, chiefly the grandparents, mother's sisters, and paternal aunts. The male infant often receives genital stimulation while nursing and in other situations. A pregnant mother should not nurse. But the mortality rate among infants is high, and after a child's death an older sibling sometimes returns to the breast and may even continue to nurse until his sixth year. Weaning of such a child is sometimes brought about by his age mates' shaming him. The mother puts chili powder or a worm on her breast to discourage nursing. Although an infant is kept on a cradleboard for the first six months or more of life, there is no evidence that this restriction results in any marked frustration or that the learning of locomotor skills is slowed thereby. During his early life, a child is often cared for by an older sister, as well as by the relatives mentioned above.

An older child sometimes shows jealousy of a nursing child. A more general jealousy among siblings also occurs later, as well as jealousy for the attention of the parent of the opposite sex. Apparently, sibling rivalry is present but is deeply repressed.

From the second to sixth year of a child's life, the general indulgent character of child care continues. By the age of two, the child is toilet trained and weaned, but he is markedly indulged with regard to food. A sister is likely to care for him outside the home. Male and female role differentiation begins later, but boys and girls are expected to show different emotional character by the age of four. Boys should stop crying by this age, but girls may continue throughout life to cry under stress.

From the age of six the Hopi child is subject to increasing discipline and responsibility. A child's minor aggressive behavior arouses far more concern in Hopi parents than in parents in our society, and requires discipline. Parents and the mother's brother are the principal disciplinary agents. An older sibling who is caring for a child must appeal to the parents for disciplining if the child fails to obey. Similarly, people of the village who have a complaint against a child may reprove him but most report his misbehavior to parents rather than threaten or command the child themselves. A father is likely to punish for some offense which is angering him at the moment. For graver discipline, however, the mother will ask one of her brothers to undertake the punishment. As an outsider, the father is glad to step aside and let the clan take over.

Techniques of punishment include scolding—perhaps the most common discipline—ridiculing and teasing, threatening to withhold favors, whipping, pouring cold water on the child or rolling him in the snow, and smoking the child over a fire of green wood, so as to stifle him. This last is considered particularly severe. A mother's brother will sometimes punish a whole group of his sisters' sons when called on to discipline one of them. The effects of this sort of group culpability have nowhere been investigated. Dennis, however, points out the parallel to the ceremonial situation, in which one man's misdeeds affect the entire group. Other techniques of coercion are those which involve the supernatural. The mildest of these is the threat that the Katcinas will not bring a child presents at a dance. Usually the presents are withheld until the fourth day of the ceremony, by which time the child has promised to reform. The presents given by Katcinas, of course, are arranged for by the parents.

A more severe form of inculcating the Hopi norms is to threaten the child that the bogey giant Katcinas, Soyoko and Natashka, will come and carry him off and eat him if he is disobedient. The occasional appearance of these figures as Katcina impersonations is used as a particularly awesome method of bringing about an obedient frame of mind.

Don Talayesva was born in Oraibi in 1890. At the end of the life-history he is fifty years of age. He lived through the Oraibi split of 1906, siding with the Friendly (pro-white) group because his family did. He attended school for ten years, three of them away from the Hopi towns, in California. He was initiated into the Wowochim society, married, and had four children, all of whom died at infancy. He finally raised an adopted child, Norman, to maturity. During his married life he underwent a six-year period of impotence, though prior to this he had numerous extra-marital sexual contacts. In spite of infidelity, impotence, early difficulties in making a living, and the death of five children, he and his wife never separated or divorced.

A prestige-driven man, he eventually gained the positions of male leader of the Sun clan, owner of the associated Sun Hill kiva, and ceremonial officer in the Soyal ceremony. He remains an aggressive, prestige-conscious, deeply mistrustful man, who has gradually become convinced that evil in the world is caused by witches, who are found everywhere. In recent years his contacts with anthropologists have afforded him much satisfaction.

From earliest childhood Don was fed with stories of his power and his promise of greatness, accepted such stories gladly, and showed continuous preoccupation with prestige from childhood to the present time. The problem of what happens to prestige strivings under the conditions of Hopi social life will be a recurrent topic in this study.

It was Don's maternal grandfather who instructed him in ideal behavior, in classic Hopi terms:

As soon as I was old enough to take advice, he taught me that it was a disgrace to be called *kahopi* (not Hopi, not peaceable). He said, "My grandson, old people are important. They know a lot and don't lie. Listen to them, obey your parents, work hard, treat everyone right. Then people will say, 'That boy Chucka is a good child. Let's be kind to him.' If you do these things, you will live to be an old man yourself and pass away in sleep without pain. This is the trail that every good Hopi follows. Children who ignore these teachings don't live long."

Here, in concise form, are embodied the ideals of being Hopi—conformity, obedience, hard work, and being good to people. The rewards offered are kindness from others and a long, healthy life following the right trail. Absent as yet are the ideas that good behavior will bring the benefits of supernatural support to the community and that bad behavior or thought has evil effects for the entire group; but these things, too, Don learned before his sixth year. Thus, he was told that dances were for rain, not for pleasure. If rain followed a dance it showed the favor of the gods, and those who danced were praised. "If a strong wind followed the dance, it was a sign that the people who had invited the Katcinas to come and dance had a bad heart or had done some evil."

Don's socialization centered about the problems raised by his insistent aggressive misbehavior toward his elders. Although his parents took a role in disciplining, they passed part of this role to relatives, and part to ostensibly supernatural scarers.

As early as his sixth year Don was preoccupied with the problems of trust and mistrust. He had "learned to pick out the people whom I could trust." Those who treated him kindly, protected him from teasing, or refrained from teasing him are included in the list of trusted individuals accompanying his statement; tacitly excluded are people who teased him or whose primary role toward him was a disciplinary one. It must be remembered that this refers to a time prior to Don's great period of misbehavior and continuous punishment. At the time that Don speaks of, his parents had punished him but little, and his maternal grandfather only twice.

Thus, at the head of the list of those he could trust was his mother; then his father, whom Don liked except for the rare punishments he gave; his maternal grandfather, who favored and taught him; his ceremonial father; his crippled uncle; and his elder sister. He knew that he could always count on his grandfather and on his ceremonial father. He also had a positive attitude toward some people whose personal contacts with him were more remote—some maternal relatives (the village officers mentioned above), who showed interest in him and did not tease him.

Ambivalently regarded were his older brother, who, he felt, was not a very good friend to him, and a paternal aunt who stood up for him when he was teased, but was hot-tempered and unpredictable. Hostiles were to be avoided. There were, of course, in the village, many people of no particular significance to him. Summing all this, Don says, "I had learned to find my way about the mesa and to avoid graves, shrines, and harmful plants, *to size up people, and to watch out for witches.*"

Those whom Don failed to include in the circle of trust, then, were the people whose motivations toward him he did not understand——those who disciplined him and claimed to love him, those who treated him very roughly and pretended high regard for him. Furthermore, Don was no stranger to the concealment of aggression. His parents always stopped quarreling when anyone came to the house. (It is of some interest that this is Don's only reference to strains in the relationship between his parents. How severe they were or of what variety he does not say.)

The next element in the pattern of mistrust was Don's growing misgivings about the Katcinas. He knew of them first as supernatural figures who came in answer to prayers, bringing good luck, singing and dancing in the plaza, and giving presents. They afforded some protection from Two-Hearts, "pleased the gods and insured our lives." But from his early years on, things happened which made Don think that there was something odd about the Katcinas. Thus, when he was four or five, he once "saw the Katcinas resting near by. It seemed that they had cut off their heads and laid them to one side. They were eating and using human heads and mouths like our own. I felt very sad to see those Katcinas without their own heads." Don's sadness, it may be surmised, was the beginning of disillusionment. Belief in the Katcinas already required effort and the ignoring of some features of reality.

The elements of discipline, mistrust, and suspicion about the Katcinas became connected during the crucial Katcina initiation, at the end of which Don became obedient but at the same time sadly disillusioned and resentful. He was just under nine at this time. Since Tuvenga, his ceremonial father, was too old to act on Don's behalf, this man's nephew, Sekahongeoma, took the role of ceremonial father; his sister was Don's ceremonial mother. Over the protests of Don's mother and his ceremonial mother, Don's father, who had the right to make the decision, insisted that he join the Katcina society instead of the Powamu, which had an easier initiation rite.

"I want him to join the Katcinas and be whipped. You have complained time after time that you are getting tired of his mischief. So you have no right to back down now. It will do him good to be whipped soundly and learn a lesson. We can pray to the Whipper Katcinas to drive the evil from our boy's mind, so that he may grow up to be a good and wise man. Don't you agree with me?"

The two women wept but consented. A stronger form of protest came from Sekahongeoma, who asked four times that the boy be admitted to the Powamu instead. Don's quieter, better-natured brother had been taken into the Powamu. During all this, Don did not cry but smiled. But as the initiation approached, he became more concerned about the flogging. Although other boys would tell him nothing after their initiation, he had seen them and knew that "it would be pretty bad." He knew that the boys were struck four times with yucca blades, but he thought he could stand the whipping. "I made up my mind that I would set my teeth to grin and bear it, for other boys had been brave enough to do it."

All details of the ceremony need not be given here. After certain rites, during which the boys were wished a long and happy life, a Katcina appeared. He ordered that the children be whipped "to enlighten our hearts and lead us over life's road." Other Katcinas made their appearance, and then came the whippers. Some children had begun to cry, but not Don. The whipping followed. Naked and protecting his genitals, Don received four blows from the Ho Katcinas without crying and thought his troubles were over. Four more severe blows, however, drew blood and made him struggle, shout, and urinate involuntarily. His godfather, who had made no effort to take the blows for him, as is sometimes done, finally pulled him away. His ceremonial mother and others in the kiva were upset and angry at the Whipper for giving more than four blows. Don was able to control his sobbing but was too upset and hurt even to watch the other floggings. He did, however, get a little enjoyment out of seeing the Katcinas flog one another. Then the children were warned never to tell uninitiated children what they had seen.

That night Don's bloody wounds stuck to his sheepskin. The next day "my mother reproached my father for his cruelty." His father had requested the double whipping and had told his ceremonial father not to protect him. The wounds caused by the whipping became infected and permanent scars resulted.

The next night came the revelation that the Katcinas were only people of Oraibi. "I recognized nearly every one of them, and felt very unhappy, because I had been told all my life that the Katcinas were gods. I was especially shocked and angry when I saw all my uncles, fathers, and clan brothers dancing as Katcinas. I felt the worst when I saw my own father —and whenever he glanced at me I turned my face away." A worse thrashing than the first was promised to anyone who revealed the secret of the Katcinas to the uninitiated. One child, they were told, was whipped to death for revealing it.

Don, as a consequence of his initiation, had a new ally: his ceremonial father, he was told, could be counted on if his father were to neglect him, and the ceremonial father would never punish him. He also gained a supernatural supervisor: the Sun god appeared to him in a dream and told Don that "he saw and heard everything I did. Although he was kind and polite, I awoke frightened." The dream followed a period of praying before sunrise, a duty Don took on himself after initiation.

It was after his initiation that the final element of distrust was introduced into Don's beliefs about witches. He found out that "our closest kin and best friends might be Two-Hearts."

It remains a curious and unexplained fact that even after initiation Don still believed in the giant Katcinas as supernatural figures. When they came into Oraibi he was terrified and fled to a kiva to ask protection.

The initiation experience was not a unique traumatic event which operated as a sole agent in creating Don's reactions.

Rather, it was the climax of a long series of experiences. The new elements brought into Don's life by the initiation, and many other attitudes, were now organized into a new product.

On the negative side Don was disillusioned, in a literal sense. He found that the immediate presence of the gods was an illusion fostered by the trickery of the adults of the community, a discovery which shocked and angered him. (That is not to say that Don became an atheist: within a short time he had absorbed the sophisticated point of view that the spirits inhabit the masks when men wear them. Belief in the power of the more distant spirit was strong in his adult life.) The disillusionment, however, was not a sudden one. Beginning with his feeling "sad" to see the Katcinas with their "heads" off, and passing through a period of acute conscious doubt, Don had found more and more reason to link the Katcinas with people, particularly with his own parents. (Either his parents or the Katcinas were stealing their presents back; his mother made red wafer bread which he thought only Katcinas gave.) The disillusionment had been long impending, though he had succeeded in staving it off for a time.

In the initiation, however, he had to find out. Not only was he disturbed by the loss of the immediate presence of gods, he was troubled because the Katcinas were not only ordinary men but his own relatives. Worst of all—the thing he could not face—was the fact that among them was his own father. This revelation is the culmination of a sequence of events: first he suspected a link between Katcinas and parents; then he discovered that the Katcinas had been severe at his father's request; last, he found that they were identical with relatives and with his father.

This discovery, together with the newly acquired knowledge that witches were to be found among one's own kin, links up with earlier experience. Don's listing of those whom he could trust was involved with the problem of deciding what were people's real motivations toward him. The people who treated him worst, as he saw it, always claimed to be well-intentioned. His parents had to some degree pushed off the administering of the worst punishments and the making of the worst threats onto other relatives and onto Masau'u, Soyoko, and finally the Katcinas. Now the parents themselves turned out to be the Katcinas. The effect of the initiation, combined with the events which preceded it, and Don's new information on witchcraft, was to confirm his suspicion that things were not what they seemed, that people were unfathomable, untrustworthy, and kept secret their true intentions.

In the Katcina initiation itself, the puzzle remained. What was done to him, he was told, was not aggressively intended but was for his own good. So not only resentment but also mistrust continued. It was impossible for him to fathom true intention.

As for Don's disobedience, his discovery that the parents are identical with the Katcinas seems to have made it clear to him once and for all that his parents' solidarity with their own generation surmounted their affection for him. It is true that his parents had previously turned him over to various relatives for punishment, and that in punishing him these relatives had acted as agents for the parents. At other times, however, in toughening Don they operated independently. And the very fact that the parents were unwilling to go as far as other relatives in punishing him indicated that in some degree he could expect leniency from them—could anticipate that their affection would prevent them from treating him as other relatives treated him. Prior to the Katcina initiation therefore, he was not up against a blank wall of adult solidarity. After the initiation, however, the parents proved to be identical with the agents of punishment —members of the Katcina society.

Thus, the revelation of the Katcina secret, as the culmination of many experiences all pointing in the same direction, operated to produce not only obedience but also mistrust, disillusionment, and resentment.

It is now necessary to discuss the problem of the relationship of Don's experience to general Hopi experience. In this study the understanding derived from Don's case will be compared with more general statements about Hopi culture. The legitimacy of this procedure finds a basis in the ethnological material.

Contact with witchcraft lore, stories or performances of Soyoko, and initiation are universals of Hopi child experience in all except markedly Christianized Hopi families. Therefore it seems fair to assume that the aspects of the behavior of parents and relatives which led to Don's puzzlement and mistrust are general in Hopi society. His experience, of course, was atypical in the amount of punishment he received as the worst boy in Oraibi. What emerges from Don's experience is a progression of discipline from mildest to most severe, depending on the resistance of the child, until finally aggression against elders was curbed. But the character of the discipline in certain of its universal aspects was always such as to create not only obedience but also distrust, disillusionment, and resentment.

During his ten years at school, beginning at age nine, Don lived in two worlds. He learned new and unaccustomed things, but because of his absence from the Hopi country he failed to learn the customary techniques for life. He passed through a clash of values principally involving religious and sexual codes, and was faced with the problem which plagued him all his life: how to maintain his self-esteem as a Hopi. And he experienced a crisis in health and belief, the resolution of which was critical in establishing his favorable attitude to a return to the Hopi country. Problems such as mistrust, insubordination, and prestige among his fellows, which were important in his earlier years, became much reduced in significance during this period.

The problem of aggression is highlighted by an episode in the summer vacation of Don's eleventh year. The crisis which occurred brings out the degree to which he had become unable to express direct aggression against his elders in the course of his socialization. He criticized his father's brother's little boy for being a crybaby. His mother, who was caring for the child, became angry and struck Don, and he went off to the foothills and dug a pit in the sand. There he lay waiting for a cave-in to kill him. He left the pit for a few minutes, and shortly after that the cave-in occurred. He became terrified and returned to the village. He found his mother very upset, since she thought he left for Oraibi, forty miles distant, as he had threatened to do. This would have been a long and dangerous trip for an eleven-year-old to make alone. He was careful to tell her where he had been and what he had done. It appears that Don's only weapon for turning against her was to attempt his own death. It may be that Don chose this passive mode of self-slaughter, simply waiting for the fateful moment, in order to avoid complete disobedience of the strong taboo against suicide.

The full effect of some of Don's school experiences can only be discussed in the context of events after his return to Oraibi. The significance, however, can be dealt with now. Don went to school relatively well socialized regarding respectful behavior toward superiors. Few of the things for which he was disciplined involved the aggression against his elders— in this case teachers—that was so apparent in his earlier misdeeds. The same is true of his actions in the Hopi setting. His behavior at the time of his suicidal attempt shows that aggression toward elders was virtually choked off. Although he fought with other boys in his early years in school, he gradually left off fighting.

During these ten years, Don acquired a great deal of information and a knowledge of English. He also learned new, direct techniques for dealing with whites, which evidently afforded him great satisfaction. Such techniques were uncommon between Hopi.

There was a clash between what he believed was the proper attitude toward heterosexual activity and masturbation, and what the school authorities believed. Nevertheless, though life was somewhat clouded by "fear of sin or a rawhide," his first sex experience as an adolescent appears to have been unaccompanied by the revulsion, disgust, fear or guilt which often typify the event for middle-class American boys. And he carried out normal Hopi courtship patterns: many affairs, payment, and full sex relations, in spite of the limitations created by school conditions.

A more severe strain was set up by his wish to be white. What the precise meaning of this was for him during this early period is not entirely clear. Accumulation of wealth (in view of his stress on earnings) appears to have been one element. In addition, it may be presumed that as a Hopi, more specifically as a nonwhite, he suffered from feelings of inferiority. For him Christianity appears to have been mainly an instrumentality for becoming white. After that, the "half-Christian and half-heathen" boy who at seventeen wished for a miracle to change his skin color, became strongly motivated "to become a real Hopi again" by the age of nineteen. One element in the motivation undoubtedly was the lack of any miracle of skin change such as he hoped

for. The channels for his passing into white society in any satisfactory way were difficult to find.

On his return to the Hopi country after leaving school, Don was faced with the problem of reacculturation as a Hopi: of experiencing and affirming his solidarity with the Hopi, denying his allegiance to the whites, and taking the normal step of adult initiation. He was much preoccupied with getting a girl, and with the question of whether or not to marry, and was involved in many cross pressures in connection with sexual adventure and marriage. Old problems of mistrust, fear of witchcraft, and desire for prestige recurred, though the control of aggression was of far less concern to him at this time than it became later in his life. He made an economic adjustment as "hired hand" on agency and other white-controlled projects, shifting more toward a role as Hopi farmer and herder as his marriage arrangements progressed. The Hopi exchange of feasts and property and the accumulation of corn and woven products which must accompany a wedding occupied his time from November, 1910, to January, 1911.

Don moved, during this year and a half, from the position of returned schoolboy to that of adult, married Hopi man. The adjustment was not made without conflict and difficulty. Further schooling and employment with the whites pulled him in one direction. His attachment to his girl friend Mettie, who had returned to school, was but one element in this pull. During this period virtually all Don's employment was with whites. Techniques learned in school were useful to him in gaining this employment; his knowledge of white ways and his ability to speak English. He hoped, too, for better jobs, such as the one in the bakeshop, which would have involved what he had learned in school. Because work with the whites meant for Don an easier time and more money, it was hard for him to give up the idea of returning to school, even when he was about to be married.

But another way had been pointed by the approval of his family and of "the old people." This approval, the need for adult status, the need for protection from witchcraft, and the need for adequate techniques to face life in the semi-desert were the most important pressures toward his resuming his place in Oraibi. The problem of dealing with the arid environment, however, did not assume as prominent a place in his thinking as it did later, when he was married and working in the fields.

In spite of his doubts and hesitations at the time of initiation and marriage, Don made his decision in favor of Hopi ways, without, however, relinquishing his wishes for an easier and more remunerative life. Once committed, he sought prestige and security among the Hopi by his ceremonial participation, even forcing his way into one ceremonial by a faked dream. As a further consequence of this mode of life, Don was once again involved in a system of beliefs which had been for the most part dormant during the last three years of his schooling: "bad hearts," arguments, and the like could ruin the prospects for agricultural success of the entire community. Within a short time, too, his concern with witchcraft, revivified during his death vision, began to take the form of definite suspicions, directed against specific individuals. He had, furthermore, little confidence that witches could be successfully combated.

Allied to the white-Hopi conflict in his mind was the conflict between freedom and marriage. If he married, school was out of the question. In deciding to relinquish schooling and to marry, Don was heavily committed to participation in Hopi society and was completely involved in Hopi beliefs.

Don's economic adjustment during the first eighteen years of his marriage was accomplished through his taking an entrepreneurial role. His insecurity at this time led to an increasing mistrust of people who he thought were witches. This feeling received further reinforcement and focus in consequence of the deaths of his children and relatives, and his own illnesses. The "double factor theory" of disease led to cycles of self-blame and to accusations of others, as well as to feelings of inadequacy in dealing with such misfortunes. Misfortunes led to increasing isolation, and in Don's case to the fear of the very people on whom he depended for support. Concealment of emotion, the best weapon to conciliate witches, was not an effective one.

Strains in the marital relationship centered about responsibility and control, relationships with affinals, philandering, and the sicknesses and death of children.

The successive deaths of Don's four children created a series of crises in his relations with [his wife] Irene and her kin. It was not the deaths which were critical, but the community's interpretation of these deaths. A cycle of accusations and counteraccusations followed. Irene's clan members implied that Don must have done something wrong to have this bad luck. He examined his own conduct and found nothing to blame. Therefore, he knew, someone must be against him. A Hopi doctor corroborated his opinion but would not identify the witch, except to say that it was a close relative of Irene's. The enhancement of distrust in Don's adult life appears with great clarity. The sorcerer cannot be detected, because he is keeping up a cheerful appearance. Don's suspicions cannot be detected, because he, too, aims at concealment of emotion to protect himself. The implications for the entire society are clear: the innocent man knows neither who may be his witch enemy nor who may suspect him, however incorrectly, of witchcraft.

Don's prestige cravings were satisfied to some degree by his success as a teamster and by his achieving the positions of chief of the Sun clan and owner of the Mongwi (Tawaovi) kiva—though Don attributed undue importance to these positions. He was unable to gain admittance into the Snake society.

As to white culture, Don rejected the whites, who made him feel inferior and helpless (since their presence interfered with the effectiveness of ceremonials). Yet he still badly wanted education and status in the eyes of the whites.

In closing his account, Don tells of his hopes for the future. Along with his optimism Don has a feeling that Hopi culture inevitably will succumb to the whites. Some of his hopes and expectations have already been discussed in connection with his attitudes toward the whites.

In a dream his Spirit Guide took him to a beautiful, big brick house with a porch and showed him a flock of more than nine hundred sheep that would herd themselves without the necessity of human labor, a large plot of land, which the Guide warned Don he must not let the whites get from him, and a good source of water. When Don recognized a grandfather of his who had been dead for many years, he knew that this was the afterlife and awakened happily.

Until he can achieve the reward promised by the Guardian Spirit, Don wants to remain in Oraibi, well supplied with food; he wants to tell his nephews and nieces about his life and continue his diary for Simmons. He hopes that, when he becomes helpless, he will die painlessly in his sleep, and that Norman [his adopted son] will bury him in the Hopi fashion and in the costume of a special officer of the Soyal. "If he wishes to put me in a coffin, he may do even that, but he must leave the lid unlocked, place food near by, and set up a grave ladder so that I can climb out. I shall hasten to my dear ones (the dead), but I will return with good rains and dance as a Katcina in the plaza with my ancestors—even if Oraibi is in ruins."

Don's economic adjustment improved. His successful rearing of Norman served to divert witchcraft accusations from him and provided him with important emotional satisfactions. His relations with his wife and with his affinal kin improved. This fact affords further substantiation of the view that witchcraft accusations do not simply serve to allow aggressions to be expressed, but create severe disruptions of social ties. If the death of Don's children had simply provided a convenient excuse for him to break with his wife's family, he would probably not have tried so hard to effect a peace treaty with his mother-in-law. His regaining of sexual potency evidently improved the situation with Irene and permitted him once again to enjoy philandering, though to a lesser degree than before.

Contacts with anthropologists allowed Don to hew out a new role for himself, a role so satisfactory that he resisted considerable social pressure in order to maintain it. Don found satisfaction in these contacts because of the financial gain they brought him, the emotional warmth of the relationships, his feeling of security in being able to trust the anthropologists as he could not trust his fellow Hopi, the high valuation of Hopi culture expressed by the anthropologists and the prestige they accorded him.

Lastly, the attitudes surrounding disease, death, and witchcraft are brought out in starkest detail in this section. By his fiftieth year, Don had suspected his "grandmother," his affinal kin, his grandfather, and finally his own mother, of witchcraft. Disease, in most cases, and death a fortiori created suspicion against the sick or dying, blame of self, and suspicion against others. To die, Don felt, was to will oneself to die, to reject the positive feelings of one's relatives, and to try to disturb them and ultimately to carry them along to the afterlife.

Any hostile feelings outside a very narrow range of permitted aggression created anxiety for his health and for the health of the object of hostility, if he was someone for whom Don had warm feelings.

Now we must face the question: "What is the significance of the findings in this case for an understanding of Hopi individuals and Hopi society?" Some of the logic of the application of the single case for general analysis has already emerged, but it is now necessary to make it more explicit. Clearly, the point of departure cannot be that the course of Don's life or the structure of his personality is typical. Not every Hopi has lost all his children, or has become impotent at some time, or has acted as an informant, or has become Sun chief. Nor does Don represent a determinate point in the distribution of such personality characteristics as aggression, suspicion, or prestige drive. The generalizations made here must be in such a form that it does not matter if Don is the most extreme in all these regards of all men in Oraibi, and Oraibi the most strife-ridden community. (Neither statement is necessarily true.)

To make our generalizations legitimate, we must return to the ethnological material with which we started. We have seen that the system of beliefs and values with which Don operated is that of other Hopi. It follows that their interpretations of certain situations will be similar to his, and the consequences will be similar in range. As W. I. Thomas had said, "If men define situations as real, they are real in

their consequences." The prestige system and the system of role allocation that Don faced are those of Hopi society. The differential locus of responsibilty and control in marriage, its tensions, and the strains of relationships to affinals are features of Hopi society. The socialization system that brought Don to conformity is to a significant degree the same for other Hopi. The uncontrollable and unpredictable features of the total environment that affected him—drought and crop failure, disease, infant mortality and other premature deaths—are chronic for all Hopi.

Lastly, relationships with American society, which caused him so much conflict, are features of the situation to which every Hopi must accommodate, though the modes of accommodation are multiple. Education in American schools and attendant value conflicts, the existence of alternatives to Hopi life in American society, American control of the stock program, the tourist trade, missionaries, and the like, are all things in respect to which the Hopi must work out a *modus vivendi*. The intensity and exact nature of the problems thus created will vary in time and will differ for individuals according to personality, social status, sex, and age. But for no Hopi can this sector of life be successfully ignored.

Although in many respects Don is a unique *person,* the beliefs with which he operates, the social system in which he lives, and the human and nonhuman environment he faces are those which our analysis of Hopi society would lead us to expect. Differences between Don's experience and his interpretations of experience, on the one hand, and our expectations on the other, are minute or nonexistent. It follows that *whenever* Hopi face certain situations, then certain typical problems arise for them. How often these problems will arise, precisely what individuals will be affected, or what solutions will be adopted, cannot be decided from this analysis. These are problems for further research. But from the ethnological material and from Don's own life a fairly satisfactory picture of the *range* of possible alternative responses to chronic features of Hopi life has been derived.

We may shift from a consideration of reactions of individuals to a consideration of the *interaction* of a group of people who share these definitions of the situation and participate in the same social system. By so doing we animate our earlier and more static picture of Hopi society. If we add variations in the situations itself—variations in weather, morbidity, mortality, and relations with American society, for example—we can see the effects of a group of individuals operating with a common definition of the situation, in a common social system, under various conditions. It is thus that we arrive at a comprehensive interpretation of the relationship of Hopi beliefs and Hopi action, and finally of Hopi society itself, in its total situation.

Hence, from what has already been said about Don I shall proceed to generalizations about Hopi reactions to recurrent situations, and from these to statements about Hopi society. In doing so, I have no intention of psychological reductionism—of "building up" Hopi society from considerations about the individual. The statements that have been made derive their meaning from the earlier summary of Hopi ethnology. But only by seeing the individual in the social network, only by understanding the range of individual reactions, can we advance to an encompassing view of Hopi society in operation.

Throughout what follows, the picture will be drawn somewhat starkly, for the sake of clarity.

The right to fill certain offices belongs to the senior families of various clans.

Among the individuals who might be selected for such offices, some will probably be insufficiently motivated or endowed for the exercise of office. The strains which might arise from such a situation are alleviated by the provision for allocating offices to the abler and more strongly motivated individuals within the families which inherit office. Of course it is possible that some persons acquire offices that they do not want. The life-history gives us no information about such individuals. It can be said, however, that if *every* available Hopi male were unwilling to take *any* office, the society would break down. This situation has not arisen.

The life-history casts light on the other side of this problem—the man who desires prestigeful position but has no legitimate access to it. There are certain alleviations to this situation, also: the prestige that comes from being a good Hopi, and that derived from participation in important religious societies. It is clear from Don's case that these provisions do not make for the alleviation of prestige strains for everyone. It might be argued that individuals like Don are rare. Against this argument it may be pointed out that it is inconceivable that in a society with a great deal of ascribed status, such as Hopi, the combined processes of socialization and selection could bring about a *perfect* correspondence of individual aims and ability on the one hand, and social position on the other. It may be that the example of competitive American society has exacerbated the Hopi situation, but only under the conditions described in Aldous Huxley's *Brave New World* is it possible to avoid the existence of frustrated individuals like Don. Hopi history —the Oraibi split— indicates that such individuals do exist. And whenever they do, whenever a person who wishes a prestigeful position is unfavorably situated by birth, he cannot easily attain it. What are the possible results?

Such a man may simply stifle his wishes, and this doubtless happens. There was a time in Hopi society when a man might find his answer in warfare and the status of "real warrior"—a peculiar, but not a disvalued status. In the old days he might have joined the curers' society, which is now extinct, and even today he might become a curer. But getting the training for such a position is probably difficult. It is not known how curers are trained today; probably they are taught informally by other doctors. The role of curer can perhaps be achieved regardless of birth, but it is regarded with great ambivalence. A curer may eventually find himself a social isolate rather than a man of status, because of accusations of witchcraft. This happened to a Hotevilla doctor.

He might, like Don, achieve a status with anthropologists as an informant, persevering in this course in spite of community opposition, isolation, and accusations of witchcraft. Similarly, he might seek other positions of status with whites on the reservation: teacher, interpreter, government employee. These, too, demand solidarity with Americans and acculturation, and cut a man off from other Hopi. He might seek a position of leadership in the community-council system of acculturated New Oraibi. He might leave the reservation. (The desire for prestige is undoubtedly not the only or even the main, reason for so doing.) He might become an innovator or inflate his importance by claiming to be a witch. These solutions, too, would cut him off from the very group in which he hoped to attain status.

Lastly, as the history of the Oraibi split and other episodes of that period indicate, he might make a claim to a position not traditionally his, justifying his claim through a reinterpretation of mythogy or a complex kinship linkage. This last solution is only likely to succeed

if there are other favorable conditions— quarrels over land, factional disputes over policy toward the whites, and the like. Then the claimant will have the backing of interested followers instead of remaining an isolated crank. This is not likely to be a common solution to the prestige problem, but it has been chosen at various times. It demands a willingness to face antagonism and accusations of witchcraft. But Yokioma, a Hopi leader of a schism, did face them, and so did Don as an informant. Once schism starts, the lack of tight political control makes its consequences for social cohesion drastic indeed.

Analysis of Don's motivations and of Hopi social structure indicates, therefore, that if a man is born into the "wrong" place, he can find only a limited number of solutions to the problems raised by his wishes for prestige. None is likely to be completely satisfactory to the individual, and one, the last mentioned, is decidedly disruptive to the group. It is not *how often* such individuals arise that interests us, but *what situations* they may create.

It is exceedingly probable that Hopi socialization techniques, effective though they are in producing conformity, leave the individual with a life-long basis for mistrust concerning the motivations of others. The behavior of joking relatives who claim to be affectionate, parents' fobbing off of responsibility for severe punishment onto other relatives and onto Soyoko, the use of the Katcina figures for rewards and the withholding of rewards, parents' concealment of aggressive feelings in the presence of others, and the initiation experience combine to create in the child's mind a grave difficulty in interpreting the true intentions of others, particularly as regards aggression. This early-created attitude is continually fed by later experience. The concealment of one's own aggression and the inability to detect the evil-intentioned and witches, who are said to conceal their own aggression, make for serious mistrust of others. The nature of witchcraft beliefs, which localize the damaging individual among one's relatives, and more commonly in the more immediate kin group—the very people on whom one depends for emotional security, economic support, and solidarity—put the area of mistrust in the most damaging possible place and tend to bring about a real psychosocial isolation. Although the character structure and life experience of individuals will make for great variations in the amount of such feelings, it is improbable that anyone can escape some situations that mobilize mistrustfulness.

The creation of hostility. In the system of explanatory beliefs, the inevitable misfortunes of Hopi life, such as crop failure, disease, and infant or premature death, are interpreted as due in part to the hostility of others: to their bad thoughts of active practice of witchcraft. (Things would be entirely different if the Hopi believed that their misfortunes came from an unknowable God, from the Devil, from breaking taboos, or from their own bad thoughts alone.) There are other situations, also, that mobilize hostility— the strains of the marital situation and of relationships with affinals, others' accusations of witchcraft or misbehavior, and the like. Thus, though the *amount* of hostility will vary from individual to individual, and from situation to situation, there are chronic features of Hopi life that mobilize hostility. This is true of any social order, but in Hopi life hostility arises not only from certain characteristics of interpersonal relations but also out of the interpretations of a variety of natural catastrophes.

The disposition of hostility. Whatever the origin of hostile and aggressive impulses in any particular case, their existence creates an insoluble problem for any Hopi. If he suppresses them,

he may damage himself: both because bad thoughts themselves are harmful— are pathogenic agents, in fact—and because they render an individual particularly susceptible to the effects of witchcraft. Furthermore, simply having aggressive thoughts may damage the object of those thoughts far beyond the conscious intent of the man who holds them. One's own bad thoughts may seriously injure or kill a spouse or a child. Worry or grief may similarly damage the person who is disturbed, and may affect the health of his children. If a bad thinker is a ceremonial participant, his thoughts may damage the whole community. Release of hostility only exacerbates these situations. It hurts the man who releases the hostility, hurts those against whom he releases it, and alienates him from the community, under the opprobrium of being *kahopi,* evil-intentioned, and the like. To express hostility or to conceal it alike may produce accusations of witchcraft, particularly since in a situation in which every man knows he conceals certain reactions it becomes very easy to impute those reactions to others.

Consequently, if one is aggressive, or if one has experienced misfortune, the easiest way out is to accuse someone else before one becomes the object of accusations. This process is somewhat curbed by the belief that aggressive behavior toward a witch does not harm the witch but helps him. This and the fear of being damaged by the witch inhibit such accusations, but under severe "provocation" the accusations break through. Thus, cycles of blame and counterblame are set up.

Gossip, on the other hand, since it is not experienced by the gossiper as direct aggression, is a safer outlet and is exceedingly common.

It is not implied that all Hopi towns and all their component individuals are continually at the boiling point. Nor is it implied that individuals react uniformly to the problem of aggression. The range of responses may run from psychosomatic illness to overt accusations of witchcraft.

Furthermore, the concept of the witch is illuminated by the foregoing. For as the Hopi see it, the witch is the person who escapes the conflict created by aggression. Although he is threatened with ultimate damnation and with possible isolation in this life, he may be aggressive without fearing to hurt himself. Under these circumstances, it is possible that the fantasies about witches have undercurrents of envy, and that a man might find certain attractions in the idea of being a witch. (There are no data for estimating how many people may actually believe themselves to be witches.)

Lastly, it is evident that illness, one's own aggression, and that of others all create great anxiety in Hopi individuals, more than in some other social systems. These situations lead to feelings of helplessness, since protection against witchcraft is slight.

In this light, it is clear how the Hopi solve the problem of conformity and of social control, at least in any ordinary crisis. The process of socialization that has been described, culminating in the initiation procedure, provides the foundation for conformity. The dangers of aggression, for oneself and others, and the possibility of social isolation through the gossip of others all direct the individual in nonaggressive, traditionalistic and cooperative paths.

The conclusion must not be drawn that life in a Hopi situation is unbearable. It must not be forgotten that adherence to the Hopi way provides insurance for health, economic security, and life; that ceremonial activity is unquestionably a rich and rewarding experience; that under favorable circumstances this way of life may give very considerable security to individuals.

Once again it must be emphasized that these conclusions do not tell us *how many* of *what kind* of reactions will occur, nor do they tell us what kind of personalities Hopi have. They entitle us only to say that *whenever* there are prestige-driven Hopi, sick Hopi, aggressive Hopi, those individuals face a particular set of problems to which there is a certain range of responses, some of which reintegrate the individual in the group, and some of which are disruptive of his group relationships.

Thus far this study has been concerned with the reactions of individual Hopi. Now the question arises: "If a group of people with these reactions lives in the kind of social system that has been described, what are the consequences?"

The Hopi social system is best conceived of as an unstable equilibrium. Its political, economic, and kinship features, its system of beliefs and values, its human and nonhuman environment, and the reactions of individual members to all these features have been examined. The products, taken together, make for a system which operates rather differently under different conditions. Good weather, plentiful crops, a low disease rate, and a minimum of pressures from American society tend to produce cooperation in a social system with minimal means of coercion, conformity to tradition, and feelings of good-will and mutual support. An increase in any area of potential misfortune will start minor cycles of blame, mistrust, and the like, within various groups, but pressures such as gossip and the isolation of deviants will still prevent the breakdown of the system. If, however, individuals arise whose deviance cannot be handled by these techniques in situations in which it becomes possible for them to mobilize factions, then very serious tensions will arise and perhaps ultimately a town will split. The factions, however, have it in their power to reconstitute new communities. The important fact is that Hopi society has no second line of defense against the innovator, the political dissident, or the like. It is this fact, together with the tendency of Hopi belief to direct blame for catastrophy toward individuals, rather than toward gods or nature, that makes us describe the society as unstable in equilibrium. Under one set of conditions Hopi beliefs and values operate to produce security, conformity and stability; under another set they produce everything from psychosomatic disease to community fission.

An analogy from American society may dispel this apparent paradox. There are elements in the American value system that emphasize independence, self-sufficiency, responsibility, and enterprise as norms to which individuals should conform. These norms also emphasize the individual's responsibility for his own fate. Under favorable economic conditions these values lead to vigorous effort, enterprise, entrepreneurial activity, and inventiveness. In an economic depression, however, they lead to self-blame, guilt, and depression. Although it is true that the tendency to blame the economic system rather than oneself may increase in an economic depression, the ideology is surprisingly persistent under bad conditions. Similarly, the Hopi react to alterations in their situation in terms of the definition of the situation, cognitive and evaluative, which participation in their society has given them.

It is in the light of this interpretation that varous accounts of the Hopi may be seen as complementary rather than divergent. If an observer studies a demoralized Hopi community, he may find witchcraft, suspicion, and hostility to be the more prominent part of the picture. In another Hopi community, under different conditions, cooperation, lack of physical coersion, and peaceful behavior will be more noticeable. Neither aspect will ever be completely absent in any community. Furthermore, the scientist may phrase his problem to concentrate on whichever aspect he wishes. In personality psychology, for example, we may choose the same case to illustrate both the constructive work of the ego and the effects of emotional stress. So, depending on the town selected for study and the problem selected for analysis, either aspect of Hopi society or the interrelationship of the aspects may be profitably examined. It is not a question of which problem is more "correct," nor is it a question of mutually exclusive alternatives. The validity of the present interpretation of the Hopi can be checked by a study of the amount of disruptive or cohesive action in the community. If we find that the community that should be least disrupted is most disrupted, or vice versa, then this interpretation is challenged. With other treatments of the Hopi, a careful evaluation of the body of data employed and the precise forms in which the problems are stated tends to show that, by and large, the studies are concerned with different things and different problems and are not actually contradictory. In the context of the interpretation of Hopi society presented here, it becomes possible to see the contribution which each study makes to the understanding of the Hopi, and the way in which the studies fit together.

Let us recall the original problem of this chapter: The Hopi are characterized in two separate ways by different investigators. On the one hand, they are seen as peaceful, harmonious, and operating with a minimum of coercion. On the other hand, child-rearing practices are repressive and adults are constrained, and they are seen as anxious and mistrustful and full of suppressed hostility.

Now there is no need to belabor the point that it is possible to identify modal personality features among the members of a society and that it is possible to observe modal personality differences between societies. Very simply, this means that there are personality features which most of the members of a society share in common and which characterize them *vis-à-vis* other societal groups. And it is generally assumed by students of society that there is usually a congruence between modal personality and the institutional systems in the society. What is more, it is often possible to infer from ongoing sociocultural processes that people strive for consistency, to paraphrase Sumner,[4] in their many institutional participations as well as between the personality features which they share in common and their society's institutional structures and systems.

At the same time that there are such modal patterns, however, there is a great danger in categorizing a people in one set of absolute or categorical terms without the qualifying awareness that observed modal patterns are part of *modal ranges of potentialities and predispositions* which are elicited or inhibited by different conditions. For example, Germany is the nation which produced both a Hitler and a Goethe; Spain has produced a Franco and a Casals; Soviet Russia its slave labor camps and some of man's greatest triumphs in exploring the universe; and so on, almost *ad infinitum*. The Hopi, too, like many other people or society, are neither "this" nor "that": they are many things, and have many qualities, some of which may appear to non-Indian Americans as contradictory.

Every human individual, to take another perspective, experiences anxiety and frustration in the course of growing up and in the course of normal living. One possible result of this can be a predisposition to aggressivity and hostility. But there is no simple or one-to-one causal relationship between anxiety or frustration and aggression, because anxiety and frustration can be coped with by other means, such as by displacement or by the use of socially provided instruments, like religion or alcohol. *Under certain types of conditions the predisposition to anxiety and aggression will be maximized and under other sets of conditions this predisposition will be minimized.*

The basic values and tenets of Hopi life demand, among other things, that feelings of mistrust and aggression be repressed. As a result, such feelings as hostility and mistrust become unacceptable to the Hopi individual, whether he experiences these within himself or in others. In turn, these unacceptable feelings become part of the basic premises of Hopi society; these premises are clearly outlined by Dorothy Eggan in her paper on "The General Problem of Hopi Adjustment," [5] and need not be repeated here. But what is especially important in this connection is that repressions *per se* do not necessarily lead to disruptive behavior

---

[4] Sumner, 1906, pp. 5-6.
[5] Eggan, 1952.

in society or to the disruption of social institutions. *It is when individuals are expected to behave—or are impelled by circumstances to behave—in a manner which is unacceptable to them that disruptions in sociological relationships will arise.* Let us illustrate this point by a slight digression. If the children of a society are raised in such a manner that they have little alternative but to repress their sexual strivings, we cannot, solely on the basis of *this* isolated datum, predict that the sociological relationships in which these individuals engage as adults will be interfered with or disrupted by their repressions. But if these individuals, as adults, are placed in situations in which they must act in a way which is unacceptable to them—in social relationships, such as marriage, which are sexually demanding—then we can safely predict that a not inconsiderable amount of intrapersonal and interpersonal conflict will arise in one way or another.

If, then, all that was demanded of a Hopi individual was that he act in a mild, beneficent, unaggressive manner—all would be well within him and between him and his fellows. But life is never that simple in any society; contradictions within the total way of life are always bound to arise, and there are, inevitably, frustrations emanating from the physical and social environments. Taught to trust people, especially clansmen and other relatives, and to cooperate with them in many spheres of life, the Hopi child is also subjected to many experiences which give rise to *potentials* or *predispositions* to tremendous hostilities to people, again especially to clansmen and other relatives. But such hostility is also tabooed, for it interferes with the ideological goals of Hopi society. Religious institutions, which are also in a central position in Hopi social relationships, not only foster social cohesiveness and rain, the latter being indispensable to effective living in the pueblos, but these institutions, especially one's initiation into them, also foster disillusionment with parents and other relatives, and such experiences serve as catalysts and reactivating stimuli to earlier feelings of mistrust and anxiety. But the Hopi also believe that these religious institutions cannot function when there is resentment and aggression in people's hearts and minds.

Are the Hopi, then, in a constant turmoil and an unceasing state of conflict? The answer is not a simple one, for it is neither in the affirmative nor in the negative. Rather, the answer would seem to be: not necessarily, as Aberle indicated clearly in the last three paragraphs of the analysis which we have just read.

With a few minor exceptions, the formulations following the selection by Aberle, as *general* descriptions, are true of all human societies, especially in Aberle's concise statement that "The products, taken together, make for a system which operates rather differently under different conditions." We can see similar relationships operating on many levels of our own society: in our recurrent post-war needs for witch-hunts; in the pre-World War II inverse relationship between the price of cotton and the frequency of lynchings in segments of the nation; in the frequencies of adolescent delinquency and adult drug addiction among Puerto Rican migrants to the mainland, where such phenomena were almost unknown in Puerto Rico itself; and the like. In the description of *any* people it is impossible to stop at simple descriptions of them as having "this" or "that" set of qualities or characteristics. As we have already seen, Americans are neither "puritanical" nor "liberal" in their attitudes toward sexuality; Russians have neither a great "need for affiliation" nor a great need for individualism or isolation; the Hopi are neither placid nor hostile; the Chinese peasant exhibits neither *anomie* nor excessive conformity. In all such instances, as we have seen, and the list of illustrations could be extended greatly, we must always understand *the specific sets of social-structural conditions* under which particular patterns arise out of modal predispositions and function within the society.

To illustrate the point just made, let us take another group of people, this time the Teton-Dakota Indians of the American Great Plains. We will illustrate this last point not only by citing another case, but also by stating our proposition in somewhat different terms: *Any behavior, custom, habit, personality system, or character structure may be, but is not necessarily, adaptive or maladaptive, normal or abnormal, healthy or unhealthy. What determines the adaptive quality of a behavior or a personality system are the* conditions *under which these occur.* To illustrate this, we will look at the Teton-Dakota at two points in their history: (1) when they lived on the Great Plains as roaming buffalo hunters, and (2) during the present era, when they are living on a government reservation.

THE TETON-DAKOTA INDIANS*

About three hundred years ago, the Tetons abandoned their agricultural way of life and moved onto the Great Plains to begin leading a nomadic existence, wandering about in search of buffalo and the scalps of enemies. Their nomadism was greatly facilitated by the introduction of the horse by the Spaniards. As we saw in Chapter 4, the group in which these people lived and in which nomadic life was conducted was the band. This group consisted of several related families who hunted together and fought together. Bands did not attack each other, but raided bands of other tribes. The manifest object of these wars and skirmishes was hunting territory; the more territory a tribe and its bands had the more buffalo they had to hunt and the more they had to eat.

But warfare and hunting had a special value for these people besides get-

ting enough to eat. The only way in which a man could attain prestige—to be respected, looked up to, desirable as a lover or as a husband, to become a chief—was to be successful on the warpath and on the hunt. For each feat of bravery a man received a war bonnet or a feather specifying exactly what he had done. Competition was between men who constantly strove to outdo each other in accumulating points and war honors. A man also attained honor and prestige in hunting buffalo, but in a special way. Generosity and liberality were some of the most esteemed virtues among the Teton-Dakota (as it was among almost all of the Plains Indians), and when a man killed a buffalo or several buffalo he was expected to divide and share his meat with everyone in the band, or at least with those who did not have enough to eat. The more he gave away the more

* The data for this section are based largely on *Warriors without Weapons,* by Gordon Macgregor. Chicago: The University of Chicago Press, 1946.

he was esteemed. Hence, a man tried to kill as many buffalo as he could. Anyone within the band who was in need, such as disabled warriors, sick people, old people, and the like, had a right to ask for food from those who had and they had a perfect right to expect to receive whatever they asked for. Visitors were always hospitably received, were given the seat of honor at the rear of the tipi, and were immediately served with great quantities of food, no matter at what time of the day they came.

For the Teton-Dakota individual, social relationships were of paramount importance, and these considerations overrode all material considerations. The specific focus or representation of these relationships resided in an elaborate network of giving and receiving. In almost all relationships an individual was supposed to consider the welfare of others before considering his own, as long as he and his family had enough on which to subsist. Thus, even his social relationships involved success and ability on the hunt.

But success on the warpath or on the hunt depended on more than mere physical prowess or bravery. A man had to have power—specifically, *supernatural power*. Such power was gotten by an individual without any help from anyone else. To achieve supernatural power a boy or young man went out alone onto the plains, wearing only a breechcloth and moccasins, fasting, telling the gods of his poverty and weakness. After several days of this he received a vision in the form of some animal or bird which then became his guardian spirit. This spirit then became the source of the individual's power. He had to obey it and do its beckoning; by this he was able to succeed on the warpath and on the hunt.

After a child was born he was placed in a cradle-board to which he was strapped until the age of about 12-14 months. He was fed whenever he cried,

and no demand he made went unheeded. He was constantly with his mother or with some older female who would respond immediately to his needs. As children grew older, the main emphasis in their training was to be generous. When children played together, they were punished for not giving up anything which any of their playmates demanded. Children were rarely slapped, but a favorite form of punishment was to pour water down their noses for disobeying their parents. Although children were constantly taught to consider the welfare of others before considering their own, this was not an attempt to teach or impose a system of self-abnegation. They were rewarded for being generous and kind to others and they also learned that they could expect to receive things from others by asking for it and that these persons were obligated to give it to them. Hence, from a very early age the individual learned that generosity was reciprocal. It was not a conditional reciprocity; that is, the rules of the game did not say: if you give to me I will give to you. Rather, the rules said: I will give to you; when I need something, you will give to me.

Finally, one of the most outstanding characteristics of aboriginal life on the Plains was a constant and consistent pattern of destruction. The first things destroyed were the buffalo. Since so much of an individual's prestige depended on his generosity in dispensing meat to his neighbors and relatives, buffalo were constantly being destroyed faster than they could reproduce themselves. By the time the white man came onto the Plains, the Indians were apparently considerably hard-pressed economically in terms of their food supply. They were apparently convinced that their supernatural powers would take care of them and would provide what they needed. They never, it seems, developed a policy of conservation of buffalo.

The other part of the pattern of destruction was to be found in the constant raids that went on between tribes. It was a rule of the Plains that every raid was responded to with a retaliatory raid. Since many tribes were involved in these raids, a vicious circle of raiding was set into motion. Fuel was added to the fire by younger men who, eager and avid for glory, often initiated a series of raids so that they could win war honors. Often, the older and more experienced people of the tribe had all they could do to restrain these young men from starting a raid when strategy or other considerations indicated that engagement in a skirmish or a fracas would not be prudent.

What ultimate adjustments would have been made by the Tetons and other Plains Indians to the depletion of the buffalo and to the self-destructive pattern of raiding is something we do not know and about which we cannot speculate with too much certainty. The coming of the American Whites precluded the completion of this experiment of nature. But it was a system which, until the middle of the nineteenth century, functioned well. There was a fine integration of the major elements and chords of the system, their attitudes toward the supernatural, material, and social worlds being in considerably good harmony with each other.

Until 1855, the Teton-Dakota were free and independent, living as nomadic warriors and hunters and following the way of life which they had developed in two hundred years on the Great Plains. By the Treaty of 1868, which terminated their wars with the American Whites, the Teton-Dakota accepted a single large reservation, where their hunting rights were to be undisturbed. There was an uprising against the Americans in 1876, in which the Tetons were soundly beaten, and this was followed by a final "acceptance" of reservation life. They really had

no choice but to accept, because the buffalo, their basic source of food, had almost vanished from the Plains.

About 1900, the Indians were given cattle and land by the government, and they built log cabins along the creeks and rivers of the reservation. (Some of the consequences of this settlement pattern were discussed in Chapter 4.) The old encampments of the bands broke up, and each family lived apart from the others on its own tract of land. Slowly, each family began to accumulate cattle and also began to prosper. During World War I, cattle prices soared and the Indians were encouraged to sell their herds. By 1916, nearly all their herds had been sold. After the sale of these cattle, the White stock-men moved into the area and rented nearly all the Indian pasture lands. By 1921, almost all the grazing lands had been sold or leased. The Indians indulged in what can only be described as an orgy of spending, for their cash incomes from the sale of their herds and renting of land appeared to be endless. Just as they destroyed the buffalo without thought to the future, so they sold their cattle and gave up their lands without thought to the implications of the destruction of their working capital.

In 1921, a postwar recession set in and most of the White cattlemen went out of business and defaulted on their leases. The Indians were now without cattle and without cash. By 1922, the cattle market had recovered and the government encouraged the Indians to sell their grazing lands to the now recovered White cattle-raisers. Apparently, no one bothered to tell an Indian that he was being defrauded when he accepted $40 and a suit of clothes for his land, believing that it was a down-payment, only later to find that he had signed a final deed of sale. From petty capitalists the Indians became poverty-stricken dependents on charity.

As among many other American Indian societies, there are today two main groups among the Teton-Dakota. First, there are the "full-bloods" who have attempted to maintain a traditional way of life. Second, there are the "mixed-bloods" who have adopted many of the ways of White society. The latter are people who have rejected traditional Indian ways of generosity and assistance to needy kinsmen. In terms of White values, they are beginning to succeed economically and they are beginning to adjust to the majority world around them. But the "mixed-bloods" have also paid a price. They have been ostracized by the "full-bloods," many of whom are relatives of the "mixed-bloods." Even the latter realize that the ostracism and criticism to which they have been subjected has been quite a price to pay for their economic success.

Two of the traditional Teton-Dakota values retained by the full-bloods are especially outstanding. The first has to do with generosity. By traditional Teton values, a man has a right to come and stay with a relative whenever he is in need or chooses to do so. Generally, these days, people come and "camp down" with relatives who have food and money. The mixed-bloods—those who are trying to amass wealth like White people do—always tell their relatives that they do not have anything with which to feed people. Although others know that they do have food and money, one has no choice but to leave and have nothing to do with such a stingy person. The full-bloods still retain the idea that it is *sinful* not to give to a kinsman when he himself has some food left. These people realize that most of their "guests" are really poachers who go from relative to relative until all the food has run out. Hence, for those who have retained the traditional values and ways of life, hospitality has become a burden and a strong deterrent to the accumulation of wealth. In the old days, a hospitable person received great honor

and prestige; and, since everyone else had food, he was certain of reciprocity. Now he is left poverty-stricken and without a social system in which the prestige which one derived from such generosity once had great meaning.

The second general value relevant in this connection is the belief that there is a providential supernatural power which will bring back the buffalo (though this is weakening) a belief which functions in much the same way as the belief once held that one secured supernatural power to assist one on the buffalo hunt and on the warpath. The full-bloods who continued to live on this belief, incidentally, are neither demented nor out of contact with reality. They live in log cabins, not tipis; they use American utensils, wear American clothes, send their children to school, and the like. Furthermore, they are fully aware of the fact that they are poor. Yet, despite their surface acceptance of things belonging to the world of White men, they are unwilling—or, perhaps, unable—to accept modern life and the facts of culture change. Instead, there is the fantasy among many of the full-bloods of an eventual return to the former Indian life. The full-bloods believe that the present situation is not here to stay. One of the ways in which they avoid accepting fully the present situation is by thinking, dreaming, and behaving as though the old life *could* be regained. To them, the old way of life is reality, and the necessity for Indians to live as Whites is still unreal, or at least to be avoided. They cling to old Indian ways and cherish the values and attitudes which supported those ways. (This picture was far more true thirty or forty years ago than it is today.)

The tremendous discrepancy and conflict between reality and fantasy must —and does—generate a terrible amount of anxiety. For example, the Indians who have clung to traditional ways and beliefs hold that a return of the buffalo and of the old tribal days will alleviate the terrible anxiety they are suffering. This inhibits their adoption of White ways and values and maintains their awful poverty; this poverty in turn generates anxiety and, again, in turn leads them to fantasy about the "good old days."

Another way in which this anxiety is expressed—and also one way in which they attempt to alleviate it—is in the taking of "peyote." Peyote is a plant which has some of the properties of a narcotic, but is definitely not a narcotic; it produces visions and a state of euphoria. It is not, however, a drug to which one can become addicted, and it appears to produce little physical injury to the individual. The taking of peyote has been ceremonialized into a cult, and has taken on some of the qualities of a new religion. Despite its relatively recent institutionalization, and its lack of physical harm to the individual, peyote does have cultural and psychological effects which, from the point of view of the predicament of the Teton-Dakota Indians, are quite harmful. First of all, it is used as a way of escaping unpleasant reality instead of coping with it on a realistic level. Often, peyote is fed to children; pneumonia is rather frequent among these children of the Tetons, and for some reason it is difficult to treat pneumonia in children who have been given peyote. Secondly, it makes the employment of general anaesthesia prior to surgery extremely dangerous, since one cannot rely on the functioning of the respiratory system of any person who has taken peyote, or any narcotic for that matter.

The cultural harm that this has wrought has been tremendous. The Teton-Dakota believe that peyote has curative values and properties. And, as a matter of fact, the Peyote Cult has also become a curing cult. Since peyote often tends to interfere with the White man's curing techniques, the idea is reinforced in the Indians that the White man has really little to offer in the way of relieving suffering and, in this way, he reinforces his ideas that the ways of the past are really that much better than modern White ways of doing things. This, again, feeds his anxieties about the world in which he is supposed to be living, and in turn leads to his escape in ways which are not conducive to learning the possible worth in White ways of doing things. He has been caught in a vicious circle.

His anxieties have other sources besides economic ones, however. Most people, no matter what their society or cultural affiliation, want to acquire prestige in the eyes of their fellows and to be admired by them. Among the Teton-Dakota Indians, prestige and honor and respect were traditionally acquired through success in hunting and warfare. *But these two sources of prestige have been taken away from him and no new sources have been provided or made available to him.* And because the full-bloods often raise their children on stories of the glorious past on the Plains, they frequently have no opportunity to learn that there are *other* ways in which one can acquire prestige, honor, and respect from others. This pattern, of course, is weakened by children's attendance at school.

SUMMARY

The case of the Teton-Dakota illustrates rather well the concept that one pattern of culture can function perfectly well under one set of sociocultural conditions and be dysfunctional under a different set of conditions. At the same time, however, we must not make the mistake of assuming that contact between cultures in and of itself produces conflict, dysfunction, and disequilibrium within a society and within its members. We will return to this point in Chapter 14.

The Teton-Dakota represent the kind of situation in which one society is engulfed within a much larger and much stronger society (here, industrialized American society). But even where such encirclement has taken prace, as elsewhere, qualifications must be introduced. There are many subsocieties in North America which possess patterns which are drastically different from those of the stronger and dominant society—such as the Amish, the Mennonites, the Hutterites, as well as other American Indian societies—but which have not met the fate of the Teton-Dakota. There are many reasons for this difference, one of the most outstanding of which appears to center around the problem of prestige-systems.

There are two dimensions to prestige, the one sociological, the other psychological; in reality, however, the two are inseparable though not equatable. Sociologically, prestige refers to a person's social status, his social influence, and the esteem in which others hold him. Psychologically, prestige refers to an important facet of the "self"—the sense of worth which a person has, the degree of self-esteem, the feeling of accomplishment and achievement and satisfaction. Where a society's prestige-system (sociologically speaking) has broken down—that is, if the society has no consistent and meaningful *sources* and material *symbols* of prestige—there can be no consistent and meaningful sense of self-esteem for the individual, no feeling of meaningful accomplishment and achievement. Without these, there is an almost ineluctable lack of fulfillment in one of the most significant aspects of the "self," and dysfunctional consequences very often result for the individual as well as for the total society.

Generally speaking, those small subsocieties which have managed to avoid the fate of the Teton-Dakota have been able either to retain an old prestige system (usually based on agriculture) or to develop a new prestige system based upon an industrial technology, as among the Menomini Indians about whom we shall read in Chapter 14. But before old patterns can be given up comfortably, new ones have to be available. The Teton-Dakota Indians, especially the full-bloods, have been unable to give up their old patterns, largely because of the absence of any rewarding tradition of farming and non-Indian business practices. But equally important is the fact that no new patterns, such as an industrial organization, have been provided which might serve as new sources of prestige.

BIBLIOGRAPHY AND SUGGESTED READINGS

Aberle, David F. "The Psychosocial Analysis of a Hopi Life History," *Comparative Psychology Monographs,* Vol. *21,* pp. 1-133, 1951.

Benedict, Ruth. *Patterns of Culture.* New York: Houghton, 1934. Especially Chapter 4, "The Pueblos of New Mexico." One of the earliest attempts by an anthropologist to characterize a society in psychological terms.

Bennett, John W. "The Interpretation of Pueblo Culture," in *Personal Character and Cultural Milieu* (3rd ed.), edited by Douglas Haring, pp. 203-216. Syracuse, New York: Syracuse University Press, 1956.

Dennis, Wayne. *The Hopi Child.* New York: Appleton, 1940.

Eggan, Dorothy. "The General Problem of Hopi Adjustment," in *Personality in Nature, Society and Culture,* edited by Kluckhohn *et al.,* pp. 276-291. New York: Knopf, 1955.

Goldfrank, Esther. "Socialization, Personality, and the Structure of Pueblo Society (with Particular Reference to Hopi and Zuni)," in *Personal Character and Cultural Milieu,* edited by Douglas Haring, pp. 303-327. Syracuse, New York: Syracuse University Press, 1956.

Haring, Douglas (editor). *Personal Character and Cultural Milieu* (3rd edition). Syracuse, Syracuse University Press, 1956.

Inkeles, Alex. "Some Sociological Observations on Culture and Personality Studies," in *Personality in Nature, Society and Culture,* edited by Kluckhohn *et al.,* pp. 577-592. New York: Knopf, 1955. A notable essay on some of the pitfalls which must be avoided in examining the relationships between personality and total social systems.

Kardiner, Abram. *The Individual and his Society.* New York: Columbia, 1939. This, and the following book, are two pioneering studies about personality and social systems to which all students of society and personality are indebted in one way or another.

Kardiner, Abram. *The Psychological Frontiers of Society.* New York: Columbia, 1945.

Simmons, Leo. *Sun Chief: The Autobiography of a Hopi Indian.* New Haven: Yale, 1942.

Sumner, William G. *Folkways.* Boston, Ginn, 1906.

Section IV

EFFECTS OF COMMUNITY SYSTEMS ON PERSONALITY

Chapter 10

WORLD VIEW

Beginning with this chapter, we are going to enter into analyses of issues which are somewhat more complex than those with which we have dealt before. The reason for this greater complexity is that we are going to deal with some of the effects on personality of the total communities in which people live and with effects of total life situations. In these discussions, we are going to bring together many of the social-structural forces—such as social distance, the differential access to culture as a function of social status, acculturation, kinship relationships, and so forth—which heretofore have been analyzed individually, and attempt to learn how they affect personality *in juxtaposition with each other*.

One of the fundamental assumptions underlying the studies to follow is that motivational systems—the impact of special forces which give impetus to the individual to move in certain directions rather than in others[1]—can be and are shaped in adulthood as well as childhood. This is not to deny the importance of childhood experiences which are, indeed, overriding. But as will be seen in the following chapters, a full understanding of motivational systems is impossible without an awareness of the ways in which childhood *and* adult experiences give rise to these psychologically structured impulsions to action.

People behave the way they do in institutional contexts for many reasons. They act in particular fashion because they have acquired certain "needs" while growing up and while being adults; because they have, in one way or another, learned that others expect certain behaviors and responses from them; because they have learned to perceive the physical universe and other individuals in particular ways; because they are often confronted with abrupt social change or catastrophe or emotional stress and must make the necessary psychological adaptations. In this chapter, we are going to focus on only one facet of motivation, namely, the ways in which people come to see or perceive the world around them. As we shall learn by reading about world views in Guatemala and in India, there is a remarkably close correspondence between the ways in which people view their social and physical worlds, that is, their ideas about man and about nature.

---

[1] See Kelly, 1958.

287

ETHOS AND CULTURAL ASPECTS OF PERSONALITY*
By John P. Gillin

Almost any short statement regarding ethos and cultural aspects of personality structure in modern Middle America made by an individual worker in this field is certain to be greeted at the present time by a certain amount of disagreement, or at least, demands for further clarification. The general concepts involved with ethos and cultural personality have not been thoroughly analyzed on a theoretical level and subjected to empirical test. Thus, at the present time there is no general agreement on terminology, concepts, or methodology in these matters. The culture, and therefore the ethos and cultural personalities, of all Middle Americans are not precisely alike, are not homogeneous throughout the area. The most important distinction is that between Indian cultures and those of Ladinos, Mestizos, or however one wishes to label the carriers and practitioners of Modern Latin American culture or civilization. Nor is either one of these two major cultural manifestations uniform throughout Middle America. The Indian cultures vary along a scale of acculturation from the less Europeanized to the more Europeanized or modernized. Also, the aboriginal bases of the original Indian cultures were by no means identical in content, organization, or cultural status. On the Ladino side of the line several forms of variation must be recognized. Some Ladino exhibits are more acculturated by the aboriginal cultures than others. These are apparently the more isolated and "folk-like" communities. Also the Ladino culture is exhibited in a variety of community situations. To mention two of the most important, the rural and the urban situations, I believe

that Redfield and his co-workers have demonstrated that, other things being equal, the rural situation produces a more homogeneous or more closely integrated culture than the urban environment. Thus, even if it can be shown that there is a general Indian ethos and personality distinguishable in pure form from those of Ladinos, each would show several sub-forms. Likewise, we may expect to encounter many mixed forms—cases, for example, in which the ethos is midway between the ideal types.

Ethos is taken to mean the constellation of acquired drives or motivations which are characteristic of a culture, plus the goals, both explicit and implicit, toward which cultural activities are directed or upon which high value is placed. The concept can and should be more thoroughly analyzed, but I shall not attempt to do so here. Considered as a whole, such a configuration of drives and goals imparts to a culture a characteristic quality which can be compared with those of other cultures.

The aspects of personality with which we are most concerned here are those which are produced or influenced by the operation of the culture and which are in some measure common to "typical" members of a community, society, or region who practice a common culture. I am aware of practically no work which has been done on depth psychology or psychoanalysis with a cultural orientation in the Middle American area, and only one series of Rorschach tests has been published which makes possible a systematic comparison of Indians and Ladinos. Thus we are not equipped at

* Reprinted with abridgment from *Heritage of Conquest: The Ethnology of Middle America,* edited by Sol Tax, pp. 193-212. Glencoe, Illinois: The Free Press, 1952.

present to discuss on the basis of data the deeper levels of personality organization and formation, although I believe that it is within the province of this symposium to make suggestions for research along these lines.

I shall take as my point of departure the community of San Luis Jilotepeque in the Department of Jalapa, Guatemala. It is the Middle American community which I personally know best, having spent three field seasons there in the last seven years. San Luis also happens to be a community which contains both Indians and Ladinos, each still preserving separate and distinguishable cultures, so that one is in a position to observe and test the differences in a situation the other components of which remain constant. Starting with this situation, then, I propose to set out certain propositions which, on the basis of reports from other Middle American studies, seem to be generally typical throughout the area, for Indians or Ladinos as the case may be. At least the propositions are intended to be amenable to research and open to investigation. It is taken for granted that it is not our function to judge the cultures and personalities in terms of our own cultural preconceptions. Our job is to understand them. No remarks herewith imply either approval or disapproval.

1. The principal and fundamental goal of Indian cultures is to effect a peaceful adjustment or adaptation of men to the universe. In contrast, the main goal of Ladino culture is to effect control of the universe by man. The Indian wishes to come to terms with the universe, the Ladino wishes to dominate it. Connected with these goals and motivations are two different sets of underlying premises. The Indian attitude is not one of abject submission to natural and supernatural forces. The basic assumptions in Indian cultures, however, do hold that man is in a world which operates according to certain laws or rules ultimately controlled by that part of the universe which we would call the supernatural or the unseen, that this general plan of things is on-going and immutable, that man must learn certain patterns of action and attitude to bring himself into conformity with this scheme of things, and that if he does so he will receive the minimum amount of punishment or misfortune and the maximum rewards of which such a scheme is capable. Some suffering or misfortune is inevitable, but the culture also provides patterns for mitigating it once it has befallen, as well as for avoiding it. These assumptions are implicit to most common men, and even uncommonly gifted men among the Indians of these days seldom raise them to the status of philosophical principles. The Ladino, on the other hand, assumes that the universe, including its supernatural department, can be manipulated by man; that control and power can be established not only over things and other animals but also over other men; that man has a will of his own and that the supernatural realm is also inhabited by beings with individual wills or personalities; that God and the saints can be dealt with on a personality basis, even though at times this necessarily must be done through the mediation of constituted priests; that in manipulating the universe human ideas or beliefs are more important tools than are material artifacts; and that destructive force, even to death, is the legitimate and ultimate technique for the removal of barriers to the individual's control. It is recognized that many persons must because of circumstances submit to frustration in this life, but the philosophy holds that this is no reason that they should not keep on trying to avoid it or remove it. Ladinos are usually much more glib, although not necessarily more explicit from a logical point of view, about the assumptions of their culture than are Indians.

In the Indian scheme of things, the individual as such counts less than the group. To put it another way, the individual exists as a member of the group which is adjusting to nature; by following its patterns he survives and prospers; but man, not any individual man, is the higher value among the Indians. In contrast, among the Ladinos, the individual personality in the abstract has the higher value. This value does not attach to all specific Ladino individuals equally. But the individual soul, ego, personality or what-have-you confronting the universe is of high value in Ladino thinking. The group, or certain groups such as the family, the clique, or the faction, exist to promote the individual, rather than the reverse. Another pair of corollaries is as follows. For Indians uninterrupted routine practice of the traditional patterns of adjustment has high value. For the Ladino such routine is intensely boring and dissatisfying. Periodic change of power locus together with constant struggle which such involves breaks the routine for the Ladino, adds zest to life. Struggle and the oscillation of power are definitely patterned in Ladino mental culture. They are part of the system.

2. The universe in any way of thinking, of course, takes in a lot of territory. However, in Middle America it is always much more restricted from the point of view of Indian culture than for Ladinos. The Indian universe is spatially limited and its horizon typically does not extend beyond the limits of the local community or region. This is not because Indians—especially Indian men—have never seen or visited other localities. In San Luis, for instance, practically all men have served in the army in Guatemala City or elsewhere, and throughout their lives they make periodic trips to El Salvador to sell pots or to the United Fruit plantations to earn money. The average man in one sample could name 14 other localities with which he was familiar. Yet these other places are not part of his universe, except in a most casual sense. The nearest analogy of which I can think is that of dream scenes for normal persons among ourselves. The Indians pass through other places, remember odds and ends about them, but do not think of them as part of their structured life experience. The result is, of course, that concepts of nationalism, of regionalism, tribal unity, One World, and the like, are beyond their ken. Tax has reported the same local focus among the Indians of Western Guatemala.

Likewise the Indians of these days live in a restricted time space. The universe of the Indian does not extend backward to a remembered past, glorious or otherwise. Even the Indians who live on the sites of the great ruins of antiquity do not connect these with their own ancestors. Nor do they project changes for the future. According to the Indian scheme of things life goes on in a timeless present, it has been this way as long as any one knows, and one will be content to see the pattern continue indefinitely. The object of life is to keep the scheme going according to expectations.

The typical Ladino, on the other hand, lives in a universe considerably more expanded both in space and time. His notions about the great world beyond the limits of his own community may be uninformed and naive from the point of view of modern science, but he does not believe that the world ends at the limits of his township or local region. Ladinos have kinship, political, and economic connections with the capital and other towns. They cultivate a concept of nationality, which may differ considerably from that held in the United States, but which enables them to see themselves as part of the Republic. The goal of control with its underlying assumptions may lead the Ladino into frequent revolutions and feuds in order to impose his will or that of men with whom he is associated in the nation, but the nation always figures in his thinking. Furthermore, the Ladinos hold the view that their ancestors came from Europe, that they are the descendants of civilized men with a long and glorious past. Historical details are usually unknown to the average Ladino, yet Ladino culture in its more intellectual circles fosters a strong interest in history, which is the only social science which, until recently, has been well-developed in Latin America. Thus the Ladino's universe takes in at least his own country, and usually he is also aware of the world as a whole, although in a comparatively ignorant way. The Ladino's strivings or drives are seldom entirely restricted to his local community, but are also oriented toward goals whose locus is in the larger outside world. In fact, the major rewards of life, from the Ladino point of view, are to be found in the provincial capital, the national capital, or even in the United States or Europe. What one achieves in his home town is merely a stepping stone to further achievements outside. Not only is the universe large, but it can be made over and manipulated for the achievement of human desires.

3. The differences between the goal of adjustment and the goal of control are seen in many details of the cultures.

a. Throughout the area consuming interest of both Ladinos and Indians is land. The Indian identifies with the land; there is a reciprocal relationship between milpa and man; a man's fulfillment in one sense comes from his opportunity to work out this adjustment between himself and a milpa. Thus, in San Luis, an Indian speaks of "my milpa," even though he and his father before him have worked it for decades on shares from a Ladino owner. Indians are interested in owning land so that they personally can work on it. Even those who own so much that they must pay other men to help them, invariably also work themselves. A man has not achieved his life goals unless he personally, with his own hands, can work milpa. If an Indian is successful in some specialized nonagricultural occupation, such as tile-making or adobe making, his notion is to give up such a business as soon as he has been able to acquire enough land to satisfy his needs. No Indian ever tries to acquire wealth or skill so that he can retire from the land, but rather the reverse. The Ladino, in contrast, personally works the land only when all other means of livelihood are unavailable. The Ladino wishes to control land—the more the better. He wishes to own it, to have other people work it for him under his orders. Control of land is a subgoal in itself for a Ladino; even if it is not financially profitable, it enables the owner to master the lives of his tenants and workmen, to exert influence in the town hall, and to bask in a certain prestige. If it is financially profitable, the return on the land places in the Ladino's hands the instrument for acquiring control in other fields.

b. The approach to things is typically more direct in Indian culture than in Ladino culture, which patterns the use of instrumentalities as a general rule. The Indian tills his milpa, cuts wood, gathers grass for house thatch, makes pottery, and so on, with his or her own hands, aided by a simple array of tools, and he transports himself and his burdens with his own feet planted directly on the ground. The weariness that comes from physical toil is one of the facts of life, not a resented punishment to be avoided at all costs, and one receives the approval of his fellows, rather than their derogation, for doing these things. Quite the opposite is true of Ladinos. Labor in the field or in the household is, from the Ladino point of view, properly performed through the instrumentality of other men or women under one's control. Toil is not only unbearably wearisome, but also disgraceful. A Ladino does not walk, if he can help it, but always rides an animal or a machine. He never carries a burden.

c. In relations with other men, the Indian pattern is adjustive and permissive, the Ladino pattern ordering, dominating. Ranking or stratification into classes is not characteristic of Indian society, is always present among Ladinos if their numbers exceed a handful. Statuses of leadership among Indians, such as *major-domos, principales,* and the like, are thought of as obligations, rather than something to be striven for competitively. Every man who follows the pathways of the culture and who gains the respect of his fellows may expect to assume some such position of prominence during his lifetime; these statuses are not thought of as a restricted group of prizes for which many must compete and few attain. Envy and competitiveness are regarded as an anomaly or a crime. One of the categories of magical illness among Indians is *envidia* (envy) which is believed to be caused by witchcraft perpetrated by an envious person. The victim has the perfect right, with the approval of the community, to kill his magical attacker if the latter can be discovered. Open expression of envy or competitiveness is unthinkable. An Indian in a position of prominence never gives orders to his fellows. He may point out the proper pattern to be followed in a ritual or suggest practical modes of action, as in building a house. But this is in the manner of dispensing superior knowledge, not of dominating others either by force of personality or by authority of position. Age gives knowledge and wisdom and is respected *sui generis.* Group decisions are taken by consensus rather than by majority rule or dictatorial fiat. Perhaps one can say that almost all patterns of social activity in Indian culture lead toward mergence

with the society, rather than toward individual distinctiveness. The approved way of doing things is to live and let live, to adjust to other human beings, to avoid conflict. This does not mean highly organized cooperation—in Middle American Indian society one does not find large work gangs among Indians (unless they have been dragooned into them by Ladinos), one does not find elaborately planned projects in which every individual or group has a clear-cut place in an explicit scheme of cooperation, one does not find communism in property. Rather one finds a picture of individuals, families, and relatively small groups each going about its business and not interfering with others. As regards Ladinos and others outside the Indian circle of society, the pattern normally calls for avoidance or submission within limits, rather than protest or conflict. Overt expression of resentment or disagreement is avoided. Political controls are regarded simply as means of keeping the system operating smoothly.

Ladino patterns of social interaction reflect the basic goals and attitudes. Ceremonial politeness with a great tenderness toward the other person's social position and ego is characteristic of Ladino behavior toward strange members of the same caste. Restriction of social contacts with members of lower groups, domineering or ordering behavior toward persons of lower status, and development of factions within the same class are common. Feuds between families and cliques occur with regularity, and in some communities the feud lines are of sufficient antiquity to be regarded as institutionalized. Gossip, character assassination, oaths, and insults are common on the overt level. Strong verbal protest against actions or attitudes disapproved by the individual is expected. The individual strives for prominence, a feat in which he is often assisted by his family. Competition or conflict is typically encountered along the road to power, and the average male must learn techniques of open or covert aggression. High status means the right to plan and order subordinates, but also demands a certain deference to their desires if one's subordinates are not to desert to a rival. The *caudillo* pattern, whether in military affairs, or otherwise, is well established in Ladino culture. But a given caudillo seldom stays in power very long because of the variant drives of his followers. Political advancement is regarded as a legitimate means of advancing one's own interests, if necessary at the expense of other members or factions of the community, including other Ladinos.

As democratic forms move into this area the goals and drives may well be changed for both Indians and Ladinos as the greater rewards of the new dispensation are demonstrated, but the foregoing features seem to be characteristic of the respective ethos at present.

d. Attitudes toward women and family on the whole are consistent with the basic orientations in the two cultures. Although the husband is officially dominant in Indian families, in actual practice the patterns require a reciprocal division of labor and of authority within the family. When a man takes a post of public responsibility, his wife shares the honors and the responsibilities. Man and woman form a cooperative partnership in the general pattern of adjustment to the universe, and to this team are added the children at about the age of seven or eight. Exploitation of one sex by the other in the family is atypical, nor are children dominated by physical or other heavy punishments imposed by the parents. Bickering and fighting between mates is not characteristic. In case of continued incompatibility one or the other mate, usually the woman, retires from the menage rather than continue in opposition to the other spouse. Again the implicit notion seems to be that adjustment without friction is the goal, and that if this proves to be impossible, withdrawal rather than domination is the answer. Several authors have mentioned their impression that sex is of no interest to Indians. My own material does not confirm this. Not only men but also women say that they enjoy the sex act. In one series of 21 women interviewed by my wife, only three, or about 9 percent, could be called cold or indifferent, but even they did not regard sex as repugnant or strongly distasteful. If I interpret the ethos correctly sex is regarded as necessary, but also as natural. It is readily available before marriage and between spouses, and dissatisfied spouses do not hesitate to fill their needs by adultery. Jealousy does occur, but I am certain that from the Indian point of view the use of sex for exploitative purposes is inconsistent with the ethos, just as are all other forms of exploitation of human beings. Sexual prowess does not add to the lustre of an individual.

Among Ladinos marriage is always a contract between families as well as individuals, and tends to be calculated with heavy attention to the social status of the prospective spouses, a feature which does not occur among Indians. The husband's authority is definitely superior in the family, according to the ideal patterns. Women's influence is exerted by devious or indirect means. The man does not expect his wife to share with him his public life in politics, business, and the like, and attempts of the woman to exert authority in these spheres are rejected. The woman participates in social life only with families whose relations with her own household are the most intimate. Double sex standard prevails. Sex is regarded as necessary for men, not necessarily so for women. It is much less easy to come by than among Indians, and prostitutes, Indian women and déclassé women provide a degree of satisfaction to men for gain. This does not mean that there are not many happy marriages among Ladinos. The Ladinos, however, as civilized Christians feel greater guilt about transgressions of the Christian sexual code than do Indians. Although the attitude of fathers toward children is not notably oppressive, children are more dependent upon the father's standing and his goodwill and advice than are Indian children. Fathers project more upon their children, because the latter are reflections of their own egos, and consequently are more insistent that children follow certain lines of conduct specified by the parent. In San Luis, at least, physical punishment is by actual count about three times as frequent for children of Ladino families than for Indians. These authoritarian patterns of family life are gradually being replaced by more equalitarian practices, but the dominance of the father and husband is still the ideal pattern, and it is of course reinforced by church doctrine.

e. The point has often been made that religion among Middle American Indians is not a departmentalized aspect of culture, but that it tends to permeate all of life, whereas Ladino culture appears much more secular. Here again I believe that the differences can be interpreted in terms of the respective ethos. Just as there is no notion of compartmentalizing society among the Indians, so likewise is the idea of compartmentalizing the universe foreign to them. What modern Western man calls the supernatural is not so distinguished in the Indian culture; the universe is viewed in these terms as a more or less integrated whole. In the less acculturated Indian communities remnants of the old gods still govern the various empirical aspects of the world—gods of the winds, of the sky, of the caves, of the game, of the maize, and so on. Among nominally Catholic Indians

who still have not been converted to Ladino culture, the same basic notion persists, although in attenuated form and often the old gods or spirits have been replaced in name by Christian saints. But the planting ceremonies, the rain-making ceremonies, the divinations and magical cures operate without any distinction between empirical and spiritual worlds.

Among nominally Christian Indians, a readily distinguishable difference in attitude and basic assumptions is apparent when compared with their official brethren in the church, the Ladinos. Of course, certain differences in participation in worship are symbols of social distance and cultural difference enforced by the Ladinos—for example, the pattern found in many churches of the Indians worshipping on the floor at the rear of the church and the Ladinos on chairs or prayer benches toward the front, the Indian women without head covering and the Ladino women obeying St. Paul's injunction with a veil over the head. But apart from these slight differences I believe that a major distinction in culturally generated attitude can be discerned. Very few Indians are accustomed to approach God or the saints alone; few Indians confess to the priest, except under Ladinos coercion; prayers and masses for the individual souls of the dead are uncommon, not only because of the cost, for quite expensive rituals are undertaken by Indians, but because of comparative lack of interest in the individual soul, as conceived by Catholic doctrine. The Indian approach to the supernatural is the group approach. In San Luis, at least, the Indians always confer with the priest in a delegation, practically never as individuals. The saints are venerated in *cofradias,* a form of organization and activity in which Ladinos show little interest. Holy water for the planting is brought from Esquipulas by a delegation; a commission carries out the rain-making and thanksgiving ceremonies. The priest is really an outsider; the real repositories of Indian religion, in a sense the effective priests, are the principales, who are also the holders of political power within Indian society and the judges of disputes and controversies which do not reach the civil authority. They symbolize in their multiple functions the intertwining of religion throughout life experience. When an Indian prays in earnest, it is necessary to have a principal, an agent of the society as a whole, do it for him. In prayers I have recorded it is interesting to note that even when a request is made of a particular saint, the saint is addressed as a member of a group. As many as forty-five saints' names may be involved in an invocation. Thus one group—the earthly society—approaches another group—that of heaven. Individuals have souls, yes; but for an Indian the soul is necessary for life in this world. Real anxiety occurs when the soul escapes from the body, as in *espanto,* or magical fright; but little anxiety is generated by contemplating the fate of the soul in the next world. Even in the recovery of the soul in espanto, the procedures require the presence of a group, and most of the therapeutic measures involve restoration of the patient to full social functioning. In short the Indians are not worried about their souls in the hereafter; but they are concerned about them here and now. The person who has lost his soul is incapable of carrying on his routine interaction with his fellows—and that is much worse than hell-fire or damnation. [We will return to this phenomenon in Chapter 16.]

For the Ladino, on the other hand, religion has somewhat different meanings. In contrast to Indian women Ladino women show more devotion than men, a fact that can probably be correlated with their more restricted roles in the home and the world of affairs. However, on the whole, organized support of the church is striking by its absence in Ladino communities. One of the prevailing complaints of the hierarchy in Mexico and Guatemala, at least, is the unwillingness of Ladinos to support the cult either by money or deeds. Cofradias do not flourish among Ladinos. Fiestas are attended for their commercial and merry-making features. Political and economic affairs tend to be separated from the religion. However, Ladinos are quite concerned about their immortal souls. Although men do not confess regularly, all men (and women likewise) are strongly impressed by the necessity of confession before death, either to a priest or by act of perfect contrition. Masses for the dead, novenas, and anniversaries of death are religiously celebrated. When a Ladino does pray it is usually as an individual. The usual approach is toward a saint or the Virgin as a supernatural personality who takes a personal interest in the supplicant. Vows are made by the supplicant, presents are made by him as an individual to the image, pilgrimages are made alone or only incidentally in company with other individual pilgrims. Priests are regarded as officials who have special powers to perform certain offices, such as the sacraments, for the benefit of the individual or for his children, land, or animals. Otherwise, in matters which do not directly involve the individual soul, the average Ladino is inclined to ignore the church, except as it may effect his social standing. It is customary to assure everyone that one is a good Catholic, very devoted, who has contributed so-and-so much to the temple, for such a show of conformity may enhance one's prestige. But the typical Ladino is not interested in the dogma of the church insofar as it does not affect him as an individual, and he is bored by most of the routine ritual. His everyday affairs are not believed to be governed by God or the saints except in a far-removed fashion, and he is skeptical of assertions by priests and old women to the contrary. In short, the Ladino cultural attitude is secular.

In the present state of our investigations any remarks about personality type for the Middle American area as a whole must be taken as strictly hypothetical or suggestive, to be validated or rejected on the basis of more detailed and intensive investigation in the future.

In San Luis Jilotepeque the Rorschach material and observational material alike show what appear to be some fundamental differences, at least, in the public, social, or cultural personalities of Indians and Ladinos, respectively. For both castes the range of the culture is distinctly limited and, as might be expected, this is reflected in a relatively restricted personality type in both castes. Neither Indians nor Ladinos show on the adult level much original intellectual ability, freedom in solving problems outside the patterns of the culture, or imagination.

On the Indian side of the line the personality of the typical individual, provided his cultural routine is not interfered with by outside individuals or forces, is relatively more secure and perhaps better integrated than that of the Ladino. In some respects the Indian personality might be considered compulsive. At any rate there is evident what would be called in other countries the compulsive following of the approved patterns of the culture without any strong motivation toward special rewards, distinctions, prominence, or the like. This is especially evident in the work patterns, and the Indians, male and female alike, follow with the utmost diligence the standard routines, such as milpa, work, pottery making, corn-grinding, palm-braiding for straw hats, and other activity patterns. The same careful following of pattern is likewise evidenced in ceremonial activities, such as fiestas, cofradia ceremonies, magical cures, and so on. For a great many reasons it seems obvious that the Indian maintains a feeling of personal security so long as he stays within the framework of his culture and is enabled to follow the pathways without deviation which it lays down for him. The adult personality is, on the surface at least, characterized by calmness and comparatively little effect, or show of emotion, in comparison with the Ladinos. However, the typical Indian personality does not show a neurotic constriction of emotion or the flat schizoid reaction. The *abrazo* is given, although not with a great show of enthusiasm; patting of the back and the arm, and handshaking are indulged in without any noticeable stiffness. Also, joking is characteristic although always in a restrained manner when the individual is sober. The belly laugh and hearty laughter of any type is not characteristic. Likewise there is normally little show of aggressiveness on the part of Indians. That Indians are capable of aggressive actions is shown by a good many incidents, however. Several cases are on record of Indians attacking each other with sticks or machetes; these cases are always precipitated by some rank breach of the code, such as a man catching a lover with his wife, gross interference on the part of a father-in-law, or something of the sort. Overt aggression usually appears only when the individuals are under the influence of alcohol. That there are aggressive feelings against Ladinos for the restrictions and punishments which the caste system has laid upon the Indians is evidenced by such things as violent attacks made by Indians on certain Ladinos at the time of the 1944 revolution in Guatemala and by the fact that several of the "devils" who are supposed to snatch souls in espanto are called by Ladino names.

Although one would expect that a constricted character structure of this sort, somewhat compulsive and not given to overt expression of emotions, would be the product of an authoritarian type of child-rearing, the fact is that the first five or six years at least of the Indian's life seem to be quite permissive. Children are nursed whenever they cry and they are not expected to develop sphincter control until able to understand language. Babies are not wrapped in constraining clothes or cradles and, in fact, do not even wear diapers as a general rule. Small children are hardly ever physically punished and are given the utmost freedom to explore their own bodies, the furnishings of the house, and their surroundings. However, they are always under supervision either of one of the parents or of an older sibling in order to protect them from accident. However, this protection is not given through punishment but simply through removing the child from the source of danger and directing its attention upon some other object. For example, if the child crawls toward the fire, he will be lifted up and placed on another part of the floor and given some object to play with, but he will not be spanked or switched. There is no weaning trauma nor, in fact, any other startling experience through which the normal child goes as he emerges from infancy to childhood.

Our Rorschach and observational material indicate that children up to about the age of 18 have a much more out-going type of personality than they develop as adults. They show more imagination than their elders and a much greater readiness to experiment with adjustive techniques not in the pattern. It has been our opinion that part of the constrictive and relatively rigid character structure of the adult is the result of inhibitions inculcated by the caste system rather than the training of early childhood. Boys and girls are inducted into

adult patterns gradually and begin to be useful workers in their respective spheres about the age of eight. Motivation based upon respect from others instigates the child to imitate the work patterns of adults, and the adult attitude is that children should not be "forced" but that they should be given responsibilities and allowed to perform activities which are commensurate with their physical and mental development.

It is, I think, noteworthy that what might be considered neuroses within the Indian framework are of two general types which can be interpreted consistently with this view of Indian personality. The principal neurotic manifestation is phrased as espanto or susto (magical fright). It is of importance that from the native point of view this personality upset is believed to be caused by a sudden fright or startle. In other words, the personality can be thrown off balance by any incident which interferes with the smooth performance of the routine patterns. In analyzing a number of cases and cures it also is evident that the person in this condition suffers from heavy anxiety regarding his social relationships, that is, the person with espanto is always out of touch in some way with his fellows and feels that he has lost integration in the social group. The other principal neurotic manifestation is envidia. This literally means envy and is believed to be caused by witchcraft whereby the victim is magically and secretly attacked by someone who is envious of him or otherwise aggressive toward him. In view of the fact that overt aggression is either repressed or constricted in the culture pattern, it is not surprising that anxiety concerning aggression should take the form of fears concerning sub rosa magical attacks. It is also of interest that whereas elaborate patterns are available for warding off, curing, and carrying out magical attacks, there are no clear-cut patterns of overt aggression in the culture. When an individual attacks another physically, he uses whatever weapon may be at hand and the attack exhibits a sort of random trial and error flailing about of the arms. This is in contrast to the very careful procedures used in witchcraft.

In summary it seems to be clear that adult Indians at the present time are little adaptable to changes in the situation. By the time they have reached maturity their habit patterns, both overt and non-overt, have been so firmly established that any deviation from the routine tends to upset the personality integration and to create an insecurity feeling in the individual. However, the young individuals are quite plastic. The fact that this is so seems to account for the comparative ease with which Indians pass into the Ladino status if they are removed from their Indian cultural environment while young and given an opportunity to learn Ladino patterns.

The Ladino personality structure in San Luis, at least, is also constrictive. This, however, seems to be the result of isolation and of the comparative poverty of local Ladino culture in areas outside its home grounds. In contrast to the manifested personality characteristics of Indians, the Ladinos show much more emotionalism. Not only are likes and dislikes more demonstratively expressed, but the average Ladino is characterized by mood swings which range from depression and helplessness to feelings of high euphoria. Consistent with this is the impression that the typical Ladino is basically much less secure than the typical Indian. He has no feeling of certainty that any of his available culture patterns will produce satisfactions which he expects and he is uncertain about their effectiveness when practiced outside the community. The result is that many Ladinos tend to withdraw from or be hesitant about interaction in the larger world

outside, but, since they wish to adjust to the larger world, this produces feelings of frustration and inadequacy. Ladinos are much more aggressive, at least on the overt level, both toward themselves and toward members of the other caste. This aggressiveness can be interpreted in the light of the frustrations which Ladinos face. Furthermore, the Ladinos show a higher percentage of hypochondriasis, psychosomatic ailments, neurotic twitches, and the like. That Ladinos habitually get more drunk more often than do Indians, seems to indicate that they find release from anxiety and frustration in alcohol as well as in hypochondriasis and aggressive outbreaks. Many Ladinos resort to cures for relief from magical fright and witchcraft, but do so with an ambivalent attitude. In other words, Ladinos only half believe in these conditions and the measures taken to alleviate them, but this tendency among Ladinos indicates again their willingness to try anything for relief from anxiety of frustration feelings.

Child care among Ladinos is fairly permissive as compared with middle class patterns in Europe or America of 25 years ago, but it is probably more authoritarian than the Indian system. Within the last few years some upper class Ladino families have instituted formula feeding on schedule, rigid cleanliness training, and so on—patterns which have been acquired from the great world outside—but these are not characteristic of the Ladino pattern as a whole up to the present. However, the Ladino child is usually dressed in diapers and underpants, earlier attempts at cleanliness training are instituted by parents than among the Indians, and the authority of the father in particular is more strict. Although small babies are given the breast whenever it is desired, the typical Ladino mother tries to wean her child by the end of the first year and does not permit the child to soil the house once it is able to crawl about. Also the higher one goes in the Ladino class system, the greater is the rigidity of child training.

Ladino children are sent to school at the age of six and subjected to fairly rigid schoolmaster's discipline which emphasizes the values of Ladino life. Proportionately fewer Indian children go to school, but for those that do so the transition from the Indian home to the school room is more of a trauma for the Indian child than for the Ladino, because the teachers have traditionally taken a negative attitude toward their Indian pupils who are frequently unable to understand or speak Spanish by the time they arrive in school. If the Indian child suffers a greater shock in going to school, he usually escapes from it within a relatively short time. Thus the school discipline has had up to now a relatively insignificant influence on the development of Indian personality patterns, because few Indian children enter school and most of those who do drop out after the first year or two. With the Ladino, on the other hand, the child goes through the three or four years of elementary school offered locally, and it is the ideal pattern then to send children away to other communities where they can at least get through the sixth year. Thus the typical Ladino is subjected to at least six years of the compulsive type of discipline which has been characteristic of Guatemalan and Mexican elementary schools up until very recently. At the end of this time most of the Ladinos come back to their home town. Indian children of this age have already worked into the adult patterns which they expect to follow throughout their lives. The boys are helping their fathers in the fields and on pottery-peddling trips. The girls have mastered the techniques of the woman's world. The young Ladino, however, emerging from school is provided with none of the patterns which he will expect to use as an adult, except literacy. The result is that there is a period of adolescent adjustment for Ladinos which does not have a counterpart among the Indians. During this time the girl receives some instruction as to how to manage a house and waits hopefully for marriage. The boy seeks to find a place for himself in the Ladino adult world. Since there are a wider variety of patterns open to the Ladino men than there are to Indians, a certain element of choice is involved here rather than merely the safe road of following one's father's footsteps. Since manual work is not regarded as desirable for Ladino males, but rather manipulative activities are valued either in managing agricultural or business enterprises, the adolescent Ladino male is often at loose ends. He is not mature enough to assume the managerial role nor are the patterns whereby he may do so clear to him, except if he belongs to an established family or is able to develop personal contacts. The rather vague and often unobtainable goals of Ladino culture have been implanted in his thinking by the school and by his fellows. Just as is the case with the Indian youngsters, Ladino youngsters also show more malleability and plasticity than do their elders. By the time a Ladino boy has reached maturity he has either found a place in the local system which usually does not appear to be entirely satisfactory to him, or he has moved away from the community to seek his rewards in the outside world. At any rate, those who remain suffer from feelings of anxiety, frustration, and insecurity which we have already mentioned. The high degree of verbosity which many observers have mentioned in connection with Ladino personality traits can, I think, be interpreted as partly related to the comparative insecurity of the real world. Even in a small isolated community like San Luis, Ladinos are given to living, as one might say, on a partly fanciful level in which argumentation and discussion about ideals and ideas takes up a good deal of time. In rural communities the ideas themselves may be comparatively naïve but they are usually discussed with great affect. As a North American would say, they are taken more seriously than would seem to be justified. Since the culture of the Ladinos does not offer many

and sure rewards when their attention is directed primarily toward things, it is perhaps to be expected that fantasy reward on the level of verbalization may serve as a compensation to some extent. If one cannot manipulate things to his own satisfaction, he can at least manipulate ideas or emotions. Thus the Ladino is often a violent partisan when it comes to any matter of opinion or policy.

THE WORLD AND THE WORLD VIEW OF THE KOTA*

By David G. Mandelbaum

The world view of a people is their characteristic outlook. It is the inside view, the ways in which a person of the group typically sees himself in relation to his world. It includes his mapping of that world, that is to say, the categories he uses in his perception of the familiar and of the strange. It includes the emphasis he places on what he sees, the choices he makes from among the alternatives he knows.

Few will deny that a statement of this inside view is a most desirable resource for anthropological analysis; more will wonder whether it is possible to make a valid and testable statement of this sort. Difficulties suggest themselves at once. Whose world view? Even in so numerically small a society as the *Kota,* there are many status positions, each invoking a somewhat different outlook. Thus there are different perceptions expected of a priest than those normally required of a layman. There are differences in typical outlook—at least in some respects—as between people from different villages, or as between a man and a woman. In one of the writer's published studies of

the *Kota,* the difference in outlook according to age was noted, and the consequences of the varying perceptions as between young men and older men in the society were indicated.

In the same study, personality differences in characteristic outlook were traced. Not the least of other possible variations in outlook are those which ensue from special environmental situations, such as dire physical deprivation. A people desperate for food may be expected to view the world about them somewhat differently than they do when hunger pangs are not so insistent.

Yet despite all these variations, a field ethnologist—no less than an observant administrator or traveler—often gains the impression that there is a characteristic way of seeing the world among the people he is studying. It is characteristic because it may be discerned through the whole range of personalities and status positions within the society and because it is expressed in a broad variety of life-situations.

The problem is to transcribe the impressions which register on the sensitized

* Reprinted with abridgment from *Village India: Studies in the Little Community,* edited by McKim Marriott, pp. 223-254. Memoir *83* of the American Anthropological Association, 1955 (*American Anthropologist,* Vol. *57,* No. *3,* Part 2), by permission of The University of Chicago Press.

observer into clear statements which can be tested repeatedly in various contexts and which can then be compared with formulations of world view among other peoples.

It might seem that the *Kota* offer a particularly favorable field for a start toward the analysis of world view. They are a small society; their seven villages together now hold about a thousand people, hardly more than a fair-sized village in most of India. Yet they clearly have a distinct society and culture, with language, religion, ceremonies, all obviously different from those of their neighbors. Within the villages there are not elaborate social stratifications, and their culture appears to be relatively homogeneous, if for no other reason than the absence of diverse caste practices.

However, it would scarcely be proper to present *Kota* society as a simple, relatively undifferentiated social organism within which the world view shines forth in a clearer, more comprehensible fashion than among, say, the manifestly complex Brahmans of Tanjore. Far from it. The *Kota* case presents many complexities, both structural and historical.

The *Kota* villages lie on a plateau in the south of India, an area which is now the Nilgiri District of the State of Madras. The plateau, some 6,500 feet in average elevation, rises quite precipitously from the plains, so much so that the trip was a hazardous one before the British put through roads and a railroad in the mid-nineteenth century. The area at the top of the hills, some 15 by 40 miles in greatest extent, supported four groups before the coming of the English and of the lowlanders who came with them.

The *Kota,* whose numbers have remained fairly stable in these years, were traditionally the artisans—smiths, potters, woodworkers—and musicians of the region. Their villages are interspersed among the settlements of the *Toda,* who still live in much the same places as of old, and of the *Badagas,* whose villages have greatly enlarged in size and number.

The *Kota* have always done some cultivation and have adequate lands of their own around each of their villages. In recent decades they have had to rely more and more heavily on cultivation for a livelihood, since their handicrafts and music are no longer in great demand among their neighbors. They now must devote most of their cultivation to a cash crop, potatoes.

A *Kota* village usually has three main streets, each street being the residence of a single patrilineal clan. Near the center of the village is a green on which stand three temples, one to each deity of an ancient triad. In the village of Kolmel, to which this discussion more specifically pertains, a new temple has recently been built to a trinity of Hindu-like gods. Around the introduction of these newest, Sanskritized deities there has crystallized a factional split in the village. The adherents of the more conservative ways are the "Old Rule" (*Ma.mul*) faction, who have resisted the innovations proposed by their opponents. The reform group is called "Cropped" (*Karap*) using the *Kota* version of the English word for haircut. Cutting off the traditional *Kota* chignon by the men of that party symbolizes their adoption of a strong reformist attitude. The two factions in this village have, as has happened elsewhere in village India, drawn apart, so that they stage separate ceremonies and do not interdine. The original issue of the factional split, the worship of the new gods, is no longer the divisive factor, since both factions worship the new as well as the old gods, although each side does so separately. One of the original reasons for the division is gone, the split remains.

For the traditional deities there are still two priests whose office is respected by conservatives and reformists alike.

The priests must be kept segregate from the other villagers in many ways. They must dress only in the old style and, in general, conduct their lives in a ritually guarded manner, guarded also from some of the technological innovations which have been adopted in recent decades. The deities are additionally served by diviners, one for each god. Through the diviners, at appropriate occasions, the voice of the god speaks and tells the villagers the pleasure of the gods. The diviners must also lead more carefully guarded lives than do other villagers.

Two important occasions in the ceremonial cycle are the first funeral, where the bodies are cremated, and the second funeral at the end of the ceremonial year. Then all who have died during the year are finally sent off to the afterworld, and mourning for them officially ends. A bone of the deceased which has been taken out of the cremation pyre at the first funeral is recremated in the second funeral. An important ritual element in both funerals is the bowing to the remains of the deceased.

It is at this point in the funeral, when the living give a parting bow of respect to the dead, that great quarrels frequently arise. All who have any claim to kinship with the deceased press forward to bow, and anyone present who is a *Kota* feels impelled to make this last bow. Not infrequently some men, usually the close relatives of the deceased, try to prevent others from bowing. Those who are thus barred strain with great argument and pushing (though rarely with blows) to accomplish the ritual gesture. Some of the men not directly involved in the quarrel try to separate the pushing melee of contenders and attempt to bring about a temporary calm which they try to transform into a workable compromise. Sometimes, not often, no suggested compromise avails, and one side or the other calls in the police, an act which brings to bear alien forces which usually must be mollified by suitable cash payment.

The study of *Kota* world view can well begin with an analysis of this recurrent situation. In so doing, we may be sure to begin with something which most *Kota* see as being highly important in their lives. If we should seek statements of world view by approaching only the more articulate and reflective persons, we may easily get a fluent and consistent formulation, but one which may not apply for many in the society. Or the observer may unwittingly select the outlook appropriate to a particular status or stratum and present that as the view of the whole people.

The selection of this situation as worthy of special note is made by the *Kota* themselves. Controversies about bowing to the dead have arisen at most funerals which the present writer has heard about or seen. Moreover, reference to such situations is made quite spontaneously in various contexts by men and women of differing ages and status positions.

Thus one man of the Cropped faction tells that he is letting his hair grow again because his father-in-law is growing old and he wants to be able to bow to the corpse when the old man dies. If he continues in the Cropped party, he may be debarred from doing so. A healer—part shaman, part physician—and a conservative from a conservative village tells how his Cropped relatives from another village tried to bow to the corpse at his brother's funeral. Violent protests ensued from his conservative fellow-villagers, and he persuaded his Cropped kin not to bow. If they forced the issue, he reminded them, he would be the one to suffer and perhaps could no longer live in his own village.

Deliberate abstention from bowing brings on societal concern as well as does deliberate exclusion. Several men become affronted during a funeral and express their grievance by refusing to participate in the appropriate gestures. The ritual proceedings are delayed until these men are persuaded to take part again. One of these men, incidentally, is a highly aberrant person—the one effeminate man in the society—but in this matter he shares the common outlook.

Why, then, is this occasion of bowing to the deceased so important to the *Kota*? Why is it the scene of personal victories and personal defeats? To which of the principal spheres of life do these victories and defeats pertain? These spheres, in the broadest sense, are the same for a *Kota* as for man generally—one's relation to the supernatural, to the material environment, and to other people.

In this brief survey the examination of one main tension point necessarily overlooks many of the more placid vistas of *Kota* world view. Yet the scene of conflict is also the setting for reward; both are in the forefront of a *Kota* man's view. The view thus sketched is the man's view. The woman's view, in so far as my relatively limited evidence on the woman's outlook goes, is not at odds with it.

Funerals are generally ritual occasions, involving the participants in some kind of relation with their concept of the supernatural. *Kota* funerals are no exception: the supernatural is clearly and prominently entailed in these rites. But the gods are not importantly involved in the controversies which boil up around the business of bowing. This central concern does not have to do with the gods, nor are very many *Kota* life-problems and dilemmas concerned with relations to gods—this despite the fact that the great factional split has been precipitated by matters of worship, that worship still brings the men before the temples every morning, and that religious ceremonies still provide the great occasions of the year.

To the *Kota,* the gods—all gods, the traditional deities and the newer Hindu-like powers—are potent beyond anyone's doubt. They have strong attributes and great power to affect mortals. But they do not often appear in the center of *Kota* concern. The supernatural is handled like high voltage. If the gods are properly served, they do not act capriciously and do not intervene unnecessarily. There are exceptions to this, it is true. And the voice of the gods is regularly heard through their chosen diviners, appraising the villagers' behavior and telling them what and what not to do. For all this, the gods are addressed and invoked more as a way of turning their attention to the affairs at hand than by way of cajoling or persuading or even of imploring them to take charge. Some specific examples will illustrate this broad impression.

The *Kota* have no great interest in the afterworld. They know that there is such a realm to which the spirits of the dead go, but the nature of that bourne is only vaguely known; little curiosity is shown about it. Once the spirits are duly dispatched after the final funeral rites, they do not return to worry men. The rites are always successful, the spirit departs, there the matter ends. This spirit may later speak through a woman medium, counsel his descendants and foretell coming events, but neither this occasional message from a departed kinsman nor the regularly heard voices of the deities themselves seem to be taken by the *Kota* as anything more than tips for the general welfare. These tips have often to do with the proper performance of ritual. Here the emphasis lies—on the successful manipulation of the supernaturals rather than on inducing in the gods a beneficent state of mind.

This mechanical mode of dealing with the supernatural is exemplified in the legal fictions frequently used in ceremonies. Thus women during their menstrual periods are abhorrent to everything supernatural. They must be secluded and return to normal status in several stages. During menstruation a woman must take care to avoid being seen by a priest and must not approach anything which is specially sacrosanct, whether it be a temple or the hearth in her kitchen. However, every soul in the village must participate in the greatest ceremony of the year, the God Ceremony. All must then be refurbished and renewed. But some women inevitably will be menstruating during the days of this ceremony and should presumably be disqualified from participating in this occasion when all the village is one sacred precinct. The *Kota* solution is simple and is typical of their relations to the supernatural. Before the ceremony begins all the women go out of the village for a time as a token of menstrual seclusion. Hence any woman who menstruates during the days of the ceremony has already been in seclusion for that month, and therefore the subsequent physical condition need not be taken as true menstruation. She may participate with all the village in the holy rituals.

The malevolent manipulation of the supernatural does cause concern, but it is a concern which is met by dealing with people rather than with the supernatural directly. The *Kota* know of the evil eye, but one *Kota* cannot put the evil eye on another. If a villager should want to bring harm to a fellow-villager, or a *Badaga* to a *Kota,* the plotter must hire a *Kurumba* to perform the evil magic. The victim, when he learns of the cause of his misfortunes, must hire yet another *Kurumba* to end the evil. Nowadays *Kurumbas* are less resorted to, although still much feared; Hindu or Muslim exorcisers and amulet purveyors are patronized. In any event, the power to use directly supernatural means in a malevolent way is not an attribute of a *Kota*. The fear of *Kurumba* sorcery is considerable, but it can be met by using guardian *Kurumbas*. People—though not your own kind—

can deal properly with this sort of supernatural power also.

In all, the supernatural must be given its great due, must be respectfully handled, but it can be handled successfully. In so far as a people's world view is focused on what troubles them, on the sources of their chief tensions as well as on the arenas of their chief victories, the sphere of the supernatural does not appear to most *Kota* to be either a prime source of tension or a major arena for reward.

As for the second great sphere of life which all world views must comprehend, that of relations to nature, we can summarize the *Kota* view briefly. There are some peoples for whom dealing with nature has magnetic interest. Some are engrossed in cultivation, think of and care for their fields with surpassing concern. Some *Badaga* groups strike me as having such an absorbing interest in their crops. Others may be heart and soul engrossed with their animals. The *Toda* are clearly so engrossed. There are artisans whose stakes in life lie in their craft. But the *Kota* share none of these absorptions. They have been and still are artisans. But they work in the smithy just to get a job done. In recent decades only one man in Kolmel village has ever been moved to lavish his skill in turning out a particularly fine and ornamented blade. Few other *Kota* have tried, as he did, to fashion an ax that would be a thing of uncommon strength and beauty. They have turned out axes in great numbers, and they have skill as smiths. But an ax for them is something to trade or use, not something which may bring special joy or prestige. It may have been different in the past; many a fine skill has in India been washed out by the flood of goods made by Western techniques. In the memory of the living Nilgiri generations, the *Kota* are professional artisans but indifferent craftsmen.

So it is with their activities in dealing

with plant and animal. They keep a few cattle, goats, buffalo, but there is nothing of the *Toda* zeal for their beasts. They cultivate and now must earn most of their living at it. But in comparison with the nearby *Badaga* fields, the *Kota* fields are not so well tilled. Their crop yield is usually lower, their attention to farming more indifferent.

Note that these are general and comparative statements. There are some *Kota* who are excellent cultivators and take pride and joy in their fields. But most are not as interested in farming as are most *Badagas*. The *Kota* do not lack industry; they can work hard and steadily on occasion. But the general occasions of cultivation do not evoke notably effective efforts. A *Kota's* main interest generally lies in another sphere; not in his relations to the gods, not in his necessary dealings with plant and animal and matter, but in his relations to other men. Around these relations cluster *Kota* concern; it is here that the matter of bowing at the funeral becomes a matter for passion and pride.

Man's prime struggle is with man: this idea comes through in life-histories, in anecdotes, in folklore. In some societies, as among the Tanjore Brahmans, there is great concern with the self: a good part of the struggle is with the self. This is not so for the *Kota*. They have little worry about their impulses. Most men and women enjoy a vigorous sex life which starts at a quite early age. While most men are much interested in sexual activities over a large span of the life-cycle, the interest is in satisfying the impulses rather than in denying them. There is something of the widespread Indic belief that overindulgence is harmful, but this belief is expressed more as an explanation for a manifest ailment than as an immediate guide to conduct.

Nor is strong drink eschewed in principle or in practice. The aversion to this means of self-gratification, common to the higher castes and now expressed in the Madras prohibition law, is not shared by the *Kota*. They grumble about how difficult it is now to get liquor and how the welfare of the people has suffered from the governmental prohibition.

Kota men generally do not question their physical needs and gratifications, and they show little sign of worry about their roles in life. They give the impression of a vigorous self-confidence; life-histories usually display evidence of what may be called a firm sense of ego-identity.

Similarly, in relations with women, *Kota* men give few evidences, direct or indirect, of special anxieties. If the main struggle is not with the self, it is also not between the sexes. Some special points of friction develop. Not infrequently a younger brother will move out of the joint family household because he does not get along with the elder brother's wife. But frequently also this brother's wife is the lad's special friend. In ritual the link between husband and wife is very close, and the two stand as one at some crucial ritual junctures. It is not with women that a *Kota* man feels he must contend.

The struggle lies among males, particularly among peers. The close kin of the older and of the younger generations are one's allies and supporters. In tales and in small talk, a man's father, his father's brothers, his mother's brothers all appear as supportive characters. The mother's brother, having no great disciplinary responsibility for his nephew, is expected to be and frequently is a kind and benevolent figure who provides emotional refuge as well as material aid. Often enough he is, in the *Kota* system of preferred cross-cousin marriage, the father-in-law as well.

A man's relations with his father, as recounted and as observed, give little indication of any strong oedipus-like reactions, such as those noted for the Brahmans of Kumbapettai in Tanjore. Nor is there any special reason why such tensions should prevail here. Fathers do

not and, indeed, cannot well dispossess
or disinherit their sons. The society encourages youths to be quite independent.
And sons are a man's most precious possession.

In the last matter, the *Kota* are at
one with the vast Concourse of Indic
peoples. Without a son, or at least a
child, a *Kota* feels himself scarcely a person. A childless couple does not often go
many years without a child in the house.
A man takes in a brother's son to feed
and raise, or an orphan lad with no close
kin is adopted, or a succession of wives
is taken until one yields a child. In some
manner a man must have someone in his
house to call him father.

Children are thus tremendously important, and a man who has none does
not rest easily until he does have a child,
preferably a son, more preferably several.
Few men remain long incapacitated on
that score. If they do not become biological fathers in due course, they manage to be sociological fathers. Once
children are acquired, however, their
rearing seems not to be a major focus of
concern. There are problems, of course,
in rearing children, in getting them healed
if they are sick, saved if they are bewitched, married if a bride price must be
scraped together. Great anxieties may be
aroused in a man's life on any or all of
these scores, but he typically meets these
problems as they turn up; he does not
keep these possibilities in the forefront
of his view.

What is central to a man's social
perception is his relation with his peers.
In the first instance it is his relation with
his brothers, both real and classificatory.
Brothers are allies. They usually work as
a co-operative group in the fields, in the
smithy, in providing music. If a man has
no uterine brothers, he generally works
with several of his classificatory brothers
of the clan.

The brothers face the world together,
as a single group. When one is threatened, all are supposed to rally to his
support and usually do so. In one rare
case in which two brothers belonged to
opposing factions, there was a dramatic
display of the strength of the fraternal
tie. Ordinarily the two do not go into one
another's house or interdine. But when
one suffered a psychotic episode in which
his life was endangered and there was no
other man willing to care for the sick
one, the well brother did drop all factional enmity, nursed and cared for his
sick brother until the man was able to
carry on in society. Since then the two
have reverted to their separate ways and
factions.

In ritual, one brother can stand as
a perfect substitute for another. When a
man goes on a formal mission, as when
he goes to take his bride from her father's house, he must have a brother
along with him. Many of the folk-tale
motifs occur as happenings to a set of
brothers.

For all that there is this brother bond,
however, there is also a sharp awareness
within the brother group of the rights and
duties of each. Each brother must have
an equal share in everything the group
attains. Though the harvest may be
pooled and the family purse and kitchen
be jointly shared, no one brother may
take a larger share than another. Elder
brothers are given due respect by their
juniors, the needs of the brothers with
more mouths to feed are duly taken into
account, but each one feels equal in
rights to every other. There must be a
fraternal equivalance in all things, and
many are the quarrels among a set of
brothers about such things as cultivation,
sharing the work of the smithy, and the
division of property. The equal sharing
occurs in sex relations as well, but quarrels about these relations are not directly
expressed.

Within a set of brothers, then, there

is strong identification and co-operation, but there is also a strong sense of individual rights. These rights are jealously guarded so that the identification with the brother group does not wipe out a man's very lively sense of his status as an individual in the group. A *Kota's* notion that he has not been given his proper due among the brothers not infrequently leads him to split off from them, to arrange some new alliances, perhaps with classificatory rather than uterine brothers, or to carry on economically only with his sons or affines.

Such procedure prevails also in the widening circles of a man's social relations. When the clan is involved, each clansman guards, as much for himself as for the clan group, those prerogatives which belong to his clan. When the villagers of Kolmel deal with men of another *Kota* village, they are quick to defend Kolmel's full measure of respect or gifts or whatever may be involved. Factional divisions now complicate the scene. A conservative from Kolmel attending a ceremony in another village may strive to bar a Kolmel man of the opposing faction from participating in the rite. Yet he may have some feeling that his own status as a Kolmel man suffers when his fellow-villager is roughly handled.

As against the *Badaga*, all *Kota* factions are as one. While some still provide music to those of the *Badaga* who want *Kota* music, all *Kota* steadily claim more from the *Badaga* than any *Badaga* is now willing to grant. This contention with the *Badaga* is very much in the *Kotas'* view, though most *Badaga* do not take much notice of the few and, to their minds, lowly *Kota*. The *Kota* sees himself as a kind of peer of the *Badaga,* perhaps not as pure as some or as wealthy as others, but a peer nonetheless in that the *Kota* believes he has certain rights and duties toward the *Badaga* and, more especially,

that the *Badaga* should have certain obligations toward him.

Whether as brother among brothers, villager among villagers, *Kota* among Nilgiri peoples, a man's chief interest is in dealing with other men in the proper way—the proper way being that way which preserves his full rights or what he deems to be his full rights. These dealings and the contention about them are the common currency of talk and the patent focus of interest among the *Kota*.

How then are men to be dealt with? The mode of confronting one's fellows may be termed "aggressive defense." A man must ever be wary lest his rights and privileges be encroached upon: if they are, defensive response must be quick and vigorous. He must react sharply to any possible slight. He must be instantly jealous of his status.

That is why bowing to the relic of the corpse is so important. In the usual course of the ceremony, everyone present expects to bow as a last gesture of respect and alliance with the deceased. The gesture symbolizes that the one who bows belongs to the social network, that he has the status of a *Kota*. Whatever factional side a man may take, he does not want to cut loose from the whole society of his people; rather he wants to bring them all to share in his ways.

On the other side, those in charge of a funeral are zealous to keep away from their deceased kinsmen anyone who is not a complete *Kota* in their view. If such a one should bow, they would all feel demeaned, their own status undermined. Hence members of one faction try to bow, those of the other try to prevent them, and great rows are precipitated.

Such quarrels commonly delay ceremonies for hours. *Kota* men, possessing as they do a strong sense of their worth and independence, carry on the arguments with great vigor. But the arguments are almost always on the verbal level only; rarely do *Kota* come to physical aggression or even to attempts at magical manipulation. This may be because each man seeks, not to undermine the other man, or forcibly to subordinate him, but rather to protect his own rights.

The use of bezoars, concretions sometimes found in the alimentary system of ruminants, illustrates *Kota* notions of how a man should conduct himself. Bezoars are ground up and fed a child so that he may have "anger and common sense." "Anger" is a straightforward interpretation of the *Kota* word; "common sense" is a translation (suggested by an interpreter) for the quality of being able to make sound, practical judgments. Why, then, "anger and common sense"? Anger so that he may fight vigorously in defense of his rights; common sense so that he may know when his rights have been transgressed.

Important to this self-defense is the avoidance of ritual pollution. A person so defiled is also socially disabled. He loses, at least temporarily, his full previous status. And he is made specially vulnerable to such loss by contact with the biological experiences of birth, menstruation, and death. There are other sources of ritual and social disablement, but these are among the most dangerous. Thus when a *Kota* dies, his closest kin are barred from ordinary social contacts. A main emphasis of the elaborate double funeral is to reinstate the mourners to normal social status. So long as a person is defiled on this account or on some lesser score, he is dangerous to his fellows. The danger is only partly thought of as supernatural; it is quite vividly the danger of degrading others to a comparable state of social paralysis.

It is as though all social relations are in delicate balance, so that any one of many ritual impairments can throw them out of balance. Once dislocated, these relations must be put back in order by proper ritual purification.

In this delicate balance, withdrawal from social relations is a main procedure, both as an individual's weapon and as the group's disciplinary means. If a man feels affronted, believes his proper rights have been slighted, he will withdraw from participation in the social enterprise in which he has felt himself disparaged. Thus in the episode mentioned earlier, in which several men refused to participate in a funeral ceremony because they felt slighted, these men believed, in effect, that they had been detracted and that further participation would signal that they accepted a lowered standing. The others involved in the ceremony were eager to have them participate—and eventually arranged a compromise which brought them back in—because less than full participation would reduce the worth of the whole ceremony and so take away something from each person who did carry on with it.

Viewed from the other aspect, withdrawal by the group from the individual is the traditional way of dealing with transgressors. One who violates the group's standards of conduct thereby demeans everyone within the group. Hence social relations with him are severed until he repairs his transgression and symbolically affirms that he is at one with the group again. This is the common Indic practice of outcasting. In Kolmel village the Old Rule people have cast out every Cropped man. The Cropped have retaliated by forming a factional group which takes the stand that it is they who have thrown out the others. However, the Cropped men still adamantly strive to bow to the corpse at funerals conducted by Old Rule men and are as adamantly hindered from doing so.

There is a certain amount of physical pushing and pulling during such encounters, but generally a transgressor is not subject to physical coercion to make him behave properly. The important note is not one of forcing the wrongdoer to conform but rather of enforcing the break of social relations until such time as the miscreant makes amends.

Positive achievements also contribute to the defense of one's status. Every man has a lively sense of his rights as a *Kota,* as an equal among equals. If an individual commands personal esteem, it is more likely that his own appraisal of his rights will be accepted by the group. There are various means of achieving personal respect. One of the qualities necessary for becoming headman is a talent for mediating quarrels, for maintaining the societal equilibrium. Other avenues to personal prestige are attaining wealth, excelling in debate, performing ritual and social obligations meticulously. We have noted above that a man without children feels himself something less than equal. But having sons does not alone guarantee the assured preservation of one's rights. Other accomplishments bolster a man's claims.

Not that there is a dead level of equality in all things. There is a very strict order of precedence, for example, in ceremonies. All men precede all women, elders precede juniors in age, secular officers go ahead of ordinary villagers, sacred officers lead all with the senior priest in front. But two men may differ as to their respective positions within this rank order. One may feel that his should be the prior place in the funeral feast because he is of closer kin than another man who may be the elder of the two. In such disputes, the one who commands greater respect is apt to have his demand supported by most people and to win his claimed precedence.

There are personality differences in claims made and in personal sensitivity to perceived slights. But even the less sensitive man, even one who gets scant regard from his fellows, nonetheless rises in sharp protest if he detects that he has not been given his just deserts.

What a *Kota* considers the world to owe him has changed in recent decades. Claims on the *Badagas* are still voiced but with not much hope of having these demands met. Claims on the government are beginning to be more prominent, but government is still too remote and awesome to be grappled directly. Meanwhile intramural struggles rage between those more ready to accept innovation and those less ready to do so. These struggles are fought out over such matters as bowing to the corpse. In these struggles *Kota* attention is not riveted on change as much as it is on the societal consequences of adopting new ways. The *Kota's* interest is in preventing any personal derogation either in the course of change or—from the viewpoint of the Cropped faction—in not changing some of the older *Kota* ways. Change can easily be accepted so long as man is assured that personal loss of status will not thereby be suffered.

This formulation of one aspect of *Kota* world view has not touched upon other aspects which could properly be included in a more lengthy discussion. It has presented what seems typically to be in the forefront of a *Kota's* perception—that man must struggle with man in defense of his social self. Like all condensed formulations, this characterization is subject to modification according to particular circumstances and personalities. But it is generally valid for *Kota* life, as are the other general views abstracted from *Kota* testimony. One such view is that the gods are potent but not capricious: they can be dealt with effectively. Nature can be recalcitrant to man's efforts, but is not the center of interest. The best man is one who does not allow himself to be deprived, one who responds vigorously to any threat of deprivation in social relations.

SUMMARY

As Gillin and Mandelbaum have shown in describing the two societies in the papers just read, there is an entire universe of objects and dimensions which is constantly impinging upon people and which must be understood within a consistent cultural frame of reference. There are, for example, the phenomena of nature—stars, winds, oceans, rain, floods, and the like. There is yesterday, and last year, and the generations of one's ancestors; and there is the future, as well. There are other lands and strange peoples, and there are neighbors and societal boundaries. And, not least in importance, there are the many mysteries and unknown phenomena of nature.

In every society, individuals are taught how to perceive the total world of nature; that is, they learn how the universe is ordered or organized and what meanings can be attached or attributed to this order. But these perceptions of nature include more than just a series of ideas about why there are stars, and a moon or a sun, or why it rains, lightnings and thunders. These perceptions of nature almost always include ideas about man's place—morally, spatially, and temporally—within the social and physical universe.

It was said at the start of this chapter that we were to study some of the effects of total life-situations and of the communities in which people live on personality. But in order to study the effects of community-systems or total life-situations on, for example, sharing or nonsharing of food or on patterns of friendship or on psychosis, the interrelationships among the ways in which people *think,* the types of communities in which they live, and the general tenor of the ways in which they *act* must first be understood. Once this general picture is obtained—and it was the purpose of this chapter to provide a broad base for such an understanding—we can then go on to detailed analyses of individual areas of behavior.

Let us attempt to clarify this further by means of an analogy. It is possible, and rewarding, to study and observe individual figures in da Vinci's "Last Supper" or individual movements in a Beethoven quartet. Each figure or musical movement has its own structure and its own meaning. But our understanding of an individual figure in the painting or movement in the quartet is enhanced immeasurably if we first know the over-all nature of the total composition—and then study or observe the individual parts against this background or within this framework. Behavior with respect to food and patterns of friendship are individual figures within the socio-cultural fresco, and before going on to study these figures we must have the broadest picture firmly in mind. This fresco is the metaphysics—or world view—of a people.

The world view shared by the members of a society is, essentially, a philosophical system with many parts; but all the parts are elements within a patterned whole. While there is no reason to assume that all of a society's beliefs about nature and human relationships are dominated by a single idea or set of ideas—and this was the most glaring theoretical error in Benedict's *Patterns of Culture,* for example—there does seem to be an interconnection between attitudes toward social relationships and ideas about the nature of society and its place within a total universe. Thus, when reading about personality in patterns of economic behavior and in friendship, and when we read about personality and cultural change, our understanding of these phenomena is enhanced if we keep in mind the ways in which social behavior is part of *and* is affected by a people's world view.

BIBLIOGRAPHY AND SUGGESTED READINGS

Benedict, Ruth. *Patterns of Culture.* Boston: Houghton, 1934. One of the earliest attempts at describing the world views of cultures by an anthropologist.

Hoijer, Harry (editor). *Language in Culture.* Memoir *79,* American Anthropological Association, 1954. No less difficult than the papers by Whorf (see below), but equally rewarding in parts.

Honigmann, John J. *Ethos and Culture in Kaska Society.* Yale University Publications in Anthropology, No. *40,* 1949. An attempt to study the world view of an Indian tribe in a comparative perspective.

Homans, George C. *English Villagers of the Thirteenth Century.* Cambridge, Massachusetts: Harvard, 1941. An invaluable study from many points of view, but especially illuminating is its description of the interconnections among the parts of a society's world view.

Kardiner, Abram. "The Concept of Basic Personality Structure as an Operational Tool in the Social Sciences," in *Personal Character and Cultural Milieu* (3rd ed.), edited by Douglas Haring, pp. 469-483. Syracuse, New York: Syracuse University Press, 1956. An approach to dimensions of world view which are not readily observable by most techniques.

Kelly, George A. "Man's Construction of his Alternatives," in *Assessment of Human Motives,* edited by Gardner Lindzey, pp. 33-64. New York: Rinehart, 1958.

Langland, William. *Piers the Ploughman.* There are many editions of this classical account of how one man saw the structure of the world in the fourteenth century.

Redfield, Robert. "The Folk Society," *American Journal of Sociology,* Vol. *52,* pp. 293-302, 1947. An ideal-type (and somewhat idealized) analysis of the philosophy and nature of life in nonindustrialized societies, but still among the best wine of its kind. Redfield's conceptualization is bottled even more delicately in the following three books by him.

Redfield, Robert. *The Little Community: Viewpoints for the Study of the Human Whole.* Chicago, University of Chicago, 1955.

Redfield, Robert. *Peasant Society and Culture.* Chicago, University of Chicago, 1956.

Redfield, Robert. *The Primitive World and its Transformations.* Ithaca, New York: Cornell, 1953.

Whorf, Benjamin Lee. *Language, Thought, and Reality: Selected Writings of Benjamin Lee Whorf,* edited by John B. Carroll. New York: Wiley, 1956. Containing some of the most germinal (and sometimes difficult) essays on the relationship of language, patterns of thought, and cultural behavior.

Chapter 11

FOOD AND ITS VICISSITUDES: A CROSS-CULTURAL STUDY OF SHARING AND NONSHARING*

By Yehudi A. Cohen

The study to be reported on in this chapter will consider some of the personality factors underlying socially patterned behavior with respect to the distribution of food. While the specific problem to be examined is extremely important in its own right, our ultimate aim is to show how social-structural forces in different types of community-systems affect personality. In other words, through the empirical analysis of one problem we are going to try to illustrate a theoretical approach to the relationship between community-systems and personality. In Chapter 12, the same theoretical approach will be adapted to an investigation of personality factors underlying patterns of friendship.

Before stating the specific issues to be investigated in this chapter, some introductory remarks are necessary as a general background. Since we will be dealing in this chapter, and again in Chapter 12, with data from a wide variety of non-Western societies, instead of from one society or social group as has been done until now, we will need some way of organizing our sociocultural units into categories or taxonomic types. To do this—and this is indispensable for the intelligible handling of so many data—

we will first, after stating the problems to be investigated, outline a classificatory scheme of types of community-systems; this taxonomy will be employed in the cross-cultural studies in the present chapter and in the next. Before going any further, it should be pointed out emphatically that this typology of community-systems is an expedient one; there are many possible ways of describing community-systems, but the scheme to be presented below was found to be the most expedient for analyzing *these* problems.

METHODOLOGY

The data to be presented in this cross-cultural study, and in the one in Chapter 12, were gathered from complete ethnographic reports for each of the groups in the sample. These were read in their entirety by the writer, who marked off pertinent passages which were then copied onto file cards by a secretary who did not know the hypotheses. This sample was originally selected for the cross-cultural investigation of systems of food distribution. Although it had been hoped to investigate a randomly selected sample of societies in which each culture area

* This chapter is adapted from an essay of the same title. It was awarded the Socio-Psychological Award of the American Association for the Advancement of Science in 1955.

would be proportionately represented, certain categories of data were required for this study; societies for which these data were unavailable were excluded from the sample. One of the problems faced at the commencement of the research into patterns of friendship was whether to retain the sample used in the first study or select a new sample which would be more representative of distributions within culture areas. The first alternative was elected in the light of some over-all and long-range goals. Simply, it is hoped that several studies like the two presented in this and in the next chapter, will aid in gaining some insight into the problem of which patterns of culture are necessary correlates of particular personality constellations. More rigorous sampling methods might yield considerably sharper insights into patterns of friendship, but at the expense of broader theoretical considerations.

Ideally, this kind of research should be carried out by one or more assistants working for the author. Under such ideal conditions, only the author knows the hypothesis to be tested while the research is in progress, and the assistant is told to find certain kinds of data without knowing why these data might be related to each other; in other words, he is supposed to be free of any knowledge of the purpose of the research so that his findings will not be influenced by the hypothesis to be tested. This is an ideal condition. The present research, however, was not carried out under such conditions. To meet the criteria of ideal conditions, especially in scientific research, a fair amount of money is required, because investigations like the present one have to be carried out several times. No funds to carry out this investigation were available. Consequently, we had to rely on our own sources of time and energy. Since becoming involved and identified with one's hypotheses is inevitable, there

is the natural danger that one will seek out the kinds of data which will support the hypotheses being tested. In the original report in which this investigation was presented, we recapitulated the data (often verbatim) for each society in the sample; to an extent, this enabled the reader to "repeat the experiment," as it were, while he was reading. In the present adaptation, however, limitations of space preclude this technique of reportage. In view of the inability to conduct our research under ideal conditions, we were faced with the alternative of presenting results as we found them or allowing them to gather dust in a drawer. At the end of this chapter, the data for a few societies will be presented to enable the reader to ascertain the kinds of data which have been used.

THE PROBLEM

When reading the ethnographic literature for societies in different parts of the world with one eye cocked for information about what people do with their food—sociologically, that is, before they eat it—one quickly notices that such behavior can be classified into categories and types. Specifically, one observes that in some societies there is a constant flow of raw foodstuffs from person to person and from family to family; in some societies, this movement of food is especially striking because the rules of that society state that a person cannot eat the food which he himself has grown, captured, or killed, and that he may die if he does. From the point of view of an urbanized American, this seems somewhat uneconomical—why should people go to all the trouble of raising food and then give it all away and eat only food which has been received from others? Similarly, why should people in other societies daily or weekly exchange equal amounts of corn, yams, or rice? And why should people in other societies give food to each other only when they are in real need; why should people in still other societies give each other economic help, but only very grudgingly and reluctantly; and why should the pattern in still other societies be that people rarely, if at all, give each other economic assistance?

There must be reasons for such behavior; the more readily apparent ones, such as scarcity and plentitude of food, do not correlate with any of the observable patterns of behavior. We assume that there are reasons for such variability in behavior regarding food, and in our search for reasons ask only "why," not "what functions does this or that behavior serve?" We further assume that the reasons for these different economic patterns are many and varied, but that some of these can be found in the emotional patterns of the people. Our task here is to learn what these emotional patterns are.

As questions begin to form concretely, so do hunches, insights, and answers. In this research, the first hunch pointed to early feeding experiences; this eventually provided a partial answer, but its limitations forced us to continue to look for other answers in still other directions. Slowly, but with increasing conviction, arrows began to point toward the social-structural arrangements of community organization, and types of communities began to emerge as correlative to types of behavior with respect to food. We shall first describe the types of community-systems which can be distinguished for the purposes of this research, then go on to our hypotheses and attempts to elicit reasons for these different kinds of economic behavior.

THE FUNCTIONALLY SIGNIFICANT UNIT OF ASSOCIATION

Four types of communities emerged out of the attempts to explain, in part, economic behavior in non-Western societies. None of these types is absolutely and rigidly demarcated from the others. They tend to shade off into each other, but they are extremely useful in classifying the phenomena under observation. We are going to call each of these types a "functionally significant unit of association" in order to distinguish social-structural units from other sociological factors, such as status, authority, distance and proximity, and the like. By the functionally significant unit of association we mean *that solidary social group which, for the individual, is the most immediate and consistent area of cooperation, reciprocity, and feelings of responsibility for others.* Such social alignments are the contexts of social control, and they are the interpersonal sources of values, goals, and emotional support for the individual. Furthermore, these alignments almost everywhere provide the primary lines of intergroup as well as intragroup communication.

The first type which can be distinguished—which is one extreme point along a continuum of solidarity and lesser solidarity—is the "maximally solidary community." This is a societal grouping having either definite social or physical boundaries, or both. It *may* coincide with the total geographic community, or it may be one of two or more societal nuclei within the community defined geographically. If the latter is the case, each of the maximally solidary groupings has its own social and geographical boundaries and, for all intents and purposes, constitutes a societal nucleus within a geographical community. Where such a situation obtains, these nuclei are not wholly autonomous or independent of each other; instead, they are almost always interdependent for political, religious, economic, or other purposes, such as a source of spouses for each other.

The maximally solidary community is generally a descent group which is frequently localized and in which is vested ultimate ownership of the land, the individual having only rights of usufruct.[1] Secondly, there is great physical proximity between households, and the component families of this localized grouping stand in given and relatively fixed physical and spatial relationship to each other. Stemming from this kind of organization is the fact that interpersonal communication is conducted in stable and consistently functioning primary or face-to-face groupings. The families of the maximally solidary community can thus be said to be socially, physically, and emotionally inbred within their respective societal nuclei and *vis-à-vis* other groupings. The maximally solidary community is sedentary, and an agricultural subsistence pattern is primary, except in such unusual instances as the Kwakiutl. In brief, the juxtaposition of highly integrated kin groups, physical proximity, and sedentary life appear to yield feelings of social proximity in extreme degree.

In this type of organization, as well as in the second type, extended family organization appears to prevail. The presence of the nuclear family in individual cases as the primary familial unit, instead of the extended family, does not appreciably alter this picture for, as Steward has pointed out, "the nuclear family may be integrated directly into a larger, multikin structure."[2]

The second type of community-system is the "solidary-fissile community." Like the maximally solidary community, this is a social grouping which has definite physical or social boundaries or both, and it, too, may coincide with the total geographical community or it may be one of two or more similarly constituted groupings within the total geographical community.

Sociologically, the primary difference between these two types is that in the solidary-fissile community the ties and alignments of kinship are not solidified into corporate kin groups. The bonds of kinship in most solidary-fissile communities, qualitatively speaking, are equally as strong as in the maximally solidary community, but these ties are not elevated to the level of exclusive, solidary groupings which own the land. At the same time, however, the ties of kinship are far from disregarded in the solidary-fissile community. Rather, two processes are operating simultaneously within it: one produces a degree of solidarity of families within the group, and the other a degree of fissility of the community.

A degree of social and emotional solidarity is produced in such a community by the strong and marked tendency to associate and interact primarily with kinsmen, real or fictive. Specifically, the members of a solidary-fissile community or band are mostly kinsmen, and occasionally entirely kinsmen. The element of fissility, and a corresponding degree of social distance, is introduced into such a community by a variety of factors. First, physical mobility and change in community-membership are usually permitted, thus resulting in the simultaneous presence within the group of kinsmen *and* nonkinsmen. Where nonkinsmen join the community, they are sometimes addressed and treated as kinsmen; consanguineal ties are the mainsprings of such relationships. But equally important, if not of greater significance, is that kinsmen have the theoretical as well as the actual right to sever relationships with the band or community and either establish or join an entirely independent band or community. While extreme per-

[1] For definitions of such terms and concepts, see Hoebel, 1958, pp. 341-365.
[2] Steward, 1955, p. 55.

sonalization of relationships is the rule in the solidary-fissile community, the degree of social proximity is proportionately weakened by physical mobility *away* from kinsmen, and by the intrusion of non-kinsmen into the community. These, it is assumed, are factors making for social distance within the community. Among many peoples, the exigencies of the food-producing environment, rather than tension or quarrels, appear to have necessitated such adjustments on the social-structural level. Be that as it may, the *effects*—in terms of fission and social distance—are similar. This seems to be the case among such groups as the Andamanese, Arunta, Bushmen, Plains tribes, Sanpoil, Witoto, and the like.

Descent groups are rarely localized spatially or geographically in the solidary-fissile community. Ownership of the means of production is either in the hands of the individual or family group, or in the hands of a territorial unit larger than the kin group, such as the paramountcy organization of the Basuto and Dahomeans. In hunting societies, each tribe has its own territory, with areas allotted to each band.

Within the solidary-fissile community it is possible to observe a process of "compromise" between those forces making for social proximity and those making for social distance. Any of these, when taken alone, are productive of either solidarity or fissility. Among the Navaho and the people of Taitou (Shantung Province, China), clanship, when taken separately, would produce a high degree of social solidarity. Similarly, the isolation of the family, geographically (and hence emotionally) among the Navaho, and almost entirely emotionally in Taitou, makes for the emotional inbreeding of the family *vis-à-vis* the community. The simultaneous operation of factors making both for solidarity and fissility produces a "compromise" between the two, and

places such peoples at this point along the continuum of social cohesiveness and soildarity rather than at the point of maximal or lesser solidarity.

In line with the absence of solidary land-owning kin groups in this type of community, the principal lines of communication are generally within the territorial boundaries of the community, rather than within the sociological confines of the exclusive kin group. In other words, interpersonal relationships in the solidary-fissile community are not confined to kinsmen or non-kinsmen.

The third type in the model is the "nonnucleated society." The functionally significant unit of association in this type is the isolated family group; socially, geographically, and emotionally isolated from all other family units, it constitutes neither a society nor a community. Nor do these several family units make up either a society or a community, structurally or functionally, when taken together. In this case, the application of the term "society" does not represent social reality and, for all intents and purposes, serves only as a classificatory device or artifact.

The primary characteristic of the nonnucleated society is the presence of relatively great distances between households and families, generally physical distance. This geographical distance sets the stage for the maintenance of clearly demarcated *social* boundaries between families; physical space or distance in the nonnucleated society serves as a boundary-maintaining force only in very indirect and incidental ways. This is an important point to bear in mind, because even when the family units of the nonnucleated society unite for temporary amalgamations, they continue to maintain their great social distance from each other. Another way of saying this, in highly abstract terms, is that the spatial relationship between isolated family groups in the non-nucleated society functions as a phenomenon of distance, not of boundedness. Although the ties of kinship in the non-nucleated society *may* be highly formalized, there are rarely any functioning kin groups outside the family, and kinship ties become increasingly diffuse as the physical distance between kinsmen increases.

In the nonnucleated society families generally live physically distant from one another for the greater part of the year, coming together for only a few months at predetermined seasons. Such fission and fusion is generally dictated by climatic exigencies, and the periodic "community-type" amalgamations are temporary in nature. This fission and fusion is quite separate from the previously mentioned process of "solidarity-fissility." In the latter, there are two separate but complementary principles at work at the same time, between which it is often possible to observe "compromises." Where fission and fusion are characteristic of the social system, divisive forces are at work without the "compromising" effects of other integrative factors.

Although the nonnucleated society is usually a nomadic one, there are occasional instances in which this type of social system can be observed in a sedentary people among whom there is also physical proximity between families and households. In such cases, however, it appears that the nonnucleated structure—an extreme and marked atomism—is a temporary or transitional phase in the society's history. Among the *zadruga* of Croatia, for instance, the social structure was characterized by maximal solidarity; for a brief period in its history, during the latter part of the nineteenth century, a nonnucleated structure arose in response to

forces transpiring throughout Croatia, specifically, a growing state structure which imposed taxes on individuals. As a result of political readjustments, the *zadruga* reverted to a maximally solidary community. The Dahomeans also appear to have undergone a shift in their social structure. Indications are that the social system of ancient Dahomey was founded on localized patrilineal clans, each of which was a maximally solidary community. The rise of a civil state structure in Dahomey, which was inconsistent with such a clan organization, appears to have precipitated a temporary shift in Dahomey from a maximally solidary community to a nonnucleated society. This appears to have lasted only a short time, and Dahomean society shifted to a system founded on solidary-fissile communities.[3] It is possible, furthermore, that many segments of American society fall within the category of the nonnucleated society, but the dearth of adequate data preclude their inclusion within the present analysis.

"Individuated social structure," the fourth type in the model, is antithetical to the first three types; that is, the first three community-systems can be thought of as different points along a single continum of solidarity-fissility. The fourth type, however, appears to be entirely discontinuous from the others and to operate on an entirely separate dimension. Individuated social structure is focussed on individuated amassment and accumulation of wealth *as an end in itself* rather than as an intervening step or means to cooperative or competitive generosity.

There are rarely, if ever, any closed groups in this type of community in which membership, feelings of belonging, and reciprocity are fixed and inalienable. Few,

---

[3] See Diamond, 1951, for a detailed reconstruction of Dahomean history.

if any, institutionally significant statuses are ascribed; authority, group cohesiveness, interfamilial support, mutual assistance, and the like, are almost always for the nonce. Similarly, allegiances are expedient and frequently contractual. While considerations or bonds of kinship appear to play occasional roles in interpersonal associations in the individuated social structure, such considerations are decidedly secondary; instead, kinsmen and nonkinsmen alike enter into the economically competitive struggle, and personal profit and success emerge as overwhelmingly predominant values. Power in this type of community generally resides among those who are monetarily powerful rather than among those persons whose social dominance might derive from ascribed high status or who have succeeded in other spheres of competition.

Societies characterized by this type of system superficially resemble the non-nucleated society in that the functionally significant unit of association in both appears to be the independent nuclear family. This resemblance, however, is but a surface one. In individuated social structures the social-emotional isolation of the nuclear family does not stem from physical distance between family units or from fractionating political forces. The principal isolating and individuating factor appears to be the central or focal condition of individuated amassment of wealth. But what is even more important, however, is that as a functionally significant unit of association *even the nuclear family is not maximally solidary in the individuated social structure.*

These four types of community-systems will serve as very important tools in the analysis of personality factors in economic behavior. As we shall attempt to show, each of these community-systems produces its own emotional or motivational forces in individuals; but there are other factors, such as the experiences of infancy and early childhood, which also produce motivations. The latter will be spelled out in the specific hypotheses of this study.

HYPOTHESES

There are two major hypotheses in this study. (1) In those societies in which infants and young children are fed whenever they cry for food or ask for food individuals will, as adults, share their food or money, or both, with other people. Conversely, in those societies in which infants and young children are not fed whenever they communicate the desire for food individuals will, as adults, amass or hoard their wealth, and there will be few enforceable prescriptions to share that wealth with other persons. (See Table 1.)

(2) Those factors which make for social proximity between households will maximize the emotional predisposition to share food or money, or both, with other persons which was created by feeding on demand during infancy and childhood. Similarly, those factors which make for social distance between households will minimize this predisposition to share which was created by feeding on demand during infancy and childhood. Thus, it is hypothesized, where infants and children are fed on demand the emotional predisposition to share will find its most elaborate expression in the maximally solidary community; this predisposition will find its medial expression in the solidary-fissile community; and it will find its minimal expression in the non-nucleated society. These relationships are tabulated in Table 2.

It will be noted that "food" and "money" are occasionally used interchangeably in the course of these discussions. This substitution is often made because it appears that food and money are

TABLE 1

Relationship between Early Feeding Experiences and Sharing

	Sharing			Nonsharing

GRATIFICATION	Andamanese
	Apache
	Arapesh
	Arunta
	Balinese
	Bantu
	  Kavirondo
	Basuto
	Bena
	Bushmen
	Camayura
	Cañamelar
	Chagga
	Chamorros
	Cenchu
	Chimaltenango
	Dahomey
	Dusun
	Eskimo
	Fiji
		Gros Ventres
		Hopi
		Ifaluk
		Kaingang
		Kaska
		Kurtatchi
		Kwakiutl
		Kwoma
		Lakher
		Lamba
		Lepcha
		Lone Hill
		Lesu
		Lushai
		Malekula
		Manua
		Mirebalais
		Moche
		Mohave
		Murngin
			Nama
			Navaho
			Ojibwa
			Okinawans
			Omaha
			Papago
			Pukapuka
			Sanpoil
			Siuai
			Slave
			Suye Mura
			Taitou
			Tallensi
			Tanala
			Tarascans
			Tetons
			Thonga
			Tikopia
			Witoto
			Zadruga
			  (Croatia)
				Sirionó

DEPRIVATION				Alor Marquesans Rocky Roads (Jamaica) Yakut Yurok

symbolically equated in most of the societies of the present sample. In nonindustrialized societies in which the family is simultaneously a unit of production as well as of consumption, and in which money is present, individuals appear to learn very early that money generally derives directly from food. In industrial societies, on the other hand, the conditions underlying the distinction between the family as a productive unit and the economic activities of individuals within the family make it difficult for a young child to grasp the near-equation of food and money. Hence, in industrialized societies, money often appears to have its own social and emotional qualities or properties; in nonindustrialized societies, apparently, such distinctions between money and the products of the soil are not made. (This distinction has considerable significance for the psychoanalytic hypothesis of the "anal character" and it suggests that the problem of the unconscious symbolization of money is probably far more complicated than its traditional treatment in most psychoanalytic writings. Unfortunately, limitations of space prevent a discussion of this problem here.)

TABLE 2

Types of Food Distribution

Recurrent Exchange and Sharing	Mutual Assistance and Sharing in Times of Need	Narrowed and Reluctant Sharing	Nonsharing
Arapesh	Andamanese	Kaska	Alor
	Apache (Chiricahua)		
Bantu Kavirondo	Arunta		
	Balinese	Ojibwa	Marquesans
Chagga	Basuto		
	Bena		
Hopi	Bushmen	*Tanala	Rocky Roads
	Camayura		(Jamaica)
Kurtatchi	Cañamelar (Puerto Rico)		
	Chamorros	*Teton-Dakota	
Kwakiutl	Chenchu		Sirionó
	Chimaltenango		
Kwoma	Dahomey	*Zadruga of	
	Dusun	Croatia	Yakut
Lamba	Eskimo (Copper)		
	Fiji		
Lesu	Gros Ventres		Yurok
	Ifaluk		
Malekula	Kaingang		
	Lakher		
Manu'a	Lepcha		
	Lone Hill (Mandan-Hidatsa)		
*Papago	Lushai		
Pukapuka	Mirebalais (Haiti)		
	Moche		
Tallensi	Mohave		
	Murngin		
*Tanala	Nama		
	Navaho		
Thonga	Okinawans		
	Omaha		
Tikopia	*Papago		
	Sanpoil		
*Zadruga of Croatia	Siuai		
	Slave		
	Suye Mura (Japan)		
	Taitou (China)		
	Tarascans		
	*Teton-Dakota		
	Witoto		

* Those groups marked (*) appear twice in the table because of historical changes in their social organizations. These will be discussed separately later on.

RESULTS

Two over-all correlations emerge as being significant and, thus, provide us with clues as to the general directions which our theoretical speculations must take. The first correlation indicates that there is a meaningful relationship between sharing and early food gratification and between nonsharing and early food deprivation. At the same time, however, the ethnographic data disclose that there is also a correlation between types of community-systems and types of food distribution. We will describe these correspondences; then, because the two over-all correlations appear to deal with the same phenomena, we shall attempt to relate them to each other.

Correlated with the maximally solidary community are several different kinds of *recurrent exchanges and sharing of food*. Putting this another way around, recurrent exchange and sharing is the pattern of food distribution which is correlated with the maximally solidary community, but it is also possible to observe variations on this theme among the societies in the sample which are characterized by the maximally solidary community. Among some peoples (such as the Arapesh and the Kwoma) this type of distribution is found in an extreme form or variation in the cultural rule that a person cannot eat food which he himself has grown, but only food grown by someone else. Among most peoples characterized by the maximally solidary community, there is a constant flow of gifts of food from household to household within the functionally significant unit of association. Among other peoples in this category, there are those whose cultures are permeated with religious ceremonial (such as the Hopi and the Tallensi); here, the recurrent distribution of food, too, takes place in a religious ceremonial context. Among still other peoples (such as

the Kurtatchi and the aboriginal Papago), there are unelaborated but repeated donations, prestations, and exchanges of small token amounts of food among kinsmen. Especially important to bear in mind is that, whatever the variations on the theme, these recurrent and repetitive exchanges of food almost always take place within the sociological boundaries of the maximally solidary community. Also important to remember is that such recurrent exchanges of food are above and beyond ceremonialized or ritualized feasts; that is, these recurrent exchanges are in addition to feasts which occur at religious occasions (with the exception of instances noted above) or at *rites de passage,* and the like. Finally, in all the societies in the sample which are characterized by the maximally solidary community, infants and young children are given food whenever they ask for it.

In the solidary-fissile community a pattern of food distribution is found which can be called *mutual assistance in times of need*. This, too, is a basic or general theme on which there are variations. In nomadic hunting and gathering societies, for example, which are characterized by the solidary-fissile community, this pattern of distribution often takes the form of the immediate distribution of meat to almost all the households of the community as soon as an animal is captured or slain, even if the recipients of the meat have also captured or slain an animal—and, therefore, also become donors themselves. Although this resembles recurrent exchange and sharing, and brings the two patterns very close to each other, what distinguishes them is the following: Where the pattern of food distribution is characterized by recurrent exchange and sharing, some food or other must be exchanged or shared at specified time-intervals, depending on the cultural rules; where the pattern of distribution is characterized by mutual assistance in times of need, and where there is immediate distribution of meat to almost all the families in the community, no other food is spontaneously shared in this manner if no meat has been captured—unless, of course, a closely related family is in great need of other food. In sedentary agricultural societies in this category, mutual assistance in times of need takes the form of aid rendered to kinsmen—real or fictional or persons to whom one stands in "kin-type" relationship—when economic help is objectively needed. Another aspect to the resemblance between mutual assistance in times of need and recurrent exchange and sharing is that mutual assistance in times of need is also present in the maximally solidary community, but in that type of social system there are *also* recurrent exchanges of one sort or another; this elaboration is not made in the solidary-fissile community.

This is not to imply that there are no feasts and exchanges whatever in the solidary-fissile community. On the contrary; these are present, but they occur only at certain specifiable occasions, such as at religious events and at the life crises marked by *rites de passage*. But there are no *recurrent* exchanges above and beyond these ritualized occasions of feasting. Nor is the *idea* of recurrent prestation unknown to societies characterized by the solidary-fissile community, but such exchange is almost always confined to gifts of goods, not food.

Finally, in all the societies of the sample which are characterized by the solidary-fissile community (with the possible exception of the Sirionó, to be discussed later), infants and young children are fed whenever they cry for food or ask for food.

In the nonnucleated society, we generally find a pattern of *narrowed and reluctant sharing*. By this is meant that whenever assistance is rendered to people, it is given very reluctantly and very grudgingly. Furthermore, whenever individuals in the nonnucleated society are willing to extend aid, they are only willing to do so within a very narrowed range or number of people. The individual cultures of peoples characterized by the nonnucleated society generally contain the ideal prescription of generosity and mutual assistance in times of need, but this ideal is rarely, if ever, achieved; in actual behavior, generosity and assistance are extremely narrowed and restricted, qualitatively and in the number and categories of persons toward whom such behavior is manifest. Another way of stating this is that behavior with respect to food in the nonnucleated society *approaches* parsimoniousness, but never quite achieves it. (It is both curious and significant, in a way, that there is so little to be said about such fragmented societies; about one such group, the Shoshoneans, Steward notes that the individual family "probably could have survived in complete isolation." [4]) Finally, among all the peoples in the sample characterized by the nonnucleated society, infants and young children are fed whenever they vocally request it.

Behavior with respect to food and money in the individuated social structure has already been described in our discussion of this type of community-system. The only factor or independent variable which characterized these societies, and which was not found in those of the other three types, was that infants and young children are *not* fed whenever they cry for food or ask for food. This is true of the Alorese,[5] the Marquesans,[6] the

---

4 Steward, 1955, p. 108.
5 DuBois, 1941, p. 274; 1944, pp. 34, 76.
6 Handy, 1923, p. 75; Linton, 1939, pp. 164-165.

Rocky Roaders,[7] the Yakut, whose infants do not get enough to eat because of their mothers' malnutrition,[8] and the Yurok, whose infants are subjected to deprivation after six or seven months.[9]

It could be asked with some justification at this point: in view of the excellent correlations between the functionally significant units of association, on the one hand, and patterns of food distribution, on the other, why do we need the psychological dimension and the experiences associated with early feeding? Could we not inquire into the problem of why people in different societies behave differently with respect to food solely on a sociological level?

The psychological dimension has been found to be indispensable here because those societies characterized by an individuated social structure *could* have been subsumed under the social-structural category of the solidary-fissile community or under the nonnucleated category. In other words, individuated social structures—*sociologically*—often resemble solidary-fissile communities or nonnucleated social structures. What differentiates the individuated social structure from the other two —that is, the factor which enables us to understand nonsharing in the absence of explanatory sociological factors—is the phenomenon of early food deprivation.

This should not be taken to mean that the individuated social structure is unilaterally or directly derived from, or is "produced" by, early childhood food deprivation. What the data do seem to imply, instead, is that nonsharing and amassment tend to covary with this early-life experience and that, *in turn, other cultural and structural features tend to covary with nonsharing and amassment.*

There is only one category of "nonsharing" while there are three categories of "sharing" behavior. It is entirely plausible to assume that, *in reality,* there is more than one "nonsharing" category and that more such categories could be uncovered by future and more extensive research. But there were only six societies in our sample which fell into a "nonsharing" category. As a result of this, we did not have enough cases of "nonsharing" which could be examined in order to differentiate several subtypes; it can be estimated, roughly, that it would require at least twenty-five "nonsharing" societies in order to make such differentiations.

It should be pointed out, if only in passing, that there were no relationships between age at weaning, method of weaning, severity of weaning, similar categories of sphincter training, and the like, on one hand, and any type of behavior with respect to food, on the other. Nor were there any correlations between scarcity and availability of food and patterns of sharing or nonsharing.

One further caveat is in order. Cross-cultural inquiries such as this one aim at uncovering particular regularities and uniformities among societies. In this instance, we are seeking such principles with respect to one dimension of economic behavior; in the next chapter, we shall attempt to do the same for friendship. To a very limited extent, it can be said that the commonalities among societies which are derived in this manner are misleading, for, as is generally accepted in anthropology and sociology, the many parts of each cultural whole are integrated and patterned according to principles which are unique to that culture. The mere fact that two societies possess "recurrent exchange and sharing of food" does not, and should not be taken to, imply that such an abstract category of

---

[7] Cohen, 1955, p. 276.
[8] Priklonskii, 1953, pp. 29:11, 32:22
[9] Erikson, 1950, pp. 285-286.

behavior has the same significance or meaning for these two societies. For example, although the Kwoma and the aboriginal Papago appear within the first category of sharing, the significance and *consequences* of Kwoma elaborations on this basic pattern are radically different from those of the aboriginal Papago. Similarly, the Chiricahua Apache variation on the basic pattern of mutual assistance in times of need has an entirely different place in Chiricahua culture than does the Copper Eskimo variation in Eskimo culture. *Despite this, however, we can seek common denominators and subsume both under the same generic subheading.*

SOCIAL-STRUCTURAL MAXIMIZATION AND MINIMIZATION OF MOTIVATIONS

At the beginning of Chapter 10, it was stated that by "motivation" was meant the psychologically structured impulsions to behavior. This working definition, of course, also implies that there are biological and physiological impulsions to behavior; but we are concerned with those psychological and emotional forces which, in part, arise out of and are engrafted onto the physical properties of the person.

The theoretical discussions which follow are based to a very large extent on two axioms, neither of which is particularly new but which must be made explicit: (1) The motivations which underlie behavior do not derive exclusively from either the biophysiological structure of the individual or from the social system into which he is born, in which he grows, and in which he participates. Instead, it is our contention, motivations within the individual derive from *both*. (2) The emotions which are aroused

during the years of growth, especially in child-parent interaction, are emotional *predispositions* to behavior. No single experience at any stage of development will necessarily lead to any single pattern of behavior. Instead, it can be posited, each of the many biological and sociological conditions under which people live creates its own emotional predispositions. It is the *combinations* of these predispositions which yield the *motivations* which, as we infer them, underlie observable patterns of behavior. In other words, no one behavioral or cultural item is the direct outgrowth of any one emotional predisposition; instead, every such item is a combination of a multiplicity of emotional predispositions which mold and catalyze each other.

Very little is known about such psychological processes; hence, the constructs just used are imprecise and descriptive. But in unravelling the threads in any one pattern of behavior, it is necessary to begin at a definite point and maintain a consistent perspective. Our theoretical predilection leads us to ask: by what means and in what manners do the emotional predispositions aroused by different social systems maximize or minimize the emotional predispositions aroused by early-life experiences? To a very large extent, our procedure in this study can be described as one in which we are holding constant the experience of early-food gratification and varying the sociological conditions. (This, as we shall see, is not the only procedure which will be employed, but it is the basic one.)

An indispensable postulate which will appear constantly in the fabric which we will attempt to weave derives from the "genetic approach" of psychoanalytic theory. This approach endeavors to "describe how any [clinical] condition under observation has grown out of an individual's past, and extended throughout his total life span. . . . Genetic propositions state how these reactions came into being and are used in the course of an individual's life." [10]

Fundamental to the "genetic approach" is the postulate that adult patterns of interpersonal behavior are outgrowths of patterns which were established in infancy, childhood, and adolescence in child-parent interaction. What is manifest throughout life are not the overt behaviors which were established early in the child-parent relationship, but rather the emotional *predispositions* which have now, in adulthood, combined with each other to become the motivations to overt behavior.

For example, hungry infants cry, whine, thrash about. In no society is such behavior acceptable for a hungry adult. At the other extreme of the fear and anxiety which such behavior in infants appears to represent is "trust." [11] When an infant is well satiated, all other things being equal, he sleeps or plays contentedly. Similarly, alternation between eating, sleeping, and playing is not appropriate behavior for a satiated and "trusting" adult in any society. The original or raw emotion is never lost, but overt behaviors appropriate to the affective feeling must be learned at different developmental stages in the life cycle. (Naturally, no one incident, event, or experience, however pleasurable or traumatic, can, by itself, establish emotional predispositions of this sort. When we talk about experiences with respect to food during infancy and early childhood, we mean a specific pattern of experience which is repeated with great consistency over several years.) Furthermore, the overt behaviors which represent or express motivations must be appropriate to the culture.

Applying this theoretical approach,

it appears that the repetitive and consistent gratification of hunger by the mother, or surrogate, instils within the maturing infant a world view predicated on the notion that there is enough food in the world, that one can always secure food when one needs it, and that other persons will give food when asked for it. Hence, people with this predisposing view of the world will be capable, psychologically speaking, of giving food to others because they "know," however irrationally, that there is always food to be gotten. Putting this in symbolic, and probably "culture-bound," terms: the imaged breast is always full and can always be secured. In terms of self-portraiture, the repetitive gratification of the demands of hunger in the infant and young child produces a sense of "trust"; [12] that is, it sets into motion a security system in which an awareness is present, albeit unconsciously, that the need for food can be realized interpersonally without the experience of threat. Because the demands of hunger have been met during the years of vulnerability in the life-cycle, the individual experiences or perceives himself as one who can fulfil his wants by mutual interaction with others. He not only views himself as gratified and satiated but he also views others as gratifying and satiating persons.

This self-perception is not necessarily "adaptive" or oriented toward the "reality" of the food-yielding environment. Rather, it is a perception which defines physical reality in terms of a previously defined "social reality." The Arapesh who have maximized the sharing of food to such an extreme degree that each person eats only food which has been grown by someone else, are a dramatic example.[13] But they are not demented; they know

---

[10] Hartmann and Kris, 1945, p. 11.
[11] Erikson, 1950, pp. 75, 80, 219-222.
[12] *Loc. cit.*
[13] Mead, 1939, pp. 28-29.

that they live in an environment of scarcity;[14] yet this knowledge is completely overshadowed by their knowledge—unconscious though it may be—that their kinsmen will always provide them with food. Here we see, in part, the functioning of that facet of the "self" which is "not only an aspect of all experience and a standard for all experience [but one which] contributes to the *quality and form of all experience.*" [15]

These emotional predispositions can be seen in clearer perspective when they are contrasted with those which appear to be produced by early food deprivation. From inadequate feeding in infancy and early childhood the individual learns that the world (represented by his mother) is a depriving place. We can postulate that when the child is deprived "of what he wants, the result is not only frustration of his wants, but a self that is less adequate because it cannot fulfill these wants." [16] In societies in which infants and young children are not fed on demand, there appears to be in adulthood a "distrust" which motivates a characterological demandingness for what had been denied originally. It can be hypothesized that stemming from the food deprivation of infancy and early childhood is the individual's perception of himself as an inadequate person, specifically, a hungry and impoverished one. Just as the individual views himself as one who "never has enough"—and this impression is inescapable in the "non-sharing" societies—so does he view the world as "not having enough *for* him."

People with this perception of themselves and of the world will want to have as much food, or *that which buys food,* as possible. Since it is difficult to hoard most foods, and people in preliterate and folk

societies cannot amass food due to lack of refrigeration and substitute techniques, individuals characterized by this affective predisposition will tend to accumulate money—be the latter gongs and mokos in Alor, dentalium shells among the Yurok, or shillings and pounds in Jamacia—as a substitute form of insurance. They cannot be expected to share their food or money with others, for they will tend to feel that neither they nor the food-producing world will have enough in the first place, and their fear of impoverishment will restrain or inhibit them from endangering or weakening the bulwark they have erected against that impoverishment. Nor can it be assumed in the case of "nonsharing" people that this perception of the human world is "adaptive" or responsive to the exigencies of the material environment. Just as there are economies of scarcity in the first two types of distribution, so are there environments of plenty in the "nonsharing" category. The Alorese, the Jamaicans, the Yurok, and even the Marquesans, do not appear to be faced by recurrent shortages of food. As for the Yakut, who are often faced with scarcity, there does appear to be sufficient material in the environment for the establishment of great differences of wealth between the social classes.

The Sirionó appear to be the most striking exception to the first hypothesis. Sirionó infants and young children appear to be fed on demand,[17] and by all other criteria it would be predicted that their system of distribution would be characterized by mutual assistance and sharing in times of need. Actually, "the distribution of food rarely extends beyond the extended family." [18] One of the important rules of the culture

---

[14] *Ibid.,* p. 19.
[15] Murphy, 1947, p. 499, italics his.
[16] *Ibid.,* p. 533.
[17] Holmberg, 1950, pp. 75-76.
[18] *Ibid.,* p. 50.

. . . is that of sharing food within the extended family. . . . Frequently, in fact, food sharing does not go beyond the nuclear family, *even though the quantity of food may be more than adequate to take care of immediate needs.* Under such conditions, one may be accused of hoarding food, but the other members of the extended family can do little about it except to go out and look for their own.[19]

It could be argued that the Sirionó constitute an indeterminate occurrence with respect to early feeding. They constantly live on the verge of starvation, and it is plausible to ask whether lactating mothers thus subsisting could ever have enough, and sufficiently nutritious, milk to give their youngsters. Be that as it may— there is also the possibility that there was a temptation to "find" an exception to the hypothesis—let us assume that the Sirionó are truly an exception and attempt to discern some of the implications of this occurrence.

The Sirionó illustrate the proposition that *the emotional results of the experiences of socialization are flexible, changeable, and mutable.* The Sirionó constitute a dramatic, albeit unique, example of this principle, for it appears that the recurrent traumata of near-starvation in late childhood, adolescence, and adulthood are sufficient to overcome the experiences of (assumed) early food gratification. One would also expect a considerable degree of psychological confusion to result from such a complete contradiction of early learning by later experiences. There is some evidence for this confusion, or "conflict," if one so wishes to label it, as can be seen in the fact that there are cultural requirements for mutual assistance and reciprocity but simultaneously patterned stealth in eating when food is available.[20]

The cross-cultural ethnographic data, however, even if we did not have the Sirionó case, provide the strongest evidence for the principle that the emotional results of early-life experiences are flexible, changeable and mutable, that they are essentially *predispositions.* This evidence is to be found empirically in the three types of "sharing." We have observed that crosscutting the general category of "sharing" are distinct *types* of sharing. If we are correct in postulating that any observable behavior and its inferred motivations result from the *totality* of experiences or conditions of life, our task is to discover what later experiences (or conditions) have combined with the early experience of gratification to produce the three types of sharing. That is, since early food gratification is highly correlated with sharing, some other factors must combine with early gratification to produce the different *types* of sharing.

Consistent early food gratification, it can be posited, produces a sense of "trust." Similarly, it can be posited, each of the different types of community-systems produces its own emotional predispositions. (We shall see what these are in a moment.) It is our contention that the sense of trust is flexed and mutated— and thus given its final shape—by the *sociologically*-produced emotional predispositions with which this sense of trust combines. It is further contended here that the emotional predispositions elicited by the different community-systems maximize or minimize this basic sense of trust. It is here, incidentally, that we observe our operational procedure of holding one factor (early feeding experiences) constant, varying the second (community-systems), and thereby observing corollary variations in a third area (types of sharing).

---

[19] *Ibid.,* p. 60, italics supplied.
[20] *Ibid.,* pp. 36, 60, 62.

The principal assumptions which seem to underlie inquiries into processes of communication in social-structural contexts appear to be predicated on the notion that social "communication in general . . . does not constitute an institution; rather does it pervade all institutional activities and makes them possible; equally it has its own autonomous structure." [21] Again, Hallowell writes: "Symbolic communication is the basis on which a common world of meanings and values is established and transmitted in human activities. Communication at this new level is a necessary condition for the operation of human societies in their characteristic form." [22]

This relegation of communication to the level of a universal process which *makes possible* almost all social interaction appears to have had a curious effect on the investigation of social processes in general. The failure to examine critically and question the postulate that communication makes institutional activities possible has, to a certain extent, inhibited inquiry into some of the more important functions of institutional structures. In the present analysis this postulate will be inverted as an operational one (still recognizing, however, that without the ability to communicate people would be unable to conduct institutionalized activities) and, in its stead, will be substituted the postulate that *the primary and significant communicative activities of human life take place along and are made possible by existing institutional lines, specifically, along the lines and according to the nature of the functionally significant unit of association.*

Emotions and motivations are learned interpersonally, and their expression is equally an interpersonal process. Speaking reductionistically for a moment, the expression of emotions and affects is a communication to other persons of the feelings one has about oneself and about them. While culturally patterned emotions and motivations generally require expression by the individual, either verbally or materially, it appears that *no society allows for their random and promiscuous expression to just anyone.* Rather, one may communicate these feelings, either verbally, physically, or materially only to certain people. These lines of communication are almost everywhere specified, structuralized, and consistent; they are, in essence, institutionalized. The operation of this principle can be observed in many areas of societal living. This is seen everyday, as in the fact that we are permitted to express and receive love only in relation to specific persons; we are permitted to exchange confidences only with particular individuals; dependency needs can be gratified by certain people and not by others; we may express hostility only to specific individuals and in appropriate ways, depending on our relationships to them; and so forth. We shall see in the final chapters of this book how the breakdown of such lines of communication is intimately tied to the development of psychosis. This principle can also be observed very clearly in societies which have undergone change in their social structures; in these societies, it is found that as sociological relationships change, feelings and emotions which previously had been expressed toward one category of people may now be expressed to entirely different categories or within different kinds of relationships. And we can also observe the operation of this principle in societies in which forces making for social proximity and those making for social distance are functioning simultaneously.

It has been postulated that social

---

21 Nadel, 1951, p. 143.
22 Hallowell, 1953, p. 603.

distance is a function of, among other factors, physical distance. As a partial determinant of behavior with respect to food, this relationship characterizes the third type of sharing as a whole. In four of the five societies in this category (Kaska, Ojibwa, Tanala, Teton Dakota), the principle determinant of social distance appears to be physical distance. As a corollary of this, we find a considerable degree of atomism in behavior with respect to food: narrowed and reluctant sharing.

Similarly, in societies in which all the factors making for social proximity are operating simultaneously, the lines of communication are continuous and solidified. Thus, in a society in which there are solidary kin groups and in which membership is relatively inalienable, we should expect to find—and this is borne out by the data—that feelings of proximity and intimacy are expressed materially in the recurrent and repetitive exchange of food.

It was also posited that such feelings of solidarity, proximity, and intimacy would be proportionately weakened as the element of personal choice in group affiliation and membership entered the picture. In other words, we are assuming that there appears to inhere in the phenomenon of physical movement away from people a force which makes for social distance in the structure of relationships within the group. (This is a rather obvious postulate, because it can be assumed that people will invest less emotional energy in people who might move away than in people who can be assumed to remain within the group permanently.) Hence, it can be posited still further that the greater the volitional or personal choice in residence and affiliation the greater will be the social distance—or the weaker the social proximity—among per-

sons. And, furthermore, this greater social distance will be expressed materially in behavior with respect to food. Thus, within the general category of "sharing"—and paralleling the continuum of the maximally solidary community–the solidary fissile community–the nonnucleated society—we find the continuum of recurrent and repetitive exchange—mutual assistance in times of need—narrowed and reluctant sharing.

Not only do emotional predispositions maximize each other—as in the juxtaposition of social proximity with "trust" —and minimize each other—as in the combination of social distance and "trust" —but opposing social-structural principles can combine to produce particular emotional predispositions. We can see this in "compromise" conditions as, for example, among the Navaho. Physical distance among Navaho families gives rise to a large degree of social distance between them; and from the physical factor alone we might predict that the Navaho pattern of food distribution would be characterized by narrowed and reluctant sharing. Clanship, on the other hand, produces a high degree of social proximity; and from this sociological factor alone we might predict for them recurrent and repetitive exchange of food. But both factors operate simultaneously among the Navaho, and the "compromise" between the two appears to produce the same relative picture which seems to characterize the other solidary-fissile groups in the sample. Correlated with this "compromise" is a pattern of mutual assistance in times of need. The dominant theme in Navaho economic behavior is a marked individualism[23] which is greatly tempered by mutual assistance among clansmen in times of need,[24] it being the clanship which "gives rise to occasional economic and other rec-

---

[23] Kluckhohn and Leighton, 1946, pp. 57-58.
[24] *Ibid.*, pp. 220-222.

iprocities." [25] At the same time, the emotional predispositions evoked by clanship are considerably weakened "by the emotional inbreeding which the geographical isolation of Navaho households makes almost inevitable." [26]

People in all societies have the need to relate to each other. By this we mean that they have the need of possessing the means—physical, material, or verbal—of expressing awareness of each other; of recognizing and gratifying each other's emotional and physical needs; of expressing the "self" *vis-à-vis* others; of realizing a personal sense of "being" through and with others. Depending on the culture, this need for relatedness is met in a variety of ways and on different levels of symbolic activity. While there is variation from one culture to another in this respect, there appear to be a limited number of techniques for the realization of interpersonal relatedness. Heterosexual intercourse, to take only one example, is everywhere a physiological as well as symbolic means of relatedness. At the same time, however, in no society of which we have knowledge has the culture delineated heterosexual intercourse as the sole area or avenue of interpersonal relatedness; as a mode of relatedness, different cultures have elaborated or minimized it. Similarly, the degree of elaboration of such modes, and their symbolic meanings, may also vary from status to status within the total society.

Another category from which all societies appear to derive modes or techniques of interpersonal relatedness is food. The reason for this apparently universal symbolic usage of food is that *food is the mainspring and the context of the very first warmth and sensed belonging—the very first sense of relating to another person—which the individual, as a neonate, experiences.* Generally speaking, the earliest experiences with the mother (as a representative of the world) through the instrumentality of food establish one important and basic pattern of relating to other people later on. The great importance of this experience is, of course, not only due to the fact that it is his first knowledge and acquaintance of relating himself to another person but also due to the fact that he is so psychologically vulnerable, impressible, and receptive at this stage of life.

Looking at food as a means of relating to people from a cross-cultural vantage, it is significant that more than eighty percent of the societies in the present sample are characterized by active interpersonal relatedness via food, recurrent and repetitive exchange and mutual assistance in times of need. In the nonnucleated society, food is reluctantly given to people, and the apparent failure of these peoples to employ food as a recurrent means of relating to kinsmen and other persons parallels the rather weak bonds among individuals and between families. In other words, the emotional isolation of individuals in the nonnucleated society and their reluctance to approach one another on various levels of intimacy is manifest materially in their reluctance to share food with one another. Landes writes that the Ojibwa individual, for example,

. . . can never free himself from the wariness proper to the winter, and at all times views the proximity of other Indians as a threat. He is achingly alive to the people about him. Unless drunk, one man never meets another with a frank relaxed manner. With a poker face he watches his companion, trying to penetrate his motivations and fortifying his own defenses. Even those

---

[25] *Ibid.,* p. 65.
[26] Kluckhohn, 1944, p. 53.

whom he calls friends he does not trust to the extent of dispensing with protective magic. . . . Just as a hunter is allowed to shoot a trespasser on sight, so a shaman strikes with evil magic anyone whom he thinks has threatened or insulted him.[27]

In the individuated social structure, a predominating cultural value or goal is the amassment of wealth by the individual. There are two intimately related dimensions to the strivings for wealth in such groups.

In these societies, a predominating cultural goal is the amassment of wealth, and individual self-portraiture is predicated on success or failure in this respect. Thus almost all activity in regard to food is alienating and divisive. A second important aspect of these societies is that interpersonal relatedness is predicated on recurrent individual comparisons with other persons. It is a "negative" mode of relatedness, in which the person experiences belongingness to and with others within a system in which the person can compare his self with other selves and in which he is accorded prestige by these other selves in the competitive struggle. The person does have the experience of belonging, for the psychological-sociological security system gives him positional standing of one sort or another in his interpersonal world. Yet such belongingness is very tenuous, and the person gives the impression of frantically attempting to climb a ladder—or at least attempting to keep from slipping down one.[28]

We have hypothesized that the sense of "trust" predisposes people to share with each other. Sociologically produced feelings of intimacy, when combined with this emotional predisposition, maximize this sense of "trust"; the juxtaposition of the two yields a system of recurrent and repetitive exchange. It can be posited that such behavior is, at the same time, *a material and symbolic expression* of such feelings of proximity and intimacy. Similarly, when feelings of proximity and intimacy are slightly attenuated to produce the structure of the solidary-fissile community, this feeling of "trust" is given a medial expression, namely, a system of distribution in the form of mutual assistance in times of need.

But this formulation is only a very limited explanation of why there are different types of food distribution. Why *do* people share with each other, in different ways, in the first place?

It appears from the ethnographic data that people in almost all societies expect or want to receive food from one another. We shall speculate as to why this is so in a moment. However, despite this common characteristic of people in most societies, we have also seen that there are several different types of food distribution—there are several different types of institutionalized forms in which this expectation or wish is satisfied. Here again, we have a *constant* factor (the wish or need to receive) and four related *variable* factors (the different community-systems and their associated patterns of food distribution).

Now, when two persons engage in what is called a social relationship, *A* expects to receive food from *B* if he has given food to *B*. The latter's return of *A's* gift in turn obligates *A* to reciprocate again *B's* gift. This is a simplistic isolation of only two persons, but on a sociological level such reciprocities are almost always extended into much broader webs. When this occurs in society, rather than between only two people, we are naturally confronted with the processes underlying rec-

[27] Landes, 1937, p. 55.
[28] Cohen, 1955, p. 293.

iprocity. At the same time, however, we are also confronted with a problem which is far more fundamental: Why should whole groups of people engage in—and institutionalize—a system in which they eat food grown or secured by someone else, or exchange identical or equivalent gifts?

It is possible, of course, that the very asking of this question is a "culture-bound" response to a totally alien occurrence. From the point of view of a Western observer, a system based on mutual assistance in times of need is somewhat more realistic. In this, food is viewed by the members of the group as an objectively necessary means of survival, although, as in the other three types, there are special occasions on which gifts are given and exchanged. From the same point of view, however, mutual assistance demands explanation as much as does repetitive exchange and sharing.

Starting out from the proposition that people in most societies appear to want to receive food from others, it can be posited that a community-system of the nature of the maximally solidary community not only maximizes the predisposition to give or share food, but it also, at the same time, *makes possible the maximal realization of the wish to receive from others.* In other words, the maximally solidary community enables the individual to gratify his wish or need to *receive* because it maximizes the predisposition to *give.* In this type of community, the constant giving-and-receiving—even in token form, as among the aboriginal Papago—is principally an expression of the "trust" and extreme proximity among individuals in the group.

This can be seen in somewhat sharper perspective by a comparison of the first and second types. In the maximally solidary community, the solidary and exclusive nature of kin groups which are generally localized, enhances feelings of prox-

imity among families and individuals. Similarly, the attenuation of such exclusiveness and solidarity makes for proportionate social distance, however imperceptible that distance may be. This seems to occur, as in band organization, because of the ability or the right of the individual to change his residence or group loyalty. It would appear that the very knowledge that a neighboring kinsman has the theoretical right of severing *immediate* ties of kinship introduces a slight, albeit significant, element of tenuousness and distance in interpersonal relationships. These dialectics can be observed with even greater clarity in the nonnucleated society, though they need not be spelled out.

These dialectics become active parts of societal systems—and not just calculus-type formulations on paper—because of several principles which are constantly at work in people; we have alluded to these principles at different points in our discussion. Most importantly, the emotional need for warmth and belongingness, first learned in connection with the receipt of food, *continues* to demand satisfaction. Furthermore, it is expressed through the matter and medium with which it was first learned—food. This repetitiveness helps to explain, in part, what appears to be a universal need or desire to receive food from others. And we have also seen that those emotional predispositions which are aroused in the early years are mutable and changeable by the emotional predispositions elicited by different community-systems. Hence, we can stipulate further that *those forces which make for feelings of proximity will make for a corresponding degree of realization of the need to receive food from others; those forces which make for feelings of distance will make for a correspondingly smaller degree of the realization of the need to receive food from others.*

The wish to receive from others in the individuated social structure appears to be predicated on a repetitive attempt to recapture and make up for the warmth and affection denied in the course of earlier inadequate feeding. Rather than employing food and money symbolically as a material means of interpersonal relatedness, it appears that the individual in such a society seeks food, money, or both, from others to add to his store of wealth for the enhancement of a self-system which revolves upon the *amount* he has amassed. Sociologically viewed, what appears to be significant here is the fact that the wish to receive from others is not gratified, and it is undoubtedly true that the deprivation of this wish in adulthood further isolates individuals from each other. As Fromm has put it: ". . . the hoarding orientation . . . makes people have little faith in anything new they might get from the outside world; their security is based upon hoarding and saving, while spending is felt to be a threat." [29]

To summarize, it appears that the willingness to share or give implies an *ability,* psychologically viewed, on the part of the donor to meet the wants, needs, and demands of another person within a total cultural and social system which impinges on both of them simultaneously and with (assumed) equal intensity. Furthermore, this ability to share or give revolves upon the individual's unconscious sense of "trust," his perception of himself as a person who "has enough" and who need not fear to "give up" some of what he has, because he "knows" that there is "enough" in the environment or in other people to make up for what he has given away. In other words, his perception dictates that just as other people

take things from him they are equally willing to give to him.

The interplay between the ability to give and the need to receive are necessary factors in understanding behavior with respect to food, but they are not sufficient because they encompass only one side of the picture of motivations in this area. The ethnographic data reveal with marked clarity that *no matter how highly elaborated a system of recurrent exchange and sharing may be, nowhere is an individual expected to give up everything he possesses. Nowhere is true "selflessness" an expected or imposed value to which the individual must adhere.* A few examples from the data will illustrate this.

Among the Arapesh, who have elaborated recurrent exchange to an extreme, personal ownership and rights in property are clearly delineated with definite notions of "mine" and "yours." [30] Among the Logoli and Vugusu, cattle do not constitute a significant part of the subsistence economy,[31] but they do constitute a form of

. . . wealth, [which] if wisely used, is a certain means of gaining prestige and influence within the clan community. The wealthy person, it is true, has the duty of being generous and helpful to the needy, but in return his homestead and thereby he himself become the center of the social life of the neighborhood or even of the entire clan community.[32]

Similarly, even within the most highly formalized areas of cooperation among the Hopi, as between sisters, there is apt to be intense competition for the possessions of a mother who has died without

[29] Fromm, 1947, p. 65.
[30] Mead, 1939, pp. 59-60; 1940, p. 217.
[31] Wagner, 1939, pp. 23-24.
[32] Wagner, 1949, p. 80.

making disposition of household owner-ship,[33] just as there are often bitter quar-rels over land within the clan.[34] Among the Kurtatchi, pigs "are entirely personal possessions, and may be owned by any-body, man, woman, or child. A man with no pigs is regarded as poor, but there is nothing to prevent him from gaining prestige in the village by other means." [35]

Although actual destruction of goods did occur occasionally in the Kwakiutl potlatch,[36] there was definitely present a quest for individual profit in addition to the prestige derived from extreme gen-erosity.[37] The Kwoma, who believe that a man would die if he ate his own har-vest,[38] simultaneously specify individual ownership of the yield of the land, each person's crop being put in a separate bin in a storehouse.[39]

Skipping several alphabetical listings in the category of recurrent exchange to the last two groups in this type, we come to the Tikopia who also have a fairly eleborate system of repetitive exchange of food. Although "there are no landless Tikopia," [40] "land is the greatest source of wealth in Tikopia. Some of the terms for a wealthy person are really references to control over land therefore over food." [41] Although such wealth does not afford an individual any particular degree of prestige, "the natives themselves em-phasize how the desire for land is a poten-tial cause of dissension. In olden times it

even gave rise to fratricide." [42] Among the *zadruga* of Croatia, where there ex-isted an extreme egalitarianism, individ-uals held personal ownership over vine-yards, some parcels of land, and movable goods.[43]

Similarly, rights of ownership over material possessions, such as instruments of agriculture and hunting, as well as other goods, are privately and individually held in all the societies of this type, as well as in the groups of the other types. For example, among the Andamanese, who strictly prescribe that all available food be shared with those who do not have sufficient food, "all food is private property and belongs to the man or woman who has obtained it." [44] Similarly, "all portable property is . . . owned by individuals. . . ." [45] Likewise, the Chiri-cahua Apache, who have formalized open-handed and generous distribution even more so than the Andamanese, stipu-late that

the products of an individual's industry, skill, and daring are, in theory at least, his own. . . . Those things which a man makes or obtains are his own, and his wife may not dispose of them with-out his permission. But if he recklessly gives away all the booty he has earned in a successful raid and leaves his own family impoverished, he is subjected to stinging criticism at home and ridicule outside.[46]

---

[33] Titiev, 1944, p. 24.
[34] *Ibid.*, pp. 181-182.
[35] Blackwood, 1935, p. 454.
[36] Codere, 1951, p. 77.
[37] *Ibid.*, p. 76; Ford, 1941, p. 123.
[38] Whiting, 1941, pp. 109-110.
[39] *Ibid.*, pp. 111, 120.
[40] Firth, 1939, p. 58.
[41] Firth, 1936, p. 373.
[42] *Loc. cit.*
[43] Tomasic, 1942, p. 232.
[44] Radcliffe-Brown, 1933, p. 43.
[45] *Ibid.*, p. 42.
[46] Opler, 1941, pp. 397-398.

The interplay between generosity and privacy of ownership is clearly expressed in the words of a Chiricahua informant: " 'When a man returns from the hunt, the proceeds are his own. He doesn't have to give anything, but even if a lazy man wants food, he would not refuse him.' " [47]

Similarly, among the Dahomeans, where there are clearly enunciated and formalized lines of mutual assistance,[48]

. . . the ownership of a very large proportion of wealth is in the hands of individuals. . . . Thus, the compound a man builds is his property; the trees he plants belong to him; the money he earns is his to dispose of as he pleases; the utensils he buys are his, as are the clothes a man possesses, his guns . . . and the like. Above all, the property he is most careful of is his money. This he keeps in some secret place, and since he will not ordinarily entrust it to a locked container in his house, he buries it under a tree. Tales abound of reputedly wealthy persons who, fearing to entrust this knowledge to another, had died leaving their heirs in ignorance of the place where they had secreted their wealth.[49]

Among the Copper Eskimo, where "if only one seal is caught, the whole of the meat must be distributed, otherwise some of the people would go hungry," [50] we again note an element of behavior antithetical, so to speak, to this general pattern of mutual assistance:

In the winter, when each wife cooks in her own hut, she can hide away some of the choicer portions of the meat for her husband and herself to eat after the visitors have left; but in the summer, when most of the cooking is done out of doors, everyone gathers round the pot to eat and no concealment is possible.[51]

Similar data can be found for each of the societies in the present sample; a few have been cited haphazardly and randomly to illustrate what appears to be a basal universal phenomenon or process.

What appears to emerge from all this is that the sharing and distribution of food and money is not the outgrowth of a simple relationship between early training with respect to food and later adult behavior. Similarly, while it is undoubtedly analytically correct to say that given cultural and sociological conditions or occurrences can maximize or minimize the degree of generosity characteristic of most of the members of a group, it appears that the matter must be stated from still another point of view: *Those sociocultural systems which maximize generosity—the dialectic of wanting to receive and the willingness or ability to give or share— equally constrict the need or tendency to individual retentiveness. Similarly, those sociocultural systems which minimize and narrow generosity equally allow for proportionately greater degrees of individual retentiveness.*

COMPARISONS WITHIN CULTURES

Hypotheses dealing with relationships between social structure and personality must not only be validated cross-culturally, but they must meet two other tests of credibility. First, they must stand the test of history; in this study, the attempt will be made to show that as the functionally significant unit of association changes, behavior with respect to food will also

---

[47] *Ibid.*, p. 323.
[48] Herskovits, 1938, pp. 51, 60, 64, 70-72, 154.
[49] *Ibid.*, p. 81.
[50] Jenness, 1922, p. 90.
[51] *Loc. cit.*

change, and in predictable directions. Secondly, these hypotheses must be tested within individual cultures in order to show that different degrees of social distance and proximity within a culture will produce the same effects as do social distance and proximity in the comparison of many cultures. We shall attempt the second test of credibility first, and then conclude this chapter with the historical test. The latter will also give us the opportunity to present the data for four societies in detail, and thereby to show the kinds of data which were used for this study.

The following statements are to be taken as nothing more than tentative allusions to certain sociocultural processes, because a complete analysis of the problem—class- and rank-differentiated behavior—is essentially a separate research task requiring its own specialized techniques.

"Culture" can be viewed along two separate dimensions. On one hand, it is employed as the designative criterion of the customs, habits, and history of a self-perpetuating group; in part, it differentiates a societal group from all others. On the other hand, "culture" has a generic meaning, namely, the commonalities of panhuman experience which people in all societies share. Operationally speaking, cross-cultural research aims at deriving and formulating universal regularities which can ultimately provide a sharper understanding of the dynamics of individual cultural systems.

Throughout this chapter, we have stressed the importance of social proximity and distance for behavior regarding food. We submit that *to the extent that the variable of social distance realistically operates in cross-cultural comparisons of behavior with respect to food, this variable should have similar effects within individual societies.* That is, we can assume that every society contains some forces, however few and small, which help to make for social distance (even in the maximally solidary community). Now, in a society in which extreme social proximity helps to produce a pattern of recurrent sharing of food we can expect that factors making for social distance *in the same society* will help to produce a proportionate reluctance to share or tendencies toward the retention of wealth. These tendencies would go beyond or would be in addition to those processes postulated at the end of the previous section which appear to make for retentiveness in the midst of patterns of sharing.

Unfortunately, we cannot discuss the experiences of feeding during infancy and early childhood in this context. Even where ethnologists do report on such feeding experiences they rarely, if ever, report whether or not there are variations from status to status within the same society. In most stratified preliterate societies there appears to be a definite continuity of culture from status to status; rarely are there any indications that the ruling classes of a society, for example, do not "understand" the social and emotional "language" of those far below them. Although there are often specialized techniques for the education of the children of these higher strata, it seems fairly safe to assume that there are no great differences in the experiences to which infants and young children are subjected throughout the entire society. Hence, we shall assume that the early experiences surrounding feeding remain constant between the statuses of the groups with which we are dealing.

For our present purposes, there is no need to enter into the possibile sources of "social classes"—whether they emerge through military conquest, from ownership and control of the means of production, through "natural" social differentiation, and the like. As a matter of fact, it is possible to question the validity of the term "classes" with respect to most of the groups in the present sample. Most students would prefer to speak simply of "social ranking" or "differentiation."

High social status, such as chieftainship, is determined in numerous ways, and the criteria vary from society to society. To illustrate the proposition being proffered, let us take one criterion of social ranking—hereditary status. It was stated earlier that *social distance not only minimizes and narrows generosity but, equally, allows for proportionately greater degrees of individual retentiveness.* It can be postulated that social distance is greater between persons of high and low ascribed statuses than between persons of high and low achieved statuses. Now, if we combine the relationships between social distance generally and behavior with respect to food with the principle of individual needs for retentiveness, it would follow that *retentiveness or amassment would covary with ascribed high status* even in societies characterized by the maximally solidary or solidary-fissile communities. In other words, it can be assumed that persons with ascribed high status in either of these societies will employ, perhaps not consciously, their social distance from the "masses" or "commoners" as a mechanism for the allowance of greater manifestation of needs or tendencies to retentiveness.

To illustrate this, let us select a few societies characterized by the maximally solidary community in which are present clearly differentiated hereditary statuses. Among the Kurtatchi, hereditary chiefs "always lived the same life as commoners, observing the same taboos, working at the same tasks, eating the same food,

and living in the same kind of huts." [52] Social distance between ascribed statuses is apparently minimized among the Kurtatchi, but it is expressed economically nevertheless. The chief

> . . . does, as a rule, own more strings of ceremonial currency than most people can boast of, either handed down on the death of former *tsunaun* or received as payment for favors shown. But he needs more than a commoner to provide for the marriage payments of the young men of his lineage, who, being themselves *tsunaun* should marry women equal to them in position.[53]

In Manua, with a fairly elaborated hierarchical organization of chieftainship, "rank had a few feudal privileges which guaranteed a high income, and was dependent upon maintaining a proper amount of pomp and circumstance. . . ." [54] At the same time, however, even chieftain wealth was kept in circulation by requirements of generous expenditure and assistance of poor people by the chiefs. [55]

Individual wealth in Tikopia is a function of hereditary status rather than a means to higher status and, as such, revolves upon the control over land and food. [56] One index of the degree of social distance between hereditary chiefs and commoners is seen in the fact that "if a commoner strikes a member of a chiefly family, he will probably have to expiate his offense by going off to sea," [57] namely, to certain death. At the same time, however, there are forces at work in the social life of Tikopia which in turn narrow this social distance, for the chiefs mingle freely with commoners, "exchanges take place between them on a basis of general

---

[52] Blackwood, 1935, p. 50.
[53] *Ibid.,* pp. 50-51.
[54] Mead, 1930, p. 79.
[55] *Ibid.,* pp. 18-19, 79.
[56] Firth, 1936, pp. 360, 373.
[57] *Ibid.,* p. 358.

reciprocity, there is no 'chief's language,' as in Samoa or Java, kinship terms are used between them, and nowadays intermarriage takes place freely between their members." [58] This narrowed social distance, or increased social proximity, between hereditary chiefs and commoners is also expressed materially, for the chiefs "have in past generations undoubtedly tended to impoverish themselves and their descendants by grants of orchards to immigrants and to destitute persons. In this way they have maintained their reputation for beneficence and care for the welfare of the population as a whole at the expense of their own economic interests." [59]

In turning to societies characterized by the solidary-fissile community, groups which are generally characterized by somewhat less social proximity in overall structural terms, we should again expect to find manifestations of individual retentiveness as covariant with greater social distance—in this case, too, as measured by hereditary high status—but in proportionately greater degrees than in societies characterized by the maximally solidary community. We read of the Basuto:

Formerly the chiefs, whose position was largely dependent on popular support, spent [their] surplus on feeding their people, helping needy but influential persons, and providing the poor with gifts, loaned stock . . . and even, in a few cases, with wives. *Now that political power is largely independent of popularity,* there is no need for them to do this and they and other wealthy people can, if they wish, expend their

wealth on advanced education for their children and luxuries for themselves, such as expensive tailor-made suits, large houses built on European lines, motor cars, travel, liquor and racehorses.[60]

Among the ancient Chamorros of Guam there were three distinct classes or social strata, namely, noblemen, commoners, and slaves.[61] After the Spanish conquest of Guam the nobility became a property-owning class through union with the Spaniards, and became even further separated from the commoners than previously.

By the end of the Spanish regime the "high people" consisted of about a dozen intermarrying Spanish-Chamorro families who formed a wealthy and powerful group cultivating a Spanish Catholic tradition. Each family controlled a relatively large amount of land, the largest of which, however, was probably not more than 1500 hectares (3706.5 acres). They . . . did not engage in any sort of manual work but hired laborers and servants to cultivate their lands.[62]

Dahomean social structure is crosscut by four social classes, the lowest, economically and socially, composed of slaves and the highest of the rulers who were also a leisure class.[63] "The economic role of the priests, like that of the rulers, was mainly one of consumption, as it is at the present time." [64] Dahomean economic organization was almost always characterized by a surplus which, through the medium of a monetary system, eventually "brought about the concentration of wealth in the hands of the members

---

[58] *Loc. cit.*
[59] *Ibid.,* p. 360.
[60] Ashton, 1942, p. 175, italics supplied.
[61] Thompson, 1941, pp. 39-40.
[62] *Ibid.,* pp. 45-46.
[63] Herskovits, 1938, pp. 99-102.
[64] *Ibid.,* p. 102.

of the Dahomean leisure class." [65] The degree of a corresponding social distance can be observed in that while tradition dictated that all Dahomeans must be workers, this tenet was "honored . . . more in the breach than in the observance." [66]

Now let us try to relate these few cases to the propositions presented earlier. What seems to emerge first is that the *over-all* tendency to social proximity in societies characterized by the maximally solidary community mitigates or minimizes those factors which tend to make for social distance within those societies; this tendency does not eliminate the distance but only abates it. By similar token, factors which make for social distance tend to lessen or abridge the over-all proximity in the maximally solidary community. Thus, since over-all social proximity is diminished, however slightly, in societies characterized by the solidary-fissile community, we can say that this sociological state of affairs allows for correspondingly greater retentiveness than in the maximally solidary community as a covariant of ascribed high or hereditary status.

This formulation is in no way meant as an exhaustive analysis of the economic chicanery, exploitation, and caballing which appears to occur in so many societies, even in the most "egalitarian" and maximally solidary ones. It has been stated because of the tenet that "laws" or principles which are uncovered by cross-cultural research must be shown to be operative within individual systems. Whether our final goal is the formulation of cross-cultural principles, or whether such inquiry is merely a means to a sharper understanding of individual cultures as, possibly, closed systems, our

hypotheses and generalized formulations must be so stated that they can serve either end.

The ethnographic data for many of the societies in the sample of the present study give clear-cut evidence that their social structures have changed. While there is still almost unlimited value in the study of social-structural change per se, our concern in this research is with the relationship between changes in the institutional organization of society and culture content. At the same time, however, there are not enough data about behavior with respect to food at both stages in all the societies for which there is information about changes in the social structure. There is, for example, an excellent reconstruction of the alterations in Dahomean social structure but the corresponding evolutions in behavior with respect to food appear to be lost in Dahomean time. Hence, we shall concern ourselves at this point only with societies for which there are data covering social-structural relationships as well as behavior with respect to food during both points in history.

There are four societies in the present sample—the Papago, the Tanala, the Teton Dakota, and the *zadruga* of Croatia—for which there are adequate data to trace the changes in behavior with respect to food paralleling the changes in the respective functionally significant units of association. Three of these—the Papago, the Tanala, and the *zadruga*— were originally characterized by the maximally solidary community. The Papago shifted to a solidary-fissile community, while the Tanala and the *zadruga* shifted to the nonnucleated society, although for different reasons. The Teton Dakota were originally characterized by a soli-

---

[65] *Ibid.*, pp. 98-99.
[66] *Ibid.*, p. 96.

dary-fissile community and shifted to the nonnucleated society. The hypothesis in this section of our analysis is that behavior with respect to food will follow the shifts in social-structural organization; the data bear out the hypothesis, as will be seen.

Before proceeding to the data, one theoretical problem must be mentioned. The four instances of shift which we shall analyze in a moment are all in the direction away from maximal solidarity toward minimal solidarity. Actually, the *zadruga* did revert from the nonnucleated society to a maximally solidary one. If any conclusions are to be drawn from the generalization of a shift from maximal to minimal solidarity, the case of the *zadruga* does not refute them. The *zadruga's* reversion took place rather shortly after the shift to the nonnucleated society. This change took place before the altered social structure could intrude into the socialization process of too many of its members and, thus, before any deeply significant changes in the basic personality structure could be passed from one generation to another.

Most of the data we possess about such changes stem from acculturative situations involving Western society, one which is not, to put it mildly, based on values of interpersonal solidarity and social-structural cohesiveness. But none of the societies characterized by the maximally solidary community were thus organized from the beginning of time. Even assuming that these social structures grew out of band-communities, it would be invaluable to know how a solidary-fissile community, for example, was transformed into a maximally solidary one. A sedentary agricultural pattern surely had to be adopted for such a change to take place, but we can only imagine the rest. In the

contemporary dominance of Western values throughout the world, it does not appear that we will ever learn through observation how maximal solidarity occurs.

Papago: Prior to their contact with white society, the Papago of Arizona and adjacent Mexico were differentiated sociologically into patrilocal extended families, patrilineal, exogamous, localized clans, and (possibly exogamous) patrilineal moieties; of these, the patrilineal clan was probably the functionally significant unit of association.[67] The Papago were agricultural and sedentary.

Paralleling this social organization was a system of distribution of food in which "they were constantly giving, as though from an inexhaustible supply. . . . The supply, meagre though it was from the modern point of view, was sufficient, for their simple needs and more." [68] Gifts of food among kinsmen were recurrent;

> there was no particular rule as to quantity. One family gave two large wooden spoonsful to every household at every meal; another cooked for each meal a four gallon pot and distributed it all, sometimes leaving nothing for the home household which subsisted on gifts. Other households sent gifts only once or twice a week or when they had something unusual. The ratio of giving was determined by custom with each group. . . . But it was kept up regularly, each gift being reciprocated with a like amount.[69]

"The center of the system was the patriarchal family which, rather than the individual, must be taken as the unit both of property holding and of gift exchange." [70] Nor was sharing confined solely to agricultural products.

[67] Underhill, 1939, pp. 31-34.
[68] *Ibid.*, p. 90.
[69] *Ibid.*, pp. 100-101.
[70] *Ibid.*, p. 90.

When a hunter brought home a deer, he went to each main house and presented a portion proportionate to the size of the family there. If there were hunters in that house, his family would soon receive a similar gift; if not, it could be any other food they could afford. But with such relatives, there was a distinct obligation not to cease giving even though there should be no return. The investment was a long term affair, to be realized on in the future if not the present.[71]

The Papago rationalized their pattern of gift-giving as an investment against periods of need, when assistance would then be certainly forthcoming.[72] Be that as it may, one did not make such an "investment" with just anyone. On the contrary, "such an investment was rarely made in nonrelatives, since they could not be trusted to repay, having their own more intimate obligations. But a relative valued his kin status and would pay, either in goods or services, now or later." [73]

The Papago no longer reside in localized clan communities.[74] "Today there is no wider kin group among the Papago than the extended family. . . . It is safe to say that no well-developed clan concept survives and that the present concept of the family and the extended family has not changed radically within the past generation." [75] In addition to the disruption of clan localization there has been a great change in the settlement pattern.

Though some houses cluster around the school or the church, there seems to be no nucleus for the village as a whole. There are no streets or other spatial regularities, nor is there a general pattern for the location of homes and fields; some families live in the midst of their fields, and others live at some distances from them. Closely related families may live fairly near to each other, but most households see the tops of their neighbors' homes over a hundred yards of creosote and cholla bushes.[76]

The dispersal of kinsmen has been furthered by the introduction of wage work at points distant from the community, and by entrance of many younger men into Civilian Conservation Corps work.

A conflict also arose, as the old men had predicted, from the money that now came in as it had never before. Young men could now buy food and need not be tied down to the fields; they could be independent of their fathers. . . . Road construction and the acquisition of cars directly abetted this new independence.[77]

The distribution of food among the Papago, and particularly the prestige from participation in the system, has shifted from a ceremonial context to one of mutual assistance to kinsmen and neighbors.[78] Those who fail to meet their interpersonal obligations of such mutual aid are subject to severe censure both by neighbors and kinsmen.[79]

Tanala: Traditionally, the Tanala, a Malayo-Polynesian people of Madagascar, were cultivators of dry rice who lived in permanent villages of from fifty to eighty families. Sociological alignment was in patrilocal extended families, patrilineal

---

[71] *Ibid.,* p. 44.
[72] *Ibid.,* p. 90.
[73] *Ibid.,* pp. 42-43.
[74] *Ibid.,* p. 34.
[75] Joseph, Spicer, and Chesky, 1949, pp. 56-57.
[76] *Ibid.,* p. 60.
[77] *Ibid.,* p. 26.
[78] Underhill, 1939, p. 210.
[79] Joseph *et al.,* 1949, pp. 54, 57-58.

lineages, and patrilineal clans; of these, the patrilineage was the functionally significant unit of association.[80] The lineage was localized in a separate ward of the village, and lineage exogamy was preferred. The ward of the village in which the lineage was localized was the property of that lineage, and the lineage owned the land used for cultivation, the individual having but rights of usufruct. The principle function of the clan was to unite for defensive purposes in time of war.[81]

The Tanala apparently did not elaborate their system of food distribution, confining that system to a fairly simple pattern in which the members of the lineage shared their food "freely." [82] Feasts appear to have been confined to ritual ceremonial occasions, such as funerals. Within such a system, there was no need to produce more than was needed or to hoard food.[83] In addition to recurrent sharing and mutual assistance within the lineage, some clans had evolved a pattern of ritual friendship or blood-brotherhood in which free access to a partner's property and mutual assistance were mutual and reciprocal.[84]

With the abolition of Tanala warfare, clan organization broke down.[85] Shortly afterward, the cultivation of irrigated rice was begun.[86] "It was at first an adjunct to dry rice carried on by individual families. But an irrigated rice field could be tended by a single family and . . . these

distant fields also became household rather than joint family affairs." [87] Hence, not only was there a breakup of the clan and a dispersal of the lineage, but even the extended family disintegrated.

Correlated with the introduction of wet rice cultivation was "an increasing tendency toward individual ownership of land." [88] The new social isolation of the individual nuclear families produced other changes within the culture. For example, "in the life cycle of the individual we begin to note important changes. The approaching birth of a child is not announced, for fear of sorcery." [89]

More pertinent to the present inquiry are the changes which have transpired in the system of food distribution among the Tanala. Even when they were a society characterized by the maximally solidary community, the system of recurrent exchanges between households of the lineage was not highly elaborated. With the introduction of new social-structural elements, even these unelaborated exchanges disappeared and there are no longer exchanges of gifts of food between persons and households.[90] There is still mutual assistance among related families when they are in need of help,[91] but there is an increasing reluctance to share with those who have not contributed to the individual nuclear family's production of food.[92] Furthermore, there has not only been a greater tendency to amass wealth, but individuals have adopted the corresponding

---

[80] Linton, 1933, pp. 24, 133.
[81] *Ibid.*, pp. 24-25.
[82] *Ibid.*, p. 134.
[83] *Ibid.*, p. 253.
[84] *Ibid.*, pp. 308-309.
[85] *Ibid.*, pp. 134-135.
[86] *Ibid.*, p. 40.
[87] Linton, 1939, p. 282.
[88] Linton, 1933, p. 129.
[89] Linton, 1939, p. 286.
[90] *Ibid.*, pp. 254-255.
[91] *Ibid.*, p. 255.
[92] *Ibid.*, p. 282.

habit of keeping secret the amount of their wealth and of hiding their money.[93] Blood brotherhood remains a highly significant context of mutual assistance, but even this relationship has undergone change, for ritual kinsmen insist on "the reservation that the help should not bring them into conflict with the government. Under this a man can legitimately refuse to help his [blood] brother if he is a fugitive from justice." [94]

Zadruga of Croatia: The *zadruga* of Croatia, a deme,[95] was originally a maximally solidary community, a self-sustaining "social and economic unit. It was composed of an extended kinship group, together with some adopted and unrelated members and families. . . . Endogamy was often practiced in the zadruga, and zadruga life discouraged migration." [96] Land was held in common by the entire *zadruga;* agriculture was the primary source of food supplemented by husbandry.

The distribution of food in the *zadruga* was founded on the principle that "individual members had only the right to share in the produce of the zadruga." [97] Individual profit and gain were virtually impossible; "the whole system of property relations . . . aimed at an equal share in income, safety and privacy." [98] Private possessions did exist, but these were limited to vineyards and household paraphernalia. This system of distribution, while almost completely egalitarian, was far from elaborated. While there were community-wide feasts, these were limited to occasions of common work involving most of the members of the *zadruga* and other similar events.[99] There were no patterns of recurrent exchange involving repetitive gifts of food, and this appears to be intimately related to the fact that

zadruga society was not in favor of strengthening the kinship ties within the community because that might have disturbed the foundations on which the zadruga system was built. All zadrugas accentuated the common zadruga goal, namely, the well-being of all. Those who showed any inclination to improve their affairs at the expense of common interests were frowned upon.[100]

In the latter part of the 19th century there occurred in Croatia a "breakdown of the feudal system and the subsequent formation of an urban class which took the power from the hands of the nobility and reorganized the state in favor of itself." [101] One of the most immediate consequences of the new state structure was a system of taxation, the demands of which the traditional economy of the *zadruga* was unable to meet.[102]

At once, many zadruga began to divide their common property and parcel themselves into "individual" family economies. The state laws tried to prevent this trend but the zadrugas violated the laws by secret divisions. Formally they kept together; *de facto* they lived apart, each zadruga being broken down into a few families managing their own separate economies.[103]

---

[93] *Ibid.,* pp. 355-356; 1933, pp. 122-124.
[94] Linton, 1933, p. 308.
[95] Murdock, 1949, pp. 63-64.
[96] Tomasic, 1942, p. 230.
[97] *Ibid.,* p. 231.
[98] *Ibid.,* p. 233.
[99] *Ibid.,* pp. 230-233.
[100] *Ibid.,* p. 235.
[101] *Ibid.,* p. 249.
[102] *Ibid.,* pp. 249-250.
[103] *Ibid.,* p. 250.

The solidarity of the community was further attacked by the departure of *zadruga* members to new urban areas,[104] and by the introduction of power relationships along lines of wealth within the community.[105] Concomitantly, the system of distribution broke down.

> The old economic stability and the feeling of security . . . were completely shaken. Not only was economic security undermined, but also their emotional security suffered greatly. The common labor, feasts and festivals, the marriage celebration, all of the old rituals and ceremonials which served to give personal satisfaction and which were channels for emotional outlet, had to be greatly reduced.[106]

Furthermore, values with respect to food and money changed radically, for individuals began to strive for personal profit, sometimes at the expense of other members of the community.[107] The requirements of taxation and the meeting of legal fees motivated individuals and families to concern themselves solely with their own interests and introduced a reluctance to come to the assistance of others.[108]

Partly because of the growing state's opposition to the fragmentization of the *zadruga* and partly because of social structural differentiations within the *zadruga* itself, namely, the limitations imposed on the flow of change by antecedent sociocultural conditions inherent in the historical development of the *zadruga* system, the nonnucleated social structure of the *zadruga* during this period was essentially a transitory phase. Eventually,

the *zadruga* reverted to a maximally solidary community.

> After the breakdown of the zadrugas a new type of peasant settlement developed. Instead of scattered zadrugas, villages were formed composed of groups of neighborhoods. In the place of former zadrugas there were groups of separate households or neighborhoods occupied by the families who formerly lived together, mostly relatives. A number of such neighborhoods formed the new village settlement. . . . The village in fact became the repetition of the zadruga on a new level.[109]

Teton Dakota: The Teton Dakota trace their descent bilaterally, and, during their nomadic state, each of the seven Teton divisions was organized into hunting bands of from ten to twenty related nuclear families. Although most band-members were kinsmen, the individual family had considerable freedom in choosing its band affiliation; paralleling a degree of vagueness with respect to matri- and patrilocality was a corresponding degree of uncertainty in predicting the band membership of any family group.[110] "Occasionally the band included other families who joined either to escape some unpleasant social pressure or to become the followers of a renowned warrior. There were also larger bands of related and unrelated extended families, which maintained social unity the year round." [111] Bands united into larger aggregates during the spring and summer for ceremonial, hunting and war purposes, but these "encampments . . . were not permanent the year round and were constantly shifting

---

104 *Ibid.*, pp. 253-254.
105 *Ibid.*, p. 251.
106 *Ibid.*, p. 250.
107 *Ibid.*, p. 251.
108 *Ibid.*, pp. 254-256.
109 *Ibid.*, p. 257.
110 Hassrick, 1944, p. 340.
111 Macgregor, 1946, pp. 52-53.

in band membership." [112] Band exogamy was practiced in marriage, and residence generally tended to be patrilocal.

Generosity, one of the most highly esteemed values in Teton Dakota life, was the principle basis of the system of food-distribution. Open-handedness was not only a cardinal criterion of behavior among kinsmen, but was extended to unrelated members of the band.

> In some cases old people had no place to go and were forced to live alone at the edge of the encampment. They were given food and supplies by the generous young men, who thereby gained prestige. They were the recipients of the wealthy men's spare horse at name-giving ceremonies. As the wards of the society they were the basis for moral-istic myths, the foundation for the philanthropist's prestige.[113]

The system of distribution included the "give-away," at which an individual distributed almost all his possessions among kinsmen and friends at such occasions as births, weddings, funerals, at feasts celebrating a son's recovery from illness, at a feast in celebration of an honored stranger, and the like.[114]

Since their "pacification" and settlement on the reservation, changes have occurred in the structuralizations of relationships among many of the Teton Dakotas with concomitant shifts in the system of distribution. Aside from the loss of the buffalo as the source of subsistence, and of warfare as the primary source of prestige, perhaps the most significant change which transpired among

the Teton Dakotas was the loss of the ancient band organization and the dispersal of individual households.[115] As a result of the American system of land allotments to individual families, individual extended families are "stretched in a line of separated homes." [116] "Family homes are geographically widely separated today in comparison with the band camp"; [117] as a result, "the family now lives with greater independence of related families in its own farm home." [118]

Concomitantly, significant changes stemming from these shifts can be observed on many levels. Not only are the "associations within an extended group . . . less frequent and intensive," [119] but energies which were formerly directed outside the family are now turned into it.

> The mother's role has also gained by the present isolation of the individual household. Formerly the family lived in a camp with several other related families, with whom the child associated freely. Now the child living in a farm-house on an allotment is forced to spend much more time with his own family and especially with his mother.[120]

In line with the status of the family as a productive unit, "the individual and the individual family can, if they so desire, support themselves on a farm or by wage work without the assistance of others and can find companionship and social life outside the community." [121]

Corollary changes have taken place in the modes of distribution. While there

---

[112] *Ibid.*, p. 53.
[113] Hassrick, 1944, p. 341.
[114] Macgregor, 1946, p. 107; Mekeel, 1936, pp. 11-12.
[115] Macgregor, 1946, pp. 60, 66-68.
[116] *Ibid.*, p. 66.
[117] *Ibid.*, p. 60.
[118] *Ibid.*, p. 56.
[119] *Ibid.*, p. 60.
[120] *Ibid.*, p. 57.
[121] *Ibid.*, p. 68.

is still no prestige derived from individ-uated amassment of wealth,[122] and indi-viduals related consanguineally and affi-nally expect and receive assistance from one another in times of need,[123] there has developed a great reluctance to share food and money with others.[124]

The conflict between the developing in-dividualism of the white man and the cooperation and sharing of the [Teton Dakota] also crops up in the difference in attitudes toward the accumulation and sharing of wealth. The second gen-eration, especially the mixed-blood members, have diverged greatly from the Indian customs surrounding gener-osity . . .

Pressure to abandon the practice of the give-away has had some effect. . . . A widow gave stacks of hay to her hus-band's relatives and said privately that she would give away all her household furnishings. Her stepfather advised her that this would be foolish, for she would need them later. The next day the widow gave away a great length of calico purchased at the store but kept her house intact. This was not entirely outside former [Teton Dakota] prac-tice, when the husband's relatives would request a woman to keep some things for herself, but such encouragement from her own relatives were formerly looked upon as selfish. Now . . . the Indians are becoming more cautious in the giving-away of goods.[125]

Relatives still feel free to seek out well-to-do kinsmen and "camp down" with them for a while, but such generosity is being dispensed more and more grudg-ingly. As a result, individuals are becom-ing reluctant to convert their money into food and many ways are being found of keeping secret the extent of one's earn-ings.[126]

With respect to the hypothesis of the relationship between early feeding experi-ences and later behavior about food, there appear to be no changes in feeding prac-tices in the shifts from one social-struc-tural type to another. Papago infants and young children continued to be fed on demand after the shift in Papago social organization.[127] There was no change in Tanala feeding practices,[128] although as was pointed out above, certain changes in Tanala socialization, corresponding to the new isolation of the nuclear family, did ensue. There was no change in *zad-ruga* feeding practices during the brief episode of the nonnucleated society. Nor was there any change in Teton feeding practices,[129] although, as among the Tana-la, there were changes in other areas re-flecting the isolation of the family group.

SUMMARY

It was hypothesized that repetitive early food gratification will create an emo-tional predisposition to share food with others and that this predisposition will be maximized or minimized by the emotional predispositions aroused by different community-systems. Conversely, it was hypothesized that repetitive early food dep-rivation will establish a predisposition to amass and not share food, money or

[122] Mekeel, 1936, pp. 12-13.
[123] Macgregor, 1946, p. 64.
[124] *Ibid.,* pp. 55-56; Goldfrank, 1943, p. 82.
[125] Macgregor, 1946, pp. 113-115.
[126] *Ibid.,* pp. 115-117.
[127] Joseph *et al.,* 1949, pp. 121, 123.
[128] Linton, 1933, p. 267; 1939, p. 261.
[129] Erikson, 1950, pp. 119, 150; Macgregor, 1946, pp. 123-125.

both. We have also seen that behind these relationships lies a basic need to receive from others, and that the gratification of this need, too, is maximized or minimized by different sociological conditions. Finally, the attempt was made to show that those factors which explain differences between societies help to explain different patterns of behavior with respect to food within societies, and that as the social structure changes, behavior regarding food will also change.

Limitations of space prevented a presentation of statistical tests of significance; all the hypothesized differences are significant by chi square tests at least at the .01 level. Statistical analyses also showed no significance for these hypotheses of toilet-training practices, weaning practices, or scarcity and abundance of food.

In brief, we endeavored to demonstrate that such phenomena as behavior concerning food can be organized taxonomically and that they are understandable in terms of personality predispositions which are created by the conditions under which people live. These are neither entirely experiences of early life, nor are they entirely experiences in the conditions of the sociocultural environment; rather, they are both. It is the totality of life which enters into any one area of behavior, not a fragment of it. Similarly, reciprocal behavior with respect to food must be looked at from the point of view of the donor as well as of the recipient, for each has his own needs, motivations, interests, and position in a structural system.

BIBLIOGRAPHY AND SUGGESTED READINGS

SUGGESTED READINGS

Abraham, Karl. "The Influence of Oral Erotism on Character Formation," in *The Selected Papers of Karl Abraham*. London: Hogarth, 1927. This classical paper contains the original psychoanalytic hypothesis on the relationship between unconscious personality factors and such phenomena as generosity.

Fenichel, Otto. "The Drive to Amass Wealth," in *The Collected Papers of Otto Fenichel*, second series. New York: Norton, 1954. One of the few attempts in psychoanalytic theory to deal with the problem within a context broader than the instinctual one.

Goldschmidt, Walter. "Review" of *Economic Anthropology* (by Herskovits), *American Sociological Review*, Vol. *19*, pp. 617-619, 1954. An important critique of one kind of anthropological approach.

Herskovits, Melville J. *Economic Anthropology: A Study in Comparative Economics*. New York: Knopf, 1952. More in the nature of a textbook, this book presents an approach to economic behavior which can be considered diametrically opposed to the one outlined in the present chapter.

Hobhouse, L. T., G. C. Wheeler and M. Ginsberg. *The Material Culture and Social Institutions of the Simpler Peoples: An Essay in Correlation*. London: Macmillan, 1915. One of the original attempts to study economic behavior cross-culturally.

Hunt, J. McV. "The Effects of Infant-Feeding-Frustration upon Adult Hoarding in the Albino Rat," *Journal of Abnormal and Social Psychology,* Vol. *36,* pp. 338-360, 1941. This and the following paper present experimental findings which are in almost complete accord with the first hypothesis in the present chapter.

Hunt, J. McV. and others. "Studies of the Effects of Infantile Experience on Adult Behavior in Rats: I. Effects of Infantile Feeding-Frustration on Adult Hoarding," *Journal of Comparative and Physiological Psychology,* Vol. *40,* pp. 291-304, 1947.

Mauss, Marcel. *The Gift: Forms and Functions of Exchange in Archaic Societies* (translated by Ian Cunnison). Glencoe, Illinois: Free Press, 1956. A quaint and interesting historical document.

Mead, Margaret. *Cooperation and Competition among Primitive Peoples.* New York: McGraw-Hill, 1937. For its time, a remarkable attempt to study such economic phenomena cross-culturally without restriction to traditional disciplinary boundaries; it still continues to warrant careful study by the beginning student.

BIBLIOGRAPHY

Ashton, Hugh. *The Basuto.* London: Oxford University Press, 1952.

Blackwood, Beatrice. *Both Sides of Buka Pasage: An Ethnographic Study of Social, Sexual, and Economic Questions in the North-Western Solomon Islands.* Oxford: Oxford University Press, 1935.

Codere, Helen. *Fighting with Property: A Study of Kwakiutl Potlatching and Warfare: 1792-1930.* Monograph of the American Ethnological Society, No. *18,* 1951.

Cohen, Yehudi A. "Character Formation and Social Structure in a Jamaican Community," *Psychiatry,* Vol. *18,* pp. 275-296, 1955.

Diamond, Stanley. *Dahomey: A Proto-State in West Africa.* Doctoral Dissertation, Columbia University, 1951. University Microfilms, No. *2808,* Ann Arbor.

Du Bois, Cora. "Attitudes toward Food and Hunger in Alor," in *Personal Character and Cultural Milieu,* edited by Douglas Haring, pp. 241-253. Syracuse, New York: Syracuse University Press, 1956.

Du Bois, Cora. *The People of Alor: A Socio-Psychological Study of an East Indian Island.* Minneapolis, Minnesota: University of Minnesota Press, 1944.

Erikson, Erik H. *Childhood and Society.* New York: Norton, 1950.

Firth, Raymond. *Primitive Polynesian Economy.* London: Routledge, 1939.

Firth, Raymond. *We, the Tikopia.* London: Macmillan, 1936.

Fromm, Erich. *Man for Himself.* New York: Holt, Rinehart and Winston, 1947.

Goldfrank, Esther. "Historic Change and Social Character: A Study of the Teton Dakota," *American Anthropologist,* Vol. *45,* pp. 67-83, 1943.

Hallowell, A. Irving. "Culture, Personality, and Society," in *Anthropology Today,* edited by A. L. Kroeber, pp. 597-620. Chicago, Illinois: University of Chicago, 1953.

Handy, E. S. Craighill. *The Native Culture in the Marquesas.* Bulletin, Bernice P. Bishop Museum, No. *9,* 1923.

Hartmann, Heinz and Ernst Kris. "The Genetic Approach in Psychoanalysis," in *The Psychoanalytic Study of the Child,* Vol. *1,* pp. 11-30, New York: International Universities Press, 1945.

Hassrick, Royal B. "Teton Dakota Kinship System," *American Anthropologist,* Vol. *46,* pp. 338-347, 1944.

Herskovits, Melville J. *Dahomey: An Ancient West African Kingdom.* (Vol. *1*). New York: J. J. Augustin, 1938.

Hoebel, E. Adamson. *Man in the Primitive World: An Introduction to Anthropology.* New York: McGraw-Hill, 1958.

Holmberg, Allan R. *Nomads of the Long Bow: The Sirionó of Eastern Bolivia.* Smithsonian Institution, Institute of Social Anthropology, Publication No. *10,* 1950.

Jenness, Diamond. *The Life of the Copper Eskimos.* Report of the Canadian Arctic Expedition, Vol. *XII,* Part A, 1922.

Joseph, Alice, Rosamond B. Spicer, and Jane Chesky. *The Desert People: A Study of the Papago Indians.* Chicago, Illinois: University of Chicago, 1949.

Kluckhohn, Clyde. *Navaho Witchcraft.* Papers of the Peabody Museum of American Archaeology and Ethnology, Harvard University, Vol. *22,* No. *2,* 1944.

Kluckhohn, Clyde and Dorothea Leighton. *The Navaho.* Cambridge, Massachusetts: Harvard, 1946.

Landes, Ruth. "The Personality of the Ojibwa," *Character and Personality,* Vol. *6,* pp. 51-60, 1937.

Linton, Ralph. *The Tanala: A Hill Tribe in Madagascar.* Anthropological Series, Field Museum of Natural History, Vol. *22,* 1933.

Linton, Ralph. "The Tanala of Madagascar," in *The Individual and his Society,* by Abram Kardiner, pp. 251-290. New York: Columbia, 1939.

Macgregor, Gordon. *Warriors without Weapons.* Chicago, Illinois: University of Chicago, 1946.

Mead, Margaret. "The Mountain Arapesh. III. Socio-Economic Life," *Anthropological Papers of the American Museum of Natural History,* Vol. *40,* Part *III,* pp. 163-232, 1940.

Mead, Margaret. *Sex and Temperament in Three Primitive Societies,* in *From the South Seas.* New York: Morrow, 1939.

Mead, Margaret. *Social Organization of Manua.* Bulletin, Bernice P. Bishop Museum, No. *76,* 1930.

Mekeel, H. S. *The Economy of a Modern Teton Dakota Community.* Yale University Publications in Anthropology, No. *6,* 1936.

Murdock, George P. *Social Structure.* New York: Macmillan, 1949.

Murphy, Gardner. *Personality: A Biosocial Approach to Origins and Structure.* New York: Harper, 1947.

Nadel, S. F. *The Foundations of Social Anthropology.* Glencoe, Illinois: Free Press, 1951.

Opler, Morris E. *An Apache Life-Way: The Economic, Social, and Religious Institutions of the Chiricahua Indians.* Chicago, Illinois: University of Chicago, 1941.

Priklonskii, V. L. *Three Years in Yakut Territory.* In *Yakut Ethnographic Sketches.* Behavior Science Translations, Human Relations Area Files, New Haven, 1953.

Radcliffe-Brown, A. R. *The Andaman Islanders.* Cambridge, Cambridge University Press, 1933.

Steward, Julian. *Theory of Culture Change: The Methodology of Multilinear Evolution.* Urbana, Illinois: University of Illinois, 1955.

Thompson, Laura. *Guam and its People: A Study of Culture Change.* Princeton, New Jersey: American Council on Education, 1941.

Tomasic, Dinko. "Personality Development in the Zadruga Society," *Psychiatry,* Vol. *5,* pp. 229-261, 1942.

Underhill, Ruth. *Social Organization of the Papago Indians.* Columbia University Contributions in Anthropology, Vol. *30,* 1939.

Wagner, Gunter. *The Bantu Kavirondo.* London, Oxford University Press, 1949.

Wagner, Gunter. "The Changing Family among the Bantu Kavirondo," Supplement to *Africa,* Vol. *12,* No. *1,* 1939.

Whiting, John W. M. *Becoming a Kwoma: Teaching and Learning in a New Guinea Tribe.* New Haven, Connecticut: Yale, 1941.

Chapter 12

PATTERNS OF FRIENDSHIP*

By Yehudi A. Cohen

I

Friendship is a highly personal affair and it arouses a wide variety of feelings and emotions in most of us. Not only are particular friendships often highly charged, but it would also appear that friendship, as an area of study, is equally so. One indirect indication of this is the relative neglect of the area as an object of study. There are certain rules governing such relationships in our society; at the same time a wide latitude is allowed in deviating from the norms of friendship. Friendships in American society are wholly voluntary; they are usually limited to members of the same sex, of the same race, of the same educational and age levels, and the like. With the exception of the voluntary nature of friendship formation in American society, deviations from all the other norms just referred to are frequent and accepted. Also important is the fact that friendships can be terminated for a variety of reasons. These terminations, somewhat more so than the friendships themselves, are also often highly charged and have been more frequently dealt with in humanistic terms—in fiction, poetry, drama, philosophy—than in scientific terms.

Inevitably, perhaps because of the purely personal nature of friendship and the wide latitude allowed in deviations from the norms, a certain degree of confusion centers about the role system of friendship in the normative value system of American society. Unrecognized by either legal or religious sanction, but viewed as one of the *sine qua non* of meaningful living, it remains a moot question whether friendship in American society is an institution. Whereas most institutions in any society overlap and flow into one another, there is a peculiar ideology surrounding friendship in American society which tends to keep it encapsulated; for example, in the prescription that economic and friendship relationships must not affect each other: although friends may occasionally assist each other economically, a friend must not allow himself to suffer in his business because of a friendship relationship. It is only at the pre-adult level, as among adolescents, that friendship in the American normative system tends to take on an institutionalized aspect. The quality of adolescent friendship, and the rules governing such relationships, differ considerably from those associated with adult friendship. This is understandable, given the unusual positions of adolescents in the total social structure of our society (for a comparable example in another society, see the discussion of adolescence in a

---

* This chapter is an original study by the author and has not appeared elsewhere.

Jamaican community, in Chapter 6).

It is the quality of friendship which is the challenging and fascinating aspect of this area of human behavior. If we look about at the people we know, it soon becomes apparent that the types of friendships into which people enter provide some of the clearest clues to the kinds of people they are and the kinds of lives they lead. David and Jonathan convey one imagery of friendship and a style of life, whereas Willie Loman's philosophy of friendship (in Arthur Miller's *Death of a Salesman*) conveys an entirely different picture. We all know people who do not, for one reason or another, enter into meaningful and significant friendships, and the styles of their lives mirror this looseness of form and flaccidity of feeling. In any psychiatric population in the United States, one is continually impressed by the friendlessness of the overwhelming majority of these people even prior to their hospitalization.

The brief and fleeting sketches made of everyday scenes, as well as our careful observations, teach that friendship, taken separately, proceeds in intimate relationship with other parameters of the totality of life. But every area of life— or every institution or role system—has its own special quality and flavor; friendship is one such area. The purpose of this chapter is to learn from which parameters of the totality of life friendship derives its own special qualities. Thus, we shall assume that a particular type of friendship not only has its specific sources but its own specific consequences.

II

In almost all societies—with the possible exception of some groups characterized by a nonnucleated social structure—individuals have the predisposition or capacity to form friendships. This predisposition or capacity derives from experiences with kinsmen and nonkinsmen during the formative and later years. It does not, however, materialize in actual behavior in the same way in all societies. The research to be presented in this chapter will focus on those social-structural forces which maximize this predisposition and those which minimize it. For the purposes of the present inquiry we shall designate as "friendship" those supra- and extra-kin relationships and bonds which are entered into voluntarily *and/or* which are culturally recognized.

There are four types of friendship which can be distinguished. The first is unique and independent of the other three; the latter, on the other hand, tend to shade off into each other along a continuum. (This is analagous to the situation in the systems of food distribution; in that study the fourth type was independent, while here the first type occupies that position.) Although these types shall be distinguished in rather arbitrary fashion, this is done for analytic and heuristic purposes.

The first type of friendship which can be distinguished is "inalienable friendship." This is a form which is entered into ritually or ceremonially, and once joined cannot, ideally, be withdrawn. Often, such bonds of friendship are governed morally by supernatural and quasi-legal sanction, and the duties and liabilities imposed upon inalienable friends, as well as the privileges and rights accorded them, are as binding as those of consanguineal kinsmen. Such friendships pervade many areas of life: sexual, economic, political, religious, and, above all, emotional. With rare exceptions, such friendships are entered into intrasexually, most often between men. Inalienable friendship includes blood brotherhood, bond friendship, best friendship, institutionalized friendship, and the like.

The second type of friendship which can be distinguished is "close friendship." The emotional and social propinquity of close friendship approximates that of inalienable friendship, but it never quite achieves it. Close friendships are not ceremonialized or ritualized, they can be broken or withdrawn without sanction, and rarely does one read that close friends are privies to each other's intimate secrets, as are inalienable friends. Close friendship is informal, in the sense that if duties are culturally prescribed and privileges defined for close friends, the performance of such obligations, and their reciprocities, cannot be enforced legally and religiously; instead, they are left to the volition of the individual friends. The element of personal choice is the dominant characteristic of close friendship, and it bears little resemblance to the bonds of consanguineal kinship which inalienable friendship does.

The third type of friendship is "casual friendship." Casual friendship is perfunctory and lax. It is never ritualized and it is rarely culturally recognized as constituting a specific social category of persons. Casual friendship does not contain within it any duties, liabilities, privileges, or rights specific to the relationship itself. Such friendship can be withdrawn at any time. Unlike inalienable, close, or even expedient friendships, casual friendship implies neither allegiance nor affiliation. It is almost without direction or intention, merely providing two individuals with a slightly focussed or accented awareness of each other vis-à-vis other persons. Social and emotional propinquity is at a minimum in casual friendship and little is shared within the relationship, socially, materially, or emotionally.

The fourth type of friendship is "expedient friendship." In friendship of this type, the temporal element in juxtaposition with the social element is of overriding importance. The element of time also inheres in inalienable friendship, but it implies permanence. Such fixity is not implied in expedient friendship. Expedient friendship is an alignment of two persons, often standing in superordinate-subordinate relationship, in which some gain, material, social, or a combination of them accrues to both parties as a direct result of their affiliation with each other. This gain need not be the same for both. For example, in the expedient friendship of a wealthy man and a poor man, the latter may receive economic benefits while the former is assured of the other's social and political loyalty. When the specific need for one or both no longer exists, or greater benefits can be achieved by one party through alliance with a third, the relationship is dissolved. To an extent, expedient friendship can be thought of as contractual; emotional propinquity is absent. While the relationship is independent of legal and religious sanction, the particular needs motivating the formation of the friendship contain within them the rewards and punishments for the maintenance and severance of the alliance.

As noted in the section on methodology early in Chapter 11, the data for this study were gathered in the same ways employed in researching patterns of food distribution. Similarly, the same sample of sixty-five societies has been used for both studies; the reasons for this were outlined in the original discussion of methodology.

III

It is hypothesized that inalienable friendship will be found in the maximally solidary community; that close friendship is characteristic of the solidary-fissile community; that casual friendship appears in the nonnucleated society; and that expedient friendship is found in the individuated social structure. (For definitions of these community-systems, see Chapter 11, pp. 314-318.)

Table 1 presents the covariants of friendship with the maximally solidary community.

The presence of inalienable friendship in societies characterized by the maximally solidary community does not, of course, preclude other types of friendship. In addition to an inalienable friend, an individual in this type of society also has extra-kin bonds which are close and casual. But it is the *concept* of inalienability of friendship, above and beyond other types, with which we are concerned here. Table 1 leaves little room to doubt that inalienable friendship, as a type, will tend to be found among peoples whose functionally significant unit of association is the maximally solidary community.

TABLE 1

Types of Friendship in the Maximally Solidary Community

Inalienable Friendship	Close Friendship	No Data
Arapesh	Kwakiutl	Kurtatchi
Bantu Kavirondo (Logoli and Vugusu)	Lesu	Papago (aboriginal)
Chagga		Pukapuka
Hopi		
Kwoma		
Lamba		
Malekula		
Tallensi		
Tanala (pre-contact)		
Tikopia		
Zadruga of Croatia		

Inalienable friendship is essentially an ideal or abstract category, a common denominator or theme, on the basis of which different societies construct variant types: blood brotherhood, bond friendship, and the like. Similarly, the rationalizations for such friendship, the functions which such friendship may serve, and the particular contexts in which it occurs vary among the societies characterized by the maximally solidary community.

The Arapesh of Northwest New Guinea are aligned sociologically into patrilineal clan communities, and one's patrilineal kinsmen constitute one's functionally significant unit of association, or, as Mead calls it, "the effective economic unit." [1] Inalienable friendship among the Arapesh takes the form of the hereditary trade friends, called *buanyin*. "Although theoretically every man may have a *buanyin*, actually only one son or nephew of a big man will take over some male heir

---

[1] Mead, 1940, pp. 211-212.

of the *buanyin* of his father, and the lesser members of the gens of each will cluster about these two leaders, and help with the prosecution of this one *buanyin* relationship." [2]

The localized clan community is the functionally significant unit among the Bantu Kavirondo (Logoli and Vugusu) who have two types of inalienable friendship. The first of these is called *omírongo* and it is entered into by two youths who have undergone circumcision together.[3] Among the Logoli, a third person frequently joins the *virongo* relationship.[4] The second type, *ovuvute,* is entered into between two clans.[5] *Omírongo* ". . . cannot marry each other's sisters, although the children would be permitted to intermarry." [6] Nor can marriage take place between members of clans in *vute* relationship.

Among the Chagga of northeastern Tanganyika, who live in localized patrilineal clans, inalienable friendship is established between youths who have been circumcised together; the bond between such friends "never ends." [7] Between them there is mutual generosity and equal sharing.[8] Furthermore, "a man and his friend protect each other. . . . You are incapable of rebuking your friend. . . . And if one friend and another quarrel . . . don't let one friend think of revenge against another friend." [9] As among the Logoli and Vugusu, the Chagga also have inalienable friendship between two

clans.[10] Inalienable friends may not marry each other's sisters or daughters.[11]

The Hopi of Arizona may well constitute an indeterminate occurrence with respect to the question of whether they possess the institution of inalienable friendship. In the score of references consulted, no mention of friendship as an institution was found; they may well have been missed during the gathering of the data. The Zuñi, who are not included in the present sample, do have an institution of inalienable friendship, but E. C. Parsons[12] believes it to be a relatively recent development. The Zuñi, incidentally, are one of the few instances of a group in which inalienable friendship can be joined intersexually.[13]

It appears not unlikely that the "ceremonial father" in Hopi is at bottom an inalienable friendship or at least a close friendship, even though it does not occur between age-mates. As F. Eggan points out, Hopi and Zuñi social structures can best be understood by compariing them to each other:

> In both, the kinship structures are organized on a similar pattern and utilize the same structural principles. The behavior patterns toward relatives are likewise comparable . . . though greater variability is apparent in the Zuñi system, and there is a lesser emphasis on the importance of the maternal uncles. The extension of kinship patterns among the Hopi is primarily

---

[2] *Ibid.,* p. 204.
[3] Wagner, 1949, pp. 345-346.
[4] *Ibid.,* p. 372.
[5] *Ibid.,* pp. 383, 389.
[6] *Ibid.,* p. 346.
[7] Guttman, 1926, p. 81; 1932, pp. 12-13, 93, 105; Raum, 1940, p. 347.
[8] Guttman, 1932, p. 93.
[9] *Ibid.,* p. 96.
[10] Guttman, 1926, pp. 251-258.
[11] *Ibid.,* pp. 81-82.
[12] Parsons, 1917, pp. 5-7.
[13] *Ibid.,* pp. 5, 8.

in terms of the clan system; Zuñi makes less use of the clan and more of society association and friendship." [14]

Both the Hopi and the Zuñi have the institution of the "ceremonial father," but it is de-emphasized among the Zuñi who select him from the father's clan, and elaborated among the Hopi, who always select a nonrelative to be "ceremonial father" (or mother) to a child. It is on the basis of this substitution between Hopi and Zuñi that the hypothesis is suggested that the "ceremonial father" in Hopi is a form of inalienable friendship. In this ceremonial relationship, ". . . kinship ties are extended *in toto* to the ceremonial father's clan and phratry, and in native theory it is an advantage to have connections with as many groups as possible." [15] Marriage restrictions do not arise out of such ceremonial relationships. The principle duty of the ceremonial parent is to sponsor his "child" in the initiation ceremony, while the latter repays his ritual parent with gifts and economic assistance. Although the formal responsibilities of the ceremonial father end with his sponsorship at the initiation ceremony, ". . . the kinship relations and obligations remain as permanent bonds." [16]

The Kwakiutl Indians of British Columbia are fishermen living in sedentary clan communities. They appear to be an exception to the hypothesis of the relationship between organization into maximally solidary communities and the possession of inalienable friendship. Charlie Newell, in his autobiography, speaks of his "best friend" who ". . . goes between me and the girls and comes back with the answer." [17] But there appears to be no ritualization or formalization of friendship. Boas notes that a different etiquette is prescribed when entertaining friends at home than when entertaining clansmen, but he does not discuss the quality of Kwakiutl friendship. [18]

The functionally significant unit of association of the Kwoma of New Guinea is the patrilineal sib. Inalienable friendship among the Kwoma is entered into in the course of initiation ceremonies, ". . . as a result of being scarified at the same time, so that their blood is mixed on the bark slab on which the operation is performed." [19]

A Kwoma's *friends* are of considerable importance to him. . . . A man's *friends,* usually three in number, are always members of another sib and unrelated to him by any true kinship ties, but after he has established blood bonds with them he treats them as though they were real relatives. He may eat at their house or invite them to eat at his, without fear that they will steal sorcery material from him. He supports them at court meetings, and in return they stand by him against those who threaten or accuse him; they may even take his side if he has a dispute with their own relatives. He is supposed to steal sorcery materials from members of his own hamlet if he is requested to do so by a *friend,* and he may ask the same favor in return. A man calls his friends' parents *father* and *mother,* their sisters *sister,* and their children *children* and behaves toward them as he does toward such relatives; incest taboos apply to their close female relatives. [20]

A friend among the Lambas of northern Rhodesia is known as an "*umulunda*

---

[14] Eggan, 1950, p. 218.
[15] Titiev, 1944, p. 13.
[16] Eggan, 1950, p. 52.
[17] Ford, 1941, p. 124.
[18] Boas, 1909, pp. 431-438.
[19] Whiting, 1941, p. 82.
[20] *Ibid.,* p. 154.

or 'halfsection.' Such friendship is always initiated with reciprocal gifts, and kept up by a constant interchange of gifts, cloth, food, fish, meat, etc. Lambas say, . . . 'friendship begins by barter.' " [21] Friendship among the Lambas does not appear to produce incest taboos.

The people of Lesu of New Ireland, in Melanesia, constitute another exception to the hypothesis of the relationship between organization into maximally solidary communities and the possession of inalienable friendship. There are friendships in Lesu, but "the friendships do not constitute a separate category of persons with special terms of address or with extended kinship terms. The choice is purely personal and has nothing to do with the boys being circumcised together. Since usually it is a younger boy and an older one who are friends, they could not have been circumcised together. Friendships are not inherited, and they can be broken." [22]

The Malekula of the New Hebrides, in Melanesia, are organized sociologically into localized patrilineal clans. Inalienable friendship takes on a very particular form in Malekula, being completely suffused with overt homosexuality. Inalienable friends are

> two men who habitually eat together, sharing a common meal, [and] come to feel that they are united by a very intense bond, by something that may be described almost as love. . . . If two men are thus closely bound together, and one of them dies, then the surviving friend is overwhelmed with uncontrollable grief; he is filled with a sense of the hopelessness and futility of all things.[23]

Such friendship is joined during the initiation ceremony. In addition to this institutionalized friendship, there is a gradation of "next best" friendship, but homosexuality is confined to inalienable friends.[24]

The Tallensi of the northern Gold Coast of Africa are organized sociologically into localized patrilineal clans which are the functionally significant units of association. Friendship among the Tallensi does not arise in any particular context, but is joined at any stage of the life-cycle.[25] The primary functions of friendship are gift-exchange and mutual assistance. Fortes records one instance in which an aged man ". . . deputed his closest friend and distant sister's son . . . to beget a child for him. . . . One might almost describe it as, from their point of view, a kind of artificial insemination." [26]

The Tanala were originally cultivators of dry rice who lived in localized patrilineages which were the significant units of association. The principal function of the patrilineal clan was to unite for defense in war. Inalienable friendship, called *mifanangena,* may be joined between two men, two women, or a man and a woman; the only restriction on the covenant is that such friendship may not be entered into by a noble and a slave. Inalienable friendship automatically invokes incest taboos between friends as well as their siblings and descendants. The principal function or duty of inalienable friendship is economic; friends must assist each other economically, and often hold property in common. "The bond is regarded with the utmost seriousness and it is thought that any infraction

---

[21] Doke, 1931, p. 128.
[22] Hortense Powdermaker, personal communication.
[23] Deacon, 1934, p. 538.
[24] *Ibid.,* pp. 260-262, 539-540.
[25] Fortes, 1949, p. 337.
[26] *Ibid.,* pp. 23-24.

will be punished supernaturally." [27] Inalienable friendship is not entered into between clans for political alliance.

"In Tikopia, a Polynesian island of the Solomons, there is an institutionalized form of friendship which constitutes a life-long bond, reinforced and expressed by reciprocal obligations, mutual trust and periodical exchange of gifts." [28] This friendship is joined during adolescence or early adulthood and is confined to men. The most clearly defined obligations and privileges of friendship are economic; friends are further obligated to give each other refuge if either has quarreled with his family or is in physical danger. Friendship is a moral obligation, but is not sanctioned supernaturally.

The *zadruga* of Croatia was a self-sustaining ". . . social and economic unit. It was composed of an extended kinship group, together with some adopted and unrelated members and families . . . Endogamy was often practiced in the *zadruga*, and *zadruga* life discouraged migration." [29] Land was held in common by the entire *zadruga*. Friendship stemmed from ". . . the institution of *kum*—godfather—and *kuma* —godmother." [30] The obligations of friendship were essentially mutual economic assistance.

Table 2 presents the covariants of friendship with the solidary-fissile community.

Table 2 leaves little room to doubt that close friendship, as a type, will tend to be found among peoples whose social structure is characterized by the solidary-fissile community.

The Andamanese, semi-nomadic hunters and gatherers, are grouped into tribes and bands, the latter composed of individual nuclear families. The bands were the functionally significant units of association; "these were the only social divisions among the Andamanese, who were without any of those divisions known as 'clans'. . . ." [31] Membership in the local band was not inalienable; although people generally belonged to the local groups in which they were born, "there is nothing . . . to prevent a person from taking up his residence with any other local group if he so wishes, and if the members of the group are willing to welcome him." [32] Friendship was joined between two men of different bands through the exchange or adoption of each other's children; "the object of the exchange was to produce a friendly feeling between the two persons concerned, and unless it did this it failed of its purpose." [33] Friends acted as go-betweens in marriage arrangements, exchanged gifts, and protected or avenged each other in case of murder. There was, however, an element of volition in performing the duties of friendship, and friendships were often transformed into strong antagonisms.[34]

The Chiricahua Apache of southeastern Arizona were organized into hunting bands in which membership was neither fixed nor inalienable. Characterized in their social structure by the solidary-fissile community, the Chiricahua Apache possessed inalienable friendship. This friendship arose in the context of girls' initiation ceremonies, but these ceremonies did not involve the formation of

---

[27] Linton, 1933, p. 307.
[28] Firth, 1936, p. 259.
[29] Tomasic, 1942, p. 230.
[30] *Ibid.*, p. 244.
[31] Radcliffe-Brown, 1933, p. 23.
[32] *Ibid.*, p. 29.
[33] *Ibid.*, p. 84.
[34] *Ibid.*, pp. 42-43, 49, 73, 84.

TABLE 2

Types of Friendship in the Solidary-Fissile Community

Inalienable	Close	Casual	No Data
Apache (Chiricahua)	Andamanese		Ifaluk
Bena	Arunta		Murngin
Dahomey	Balinese		Sanpoil
Gros Ventres	Basuto		Sirionó
Nama	Bushmen		Slave
Navaho	Camayura		Witoto
Omaha	Cañamelar		
Teton Dakota (Precontact)	Charmorros		
	Chenchu		
	Chimaltenango		
	Dusun		
	Eskimo (Copper)		
	Fiji		
	Kaingang		
	Lakher		
	Lepcha		
	Lone Hill		
	Manua		
	Mirebalais		
	Moche		
	Okinawa		
	Papago (Postcontact)		
	Siuai		
	Suye Mura		
	Taitou		
	Tarascans		
	Thonga		

inalienable friendships among the girls. Rather, their fathers became involved in such extra-kin relationships as a result of the *rites de passage*.

The most conspicuous ritualist of the [girl's puberty rite] ceremony is one who will be called "the singer" because it is his primary task to superintend the erection of the sacred shelter in which the songs of the rite are chanted and to sing the songs. . . . In the selection of a singer the greatest forethought is exercised: "Well, suppose you were an Indian here and you had a granddaughter who was growing up. You would come around and say that you wanted your granddaughter to be White Painted Woman. You know me very well, and you say to me, 'There are three or four men who know how to sing for this ceremony. Just between you and me which one of these men do you think should sing for my granddaughter? Which one should I make my friend?'

"And right there you want to be very careful. If you choose one of these men, you are brother to him all your life, even if you are not related to him. You call him friend, but you think just as much of him as you do of your brother. He thinks of your children as his children." [35]

[35] Opler, 1941, pp. 85-86.

The Arunta of Central Australia, nomadic hunters and gatherers, are aligned sociologically in loosely organized local bands each of which occupies a given territory. Friendships are formed between members of neighboring bands, and such ties serve two purposes. First, the lending of *churinga* follows friendship lines. Secondly, while visits between groups are marked by formal etiquette, informal visits could be paid by friends.[36]

The Balinese of the Malay Archipelago are primarily agricultural and reside in permanent villages; kinship is reckoned bilaterally with a slight emphasis on patrilineality. Sociological alignment is into castes and villages; it is within the latter that significant associations occur. Caste differentiation is not of paramount importance in ordinary everyday relationships, for "more than ninety percent of the Balinese are Sudra, the fourth and lowest Hindu caste, called in Bali . . . outsiders."[37] Friendship in Bali occurs principally within the context of the *bandjar,* the cooperative society. There are several *bandjars* within a village, and although they are bound to assist each other, each is relatively autonomous within its own ward. Membership in the *bandjar* is compulsory after marriage and failure to join in its economic activities can result in ostracism from the community.[38] A friend also provides a man with a place to sleep while his wife is menstruating. Friends address each other informally except when there is a disparity in caste membership.

Among the contemporary Basuto of South Africa, the functionally significant unit of association is the patrilocal extended family; land is nominally owned by the Paramount Chief, not by the clan. Friendship among the Basuto is an informal affair, its principal function being economic. Friends customarily share their labor, ploughing each other's lands in rotation, and care for each other's cattle ". . . to save hiring herd-boys, to take advantage of good grazing in areas in which they might otherwise be denied access, and above all to cement personal and political loyalties."[39]

The Bena of Tanganyika no longer live in localized patrilineal clans, but are divided into territorial tribal areas or units, each of which is a petty kingdom. Friendship takes the form of blood-brotherhood which is sworn ritually between two men. These inalienable friends are included within the sphere of one's kindred:

> A man's *walongo* are all his blood relatives, both maternal and paternal, his and their connections by marriage, those with whom he has sworn blood-brotherhood, and lastly any particular friends on whom he may rely for help in time of need, and who will similarly look to him for aid. It is a Mutual Service Society. An *mlongo* is described as "one who will feed you ungrudgingly and from whom you can borrow." He is the friend who is the friend in need. The practical convenience of such a group in aiding the absorption of aliens into tribal life is obvious. Its existence also partly explains the mutual obligations still existing between the families of freed slaves and their former masters.[40]

Inalienable and intimate friends habitually swear at each other and insult each other upon meeting, and inalienable friendship initiates classificatory incest taboos.

---

[36] Baldwin and Spencer, 1927, pp. 12-13, 135; Strehlow, 1947, pp. 52-53.
[37] Belo, 1936, pp. 15-16.
[38] Covarrubias, 1947, pp. 60-61.
[39] Ashton, 1952, p. 181.
[40] Culwick, 1935, p. 186.

The Bushmen of South Africa are nomadic hunters and gatherers who are aligned sociologically into small bands which are fluid in their membership. There appears to be no ritualization of friendship among the Bushmen, but there does appear to be a recognition of friendship as occupying a role within the institutional structure of the society. For example, ". . . a young man eligible for marriage is known as a *!gari-khoib.* When he desires to marry he first speaks about the matter to his best friend (*/hosab*) who then approaches the parents of the prospective bride. The latter will reply: 'We are poor, we cannot afford to give our daughter away.' Thereupon the */hosab* returns to the suitor and tells him to go and speak to the mother himself." [41]

The Camayura of northern Matto Grosso, Brazil, move from area to area as they deplete the soil. The small village grouping, composed of extended families, is the functionally significant unit of association. Friendship within the community is close and is expressed primarily through economic assistance and exchange of gifts. Between communities relationships are tense and are founded on deep-seated suspicions, often giving rise to ill-feeling.[42]

The Puerto Ricans of Cañamelar reside in independent nuclear families each of which is ". . . tied by a wide variety of blood, ritual, and marriage relationships to many houses in the Barrio." [43] Friendship in Cañamelar takes the form of *compadrazgo* (co-parenthood). These bonds function first as ceremonial sponsorships and, secondly, but at least as importantly, as sources of economic assistance; ". . . the important function of *compadrazgo* is to bind contemporaries. Thus, while it is based on a relationship between adults and infants (that is, between godparents and godchild), it serves a more important purpose by binding together persons of about the same ages." [44] These bonds can be broken;

> whether the *compadre* relationship will survive a financial exchange will depend, of course, on the solemnity with which *compadres* view their bond. There are cases . . . where a *compadre* tie was destroyed by excessive borrowing and failure to pay through cynicism and carelessness. It is not the failure to pay as such which will injure the relationship, but failure to pay when the means are available.[45]

The Chamorros of Guam have become bilateral since American rule was established, and ownership of land is now entirely individual. They are grouped into matrilocal extended families and village communities in the rural areas and into barrios in the city. Friendship among the Chamorros, too, takes the form of *compadrazgo,* and its content largely repeats that of the people of Cañamelar.[46]

The Chenchu of Hyderabad, in the Deccan of India, are bilateral, and the village community is the functionally significant unit. The individual ". . . has no pride of belonging to one particular . . ." group of kinsmen or the other.[47] Nor does he consider himself more bound to the welfare of kinsmen than to that of the total community. Friendships are made within the village community, and their most explicit function is to provide

---

[41] Fourie, 1928, p. 93; Schapera, 1930, p. 106.
[42] Oberg, 1953, pp. 41, 45, 52.
[43] Mintz, 1951.
[44] Mintz, 1956, p. 390.
[45] *Loc. cit.*
[46] Thompson, 1941, pp. 41, 43-44, 73-78.
[47] Furer-Haimendorf, 1943, p. 94.

persons who will prepare a deceased's funerary feast.[48]

Santiago Chimaltenango, a Guatemalan *municipio,* is divided into four wards (*cantones*); within the ward, the sociological alignments are patrilineal kin groups resembling lineages. At about twelve or thirteen years of age boys enter into intimate and intense friendship, two such friends spending most of their leisure hours together, sleeping together, acting as go-betweens in arranging trysts for each other, and are generally inseparable. This relationship lasts until the marriage of one of them brings the friendship to an end.[49] Adult friendship takes the form of *compadrazgo.*

The relationship between the parents of the child and the godparents, the *compadres* and the *comadres,* is . . . more important than the relationship between the godparents and their godchild. . . . The relationship between *compadres* and *comadres* is more formal than the relationship between close relatives, but the reciprocal obligations and the rights established provide an important extension of security beyond the family and kinship group.[50]

The Dahomeans of West Africa are organized sociologically into patrilocal extended families, patrilineal clans which are no longer localized but which cross-cut many villages, social classes, and mutual-assistance associations. Friendship is an elaborately institutionalized affair in Dahomey and, "in its institutionalized form . . . is . . . a basic element in the social structure." [51] Both men and women enter into inalienable friendships, albeit

intrasexually, though this friendship plays a far more important role among the men. Ideally, each person is supposed to have three such friends, but of the three the first is by far the more important than the second, and the second more important than the third. The strongest of these friendships are entered into during the initiation ceremonies, and such friends regard each other as "brothers by the same knife." [52] Inalienable friends in Dahomey play three important roles. The first of these is the role of intimate friend and confidant, and it is said that even ". . . the King had his best friend, whom he would visit under cover of night, and with whom he would discuss his problems until break of day." [53] The most elaborated role played by an inalienable friend is in the conduct of funerary ceremonies. Equally important, however, is the fact that a third function of such friendship is ". . . that the best friend of a deceased man or woman state the will of the dead to the survivors." [54]

The Dusun of North Borneo reside in self-sufficient agricultural communities which are loosely organized and which do not appear to be kin-communities. Friends address each other as brothers-in-law and provide protection for each other against enemies.[55] However, accepting the hospitality of a friend's enemy destroyed the friendship and made the former friends enemies.[56]

The Copper Eskimo of north central Canada are hunters and fishermen who reside in semipermanent settlements. Although most members of a settlement are related either by blood or marriage,

---

[48] *Ibid.,* p. 157.
[49] Wagley, 1949, p. 35.
[50] *Ibid.,* pp. 18-19.
[51] Herskovits, 1938, p. 239.
[52] *Ibid.,* p. 299.
[53] *Ibid.,* p. 88.
[54] *Loc. cit.*
[55] Staal, 1923-24, p. 974.
[56] Rutter, 1929, p. 183.

strangers to the group may attach themselves to the community either by marriage or ". . . by establishing definite ties with individual members. Even temporary visitors do the same. . . . In this way a permanent tie was established between the two men, to last till one of them died or a violent quarrel caused their estrangement." [57] Close friendship, called "flipper associates," is established by two nonkinsmen through the exchange of gifts of seal flippers.[58]

The Fijians of Polynesia are sedentary agriculturalists residing in permanent villages. A person has automatic rights to membership in a village, ". . . which may or may not be taken advantage of at the option of the individual." [59] The primary kinship unit is the matrilineal moiety which crosscuts villages and which is generally, but not always, exogamous. Moiety membership does not provide an individual with an inalienable grouping of kinsmen but rather provides a kin baseline within his village from which he can choose kinsmen with whom he will affiliate and cooperate. Although the Fijians do have initiation rites, and lads who are circumcised together are henceforth known as "age-mates," these do not provide a context for the joining of friendships. There are two types of friendship; both are joined later in life and between nonkinsmen. The first is a trade-partnership between two men of different villages; this is a quasi-competitive relationship in which "they vie with each other in displaying their wealth." [60] The second type is called "gummed together." [61] These friendships can be and are broken, especially where mutual trust

has been violated. Friends may serve as go-betweens in love affairs, but this is usually a sister's function. "Friends provide relief from the strain of gaiety and politeness which cross-cousins require. Friends are also free from the property obligations and status distinctions which may cause tension among brothers." [62]

The Gros Ventres of Montana were nomadic buffalo hunters in their aboriginal lives on the Canadian Plains. Friendship among the Gros Ventres took several forms, two of which were outstanding. The first was the institution of "inseparable-friends."

> If two men are *inithiha* this means that they have grown up together and are the same as brothers although they are not really kin to each other. The children of these two men would be the same as brothers and sisters to each other and could not marry. All relatives of "inseparable friends" were considered as own relatives. . . . A woman could tease the "inseparable friend" of her husband in just the same way she could tease her brother-in-law.[63]

The second major form of friendship taken among the Gros Ventres was the relationship known as "enemy-friendship." [64] This was a joking relationship in which the two friends could say anything to each other (which they would have to bear with equanimity) that would otherwise provoke murderous rage. "Enemy-friends" played practical jokes on each other, and their freedom to insult each other often served as a mechanism of social control.

The Kaingang of southeastern Brazil live in nomadic bands of from fifty to

[57] Jenness, 1922, pp. 86-87.
[58] *Ibid.*, p. 87.
[59] Quain, 1948, p. 181.
[60] *Ibid.*, p. 295.
[61] *Loc. cit.*
[62] *Ibid.*, p. 296.
[63] Flannery, 1953, p. 125.
[64] *Ibid.*, pp. 102-103.

three hundred people. Bands are endogamous, not because of kinship regulations but because of the fear and hatred in which all other groups are held. Friendships tend to be inherited, but they can also be broken.

The inheritance of paternal loyalties is very important in Kaingang society. If two men have been close associates for years, their sons will be close companions by the pure accident of their fathers' association. To the Kaingang such a relationship has a special warmth because it is a reminder of their parents. . . . As long as the nightmare of vendetta has never raised barriers between them, the members of the group live without serious conflict. . . . Stability is maintained by yielding to the aggressor, but grumbling under one's breath, and, at last, by going away—that is the end of all tension.[65]

The Lakher of Assam in eastern India are aligned sociologically into patrilineal clans, only the numerically weakest of which are localized. Friendship is formalized among the Lakher, but it is not inalienable:

Lakher men generally have some special formal friend. . . . Such a friend is known as *Kei*. There are two grades of formal friends: the *kei macha,* the principal friend, and the *kei hawti,* the secondary friend. Every Lakher has a *kei macha,* but the majority of men do not bother about making a *kei hawti.* . . . If a friendship is broken off, no claims can be made between friends on account of benefits given or received. If after breaking off a friendship either of the friends publishes any confidences that have been made him by his friend he would be fined.[66]

The Lepcha of Sikkim in the Himalayan Mountains are sedentary agriculturalists who are aligned sociologically into patrilocal extended families and exogamous patrilineal clans which were at one time localized but no longer are. The Lepcha once possessed a form of inalienable friendship which was a trade-relationship entered into with foreigners.

In order to be able to trade continuously and to receive hospitality and protection in foreign countries a formal relationship with religious sanctions was instituted. This relationship, and the two parties who entered into it, were called *ingzong,* which means literally "like a younger brother". . . . Once the full ceremony [formalizing the relationship] has been performed the two *ingzong* are regarded as being in truth sons of one father, and intermarriage between their descendants is forbidden as incestuous for nine generations.[67]

Once such foreign trade ceased, this institution lapsed. Today the term *"ingzong"* is applied only to close friendship among the Lepcha themselves.

Two reasons are advanced for setting up this inter- and intra-village relationship: either because the two men love one another, or because one or both lack anybody they can call "brother" and wish for somebody to look to for help in emergencies and who will care for their dependants in the event of untimely death. . . . These Lepcha relationships are not very stable and are often allowed to lapse; this is of no importance as the relationship has no religious sanctions.[68]

The Mandan-Hidatsa of Lone Hill, North Dakota, retain much of their aboriginal cultural values, but the social structure has been considerably weakened. The age-grading system has disappeared as has ritualized friendship.

---

[65] Henry, 1941, pp. 97-98.
[66] Parry, 1932, pp. 274-275.
[67] Gorer, 1938, p. 119.
[68] *Ibid.,* p. 120.

Within the peer group, certain individuals would "pair off" and would be recognized by others and themselves as especially close to one another. In a real sense these friendships, which were in almost all cases supported by a kinship relationship, were much closer than "friendship" in our society. Two "friends" would cooperate economically, even merge their cattle herds, would . . . eat together at one or the other's house, and the like.[69]

The Manua of Samoa are aligned sociologically into exogamous bilateral kindreds. Young men form friendships—*soa*—from among those with whom they are circumcised. These friends are employed as ambassadors in arranging love affairs and marriages. In arranging trysts and love affairs, a youth does not always trust his friend, who may himself win a girl's favors, and so employs several *soa* to spy on each other.[70]

The Haitians of Mirebalais, a commune in central Haita, are peasant farmers who reside in a permanent village. Friendship takes several forms, foremost among which is *compadrazgo*. In Mirebalais the emphasis of this institution is on relationships between generations, rather than between contemporaries.

A man may turn to his godparents for aid before asking it of his family, for they are regarded as truest of friends. Nor does he stand in awe of them as he does of his older relations. There is a free joking give-and-take between godparent and godchild, which reflects this attitude of warm affection. A person even stands in a special relationship to the children of his godparents, calling them "baptismal brothers" or "baptismal sisters." [71]

Other friendship associations are the *mira, coup de main,* and *combite,* groupings of various sizes in which labor is pooled and which are sources of other economic aid. Friends also serve as mourners and as a context for the exchange of children.

The community of Moche lies near the coast of Peru and is composed of sedentary farmers. Mochero social organization does not possess either extended families or unilinear kin groups of any sort. "So far as its structural features are concerned, the Moche family and kin are very much like those of North America, except that they and the individuals involved are less mobile, both physically and socially." [72] Every individual is supported by three sets of social bonds, namely, consanguineal and affinal relationships and by ties of *compadrazgo.* "The emphasis in [the *compadrazgo* of] Moche is upon the relations between sponsors (*padrinos, madrinas*) of an individual or thing, and between them and other persons (the parents of the godchild or the owners of the thing sponsored)—in other words, relations between adults rather than between adults and children or things." [73] There are two categories of *compadre* relationships: spiritual *padrinos,* who sponsor persons, and friendship *padrinos.* "In the 'friendship' type of sponsorship, the *padrino* is said to sponsor a thing, but he is actually sponsoring or aiding the thing's owner or proprietor." [74] *Compadres* are generally nonkinsmen, and in addition to their religious functions they assist each other socially and economically.

The Nama Hottentot of Southwest Africa are nomadic pastoralists who

[69] Edward M. Bruner, personal communication.
[70] Mead, 1930, pp. 35-36; 1939a, pp. 69-70, 90.
[71] Herskovits, 1937, p. 98.
[72] Gillin, 1947, p. 101.
[73] *Ibid.,* p. 104.
[74] *Ibid.,* p. 105.

are divided sociologically into tribes and exogamous patrilineal clans. Friendship among the Nama appears to be inalienable. Schapera, quoting Tindall, points to some of the ways in which individuals exploit the sense of obligation and responsibility of such friendship and impoverish their friends.[75]

Wikar, himself a party to such a compact, speaks of it in far more generous terms. "An old father and captain of the Bushmen [sic] named Ougaa came to me this evening and proposed to take me on as his bond brother (opligtbroer), to which I was agreeable, but I said I had no cattle to give him. He replied however that tobacco would do just as well as cattle from me. If I got cattle during his lifetime then we could give them to one another, if not he would still be my brother and never leave me in the lurch but would help me and be faithful to me. And this was indeed the case, for I must acknowledge before God and man that he was to me not merely as a brother but even as a father in all my sorrow, distress, hunger and bodily danger. According to Hottentot practice I might now refuse him nothing for which he asked me and which I had, I must help him and stand beside him in everything, and so too must he act towards me." [76]

The Navaho Indians of Arizona and New Mexico are sedentary pastoralists who are aligned sociologically into matrilocal extended families and matrilineal clans which are further grouped into phratries; clans are not localized and considerable distance separates households. "There is definitely a Navaho term for friendship as a social category separate from kinsmen. It can very properly be translated into English as 'friend.' There

is another term usually translated as 'partner' which embraces a conceptual territory somewhat different from anything we have in English. It is sometimes used in a semijocular way to refer to one's wife. But it is also used to designate any person—whether related or not—with whom one habitually hunts or travels or works." [77] Father Haile refers to inalienable friendship among the Navaho, and states that ". . . it is reprehensible to marry a woman with whom one has concluded a friendly relationship . . . as this is equivalent to consanguinity with her." [78]

Okinawa is the largest island in the Ryuju Archipelago in the Western Pacific. The Okinawans reported on here are sedentary farmers.[79] Sociological alignment is into patrilocal extended families and nonlocalized exogamous patrilineal clans; the latter crosscut the entire island. Close friendships are formed among young schoolmates and tend to persist as long as friends are geographically close. During adolescence friends indulge in sexual escapades together, masturbate in each other's company, and in adulthood constitute a significant source of mutual economic assistance in times of stress.

The Omaha, Plains Indians of Iowa and Nebraska, were primarily buffalo hunters in their aboriginal state. Kinship was traced patrilineally, and kinsmen were grouped sociologically into patrilineal clans the principal function of which was the regulation of marriage by clan exogamy.

Friendships played an important part in the lives of both men and women and the intimacies begun in childhood often extended throughout life. The friendships among the women had

[75] Schapera, 1930, pp. 321-322.
[76] Ibid., p. 322.
[77] Clyde Kluckhohn, personal communication.
[78] Haile, 1910, p. 433.
[79] From my personal field notes.

seemingly fewer dramatic incidents than those between young men, the lives of the former being less exposed to the stirring incidents of the warpath and the chase. . . . Friends were apt to be confidants and few secrets appear to have been withheld from one's intimate companion. A man would cleave to his friend, follow him in the face of danger, and if necessary protect him with his life. To be false to a friend in either love or war marked such an individual as without honor and especially to be shunned.[80]

The Papago of Arizona and adjacent Mexico were characterized in precontact times by the localization of the patrilineal clan. "Today there is no wider kin group among the Papago than the extended family."[81] It appears that there were strong pressures against the formation of extrakin ties in precontact times, but such affiliations are permissible today. In addition, the Papago have adopted the institution of *compadrazgo*.

A warm and close relationship is established not only between the child and his godparents but also between the two families. . . . One pair of godparents serves for all the children of a family. . . . The rights and obligations of relatives are extended to godparents and their children, but these extensions are not so vital a part of the family system as among the Arizona Yaqui, who have a similar arrangement.[82]

The Siuai of Bougainville in the Solomon Islands are sedentary agriculturalists who reside in hamlets of from two to nine families. Aligned sociologically into matrilineal sibs and independent nuclear families, the latter are the

significant units of association. Friendship in Siuai is wholly unelaborated, ". . . there are no mechanisms for formalizing such friendships, and in fact there is probably less emphasis on friendship in Siuai than in most societies."[83] The most explicit extrakin relationship is the *Taovu*-partnership or exchange relationship. These partners may never haggle over the goods which they exchange, but in reality there are ". . . cases of litigation between Taovu based on complaints of delayed or nonequivalent reciprocation of 'gifts.' And some of the most bitter political rivalries, including cases of outright enmity, involve former Taovus. In fact, several successful natives . . . expressed cynicism about the Taovu relationship, considering it a vehicle for fraud and trouble."[84]

Suye Mura is a peasant village on the main Japanese island of Honshu. It is subdivided into clusters of farmhouses, *buraku,* which are the functionally significant units of association.

At school the children, especially the boys, form close friendships with their own classmates, children mostly of the same age. Classmates are called *dōkyosei;* people of the same age, *dōnen.* It is the *dōnen* tie which is more important. All through life *dōnen* remain close. . . . The ties of *dōnen* increase with age. As a man grows old and the sexual desires die down, parties of *dōnen* are the only true pleasures left in life, and the farmers of Suye say that a *dōnen* then becomes closer than a wife.[85]

These age-mates form *kō,* cooperative credit clubs, which are a source of mutual economic assistance. "Richer men

---

[80] Fletcher and La Flesche, 1911, pp. 318-319.
[81] Joseph, Spicer, and Chesky, 1949, p. 56.
[82] *Loc. cit.*
[83] Oliver, 1955, p. 333.
[84] *Ibid.,* pp. 299-300.
[85] Embree, 1946, pp. 141-142.

join expensive *kō,* while a group based more on friendship forms a less expensive one." [86] A close friend will adopt another's child if the former is childless or if his friend is in poverty.

The village of Taitou lies in Shantung Province, China. The villagers of Taitou are peasant farmers who are divided into four patrilineal clans, each of which forms one of the four divisions of the village. The patrilocal extended family is the significant unit of association. Friendships are formed during the school years, and in many cases these supersede extrafamilial kin relationships.[87]

The Tarascans of Mexico trace their descent bilaterally; the independent household is the significant unit of association. Friendship takes the form of *compadrazgo.* "Ordinarily this could be translated as simply the godparent system, but at Cheran the relations between parents and godparents are often as important as those between godparents and godchildren and may be entered into in some cases without children being involved." [88] In addition to its religious functions, *compadrazgo* serves as a source of economic assistance in time of stress.[89]

The Teton Dakota, a Siouan Plains Indian tribe of South Dakota, trace their descent bilaterally, were organized into hunting bands of from ten to twenty related nuclear families in their aboriginal state. Friendship was inalienable; "thus toward one's blood brothers and those who became blood brothers through ceremonial adoption, respect was shown in affection and in complete loyalty on all occasions." [90]

The Thonga of southern Mozambique are sedentary farmers. They are grouped into one nation under a paramount chief, and kin groups are not localized. Friendship is neither ritualized nor inalienable. One of the principal functions of friends is to assist in making arrangements for a marriage.

When a young man has made up his mind to get married, and when he is in possession of the necessary lobola cattle, he starts, one fine day, with two or three of his friends to look for a wife in the villages. He puts on his most brilliant ornaments and his most precious skins. Here they are, arriving on the square of the village; they sit down in the shade. They are asked: "What do you want?" "We have come to see the girls," they answer bluntly. And the reply is: "All right. Look at them." [91]

Table 3 presents the covariants of friendship with the nonnucleated society.

TABLE 3

Inalienable	Close	Casual	No Data
Tanala (postcontact)		Kaska Ojibwa Teton Dakota (postcontact)	Zadruga (transitional period)

---

[86] *Ibid.,* p. 122.
[87] Yang, 1945, pp. 151, 221.
[88] Beals, 1946, p. 102.
[89] Foster, 1948, p. 264.
[90] Macgregor, 1946, p. 55.
[91] Junod, 1927, p. 102.

Kaska social organization is dominated by "the social isolation maintained by the family," [92] since "interpersonal relations are primarily restricted within the [isolated] family during six or seven months of the year." [93] Friendship appears to occur most frequently among unmarried youths.

"Fluidity tends to be a feature of such friendships, but during the period when a particular relationship exists it is often marked by close affection and exchange of confidence. The emotions of friendship are rarely expressed verbally, but are abundantly demonstrated tactually. Such expression is most strongly developed in girls, who are often seen holding hands, sitting close together, hugging and wrestling. Boys, too, often sit resting against each others' bodies. Sometimes a boy creeps up behind a friend and embraces him tightly from behind, whereupon the other tries to lift him up or shake him loose. Such horsing around often leads to wrestling for sport." [94]

In a different context, Honigmann suggests that this behavior, which may be ". . . indicative of repressed or inhibited homosexual tendencies," probably stems from sexual deprivations.[95]

Among the northern Ojibwa, whose ". . . households are always isolated, and for most of the year one lodge is separated by miles of forest from the rest of the world," [96] it is necessary to distinguish between the formalized or idealized rules of friendship and actual behavior. Although gift-giving and exchange is un-

elaborated among the northern Ojibwa and restricted to a narrow range of persons, the formal rules of the culture dictate that exchange is one of the functions or duties of friendship. But even the formalization of this relationship must be qualified, for it is a "very amorphous one in which friends privately engage. . . ." [97] Friends, however, not unlike even primary kinsmen, have no automatic rights to each other's property and the privileges of friendship are ". . . contingent upon the owner's grant of permission." [98] In actual behavior, such privileges are generally granted to avoid the threat of sorcery. In more significant, albeit subjective, terms the Ojibwa

. . . can never free himself from the wariness proper to the winter, and at all times views the proximity of other Indians as a threat. . . . Even those whom he calls friends he does not trust to the extent of dispensing with protective magic.[99]

The Tanala, as already indicated, were originally characterized by the maximally solidary community. With the abolition of warfare, clan organization broke down and shortly thereafter the cultivation of irrigated rice was begun. "It was at first an adjunct to dry rice carried on by individual families. But an irrigated rice field could be tended by a single family and . . . these distant fields also became household rather than joint family affairs." [100] Ultimately, the individual nuclear family became isolated from other families. The Tanala have retained in-

[92] Honigmann, 1947, p. 125.
[93] *Ibid.,* p. 136.
[94] Honigmann, 1949, p. 191.
[95] *Ibid.,* p. 165.
[96] Landes, 1938, p. 9.
[97] Landes, 1937a, p. 142.
[98] *Ibid.,* p. 88.
[99] Landes, 1937b, p. 55.
[100] Linton, 1933, p. 282.

alienable friendship, but it has already begun to show signs of becoming highly attenuated.

> The bond is regarded with the utmost seriousness and it is thought that any infraction will be punished supernaturally. An interesting modern development is that [blood] brothers may now promise to help each other with the reservation that the help shall not bring them into conflict with the government. Under this a man can legitimately refuse to help his [blood] brother if he is a fugitive from justice.[101]

The Teton Dakota, like almost all other Plains Indians, were once characterized by the solidary-fissile community in which the band was the significant unit of association. Concomitant with the separation of households attendant upon the American system of land allotments, significant changes stemming from this alteration of social structure can be observed on many levels. Not only are the "associations within an extended group . . . less frequent and intensive,"[102] but energies which were formerly directed outside the family are now turned into it. Blood brotherhood, age-grading, and associated institutions have been lost or remain only as vestiges of the old order of things. Casual friendships are now formed at school, and there is little stability or permanence in social relationships. "By the time the child has reached his twelfth or thirteenth birthday, his home is still the only place of security. Within his Indian society, there are no other groups and few activities in which he can participate and form any bond of close relationship." [103]

Table 4 presents the covariants of friendship with the individuated social structure.

TABLE 4

Types of Friendship in the Individual Social Structure

Inalienable	Close	Casual	Expedient
	Marquesans		Alorese
			Rocky Roads
			Yakut
			Yurok

The Alorese are sedentary farmers who live in permanent villages. Within the village the principal unit is the family group. Descent is reckoned patrilineally and the Alorese do possess lineages, but these are not cohesive groupings. Individuated wealth is the primary source of prestige within the community and ". . . must be validated by individual effort." [104] In economic and noneconomic spheres "expediency and interpersonal relationships outweigh theory and dictate arrangements." [105] But economic relationships set the tone for almost all social patterns:

> Status and finance on the institutional side reflect and reinforce the uncertain-

---

[101] *Ibid.*, p. 308.
[102] Macgregor, 1946, p. 60.
[103] *Ibid.*, p. 139.
[104] DuBois, 1944, p. 116.
[105] *Ibid.*, p. 22.

ties involved in trusting other people; yet certain aspects of the culture reveal the need for their good will. . . . There is no room for sentimentality but there is every opportunity for expediency. Aside from external pressures for the maintenance of social equilibrium, the only internal barriers that prevent the Atimelangers from being a group of utterly ruthless individualists is the fact that there has been no building up of self-assurance comparable to the demands of being self-reliant.[106]

The Marquesans of eastern Polynesia are sedentary farmers and fishermen who appear to be in social and cultural transition; structurally, they are now largely non-Polynesian. All that remains of the former system are loose survivals of ties between an individual and his mother's brother and father's sister. Households and individuals are graded in a prestige system based on manpower and derived wealth. The Marquesans possessed a form of friendship, called *e inoa* or *enoa,* which reflects the over-all state of transition; it was entered into ritually. It ". . . consisted of a formal union between two individuals of the same sex, which was accomplished by an exchange of names, the two thus becoming namesakes. The . . . intimate connection or identity of the personality and the name indicates how complete a bond this made for the native." [107] This was not inalienable friendship, however, for ". . . the bond was easily terminated." [108]

Rocky Roads is a small community of peasant farmers in Jamaica, B. W. I., whose households are relatively isolated in a scatter-pattern. Economic relationships are entirely competitive; money is to be amassed and the goal of individ-

uated wealth is the chief and uncompromising end of every adult. The Rocky Roaders say that every man should have a "best friend," but there are no such arrangements. The only patterned extra-kin relationships are exchanges of labor by two men.[109]

The Yakut of northeastern Siberia are semi-nomadic pastoralists aligned sociologically into patrilocal extended families and patrilineal clans; the principal functions of the latter are to regulate marriage and perform occasional religious ceremonies. The Yakut are further grouped into social classes which tend to be endogamous. Class divisions are almost entirely dependent on individually amassed wealth, and differentiations between rich and poor are great. Extrakin relationships are entered into principally to preserve and increase wealth, and the rules of clan exogamy are often violated in attaining this goal.[110]

The Yurok are hunters, fishermen, and gatherers who live near the Pacific Ocean in extreme northern California. Yurok finance is not too highly elaborated but "the persistence with which the Yurok desire wealth is extraordinary." [111] The individual concerns himself with little else beside the quest and desire for personally and individually amassed wealth. Status was determined almost entirely by economic position. Extrakin relationships appear to have been economically expedient:

Life was evidently so regulated that there was little opportunity for any one to improve his wealth and station in society materially. The poor, therefore, accepted more or less gracefully the patronage of a man of means, or

---

[106] *Ibid.,* pp. 150-151.
[107] Handy, 1923, p. 89.
[108] *Ibid.,* p. 90.
[109] Cohen, 1955, p. 292.
[110] Jochelson, 1933, p. 134.
[111] Kroeber, 1925, p. 40.

attempted to win for themselves a position of some kind not dependent on property. A savage temper, and physical prowess to support it, were perhaps

the only avenue open in this direction; shamans were women, and priests those who had inherited knowledge of formulas.[112]

IV

One cannot read the ethnographic data for sixty-five or so societies with respect to a specific problem without arriving at some over-all subjective conclusions about the problem for which information is being gathered. Since these subjective conclusions will assuredly affect the discussions to follow, they are best stated at the outset.

Friendship, irrespective of type, obviously provides an individual with a range of different kinds of "supports" and relationships outside the social and physical realms of his community of kinsmen. But what is especially curious about friendship is that—at least in its institutionalized or inalienable form—it is not a sociological or cultural imperative. There is little that an inalienable friend manifestly performs which any other category of person cannot perform. Why, then, do some peoples go to the "extreme" of institutionalizing and ritualizing friendship?

Let us put this another way. There are many "functions" which can be read into or attributed to patterns of food distribution. Food is indispensable to the perpetuation of physical life. It is ongoing, and its daily availability is a requisite for survival. It is so absolutely necessary to the maintenance of the social fabric; its possession, or lack, seems capable of arousing such intense emotions and feelings; and its availability— if only in terms of avoiding physical discomfort or irritability—appears so essential to the smooth functioning of so many different types of activity that it could be hypothesized that every society

"recognizes" the need for predictability and regularity in the distribution of food as well as in its acquisition.

Perhaps because food is crucial to the survival and effective functioning of a society, its pattern of distributing food appears to be extremely sensitive to its structure of social relationships. But friendship, as a social and cultural category, does not occupy the same kind of imperative cultural position as does food distribution. That is, as the data in the foregoing section demonstrate clearly, many societies can function with smooth regularity without an explicit formalization and institutionalization of friendship. While we may feel differently about this in our *personal* philosophies, it can be argued that friendship is not indispensable to the *institutional structure* and fabric of society as is the distribution of food. What does emerge—and this will serve as the major guide-line for the discussions to follow—is that friendship constitutes a major avenue by which can be learned a great deal about the effects of social structure and community systems on personality. Specifically, we are going to see that there are strengths and weaknesses in these different community-systems, and we shall learn how these strengths and weaknesses, too, have their effects on personality.

The data gathered for this study reveal that there are seven major functions or duties, among others, which friends can perform for each other. In the societies characterized by the maximally solidary community for which

---

[112] *Loc. cit.*

there are data on friendship, the following distributions of societies were found for each of these functions; naturally, there are instances in which more than one of these functions will be included in the friendship pattern of a society:

Material exchange and/or economic assistance: Arapesh, Bantu Kavirondo, Chagga, Hopi, Kwakiutl, Lamba, Lesu, Malekula, Tallensi, Tanala, Tikopia, *zadruga* of Croatia.

Sociopolitical and emotional support: Kwoma, Tanala, Tikopia, *zadruga* of Croatia.

Go-between in love affairs and marriage arrangements: Bantu Kavirondo, Kwakiutl.

Homosexuality: Bantu Kavirondo (inconclusive), Malekula.

Sponsorship in rites de passage: Hopi.

Mourning obligations: Malekula.

Exchange of children: Tikopia.

In those societies characterized by the solidary-fissile community for which there are data on friendship, the following distributions were found with respect to the apparent manifest functions of friendship:

Material exchange and/or economic assistance: Andamanese, Apache, Bali, Bena, Camayura, Cañamelar, Chamorros, Chimaltenango, Eskimo, Fiji, Gros Ventres, Lepcha, Lone Hill, Mirebalais, Moche, Nama, Navaho, Okinawa, Omaha, Papago, Siuai, Suye Mura, Tarascans, Teton-Dakota.

Sociopolitical and emotional support: Andamanese, Apache, Arunta, Basuto, Bushmen, Dahomey, Dusun, Fiji, Gros Ventres, Kaingang, Moche, Okinawa, Omaha, Suye Mura, Taitou, Teton Dakota.

Go-between in love affairs and marriage arrangements: Andamanese, Bushmen, Cañamelar, Chimaltenango, Manua, Thonga.

Homosexuality: Dahomey, Manua, Nama.

Sponsorship in rites de passage: Apache, Cañamelar, Chamorros, Chimaltenango, Mirebalais, Moche, Papago, Tarascans.

Mourning obligations: Chenchu, Dahomey, Siuai.

Exchange of children: Andamanese, Mirebalais.

Casual friendship is generally geared to informal social contact; economic assistance plays a decidedly secondary role and other functions appear to be absent. The economic function appears to be exclusive in expedient friendship.

Almost the same proportion of societies characterized by the maximally solidary and solidary-fissile communities use friendship as an extra-kin *economic* relationship of one sort or another: 81 percent in societies characterized by the maximally solidary community and 77 percent in societies characterized by the solidary-fissile community. The greatest difference between these two types of social structure, however, is to be found in the use of friendship as a source of *sociopolitical* and *emotional* support. In 25 percent of the societies characterized by the maximally solidary community, sociopolitical and emotional support is one of the major functions of friendship. But this function is found in 52 percent of the societies characterized by the solidary-fissile community.

There can be little doubt, as seen in Chapters 10 and 11, that the social-structural alignments of a group—according to which persons are ranged along continua of social-physical proximity and distance—somehow become part and parcel of the equipment of the individual. Nor can there be much doubt that these alignments are internalized within the individual as emotionally predisposing forces which are as strong as the religious values of his society, its ideas of sexual propriety, its ideas of good and bad, desirable and undesirable, right and wrong, and the like. It is true that we know far less about how the social structure of a society is learned than about how these cultural values are internalized. But we can accept as axiomatic the proposition that a social structure is one organ of the individual's makeup or constitution, specifically, of his motivational and perceptual apparatus.

The individual in the maximally solidary community is almost invariably provided with a set of inalienable consanguineal relationships which, very often, are geographically and socially localized. The material symbolization of this extreme solidarity is, among other things, corporate ownership of the land by the localized group. If it is indeed true that the social structure of a group becomes part of the individual's self-system, it would be insufficient merely to say that he is "provided with" inalienable kin relationships in the maximally solidary community. Instead, it would seem more precise to speak of the individual as *having* or *being possessed of* inalienable ties, in terms of his personality functioning as well as in terms of formal and external social structure. The possession of such ties connotes a particular kind of "knowledge" about the social world; it suggests a basic set of implicit moral premises about the nature and quality of human relationships. It is a moral standard of affective quality, a personality predisposition. The *world view* of the maximally solidary community is one which pictures human relationships as ideally permanent, intense, and irrevocable. Thus, in the cultures of these societies, such standards are applied *even to extra-kin relationships*. This, it would appear, is the general and thematic process underlying the existence of the *concept* of inalienable friendship within a society. (It would be tempting to understand this in terms of the behaviorist psychologists' concept of "generalization"; but to apply this concept to such an over-all and meaningful process is too mechanistic, too simple, and too "pat." The concept of "world view" or *Weltanschauung* seems more appropriate.)

A paradox, but one which is easily resolvable, seems to inhere in this picture. But to fully understand this paradox, it is necessary to point to an additional fact characterizing inalienable friendship. There are two kinds of inalienable friendship. One occurs *within* the community of kinsmen. The second is joined *outside* the solidary group of kinsmen—between nonkinsmen, consanguineal or affinal. Among some peoples, both types are found, an option for one or the other being exercised by the individual. No attempt was made in this research to determine what factors might instigate one type of inalienable friendship or the other, in part because of insufficient data.

The paradox just mentioned refers to the fact that in the maximally solidary community the individual is possessed of a complex web of kin relationships which, the attempt has been made to argue, constitute the basis for a world view which is applied as a standard to kin as well as nonkin relationships. At the same time, however, one enters into inalienable friendship with *one* person, and rarely with more, be that person a kinsman or not.

This paradox seems resolvable when it is borne in mind that in most societies consanguineal kinship supersedes all other bonds, especially in the maximally solidary community. To extend the limits of inalienable friendship beyond one person would establish a set of relationships *in competition with those of the maximally solidary community*. Where inalienable friendship is joined with a consanguineal kinsman, usually a cousin, the individual is accentuating and discriminatingly exhibiting a preference for one kinsman as opposed to all others. Where inalienable friendship is joined with a nonkinsman, he is setting himself off from his community of kinsmen. In either instance, he is arrogating to himself the right of intensifying one social relationship, or set of social relationships, at the possible expense of others.

Another function which might be served by limiting the number of inalienable friends can be found in relationships *between* neighboring maximally solidary communities. Where such a friendship is formed with a person in another community, the friends are representatives of their respective groups entering into a symbolic tie of amity or fraternity. Where such bonds exist, they often help to keep intergroup conflict at a minimum. If, on the other hand, this friendship were entered into with an unlimited number of persons, such a set of relationships might constitute an actual alliance and a conflict of loyalties in the event that overt aggressive action had to be taken by one group against the other.

The separateness of inalienable friendship and the ties of consanguineal kinship are to be seen, in part, in the fact that an inalienable friend is often privy to secrets which are not disclosed to one's kinsmen (or to any other kinsmen where such a friend is already a relative). Now, every social system has strengths as well as weaknesses; these exist at all levels, including the boundaries of the community. But such strengths and weaknesses do not necessarily stem from the same source in all types of communities. In the maximally solidary community, in which an extreme emphasis is placed on kin ties, part of the vulnerability and tensility of its boundaries is to be found in the "negative" component of the am-

bivalence which inheres in most kin relationships. Generally, where an inalienable friend is also a kinsman the two are tertiary relatives; sometimes they are secondary relatives, but never primary ones.[113] Obligations to primary relatives are greater and more important to the functioning of society than are obligations to tertiary kinsmen; but a person is generally far more ambivalent towards primary kinsmen than toward others. He is also far less ambivalent toward an inalienable friend who is not a kinsman. Thus, there is always the potential danger that inalienable friendship of either type —with a nonkinsman or a distant kinsman—might supplant primary kin ties and their attendant duties and liabilities. *In establishing the emotional propensities which are actualized in inalienable friendship, the maximally solidary community also creates a threat directed at itself; but it protects itself against this threat by arbitrarily limiting the range and extent of inalienable friendship.* And this relationship between friendship and the structure of the maximally solidary community provides one of the most striking examples of ways in which the boundaries of a social structure not only create emotional predispositions but also set limits for them.

In more than three-fourths of the societies characterized by the maximally solidary community the principal function of friendship is economic exchange and assistance. In this connection, it is important to bear in mind that trade relationships are generally across group lines; often, such exchange involves goods and foods not produced in one of the groups but essential to its diet or technology. Such barter, for this is what it essentially is, can take place outside the context of friendship, but once such friendship ex-

---

[113] For definitions of these terms and categories of relatives, see Murdock, 1949, pp. 94-95.

ists it is culturally exploited to the maximum and economic exchange is often included within it.

The sociopolitical and emotional belongingness and support of the individual is at an extreme in the maximally solidary community. (Of course, the ascription of such a feeling of belonging in this type of community is not meant to imply an idyllic, conflict-free existence. From the vantage of American culture it is possible to err in assuming that maximal belongingness precludes competition, mutual exploitation, chicanery, and the like. On purely *logical* grounds, however, there is no reason for assuming that the dimensions of belongingness and competitiveness are mutually exclusive. That we understand little of the ways in which both can exist side by side is but one illustration of the limits imposed by our own culture on our understanding of cultural processes in other societies.) Most expressive of the belongingness and emotional support accorded the individual in the maximally solidary community is joint legal liability. Since the fundamental human need for a sense of belonging is met at an apparently optimal level in the maximally solidary community, it is not at all surprising that sociopolitical and emotional support emerges as a manifest duty in the friendship patterns of only a few (25 percent) societies characterized by this maximally solidary community. But there *is* inalienable friendship in these societies nevertheless; the yardstick of human relationships is still applied, even though they find it necessary to set limits for such friendship.

It appears that we can better understand the functions of friendship in relationship to social structure when we compare friendship in the solidary-fissile community with friendship in the maximally solidary community. The greatest difference between the two community systems is that in the latter kinship ties are elevated to the level of exclusive and solidary groupings which own the land; in the former they are usually not. In the solidary-fissile community, the individual brings to bear a world view which does define human relationships in terms of propinquity, intimacy, and solidarity— but not of inalienability. The absence of inalienability in the solidary-fissile community appears to stem from the intrusion of forces making for a degree of tenuousness in social relationships, such as physical mobility and nonlocalization of kin groups. Thus, since the individual in this community-system is possessed of a world view or Weltanschauung of close interpersonal bonds *but not of a complete or full degree of sociopolitical and emotional support,* friendship in the cultures of this community-system tends to continue to retain the function of economic assistance *but it adds the function of sociopolitical and emotional support in 52 percent of the cases.*

We have singled out the functions of friendship for exploration because they seem to indicate relative *trends* of particular sorts within the different community systems. The fact that emotional support is a function of friendship in less than half the societies of one community type and slightly more than half in the other type does not mean that it is absent in the societies for which it is not reported. Economic assistance surely gives rise to emotional support even though an ethnographer does not report it. And it can be assumed that the other functions of friendship also give rise to emotional support between friends. If our foregoing theoretical speculations have been correct, then it appears that we can say that emotional support is reported as a function of friendship in the solidary-fissile community more often than in the maximally solidary community because the cultures of the former have *had* to elaborate this function formally because of the world view precipitated by the nature of the solidary-fissile community. The cultures of the maximally solidary community have not had to elaborate this function formally because it is so clearly met through other institutionalized relationships.

Before proceeding, let us look into the exceptions to the hypotheses for the maximally solidary and the solidary-fissile communities.

In the category of the maximally solidary community there are two instances in which inalienable friendship is absent. All other things being equal, we would predict that the Kwakiutl possess some form of inalienable friendship. What renders "all other things not equal" is the potlatch. Extra-kin relationships among the Kwakiutl, that is, those with whom inalienable friendships might be formed, constitute the lines of communication for potlatching. But potlatching is a competitive affair and inalienable friendship, ideally, is devoid of competitiveness. Since potlatching is central to Kwakiutl values and social structure, and since inalienable friendship, it would appear, is not an imperative of either culture or social structure, there can be no question but that inalienable friendship would be expendable. As for the second exception, all other things being equal, it would have been predicted that inalienable friendship existed among the people of Lesu; we are unable to explain this exception.

Within the category of the solidary-fissile community, for which we predicted "close" friendship, the exceptions to the original hypothesis can be grouped into two classes. The first group consists of the Chiricahua Apache, the Gros Ventres, the Omaha, and the aboriginal Teton

Dakota. Central to their cultures and social structures was the pattern of warfare with which was associated an age-grading system; it was in the context of the latter that inalienable friendships were joined. Among the Chiricahua Apache inalienable friendship was joined through a man's affinal associations or by a girl's father and the man who "sang for her" at her puberty rites.

The second group of exceptions consists of the Bena, the Dahomeans, the Nama, and the Navaho. The social structure of each of these four groups was apparently once characterized by the maximally solidary community; for one of these, the Dahomeans, there is an excellent historical reconstruction of the original social structure and its subsequent attenuation.[114] The values of clanship seem to have survived within the world views of these peoples, even though the external and formal structure of clanship has been weakened in each by various historical forces. These events have resulted in a solidary-fissile type of social structure; inalienable friendship in these four societies can be viewed as a possible survival from the original social structure, but reflecting a persisting *Weltanschauung*. Inalienable friendship among the Navaho, too, can be attributed to the forces of clanship; the latter also mitigate the isolation of households. Inalienable friendship among the Navaho is joined between clans or between a man and a woman who are thenceforth sexually taboo to each other.

These exceptions to our hypotheses about friendship in the first two community types help to reinforce the assertion that inalienable friendship is a manifestation of the *Weltanschauung* of the maximally solidary community and that close friendship mirrors the world view of the solidary-fissile community.

---

[114] Diamond, 1951.

Before turning to a consideration of friendship in the nonnucleated society and in the individuated social structure, we would like to digress into a detailed discussion of one variety of friendship which has long held considerable fascination for anthropologists: *compadrazgo*. This slightly technical digression is not only addressed to the anthropological specialist; it will also serve the general reader as an illuminating example of some of the ways in which certain kinds of cultures can, independently of each other, take an institution from an alien society and mold, refashion, and incorporate it into a local setting.

Many writers have tended to equate ritual kinship or coparenthood (*compadrazgo*) with what has been termed here inalienable friendship. Exception is being taken to this widely held view by subsuming *compadrazgo* under the category of "close friendship." Seven societies in our sample which are characterized by the solidary-fissile community share the institution of *compadrazgo*. This institution of ritual coparenthood refers to the set of relationships between individuals placed in motion (generally, but not always) through their participation in the Roman Catholic ritual of baptism. In addition to their type of social structure and their possession of *compadrazgo,* these societies share one other characteristic in common—they have all been converted to Roman Catholicism within the past few hundred years. Mintz and Wolf, in their authoritative study of coparenthood, point out that

> *compadrazgo,* once accepted by a social grouping, can be moulded into the community way of life by many means. It is a two-way social system which sets up reciprocal relations of variable complexity and solemnity. By imposing

automatically, and with a varying degree of sanctity, statuses and obligations of a fixed nature, on the people who participate, it makes the immediate social environment more stable, the participants more interdependent and more secure.[115]

There are several indices supporting the interpretation of *compadrazgo* in these societies as a form of "close" rather than "inalienable" friendship. The first is an historical one, namely, that *compadre* relationships in their original settings appear to have supplanted inalienable friendship during the latter stages of European feudalism.[116]

Second, the quality of *compadrazgo* appears to be more diffuse than the bonds of inalienable friendship. There seem to be two reasons for this. First, whereas inalienable friendship is almost invariably joined with only one other person, *compadrazgo* permits an individual to maintain effective *compadre* relationships *with an indefinite number of persons.* Secondly, *compadre* relationships generally tend to lapse upon an individual's removal from the community; this has been further extended to permit the nonfulfillment of duties of *compadrazgo* if privileges, especially of economic assistance, are abused.

Third, inalienable friendship must be viewed in juxtaposition with the structure of consanguineal kinship. Aside from the fact that inalienable friendship may pose a potential threat to the maximally solidary community, the latter two continue to exist side by side; and it can be hypothesized still further that inalienable friendship derives its strength from existing consanguineal bonds. *Compadrazgo,* on the other hand, might well be a substitution for solidary kinship groupings which have been severely attenuated. As Foster writes for Tzintzuntzan:

---

[115] Mintz and Wolf, 1950, p. 355.
[116] *Ibid.,* pp. 346-347.

An interesting speculation—and it can be no more than a speculation—is to what extent the *compadrazgo* system may be compensation for a former extended family or other kinship grouping. Its great importance in all aspects of life suggests that it may fulfill the function of some previous complex now disappeared. Parsons believes that the *compadrazgo* system among the Zapotecs may replace a former more comprehensive category of relatives, though she does not equate this category specifically with a clan or lineage organization . . . I suspect that lineages may have been the rule among all pre-Conquest Tarascans. If this supposition is correct, it is by no means improbable that the *compadrazgo* relationship is the functional equivalent of one aspect of pre-Conquest social organization.[117]

An understanding of *compadrazgo* and inalienable friendship in relation to consanguineal kinship must begin with this question: to what extent does either *compadrazgo* or inalienable friendship incorporate one of the salient features of consanguineal bonds—the setting into motion of incest taboos? Those writers who have assumed that the various forms of inalienable friendship ". . . tend to take on the attributes of kinship," [118] have usually included *compadrazgo* within this form of friendship; in making this equation, they logically have to assume that one of the major attributes of consanguineal kinship—the incest taboo—appears with almost the same regularity in *compadrazgo* and inalienable friendship. If, on the other hand, there is a decided and marked difference between the two in this respect, then their juxtaposition with the bonds of consanguineal kinship would provide one index for a qualitative difference between them.

What do the data reveal? Incest taboos are instituted in less than half (45 percent) of the cases of inalienable friendship, but incest taboos are set into motion in almost all the cases of *compadrazgo*.

Actually, one of the original working hypotheses of this study in patterns of friendship was that inalienable friendship incorporates or initiates sexual taboos between siblings and probably the offspring of such friends. That such taboos do not occur in even half the cases is obviously important in itself. But this finding raises several other questions. If non-genealogical extensions of the incest taboo are simply extensions of or generalizations from consanguineal relationships, we should anticipate that these extensions or generalizations would occur most often in the maximally solidary community with its intricate network of kin ties—with which inalienable friendship is associated —and in which kin-community exogamy is generally the rule. Questions such as this, of course, explain nothing, and further research would be required to determine why the incest taboo is not generally characteristic of inalienable friendship. Another question raised by this finding— as well as by other kinds of data—is the role of such taboos in friendship relationships. We know very little about the reasons (functions) of incest taboos in general, and their regular appearance in conjunction with one type of ritualized relationship and irregular appearance in the context of another kind of relationship lend even more perplexity to the over-all problem of the incest taboo.

But, these intriguing ancillary problems aside, one inescapable conclusion confronts us. Incest taboos are a direct outgrowth of consanguineal relationships. Inalienable friendship only infrequently

---

[117] Foster, 1948, p. 264.
[118] Redfield, 1947, p. 302.

initiates and incorporates incest taboos. Therefore, inalienable friendship must grow out of societal forces which are broader and more inclusive than consanguineal and genealogical relationships. It is the contention of this discussion that inalienable friendship is a logical expression and concomitant of the world view or *Weltanschauung* produced by the relatively closed boundaries of the maximally solidary community, in which kinship plays only *one* role, albeit an important one.

Thus, it seems possible to differentiate *compadrazgo* from inalienable friendship with considerably more certainty. The two types of relationship, as types, fail to share an important societal process. The societies in which *compadrazgo* appears as an institution do not appear to be characterized by the intricate webs of consanguineal kin relationships suffused by incest taboos which are found in societies in which there is inalienable friendship. It is therefore difficult to maintain the hypothesis that *compadrazgo* is an outgrowth or extension of kinship bonds, pure and simple. Rather, several interwoven principles seem to obtain in *compadrazgo*. First of all, it must be remembered that the ties of *compadrazgo* can be broken as a result of nonfulfillment of obligations; it is not an inalienable relationship. Second, *compadrazgo* can, in part, be attributed to the acculturative influences of Roman Catholicism, and can thus be viewed as a specific cultural variation or elaboration on the general process of close friendship in the solidary-fissile community. Third, because so many individuals are involved in a set of *compadre* relationships, *compadrazgo*, by virtue of the fact that it appears to be more diffuse than the bonds of inalienable friendship, emerges as qualitatively separate from inalienable friendship. Fourth, and perhaps most importantly, *compadrazgo* can be viewed as a possible substitution for solidary kin groups which have tended to disintegrate, or at least become highly attenuated, under the impact of acculturative forces.

Let us now turn our attention to the relationship between friendship and the nonnucleated society and the individuated social structure. (See Tables 3 and 4, and the data following them.) There is, as the attempt has been made to show, a subtle but distinct difference between the world views of the maximally solidary and solidary-fissile communities. The *Weltanschauung* of the nonnucleated society, however, stands apart from those of the first two, and there is no mistaking its content. The functionally significant unit of association in the nonnucleated society is the independent and isolated nuclear family; beyond it, there is usually a void of distance separating the individual and his family from all others. In his view of the social world, the individual in the nonnucleated society does not confront persons outside his family directly, but instead views them as remote, kept this way by either the profound social or physical distance, or both, which mediates his relationships to them. It is not so much that he handles and makes contact with people in distance-getting ways, but rather that his "self" is threatened by contact with others; its defense against contact is a cloak of distance and remoteness.

While the individual in the nonnucleated society sees himself as removed and apart from others, there are temporary "community-type" amalgamations of independent family units, generally during the summer months. It is during these periodic unions of family units that friendship takes form, but its content is a mirror of the world view of this type of social structure. The weakness and forcelessness of casual friendship—flaccid friendship may be a more appropriate term—is also indirectly observable in the infrequency with which functions or duties are assigned to casual friendship. Furthermore, friendship in these societies appears to occur most frequently among unmarried youths.

In view of the distances between households in the nonnucleated society and the attendant isolation within which individuals grow up in such societies, it can rightly be asked whether the initial postulate of this study can be applied to such peoples. It will be recalled that it was stated, as the point of departure for this chapter, that the predisposition or capacity to form friendships derives from experiences with kinsmen and nonkinsmen during the formative years. It was also suggested that these nonnucleated societies might constitute an exception to this generalization. An examination of the data, however, reveals that the ethnographers of these societies speak of friendship among them directly or by inference.

Unless we are in error in our postulate of the source of the predisposition to friendship, the presence of friendship in the nonnucleated social structure raises several questions, none of which, however, is answerable by the available data. First, is it possible that these ethnographers have employed a Western term with implicit Western concepts and standards to non-Western peoples? This is a doubtful possibility, but one which cannot be discarded. Second, is it at all possible that *all* people have the predisposition to form friendships regardless of their early experiences in different kinds of social systems? Is this predisposition an integral part of social human nature? Third, assuming that the initial postulate of this investigation into patterns of friendship is correct, does the predisposition to the formation of friendships in the nonnucleated society arise from contacts with nonkinsmen in the periodic or seasonal "community-type" amalgamations of nuclear families? This would seem to be the most plausible of the three possibilities, for if we assume the necessity of prototype situations in the earlier years for later adult relationships, the seasonal amalgamations would serve as the context for such prototype situations.

It may appear to be stretching a point when we refer to extra-kin relationships in the individuated social structure as friendship. The insistence on isolating a type of friendship in the individuated social structure stems, in part, from one of the theoretical biases underlying these cross-cultural investigations, namely, the belief that an attempt should be made to view an element of culture along a continuum of maximization-minimization, this continuum paralleling the one presented in the model of social structure. It could be argued that, in its uniqueness, inalienable friendship cannot be compared with close or casual friendship, to say nothing of expedient friendship. This is a question of definition and there is admittedly a measure of arbitrariness in its application.

The *Weltanschauung* of the individuated social structure is composed primarily of three elements: (1) an exclusive emphasis on competitive individuated wealth; (2) the absence of inalienable membership in any social grouping, for even the family is not maximally solidary; and (3) an individuated moral responsibility or puritanism. The goal of life in this social system is the amassment of wealth as an end in itself by individual effort and personal initiative. It is difficult to say whether the isolation of the individual is any greater in this type of social structure than in the nonnucleated society. The greatest difference between the two systems, however, is that in the individuated social structure the individual is devoted to a *competitive self-validation* through wealth. This goal is not only a

dominant theme; it is the principal determinant of social position and is the articu-
lating principle of this type of social
system. All else is a means to the realization of this goal, and wealth is a barrier
between people just as spatial distance is
a barrier in the nonnucleated society.
But space is not a goal; individuated

wealth can be converted into a goal under
special conditions, and where it occurs all
else, especially social relationships, is
transformed into an instrument of achieving it. It is the latter element of the individuated social structure's world view
which gives its extra-kin relationships a
separate quality.

SUMMARY

We have compared sixty-five societies in two cross-cultural studies in order
to learn how different community systems help to give form to personality factors
underlying behavior with respect to food and friendship. A model of community-
systems was devised for these two studies; paralleling the four types of social structure are four modes of distribution and four modes of friendship. The conclusions
of these studies, taken either separately or together, can be looked at from two
separate, but interrelated, points of view.

From one point of view, these studies provide a rather clear picture of what
a few dimensions of life are like in these many societies. In what has been called
the maximally solidary community, we find recurrent exchange and inalienable
friendship. In the solidary-fissile community, we find mutual assistance in times of
need and close friendship. In the nonnucleated society, we find narrowed and reluctant sharing and casual friendship. And in the individual social structure we find
amassment of wealth and expedient friendship. These combinations throw into focus
distinct world views and patterns of human relationships. There are surely other
patterns of behavior which can be correlated with economic and friendship behavior,
but these will have to emerge from further research.

From a second point of view, and this has been our principal intent, we have
presented these two studies to illustrate a particular theoretical approach to show
empirically that the emotional or motivational forces underlying observable behavior are never composed of single factors or elements. The ways in which people
"share" or "are generous" or even "trust" are not the results of either early experiences or of the social systems in which they live. They are combinations of at
least both—and perhaps of other factors which were not uncovered in these researches. Similarly, the kinds of friendship into which people enter are not only
the results of their predispositions to acquire friends but also of the kind of society
in which they live. As we proceed with such studies and gather more data, we shall
learn about other determinants in these patterns of behavior as well as in others.

While one of the major foci of these two studies has been the role of the "self"
in institutional behavior and practices, this has not been made explicit in the course
of Chapters 11 and 12. The reason for this was stated in the Preface, and need
not be repeated.

BIBLIOGRAPHY AND SUGGESTED READINGS

SUGGESTED READINGS

Eisenstadt, S. N. "Ritualized Personal Relations: Blood Brotherhood, Best Friends, Compadre, Etc.: Some Comparative Hypotheses and Suggestions," *Man,* Vol. *56,* pp. 90-95, July 1956. An anthropological approach to the study of friendship which is completely contradicted by the results presented in the present chapter. Eisenstadt's paper contains an excellent bibliography which need not be reproduced here.

BIBLIOGRAPHY

Ashton, Hugh. *The Basuto.* London: Oxford University Press, 1952.

Beals, Ralph. *Cheran: A Sierra Tarascan Village.* Smithsonian Institution, Institute of Social Anthropology, Publication No. *2,* 1946.

Belo, Jane. "A Study of a Balinese Family," *American Anthropologist,* Vol. *38,* pp. 12-31, 1936.

Boas, Franz. "The Kwakiutl of Vancouver Island," in the *Jessup North Pacific Expedition.* Memoir of the American Museum of Natural History, Vol. *5,* pp. 301-522, 1909.

Cohen, Yehudi A. "Character Formation and Social Structure in a Jamaican Community," *Psychiatry,* Vol. *18,* pp. 275-296, 1955.

Covarrubias, Miguel. *Island of Bali.* New York: Knopf, 1947.

Culwick, A. T. and G. M. *Ubena of the Rivers.* London: Allen & Unwin, 1935.

Deacon, A. Bernard. *Malekula: A Vanishing People in the New Hebrides.* London: Routledge, 1934.

Diamond, Stanley. *Dahomey: A Proto-State in West Africa.* Doctoral Dissertation, Columbia University, 1951. University Microfilms, No. *2808,* Ann Arbor.

Doke, Clement. *The Lambas of Northern Rhodesia: A Study of their Customs and Beliefs.* London: Harrap, 1931.

Du Bois, Cora. *The People of Alor: A Socio-Psychological Study of an East Indian Village.* Minneapolis: University of Minnesota Press, 1944.

Eggan, Fred. *Social Organization of the Western Pueblos.* Chicago: University of Chicago, 1950.

Embree, John. *A Japanese Village: Suye Mura.* London: Kegan Paul, 1946.

Firth, Raymond. "Bond Friendship in Tikopia," in *Custom is King: Essays Presented to R. R. Marett,* edited by L. H. Dudley Buxton, pp. 259-269. London: Hutchinson, 1936.

Flannery, Regina. *The Gros Ventres of Montana: Part I. Social Life.* The Catholic University of America Anthropological Series, No. *15,* 1953.

Fletcher, Alice C. and Francis La Flesche. *The Omaha Tribe.* Washington, D. C.: 27th Annual Report of the Bureau of American Ethnology, pp. 17-654, 1911.

Ford, Clellan S. *Smoke from their Fires: The Life of a Kwakiutl Chief.* New Haven, Connecticut: Yale, 1941.

Fortes, Meyer. *The Web of Kinship among the Tallensi.* London: Oxford University Press, 1949.

Foster, George M. *Empire's Children: The People of Tzintzuntzan.* Smithsonian Institution, Institute of Social Anthropology, Publication No. *6,* 1948.

Fourie, L. "The Bushmen in South West Africa," in *The Native Tribes of South-West Africa,* pp. 79-104. Cape Town: Cape Times Limited, 1928.

Furer-Haimendorf, Christoph von. *The Chenchus: Jungle Folk of the Deccan.* London: Macmillan, 1943.

Gillin, John. *Moche: A Peruvian Coastal Community.* Smithsonian Institution, Institute of Social Anthropology, Publication No. *3,* 1947.

Gorer, Geoffrey. *Himalayan Village: An Account of the Lepchas of Sikkim.* London: Michael Joseph, 1938.

Guttman, Bruno. *Das recht der Dschagga.* München: Beck, 1926.

Guttman, Bruno. *Die stammeslehren der Chagga.* München: Beck, 1932.

Haile, Rev. Berard. *An Ethnologic Dictionary of the Navaho Language.* St. Michaels, Arizona: The Franciscan Fathers, 1910.

Henry, Jules. *Jungle People: The Kaingang Tribe of the Highlands of Brazil.* New York: Augustin, 1941.

Herskovits, Melville. *Dahomey: An Ancient West African Kingdom.* New York: Augustin, 1938.

Herskovits, Melville. *Life in a Haitian Valley.* New York: Knopf, 1937.

Jenness, Diamond. *The Life of the Copper Eskimos.* Report of the Canadian Arctic Expedition, Vol. *XII,* Part A, 1922.

Jochelson, Waldemar. "The Yakut," *Anthropological Papers of the American Museum of Natural History,* Vol. *33,* Part II, pp. 35-225, 1933.

Joseph, Alice, Rosamond B. Spicer and Jane Chesky. *The Desert People: A Study of the Papago Indians.* Chicago: University of Chicago, 1949.

Kroeber, A. L. *Handbook of the Indians of California.* Bureau of American Ethnology, Bulletin *78,* 1925.

Linton, Ralph. *The Tanala: A Hill Tribe in Madagascar.* Anthropological Series, Field Museum of Natural History, Vol. *22,* 1933.

Macgregor, Gordon. *Warriors without Weapons.* Chicago: University of Chicago, 1946.

Mead, Margaret. *Coming of Age in Samoa,* in *From the South Seas.* New York: Morrow, 1939.

Mead, Margaret. "The Mountain Arapesh. III. Socio-Economic Life," *Anthropological Papers of the American Museum of Natural History,* Vol. *40,* Part III, pp. 163-232, 1940.

Mead, Margaret. *Social Organization of Manua.* Bulletin, Bernice P. Bishop Museum, No. *76,* 1930.

Mintz, Sidney W. *Canamelar: The Contemporary Culture of a Rural Puerto Rican Proletariat.* Doctoral Dissertation, Columbia University, 1951.

Mintz, Sidney W. "Canamelar: The Subculture of a Rural Sugar Plantation Proletariat," in *The People of Puerto Rico: A Study in Social Anthropology,* edited by Julian Steward, pp. 314-417. Urbana, Illinois: University of Illinois Press, 1956.

Mintz, Sidney W. and Eric R. Wolf. "An Analysis of Ritual Co-Parenthood (Compadrazgo)," *Southwestern Journal of Anthropology,* Vol. *6,* pp. 341-368, 1950.

Murdock, George P. *Social Structure.* New York: Macmillan, 1949.

Oberg, Kalvero. *Indian Tribes of Northern Matto Grosso, Brazil.* Smithsonian Institution, Institute of Social Anthropology, Publication No. *15,* 1953.

Oliver, Douglas L. *A Solomon Island Society: Kinship and Leadership among the Siuai of Bougainville.* Cambridge, Massachusetts: Harvard, 1955.

Opler, Morris E. *An Apache Life-Way: The Economic, Social, and Religious Institutions of the Chiricahua Indians.* Chicago: University of Chicago, 1941.

Parry, N. E. *The Lakhers.* London: Macmillan, 1932.

Parsons, Elsie Clews. "Ceremonial Friendship at Zuni," *American Anthropologist,* Vol. *19,* pp. 1-8, 1917.

Quain, Buell. *Fijian Village.* Chicago: University of Chicago, 1948.

Radcliffe-Brown, A. R. *The Andaman Islanders.* Cambridge: Cambridge University Press, 1933.

Redfield, Robert. "The Folk Society," *American Journal of Sociology,* Vol. *52,* pp. 293-308, 1947.

Rutter, Owen. *The Pagans of North Borneo.* London: Hutchinson, 1929.

Schapera, I. *The Khoisan Peoples of South Africa.* London: Routledge, 1930.

Spencer, Baldwin and F. J. Gillen. *The Arunta.* London: Macmillan, 1927.

Staal, R. F. "The Dusuns of North Borneo," *Anthropos,* Vol. *18-19,* pp. 958-977, 1923-1924.

Strehlow, Theodor, G. H. *Aranda Traditions*. Carlton, Australia, Melbourne University Press, 1947.

Thompson, Laura. *Guam and its People: A Study of Culture Change and Colonial Education*. Princeton, American Council on Education, 1941.

Tomasic, Dinko. "Personality Development in the Zadruga Society," *Psychiatry*, Vol. *5*, pp. 229-261, 1942.

Wagley, Charles. *The Social and Religious Life of a Guatemalan Village*. Memoir No. *71*, American Anthropological Association, 1949.

Wagner, Gunter. *The Bantu Kavirondo*. London: Oxford University Press, 1949.

Whitings, John W. M. *Becoming a Kwoma: Teaching and Learning in a New Guinea Tribe*. New Haven, Connecticut: Yale, 1941.

Yang, Martin C. *A Chinese Village: Taitou, Shantung Province*. New York: Columbia, 1945.

Section V

SOCIAL CHANGE, ACCULTURATION, AND PERSONALITY

Chapter 13

VALUES IN PERSONALITY:
ACCULTURATION
AND ASSIMILATION

The purpose of this chapter and the next is to discuss some of the personality factors which are of great significance in sociocultural change. This chapter will treat some of the personality factors which, among other things, facilitate or impede successful acculturation by immigrant groups in the United States. Chapter 14 will discuss some of the social-structural conditions which appear to produce different personality responses in two American Indian groups which have come into contact with Western culture.

The processes involved in sociocultural change are complex and deep. So intricate are the problems in this area of study that they have long constituted a field of heightened specialization in anthropology and sociology. Most often, social and cultural changes take place slowly and over long periods of time. Thus, it is extremely difficult to investigate such transitions in terms of their meanings to the people involved or in terms of the psychological factors which make such transitions emotionally easy or difficult, for the actual events and processes are often lost to sight. Usually, we have only the end results of gross evolutions to observe and can only speculate about what went on inside the people themselves.

There are, however, instances of sociocultural change which can be observed almost at the time at which such transformations are taking place. From these, we can often learn about the meaning of such change to the members of a group and about the personality factors which impede or facilitate such change. We cannot hope, in so short a space, to consider acculturation and assimilation into all types of societies; as a result, we shall confine ourselves to two instances of acculturation and assimilation to American society—one successful and the other relatively unsuccessful. By similar token, our guiding hypotheses will be specifically relevant to the American situation, although extrapolations can be made from them to fit situations in other societies.

As Florence Kluckhohn points out in her paper on "Dominant and Variant Value Orientations," it can be hypothesized ". . . that *the rate and degree of assimilation of any ethnic group into general dominant American culture will in large part depend upon the degree of goodness of fit of the group's own basic value orientations with those of dominant American culture. . . .* It is assumed at the start that there is a dominant class—in the case of the United States, the middle class—in which adherence to dominant values is marked, but also that there are other classes which hold to variant values in much of what they do and believe." [1]

This will be our guiding hypothesis, too. In this chapter, we shall consider two ethnic groups (the Japanese and the Poles) among whom can be observed varying degrees of "fit" into the general value system of the United States. Specifically, we shall attempt to see how a relatively high degree of such "fit" facilitated the acculturation (or assimilation) of Japanese immigrants to the United States, while in the situation of the Polish immigrants the relative lack of such "fit" impeded smooth acculturation. Similar to the Japanese instance is the relative ease of acculturation of Jews into American culture; comparable to the Polish instance is that of immigrants from southern Italy.

Values can be conceptualized in many ways. Despite the variety of conceptualizations, however, there is a consistency among them, and they emerge to provide a composite picture of the nature of values and of the roles they play in social life. Values are the postulates or premises which people hold about the ways in which the world *should* be ordered in its sociocultural dimensions; thus, they are always integral parts of a society's world view. These postulates or premises exist within the individual members of a group and they define what is desirable to achieve in the world. *"A value is a conception, explicit or implicit, distinctive of an individual or characteristic of a group, of the desirable which influences the selection from available modes, means, and ends of action."* [2]

There are many desirable ends and goals about which different human societies orient their sociocultural lives. But from these, each society chooses but a limited number, either rejecting all the others or even defining them as particularly undesirable as bases for action. And, as we have noted throughout our discussions thus far, behavior is always motivated or impelled from within the individual by virtue of, among other things, his positional standing within a social system.

Commencing with Chapter 7, it has been contended that the self-system of the individual, or of a group of individuals, constitutes the primary mechanism through which we can understand and evaluate the degree of "fit" between the person and an institutionalized role system. It is by means of the instrumentality of his self-system that an individual selectively perceives and weighs the pressures and demands in his environment; through this instrumentality he selects those to whom he will respond in one way or another and he selects those—and this is not necessarily conscious—to whom he will remain relatively impervious and insulated. It is also within his self-system that an individual experiences a sense or feeling of adequacy or inadequacy with respect to particular people and particular goals; it is within his self-system that he experiences success or failure, proximity or distance to others. His sense of adequacy and success, or inadequacy and failure pivot directly upon his performance in striving toward those cultural goals which he has defined for himself—within his "self"—as both desirable and attainable.

---

[1] F. Kluckhohn, 1952, pp. 354-355.
[2] C. Kluckhohn, 1951, p. 395.

"Defined for himself" is not quite accurate, however. It is more precise to say: "those cultural ends and goals which have been defined for him as both desirable and attainable, and which he has been taught are desirable and attainable." We have to make this elaboration because these desirable ends, as well as the means to them, are not randomly selected out of the air; rather, as we have seen in our discussions of social structure and socialization, they are selected or filtered out of that part of the general culture to which the parents or socializers of growing individuals have access by virtue of their status positions in the structure of society. More specifically, the ends or goals toward which an individual orients himself are filtered out of the total spectrum of the culture's general value system and are transmitted to him as pressures which others, especially his parents, expect him to meet and in the achievement of which they expect him to succeed. *In the course of his growing up, these value-pressures and goals or means to ends become engrafted onto his motivational structure in such a way that what others expect of him he comes to expect of himself.*

These engraftments of cultural values onto the personality come to make up a large and central portion of the self-system. This added dimension of values-in-personality necessitates a distinction between the general value system of a *culture* and the *selected* (or sociologically relevant) values from that culture which have become part of the modal motivations of individuals or groups of individuals within a society. We have to make such a distinction because *values or ideas do not impel, precipitate, or lead to behavior unless they have been internalized within the individual self-system.*

The following analysis of the acculturation of Japanese in Chicago is an excellent portrayal of the interplay between values in personality and social structure. Simply, the operational problem of this case study is: What values in traditional Japanese culture facilitated the acculturation of the Nisei of Chicago into the American middle-class culture? Similarly, when we turn subsequently to the problem of the immigrants from Poland, we shall ask: What values were there in traditional Polish culture which interfered with and impeded their acculturation in the United States?

ACHIEVEMENT, CULTURE AND PERSONALITY: THE CASE OF THE JAPANESE AMERICANS *

By William Caudill and George de Vos

Much of the literature on achievement has focused on the importance of hereditary or learned individual abilities, as in the relationship between IQ scores and educational or occupational success. In these studies, when discrepancies occur in expected predictions, the discrepancies are attributed to "other factors." For ex-

* Reprinted with abridgment from the *American Anthropologist*, Volume 58, pp. 1102-1126, 1956.

ample, Terman and Oden use the added factor of individual personality traits to distinguish between otherwise matched groups—their high achievers being greater in "prudence and foresight," "self-confidence," "will-power and perseverence," and "desire to excel." Recent workers have gone on to emphasize that such traits should be seen not only within the framework of the individual personality structure, but that these traits are also related to cultural values receiving very different emphases in lower and middle-class levels of American society.

Some attention has also been given to the factor of ethnic background in accounting for differences in achievement. For example, Terman and Oden found that their Jewish subjects, while not differing significantly in mean IQ scores from the total group, had higher grades in college, received a higher income, and were concentrated more heavily in professional occupations. Thus, the indication is for something specific in Jewish culture to account for these differences, but beyond allusion to its probable importance, this factor has received little systematic elaboration.

Early psychological studies of Japanese American children compared with other social and racial groups in California public schools give indication of a cultural factor at work which was not fully recognized or explored at the time. Strong, in summarizing the achievement tests, grades obtained in school, and Binet IQ scores of Japanese American pupils in comparison with other groups in California schools, asks: "How shall we explain the fact that the Japanese pupils in Los Angeles have about the same IQ as the average pupil and score about the same on educational tests but obtain strikingly better grades? It may be that they possess to a greater degree than whites those qualities which endear pupils to a teacher; that is, they are more docile,

occasion less disciplinary trouble, and give the appearance of being busy and striving to do their best . . . Another explanation would be that they come from poorer homes than the average and early realize that they must make their own way in the world; in consequence, they are better motivated to do their best." Strong does not develop the further question of why the Japanese Americans, out of the numerous low income ethnic groups in California at the time these studies were done, should show this remarkable striving and intensity of purpose.

The burden of this paper is that much further study of the cultural variable in achievement is needed in terms of understanding: (1) the achievement goals that are emphasized in the value system of the specific culture from which the subjects are drawn; (2) the processes by which these goals are implemented in the interpersonal behavior of individuals in the family, the peer group, the school, on the job, and in leisure time activities; and (3) the range and most frequent types of individual personality adjustment to these goals within the context of the specific culture, rather than a consideration of personality traits solely as an independent variable. The methods used in the research reported below were both quantitative analysis of data on the groups in question, and intensive clinical analysis of testing, interview, and psychotherapeutic data on specific individuals.

Between 1943 and 1946, approximately 20,000 Japanese Americans arrived in Chicago from relocation camps set up by the federal government when all persons of Japanese ancestry were evacuated from the Pacific Coast shortly after the United States entered World War II. Roughly a third were Issei—first generation immigrants who came to America during the early part of the century; the other two-thirds were Nisei—

second generation, who are American citizen children of the Issei. The cultural and personality adjustment of this group to life in Chicago was studied for three years (1947–1950) by an interdisciplinary team from the University of Chicago. Although the problem of achievement was not a central focus of the research, the data serve to point up the success of the Japanese Americans in this regard, and to show the necessity of a thorough consideration of cultural factors in the further study of achievement.

In terms of the usual sociological or anthropological approach, there are many reasons why the 342 Japanese American families represented in the Chicago research, or the Japanese American group in general, should experience great difficulty in achievement in the United States. Traditionally, Japanese culture, social structure, values, and religion are thought of as alien to those of America. Moreover, the Issei had a background of rural, peasant, subsistence farming, and came to the United States with only temporary settlement in mind. Most important of all, the Japanese are a racially visible group to race-conscious Americans.

Yet the data show that by 1947 the Nisei, almost as a group, held white collar and skilled trade jobs within the general employment market of the city. White employers and fellow employees accepted the Nisei and were enthusiastic in their praise of them. The median level of education for the Nisei in Chicago was, as it had been on the Pacific Coast, beyond high-school graduation. Almost all who did not go on to college took vocational training in order to become secretaries, laboratory technicians, beauty operators, or skilled workers. It must be noted, however, that the Issei had a surprisingly high level of education for immigrants—a median of ten years. A summary of Japanese American educational data may be seen in Table 1.

TABLE 1

Education of Japanese Americans Compared with American Sample

Education Level	Issei (277 persons) Percent	Nisei (488 persons) Percent	Chicago Americans (60 persons) Percent
Elementary School			
Uncompleted	7	0	0
Graduated	34	2	12
Secondary School			
Uncompleted	10	8	35
Graduated	32	56	40
College			
Uncompleted	11	21	10
Graduated	6	13	3
TOTAL	100	100	100

NOTE: Includes all persons who had completed their education as of January 1, 1947 from 342 Chicago families. Vocational and Trade School training not included. Right hand column is a normal control sample.

The Japanese Americans first found housing in some of the least desirable sections of Chicago. However, they disliked living in these sections and many families soon moved into predominantly white upper-lower and lower-middle-class neighborhoods. The Japanese Americans were accepted in these areas. Neighbors and landlords liked them because they improved the property, paid their rent promptly, and were quiet and courteous. In their clothing and general appearance the Nisei were almost stereotypes of the American middle class. This was particularly true for the women, who invariably appeared well-groomed, in conservative but chic dresses, blouses always snow white, nylons, and high heels. In their attitudes and aspirations the Nisei were oriented toward careers, white-collar work, or small businesses. They wanted little to do with factory jobs. They saw in unions a block to rapid advancement through individual achievement. In their social life the Nisei tended to stay within their own group. While they interacted freely with their white fellow workers on the job and in casual social intercourse at lunch, they had not yet achieved close intimate social contact with the white middle class they emulated. Yet they had achieved more in the space of four years in Chicago than other ethnic groups who had long been in the city, and who appear far less handicapped by racial and cultural differences.

Since occupation (as well as education) is a major avenue to achievement in America, it is worthwhile to look in a little more detail at the Japanese American data in this respect. The jobs the Japanese Americans were first able to obtain in the city were menial, unskilled, and poorly paid. Very shortly they left such jobs for semiskilled factory and service work at which the Issei stayed, while the Nisei, having higher aspirations, moved on rapidly to better employment. By 1947, the Japanese Americans showed the occupational distribution presented in Table 2, where it can be seen that 19 percent of the Issei and 60 percent of the Nisei fall in the categories of skilled workers, white-collar workers, small business owners, or managerial and professional jobs.

TABLE 2

Occupations of Japanese Americans

Occupational Category	Issei (197 persons) Percent	Nisei (383 persons) Percent
Unskilled Workers and Laborers	1	1
Domestic and Service Workers	24	7
Semi-skilled Workers	56	32
Skilled Workers	2	10
White Collar Workers	2	35
Small Business Ownership	13	6
Managerial and Professional	2	9
TOTAL	100	100

NOTE: Includes all members from 342 Chicago families who were employed as of January 1, 1947.

There were some interesting job differences between men and women. The Issei men were concentrated in semi-skilled factory and service jobs. In the factories they worked on the assembly lines, as machine operators, or at such jobs as carpentry workers in trailer manufacture. Their service jobs were as kitchen helpers, cooks, waiters, elevator operators, and janitors. There was also a considerable percentage of Issei men in building ownership and management, but the buildings were deteriorated and were operated as cheap hotels, or rooming and boarding houses. Even more than the Issei men, the Issei women were found in semiskilled factory and service jobs. Forty-three percent of all Issei women in the sample worked in the garment trades.

The Nisei men tended to be spread throughout all occupational divisions. Their major concentration was in apprentice and skilled trade jobs, and also in the white collar field. In the skilled trades the Nisei men worked as printers, welders, electricians, mechanics, and jewelry and watch repairmen. Some of these Nisei men had achieved jobs as foremen and supervisors, where they had authority over white workers. In the white collar field the Nisei men worked as clerks, draftsmen, laboratory technicians, commercial artists, and studio photographers. The percentage of Nisei men in managerial and professional positions was of considerable significance. As managers they worked in personnel departments, as laboratory heads, and as editors. As professional men they were doctors, dentists, lawyers, pharmacists, research workers, and teachers.

Nisei women were concentrated in white collar work, with 49 percent of the sample so employed. Here they were evenly distributed between secretarial-stenographic and clerical duties. Nisei women were also in the garment trades, but much less so than Issei women. Other important jobs for Nisei women were beauty operators, social workers, and registered nurses.

The aspirations of the Nisei indicated that small businesses would become increasingly important. In the sample, Nisei men owned grocery stores, garages, and cleaning shops, while the Nisei women owned such businesses as beauty parlors. All of these served the general public rather than merely the Japanese American community.

It must be remembered that the sample had been in the city for only a few years, and that the Nisei are young—clustering between twenty and thirty years of age—and have not yet reached their occupational peak.

Alan Jacobsen and Lee Rainwater investigated employers' evaluations of their Japanese American employees from 79 firms. These were owned by white businessmen, within the general economic and industrial structure of the city, and drew their employees from the general employment market. Firms owned by Japanese Americans were excluded, as were such organizations as social agencies, which might be expected to be somewhat more liberal in their employment policies. Better than two-thirds of the employers were very positive in their evaluations of Japanese Americans as workers; they considered them to be as good as the best employees they had ever had. The remaining one-third of the employers considered Japanese Americans to be no better and no worse than their average employees. An occasional negative evaluation usually took the form of criticizing the Nisei for being too ambitious and wanting to move on to a better job too quickly. In general, Japanese Americans were praised for their technical abilities such as speed and efficiency, and for their character traits of honesty, punctuality, willingness to work overtime, general moral standards, personal appearance, and so forth. They were also praised for the way they got along with other workers in informal relations. Japanese Americans had been up-graded in job and salary in 46 of the 79 firms, and in 5 others in salary alone. Seventeen Nisei were promoted to jobs which gave them authority over white workers.

Why was this so? How was it possible for the children of an immigrant group to succeed as well as the Nisei have in Chicago in approximating the American middle-class way of life, when the culture of their parents seems to diverge in so many respects from the American pattern?

Certainly relocation was a factor. No matter how well the Nisei were prepared in attitudes, behavior, and education for living a middle-class life, it seems unlikely that they would have been able to do so on the Pacific Coast because of anti-Oriental prejudice. Also, the Japanese Americans on the Coast had formed tight, self-contained communities controlled by parental authority and strong social sanctions, from which it was difficult for the Nisei to break free. Secondly, Chicago had had a Japanese population of only 390 persons, and had no social techniques for dealing with this group. Thirdly, with the scarcity of labor during the war, the highly trained Nisei were in a relatively favorable position in terms of the employment market.

These reasons may help to explain why the Nisei got their jobs, but will not satisfactorily explain why they were able to keep them and to please their employers and fellow workers.

A major hypothesis used as an orientation to our research was: there seems to be a significant compatibility (but by no means identity) between the value systems found in the culture of Japan and the value systems found in American middle-class culture. This compatibility of values gives rise to a similarity in the psychological adaptive mechanisms which are most commonly used by individuals in the two societies as they go about the business of living.

It is necessary to be aware that the hypothesis does not say that the social structure, customs, or religion of the two societies are similar. They are not, and Japan and the American middle class differ greatly in these respects. But the hypothesis does say that it is often overlooked that the Japanese and American middle-class cultures share the values of politeness, respect for authority and parental wishes, duty to community, diligence, cleanliness and neatness, emphasis on personal achievement of long-range goals, importance of keeping up appearances, and others. Equally, the hypothesis does not say that the basic personality or character structure of Japanese and middle-class American individuals is similar; but it does say that, for example, both Japanese and middle-class Americans characteristically utilize the adaptive mechanism of being highly sensitive to cues coming from the external world as to how they should act, and that they also adapt themselves to many situations by suppression of their real emotional feelings, particularly desires for physical aggressiveness.

Given this sort of relationship between the two cultures, when they meet under conditions favorable for acculturation (as in Chicago) Japanese Americans, acting in terms of their Japanese values and personality, will behave in ways that are favorably evaluated by middle-class Americans. Nevertheless, because the values and adaptive mechanisms are only compatible (and not identical), and because the social structures and personalities of the two groups are different, there are many points of conflict as well as agreement for the Nisei individual attempting to achieve in American middle class life. Certain points of conflict are made all the more poignant by the fact that the points of agreement are sufficiently strong to hold out much promise to the individual that he will succeed.

The direct relation of the general hypothesis to Japanese American achievement involves the problem of variant cultural orientations. Whenever cultural values are considered in current research studies on achievement, it is usually in terms of the dominant cultural values, whereas there may be many subgroups and individuals who do not subscribe to these values and who are, in this sense, variant. As Orville Brim says in an unpublished paper, "What is necessary is some systematic knowledge of differences between groups in the acceptance of the goals of the larger society, and it is of high importance that research operations be developed which will enable us to appraise the hierarchy of goals perceived as desirable by different *segments* of society, whether these be religious, ethnic, economic, or the like. Once accomplished, future studies could be directed toward relative individual achievement within discrete subcultures, with each of these sharing homogeneous goals."

The Japanese Americans provide an excellent example for Brim's argument. The fact that they succeed in approximating middle-class American standards in education and occupation does not necessarily mean that they are motivated by middle-class values and goals, nor that their achievement orientation should be thought of in these terms. What is needed is an analysis of Japanese American values and psychological adaptive mechanisms underlying those goals that are of crucial importance to Japanese Americans in their conception of what constitutes achievement.

From the foregoing, it appears that much more than a surface evaluation of behavior is necessary for the understanding of achievement. Japanese American and white middle-class behavior looks very much the same in many areas of life, but the psychological motivations underlying such behavior may occur within quite different cultural matrices. The following sections of this paper will present material illustrating this problem, as well as the further problem of individual differences in achievement within the Japanese American group itself.

In order to further the understanding of the success of the Japanese Americans in Chicago, Thematic Apperception Tests, Rorschachs, and psychoanalytic and social agency case studies were used. This paper, however, limits itself to the projective material pertaining to those aspects of personality dynamics that seem most relevant to achievement among Japanese Americans.

TAT material will be discussed before the Rorschach analysis because it tends to provide data on the more conscious aspects of the personality structure —internalized values, goals, and preferred ways of relating to others and to oneself. The Rorschach provides data concerning more generalized, and perhaps deeper-lying and unconscious attributes of the content and structure of the personality. Thus, the TAT can be useful in indicating the manner in which an individual approaches problems of achievement, while the Rorschach can suggest related, but often hidden, motivations and conflicts in this area.

A random sample of TAT records was gathered from Japanese Americans and compared with samples of white Americans from several socioeconomic levels. In this paper only the material from TAT pictures 1 and 2 will be presented in detail. The manifest content of these pictures is such that they usually elicit stories concerning achievement. Picture 1 is of a young boy looking at a violin on a table in front of him. Picture

2 is a country scene: in the foreground is a young woman with books in her hand, while in the background a man is working in the fields and an older woman is looking on.

Table 3 shows that the rank order of positive achievement responses to both pictures goes from the Issei who have the highest proportion, through the Nisei and white middle class, who are roughly equivalent, to the white lower class who have the lowest percentage of positive responses.

In rating the stories told to picture 1, responses were considered to be positive achievement oriented when: (a) the boy wants to be a violinist (a long-range goal) and succeeds by working hard; (b) he is puzzled how to solve the task but keeps working at it; (c) his parents want him to become a violinist and he does so successfully, etc. Stories were considered to be negatively achievement oriented when: (a) the boy openly rebels against his parents' wishes for him to play the violin (against a long-range goal) and seeks im-

TABLE 3

Positive Achievement Responses on TAT Pictures 1 and 2,
By Cultural Group

Group	Total Cases	Percent Positive on:	
		Picture 1	Picture 2
Issei	30	67	83
Nisei	40	43	55
White Middle Class	40	38	48
White Lower Class	20	0	30

mediate pleasure gratification in baseball or in breaking the violin; (b) he negativistically complies with his parents' demands and does poorly; (c) he engages in great fantasy about becoming a famous violinist, but gives no indication of how he will realistically reach this goal, etc.

Positive achievement-oriented responses on picture 2 were scored when: (a) the girl wants to leave the farm for a career, does so successfully (with or without the help of her parents), and either returns later to help her parents, or is of benefit to society elsewhere; (b) the farmers in the picture are continually striving to do a better job, etc. Negative achievement-oriented stories were when: (a) the girl wants to leave, but feels she cannot and so she stays and suffers; (b) she is disgusted with farm life and wants

to go see the bright lights of the city, etc.

Picture 1 reveals a second point: whether the boy is seen as self-motivated to work on a task, or whether he is assigned one by his parents or other adults. The distribution of the four cultural groups in this respect is shown in Table 4. The rank order here is the same as with reference to positive achievement responses.

On picture 1, then, the Issei are high in positive achievement orientation and self-motivation. Taking these characteristics with a content analysis of the stories, a major value and psychological adaptive mechanism found in the Issei is to strive for success at all costs. Even if one is tired and puzzled, and the outer world presents many difficulties in living, one must keep on and never give up. Such a

TABLE 4

Self Motivation and Task Assignment Responses on TAT Picture 1, By Cultural Group

Group	Total Cases	Self Motivated Percent	Task Assigned Percent
Issei	30	93	7
Nisei	40	62	38
White Middle Class	40	75	25
White Lower Class	20	35	65

characterization is frequent in the literature on the Japanese, and is often referred to as "the Japanese spirit" or *yamato damashii*. The Issei attempt to live up to this value by hard realistic work with little use of fantasy or magical thinking, as can be seen in the following story:

What is this? A violin? He has a violin and he's thinking, "How shall I do it?" It looks very difficult and so he rests his face on his hand and worries. He thinks, "I can't play it yet, but if I study hard, someday maybe I'll be a good musician." In the end because he holds steady, he becomes a good player. He'll grow up to be a fine persevering young man.

Like the Issei, the Nisei see the boy as positively achieving and self-motivated, but they also often see him as assigned a task and in conflict with his parents. In the latter case, the adaptive mechanism is one of negativistic compliance and self-defeat. As will be seen later, this method of adapting is in considerable contrast to that used by the white lower class who tend to be openly hostile and rebellious. Typical Nisei stories are:

Probably gifted along musical lines. . . . Perhaps mature enough to realize it isn't a plaything but something that, well, takes both skill and practice to master. . . . Perhaps he's been play-

ing but still can't get the same tone or master it with such ease as an accomplished musician could. Doesn't seem to be thinking of baseball or anything like that, that would be keeping him away. . . . Well, if he had real talent, lived for music and is guided and counseled in the right manner by his parents and teacher, he might have the making of a musician in the real sense, toward classical rather than modern big name dance orchestras. . . . Probably strive more for immaterial things to make his life satisfactory in a spiritual sense rather than purely monetary, economic. Probably would be a musician in some large municipal symphony orchestra or through his love of music be a teacher in some university. He never would be very rich, but probably won't regret it and through his music he will be living a full rich life. That's about all.

Is he supposed to be sleeping? Probably practicing. I guess the mother must of . . . something the mother is forcing on him. He's a little bored and disgusted, but he can't go against his mother's wishes. He's probably just sitting there daydreaming about the things he'd like to do rather than practicing. Something that was forced upon him. He'll probably be just a mediocre player.

The white middle-class stories are very similar in their emphasis on self-motivation toward long-range goals, to those told by the Nisei. The situation is reversed in the lower-class stories where such goals are not valued, and where the boy is largely seen as assigned a task. When parental pressure is applied in the lower class stories, the reaction is either one of open rebellion and refusal, or doing only what one has to and then quitting.

An example of a white middle-class story is:

> He is an intellectual looking young man. He probably has had an inspiration from some other violinist. He is intelligent. There seem to be two possibilities. Either he isn't too well prepared or he wonders why he isn't getting the same results from his violin that greater musicians get. He doesn't seem to register despair of any kind. Probably making an analysis of why he doesn't get the results although he seems rather young for much in the way of analytical work. He will probably go on with his studies of the violin and do quite well.

Whereas, in the white lower class:

> Doesn't want to play his violin. Hates his music lessons. His mother wants him to be a musician but he's thinking about breaking the violin.

> It strikes me as if he isn't thinking about the music there. He is thinking about a swimming hole, something like that. He has a violin there but he has his eyes closed and he's thinking about something else, probably what the other kids are doing out on the playground. He'll probably grow up to be a fiddler like Jack Benny. Probably grow up to drive a milk wagon [which is the subject's job]. When his mother quits pushing the violin on him, he will break away from it altogether.

In general, it may be said from an analysis of picture 1 that the Issei, Nisei and white middle class are self-motivated and achievement-oriented, while the white lower class are not. The determination to push ahead no matter what the obstacles, which is evident in the Issei stories, is a part of the Japanese value system and character structure, and it is this orientation that has been passed on to the Nisei in somewhat attenuated form. In addition, the Nisei give evidence of being in some conflict with the Issei parents, although they cannot openly express this. A further aspect of this conflict can be seen in the stories to picture 2, and is summarized in Table 5.

When the Issei tell stories of the girl leaving the farm to further her ambitions, it is usually in a positive manner. This is because it is a Japanese value that parents should help their children achieve long-range goals since it is (for the Issei) the unquestioned expectation that the children will then return to fulfill their obligations to their parents. For example:

> This child is going to school. It's morning and her parents are farmers and they work and she's off to school. Her mother wants her to do well in school. In the end this girl goes to school to improve herself, and she wants to grow up so she can repay her obligation to her parents.

As on picture 1, the Issei are primarily concerned with working hard in a difficult environment in their stories to picture 2, and such stories make up the bulk of "other responses" for the Issei in Table 5. A typical story is:

> Papa and Mama is working hard. One girl is about to go to school, I think. This picture mother work hard. She is working hard at something. This life is pretty hard. That's what these two are thinking—look like girl must see this situation and decide she must study diligently because Papa and Mama are concerned over her. Finally the girl becomes a nice girl, looks nice.

TABLE 5

Responses on TAT Picture 2 Indicating "Ability to Leave Farm" By Cultural Group

Group	Total Cases	Leave Positively Percent	Leave Negatively Percent	Other Responses Percent
Issei	30	37	7	56
Nisei	40	35	25	40
White Middle Class	40	35	28	37
White Lower Class	20	10	50	40

The Nisei, unlike the aging Issei, must find achievement and success within an American white middle-class world. The Japanese values and adaptive mechanisms learned from the Issei help the Nisei in such achievement, but they cannot both live up to the expectations of the American world and, at the same time, fulfill their Japanese obligations to their parents. Therefore the Nisei tell stories to picture 2 which are indicative of this conflict:

Well, let's see. This older woman over by the tree is watching her son till the soil. The younger girl with the books is this woman's daughter and this boy's sister. She sort of has disdain for this life in a farm community, it's so limiting. So she goes to a nearby school in hopes of emancipating herself from this environment. But in her face you could see that she feels a very real sense of responsibility to her family and almost a guilty feeling for not sharing the life that her family had tried to create for her. And her feelings are always changing. She feels one day that she should stay and be contented with this life, and the next day that she should go on and seek a new life, but she is committed to school, so she guiltily looks back at her family and proceeds to school.

Like the Nisei, the white middle class see the girl in picture 2 as leaving the farm to achieve a career or higher education. Almost no lower class subjects see the picture in this manner. Unlike the Nisei, the white middle class do not see the girl so much in conflict with her parents as they see her neither being helped nor hindered by the parents, but simply leaving and becoming successful. Often this success is stated in too pat a fashion to be realistic. This reflects the American lower-middle-class overevaluation (particularly in the women's stories) of education as morally good in its own right; also, one "gets an education" as a status symbol in much the same sense as one buys a new car or a house. Education is likewise valued as a status symbol by Japanese Americans, but the emphasis is more on the knowledge and learned background it gives one, or as a down-to-earth means to further achievement. A representative middle-class woman's story to picture 2 is:

The daughter was brought up on a farm. She is striving for better things. She wants to read books, go to school, see the rest of the world. She is now in the process of going away from the farm, the early things you see on the farm. She will succeed in her book learning and will become a very successful author, authoress.

The lower-class responses to picture 2 are quite distinctive. When they see the girl leaving the farm, it is not to seek a long-range goal, but instead she leaves the farm because she is "disgusted with farm life" and wants to go to the city:

> What kind of a field is that? It must be a wheat field. Girl is coming home from school. She's disgusted with the farm, doesn't like the farm. Like to get away from it all to the big city. Woman standing by the tree is her step-mother. She's very selfish. Father is a nice person. Looks to me like a very disgusted girl.

The TAT material just presented has shown some of the similarities and differences in Japanese and American achievement orientations in the area of life concerned with education, occupation, and other long-range goals. It would also be possible to make the same sort of analysis for parental, sexual, general interpersonal, and other aspects of life.

The Rorschach data offer a complementary analysis of Japanese American personality structure. The areas of mental striving and ambition drive as usually reflected in the Rorschach Test can be seen by comparing representative samples of 50 Issei and 60 Nisei with 60 American Normals ranging from lower to middle class socioeconomic status.

The perceptual organization of both the Issei and Nisei, when compared with the American sample, proves to be much more concerned with a straining to produce some over-all response to a Rorschach card (scored as W), with a neglect of both the easily perceived details (scored as D), and the smaller, usual detail responses (scored as Dd). . . . This sort of approach, along with an effort to organize the blot into complex concepts or configurations, indicates a great deal of striving in the intellectual sphere. The results also show a significantly large number of individuals among the Japanese Americans who exhibit an imbalance between an ability to be freely creative and spontaneous (as measured by movement responses on the Rorschach) and their intellectual strivings (as measured by whole responses). This finding suggests that the strong drive to accomplish outstrips, in some cases, the actual capacities available to the individual.

Although there is an over-all agreement as to striving among both Issei and Nisei, the personality context in which this striving is manifested is markedly different between the generations. The indications for a somewhat extreme intellectual constriction among the Issei are not as readily found in the Nisei. In both groups, where this constriction appears it sometimes leads to excessive associative blocking (refusal to continue responding to a particular Rorschach card) that suggests a lack of liberation of intellectual abilities, and in other cases to intense preoccupation with bodily functions, and a considerably narrowed range of interests or contacts with the outer environment. The associative blocking prevalent in the Issei was frequently accompanied by verbalization of a sense of defeat when the individual could not give an over-all response. When in a test of limits the examiner attempted to have the individuals respond to the details, in numerous instances they would not respond, feeling that they had already failed the task. They would, in many cases, only say, "*Ammari muzukashii* (it's too difficult)." This trend among the Issei is similar to their refusal to use fantasy or magical thinking even in the face of defeat as described in the TAT analysis. The American Normal group, on the other hand, shows more of a tendency to caution and momentary blocking in associative functioning. Rather than the severe blocking found in the Issei, those in the American Normal sample who show some sign of blocking recover and give responses, whereas in many cases the Issei totally reject the stimulus material.

The data suggest that oppositional trends (as measured by the frequency of white space responses) are most prevalent in the Nisei women, less common in the Nisei men, and notably lacking in the Issei group. Psychotherapy material in three of the extended treatment cases of Nisei women supports this conclusion. A strong theme running through many of the therapy cases was to oppose the mother to the extent of acting out rebellious behavior in various subtle ways. In none of the cases treated, however, was continuing difficulty with authority or supervisory figures expressed through direct opposition, probably because such direct opposition is not allowable in Japanese values. Instead, opposition was more indirectly manifested in the ways that assigned tasks would be done. The rebelliousness toward authority was prompted more toward women than men. In these cases, some break with the family always appeared, with the girl determined to make her own way, but with considerable turmoil and strong guilt feelings over neglecting the internalized obligation of obedience to family.

The kind of breakdown in ego controls observed in the Japanese American records often seems to be related to their sense of striving. The tendency to respond to the Rorschach cards in terms of confabulatory wholes found in both Issei and Nisei, the presence of vague abstract responses, the use of poorly conceived anatomy responses in which the parts were ill-defined at best, all serve to confirm the implication of an overstraining to accomplish. This strain to accomplish in spite of severe limitation is particularly present in the Issei. The observed selectivity of immigration from Japan does not allow one to infer that our results would hold true for all Japanese, and controlled studies in Japan should substantiate or modify these findings. The American normal group used here, in comparison with whom the Japanese tendency toward striving seems so marked, may on the other hand reflect a certain environmental selectivity related to their occupational framework. There is a tendency for this group to show a certain sluggishness of intellectual drive in comparison with the usual expectations of Rorschach workers. However, since the American normal group used as a sample in this study is composed of lower as well as middle class persons (unskilled and semiskilled, as well as skilled and executive groups), the results in terms of the greater striving shown in the Nisei adjustment would indicate that the orientation of the Nisei is more of a middle-class sort than is that of the Normal sample itself. The Japanese American Rorschach material has yet to be compared with Rorschach data gathered from a group of subjects with a strictly middle-class background.

In general, the over-all results of the research on Japanese Americans in Chicago seem to bear out the hypothesis that the values and adaptive mechanisms of the Japanese Americans and lower middle class are highly compatible, while the upper lower class diverges from both these groups and presents a different psychological adjustment. Where Japanese American values differ in emphasis by comparison with middle-class values, these differences are not of such a nature as to draw unfavorable comment from the middle class. Indeed, the differences would probably be considered praiseworthy by the middle class, if a little extreme, as in the extent of duty to one's parents, and the need to be of benefit to society.

The Issei place a high value on the attainment of such long-range goals as higher education, professional success, and the building of a spotless reputation in the community. These goals the Issei have passed on to their children, and the Issei willingly help the Nisei to achieve

them because it is the unquestioned expectation of the Issei that their children
will in turn filfill their obligations to their
parents. It is this "unquestioned expectation" that is the source of greatest conflict
for the Nisei, who feel deeply their obligations to their parents but who also are
striving for integration into American
middle-class life.

What appears to have occurred in the
case of the Japanese Americans is that the
Nisei, while utilizing to a considerable
extent a Japanese set of values and adaptive mechanisms, were able in their pre-
war life on the Pacific Coast to act in
ways that drew favorable comment and
recognition from their white middle class
peers and made them admirable pupils
in the eyes of their middle-class teachers.
This situation repeated itself in Chicago,
and personnel managers and fellow workers also found the Nisei to be admirable
employees. What has happened here is
that the peers, teachers, employers, and
fellow workers of the Nisei have projected their own values onto the neat,
well-dressed, and efficient Nisei in whom
they saw mirrored many of their own
ideals.

Because of this situation, the Nisei
tend to be favorably evaluated by the
American middle class, not only as individuals but as a group. Hence in Chicago,
where they are removed from the high
level of discrimination to be found on
the Pacific Coast, the Nisei can be thought
of as an entire group which is mobile
toward, and attempting to achieve in, the
American middle class. They are tremendously helped in this process by the praise
both of their parents and of the white
middle class; conversely, they are thrown
into conflict over their inability to participate as fully as they would like in the
middle class way of life, and at the same
time fulfill their Japanese obligations to
their parents.

A simile is useful in pointing up the
similarities and differences between Japanese American and white middle-class
achievement orientations: the ultimate
destinations or goals of individuals in the
two groups tend to be very similar; but
Japanese Americans go toward these destinations along straight narrow streets
lined with crowds of people who observe
their every step, while middle-class persons go toward the same destinations
along wider streets having more room for
maneuvering, and lined only with small
groups of people who, while watching
them, do not observe their every movement. In psychoanalytic terminology, this
means that the Japanese Americans have
an ego structure that is very sensitive and
vulnerable to stimuli coming from the
outer world, and a superego structure
that depends greatly upon external sanction. This tends to be true of middle-class
Americans as well, but not nearly to such
an extent. For example, individuals in
both groups are interested in acquiring
money in amounts sufficient to be translated in the achievement of social-class
prestige; however, every move of a Japanese American toward amassing money
is carefully watched, and the way he does
it and the ultimate use he makes of it in
benefiting the community are equal in
importance to the financial success itself.
This is less true of the American middle
class, where an individual can make his
money in a great variety of ways and, so
long as these are not downright dishonest,
the ways are sanctioned because of the
end product—the financial success.

The Japanese Americans provide us,
then, with the case of a group who, despite racial visibility and a culture traditionally thought of as alien, achieved a
remarkable adjustment to middle-class
American life because certain compati-
bilities in the value systems of the immigrant and host cultures operated strongly
enough to override the more obvious
difficulties.

The foregoing summary should by no means be taken to imply that all Japanese Americans will meet with success in the achievement of their goals. What is meant is that, because of the compatibility between Japanese and American middle-class cultures, individual Nisei probably have a better chance of succeeding than individuals from other ethnic groups where the underlying cultural patterns are less in harmony with those of the American middle class.

Unfortunately, there are as yet no studies of *un*successful acculturation to American middle-class life which use the same kinds of data and the same instruments of investigation as those in the study by Caudill and de Vos. Therefore, if we wish to analyze a situation of unsuccessful acculturation we will have to use information which is more descriptive and less empirical, and we will have to draw inferences about the self-systems of the individuals involved from the available data.

Despite the differences, there are several similarities between the Japanese and Polish immigrants. Most outstanding of these similarities is the patrilineal extended family. This similarity, however, is a superficial one, for it has entirely different meanings to the Japanese and Polish person. As Caudill and de Vos pointed out, traditional Japanese values clearly emphasize the individual's subordination to his *parents;* his sense of belonging, his sense of shame and guilt, his sense of pride, and his primary feelings of obligation focus most intensely about his parents. To a limited extent, the Japanese family is thus set off from the community at large, although it does have important connections with the community. But what is important is that the Japanese family's solidarity, and the individual's position within it, derives its greatest strength from the internalization of values within the individual self-system. Its functioning depends most directly on the effectiveness of the individual conscience. Overriding the differences in emphasis between Japanese and middle-class American values is a sufficient similarity and overlap to facilitate Japanese acculturation in the United States.

One of the most significant factors in the structure of the peasant Polish family is that it was almost always larger than the traditional Japanese family. Even more important, however, is the fact that since the Polish extended-family group was so large, the nuclear-family unit of parents and children derived whatever strength it possessed from the extended family, while the extended family itself derived its solidarity from the supports afforded by the village group. This latter dependency stemmed from, and was reinforced by, a complex network of mutually supportive economic relationships involving and uniting all the extended families of a community. In turn, this web of economic interdependencies rested squarely on an agricultural base. For example, relationships in the market between members of the same community were radically different from relationships between members of different communities. There were clearly prescribed areas of mutual assistance within the extended family as well as within the community. Social control derived principally from the community, secondarily from the extended family, and only minimally from the nuclear family unit. The structure, organization, and functioning of the village stemmed from its territorial unity and from its agricultural fulcrum.

While being reared as a Polish person, the child was taught throughout the years to respond to the needs and pressures of the *extended* family and of the *community*. Peasant Polish culture had not evolved any techniques for socializing children in a social context within which the nuclear family was an independent and relatively autonomous unit. Hence, when confronted with a situation in which the extended family and community structures were no longer functioning—and could not really function—in an American setting, the major and significant sources of values and controls also could no longer function. With these structural supports gone, it is not at all surprising that Polish immigrants and their children frequently responded to the American social system with maladaptive patterns of behavior, highlighted by frequent family and personal disorganization, delinquency, crime, prostitution, and the like.

These were but some of the factors which impeded the acculturation of the Polish peasant in the United States. There were other factors as well, however. Two of these relate directly to the general value system of American middle-class culture. First, the Polish immigrant, not unlike most people generally, actively desired to accumulate wealth. But here he differed from the Japanese and other successful immigrants. The Japanese, as shown, also had a great interest in accumulating money, but with the primary goal of *converting* it into prestigeful material symbols. Secondly, the *ways* in which he earned this money were extremely important; these means and ends were defined in terms of prestigeful occupations. The Polish immigrant, on the other hand, usually did not bring with him the internalized value that money must be accumulated *so that* it could be converted into socially meaningful symbols. Rather, it had its own value for him and was often accumulated for its own sake. As we shall see, this was paralleled by the lack of any strong internalized values for education which would impel the immigrant to strive for his children's acquisition of industrial skills and professional status.

Let us consider briefly the Polish peasant's attitudes toward education as part of his perception of himself as a member of a particular kind of community. Addressing themselves directly to this problem, Thomas and Znaniecki wrote in their classic study of *The Polish Peasant in Europe and America* as follows:

> The general unwillingness with which a conservative peasant group usually greets the appearance of intellectual interests in any one of its members can probably be best explained by its aversion to individualization in any form. A man who reads in a nonreading community has interests which the community does not share, ideas which differ from those of others, information which others cannot obtain; he isolates himself in some measure from his environment, lives partly in a sphere which is inaccessible to others and—what is worse—strange and unknown to them; thus, he in certain respects breaks away from social control. The situation is aggravated by the fact that learning has been associated with other social classes. There may perhaps be also some remnant of the medieval attitude toward booklore as having magical connections, either divine or devilish; thus

praying from a book in church is highly considered even in communities which are otherwise most averse to education. . . .

It is not strange, therefore, if an average member of a conservative peasant community, knowing what reaction to expect from his environment, is not easily induced to become a "paper-man" or "bookworm," *unless he has been already made partly independent of social opinion.* And even without social pressure, there is not much in learning which appeals to his traditional attitudes enough to justify in his eyes the effort necessary for its acquisition. His average curiosity is satisfied by the traditional channels of personal intercourse with newsbearers and "wise men" to whose information he can apply old and known standards and whom therefore he is often more willing to believe than papers and books, which require standards unknown to him. He does not see how he could apply knowledge to the practical questions which interest him, for this application would mean in most cases a radical change of his traditional methods which he is not prepared to face. In general, as long as he is satisfied with the old type of life there is no inducement for him in new intellectual values.[3]

At this point, let us turn to a description of the European background of the Polish peasant and his first adaptations to the American scene.

THE POLISH AMERICAN *

By R. A. Schermerhorn

During the nineteenth century the Polish people were living under three regimes—these had been established by the third partition of Poland in 1795—the largest group under Russian domination, the second largest under Prussia, and the smallest group in Galicia ruled by Austria. Although the land was fertile, the [second group of] Poles were in the position of either small proprietors or landless peasants living under feudal subjection to Prussian lords. During the middle and late 1870's there was considerable persecution under the Bismarck "Kulturkampf" policy, a crop failure in 1876, a new Prussian conscription law, and general unsettled conditions. At the same time knowledge about the successful migration of many Germans and a few Poles to the United States added

fresh stimulus to the desire of the landless peasant to escape. The movement spread from Prussian Poland to Russian Poland and finally to Galicia.

For the most part the Poles from Russian areas came with the fewest advantages. Educational standards were low and poverty was severe. The Russians pursued a policy of denationalizing their Polish subjects so that the latter were usually unable to read and write their own language, having gone to Russian schools when they went at all. At the opposite end of the scale were the Austrian Poles, who had greater advantages, went to school longer, and were given semiautonomy in the Austro-Hungarian Empire so that they sent representatives both to their territorial government and to the Parliament in Vienna. Politically

---

[3] Thomas and Znaniecki, 1927, pp. 1361-1363.
* Reprinted with abridgment from pp. 265-290, Schermerhorn, R. A., *These Our People: Minorities in American Culture.* Copyright 1949—D. C. Heath and Company.

they were the most self-conscious and articulate of all the Poles, and Galician leaders formed the spearhead of later Polish nationalist movements. The Prussian group, forming a kind of median position, were neither as underprivileged as the Russian Poles nor as strong in leadership as the Galicians.

The actual number who migrated to the United States is somewhat in doubt, because of the fact that they did not come with passports from Poland but from Prussia, Austria, and Russia. There were also a considerable number of Polish Jews that migrated at the same time, some of whom were counted in with the Polish Christians. This group will not be considered here. The greatest number [of Poles] arrived in this country in the period from 1900 to the first World War, in this respect paralleling the Italian entry. The year 1912-1913 was the peak of immigration in which 174,365 Poles were admitted into the United States. There was, however, a larger bulk of earlier immigrants among the Poles than among the Italians, and a greater number of the former went into agriculture on their arrival. It is estimated that 90 percent of the Poles who migrated to the United States since the Civil War came from agricultural regions. Even today 75 percent of the population in Poland is agricultural.

In the United States the Poles have settled most thickly in the area from Wisconsin east along the Great Lakes region through Pennsylvania and New York State to New England. The city with the greatest number of Polish inhabitants is Chicago, with more than half a million. At the opening of the second World War it was the second largest Polish city in the world, led only by Warsaw; today it may well be the largest. Other cities with large Polish populations are Buffalo and Detroit with about a quarter of a million each, Milwaukee with 150,000, and Cleveland

with 100,000. The mining areas of Pennsylvania are also thickly dotted with Polish settlements.

Whether they came from Prussia, or Austria, most of the Polish agriculturalists had lived in regions where a feudal economy was still largely practiced. Even though serfdom was practically abolished, the land had chiefly three classes: (1) estate owners who had from four hundred to one hundred thousand acres each; these landlords did not do manual labor but managed their estates with considerable personal supervision; (2) the small landowners, heads of families with from three to several hundred acres; some worked their lands with only the help of their own family members and a few hired hands; (3) at the bottom of the social scale, the landless agricultural workers who had nothing of their own but were hired at a pittance by the owners of estates or small farms. It was members of the two lower classes who migrated in greatest numbers. Perhaps the enumeration of the emigrants from Russian Poland in 1912 may be taken as fairly typical. In that year about 50 percent of those who left for America came from the landless peasants, while something like 27 percent belonged to the small landowning class.

Sometimes a landless peasant would work on one of the Prussian estates and be allowed an acre and a half for his own use so that he could raise enough vegetables to supply his family. For working on the estate he would receive in addition $20 a year and at harvest time a bushel of wheat, a bushel of peas, and twelve bushels of rye with which to make bread, etc. He and his entire family would live in two rooms of a large, square eight-room house, divided into four portions, each of which would be occupied by a different family. This house would be built of clay and straw, with one window to a room. The larger of the two rooms for each family would center on the fireplace, which would furnish all the heat available; in the creek, the clothes were dipped in the water and then flailed with a wooden paddle. During the winter this process would be more difficult since the ice had to be broken in order to get at the water. The food from day to day was monotonous, usually black bread with soup made of the vegetables the family raised, or some of the year's supplies taken at the harvest. The whole family ate out of the same soup kettle, and often enough there were no plates at all. Easter and Christmas brought white bread with potatoes, cabbage, and peas, or if the family were lucky enough to have a pig, some ham, smoked inside the fireplace. The white bread was not from pure white flour, however, but from "middlings," the best flour going to the Pan** or shipped abroad. From a nutritional point of view, however, this was an advantage.

The only break in the steady round of daily toil came during the holidays— at Christmas or Easter when there were special celebrations, at havest time, or when someone in the family was married. At such times the feasting was carried on with abandon.

Among the landed peasants, conditions were somewhat better. Of course the farms, unlike American ones, were never entirely in a single piece but were scattered in fragments over a considerable area. Even though the peasant lived in a small village and was forced to go from one section of his farm to another, this did not seem to be, from the standpoint of the community, any great handicap. It was the way things always had been, and it was accepted passively after the manner of the peasant.

On the whole the peasant seems to have been less isolated in his own village or community than the southern Italian.

Villages were closer together and the system of transportation was more developed. One result was that the dialect differences between Poles of one region and those of another were much less marked than they were among the Italians and therefore the tendency to settle in America in terms of the old geographical units was much less important. In other respects, however, the parallel between the two groups is instructive in spite of the differences.

Whereas the south Italian was a member of two main primary groups, the family and the village, the Pole in Europe had membership in several primary groups with different functions: the family, the village, the parish, the commune, and the *okolica* or "the country around," which for convenience sake is termed the community. The Polish family emphasized all blood and law relationships usually to the fourth degree, while the husband, wife, and children formed only a single element in this larger group. In this greater unit (even larger than the consanguine, since it emphasized law relatives) the individual with the most power and authority was the husband of the oldest couple having the most children and grandchildren. In other conjugal groups belonging to the large family the husband and wife were controlled by those of the superconsanguine group; a strong feeling of family solidarity kept them together since the group as a whole was judged by community opinion. Within the conjugal units the parents were responsible for the actions of the children and exercised strong authority over them, the relations generally being based on respect rather than love. (In general it has been only bourgeois or higher class societies that could afford the luxury of romantic love as a regular norm.) Here too the father retired when one of his

** Lord or proprietor; equivalent of German "Herr."

sons was better able to manage the homestead than he was; the favorite child took over the management of the farm—in central Poland the eldest son, in the southern mountain areas the youngest son, and in some cases the one with the strongest personal qualities. The result was a smaller stem-conjugal family within a larger superconsanguine family.

Since Polish society is mainly patriarchal, the life history of the son is important for an understanding of the whole culture pattern. The first stage of his life is that of childhood, in which he has practically no rights but is under the tutelage of his parents. In the second period he is able to do the work of an adult but is still unmarried; during this time his work contributes to the family support and any earnings he has must be turned unhesitatingly to the father. When he proceeds to the third stage and marries, if he is the one to carry on the family farm he then receives a considerably higher status, his private life is less controlled, and he begins to share responsibilities with the father. His brothers also have a higher status when they are married; but since they often move from the circle, they do not share in all the planning. Finally when the father retires, the son takes over the entire supervision of the farm and begins to exercise a more and more potent authority, culminating in an absolute supremacy by the time of the father's death. Every young person is supposed to marry, and his mate is chosen by the family in accordance with their status. Sometimes the marriage is arranged by friends, relatives, or the *swaty* or professional matchmaker. It is permissible, though not highly approved, to marry someone in an adjoining village but exogamy with respect to nationality or religion is regarded as a grave offence.

Promiscuous sexual relations are not tolerated by the Polish peasant community, and all conversation between a boy and a girl when there are no others present must be free from sexual allusions, though in a group ribald remarks are considered permissible. There is not the extensive chaperonage system for young women so characteristic of southern Italy, and the patriarchal tradition seems to be somewhat weaker. Illegal sexual relations before marriage are condemned and marriage is usually insisted upon if they occur. Extramarital relations are severely prohibited, whether for men or women, and it is bad form to speak in public about sexual relations within marriage itself. On the whole, sex is not considered impure but a matter of private interest within the conjugal unit which, as a part of newly developed adulthood, is kept from public discussion entirely.

Besides the family the peasant participated in other primary groups. (1) First was the village, in which relatives and lifelong acquaintances formed a natural unit of interest; where talk of crops, weather, family relations, unusual happenings, and events of supernatural importance formed the daily round. (2) Partly coextensive with the village was the parish, a larger replica of the patriarchal family, in which the priest was the natural leader. Regular meetings at the church kept alive the religious emotions and a social solidarity that was renewed on Sundays, saints' days, Christmas, Easter, christenings, weddings, and burials. The religious societies of the parish gave the individual a greater sense of participation than he had in other social groups outside the family. In general Polish Catholicism is predominantly social rather than mystical in character. It is true that the church was largely state supported and hence did not depend too directly on the gifts of its parishioners. This fact, however, did not seem to have the effect of loosening the tie between the individual and the ecclesiastical organization even when the latter was transplanted to America, where continual support was necessary. The large numbers of men as well as women who were devout worshippers, in the home as well as in the church, indicate that Polish piety was a deep-seated attitude.

While a considerable amount of superstition and magic remained in peasant religion, it was always kept subordinate to the power of the priest, who was obeyed implicitly, for his words were those of Jesus and his authority inviolable. Lacking political training on the whole, the people regarded the priest as the only leader they could trust, and this attitude they brought with them to their adopted land. It is perhaps significant also that Poland did not experience the Counter Reformation as the western European countries did; the type of Catholicism developed in Poland was therefore more authoritarian and appealed more to faith and less to reason than the type developed in France, Belgium, and western Germany, where competition with the forces of the Reformation and the Enlightenment gave it a different cast.

Two results of this religious pattern are significant for the immigrant. One was that the priest resisted any efforts on the part of his parishioners for an accounting of the money donated to the church, not because he could not give it but because it would somehow be a questioning of his authority. The other was the tradition that the church belongs to God and then to the saint for whom it is named, not to the parish. This view strengthened hierarchical control not only in Poland but later in the United States.

In addition to parish activities the peasant took a limited part in the life of the commune or restricted local government in Russian Poland. Although theoretically this was supposed to be a kind of limited political responsibility, in practice it was circumscribed by bureaucratic controls of the larger state. It functioned only in a routine way. Much more important, from the standpoint of social control, was the *okolica,* which included all those villages and groups near enough to each other to permit public opinion to operate through face to face contacts and gossip. To flout such opinion was equivalent to social suicide.

As for Russian Poland and to a lesser extent Prussian Poland as well, the political regime was conceived as a distant, mysterious, and arbitrary order that could be influenced only by personal manipulation and was even then unpredictable. As soon as emigration began, the state asserted its repressive power by attempting to prevent any outflow to America. Generally, the Pole, like the southern Italian, regarded the government as a coercive force operating from a distant source, and his antipathy toward it was increased because it tried to assimilate him forcibly into an alien culture and to forbid him the use of his own language and institutions.

As the number [of immigrants] kept increasing, a tendency toward more male immigration and scattered settlement became characteristic. The trend toward the cities began in the seventies and eighties, and 90 percent of the Polish Americans live in cities today. Before long individuals from the same provinces began to draw together in nucleated centers, occasionally forming the boarding-house complex which we have noted already among the Italians. These centers gradually formed in each city a Polish colony known as the Polonia. Engaging in manual labor of an unskilled type and knowing little of the language or customs of America, the immigrant was naturally drawn toward others of his own kind. Even though he endured some of the discrimination shown to all foreign groups, he nevertheless actually found freedom in relative absence of pressure to assimilate him, and he began to organize with great fervor. At first in many cases he imagined himself an exile from the old world rather than an immigrant in the new.

The Polonia was organized in two chronological stages. A preliminary period of transition and orientation gave way to the forming of a mutual benefit organization or "society." The members of the community who had forged ahead economically were often the leaders in the new group. Before its formation there were often collections for the poorer members of the colony bereft by death or misfortune; naturally the affluent were expected to give more substantially. The impulse to put this benefit on a more businesslike basis (parallel with the development of the community chest) motivated the leaders to form, with all other members of the colony, a society to which each person would contribute a regular share of his earnings and from which he would have the privilege to collect benefits as a matter of right rather than favor when conditions became too difficult for him to manage alone. This insurance principle, however, did not eventually constitute the main purpose of the organization but only its formative principle.

In time the society became a sort of social club that arranged dances, musicals, dramatic entertainments, lectures, and other events in which members of the colony could participate, using their own language and customs. As the community grew, Poles from all three sections of Poland came together and found a common life, thus enlarging the boundaries of the villages or province in the old world. As the group began to congregate more and more in a single area, other nationalities would gradually move out and leave homes or tenements vacant, dwellings which were soon appropriated by more incoming Poles. In some cases Polish real estate agents hastened the process by organizing a campaign to buy up more property for Polish families.

The second step of the colony was to organize the Polish parish. Like other nationality groups predominantly Catholic, the Poles on their arrival in America found themselves attending churches in which their own language was never heard and which were often shepherded by Irish priests. Sometimes, as for example in Detroit, the incoming Poles who migrated from Prussia to get away from German dominance could find no other Catholic churches in which they might worship except German parishes. Paradoxically their very familiarity with German made even this an advantage during the early years of adjustment to American life. The colony did not consider this any more than a temporary arrangement, however, and soon began to press for their own priests. The benefit society now became the foundation for the parish and this formed a new primary community with the church at the center, somewhat like the older parish in Poland. The devout parishioners soon furnished the money to erect a church of their own, and relations became more stabilized. The sacrifice necessary to build a national church in the Polonia seems incredible today. A not untypical example occurred in St. Joseph's Parish of South Bend, where unskilled laborers in 1877 contributed $22 per family to the church. In a good many cases this amount represented something like one half of the monthly income for the family.

The tendency to congregate grew even stronger. A large number of saloons, banks, stores, steamship agencies, and undertaking parlors came into being to serve Polish customers. In passing it is of interest to note that Polish Jews do not usually move into Polish neighborhoods even though the ties of language might naturally take them there. This may be due partly to the fact that they do not care to restrict their clientele to a single nationality group and partly to the tendency in Poland to keep them restricted or segregated from other aspects of Polish life, a tendency they could escape in their new environment.

The pattern of cooperative family work was modified to suit American conditions. As soon as possible each child would have a job of his own, contributing all his earnings to the family pool. Many Poles were thus able to forge ahead economically at an accelerated rate. Many working hands in the same family would sometimes bring in a weekly income of $135 to $150 at a time when wages were low by present-day standards. The head of the family with a peasant background often showed a passion for saving and thrift which enabled him to own property or a small business in a few years. Agricultural habits aided this process when the city-dwelling immigrant would find a small piece of land on the outskirts, work with his sons in the factory or foundry, and spend his spare time raising a garden or a few chickens and perhaps a hog. Autumn would find the family laying in provisions for the winter: twenty to forty bushels of potatoes, a barrel of flour, a barrel of herring, and a whole dressed hog. These staples would enable the family to save still more for the future.

While the advantages of this style of living were obvious to the transplanted peasant, *he did not always realize its results in terms of the children's future.* Leaders of the Polish press complained that *children would leave school early and go to the factory,* that some of them went as early as eleven and thirteen. *Accordingly, the number of youth entering higher educational institutions or the professions was considerably curtailed,* with results that can still be observed. Furthermore the custom of turning over all earnings to the head of the family became a bone of contention between child and father as soon as the former became Americanized and demanded new rights. [All italics in this paragraph added.]

Among the institutions in the Polonia one of the most important was the parochial school, which was usually built soon after the church. The parents frequently took the position that children grew too rapidly away from them and from the stabilizing influence of Polish customs when they entered public schools. Desiring some means of cushioning the sudden culture shock to the younger generation, the parents and the priest saw to it that the Polish language was taught as well as something of the history and culture of the home country. The efficacy of the parochial school in keeping the children under control of the parents is not to be minimized, though the Polish content in the curriculum gradually decreased as the community became more Americanized.

One of the criticisms leveled against the parochial school was that a disproportionate amount of time was given to learning the catechism and a much shorter time was allowed for reading, writing, arithmetic, and geography. As a result many children who spent six or seven years in a parochial school could hardly pass an examination for the fifth grade in a public elementary school.

Although the Polonia was to outward observation a united community, still its hold on the people did not have the coherence or force of the old peasant village or *okolica.* The members of the Polonia had frequent contacts with each other but they were also immersed in a wider society with different values, ideals, and purposes. Its members spent many hours a day in factory, shop, or place of business, in high school, or in casual contact with members of the larger American community. *What served as a strong social control in Poland became weakened in America by the loss of social reinforcement outside the local group.* Even within there were also members whom Znaniecki calls "secessionists," whose interests differed from those of the majority. Many a national home or *Dom Polski* was founded by a group of these secessionists, but the institution was more like an American club with ballroom, assembly rooms, a bar, and perhaps a theater. [Italics added.]

Before long the purely local character of the Polonia was no longer sufficient, and the demand to combine all Polish Americans in a common body of interest began in the latter part of the nineteenth century. From the first the strongest of these organizations was the Polish National Alliance, which in 1880 united the efforts of local fraternal orders or societies by giving them a rallying point. Its purposes as originally stated were, "To lay [the] foundation for an institution that would work for the material and moral amelioration of the Polish element in the United States by means of a reserve fund. To such institutions belong the Polish homes, schools, and all welfare organizations. . . . Protection of the Polish immigration. . . . Adaptation of the immigrant to American citizenship. . . . Commemoration of Polish historic events." In addition there were death benefits—$500 at the death of a member and $300 at the wife's death.

The Alliance was organized as a secular and nonsectarian group with no religious qualifications for membership. In addition to its stated aims, it seems to have promoted a patriotic national (if not nationalistic) Polish spirit. One of the main difficulties of the often untutored immigrant was ignorance of the culture and historic past belonging to his own people; for self-respect he needed a fuller knowledge of the importance which his own background had for him. Besides giving him this, the Alliance furthered the idea that the Poles in this country could in a sense be a strong and integral part of

the Polish nation that was to be reborn. This did not mean lack of allegiance to the United States but rather a demand, growing out of political freedom in this country, that this be utilized for the benefit of Poles in Europe who were still under the yoke of foreign domination. Both in Europe and in America the Poles of the new world were referred to as "the fourth province of Poland," and it was the only province where political agitation for Polish independence could operate without hindrance. Economically it was best able to furnish funds in behalf of the Polish cause. In the freer air of America the Polish National Alliance took the immigrant, often without a well-developed Polish national spirit, and helped to create in him a new patriotic consciousness. As we shall see, this process was tremendously aided by the Polish press in the United States.

Significantly enough, the Alliance was led by the intellectual elite who, as remarked before, enjoyed considerable prestige and respect among the Poles in the homeland for their service in keeping Polish culture viable. In America they continued the same function, had a superior press, and founded a college of their own, Alliance College, at Cambridge Springs, Pennsylvania, in 1912. Their chief newspapers are the *Dziennik Zwiazkowy* (*The Polish Daily Zgoda*) and the weekly *Zgoda* (*Harmony*) which is distributed to all its members throughout the country. By the late 1930's the Alliance was still the largest Polish organization in America, having 300,000 members.

Although something like 90 percent of all the Poles in America are Catholic, so that the membership of the Alliance was overwhelmingly in the church, many clerical leaders were not satisfied with an organization in which the religious element was not pre-eminent. In 1873 an informal federation of parish leaders came together to join their efforts in promoting religious unity among the Poles. They called themselves the Polish Roman Catholic Union. At first the Union failed to thrive and became inactive. A few months after the Alliance started its career in 1880, however, Rev. Vincent Barzynski with several other priests revived the Union at least partly to balance the secular influence of the Alliance. Its purpose, however, was not purely negative; its position aims were to preserve Polish national culture in its religious forms, to keep the integrity of Polish parishes from absorption by the hierarchy, *and to resist a too rapid Americanization of church members* which might result in a neglect of familiar religious usages [italics added].

From the time of the Panna Maria settlement in Texas, there have been Polish agricultural colonies in different parts of the United States, chiefly in the Middle West and New England. Since the Polish farmer had a natural love of the soil, he usually made a marked success in the new environment. Bercovici remarks that second generation Polish youth in the agricultural regions of Michigan, Wisconsin, Minnesota, and Dakota planned to stay on the farms and were attending agricultural schools in large numbers so as to prepare themselves to carry on more efficiently. This situation contrasts with the usual native American pattern of leaving the farm for the city at the earliest opportunity. Furthermore, Polish farmers did not sell their land in times of inflation, believing that the soil would eventually be worth more to them than the money they would receive for it.

Polish farmers have cleared an estimated area of two million acres throughout the United States. Accustomed to back-breaking labor in old Poland, the immigrant came with a willingness to work painstakingly in a manner usually surpassing that of his neighbors. Content at the same time to live on a standard simpler than that of the native American,

he frequently accomplished feats that seemed almost miraculous to those of a different tradition. His success with truck gardening near the large cities appears in the history of a small colony like Florida, New York, where the Poles built up an onion industry unparalleled in that area. Here they have also kept many of the traditional ceremonials and festivals of old Poland. The farmers, for instance, bring their seeds to be blessed in a springtime ceremony at the local Catholic church. Then each family tries to get its seeds planted first. With the 1939 harvest the community began a traditional festival called "The Festival under the Trees," with dancing, feasting, and merrymaking in old colorful peasant costumes.

One of the most striking successes came in New England, where the local farms had been largely exhausted and the flight to the city had seriously depleted the supply of farm labor. A few enterprising landowners discovered that by recruiting Polish laborers they could keep their farms productive because the newcomer was accustomed to hard work and did not make the same demands for easier conditions that the native born often did. Beginning with 1908 more and more Polish immigrants were recruited for such labor. Although at first they were hired help, they soon inferred that the increasing prosperity of the Yankees was due to Polish efforts and thus began to ask themselves the question, "Why not work for ourselves?" With savings they would buy a few acres of unimproved land and by dint of persistent labor bring these scrub areas into cultivation. They soon began to make a success out of crops best adapted to the soil, such as tobacco or onions, both of which require a great deal of individual cultivation. Throughout the Connecticut Valley from 1909 to 1921 the foreign stock (most of which was Polish) increased by 38 percent while the native population remained stationary.

Under these conditions the standard of living changed slowly while the immigrant consolidated his economic forces, increased his holdings, and established a regular relation with the market. By 1929, only one-third of the Polish inhabitants of Sunderland, Massachusetts (a more or less typical community) had attained a plane of living where they used birth control or opposed women and children's working in the fields. But through the years, large areas of New England once counted uninhabitable had been reclaimed by Polish labor.

During the depression of the 1930's, lower prices of farm lands enabled many Polish Americans to escape from the city and its more restrictive form of industrial labor. Using their small savings, they made down payments on farms on Long Island, in New York state, and in New England and worked hard and were satisfied with a fairly low standard of living so long as they could be on their own soil. Soon they were paying off their mortgages and becoming independent. One generalization often made about the Polish American is that he has, more frequently than not, a desire to own land. It appears likely that this applies with more force to the first generation newcomer than to his children, who are brought up in an urban environment and subject to the diversified cultural influences of American life.

The discerning reader will have noticed that the Polonia in America was not a purely Polish institution. It was really an amalgam of Polish Catholic institutions and values on the one hand and American urban, industrial, and democratic conditions on the other. From the very first the Pole had a fierce, even pugnacious love of his new country. So long ago as 1879 Henryk Sienkiewicz wrote that it was dangerous to speak disparagingly of America in the presence of an American Pole. It may be conjectured that the full range of his patriotism and nationalistic

feeling for Poland did not reach its height until it was stimulated by Polish organizations and the press in the United States. From the first, however, the immigrant's cultural heritage was soon reduced to a minimum.

On the other hand, it must not be supposed that this acculturative process was purely one sided. Culture elements from the Polish American community had had silent and largely unrecorded effect on American life as well. The strong religious devotion that the Pole has for his own type of Catholicism has had its influence on American ecclesiastical organization, forcing it to recognize a wider diversity and flexibility in its activities than would otherwise have been the case. The fact that 80 percent of the Polish families in Chicago owned their own homes before the depression of the 1930's and most of them still had these homes afterwards is not without its effect on economic mores. And to take a more trivial example, Cameron claims that after the large influx of Poles to Detroit, they were influential in changing the style of hats from derbies to soft felts. If this can be independently substantiated, it should give American males reason to be unusually thankful for Polish influence!

Since the majority of the first Polish immigrants were unskilled workers in factories, foundries, mines, or construction trades, they naturally came into early contact with the American labor movement. On the whole, except perhaps in the mining areas, they have been somewhat resistant to participation in labor unions. In 1911 it was estimated that out of 300,000 Polish Americans in Michigan, only 5000 had labor union membership, and this is not untypical. Several elements in the background help to account for this: an unsympathetic attitude toward non-Polish organizations, an antipathy toward high dues that would make a cut in personal savings, and the unfriendly attitude of many priests toward labor, which was assumed to have socialistic leanings—all of these had their influence.

In the mining towns, however, where the need for labor solidarity is great, Polish elements have joined other foreign groups to strengthen labor unions. In one area where they predominated, they formed a "singing union" and marched along the valleys to and from work singing Polish songs. Even here loyalty to the labor group is merged with love of Catholicism. In many homes the picture of John Mitchell, head of the United Mine Workers, used to hang on the wall along with pictures of the saints. At a later period the saints shared one wall with President Franklin D. Roosevelt.

Some of the early influences of the slum areas of American communities had their inevitable disorganizing effects on both first and second generation. On the first, the change from a peasant primary community to the impersonal atmosphere of an urban community loosened controls so rapidly that even the Polonia did not offer a sufficient substitute. Znaniecki maintains that the disappearance of the large family, weakness in controlling all aspects of the individual's life and the novelty of American legal standards were most influential in making many families unstable. The loosening of old controls and a new mobility hastened the emancipation of the sexual interest in the direction of promiscuity, while American law, interfering between husband and wife, enabled one or the other to use legal means in a quarrel against the other. Divorce and separation consequently increased.

As for the second generation, the children in America did not always or even frequently engage in common work occupations with the parents as was the custom in Poland. Diversity of occupation brought with it diversity of interest, and a division in the home began. Where the child was closer to American cultural standards and values, as in areas where he attended the public school rather than the parochial, he had to mediate between the parents and the community. This gave the child a sudden authority and dominance quite out of line with usual parental discipline, and the home lost its educational influence. Cut off from this restraining control, children too easily found an outlet in delinquency, which was fairly common in the younger members of the second generation. The girl who was forced to turn over her earnings in Poland understood the reason why: it would eventually be returned to her in the dowry and in the meanwhile the custom was part of life in the cooperative large family. In America the large family disappeared, the tradition of cooperation was often shattered, and assurance of a dowry at the time of marriage became problematical. The increased stimulation of city life also made home and "foreign" culture uninteresting. Since it was possible to have a separate life outside the home, the desire for recognition of "getting even" with parents gave rise to defiant behavior in seeking new experience that was often illicit.

In the meantime those who devoted themselves to the delinquency problem among second generation youth were often forced to put pressure on both the Polonia and the American community. Mrs. Josefa Kudlicka of Buffalo reiterated tirelessly to the native-born Americans that in twenty years not a single *adult* Pole had been arrested there. Most important of all she made the point that the better elements of the native American stock and of the immigrant stock never met each other and hence could not cooperate on any program for dealing with second generation delinquency. Giving a sidelight on the devious ways of acculturation she told of one boy who bragged to her one day, "We're getting Americanized real fast now. D'you hear about the two Polish boys that got arrested for counterfeitin'?

You didn't? Why all they used to get us guys for was stealin' coal. We sure are gettin' somewhere!"

Evidences of the increasing incorporation of American elements into the cultural experience of the second generation were accumulated for a sample of Polish American young people (American born) of eighteen years or over in 1929. In this study Carpenter and Katz showed that their sample group obtained about half their schooling in the parochial and half in the public school. About 70 percent of the youth approved the complete authority of parents over adult children and yet 90 percent asserted that the child should be independent in choosing his vocation. As the investigators assert, "Culture behavior changes more rapidly than rationalized culture attitudes."

Probably the same influence is at work in another response of the younger group, since three-fourths declared themselves in favor of separate Polish community life while only one-fourth maintained that the Poles should spread out and lose their identity in the larger American scene. Fifty-six percent of the group agreed to this statement: "Poles should speak Polish in their homes, subscribe to both Polish and American books, and speak English in their business and daily contacts." On the other hand 37 percent subscribed to the following: "The Poles should speak mostly English, subscribe mostly to American newspapers, read mostly American books, but should retain some Polish from the value it has in maintaining Polish culture and traditions."

Now, twenty years later, would this or a third generation group reverse these percentages? We have no definite study to inform us, but acquaintance with third-generation Poles shows them to come nearer to the second of these two ideals. Even in the 1920's the younger people of Polish descent were not in favor of endogamy; only 10 percent said that a Pole should not marry anyone but another Pole, while 41 percent said there should be no restrictions, provided the individual married a white American or another Pole. The group as a whole were more familiar with American than with Polish history, though 56 percent observed several typical Polish customs.

From the standpoint of group survival, perhaps the most significant of the assimilative factors is the reduction in the size of family and increasing exogamy. In 1935 Stouffer showed that the Catholic birth rate was dropping more rapidly than the non-Catholic. The following year Robinson's study of the birth rate in Polish and Italian colonies indicated that the reproduction rate in the first generation was twice as large as in the second generation. In Robinson's data it appears that the decline among native whites of Polish descent is more rapid than among native-born whites of Polish as a whole. When this tendency is coupled with the trend toward marrying outside the group, it does not take much imagination to conceive the end result or its effect on Polish institutions. The preservation of Polish culture and values today is being carried on largely by older members of the community.

When Paderewski visited the United States during the First World War to obtain funds for the rehabilitation of Poland, he commented ruefully that there were four million Poles in America but not one millionaire. Whether this is true after the Second World War it is difficult to ascertain, but superficial observation leads the onlooker to conclude that the accumulations of great wealth in Polish America probably do not equal those among the Italians, for example.

The lack of a well-established middle class in Poland has already been remarked, as well as the consequent attitude that manual labor has more dignity than commercial occupations. This cultural pattern tends to repeat itself in the United States; as a Polish farmer said of a Polish grocer in Sunderland, Massachusetts: "I don't see why he should work easily and not raise onions and soil his hands as I do and why his wife should sit around on the porch while my wife works in the field."

SUMMARY

The foregoing descriptive analysis by Schermerhorn presents a clear picture of a value system which helped to impede the acculturation of an immigrant group to American society. We stated at the outset of this chapter that our guiding hypothesis, taken from Florence Kluckhohn, was that the rate of assimilation of a group would pivot on the extent to which that group's values fit in with those of the dominant segment of American society. And we also pointed out that in such an analysis the attempt has to be made to determine those values which have been incorporated or internalized in the modal self-system of the group.

The materials by Caudill and de Vos on the Japanese in Chicago (a racially distinct group) clearly illustrate the concept of values-in-personality, and these authors have shown how the original Japanese value system helped to facilitate the assimilation of the Japanese into American society. Correlatively, the portrayal of the Polish immigrant's perception of himself in relation to the world around him—especially his values concerning manual labor, which are so markedly in conflict with the normative American values in this sphere—help us to understand some of the personality factors which inhibit or retard acculturation to a "host" society.

It is often possible to find a clue to the modal self-system in a group through an examination of its religious orientations. The dominant religious motif in the American middle class appears to revolve around the "Protestant ethic," a value system in which is found, among other things, a strong individualistic orientation, a high premium put on personal effort and individual validation of status, and a strong sense of personal responsibility in religious as well as secular affairs. The Polish church, as Schermerhorn observed, was authoritarian to an extreme degree, and the long history of the peasants' relationship to that church obstructed the development of techniques for personal and flexible adaptations to new sociocultural exigencies.

Another facet of the problem of assimilation and acculturation is to be found in a group's family organization and the latter's contribution to the development of a particular kind of self-system. It will be recalled that William Henry noted, in his analysis of middle-class executives, in Chapter 7, that success and upward mobility in American industrial bureaucracy depend to a large extent on a man's ability to maintain a strong psychological identification with his father. The issues involved in the development and maintenance of this identification are numerous and complex. But from a *sociological* point of view it can be hypothesized that the ability to develop such an identification depends to a large degree on the structure of the family in relation to the total community. Where the emotional investments of the growing individual are concentrated principally within the nuclear family, there exists the potentiality for a strong identification with the parent of the same sex. Where the emotional investments of the growing individual are diffused outside the nuclear family, it can be hypothesized that a strong emotional identification with the parent of the same sex would be difficult to establish. In the first instance, which the Japanese approximate, there is generally one adult male who serves as the ego-ideal or model for the growing child; in the second instance, more characteristic of the Polish peasant, there are many adult males who serve as ego-ideals, the identification with no one of them being as intense as in the first instance. (There are, of course, other social-structural factors which affect this identification, such as the isolation of the family, matrilineal descent, and the like. But such factors do not appear to be as relevant to the Japanese and Polish situations as the family's size and position within the community.) If this hypothesis has any merit or validity, then we could go on to speculate that *one* of the factors involved in the successful assimilation of the Japanese is their possession of the kind of identification-pattern which appears to be necessary for success in American industrial society; by similar token, it can be hypothesized that *one* of the factors involved in the less successful acculturation of the Poles was a wanting pattern of identification which appears necessary for success in this technological social system.

The materials which we have considered in this chapter give us an opportunity to observe another application of some principles discussed in other connections. We saw in Chapter 3 that in order for parents to be able to transmit a set of values to their children they must not only have access to those values but they must have themselves experienced some measure of success with them. The Japanese, having experienced and lived with these values in Japan, had little difficulty in applying and making use of them in the United States; this, in turn, enabled them to achieve the social status which would give them continued access to these values and to transmit them to their children. The Poles, on the other hand, had not experienced these values in their home society and thus could not make effective use of them in the "host" society; largely because of this, they were unable to acquire the kinds of occupational and other positions which are commonly associated with middle-class status. This, in turn, helped to block their access to middle-class values and their transmission of these values to their children.

BIBLIOGRAPHY AND SUGGESTED READINGS

Belshaw, Cyril S. "The Identification of Values in Anthropology," *American Journal of Sociology,* Vol. *64,* pp. 555-562. A review of different conceptualizations of values in anthropological writings.

Gillin, John. "National and Regional Cultural Values in the United States," *Social Forces,* Vol. *34,* pp. 107-113, 1955. A listing of the major value-orientations in the United States and their distributions through six culture-areas in contemporary American society.

Keesing, Felix. *Culture Change: An Analysis and Bibliography of Anthropo-*

logical Sources to 1952. An extremely important source book for research involving any aspect of culture change and acculturation.

Kluckhohn, Clyde. "Values and Value-Orientations in the Theory of Action: An Exploration in Definition and Classification," in *Toward a General Theory of Action,* edited by Talcott Parsons and Edward A Shils, pp. 388-433. Cambridge, Massachusetts: Harvard, 1954.

Kluckhohn, Florence. "Dominant and Variant Value Orientations," in *Personality in Nature, Society and Culture,* edited by C. Kluckhohn *et al.,* pp. 342-357. New York: Knopf, 1955.

Shuval, Judith T. "The Role of Ideology as a Predisposing Frame of Reference for Immigrants," *Human Relations,* Vol. *12,* pp. 51-63, 1959. A Study of immigrants to Israel; important more from a methodological point of view than for its contribution to the personality factors involved in successful assimilation.

Thomas, William I. and Florian Znaniecki. *The Polish Peasant in Europe and America.* New York: Knopf, 1927.

Worsley, Peter. *The Trumpet Shall Sound: A Study of "Cargo" Cults in Melanesia.* London: MacGibbon and Kee, 1957. An excellent survey of the literature on an exotic form of culture change which has generally suffered considerable neglect from a personality point of view.

Yinger, Milton. *Religion, Society and the Individual.* New York: Macmillan, 1957. Especially the sections on religion and social change.

Chapter 14

VALUES IN PERSONALITY:
NATURE'S EXPERIMENTS

In this chapter, the discussion of personality and sociocultural change is to be continued. This time, however, the problem will be studied from the point of view of total societies which come into contact with each other; in the previous chapter, we considered situations in which very small segments or fractions of one society enter another society and have to adapt to the latter's dominant value system. Our point of departure in the present chapter will be a slight but important contrast between two hypotheses, and each of the two studies which will be read is devoted to a demonstration of its respective hypothesis.

In the first paper, Hallowell offers the hypothesis that under conditions of acculturation ". . . the modal personality structure of a society would be expected to persist until conditions arose that *enforced* some change," and he presents data from the Ojibwa Indians in support of his contention. In the second selection of this chapter, however, we will read a condensation of Spindler's study of acculturation among the Menomini Indians where a complete personality reformulation has taken place at certain levels of the population. Spindler suggests that the reason for the difference between the Ojibwa and the Menomini is that "certain conditions must exist among the Menomini that do not exist among the Ojibwa, or among other American Indian populations so far studied. . . . When conditions are created that make it possible to identify with (to internalize) the values of the dominant population—and when those conditions contain means to attainment of those values as well as the possibilities of identification with them—then a successful psychological adaptation to the demands of those values may occur."

(We are presenting these contrasting points of view in order to illustrate the great necessity for specifying the actual sociological conditions under which psychological phenomena appear. Hallowell's original research was carried out several years before Spindler's. Since the latter's report of his findings, Hallowell has completely accepted the conclusions of the Menomini study.[1] In other words, while there may be a slight conflict of hypotheses as they are presented here, the proponents of the two points of view are in agreement today.)

The comparison of the Ojibwa and Menomini Indians with respect to acculturation indeed comprises an experiment in and by nature. First of all, both societies shared a similar aboriginal culture, coming into contact with Western culture at

---

[1] Personal communication.

about the same time. Both are part of the Northeastern Woodlands culture area, and Hallowell has been able to reconstruct the modal personality structure of the peoples living in this area during aboriginal times.[2] Second, both Hallowell and Spindler employed the same instruments of investigation—standard ethnographic procedures and projective tests, such as the Rorschach.

The validity of using the Rorschach Test as a research instrument among non-Western peoples is still open to debate among anthropologists as well as psychologists. However, we can avoid this debate entirely if we view the Rorschach in the following manner: The blots on the ten Rorschach cards are constant and standard stimuli. They are presented to Ojibwa and Menomini Indians; these are people who have shared a similar cultural heritage for several hundred years as well as, according to Hallowell's reconstruction, a modal personality structure in their aboriginal states. Thus, they are comparable groups. They have both come under the impact of Western culture and, as will be seen, have tended to respond culturally (with some exceptions) in much the same fashion. Therefore, instead of viewing the Rorschach Test in the usual fashion of being a psychological diagnostic procedure, let us think of the test in these two studies as a constant "X" factor or stimulus presented to two highly similar groups. In seeking to learn how they respond to this constant "X," we can attempt to see how and why they respond similarly and how and why —that is, under what conditions—they respond differently.

Anticipating some of the data and conclusions of this chapter, we shall see that many Ojibwa and Menomini Indians respond similarly to these constant "X" stimuli. At one point, however, two small groups of Menomini Indians respond to these constant stimuli differently from all other Menomini groups and differently from all the Ojibwa groups. The two "atypical" Menomini groups live under social-structural conditions sufficiently different from all the other groups to make their divergence easily understandable.

OJIBWA PERSONALITY AND ACCULTURATION *

By A. Irving Hallowell

In recent years anthropologists have devoted increasing attention to problems of acculturation, or contact between peoples with different modes of life. The cultural consequences of such contacts have been found to be highly variable and often unpredictable. Cultural changes may range all the way from the adoption, by one people, of a few borrowed traits which they easily fit into their own pattern of life, through cases where whole areas of a traditional culture pattern have been

---

[2] Hallowell, 1946.

* Reprinted with abridgment from *Acculturation in the Americas: Proceedings and Selected Papers of the XXIXth International Congress of Americanists,* edited by Sol Tax, pp. 105-112, by permission of The University of Chicago Press. Copyright 1952 by The University of Chicago.

affected, to those instances in which a sweeping transformation in the life of one people have resulted from their intimate contact with another.

So far, much more attention has been paid to *what* has happened than to the acculturation process itself. The latter, of course, is exceedingly complex, since it involves all the various readjustments in the habits, attitudes, goals, and motivations of the individuals through whom the novel cultural patterns that emerge are mediated. For if there were no personal readjustments in the lives of the people concerned, there would be no subsequent changes observable in the culture pattern of any group. Consequently, one of the crucial questions is the nature, character, and psychological depth of such readjustments. A comprehensive understanding of the acculturation process, therefore, demands an approach that is psychologically, as well as culturally, oriented. Yet so far even the most obvious psychological aspects of acculturation have received but scanty attention.

If we pursue our inquiries into the psychology of acculturation still further, however, we are faced with another type of problem. This further problem naturally arises out of the recent studies whose major focus has been the relations between culture and personality structure. If contact between peoples with different modes of life may sometimes be the source of basic cultural changes, it seems reasonable to inquire whether, as a result of the same set of readjustments, a parallel reconstellation occurs in the typical psychological characteristics of the people so affected. In other words, are changes in the modal or typical personality organization of the individuals of a society a necessary and intrinsic part of the readjustments that acculturation implies, or can acculturation take place under certain conditions without radical changes in personality structure?

In the first place, it is obvious that we cannot initiate an inquiry of this sort by asking: What are the incentives to personality change? We cannot go out and investigate this question in the same way that we might study the conditions that led to the borrowing of new types of tools or motivated people to acquire a new language or attend the local mission.

Indeed, we may better ask ourselves why the structural basis of the personality should undergo a change at all, so long as individuals can manage to get along without any such change. Furthermore, if the set of personality structure in man is acquired and stabilized early in life and is not under conscious control, we can hardly adopt the hypothesis that changes in personality organization throughout a society would be among the earliest effects of acculturation. In fact, it is hard to imagine how a psychological change of this order could be brought about in less than three generations. Therefore, it seems reasonable to conclude that personality structure, once established, is highly resistant to change. If this is so, then one of our fundamental hypotheses might be that the modal personality structure of a society would be expected to persist until conditions arose that *enforced* some change.

Thus, while all acculturation may be said to involve some psychological readjustment in the sense that, among other things, new habits must be learned or new attitudes or values acquired, there is no reason to assume that such readjustments *in themselves* involve the psychological core of the personality. Surely iron tools may be substituted for those made of stone, or guns replace bows and arrows, or pidgin English be learned, without any effect upon the personality organization. Let us say, then, that the culture of one group of people may be influenced by that of another in *some* respects without the people of the borrowing group undergoing any necessary change in personality organization.

The crucial question is how far can one language displace another, a new world-view or new religion be acquired, moral values be reconstituted, and sweeping changes in technological and material culture take place without deep and penetrating psychological effects? Certainly the polar case would be one in which people *A* in intimate contact with people *B* had been so transformed in their mode of life that they were culturally indistinguishable from *B*. In such an instance we might well infer that in modal personality structure they were likewise the equivalent of *B*.

But in any actual study of acculturated groups this is hardly the situation. What we are usually faced with concretely are differential effects of acculturation processes. This is what complicates the psychological problem and even makes it difficult to compare one acculturated group with another. Especially where there have been continuous contacts over a long period of time, as in the case of the North American Indians and Euro-Americans, varying levels of acculturation are discernible not only in different tribal groups with different cultural backgrounds but among peoples belonging to the same ethnic unit who once shared the same aboriginal culture. Although we have not developed precise measures of acculturation to compare one group with another, nevertheless, it is possible to distinguish roughly between different levels of acculturation. This is particularly the case in those instances where we know what the native culture was like and where it is apparent that the source of acculturation was Western civilization in its most recent and familiar phases.

The Ojibwa Indians, a food-gathering people originally and now living in communities scattered over a considerable geographical area, represent an ethnic group with a common cultural background but now exhibit varying levels of acculturation. None, of course, live in a purely aboriginal state and few if any have been completely assimilated to Western culture, although some of the Ojibwa in the Province of Ontario closely approximate this situation. In between these extremes four levels of acculturation can be distinguished, on a more or less impressionistic basis, for the purpose of further discussion.

Level 1. The Ojibwa of certain parts of Western Ontario (Canada), *e.g.,* Deer Lake, Sandy Lake, etc. They represent the *least* acculturated groups about which I have any knowledge. No one has studied them, but even the Berens River Indians thought them "primitive."

Level 2. The Inland Ojibwa (Saulteaux) of the Berens River (Canada), whom I first visited in 1932. Some of these Indians are not Christianized and speak no English.

Level 3. The Lakeside Indians of the Berens River. These people are Christianized; they use no aboriginal dwellings, and no former rites or ceremonies persist. As contrasted with the Inland group, no drum is ever heard in this community. Some speak English. About 20 percent are mixed white and Indian.

Level 4. The Lac du Flambeau Ojibwa (Northern Wisconsin). About 80 percent are mixed white and Indian. Practically all of them speak English; the children attend an excellent government school; some have radios, etc. This group was in close contact with whites during the lumbering period in Wisconsin and today their reservation is in the midst of a summer tourist area. Nevertheless, a small group still cling to the Midewiwin [Medicine Lodge].

What have been the psychological effects of acculturation upon the Ojibwa? In what respects are they similar to or different from their aboriginal ancestors? Has there been a complete psychological break with the past at one of these levels of acculturation, or is there a demonstrable psychological continuity in personality structure? Is it possible that the psychological readjustments that the acculturation process, or certain stages of it, imply can take place without any radical change in the personality organization of the people involved? If there are modifications, what is their nature? How is the actual behavior of these people affected?

One of the intrinsic difficulties in answering such questions has been the necessity of obtaining the kind of personality data that furnishes a reliable collective picture of a group of individuals, or segments of such a group (men, women, children), as well as data on intragroup variability. In my studies I have found such projective techniques as the Rorschach and TAT to be highly useful instruments. They provide independent psychological data with which other types of observation may be correlated.

Another methodological difficulty has been the necessity of establishing some kind of psychological base line from which changes in personality organization can be measured. Suppose we do manage to obtain reliable information on the modal personality structure of a group of acculturated Indians. How can we tell whether this psychological picture is a function of some stage in the acculturation process or whether it represents the persistence of the same personality organization that was characteristic of people of this ethnic group before acculturation took place? In short, how can we infer change, or continuity, or modification in personality structure without a psychological base line that represents either the precontact period or its nearest equivalent?

In my studies of the Ojibwa during the past few years, I have attacked the problems mentioned by taking the following steps:

(a) In order to obtain some kind of psychological base line from which subsequent changes could be measured, the accounts of observers who had intimate contacts with the Indians of the Eastern Woodlands in the seventeenth and eighteenth centuries were examined. A generalized characterological picture was pieced together which seemed to make psychological sense. Briefly stated, the psychological picture that emerged was that of a people among whom emotional restraint, stoicism, fortitude under torture, the inhibition of all expression of aggression in interpersonal relations, a culturally demanded amiability and mildness in the face of provocation to anger, and suppression of all open criticism of one's fellows are typical characteristics. The whole psychological picture is one that suggests a suffusion in anxiety—anxiety lest one fail to maintain the standard of fortitude required no matter what the hardship one must endure, anxiety lest one provoke resentment or anger in others. This pattern of inhibition was coexistent with an absence of superordinate authority, and, despite the minimal power of chiefs, open conflicts were rare. But *covert* slander was a constant expression of the inhibited aggressive impulses. There was also an institutionalized means of covert aggression—sorcery.

Since there were no highly institutionalized agencies of reward and punishment, individuals functioned in terms of a highly internalized conscience. It is an introverted picture, with individuals highly sensitive to others and friendly only in a reserved way, for they are always wary of the powers of others that may menace them through witchcraft. Any fancied rebuff could be taken as a slight. With so little real give and take on an open, confident, and genuinely friendly basis, there was a high degree of projection in interpersonal relations.

(b) Field work over a period of

years among the Ojibwa of the Berens River, buttressed by the collection and interpretation of a sample of 151 Rorschach records (102 adults, 49 children) was made the basis of a personality characterization of these Indians. The results were similar to those derived from a study of the records of the earlier observers mentioned. There was no evidence to suggest that the levels of acculturation (2 and 3) reached by these Indians had affected the most typical aspects of their personality organization. As already pointed out, however, a cultural gradient was observed among these groups. The Indians who lived close to Lake Winnipeg (the Lakeside group) and who were more closely and continuously in contact with whites were *more* acculturated than the Indians one hundred to two hundred miles up the river (Inland group).

(c) Because of these observable cultural differences, the next step was to inquire whether there were any concomitant psychological differences between these two groups (Levels 2 and 3). For this purpose a detailed analysis and comparison of the Rorschach protocols of the adults of the two groups was made. Certain differences were clearly discernible. The Lakeside Indians made their responses much faster than the Inland Indians, thus approaching closer to white norms. Some of the Lakeside Indians also showed signs of developing a much more extroverted adjustment, as contrasted with the quite generalized introverted picture presented by their Inland kinsmen. . . . But the personality core in both groups is the same. No radical psychological shift has occurred. There is an essential continuity in personality organization, with some modifications. What is particularly significant, however, is that the nature of some of these modifications indicated that some serious, if not actually neurotic, strains were developing within the personality structure.

On the basis of the steps taken up to this point it seems reasonable to infer (1) that the personality structure of the Berens River Indians, considered as a whole, approximates, if it is not fully identical with, an aboriginal type of modal personality structure which was characteristic not only of the Ojibwa but of other Indians of the Eastern Woodlands; (2) that a considerable degree of acculturation could occur (*i.e.*, up through Level 3) without any radical change in this personality structure; (3) that in the most highly acculturated group thus far examined the readjustment demanded in the acculturation process did produce stresses and strains that were leading to certain modifications in the modal personality structure; and (4) that, while some individuals, especially women, were making an excellent social and psychological adjustment, there were other individuals, men in particular, who were much less successful.

(d) The last step of interest here is an investigation that was undertaken in the summer of 1946 among the Ojibwa of Lac du Flambeau in northern Wisconsin. On a brief visit to this reservation during the previous summer I was much impressed with the extent to which their mode of life had been affected by acculturation. The Berens River Indians seemed positively aboriginal by comparison, and, in talking with some of the older men at Flambeau, I found that I had seen some of the things that they knew about only by hearsay. As a consequence of these impressions the investigation referred to was initiated. It must be confessed that I anticipated results quite contrary to those being expounded here. At that time I expected that the Flambeau Indians would exhibit a radically different personality picture from that of the northern Ojibwa, somehow skewed in the direction of white Americans. . . .

William Caudill, who collected TAT material on children, recently published a summary of his results. His major conclusion is that these Flambeau children exhibit the same *basic* type of characterological structure as the less acculturated Ojibwa just described. Caudill's conclusion is of special interest because the data pertain to children six to sixteen years of age, rather than adults. One might have thought that these children, many of whom do not speak and scarcely understand Ojibwa, would *not* exhibit a typically Indian pattern.

Parallel Rorschach data on the Flambeau children collected by Mrs. Blanche Watrous support the conclusions of Mr. Caudill. The conclusions of Mrs. Watrous, moreover, are based on a precise comparison with the series of protocols of Berens River children which I had previously collected. She established the significance of the similarities and differences that appeared at the successive age levels studied in terms of approved mathematical devices.

These two studies of the Flambeau children, along with the data already cited, furnish a considerable body of evidence that all points in the same direction —a persistent core of psychological characteristics sufficient to identify an Ojibwa personality constellation, aboriginal in origin, that is clearly discernible through all levels of acculturation yet studied. For this reason all the Ojibwa referred to are still Indians in a psychological sense, whatever clothes they wear, whatever their occupation, whether they speak English or not, and regardless of race mixture. While, culturally speaking, they appear more and more like whites at "higher" levels of acculturation, there is no evidence at all for a basic psychological shift in a parallel direction. Thus terms like "borrowing" and "diffusion" which are entirely appropriate to describe the

acculturation process in a cultural frame of reference are misleading and inappropriate if the acculturation process is viewed from the standpoint of a psychological frame of reference. At least in the situation described, no identifiable constellation of psychological "traits" has been "borrowed" by the Ojibwa or "diffused" to them as a result of their contacts with whites.

All the evidence points to far more complicated psychological processes than those which have led to the acquisition of the culture traits which I have used as empirical guides to different levels of acculturation. Consequently, descriptive facts of this order are no direct index to facts pertaining to personality adjustment and personality organization.

Perhaps I can best indicate the nature of this more complex psychological problem by clarifying another fundamental point in the data. While these show, as I have said, the persistence of an aboriginal character structure among the Ojibwa, this must not be interpreted to mean that no psychological modifications have been produced in the acculturation process. Actually, quite the contrary is true. Personality structure is a dynamic construct, not a substantive one. When the data at hand are viewed in terms of the actual life-adjustments which individuals have been making, the nature and dynamics of these modifications are fairly clear, although all the evidence is not yet assembled. But it is a striking fact that all through the Rorschach data there are common trends. These are evident whether we compare the Lakeside Indians with the Inland Indians of the Berens River, or the Flambeau children as a whole with the northern children, or the Flambeau adults with the Berens River adults. The impression one receives is of a personality structure which, under the varying pressures of acculturation in the two localities, is being pushed to the limits of its functional adequacy. If, for example, we compare the Indians of Level 2 (Inland group in the Berens River) with those of Level 4 (Flambeau), we obtain a psychological picture in which the latter represent a *regressive* version of the northern group. Many psychological characteristics which in the north bear a positive relation to the adjustment of the individual have been exaggerated to a point where they assume a negative role at Flambeau. The general introverted balance in the north, for instance, is fully integrated with the belief system and other aspects of the old culture. An even greater withdrawal may appear in individuals at Flambeau under conditions where such an adjustment has a negative effect.

What seems to have happened is that the acculturation process at Flambeau has generated a situation in which the personality structure is breaking down, rather than undergoing reintegration on any new or positive level. The individual has been thrown back on his psychological heels, so to speak. He lacks the cultural fulcrum which is necessary for full psychological maturity in any society. The situation might be characterized as one in which there is a frustration of maturity. From the northern Rorschach data we can see what the steps in this process of psychological maturity are. At Flambeau it is a striking fact that the protocols of adults are so much like those of the children. This means that regressive trends in their personality structure make an optimum adjustment impossible under the conditions that now confront them. In this respect they are the antithesis of the Inland group on the Berens River, who are quite well adjusted on the whole. The over-all picture at Flambeau is one that indicates a paucity of internally integrated psychological resources. In the old culture this was largely achieved through the psycho-

logical support offered by an aboriginal type of religious belief, which laid a prime emphasis on self-reliance through direct supernatural aid. There has been no real substitute for this in a superficially acquired Christianity. Perhaps this explains why even now a few Indians at Flambeau cling to the Midewiwin, which epitomizes this aboriginal outlook.

The old Ojibwa character was also built on a psychological foundation which required a maximum of *inner* control, since, from the standpoint of their social organization, highly institutionalized outer controls and sanctions were practically absent. This psychological feature of the Ojibwa is also at the basis of the so-called "social atomism" of their aboriginal society. While this inner control is still present, it has been modified in a regressive direction so that it easily breaks down. In actual behavior evidence of this is to be seen in the tremendous incidence of drunkenness and juvenile delinquency on the Flambeau Reservation. Such behavior may also be interpreted as a sign of the terrific psychological struggle which many individuals are experiencing in reacting to the apathy which the paucity of inner resources, brought about by the regression I have spoken of, produces. They are attempting to survive in a situation which, as yet, offers them no culturally defined values and goals that they have really made their own and which have become psychologically significant for them. Their advanced stage of acculturation as externally viewed is thus deceptive. From a psychological point of view they are not yet *acculturated enough*, in the sense that, while contact with the version of Western civilization available has enabled them to acquire innumerable culture traits, so far at least it has not provided the psychological means that might implement a satisfactory basis for personal adjustment.

Now let us turn to Spindler's analysis of acculturation and personality among the Menomini Indians. This study is presented in considerably greater detail than Hallowell's, and it will serve several functions for us. First, of course, it will give us more insight than any other study conducted thus far into the relationship between the social-structural conditions of acculturation and the processes of psychological functioning. Second, Spindler's study portrays in very fine detail some of the ways in which the Rorschach test can be used in the study of institutions, whether it is used as a diagnostic instrument or whether it is viewed as a constant "X" stimulus presented to comparable groups. Third, in the course of attempting to describe a psychological continuum parallelling a social-structural continuum in a society undergoing acculturation, we can also see many of the ways in which personality processes are relevant to, or "fit" into, social-structural and cultural categories.

It should be pointed out before proceeding that while Spindler's groups are small, sometimes numbering only about a dozen persons, and although his findings are not derived from the most solid statistical results, his conclusions are more than plausible, internally consistent, and in line with other social-scientific bodies of knowledge.

MENOMINI ACCULTURATION *

By George D. Spindler

This is a study of sociocultural and psychological adaptation on the part of a contemporary native population to the conditions of life created by the impact of Western civilization. It attempts to demonstrate the relationships existing between these two processes in an acculturating American Indian tribe, the Menomini of Wisconsin, which has been subjected to three hundred years of Western influence. This tribe has been selected for study because special circumstances existing in the reserve have made successful achievement in terms of Western values possible for some of its members, while others have clung to an essentially native-oriented way of life, and still others have been unable to accept either form of adaptation.

The continuum of sociocultural adaptation represented within this population thus ranges from a native-oriented group still clinging to much of the aboriginal pattern of life, to a sociopolitical reservation elite who approach most closely a middle-class American culture type. This continuum has been divided, for research purposes, into five segments that represent four levels of adaptation to the impact of Western culture: (1) the native-oriented group, in which the Medicine Lodge and Dream Dance organizations are maintained, and patterns of life from the aboriginal culture survive to the greatest extent; (2) the Peyote Cult group, in which the members have found a special solution to the strains created by the adaptive process; (3) the transi-

* Excerpted from *Sociocultural and Psychological Processes in Menomini Acculturation,* by George D. Spindler, University of California Publications in Culture and Society, Vol. 5., University of California Press, 1955. Dr. Spindler graciously checked this excerpt, and has made some editorial changes in the text.

tionals, who have had experience with both native and western-oriented religious groups but who maintain clear-cut identifications with neither, and in general indicate that they are culturally and socially suspended between two ways of life; (4) a category of persons who appear to have adopted a thoroughly Western way of life but who do not occupy a high position in the occupational or power structure of the reservation; (5) a category of persons who approximate an American middle-class pattern of life, and who receive the occupational, monetary, and prestige rewards available in the reservation community in the greatest degree.

A sample of persons representing each of these segments has been given the Rorschach personality test. The distribution of scores and patterns for each segment of the continuum has been compared with that of every other segment in order to discover what differences may exist. These differences have been given psychological meaning with the use of interpretive hypotheses standardized in Western clinics and experimental situations. The psychological adaptations thus revealed and related to the sociocultural positions on the continuum have been placed in context with data gained by participant observation. A control group of whites living and working on the reservation has been used.

The study has thus focused on a limited aspect of the acculturation process and builds upon the model provided by Hallowell's research on the Ojibwa. It reveals that there is a definable personality type characteristic of the least acculturated group which is appropriate to the patterning of the old culture as it survives in the present and extends back into the past. It also reveals that this personality type resembles that of the Ojibwa, with whom the Menomini share a cultural fundament. It further shows that significant changes away from this psychologi-

cal base line have occurred in the transitional segments of the continuum, and that these changes appear to represent a breakdown of the native-oriented personality structure. Lastly, the study indicates that the Rorschach patterns most characteristic of the elite acculturated segment suggest that a reformulation of personality has occurred here which clearly departs from that of the native-oriented extreme of the continuum of sociocultural adaptation.

SOCIOCULTURAL DIMENSIONS

The aboriginal Menomini culture was based upon an essentially hunting and gathering subsistence with modifications due to the use of maritime resources, including wild rice, and the presence of rudimentary horticulture. The material culture was moderately elaborate, and typical of the Woodlands. The sociopolitical structure gives some evidence of elaborations in moiety, phratry, and lineage groupings with hereditary chieftainships, but was changed drastically by the impact of the fur trade and colonial wars. Interpersonal relationships at a direct level were apparently characterized by controls on overt aggressive actions and avoidance of antagonism-arousing situations. The system of beliefs concerning the supernatural was fairly complex, but the fundamental relationships between man and the supernatural were mediated by individual power-gaining and dreams. Elaborations were introduced in the postcontact period by the development of ceremonial organizations. Witchcraft activities were formalized and probably acted as another means of social control. There was an elaborate mythology with thematic emphases on individual power given by supernatural forces, the loss of that power, the miracle-producing buffoon, and the valued characteristics of the good man—one who was brave, but prudent, quiet, and modest. Child training emphasized the development of constraint and self-control with consistent reward for desired behavior and sanctions against aggressive behavior by parents toward children. The language was characterized by a softening of declaratory decisiveness.

The culture described here represents a nondated construct taken in part from historical accounts written during the period of early contact, and in part from the ethnographies produced by men who knew the Menomini during the earlier part of the reservation period when much of the native culture was still intact. Its outlines still exist today among the least acculturated Menomini group, but in greatly modified form.

The reservation area and its resources, and the population, economy, educational system, and sociopolitical structure of the modern Menomini community have occupational and economic opportunities afforded by the lumbering industry which make possible an unusually successful degree of adaptation to the value system of Western society, and the contributions of other subsistence activities are of secondary importance. In political action, it appears that a radical-conservative cycle occurs and that aggressive leadership capitalizes on a reservoir of general dissatisfaction and hostility that seems to be available in the mass of transitionals. The following is concluded in respect to social structure: (1) the symbolic representation of status is on the same socioeconomic basis as in the "outside" society and the elite sociocultural category represents this system of symbols most successfully; (2) the lower-status acculturated share some value orientation with the elite acculturated but are only marginally associated with the latter's groups and cliques; (3) the transitional category as a whole is not clearly defined by group identification, and, in this respect, appears to constitute a "mass"; and (4) the Peyote Cult is a defined group, unlike the rest of the transitionals; (5) the Medicine Lodge-Dream Dance group is also sharply defined and occupies low socioeconomic status in terms of the dominant criteria within the reservation community.

The Medicine Lodge-Dream Dance group furnishes continuity between the old and the modern Menomini ways of life, however much the patterns of behavior in this group may represent modifications of the aboriginal culture. This group is, indeed, native-oriented.

One of the factors complicating adequate description and analysis of the contemporary way of life of the native-oriented group is that the present culture of this remnant is not simply the result of assimilation of elements of Western culture. The way of life of these people is structurally modified Menomini, but the elements of which it is composed are in significant part shared with contemporary native-oriented enclaves in other tribes. And this significant part in turn is composed of both an indigenous Algonkian core of long standing and what can be best described as a "pan-Indian" cultural development in all of North America, but particularly in the North Central states.

Continuity between the aboriginal way of life and that of the Medicine Lodge-Dream Dance group can be demonstrated but much cultural disintegration, as well as amalgamation, has occurred. Except in specific patterns of language, certain characteristics of ceremonial structure and behavior, and some aspects of religious belief, there is little that distinguishes this conservative element of the contemporary Menomini from similar segments of other tribes of the area. The basic orientations of man to the supernatural, as well as the values mediating direct interpersonal relationships, survive most strongly, though modified in form. The first is represented in the attitude of dependence upon power received from supernatural agencies for accomplishment or faliure in the acts of life. The acceptance of fate—of the inevitability of whatever happens—is corollary to this. The second is expressed in the careful aggression-limiting constraints imposed upon interpersonal relations, in the self-control, humility, and concern for others held up as ideals by the elders in their public exhortations, in the interpretation of these same values in admonishment and practice in child training, and even in the structure of the language. These two general orientations may be considered as themes characterizing the present culture of the native-oriented group. These themes, in all of their various expressions and together with the economic, occupational and other objective aspects, constitute the conditions of life to which the members of this group adapt. The effect of this adaptation upon the personality structure will be analyzed when the Rorschach data are discussed.

The Peyote Cult personnel earn their livelihood by working in the mill or forest, in eleven cases, and by hunting and fishing, as well as gathering and cutting ferns and greens, in two cases. Of the eleven who work for wages, seven are regularly employed at semiskilled or unskilled labor, and four are only occasionally employed in these same capacities. The cash income is less than $2,000 per year for all but one man, whose total family income is higher ($2,500 to $3,000) owing to the successful operation of a small roadside stand. Most members of this group, and their families, work in the cherry orchards and potato fields outside the reservation during the late summer and early fall. The economic activities of the Medicine Lodge-Dream Dance and Peyote Cult groups are not different, except that a few more persons in the latter category are committed to a wage economy, and a few less to hunting, gathering, and handicraft.

This cult body does not constitute a living group of the same sort as the Medicine Lodge-Dream Dance membership. Its members are drawn from a fairly diverse population of transitional character with varying degrees of experience and identification with native and Catholic religious institutions. They are likewise a group of less definite locale, though the meetings are all held at the homes of the members near Zoar. They derive their unity from their cult identification.

The ultimate declared purpose in taking peyote is to acquire the power with which it has been invested by the Great Spirit. This power cannot be obtained by merely consuming peyote. It comes to one only when the person approaches it in a proper spirit of humility and after long preoccupation and concentration. If the person is "filled with sin," the medicine will only make him ill, but once Peyote power is acquired, it will enable him to do wondrous things and serves to protect him from evil, including sorcery. The humility of approach and concentration for the purpose of attaining power is very reminiscent of the native orientation, but this humility among the Peyotists is accompanied by declarations of worthlessness. Likewise, the intense concentration during the meeting—each individual turned in upon himself with the aid of the narcotic and the fire into which he stares—is not only concentration upon the nature of the power to come to him or upon the spirits of heaven, but also upon the personal self and its conflicts.

The atmosphere during the first half of the meetings is serious, intense but quiet. Toward midnight, however, the voices become more emotional, and the drumming more rapid. The songs become a cry for help. The prayers become a plea for salvation, for aid and relief from manifest doubts, fears, and guilt feelings.

The atmosphere then becomes something very different than that found in the Medicine Lodge or Dream Dance. The constraints break down and the individual throws himself upon the mercy of the Saviour and the power of Peyote in a manner that parallels, though does not duplicate, the behaviors displayed in revivalist meetings in white society. Men pray aloud, give testimonials at certain periods in the ceremony, and frequently break into tears. But even though the atmosphere is intense and deep emotions are stirred, the ceremony is conducted with solemnity, and the members, who remain throughout it all in their places, treat each other with marked consideration and courtesy.

Each man seeks his revelations and salvation, and gains power individually. There can be, it is claimed, no instruction in the Peyote way; this must come to the individual through his own experience in meetings. It is the Indian's own religion and was here "before Columbus," and must be learned the "Indian way," it is said. Much of this instruction is gained in visions, and some in dreams. These instructions are sometimes very detailed but more often highly symbolic, and can be interpreted only after long study and discussion with other more experienced and dedicated members. But all members are aided in their striving for revelations, knowledge, and "cleansing of sins" by the efforts of the group in concert—through collective and individual prayers, singing and drumming, and the maintenance of a sacred atmosphere during the meeting.

Of all the esoteric aspects of Peyotism, that of visions has received the most attention. Full-blown visions with complete visual imagery are not too frequently experienced. Some of the members stated that they could remember only three or four in years of participation. Three claimed they had them nearly every meeting. Thirty-nine verbatim statements of visions were collected, and every member contributed at least one. These were all events of significance to the individual and given with great care and detail.

Visions are a significant and striking aspect of the cult behavior, but the curative function of Peyote is probably more important to the participant, and visions are frequently simply a part of such curing. To the members, "curing" includes not only relief from or elimination of bodily ills, but therapy for despondency and anxiety, a means of absolution of sins, and a process of salvation.

The Peyote Cult represents a systematic deviation that distinguishes its members from the amorphous and unorganized mass of transitionals that have few, if any, clear-cut group identifications, and from the groups at the extremes of the sociocultural continuum that have accepted an ordered but quite different form of adaptation to the conditions of life created by the impact of Western civilization upon Menomini culture. The cult is clearly deviant, from the viewpoint of all other groups in the reservation community. It has a high degree of visibility in this community, and the members are very self-conscious about their identity. It is systematic, because rapport has developed between the deviants, and a content of rationalizations for the deviation is held in common. The culture conflict experienced by all transitional personnel has been resolved for these persons in a way that has been formalized and institutionalized, and is supported and expressed in a shared set of symbols, roles, and behavior patterns. In these respects, it is fundamentally no different in function or origin than the religious sects that proliferated on the American frontier during the nineteenth century, and exhibits common process with all other organized deviant groups. Like many of them, it is a tightly knit, cohesive social microcosm that dominates the other social actions of the members.

The hypothesis is now posited that because this deviant group has been systematized and tightly organized, and owing to the background of culture conflict and self-doubt shared by its members, this group may represent a unity of personality. The intense self-searching and deep introversion supported by the particular ritual forms, the rationale, and the position of the cult group in the reservation community may produce a systematized and narrowly defined variant of a transitional type. So the systematic deviation apparent in cult-defined behavior of this group may appear, it is hypothesized, as a systematic deviation in personality type. This, it is suggested, now, will tend to be true, regardless of variability in other life experience, including child training. The intensity of the shared and symbolically supported systematic deviation, it is suggested, is such that all other factors, past or present, tend to be overridden. This will be tested by subsequent analysis of Rorschach data.

"Transitional" position is ascribed to persons whose life experience has included direct contact with the old culture in identification and participation with groups carrying on the native-oriented religious forms, but who are not actively identified with any such group at present and have shifted toward Catholicism. All but two cases in the sample of fifteen transitionals have become at least nominal Catholics during their lifetime, but none attend services more than occasionally and eight said they "never" went.

Speaking more broadly, the persons here defined as "transitional" represent only a minority in a larger population. Even persons whose parents were born Catholics, and who have had no identifiable experience with native-oriented

groups, are frequently transitional in the sense that they have been raised by, and still carry with them, certain assumptions, attitudes, and patterns for behavior that are native-oriented. A transitional category, in this sense, would include a majority of the present reservation population. Except where the contrary is noted, all subsequent remarks apply only to the sample of cases more narrowly defined.

The persons in the sample live in frame or log houses of varying but generally poor, condition. The majority live in the poor parts of Nepoit, but a number are scattered widely about the reservation.

It is apparent that the transitional personnel are culturally dislocated. Their way of life consists of a medley of patterns, traits, and values adopted from a generically native American and a broadly Western, but internally differentiated, culture. This way of life, further, lacks formalization to such a degree that it is scarcely definable. It is precisely this condition of disorganization that most particularly characterizes the transitional category.

Exactly what resolution of this cultural disorganization the individuals in the transitional sample or their offspring will make cannot be predicted. Since the conditions of their lives today most closely approximate those of poor working-class whites it is apparent that the majority are already adapting to that standard. But a few who are mobile and ascendant-oriented will probably achieve an approximation of middle-class status—just as some working-class whites do. Therefore they are in transition to a Western way of life, but in which segment of that way of life their transition will be finally resolved will vary according to factors that cannot be anticipated at present. Since the object of this study is to demonstrate the relations existing between the socio-cultural and the psychological adaptations of individuals in the categories of the continuum, the relevant facts are what the conditions are now.

The acculturated position on the continuum of sociocultural adaptations is reserved for individuals who were born into membership in the Catholic Church and give no evidence of ever having been identified with any native-oriented religious group. The sample is subdivided into a lower-status category consisting of ten persons who attend church irregularly and are not members of the high-ranking Holy Name Society, and a higher-status category consisting of thirteen individuals who do attend services regularly and are members of this society. Neither the definition as acculturated nor the subdivision into status categories rests upon this preliminary criterion, since a number of observable differences in group identifications, occupation, income, housing, and other defined attributes and behaviors likewise serve to distinguish them.

There are no adult Menomini living on the reservation today that have not been brought into some measure of con-

tact with surviving remnants of the old culture. This flat statement rests upon the assumption that the entire reservation community is affected by the existence of any patterns of group life within its structure identifiable as native-oriented, and that the parents or grandparents of the present generation must themselves have been in some degree of cultural transition.

In group identifications, social interaction, wielding of political power, occupation, and conditions of residence, the category of Menomini personnel designated as acculturated appear to be internally differentiated into two segments of higher and lower status. Further, these segments approximate a similar broad division of the American population as a whole. Identity with any particular local or nonlocal socioeconomic stratum or social class in American society is not claimed. The segments approximate, however, a general middle-class American condition of life in the one instance, and a generally lower- or laboring-class condition in the other. Insofar as middle-class

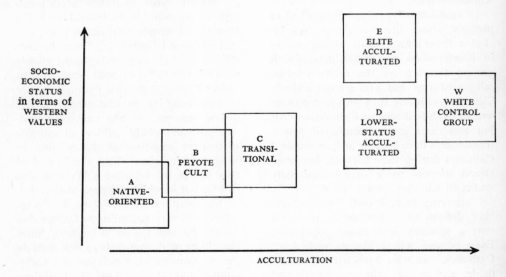

Acculturation and socioeconomic status

status in American society represents a higher level of achievement in an economically oriented hierarchy of values, the Menomini elite acculturated represent this achievement most adequately. In comparison with the other categories of Menomini personnel in the sample these two segments represent the end points of a synchronic acculturative series, seen in its sociocultural dimensions. The rest of the Menomini population as a whole, insofar as the sampling is adequate, may therefore be considered as transitional to one or the other status. Predictions of differential transition for any given group or individual are not possible within the limitations of the problem and the research design.

PSYCHOLOGICAL DIMENSIONS

The typical native-oriented Menomini personality appears to be highly intratensive, sensitive to the environment but able to maintain equilibrium despite its variations, lacking generally in overt emotional responsiveness and exhibiting a high degree of rational control over it when it does appear, motivated more by biologically oriented "survival" drives than by self-projective imaginatively creative ones, intellectually uncomplicated but adequate in terms of its setting, lacking in rigidity or constriction, without evidence of the usual forms of anxiety, tension, or internal conflict, and, in general, psychologically adequate to the demands placed upon it within its own sociocultural setting.

The typical personality structure established for the native-oriented group is apparently appropriate to the conditions of life in this category. The culturally prescribed requirement of control over overt expressions of interpersonal aggressions seems to be internalized as a psychological prescription in the general lack of overt emotional responses and high degree of control over those that do appear—if

it can be assumed that overt expression of aggressions requires overt emotional expression. This psychological characteristic, as well as that of the functionally related sensitivity to the interpersonal environment, is also appropriate to culturally prescribed constraints on the exercise of authority, to the concern about giving offense, and to the softening of declarativeness characteristic of the language.

This general psychological configuration also appears to be a psychological complement to the self-control and respect for others represented in the directives and ideals impressed upon children by direct injunction, storytelling, and culturally prescribed rewards for desired behavior.

The lack of any clear-cut indications of anxiety or tension in this highly intratensive and overtly emotionally unresponsive psychological structure may be in part a function of the dependence upon supernatural power in the exigencies of life, and of the acceptance of fate as irrevocable, as something to be accepted. Although this intratensiveness denotes social independence and self-reliance, in this case the psychological consequences that might ensue from relative emotional isolation do not occur because, it is hypothesized, the individual does not bear full personal responsibility for the consequences of his own acts. And he is probably not given to self-doubt because his power is derived from an external source that he controls only in the degree that he may lose it by failing to carry out the supernaturally prescribed observances for keeping it. The person is placed in a "passively" acceptant, rather than actively "manipulatory," relation to life.

The general congruency of the relationship between the cultural aspects of the conditions of life and the personality structure appears to be great. The continuity between the aboriginal cultural configuration and the themes expressed in the present way of life in the native-oriented group suggests that this typical personality structure has probably exhibited considerable stability through time.

The Peyote personality tends to be one in which there is a high degree of self-projective fantasy, which in a setting of anxiety, introspection, and looseness of affect control is interpretable as self-doubting rumination, however much it may represent a relative increase in creative imagination. This type of projection appears at some cost in the freedom with which biologically oriented drives are expressed. The personality tends to be subject to unsystematized anxiety, and apparently there is a tendency to attempt resolution of it by introspection. There is relative looseness of control exerted over emotional responses and some tendency for reality control, with the reservations stated previously, to disintegrate.

Evidence from the conversion statements of members indicates that the individual comes to the cult torn by the conflict of cultures, interpreted by him as a personal conflict. He is searching for a means of self-maintenance, for relief from self-doubt. Once he becomes a member, however, his concern over self is not diminished; it is, rather, given sanction in symbolically supported rumination and introverted concentration upon the relation to grace, power, and salvation which are so vital a part of the cult's esoteric emphasis. This seems to be manifest in the procedure in meetings, the search for the power which Peyote is vested as a sacrament by the "Holy Spirit," the declarations of worthlessness and feelings of being "filled with sin," the pleas for salvation, the search for psychic and physical cures, and the content of visions.

These processes seem to be directly expressed in the configuration of Rorschach indices that have been isolated as typical for the Peyotists and serve to differentiate them from the persons in the rest of the Menomini sample. Self-concern and doubt are apparently represented in the strong emphasis on human movement responses. This self-concern frequently seems to take the form of self-doubting rumination. Usually, high production in human movement responses is interpreted as indicating "self-projective creative imagination." It seems clear, however, that any imaginative creation in which the self is projected must be appropriate in character to the quality of the self, the fantasy surrounding it, and the context of the rest of the personality. The fact that the elite acculturated and the Peyote group are not clearly differentiated statistically in the human-movement factor does not necessarily mean, then, that the function of the psychological characteristics revealed by this determinant is the same in both personality types. The former group lacks evidence of anxiety and introspection that is characteristic of the latter, and the qualitative characteristics of the projected self are different.

The diffuse anxiety and the introspection are likewise appropriate to the cult context. The personal conflicts and self-doubt that must be accompanied by anxiety, and that seem to lead individuals into the cult, are apparently not resolved, but are, rather, systematized in the group search for salvation and grace. Introspection is literally sanctioned in the ritual procedure as each man stares into the fire, consumes peyote, and seeks the vision that will instruct him in the sacred lore, give him protection against threats to his life and security, or convince him that he is "saved."

But apparently the individual does not succeed in gaining confidence in himself, and he must constantly seek reassurance that he is "saved," for he symbolically repeats the conversion path from dark to light and from despair to hope by repeated experiences in vision and cures—and in the symbolism of the ritual itself. This contrasts to the situation for the native-oriented personnel, and apparently for the aboriginal Menomini, because there is assurance in their ideology that power or supernatural favor, once gained, can be depended upon unless the individual loses it by failure to observe clearly defined cultural directives. And further, the individual has not been subjected to the processes of cultural dislocation that caused the Peyotists to seek salvation and power in the first place. The native Menomini apparently regarded power from supernatural beings as a cultural heritage, and individuals could—and still do—inherit such power from parents and other relatives. The Peyotists seek power in a search for salvation and relief from doubts and fears.

This bears directly upon the looseness of emotional control exhibited by the Peyotists, and it is here that they share a crucial characteristic with the transitional personnel. The persons in both groups have been culturally dislocated. The role prescriptions and cultural directives of the native culture do not serve them effectively in their changed conditions of life, but prescriptions and directives from Western culture have apparently not become fully meaningful. The native-oriented directives and roles embodied in values, ideals, and sanctioned behavior supporting stoicism and self-control cannot function effectively in this situation, and the result appears to be loosening in control. For them this predicates a disintegrative process, however much looseness of affect control might be sanctioned and be appropriate to other cultural settings.

Although the Peyote Cult group has demonstrably shifted fundamentally away from the native-oriented personality type, this has apparently been a function of the deviant character of the cult with which its members identify. The persons in the transitional category have no such identification but have been subjected to the same kind of social and cultural dislocation. This suggests that the individuals in the transitional category should exhibit evidence, as they do, of some of the same psychological processes as do the Peyote personnel, but that the outlines of the native-oriented personality should be somewhat more identifiable.

The transitional persons in the sample exhibit statistical differences in comparison with the native-oriented group in five Rorschach indices. The differences are these: a relatively lower proportion of animal content in the total record for the transitionals, relatively fewer animal-movement responses, the presence of inanimate-movement responses, more frequent domination of uncontrolled over controlled color responses, and more frequent presence of percepts using bright color as the main determinant.

These differences are interpreted as follows. The most psychologically significant distinctions are that the transitional personnel give evidence of being more affectively open in a modal number of cases, as indicated by the presence of responses using bright color, and that this affect openness tends to be relatively uncontrolled. The other differences consist of evidence that the range of intellectual interests is broader on the part of the transitionals; they produce fewer responses in the easily perceived animal content area and are somewhat less motivated by biologically oriented drives. But there is no statistically significant relative increase in self-projective fantasy to compensate for this reduction in biologically oriented drives. And there is also evidence of tension or feelings of conflict, but this tension is not usually accompanied by direct signs of unsystematized anxiety.

It is apparent that there has not been as great a shift in psychological adaptation, by the transitionals, away from the native base, as was exhibited by the

Peyote group. The evidence indicates that a modal number of individuals in this category are functioning with the native-oriented personality type, but operating under some stress and undergoing a disintegrative shift in the direction of loss of control over open affect. This trend can be termed "disintegrative" only in the sense that it represents a breakdown of control in a personality structure that has been predicated on the basis of emotional stoicism and self-control, but in this comparative sense the term seems appropriate.

The evidence suggests that the transitionals definitely occupy a position of transition psychologically as well as socioculturally. The range of their intellectual interests is broader than that exhibited by the native-oriented group, but less broad than that of the elites. They are apparently less motivated by biologically oriented drives than the native-oriented personnel, but are not distinguished from the elites in this respect. They exhibit evidence of tension or conflict feelings that differentiate them from the native-oriented group, but not from the elites, with whom they share this characteristic in a modal number of cases. The marked differences between the native-oriented and transitional records in the latter two indices suggest a definite psychological shift toward the acculturated, away from the native-oriented psychological position, that is great enough so that the transitionals and the acculturated of both status levels (lower status and elite) exhibit some shared psychological characteristics. On the other hand, the first index (intellectual interests) suggests that the transitionals have shifted away from the native base but are in an intermediate psychological position in respect to this attribute. In intellectual productivity, they stand in somewhat the same position. They have shifted away from the native base, with an average of 21.60 responses as compared to 16.47, but produce fewer responses than do the

elites, who show an average of 27.08.

The most critical aspect of the relative position of the transitionals, from the psychological viewpoint, is in the balance of emotional controls. They are more open emotionally than are the native-oriented personnel as a group, but share this openness with both acculturated categories. They are different, however, from both the native base and the elite acculturated, for they tend to be relatively looser in their emotional control than either. This suggests that they have shifted away from the native base in the direction of a form of emotional adaptation characteristic of the elites but have not developed the same degree of control over these emotional adaptations. This is psychologically critical, because the comparative lack of open emotional response and the control over the little that does appear is especially characteristic of the native-oriented personnel, and it is in respect to this configuration that some of the most consistent adaptive changes have occurred in the other Menomini groups.

The comparisons between the transitional category and the rest of the Menomini sample have demonstrated that a psychological shift away from the native base has occurred, especially in the direction of a breakdown of the emotional stoicism and a development of relatively loose affect control that has been termed disintegrative, but that the outlines of the typical intratensive native-oriented personality structure do not appear to have disintegrated as a whole. It has been further demonstrated that this relative looseness of affect control is shared with the Peyote Cult group, and that therefore this process seems to be characteristic of the generically transitional segments of the continuum. And finally, it has been demonstrated that the transitional category occupies an intermediate psychological position between the native-oriented and elite acculturated groups that suggests a psychological as well as sociocultural process of transition, as seen within a synchronic continuum.

The relationships between the psychological processes exhibited by the transitional personnel and the conditions of life within this category have been anticipated in the discussion of the Peyote Cult group. It has been indicated that a looseness of emotional control characterizes both of these categories, and that this is an attribute not shared with either the native-oriented or elite acculturated groups. And further, that this is functionally related to the cultural and social dislocation suffered by members of both categories in the displacement of persons and the breakdown of meaningful role prescriptions and cultural patterns that occur as one phase of the total acculturative process as it applies to the Menomini.

In general, the relative lack of organization in regularity of occupation, in home situation, and in group identifications and social interaction, which characterizes life in the transitional category, appears to be reflected in the psychological adaptations of a statistically significant number of persons in the transitional sample group. A relative looseness of emotional control is exhibited by the transitional group in comparison to both the native-oriented and elite acculturated groups—even though these latter two groups in turn have adapted emotionally in different ways. There are also drops in the effectiveness of reality control, greater indications of tension or conflict appear, and there are less optimal relationships between sensitivity and formal control than is characteristic of either of the extremes of the continuum.

The lower-status group is in the ambiguous position of not being clearly differentiated from either of the two segments of the sociocultural continuum to which it is adjacent. The consistent trends are revealed more by the relative positions of the adjacent segments and the lower-status group in relation to the other Menomini categories.

The lower-status acculturated group and the transitional category exhibit no clear-cut statistical differentiation in psychological characteristics. But this acculturated group is differentiated from the native base in a number of ways, some of them of crucial significance. Likewise, the lower-status group is differentiated from the elite acculturated in only two indices, but the transitionals are distinguished from the elites in respect to five indices. These relationships support the contention that the lower-status group is in an intermediate psychological position between the transitionals and elites. This also bears upon the question of the persistence of the native-oriented personality structure. Persistence of such a structure does not seem to characterize the lower-status acculturated—despite lack of differentiation between the transitionals and the latter category. The basic shifts from the native-oriented base that the acculturated group exhibit indicate that relatively little of the native-oriented structure could be reconstructed from the evidence.

The ambiguous position of the lower-status acculturated category makes it difficult to posit clear-cut relationships between psychological process and sociocultural context.

The lower-status and elite acculturated share a sociocultural distinction from the rest of the Menomini sample in the degree to which they give evidence of departure from any native-oriented culture patterns. This is accompanied by distinction in psychological processes in that the two groups show less differentiation from each other than each does from the native base. But the lower-status and transitional categories are even less distinct psychologically, and they are differentiated in degree of native cultural retentions, but share an approximately equivalent socioeconomic status.

Commitment of the personnel in the lower-status group to a Western-oriented value system, shared with the elite acculturated, is reflected in a lack of critical psychological differentiations from the elites. The greater achievement of the elites on a scale of such values is reflected in the development of psychologically adaptive trends that serve to differentiate them as a group from the transitionals, whereas the lower-status acculturated are not.

The elite acculturated group is differentiated from the native-oriented group in the following respects. The elites as a group exhibit a faster reaction time, a larger total number of responses, fewer percepts in the animal-content area, a larger absolute number of human-movement responses, proportionately fewer animal-movement responses in the total record, more inanimate-movement responses, a more frequent emphasis on the bright color component in the shading plus achromatic color to bright color ratio, and a more frequent use of bright color in percept formation.

These differences are interpreted as follows. The elite group reacts more quickly to new problem situations, is intellectually more productive, and exhibits a broader range of interests. The elite exhibits more self-projective imaginative creativity, with a relative decrement in the free expression of biologically oriented drives. They reveal more tension, or conflict awareness—but there is no accompanying context of unsystematized or intellectualized anxiety. The elites less frequently exhibit what is usually termed "contact shyness" in Rorschach literature —which means that they produce responses displaying open affect in the use of bright color more frequently than they tend to pull back from this emotionally laden percept area to the more subtle stimuli presented by shading and achromatic color. And finally, the elites follow through with a consistent psychological shift from the native base exhibited also by the Peyotists, transitionals, and lower-status acculturated—that is, in the more open affect denoted by use of bright color as a main determinant.

The psychological differences between the elite and native-oriented group are consistent, in certain areas, with those exhibited by the other Menomini categories. These consistent differences are as follows: less restricted range of content in percept formation, less emphasis on the biologically oriented drives, more indications of tension, or conflict awareness, and more open emotional responsiveness. The elites share also with the transitionals and lower-status group the greater frequency of extratensive orientation discussed previously. Apparently there is a common core in the various psychological adaptations away from the native base in the Menomini sample as a whole, and the elite acculturated share in it.

There are certain indications that the elites represent the end point of a process that began with the Peyotists, and continues in varying degrees and ways through the other two intermediate categories. All of the Menomini categories except the native-oriented group exhibit tendencies toward relatively open emotional responsiveness in the use of bright color in percept formation. But the elites, unlike the Peyotists and transitionals, exhibit control over this more open emotionality. And although the elite and lower-status acculturated groups are not statistically differentiated from each other in this respect, there is some evidence that a trend toward emotional control begins in the lower-status group and culminates in the elite category. The elites are statistically differentiated from the transitional category in that they exhibit more control, but the lower-status group is not; and the latter group is differentiated from the native base in relative frequency of lack of control, but the elites are not.

This cumulative evidence therefore suggests that the native-oriented group and the elites do represent the respective end points of a psychological process set in motion by acculturation among the Menomini. A general lack of overt emotional responsiveness, and a control of that which does appear, are characteristic of the native personality type. The culturally and socioeconomically intermediate categories exhibit an increase in overt emotional responsiveness which is accompanied by looseness of control over it. The elites exhibit the emotional openness, but they have developed control of it. This constitutes what may be called a reformulation of personality structure on the part of the elites—in contrast to changes that tend to be comparatively regressive and disintegrative in the intermediate categories.

The hypothesis that this process indicates a reformulation of personality structure in the elite category has further support: the members of this group modally exhibit what is regarded in standard interpretations as more than adequate balance for emotional responsiveness in the factor of self-projective creative imagination. Seven of the thirteen persons in this group produced four or more human-movement responses. Although this does not provide statistical differentiation from the Peyotists and the transitionals, the configurative assumption of interpretations suggests that this factor plays a more positively creative role in a setting of controlled emotionality than in an emotionally uncontrolled setting, where it more probably represents ruminatory self-involvement.

This last condition is especially true, it has been posited, in the case of the Peyote group, where the indications of anxiety, tension and conflict, and introspection present further a complex of comparative disintegration. It is less true of the transitionals, where the hypothesis rests upon the assumption that emotional breaks, in a personality structure that has been predicated on a high degree of self-control, must create internal conflicts. That these conflicts have not been expressed more frequently in direct indications of unsystematized anxiety or introspective tendencies in the transitional group suggests that the personality structure predicated along native-oriented lines maintains considerable over-all integration despite the disintegrative process in control features.

Among the elites, indications of unsystematized anxiety appear in psychologically significant amounts in only four cases, and introspective tendencies in five cases. In view of the other aspects of the configuration, this further supports the hypothesis that an organized personality structure is modally represented in this group. There are, however, indications of what have been interpreted as tension, or conflict awareness, in ten of the thirteen cases. These indications are present in a modal number of cases in every category except the native-oriented. Apparently the production of this tension is also one consistent effect of the acculturative process that finds full expression among the elites. It appears that the process does not occur without some cost even in a reformulated personality structure, but it may also be hypothesized that this tension itself plays an adjustmental role.

The personality organization has a different content in the two extremes—the native-oriented and elite acculturated—as denoted by clear-cut statistical differences between these two groups. But the control features of both, and the psychological adequacy of each in its respective setting, denote a shared process of psychological integration.

The native-oriented personality is organized around cultural directives of self-control, restraint of overt interpersonal aggression, and a passively acceptant attitude toward the blessings of supernatural power and the exigencies of fate. The elite acculturated personality structure—insofar as the configuration isolated by analysis of differences is modal—is organized around the demand for goal achievement on a Western-oriented scale of values represented in comparatively high-level occupation, better homes, and social respectability. Along with this scale of values comes in some degree the belief that every man makes his own way, aggressively using his personal skills and unique attributes. Acceptance of fate and dependence upon supernatural power for accomplishment will not do for individuals who accept this value system, and it is necessary for them to marshal their emotional and imaginative resources in the aggressive competition required for achievement on these terms. These demands seem to be reflected directly in the open but controlled affect, more than adequate imaginative creativity, presense of tension, lack of unsystematized anxiety, and over-all psychological integration of the personality structure that seems to be most fully developed in the elite acculturated category—as seen within the framework of adaptive shifts away from the native base.

INTERPRETATION

Anthropologists who have accepted psychoanalytic premises have been inclined to see childhood training as the single determinant of personality structure. This predilection has consequences for the interpretation of any adaptive sequence in a field of culture change, since it points to certain experiences and certain cultural forms as the ultimate source, psychologically speaking, of both stability and change. There is nothing in the data that contradicts an assumption that childhood experience is a general determinant of personality structure. But the Menomini data indicate very clearly that the situations occurring in adult life are determinants of equal significance and that personality structure is perhaps more flexible, in its group dimensions, than we might presume. The situation in which each of the acculturative groups functions appears to be, in fact, the source of the concrete elements and unique configurations most sufficiently characterizing the modal adult personality in each group. This is particularly true of the Peyote group, where the nexus between the sociocultural dimension and adult personality is particularly tight, irrespective of probable variations in early childhood training. To be sure, this is not the first time that such a connection has been discovered in anthropologically oriented field research. Systematic attention to such relationships will make it possible to point with certainty to the areas of human experience most significantly affecting personality development, and will define alternative possibilities in the relationship of such experience to the psychological aspects of culture change.

Without attention to qualitative aspects of the personality, or to the particular ways in which the psychological components are put together to form group-defined configurations, it is clear that the emotional-control factor is the one in which the greatest and most significant shifts occur as a consequence of acculturation. The sequence is from the passively acceptant, emotionally limiting native-oriented type, through the regressive-breakdown characteristic of the transitional type, to the emotionally focused, aggressively oriented but highly controlled elite-acculturated type. That such a shift should occur, and that it should be the most significantly generalizable one, is logical in view of the fact that the emotional processes directly relate the individual to other men and to the symbols of value that must be manipulated within any given context. The sharp differences between the two juxtaposed cultural contexts in which these social and symbolic manipulations must occur is given representation in the psychological configurations exhibited by the extremes of the acculturative continuum. The intermediate position in this continuum represented by the transitionals (a position in which the differences have their fullest impact on the adapting individual) is inevitably one in which disturbance in emotional balance will occur.

Generalizations of this kind for the transitional group should be seen, however, in the light of the psychological variability exhibited within this category. Several persons in this sample exhibit a personality structure that is essentially no different than that most characteristic of the native-oriented group. They are all people that have maintained relatively close social relationships with members of the latter group through parents who are operating within its context. Qualitatively, their records are different from those of the native-oriented group only in that they tend to be sparser, and give some evidence of anxiety, for example, in failure to respond to certain Rorschach cards. Other persons in this sample of transitionals appear to be withdrawn, passively "hopeless" (they seem to have given up). They are not fighting back psychologically. A few give evidence of good over-all personality integration—in terms of the pattern established for the elite acculturated group. They could be termed successfully transitional. But the largest number of persons are characterized by varying degrees of diffuse anxiety, emotional blocking and potentially explosive aggressiveness, and distortions of reality perception.

The variability spelled out in these typological characterizations is expectable in a culturally transitional context. Though each man in a small group sharing a common cultural heritage may start with a roughly similar set of experiences in childhood, the personal impact of culture conflict will vary with idiosyncratic experience in adult life. Stability of friendship patterns, economic opportunity, choice of marital partner—many and complex variables—will create highly personalized contexts in which the impact of culture conflict will be differently mediated in psychologically adaptive process. In this respect, the situation of the ungrouped transitionals presents a clear and significant contrast to the situation in the Peyote Cult group, where the sociocultural context for psychological adaptation to the impact of culture conflict has been systematized.

With due regard for the psychological variability found within the transitional category, the qualitative features most adequately characterizing the transitional modal personality configuration may be described. One characteristic met before in the Peyote group is that of self-conscious "Indianism." This is coupled, in some cases, with a deep and explicit nostalgia for the old way of life. These two aspects together suggest, in very simple and direct fashion, the degree to which there is a search for cultural identity. Another phase of this same process, but with the orientation in the opposite direction, is the projection of explicit symbols of Western culture, such as "a picture of George Washington," the "atom bomb," "X-ray," and a "biology slide." And some degree of awareness of contemporary events is indicated by responses like "a picture of Stalin"—in which a member of the native-oriented group sees only "an old man." These projections all appear to be directly expressive of the intermediate sociocultural position of the transitional personnel.

A clue to the character of the self is seen in the projections of human movement. Although this expressive category of percept was characteristically "passive" in the native-oriented personality configuration, among many of the transitionals human beings are seen more often in aggressive action, such as "fighting," "doing a balancing act," "whirling around," "promenading," or "dancing." This shift mirrors the difference in context of adaptation for the two groups. In the native-oriented milieu, social acceptance and even success in subsistence—as made possible by the use of supernatural power—are gained through nonmanipulatory passivity. In the transitional context, passivity means loss, in part because the mechanisms for the gaining of goals through supernatural power are broken, and the person must operate within the framework of a competitive wage economy with only the tenuous support that nominal Christianity can give, with its emphasis on individual responsibility and sin. The result is that the self must change to a more activistic orientation—or give up. But this creates disturbance, which is mirrored in various anxiety symptoms and breakdown in the rational control of emotions.

The Peyotists deal with this disturbance by group-sanctioned introspection, and rumination about the self. This process has no support in the social context of the transitionals, and consequently, no systematic psychological expression. When the transitionals, by way of contrast, attempt to deal with the disturbance of self, they do so in a way that stops just short of introspection—such as the projection of anatomical content. This is usually interpreted as indicating a self-concern that is a symptom of anxiety without the creative component present in true introspection, and given the context of indecision and hazy form discrimination in which the anatomical responses occur in transitional records, this seems to be a correct interpretation here. The disturbance in concept of the

self, and the disintegrative shift in emotional controls characteristic of the modal transitional personality configuration, are given an added dimension by various and pervasive indications of anxiety in the Rorschach records. Others are seen in projection of "clouds," "maps," and "X-ray pictures"—all concepts of a noncommittal type that suggest anxiety because of their evasive quality. Other more clear-cut indications are seen in numerous delays in response to certain cards, or complete rejection of them, in circumlocution and verbalized rationalization, and in remarks that denote discomfiture. Any given record may contain all, or only some of these indications, and this fits the picture of variability in configurative trends in this category of personnel.

With the qualitative characteristics already described for the transitional configuration, it is expectable that there also should be indications of direct hostility —a feature lacking in the native-oriented records. These take the form of percepts like "sting-ray," "beetle," and weapons of various sorts. And this is coupled with a literally explosive quality that is expressed in responses such as volcanoes, and atom-bomb explosions. This latter type of response is usually accompanied by use of color without much attention to form. In this combination there is an indication that aggressive breaks in behavior occur, which is documented in the wife-beatings, open brawls, and occasional shootings that takes place in the transitional group.

The psychological and sociocultural condition of the transitionals represents a phase in the adaptive process that must be shared in some degree by most culturally differentiated population enclaves that are responding to the impact of a dominant civilization. Practically the same picture has emerged in Hallowell's work with the more acculturated levels of Ojibwa, and the research done on the

Teton-Dakota by Mekeel and MacGregor clearly indicates processes of the same shape at work. Suggestions that parallel developments are taking place, or have taken place, among other American Indian enclaves, are seen in studies of the Navaho, Papago, Hopi, and Zuni. Studies of acculturation in Africa and the Pacific have not been oriented sufficiently in this direction to permit a generalization of this kind to be extended to those areas, but the rich data collected and analyzed with rather different problems in mind suggest the probability that processes parallel to those isolable in the field provided by the contemporary American Indian have occurred there also.

On a microcosmic scale, and in a seemingly very different frame of reference, the Menomini transitionals represent a complex of processes that parallel the emergence of a "mass" in American society. In the "mass" the person is alienated from society. He is in it but not of it. There is superficial adherence to stereotyped values that have little meaning, because these values are not effectively mediated by symbolization at the primary group level, where internalization can occur and implicit understanding of value symbols is derived. The person is unstable, compulsive about some symbols as a means of seeking security in identification, but easily manipulated and swayed—particularly where aggression can be released.

This is a description of our own urban mass that many sociologists would accept, and it characterizes the Menomini in transition as well. The characterization finds some psychological parallel in Rorschach samples recently collected for purposes of standardization from American urban populations of predominantly lower socioeconomic rank. Both of the samples now available indicate a looseness of affect control that is unlike that presented as "normal" in Rorschach literature, and

that suggests a personality type that functionally fits the character of the mass as postulated here. Though generalizations are premature, in view of lack of knowledge concerning differential distributions of Rorschach patterns in social strata and urban or rural areas in American society, it seems probable that this looseness in affect control represented in what may be considered a sample of a "mass" population stems from processes of dislocation and cultural attenuation that parallel those represented among the Menomini transitionals. Whether this is demonstrable or not at present, there is the suggestion here that generalizations concerning so-called "culture" change and adaptation may eventually become statements of process without limiting boundaries set up by cultural specifics or by the locus of phenomena.

The lower-status acculturated group is in the position of not being markedly distinguished from either the transitionals or the elites as far as statistical comparison of segmentalized Rorschach indices reveals. And yet this group is differentiated from the native-modified group in certain ways in which the other two categories are not, suggesting that the psychological shift from the native base represented in this sociocultural category has some distinction within the continuum as a whole. Without regard for specific indices, the lower-status personnel appear to share certain features with the transitionals and share enough other features with the elites so that clear-cut segmentalized differentiations with respect to either group do not occur. But this does not deny the existence of configurative trends within the group itself. The lower-status group does present a configurative trend in psychological adaptation that merits attention. There is a modality of extratensive orientation, which means that an extroversional adjustment is occurring which brings the individual into closer relationship to variability in the environment than to his own inner fantasy life; he is motivated more by the expectations of others, by surface emotions, than by internalized self-directives. But this extroversional adjustment is accompanied by conflict between the more fully developed extroversive tendencies and certain latent capacities for an introversive adjustment. In short, there is evidence that a modal number of the persons in this group are adapting to their context through a shift toward extroversion, at the same time that there are other forces pulling them back to an introverted adjustment that is more typical of the Menomini population as a whole, and that is especially characteristic of the native-oriented group.

This configuration of conflict between extroversive and introversive forces is reflected in other functions of the personality structure. The reaction time is relatively short (fourteen seconds), and this is appropriate to the extroversive orientation; this personality tends to be motivated more by consideration of immediate environmental pressure than by need to structure responses internally. This tendency to be impressed directly and immediately by environmental variability is also expressed in the Rorschach color determinants. The persons in this group are much affected by color in the inkblots. In all but one case, color is used as a main determinant. The quality of the responses using color as a determinant suggests impressionability without a fully developed ability to control it intellectually. Apparently the stress created by conflicting adjustmental trends is reflected in some lack of balance in emotional functions, though the disturbance does not often reach as far as it frequently does among the transitionals and Peyotists.

The functional fit of this configuration of psychological processes to the particular sociocultural position of the lower-status acculturated group is inde-

terminant but suggestive. These persons share with all other Menomini some generalized impact from the old culture. Their parents, in some cases, and their grandparents in others, were in large degree native-oriented. But these people have moved far toward an acculturated state, and in this state they occupy a low-status position—in comparison with the elites. They are committed to a competitive-wage economy and Catholicism, and they have laid aside the old subsistence attitudes and the power concepts of the native religion. With this shift, they have accepted the competitive goals and values of a market-oriented Western culture, but find themselves short in attainment. They recognize the same goals as do the elites, but they have not been as successful in reaching them. They are outward oriented, figuratively reaching for goals external to them, attainable to only a limited extent, and foreign to the cultural heritage that must have affected each one in some degree. This orientation creates psychological stress that is not compensated for, as in the case of the elites, by the stabilizing factors implied by a pattern of success.

As indicated by the projections of human movement in the Rorschach protocols of this group, the self is actively, not passively, oriented, for human beings are frequently seen in vigorous action. This action is not usually particularly aggressive, and clear-cut signs of deep disturbances are infrequent. There are some indications of defensiveness, such as is possibly indicated in the equation of "Africans" and "Menomini." This may be an indication of some sensitivity concerning status as a minority group, a position that is meaningful to lower-status acculturated Menomini because they operate within the framework of Western-oriented goals without full acceptance by either middle-class whites or elite Menomini.

Their cultural position is directly reflected in the relative absence of self-conscious "Indianism" and in the frequent projection of American schoolbook culture and items taken directly from the material complex of Western civilization, such as "ashtray stand," "ribbon at a dog show," "war medal," "microscope," and "chairs."

Another qualitative feature of some significance in the lower-status acculturated personality configuration is seen in the tendency to produce percepts without much in the way of elaboration or integrative organization. With reference to their sociocultural position, this relative lack of elaboration and integration may be a function of unfulfilled realization of values to which the lower-status personnel are committed. Ability to produce abstract organizations of perceived elements is most likely to develop, it would seem, where this organizing capacity is called for in the occupational and social role—as it must be in managerial and supervisory capacities most characteristic of the elite positions. And further, it is probable that failure to reach goals, if interpreted as failure by the individual, has in itself a reductive effect on the drive to organize or elaborate intellectually.

The lower-status acculturated may be seen, therefore, as a group with a special problem. The members of this group infrequently exhibit the relatively deep-seated disturbances characteristic of a majority of transitionals and Peyotists but do exhibit a modal conflict in introversive–extroversive adjustment that is accompanied by various indications of anxiety, defensiveness, impressionability, and undeveloped organizational ability and intellectual control. This configuration appears to be related to their unique position of being acculturated—therefore committed to a Western system of values—at the same time that the social and economic goals defined by this system are not attained in full measure. The significance of this relationship will become clearer as the psychological configuration most sufficiently characterizing the elite acculturated is discussed.

The elite type reacts directly to environmental pressures and does not withhold or lack emotional expression. The elites are not stoics like the native-oriented people. But they are not emotionally disturbed like the transitionals and Peyotists. They are able to use their emotions in the attainment of goals they hold important. Where the Peyotists and transitionals exhibit explosiveness, irritability, and anxiety in their emotionality, the elites control and channelize it. Where these intermediate types exhibit what can be called regressive trends, in respect to control functions, the elites exhibit what has been called elsewhere in this analysis a reformulation of personality structure, in respect to these same functions.

Certain other objectified characteristics of this personality configuration sharpen this central emphasis. The reaction time is comparatively low (twenty-three seconds), and indicates a readiness to respond that supports the interpretation of the use of bright color. The configuration also includes indications of tension that in this context are not destructive, but rather suggest further a readiness to act. But all of these indications of responsiveness, of quick focus of action in response to demands from the world outside the person, are balanced in this configuration by two other processes. The first of these processes is the rational control exercised directly over emotional response. The second process is expressed in the self-projective fantasy in human-movement percepts, that are given comparatively frequently by the elites. This capacity to project the dynamic self into percepts constructed in response to lifeless inkblots is thought to indicate introversive processes that balance the more externally or extroversively oriented responses concerned with color that suggest capacities for immediate and overt response to environmental variability or press. If the character of these self-projections in morbid, depressed, or disturbed, as it frequently is among the Peyotists and transitionals, the balancing factor in the introversive capacity is not effective. But among the elite acculturated, the projections of human movement do not have this character and may be presumed to indicate functionally effective mediation of action in the individual's reality system.

The content of these human-movement percepts is vigorous, in contrast to the passivity or quiescence expressed in the native-oriented responses of the same type. But since this content does not suggest personal disturbance, as it does among the transitionals and Peyotists, there is again an indication that the elite personality type represents a reformulation—a successful adaptation to the exigencies of life under conditions brought about by the impact of Western civilization.

The range of content expressed in responses to the inkblots is wider than that of any other group. Objects, places, names, and concepts are given that indicate an experience with, or an orientation toward, life outside the reservation. Some of this expression content seems to indicate a desire to provide proof of this experience, as though the individual were trying to act in a self-consciously acculturated way.

Another significant qualitative aspect of the records of the elites is the degree to which spontaneous elaboration of detail and of relationships between parts of the inkblots occurs in the statement of percepts. Though few of the Menomini are given to verbosity, the records of the elites approach most closely the verbal character of the responses given by many middle-class white Americans. The native-oriented Menomini do not usually state the obvious nor concern themselves with much detail, and never express concern over elements in the blot that they cannot integrate into their concepts, whereas the elite acculturated do all of these things. The Peyotists and transitionals sometimes use many words to describe their percepts, but this elaboration appears more often to be a function of disturbance, confusion, or haziness than a function of the desire and ability to specify.

This tendency toward elaboration of percepts is logically supplemented by a greater productivity in number of responses in each protocol. The elites stand high in this respect and appear sometimes to attempt to outdo themselves in producing a long and varied series of percepts for each Rorschach card. This characteristic, indeed, bears upon a qualitative aspect of their behavior that is difficult to define precisely but which seems significant. They appear to regard the taking of the Rorschach as a true test situation, as such situations are conceived of in our Western culture. They respond to it as a challenge to their ability, and self-consciously try to achieve as high a "score" as possible. They are reluctant to give the cards up until they have extracted every possible response, and they try different combinations of elements to produce more responses. This interpretation of the situation is not met with among the native-oriented personnel, and only occasionally among transitionals and Peyotists, but more frequently among the lower-status acculturated. It may be regarded as one expression of an "achievement drive" that can be seen as an aspect of the "normal" middle-class American personality.

In both structural and qualitative aspects the most typical elite acculturated personality configuration thus represents an end point of the acculturated continuum represented within the contemporary Menomini population, as contained within this sample of male personnel. The progressive shift from something that may be called quiescent stoicism, represented by the native-oriented personality configuration, through the disturbed emotionality and regressive breakdown of control functions characteristic of the Peyotists and transitionals, to the controlled and channelized emotion responsiveness characteristic of the elites, appears to be the most consistent and dramatic aspect of the psychological adaptation accompanying the sociocultural changes represented in this synchronic continuum of acculturation. *The effectively functioning self-projection, readiness to act, wide range of perceptual content, and the drives to produce numerous and elaborated concepts, characteristic of the elite acculturated configuration, are logical corollaries of this central theme in successful adaptation of the elites to modern conditions of life.* The modal elite acculturated Menomini type is, in effect, a successfully adjusted middle-class American, with practically nothing logically identifiable as "Indian." This is so despite the fact that all of the elite must have felt the impact of the old culture in some degree—simply because they grew up on the reservation and were born of Menomini parents who could hardly have been as fully acculturated as their children are now. [Italics added.]

Despite the extensive research made with the utilization of Rorschach and other projective techniques on acculturating American Indian populations, no group has been isolated that represents a parallel psychological reformation comparable with that represented by the elite acculturated Menomini. Hallowell, for instance, comes to this conclusion concerning the psychological adaptations occurring through three levels of acculturation among the Ojibwa of Canada and Wisconsin:

There is a persistent core of psychological characteristics sufficient to identify an Ojibwa personality constellation, aboriginal in origin, that is clearly discernible through all levels of acculturation yet studied. All Ojibwa tested (including children six to sixteen) are still Indians, in a psychological sense, whatever clothes they wear, whatever their occupation, whether they speak English or not, and regardless of race mixture. While culturally speaking they appear more and more like whites at "higher" levels of acculturation there is no evidence at all for a basic psychological shift in a parallel direction.

Nothing directly comparable with the psychological shift represented by the elite acculturated Menomini was found among the Ojibwa, who share an aboriginal cultural background of the same general type and, at the more advanced levels of acculturation, have been subjected to approximately the same impact from Western civilization and its culture-carrying population.

It is apparent that certain conditions must exist among the Menomini that do not exist among the Ojibwa, or the other American Indian populations so far studied. It seems clear that this difference lies in the degree to which Western-oriented values are accepted and attainable in the Menomini situation.

American Indian reservation populations are, on the whole, depressed minorites. Avenues to successful economic adaptation, and therefore to successful adoption of a congeries of associated values in an economically oriented society, are largely denied them. The Menomini situation is relatively favorable, due to the lumber industry on the reservation and attendant possibilities for responsible self-government. It is possible for a member of the tribe to occupy a social and economic position that is comparable in many respects with that of the "successful" middle-class white American represented in the nonreservation areas close to the Menomini community. Menomini who have so succeeded interact socially with such middle-class whites, and both in their struggle for success and in their association give allegiance to middle-class oriented goals and means. It must be upon this experience and identification that the reformulated personality configuration of the elite acculturated is based.

The record of the impact of Western civilization upon native enclave populations has been depressing. Disturbance and breakdown, both social and psychological, are its usual attendants, and this is true of those segments of the Menomini population which are still culturally transitional. But the data on the elite accul-

turated suggest that when conditions are created that make it possible to identify with (to internalize) the values of the dominant population—and when those conditions contain means to attainment of those values as well as the possibilities of identification with them—then a successful psychological adaptation to the demands of those values may occur. These necessary conditions include, it seems, presentation of the value system as desiderata, availability of the institutional avenues to their attainment, and opportunities for participation within the social structure of the dominant society on a nonprejudicial basis. Where these conditions do not exist, there is little reason why a native population should undergo a reformulative psychological adaptation, despite whatever changes in dress, speech, or habitation should take place, and there is nothing to prevent what psychological changes do occur from taking a regressive and disorganizing form.

SUMMARY

There are so many implications and conclusions to be drawn from Spindler's study of acculturation among the Menomini, and from a comparison of his study with Hallowell's of the Ojibwa, that we can only list and point to those which appear to be the most significant. First of all, and to reiterate what was said at the beginning of this chapter, both these studies of acculturation have been presented as examples of conflicting approaches, and not as an example of a continuing conflict between two investigators. A comparison of Spindler's study with Hallowell's underscores the indispensability of clearly specifying the *conditions* under which events transpire instead of just knowing *what* has happened.

Second, both studies taken together point to two facets of another principle. One of these is that personality development never ceases. There are, of course, sociocultural conditions under which personality or character structure are more or less fixed by a given age; but even though we do not have the data to substantiate this, it could be speculated that as instruments of research are sharpened, more instances of continuing personality development will be uncovered and documented. What is probably more to the point is the hypothesis that while the essential and basic predispositions are usually established at some point in early adulthood in most societies, people in most groups are regularly confronted by new conditions of life which require new kinds of adaptations. A full awareness of this factor is especially important in a world in which whole ways of life can be revolutionized almost overnight by decisions made by governments thousands of miles distant. The second facet of the same principle, to which we alluded in the summaries of Chapters 9 and 12, is that specific motivations may be, but are not necessarily, adaptive under different conditions. The personality structure of the elite acculturated among the Menomini is well suited to contemporary Western sociocultural conditions; but it would have been grossly maladaptive in the aboriginal setting. Thus, to carry on the point made at the end of Chapter 12, we not only have to know the cultural antecedents of a group of people but, even more importantly, we have to know their *present* memberships and environments.

Spindler's data on the Menomini, especially when they are compared with the data gathered by Hallowell among the Ojibwa, further support and bring us back to the very first set of principles which were applied in our discussions of socialization—people only have access to the values of a culture depending on where they are located in the social structure of their society. The Menomini and the Ojibwa, like the Polish immigrants discussed in Chapter 13, have come under the impact of Western civilization. But the Poles were caught in a particular kind of vicious circle: not having experienced dominant American values in their home society, they were unable to acquire the kinds of social-structural positions which, in turn, commonly provide access to those values. The Ojibwa about whom Hallowell wrote are characterized by a set of values-in-personality which are maladaptive; they are not adaptive for the modern technological world, and the sociocultural environment for which they were once adaptive no longer exists. Furthermore, not only does the old sociocultural environment no longer exist but the Ojibwa have not been provided with any new prestige system or other sociocultural conditions which would give them any direction in which to change. They are largely at sea without a consistent frame of reference. We, reading about them, know the directions in which they should change; they do not. As maladaptive as the old patterns are, they are comfortable and safer than no consistent motivations or patterns of behavior. In brief, without a consistent frame of reference and access to new goals, why should they change?

That segment of the Menomini population which has been called the elite acculturated has been fortunate in being provided with an industry—lumbering—which can succeed, given the nature of American technology, only if it is conducted along lines which are consistent with dominant American values. This industry contains within it not only the value system itself but access to those values as well. Instead of having to work their way into this set of sociocultural conditions, the people who became the elite acculturated were placed in these conditions. Thus, they had a choice—whether to hold on to the old personality patterns or change. American cultural values are desirable and admirable goals for most Indian populations, but if they do not have direct access to them in one way or another they will not change. The elite acculturated were given access to this value system, and thus had good reason to change.

BIBLIOGRAPHY AND SUGGESTED READINGS

Hallowell, A. I. "Some Psychological Characteristics of the Northeastern Indians," in *Man in Northeastern North America,* edited by Frederick Johnson, Papers of the Robert S. Peabody Foundation for Archaeology, Vol. *3,* 1946, pp. 195-225.

Hallowell, A. I. "Values, Acculturation, and Mental Health," *American Journal of Orthopsychiatry,* Vol. *20,* pp. 732-743, 1950. (Reprinted as Chapter 20 in Hallowell's *Culture and Experience.*) Further theoretical speculations on the Ojibwa materials presented in this chapter, and a good bridge between this chapter on acculturation and the next on psychosis.

Henry, Jules. "Culture, Personality, and Evolution," *American Anthropologist,* Vol. *61,* pp. 221-226, 1959. An interesting attempt to combine personality and acculturation with physical anthropology.

Kardiner, Abram. *The Individual and his Society.* New York: Columbia, 1939.

Kardiner, Abram. *The Psychological Frontiers of Society.* New York: Columbia, 1945. Both books by Kardiner are inquiries into the problem of psychological adaptation to the institutions of society.

Spindler, George and Walter Goldschmidt. "Experimental Design in the Study of Culture Change," *Southwestern Journal of Anthropology,* Vol. *8,* pp. 68-83, 1952. The theoretical approach underlying the study of the Menomini presented in this chapter.

Spindler, Louise and George. "Male and Female Adaptations in Culture Change," *American Anthropologist,* Vol. *60,* pp. 217-233, 1958. Using the same approach as in the study presented in this chapter, this article shows the differences between Menomini men and women in the acculturation situation.

Section VI

THE SOCIOLOGICAL CONDITIONS OF PERSONAL DISORGANIZATION

Chapter 15

SOCIAL STRUCTURE
AND PSYCHOSIS

This book began with the tenet that personality cannot be fully understood apart from the context of the social structure in which it has its being. We have attempted to apply this principle by tracing the ways in which the social structure of a group affects the development of personality; the ways in which personality and institutions fit into and maintain each other; and the ways in which social structure mediates the role of personality in acculturation and assimilation. But if we really wish to demonstrate the crucial importance of social structure to personality development and functioning, we have to be able to demonstrate empirically what happens to the individual personality when his social-structural relationships are severely disturbed, or even destroyed.

It is in personality disorganization that we can observe in sharpest detail the social structure's function as a linchpin in the individual's existence and functioning. This principle could not be fully understood without first observing the role of social structure in deviant behavior, in the development of child-parent identification, in adolescence, in the maximization and minimization of emotional predispositions, and so forth. Nor, by similar token, can the role of social structure be fully understood in these various contexts without truly understanding the individual's relationship to the social structure when (and if) he becomes disorganized.

Our goal here is therefore not only to learn about psychosis but also to gain some further insight into the nature of social structure. Thus, we are going to devote and gear our inquiry into psychosis to an illustration of the proposition that, all other things being equal, if an individual's sociological relationships are unsparingly deranged he can become psychotic, or he might even die.

In this chapter, we are going to concern ourselves with some important definitions and principles involving both social structure and psychosis. In Chapter 16, we shall explore and illustrate by means of case materials the hypothesis that a severe disturbance in social-structural relationships can precipitate psychosis and even death, all other things being equal.

The qualifying phrase "all other things being equal" has been used in the foregoing statements although its use has been studiously avoided throughout most of this book. The reason for this is that when we come to psychosis, we are often

457

dealing with indeterminate variables which almost completely preclude the assumption that all the links in a chain of condition, consequence, cause, and effect can be specified. For example, biochemical, genetic, and physiological research, together with psychiatric inquiry into psychosis, have been proceeding with such leaps and bounds,[1] that it is now possible to make some rather stringent generalizations. Of foremost importance is the steadily growing conviction among researchers that not everyone can become psychotic. One has to have the constitutional equipment to become psychotic. This equipment includes an array of genetic (chromosomal) features, biochemical functions, and the like. These factors are many and complex, and they need not be gone into here.

But it is also clear from the work of many investigators, that even if a person *does* have the constitutional predispositions for one psychotic pattern or another, he will not necessarily become psychotic unless other conditions are present. These latter conditions are sociological and psychological, and it is not possible (at least at the present time) to state specifically which combination of precipitating factors in juxtaposition with physiological predispositions will give rise to psychosis.

Let us take a hypothetical example. John Doe is diagnosed as being acutely schizophrenic. It is established that he has the physiological predispositions for schizophrenia, and it also emerges that three months prior to the onset of his illness his business became bankrupt. It can be hypothesized that there is a definite relationship between the onset of his psychosis and his financial failure. But another fact of significance is that John Doe has recently entered his climactarium. All other things being equal, would he have become psychotic if his business had failed while he was at the height of his sexual capacities? The answer may well be in the negative, but it is also possible that a combination of other factors might have precipitated a psychotic episode twenty years earlier.

Thus, it could be generalized that any psychosis is a product of a combination of intricately related physiological, psychological, and sociological factors. In the discussions to follow, where we shall be dealing almost exclusively with psychosis in other societies, it will be necessary to assume that the constitutional predispositions for psychosis are present, and then go on to examine the sociological and psychological data which are available.

Another indeterminate variable in our discussions will be the severe disturbance of social-structural relationships as *one* set of predisposing or precipitating factors to the onset of psychosis. How severe is severe? it can be asked. Plainly, we cannot answer such a question. There have been people whose social lives have collapsed so catastrophically that the imagination is staggered, but who have not become psychotic. And yet there are people who become psychotic upon the loss of a friend or of a job or even upon material success. Here, again, we have to proceed upon a set of assumptions. We have to postulate that the disruption of social relationships can serve as a precipitate to psychosis when its personal and subjective psychological meaning to the individual is such that it represents for him a total collapse of his world. Similarly, since material or other kinds of success often involves readjust-

[1] Jackson, 1960.

ments in sociological relationships in one way or another, it, too, can lead to a perception of loss of social relationships. Such subjective meanings of experience are not measurable, but the individual suffering a psychotic episode can portray their reality when there is someone willing and able to listen.

In the course of growing up—which, as we have tried to show, is a process which never really ends—every individual in every society acquires a social-structural "map" which is internalized into his self-system. This map serves many functions. It tells the person which statuses and roles are open to him, which are imperative for him to assume, and which ones constitute alternatives. More importantly, however, a human being's social-structural map pinpoints the people in his environment to whom he can turn for assistance in the solution of the myriad problems which arise daily.

In getting from one social-emotional place to another—which is only one way of describing the normal course of daily events for a person in any social system— this social-structural map, with its symbols, provides the individual with a repertory of problem-solving responses. It tells him with whom he may eat under particular circumstances, for in some societies members of different categories (such as classes or castes) may not dine together. It tells him with whom he may have sexual intercourse, in whom he may confide, to whom he may turn for help in the solution of mechanical problems, and the like. Thus, while the social-structural map provides alternative social routes, it also contains implied sanctions or penalties in the event that the individual does not follow the permissible channels. With respect to sexual behavior, there are rules and sanctions governing incest, endogamy and exogamy, age, privacy, marital status, nudity, and so forth. With respect to confiding in others, most societies seem to discourage confiding in someone who is lower in status or in age; sometimes people are permitted to confide only in members of their own sex. A person in a professional occupation is taught, in the course of learning his occupation, that he may seek professional advice only from a colleague. Thus, a social structure not only provides for alternative modes of interpersonal relationships, but it also provides for a degree of predictability in the sense that an individual knows that if he turns in the proper sociological directions, all other things being equal, he will find the social contact-points which he seeks.

A social structure also supplies individuals with alternatives and standards for choosing modes in earning a living, in dress, in recreation, in decoration, and the like. As has been stressed in earlier chapters, people have access to standards of behavior depending on where they are located in the social structure of their society. Inevitably, for the effective functioning of his self-system, every individual has to believe that the choices he makes and the standards he applies are his own no matter how aware he is of the limits imposed by his society; similarly, even when an individual justifies his behavior by citing custom and tradition, he implicitly believes that he is behaving voluntarily and as a responsible agent. No person feels comfortable in the belief that he is an automaton or a slave to the dictates of others or that his choices and actions are guided by forces over which he has no control. But it is also true that *at the point at which a person cannot—for one reason or another— make use of socially or culturally provided alternatives and standards, he is in serious trouble in terms of his adequate functioning as a member of society.*

One ubiquitous area of behavior in which choices must constantly be made is in the solution of emotional conflicts. It is safe to say that all people in all societies regularly and repetitively face emotional conflicts which must be solved. Most often, such problems are resolved "without even thinking." It appears that they are most often solved with little or no conscious effort because every individual has within him a repertory of techniques, engrafted onto his self-system, with which to resolve such problems. What is more, every social system "proceeds on the assumption," as it were, that most such conflicts will be solved or dealt with effortlessly and without interrupting the smooth flow of sociological relationships.

Another aspect of the normative relationship between social structure and emotional conflicts is the fact that the emotional problems which people in a society face are patterned and similar, just as are ways of dressing, eating, walking. In other words, most people in a society generally face similar kinds of emotional conflicts, and they characteristically tend to resolve them in similar ways and by similar techniques. It is probably as a result of this commonality of emotional experience within a society that most members of a group can make use of the same social-structural map and the same symbolic language in "sharing" their problems with each other. For example, in a preliterate or peasant society, one can often observe a group of men discussing their anxieties about sorcery in indirect and symbolic ways which include, among other things, uncomfortable laughter, references to others' experiences, anger, and the like. Such circumlocutions are not only intended to keep an ethnographer in ignorance; they are essentially modes of handling anxiety, for most anxieties are difficult to deal with directly. Similarly, in Western society, a group of women at afternoon "bridge" or tea (or men in comparable situations) will discuss their sexual or status conflicts and anxieties in roundabout and symbolic ways which might be quite unintelligible to their spouses. Such symbolic modes of communication serve many functions, not the least important of which is the goal of feeling that one is not alone in one's problems and that others "understand."

Most contemporary psychologies emphasize the mechanisms existing *within* individuals by which they cope with the minor and major emotional crises which they recurrently face. Thus, these psychologies stress the weakness or rigidity of repressing mechanisms, the weakness or strength of the ego, the failure of obsessive and compulsive defenses, the control of instinctual impulses, and so forth. Without denying the reality or utility of these concepts, it appears that these psychologies often tend to lose sight of the extreme importance of social-structural relationships in healthy or pathological resolutions of emotional conflicts. One need not spend much time in a psychiatric clinic, for example, to note how friendless, how alone, and how socially isolated are the individuals who seek therapeutic help. Often, *these are people who have no consistent and meaningful relationships through which to resolve their emotional conflicts.* This is not to say that their loneliness is the source or cause of their problems, but for some reason—and this is often a core part of their difficulties—they are no longer able to use the lines of communication to other people which are provided by the social structure.

There are two major highways on any social-structural map leading *from* a person who is facing a major emotional problem. The first leads to a corner, figuratively, where the individual is alone and has only the closed system of his own confusing thoughts to guide him into a complete and vicious circle from which it is difficult to escape. The other leads to other people of socially appropriate categories, with and in association with whom, if he can use them, he is able to unravel the complexities of his problems. These appropriate categories include kinsmen, friends, colleagues, clergy, and psychotherapists.

To illustrate the concept of the social-structural map, we shall read a description of an incident on the island of Tikopia in Polynesia. This selection is an excellent account of the ways in which an individual, who is facing a crisis which is both social and emotional, exploits the social structure of his society in order to resolve his problem. In tracing the steps taken by the protagonists of this drama, we can easily see the consequences of different alternatives.

A CRISIS IN TIKOPIA*
By Raymond Firth

The event, in which I was at one point a participant as well as an observer, was of a dramatic, though not unique, kind. The initial stimulus was a tragedy. The eldest son of the chief of the village where I was living was a man of middle age, by name Pa Rangifuri, who was a friend of mine, and a kindly, honest, simple man. Shortly before I arrived in Tikopia he had the misfortune to lose his elder son at sea. The boy, called Noakena, was a self-willed, headstrong lad, resentful of discipline, and imbued with the idea of his position as the virtual heir ultimately to the title of his grandfather, the chief. It was generally thought in the village that the lad had taken a canoe and gone off to sea to seek his fate because his father had scolded him, and he had refused to accept the criticism. His father gave an additional reason. One of the popular recreations of the Tikopia

is the dart match, a formal competition between two groups of men, each side striving to produce the longest throw of a dart on a long open space rather like a cricket-pitch. One side is called the Bachelors, the other the Benedicts, though these terms have no literal meaning, and the sides really reproduce the traditional rivalry of districts and clans already referred to. Noakena had gone to a dart match as a novice on the day of the evening he went off to sea. In virtue of his social position, he might have expected some recognition, since novices in Tikopia often get special treatment at dance festivals and other public occasions. One of the other chiefs present did indeed call out to his side to let the dart of his nephew win. But the players disregarded this, and the boy had no success. He came back to his father in a rage, cursing, "May their fathers eat filth, the Benedicts; they didn't

* Reprinted with abridgment from *Elements of Social Organization,* by Raymond Firth, pp. 61-75, New York. The Philosophical Library, 1951, and London, C. A. Watts & Co. Ltd.

let my dart win. Why, the dart pitch there, does it belong to them? . . ." and more to the same effect. He had this much on his side, that the game has a ritual as well as a recreational significance, and his clan gods were believed to have a prime responsibility for the dart pitch. His father told me he thought this affair probably spurred the boy on to be fractious, so that when scolded he flung out of the house, took his canoe, and went off. He was never heard of again. The painful associations of the dart game were such that the father did not go to it any more when the period of mourning was over.

The custom in Tikopia when anyone has been lost at sea is for the relatives to wait for a year or so until some vessel from abroad has arrived. If it brings no news, it is almost certain that the lost one has been drowned. They then carry out burial rites as if for a corpse, but with mats and bark-cloth only, in an empty grave. This is called "spreading the grave-clothes, to make the lost one dry." The symbolism is that the grave-clothes provide dry garments for the spirit of the dead, whose body has gone to its last resting-place in the ocean with wet garments clinging round it. The time had now come, according to the talk in the village, to think of "spreading the grave-clothes" for Noakena. This was very much in the mind of Pa Rangifuri, as subsequent events showed.

At the same time, there was also talk in the village about a ritual dance festival which was going to be celebrated by the old chief, father of Pa Rangifuri and grandfather of the drowned boy. The feast was to be one of the series which every chief should give as his seniority advances. As such it would be a celebration of the clan gods, a grand entertainment to his fellow chiefs and the public. It became increasingly clear that it would not be possible to carry out both the funeral rite and the dance festival in close

succession because of the very large quantities of food and bark-cloth which each would need. The resources of the group, though considerable, could not stand the strain. So an important question of public interest was—which would take place first? Pa Rangifuri, naturally, wanted the rite for his son performed first. His structural obligations imposed this upon him. He had been in mourning, with food taboos and abstention from public affairs, for about a year, and wanted to be free. And, finally, he had been very fond of his son, and his sentiments were deeply engaged on the side of doing what was proper by him. Moreover, he argued, very reasonably, that he preferred to wail for his son first, and then stand up and dance in the festival later, rather than to get his mourning lifted and dance, and then have it reimposed. How could he dance with tears still unshed?—he said.

But Pa Rangifuri had five brothers. In Tikopia relations between brothers are expected to be equable. They are sharers in the family property, of which the most important item—land—is held jointly, though they may divide it on the death of their father. Hence they are all interested in any event, such as a feast, which will draw on family resources and involve all of them in contributions of labor as well as of private goods such as bark-cloth. But while in general affairs they are on an equal footing, it is the eldest who has normally most influence. He is distinguished by a special term, indicating his seniority, and he tends to be the administrator of the joint property after his father's death if the brothers keep together. With a chief's family these distinctions are sharpened because of the problem of succession. In theory, succession to chieftainship is open. In practice, if the chief has grown sons, the system is one of primogeniture. Hence beneath the superficial good relations between brothers and their general structural equality there are possibilities of jealousy and intrigue developing. In this case the brothers of Pa Rangifuri were suspected of wanting to hold the dance festival first. To them this would be the more exciting affair, with probably more opportunity for personal assertion, in dancing, in organizing roles. It was thought that they wanted to skim the cream of the food supplies available, as it were, rather than have to put up with a mediocre quantity after the funeral rites. It was thought that since they lived closer to the old chief, they were secretly trying to influence him to follow their wishes. The attitude of the chief himself was not publicly known— nor indeed apparently to his sons. But if the public estimates were correct, a decision would evidently have to be made soon.

A dramatic incident brought matters to a head. As I was writing in my house one morning, people called me out. They said that Pa Rangifuri had gone striding to his house in great anger—they did not know why. I went to his dwelling, and found him there, very angry and in a state of great excitement. We pressed noses in the usual Tikopia greeting, but he hardly paid me any further attention, though he was usually solicitous. A few of his close kinsfolk were beside him. All of them were clearly very much disturbed. One of them lay with his nose pressed to Pa Rangifuri's thigh. This was a conventional token of sympathy, expressing also a rather flattering respect. Pa Rangifuri was uttering broken, almost incoherent, statements in a high voice. Tears were streaming down his cheeks. His body was quivering. He kept bursting out with wild remarks. "I am going to leave the island and commit suicide. I only wanted to cut bark-cloth for my child. They said that *their* axe should cut first, but was it for a dirge? No! it was for the dance!"—and the like. More people came into the house, including a couple of older men.

Gradually, as they asked him what was the matter and spoke soothingly to him, he calmed down, and made some explanation. We then began to understand what had happened. He and his wife had intended to go and cut paper-mulberry trees in one of the family orchards in order to prepare some bark-cloth against their son's funeral rites. They had gone to the chief to tell him in the ordinary way— in effect, to get his permission. The old man had been very curt, and had snapped at them without giving any clear idea of whether he approved. He was so short that Pa Rangifuri thought his brothers must have been successful in persuading the old man to give priority to the dance festival and postpone the funeral. So, he explained, he felt anger rise up in his body. He wanted to show fight to his father. He wanted to drag out of the house the brother whom he suspected of being the ringleader in influencing the chief against him. But in Tikopia the person of one's father is sacred. And when one's father is a chief one must be especially careful not to show violence before him. So instead he got up, threw himself out of the door, and stalked back to his house. This was the gist of his account. But his gesture of flinging away in a rage, though it avoided an open breach, was impolite enough to offend the chief seriously, and to cause the whole village to be deeply concerned.

What could the people of the village do? Would they take sides? Would they cower away and let the principles settle the matter between them? Tikopia conventions do not operate in that way; patterns of *rapprochement* are laid down.

Some of the people were with the chief, soothing his outraged dignity. Others were with Pa Rangifuri. The people in his house were very tactful. They agreed with him about the correctness of his wanting to cut bark-cloth. They said it was right to want to hold the funeral rites before the dance festival. But when he spoke about going off to sea, or cutting himself off from his brothers, they respectfully dissented. They told him not to speak like that. They took the pathetic line. They appealed to his affection for them, who would be left behind if he went to sea. They would be without protection—not entirely an empty form of words, since the eldest son of a chief has traditionally an important role in looking after the welfare of commoners. This type of talk is customary when a man of rank has taken offense—or indeed when any person is seriously disturbed. People sit near him with sad, serious faces, listen to him, agree with his self-justification, but dissuade him from any talk of violent action. They do not adopt any ethical attitudes. They do not say that suicide is wrong, or talk of it as silly; they do not say that the man is exaggerating the whole affair.

After Pa Rangifuri was calm, people suggested *rapproachement*. They asked him to go and see his father—in effect, to make his apology. At the same time they suggested that I, as his bond-friend, should conduct him there. This is also the custom, that some neutral party of rank should play the part of mediator and escort. If I had not been present, then one of the elders, or the son of another chief, would have been drawn into service. After a time Pa Rangifuri agreed. I took him by the wrist, he rose, and we went to the chief's house. (When I heard him narrate this part of the incident later, he said that I gripped him by the wrist and dragged him to his feet, otherwise he would not have gone! Such is the function of the escort: to save the *amour propre* of the principle.) When we entered the chief's house I sat down without a word, to see what would happen. The old chief sat with set stern face, and head averted from his son. Pa Rangifuri took on a very humble air. He crawled over the floor-mats in abasement, touched his father's knee with his nose in respect, and began to wail a dirge. This was his formal apology. The old man sat like a statue, not moving a muscle except to suck at his pipe. Then, after a few minutes, he turned and said to his son, "Why are you crying? Keep still!" He lifted up Pa Rangifuri's head and pressed noses with him in token of forgiveness. But Pa Rangifuri continued his wailing in spite of repeated commands to stop, thus demonstrating his contrition. At last he stopped, blew his nose, wiped his eyes, and sat up.

Then he consented to chew betel offered him by his father. His mother and other people in the house began to reproach him for his hasty action. "Why did you not wait to listen to further talk? Your father was only waiting for you to ask him to come with you and cut trees for bark-cloth." Then the chief himself began to speak—not reproachfully, and in a gentler, more reasoning tone than I had ever heard him use with his sons before. He explained that he was only waiting for Pa Rangifuri to come and give him the word. But one of his nephews had made him angry. This man had stolen a march on him by cutting the first tree in one of his orchards—where the chief had intended to fell the first tree himself with his own axe to make bark-cloth as an offering to his principal god. That was why he had spoken sharply—he had not been angry with Pa Rangifuri, nor had intended to block his plans. The old man concluded by asking his son if he would go and fell trees for bark-cloth in the orchard that very day. After some hesitation, Pa Rangifuri, who had not tried to justify himself at all, agreed. He was then lent his father's new axe, which had not been used before, and which it would be a privilege for him to handle. So the matter was settled.

The funeral was then tacitly agreed upon. The next day I had more talk with

Pa Rangifuri, who soon brought up the topic of his dead son. He said rather bitterly, "He abandoned me and went off to sea." He told me that his father had now set aside valued neck ornaments, that his brothers and some other kin had given beads and cloth, and that all these things were to be buried in the grave the following night, during the ceremony. He was now satisfied that the correct course would be followed. His personal outburst had precipitated a decision which meant the fulfilment of structural obligations.

Why should his outburst have occurred at that particular time? There is nothing laid down in the structure of Tikopia kinship rules enjoining protest of this type if the fulfilment of kin conventions is delayed. On the other hand, though Tikopia are easily moved to the open expression of emotion, and see no shame in what to an Easterner would be a lack of restraint in their public behavior, to give an explanation simply in terms of Tikopia temperament, or the personality of the father himself, is inadequate. Some trigger action is needed to explode the emotional charge which is there in a situation of the type described. This trigger action was supplied by Pa Rangifuri himself, unwittingly, through a dream.

In my talk with him he proceeded to describe to me a dream he had had during the night before he had quarreled with his father. He said that the spirit of his son had come to him—it was the first time since the boy had been lost, months before. He said that in his dream he had been in one of the family orchards. His son had climbed a coconut palm and was twisting off a coconut. He called to him, "Noakena, Noakena." The boy answered, "What?" "What are you doing?" "Plucking coconuts for the store-place." "Hand me a coconut" ("and I reached out my hand," Pa Rangifuri said to me.) "Leave it till I throw it down," the lad replied. "Oh! Hand it to me," said the father.

"Leave it till I throw it down." The boy then came down the palm, went some distance away, and climbed another tree. The father called out to him again by name, several times, but there was no reply. "Again I called, 'Noakena, curse you! Why don't you answer me?' And then I heard him grunt at me, 'Ngu! Ngu! Ngu!' in a high tone, and then he was gone away. I then returned to my house—but I was already sleeping in my house; it was only my dream that was going on."

Pa Rangifuri then described how two women appeared to him in the dream. One of them was his sister, who had died in Anuta, the neighboring island, but who in the dream had assumed the form of a girl living in a near-by house. Each woman had a basket under her arm. He called to each woman in turn, but neither would answer. One turned her face away. Here Pa Rangifuri's wife, who was listening to the story, interjected, "A pair of female deities" (who bear the baskets of disease). "They are evil. Look at So-and-so, who saw them; a death occurred soon after in his house." "Be quiet," said Pa Rangifuri, "while I tell my dream." He continued, "Then I came to my house and slept— but I was already asleep all the time. Then Noakena came to me, crawling through the doorway like this." (He illustrated the action—the Tikopia doorways are very low, and make it necessary for one to come in on hands and knees.) "He came to my side, and I looked on his face and body. He crawled to where I lay, and leant over and said to me, 'Have you said that I shall be made dry?' Then I stirred. I stretched out my arms to embrace him, and called out, 'Oh! Alas! My baby!' And then my hand hit this box" (standing by his bed mat). "I awoke, I sat up and grasped the bark-cloth—here it is" (displaying it at the head of his mat). "I unfolded it and laid it out" (as an offering to the dead boy's spirit) "saying, 'Thy making-dry is there.' And then I sat down and wept for him. . . . Next day I said to my wife, 'Let us go and cut some bark-cloth for the two of us'—meaning to make preparation for the funeral."

I wrote down the salient features of this dream episode on the spot, as Pa Rangifuri was talking, and added further notes immediately afterwards. And although concerned in the first place with the scientific record and interpretation, I could not help being moved by the story. The man was full of sincerity, and obviously had been deeply affected. His face showed his emotion, and his voice was husky and broken, and near to tears. His cry as he opened his arms to demonstrate how he tried to hug his son to him and struck only the wooden box was poignant in its recollection of the incident. It can be understood, then, that when Pa Rangifuri went to see his father the morning after his dream he was in a highly emotional state, ready to react violently to any opposition to his impulsion to proceed with the funeral rites. He said of his acts then, "My belly was like as if a fire had entered into it."

This case raises a number of psychological issues. The dream was obviously an expression of the dreamer's paternal sentiments. It expressed also his sense of conflict and frustration, not only at apparently being thwarted and opposed by his brothers, but also at being deserted by his son. It reflects both aggression and remorse in regard to the boy. The dream symbolism, which is elaborate, can only be touched on. The coconuts and the tree are probably sex symbols. But overtly, they have significant ritual associations. They are a symbol for the head of the principal god of the clan. The wordless *ngu ngu* uttered by the boy in the dream is conventionally the typical sound of a certain type of sea spirit in the Tikopia religious system. The dream as a whole dramatized the belief that the boy is now

a spirit. From the point of view of social organization an important feature of the dream is the way in which it serves as a galvanizer or propellant to the dreamer, inducing him to take action to redress his unbalanced emotional state. The psychology is not our concern here, but its social effects are significant for our analysis.

The analysis has shown how unreal is the concept of group solidarity if applied without qualification in the examination of social process. The family, the lineage, for many public affairs do act as a unit. But in others the members supply separate forces of influence which may operate in opposition as well as in harmony. Fortes remarks of the Tallensi that in all social activities in which brothers take part as the sons of their fathers they are merged, as it were. Our example has indicated how far from the truth this would be if applied to the Tikopia. Fraternal clash of interests, breach of etiquette between father and son are uncommon enough in public expression to be dramatic when they occur, but they are recognized among the frictions of Tikopia social life.

Social organization, the handling of personal relations, includes mechanisms for dealing with such frictions. Some societies have legal mechanisms available in the last resort. But in the small community we have taken for analysis it is difficult to classify or separate out specifically legal procedures, if only because one commonly cited criterion of law— the politically organized force of the society—is lacking in a unified form. But what concerns us here is not a nominal classification of procedures for dealing with conflict, but the means of operation and their efficacy. In a small community, with a high degree of interpersonal contact between all its members, comparatively informal procedures can be very effective. In a community of larger scale, where it may be difficult to find individuals with personal knowledge of both parties to a dispute, more formal procedures of settlement must be adopted. The case we have cited shows a prominent member of the community, under emotional strain, breaking rules of etiquette towards his father and his chief, and indulging in extravagant language, including threats of suicide. Other members of his community, though disturbed, are not at a loss. Their actions follow a defined pattern—which could be seen if space allowed the description of other cases of social conflict. Let us consider the outstanding elements, expressed in the behavior of various individuals, jointly or severally.

The people give social support to the distressed man. They do not leave him alone; they rally round him. They call upon the structural principles of the society by mobilizing those to whom, by closeness of kinship or seniority of status, he is most likely to listen. To begin with, they are quiescent, showing only by small signs that they are beside him, and sympathetic; they behave to him in ways which emphasize his position as the centre of the scene, and his status. They treat the whole matter as one of great concern. They proceed to gather its full import, by questioning, and they stimulate the person to express himself freely, to talk himself out. They agree with his self-justification. What they reason with are his proposed actions. They neither scoff nor contradict; they accept his standpoint to some degree, but appeal to his affection for them, and to his vanity, not to press his proposals to the full. In effect, they purport to attack his rational arguments by the arguments of sentiment; in reality, they subdue his emotions by reason. If necessary they call in a neutral party to lend weight to their case, and in particular to enable the per-

son concerned to redress the situation without losing self-esteem. In this way a person who is socially displaced is helped to restore himself. He is allowed to expand his emotion, gather indirectly the opinion of his fellows, and regain his position by appearance of concession rather than compulsion. Catharsis and sentimental appeal are used as levers of reorganization of relations.

These levers vary in effectiveness, one of the important factors involved being the amount of time available. The Tikopia, like most Polynesian peoples are prone to suicide attempts. "The tendency to depart from situations of personal shame," as it has been called, is marked among them. This refusal to face the full implications of a social situation may take one of several forms. Hanging with a cord is a suicide method adopted by men and women. But the commonest method used by a man is to take a small canoe and put off to sea, perhaps with paddle and mat sail and a few coconuts, perhaps without provisions. A woman, who ordinarily never enters a canoe, simply swims out to sea until she is drowned or the sharks get her. When the suicide attempt is known, rescue parties go out, and not uncommonly are successful in recovering the person, whose desire for self-sacrifice has possibly abated with the nearness of death. In fact a suicide attempt can be a means of exerting social compulsion on the community, of throwing the onus of responsibility upon others, of securing rehabilitation as through a purge, by offering all that one has, even life itself, to fortune. Morselli, Steinmetz, and above all Durkheim, have examined the sociological aspects of suicide, and shown how, despite its private, intimate nature, the practice is not to be regarded as a purely personal decision. It reflects to a considerable degree other social factors. Said Morselli, "The psychical life of the individual is but the reflex of the nature and characteristics of the social aggregate in the midst of which it thinks, wills and acts." But there is some difference of opinion as to what this relationship is. Durkheim went so far as to argue that the rate of suicide of a community is an index of its social cohesion. On this view, the greater the incidence of suicide, the weaker the social integration. An alternative view is given by Nadel, who argues for a correlation between social rigidity or inclusiveness and the incidence of suicide. The less the latitude given to misfits, the fewer legitimate alternatives of living offered, the more is the predisposition to suicide. The Tikopia evidence shows that a distinction of significance is that between suicide attempted and suicide accomplished, and that the incidence of suicide accomplished has to be interpreted in relation *inter alia* to factors of social organization. Tikopia is a society which can be said to have a high degree of social cohesion, through its interlocking mechanisms of social cooperation and very distinct community consciousness. Yet its suicide attempt rate is high. On the other hand, it is not a society which can be called rigid in not offering outlets for abnormal behavior. Institutionalized roles, such as that of spirit medium, and institutional persuasion procedures, such as that just described, may give people ample opportunity to redress their social balance. The actual suicides that occur are a function of time and opportunity as well as of disposition. Suicide in Tikopia is not condemned, but neither is it encouraged by public opinion—as in Japan. Mobilization to prevent it is quick once the attempt is discovered. The social organization then acts as a distinct restraining influence on suicide, both by providing cathartic mechanisms to turn aside an attempt and rescue mechanisms to render an attempt unsuccessful.

In order to understand the consequences of different alternatives in this case study, let us bear in mind that one of the principal crises centered around a father-son conflict. Noakena committed suicide because, ostensibly, his father had scolded him. Pa Rangifuri, too, felt that his father criticized him, and also threatened to commit suicide. But as Firth pointed out, in most Tikopia social crises, "patterns of *rapprochement* are laid down." After his humiliation in the dart match, Noakena went to his father who did nothing to soothe the former's ruffled feelings. Seeing this as a criticism, Noakena stalked out and went straight out to sea. This is one alternative provided by Tikopia social structure for such a situation. But it is not the only one. Pa Rangifuri, too, felt criticized by his own father. He would have been using an alternative of Tikopia social structure if he followed the path taken by Noakena. But instead, he was able to make use of another alternative route on the Tikopia social-structural map. He publicly threatened suicide, a warning which is never taken lightly in this society. When this happens, Firth tells us, "the people give social support to the distressed man. They do not leave him alone; they rally round him." Whether Pa Rangifuri's father was telling the truth in saying that he was really angry at someone else is beside the point; the path which Pa Rangifuri did select almost ineluctably led to a reconciliation with his father and obviated the "need" for suicide.

PSYCHOSIS

With this illustration of the concept of the social-structural map in mind, let us now turn our attention directly to one aspect of the relationship of psychosis to social structure.

The use of the word "psychosis" immediately raises the problem of definition. Simply put, there are no definitions of psychosis which are universally valid. We generally tend to think of psychotics as people who are confined to a psychiatric ward or hospital. This is a misconception, since psychiatrists generally hospitalize a psychotic only when he is in danger of hurting himself or others or when he is incapable of functioning by himself. There are many people labeled by psychiatrists as psychotic who are perfectly capable of performing everyday functions, including earning a living, and for whom hospitalization is not required. Because there is no definition of psychosis which is universally applicable, we must have an operational criterion of psychosis which is meaningful in the context of the data which *social scientists* are capable of gathering. Hence, we shall say that a person is psychotic when, because of personality or psychological factors, he is unable to perform his roles as a member of the society or group of which he is a member.

Before proceeding to the actual analysis of data pertaining to the relationship between social structure and psychosis, we need one other proposition which will enable us to sharpen our operational criterion of psychosis. This will be fashioned as a descriptive, and not as an explanatory, formulation: *To the extent that an individual is a functioning member of a bounded societal group his behavior will be similarly bounded—irrespective of the culture of that group.*

For some reason which is not clear, membership within a bounded group or subgroup tends to keep items of behavior encapsulated. One example, which could be multiplied many times, will illustrate this. There can be little doubt that the hallucinatory experiences of a Plains Indian young man in quest of personal supernatural power is as much a "clinical" manifestation or entity as are the hallucinations of a hospitalized psychotic. Somehow or other, however, the Indian's membership within a bounded societal group keeps this hallucination encapsulated so that it remains within its proper cultural place and does not intrude upon or flood the rest of the personality. Similarly, the loss of such group membership would rupture this encapsulation, and the particular clinical entity would subsequently grossly affect the balance of the total personality system and the position of the behavioral entity within that balanced system.

One possible reason for the ability of the boundaries of a societal grouping to encapsulate such behavioral entities is that there tends to be little chance of demands upon the individual to behave contrarily within that group. If, *for the sake of argument, and nothing more,* we assume that an Indian is brought up for the first dozen or so years of his life in close contact with mothering, succoring, and protective people so that he develops a security system centering about quick and full gratification of his needs and demands by others, we could expect that he would experience great emotional turmoil in suddenly being thrust into a highly competitive and dangerous world in which prestige is gained almost entirely through hunting and warfare. Now let us assume further, again, only for the sake of argument, that his hallucination of a protecting deity is an unconscious or symbolic attempt to make some restitution for what he perceived as a social loss, since it is held in this society that as long as he follows the dictates of this deity, he will be successful in the hunt and on the warpath; that is, he will have enough to eat and will be noticed and paid attention to by others. If this is true, and if this is part of the culture of a bounded group, his hallucination will remain encapsulated as long as there are no demands on him to remain in a dependency relationship to, let us say, his mother or as long as no demands are made on him to be fully independent of people and of gods and entirely make his own way in the world.

To cite another illustration, it is possible that *one* of the forces maintaining paranoid processes, as "a way of life," in Rocky Roads, Jamaica, is the fact that almost everyone in that community anticipates, and often elicits, such behavior; rarely, if ever, do people expect or demand that neighbors will behave in such fashion as to exhibit or manifest trust, warmth, or cooperativeness.[2] Furthermore, as was noted before, within a bounded societal grouping, there appears to be a considerable degree of emotional security in the knowledge, however unconscious it may be, that others feel, believe, and act similarly.

Just as there are patterned ways in every society for solving emotional problems, so are there patterned ways in every society of becoming psychotic. Non-organic psychosis, however it is defined, is an attempt by an individual to adapt to or to cope with painful and overwhelming pressures which he cannot handle in the *normative* fashion prescribed by his society or social group. These pressures can arise from the external world or from within the individual's own personality makeup; usually, however, they appear to result from a combination of both sources. (These generalizations will be illustrated below.) Psychosis is, to oversimplify the matter, a way of solving certain kinds of problems; and, as in the case of most problems, the members of any society have a limited number of ways of solving them, be these technological, social, or personal. As a result, there are a limited number of ways in which a person can become psychotic, and in only very few societies do we observe the entire range or gamut of all the psychoses known to students of human behavior.

The next paper, by Aberle, is a thorough analysis of the cultural, social, and psychological factors which possibly enter into the development of some of the unusual psychoses. In addition to the fact that Aberle's analysis clearly illustrates some of the adaptive characteristics involved in the development of a psychotic pattern in non-Western societies, his paper can well serve as a model for future studies of the relationship of psychosis to the sociocultural environment.

---

[2] Cohen, 1955.

"ARCTIC HYSTERIA" AND LATAH IN MONGOLIA*
By David F. Aberle

We do not yet understand why certain forms of mental disturbance appear in some cultures and not in others, nor what function is served by the symptoms of various non-Western disorders for the people who manifest them. The data and interpretations offered here can do little but challenge existing theories regarding the first of these questions. They may, perhaps, help to illuminate the second. This paper tries to show that a mental abnormality found in several Mongol groups is identical with Malayan latah, one form of so-called "arctic hysteria," a North African condition, and the "jumping disease" of Maine. . . . Finally a tentative explanation of the psychodynamics of the latah-like condition is offered.

The symptom patterns which can be grouped under latah or latah-like behavior are so similar, from one area and one reporter to another, that they can be characterized in general terms before dealing with the Mongol data. There are two basic groups of symptoms, which may be variously combined.

(1) *The Imitation Reaction.* The most striking feature of latah is the symptom of imitating the actions and words of others (echopraxia and echolalia). Appropriately stimulated, the latah says or does what his tormentor says or does. He may go much further: he may complete a behavior sequence—even one which will injure him—which the instigator merely initiates. He may put his hand in the fire when the instigator merely gestures toward it, or undress completely when some one takes off an outer garment, or jump in the river when some one pretends to start to jump. Or he may carry out a sudden command, even when a person who gives it does not provide the latah with any behavioral cues to imitate. The appropriate stimulus may be poking the victim, startling him, or frightening him. It may be enough simply to get his attention.

A severe latah may react imitatively in any novel or disturbing situation, such as meeting a stranger or a superordinate, even when the other person has no wish to provoke imitation. The latah may imitate natural objects or animals, in the absence of any human audience. The latah is powerless to resist the impulse to imitate (there are rare exceptions) and, according to most authorities, is fully conscious, and aware of the absurdity of his behavior. There is no hypnotic preparation. Tic-like behavior is rare or absent (the importance of this point will emerge later).

(2) *The Startle Reaction.* The severe latah seems always to show a strong reaction to being startled or frightened. He may jump violently, or freeze, or flee, or turn on the source of his surprise and attempt to destroy it. He may utter a cry and, very commonly, shout obscene exclamations (coprolalia), mostly involving words for male and female genitalia. Objects of fear are variable, but phobic reactions are common: fear of mice, spiders, or snakes, or fear of the words for these animals and alligators, tigers, etc. Some people fear the word but not the object. This startle reaction, especially when there is coprolalia, is considered a mild form of latah. Severe latah may first

---

* Reprinted with abridgment from *Transactions of the New York Academy of Sciences,* Series II, Vol. *22,* No. *4,* pp. 291-297, 1952.

respond to stimulus with the startle reaction alone, on occasion, and some pass into imitation without first being startled, on occasion.

All reports mention the timidity, passivity, and easy fright of the latah. Frequently severe fright is considered the genesis of latah. For the Jumpers of Maine, the practice of tickling each other in the woods is considered pathogenic. Rarely is the latah psychotic and, if he is, the psychosis is likely to be episodic. Ordinarily he is a person of normal intelligence who otherwise performs a normal social role. In the arctic, the latah seems to be devalued and derogated but elsewhere this is not characteristic. Latah seems to begin in late adolescence, early maturity, or even later. For every group except the Manchus and, apparently, the Jumpers, more women than men are afflicted.

Keeping in mind this general picture, derived from Siberian, Manchurian, Malayan, North African, and American materials, let us turn to the Mongol data. The condition is known in Outer Mongolia, in Chahar in Inner Mongolia, in Jehol, and among the Dagors of Botkha in Manchuria. It is known to Kalmuk informants from the Lower Volga, but no detailed information was received. What follows is based almost entirely on materials provided by three Mongol informants at the Page School.

Here is an example of the full-blown condition. A Khalkha man was known to be very ticklish. People teased him by tickling him. In time, as a result of this (the informant believes) he became latah. The tendency to imitate words or actions was strongly developed and could be provoked by startling or joking with him. Given a lighted cigarette, he could be brought to write with it on the back of his hand, in imitation of a person who pretended to write on his own hand—even though he got burned in the process. If some one

pretended to drink water, this man drank until he vomited. Once, slightly drunk, he tried to mount a balky horse, which began to buck. He grabbed the horse's ear, and when people heard the commotion and ran out, they found him holding the ear and jumping frantically along with, and in imitation of, the horse. He could not stop until he was caught and pulled away. He was then deeply grateful for this assistance.

Easily startled, he shouted obscenities, usually the word for male genitals, regardless of the situation. Once, during the consecration of a young Living Buddha, age four or five, the little boy moved from a sitting to a squatting position. The latah correctly assumed that this was a preliminary to urination and began to shout, "Oh, oh, he's going to urinate!" using an obscene epithet for the Living Buddha—one which my interpreter could not translate. Here we find marked imitation of others, and of animals, and the startle reaction and coprolalia occurring in the absence of imitation.

who tipped over a skin bottle full of fer-

Other Khalkha cases involve: a lama mented milk, wanted passionately to right it, but instead had an irresistible impulse to imitate the sound of the milk running out, until it was all gone; a nun who swayed to and fro for a long time, imitating the swaying of a weed with a tuft of camel's hair caught in it, unable to stop until some one came along and removed the wool. Again, there is imitation of natural objects, without immediate interpersonal stimulation.

The Chahar informant knew but one latah in the population of 3000. Marked echolalia and echopraxia could be evoked by croaking like a frog, or by getting her attention. She was a middle-aged woman, poor but well-esteemed. The informant's family restrained him from teasing her: it was unkind, they claimed, she might hurt herself, or he himself might become latah from teasing her. The informant does not know if she was coprolalic. Her tormentors were fond of getting her to undress, but some one always stopped her before the process went too far. She recognized her difficulties and begged people not to tease her. She claimed that the condition began when a boy suddenly said, "Look, what a big frog!" She looked, and the frog seemed as big as a sheep. She fainted and was latah thereafter (age at onset is unknown). She had a phobic reaction to frogs.

The Dagor informant tells of a midwife who responded to negative commands. The only way to incite imitation was to do something, or start to do it, and say, "Don't you deliver it, I will." A boy might squat down in the street and shout "I'm having a baby." Another boy would shout at the midwife, "Don't you deliver it, I will." "No, no," she would say, "I'll do it," and she would rush to minister to the boy. After a moment she would stop and say, "Boys, boys, you shouldn't do that." This trick was played often. She got angry, sometimes reported the boys to their parents, but never struck them. She could be made to run, to bow repeatedly, or to drop objects, by negative command. Once she dropped a child, without serious consequences. Without negative command, she would not imitate and did not imitate animals or things. She had a marked startle reaction and would shout, but the informant does not know whether she was coprolalic. She was otherwise healthy, normal, and an esteemed midwife. She said that she became latah after a severe shock: her husband died during the winter. His body was kept in a storage shed because the ground was too hard for a burial. One evening she climbed up in the hut to get some food, fell back on the body, shouted for help, fainted, and thereafter was latah.

There is another group of behaviors which the Mongols separate somewhat from the fully developed syndrome, though in Yukaghir and Malay, at least, they are considered mild forms of latah. These are the phobic and startle reactions, if there is no imitation. . . . There are Khalkha cases of people with mouse phobia who go into a frenzy if they are shown a ball of wool and told that it is a mouse. They lash at it and try to destroy it. One man feared a particular insect so that if he saw one on his horse he stabbed at it, even though he might wound or kill the horse. He attacked any one who named the insect. Sometimes, even he was teased—if he were unarmed and there were a large crowd present. . . .

On the basis of rather limited data, I would say that, besides latah, the following mental pathologies are known in various parts of Mongolia: psychotic depressions with suicidal trends, schizophrenic reactions, hysterical paralyses, compulsions, obsessions, phobic reactions, spirit possession, abnormal rages, and mass hysteria. There are no cases of mass latah. Latah is not considered a form of spirit possession. None of these seems to be common. Abnormal rages fall into three classes: human rabies, delirium, and a psychic condition which sounds a little like Malay amok. The Khalkha informant says that some people brood for several weeks and then go out and kill others. He can give no details, and the pattern sounds less elaborated and less a source of concern than in the case of Malayans. Comparisons of accounts of Malay latah, the imitative form of "arctic hysteria," the North African condition, the French Canadian (more mixed French-Canadian and American) Jumpers of Maine, with the Mongol *belenci,* etc., and "acting *belenci,*" etc., indicates that all of these syndromes are identical, symptom by symptom, except that coprolalia is not mentioned for the Jumpers or for North Africa. The condition is found in Arabs, Negroes and "mixed" (Arab-Negro?) individuals in North Africa, as well as in one Maltese. Latah is said to exist in

Siam, Bengasi, Lapland, the Philippines, and among the Buriat Mongols. Observers claim to have seen Tamil, Bengali, Sikh, "Nubian," "abyssinian," Eurasian, and "Russian" (non-Siberian?) cases. One writer mentioned afflicted Europeans in the Dutch East Indies. I have not seen accounts of the condition from these areas or groups. In the case of Malay latah, of the Tungus and Manchu behavior, and of the Jumpers, the condition is differentiated terminologically from all other mental conditions, as is true for the Mongols. Authorities on the arctic tend to group latah with other conditions and call them all "arctic hysteria." But Jochelson, Bogoras, and Czaplicka use subcategories, of which the imitative and startle condition is one, and Jochelson and Bogoras clearly indicate that native vocabulary treats the latah-like condition as a single and separate category. I have found no evidence that the imitative phenomenon is known among the Eskimo. . . .

Let us now consider the problem of interpreting the psychodynamics of latah. It would seem plausible to understand the imitative behavior as a defense, and more specifically as a very simple form of "identification with the aggressor." Anna Freud says that this mechanism may be used for defense against either external dangers or instinctual stimuli, and that it involves assimilating oneself to, or identifying oneself with, the dreaded source of danger. One example sounds a little like latah. A teacher noted that when he scolded one of his pupils, the boy made faces which amused the entire class. The teacher noted this and thought that the boy was mocking him, or perhaps that he had a tic. It developed that the boy's faces caricatured the teacher's expressions during the scolding: that when the boy had to face the scolding "he tried to master his anxiety by involuntarily imitating" the teacher. If we examine latah behavior with this in mind, we may find ourselves closer to a solution. *It would appear that the latah is defending himself in various ways against the fear of being overwhelmed.* The defense takes four forms: imitation (identification with the aggressor), destruction of the stimulus, flight (not exemplified here), and coprolalia. Discussion of this last defense will be deferred. The onset of latah suggests its defensive character. Some victims suffered a shock, some women date the onset from traumatic sexual dreams of being attacked by men or by male genitalia, and some were unable to tolerate being tickled. In this last event, it must be noted on the one hand that being tickled is a somewhat erotic experience, and on the other that it renders the victim helpless and usually results in his begging for release. The traumatic dreams are a similar fusion of the erotic and of something overwhelming, *i.e.* an attack. The phobic reactions, and the Mongol data in general, are more refractory to direct interpretations, but without stretching the point we can be quite confident that the phobia, like the dream, indicates not just a fear of the external object, but the presence of an internal danger, arising from disturbing unconscious material. It is in this connection that we should consider the defense of coprolalia. Apparently, the latah faces a double danger: a threat which is evoked by certain stimuli in that outside world. In coprolalia there may be a compromise technique: the shout seems to drive back the unconsicous material, and on the other hand the material is allowed a partial, but involuntary and "meaningless" expression in the very choice of words. . . . To reformulate, latah cases seem to fear being overwhelmed by the outside world, or being surprised into betraying some forbidden but urgent inner need. Their bizarre behavior is a defense against a chaotic reaction. They "go over to" (identify with) the stimulus, flee from it, destroy it—or stifle the unconscious material with a cry.

Why this defense, so uniform in

symptoms, is found in so many areas and is apparently absent in so many others; why one person, rather than another, falls prey to latah; why the condition is common among Yukaghir, Yakut, and Malay and rare in Mongolia; and what social roles claim most of the victims, are questions which still clamor for answer. Perhaps later research will shed light on these problems. My present guess (and it is only that) is that the latah's problem is one of disturbance and ambivalence with respect to submissive behavior, that this disturbance is based on an unconscious connection between submission and a dreaded and desired passive sexual experience akin to being attacked, and on the idea that the world stands ready to "overwhelm" the victim in this double sense.

This approach to latah as a defense mechanism seems to offer promise for a more encompassing interpretation which will give due attention to social and cultural factors. For example, this analysis can be related to the observation that in many areas most of the cases are women, and to the apparent fact that latah occurs more commonly among individuals in a subservient or submerged social position, and is particularly easy to evoke when the instigator is a person of authority or prestige. But what has been said here must be considered speculative and subject to correction—presented, as it is, in the hope that it may be of some assistance in further explorations of the problem.

In line with Aberle's observation that "latah" seems to predominate among the lower-status segments of the population, similar findings have emerged from the work of other researchers. The determination of the sociological relevance of psychosis must begin with the frequencies of different psychoses in different sociological settings; at the same time, however, reported frequencies of psychosis are often unreliable and, at best, indicate trends. First of all, it is of the utmost importance to bear in mind that

> Diagnosis is no mere plaything of state hospital psychiatrists. . . . It would appear from the few papers dealing with the reliability of diagnosis that variation even between experienced clinicians is so great that comparisons between groups used by different investigators are subject to large error. In one study, three psychiatrists agreed in only 20 percent of their cases and had a majority agreement in only 48 percent. Another study revealed that the widest disagreement occurred among the most experienced clinicians.[3]

In many societies, for example, psychotics are hidden, and where statistics are being gathered by psychiatrists one cannot attach too much credence to their findings, since psychiatrists (and others) are generally unversed in such techniques as matching genealogies against household censuses in order to discover hidden psychotics. Similarly, social scientists are generally unversed in the manners of making psychiatric diagnoses and are often unaware of the items of behavior, and the other criteria, which are necessary for establishing diagnoses.

The problem of frequencies is closely tied to the issue of definition. One working rule which can be followed in gathering statistics in other societies is that if a society labels a person as psychotic, he probably is psychotic. However, this is not to say that a society's failure to define a pattern as psychotic is *ipso facto* evidence that the pattern is not a psychotic one.

---

[3] Jackson, 1960, p. 11.

Another source of difficulty especially in evaluating the significance of rates of psychoses, is the fact that the *absences* of certain types of disturbances are sometimes given especial prominence without relating these absences to a total socio-cultural context. For example, mention is often made in psychiatric and medical discussions that hypertension was absent in pre-Communist China. Admittedly, this is an important fact, but those who are impressed with this datum often fail to ask, "What did they have instead?"

Although there are some minor disagreements among those who have surveyed the frequencies of different psychoses in various societies, almost all are agreed on the major trends. The latter have been traced out carefully by Leacock, who has distilled five major findings from the studies of psychosis in different groups.

THREE SOCIAL VARIABLES AND THE OCCURRENCE OF MENTAL DISORDER*

By Eleanor Leacock

The most important findings of the studies themselves can be summarized as follows:

1. Urban living per se is not more conducive to mental illness than rural living. Were prevalence rates equal for given urban and rural areas, hospitalization rates would tend to be higher in the city. However, urban hospitalization rates are not considerably higher than rural rates in different countries and different parts of the United States. Apparently the type of city and its relation to the countryside around is more important to illness rates than the fact that it is a city. Thus it is inadequate to define an area in terms of a simple rural-urban continuum. Instead, the area being studied must be defined in terms of its specific socioeconomic structure and development, its relation to the total national scene, and its dominant value systems and goal orientations before epidemiological data can meaningfully be analyzed.

2. Studies of migrant populations within a city or country, as well as studies of immigrant populations, indicate a relationship between geographical mobility and emotional difficulty which involves more than the adverse effect of the situational stress which may result from the move. The relation can be expressed neither in the simple proposition that "mobility causes mental illness" or that "mental illness causes mobility," but at least it is clear that the types of persons among whom migration is intricately related to personality disturbance are important and definable enough to affect the ecological distribution of mental illness. As Thomas writes of the Malzberg and Lee study, this raises an important question "about the validity of epidemiological analyses of differences in the incidence of mental disease among population groups classified by urban-rural residence, by sex, age, marital status, occupation, education, and color or race, unless control of what may well be a major intervening variable —migration status—is introduced.

3. Incidence data on mental illness in relation to cultural background, although thin, do indicate that culturally patterned outlets for stress can affect the relative

* Reprinted from *Explorations in Social Psychiatry*, edited by A. H. Leighton, J. A. Clausen. and R. N. Wilson, pp. 336-337. New York: Basic Books, 1957.

distribution of different illness categories in a population. However, at this stage this can only be said to apply at a relatively superficial level. Cross-cultural comparative studies have not reached the place where statements can be made about cultural background and personality malfunctioning on deeper levels.

4. Although the studies of socioeconomic status and mental illness are not strictly comparable (some employ occupation, some income, some neighborhood or style of house as their criterion, depending upon the data available), the general trend is clear and consistent enough to be meaningful. Rates for all illness increase as one goes down the socioeconomic scale. However, the availability of good treatment varies so markedly by class that it is hard to say (1) what relation these incidence findings have to prevalence, and (2) how differential treatment affects prevalence. This is particularly significant in relation to the hypothesis that neuroses are higher in the upper classes and psychoses in the lower. It is less likely to affect rates for schizophrenia as compared to those for manic depressive psychoses, which show consistently different patterns of distribution. Rates for schizophrenia, like rates for all mental illness, go up in situations associated with situational stress—lower socioeconomic status, living in disorganized urban areas, immigration or migration—whereas rates for the manic depressive psychoses remain more constant and hence are relatively higher than rates for schizophrenia in the upper socioeconomic strata and to some extent in rural areas. The contrast between these two functional diseases has often been pointed out as of considerable promise for research into the physical and social components of mental illness.

5. Even where a correlation between higher rates for mental illness and a sociologically defined group can be established, it does not tell us much about etiological factors involved. For this reason, community oriented research is necessarily the most fruitful field for studying the relationship between social environment and mental illness. It allows for the use of both broad epidemiological techniques and intensive depth interviewing of selected cases and offers the possibility of evaluating findings against the background of a definable social context.

THE SOCIOLOGICAL RELEVANCE OF SCHIZOPHRENIA AND DEPRESSION

With these indices of differential frequencies in mind, let us turn to two of the most frequent types of psychoses in Western society—schizophrenia and psychotic depression—and attempt to link them with the social-structural contexts in which they predominate. In order to make such links, we will first have to have a picture of what these psychoses are. The thumbnail sketches of schizophrenia and psychotic depression which we will give are not intended to be definitive statements. They are, in a way, highly abstract "ideal-type" depictions. There are many different types of schizophrenia, and psychotic depression can take many forms; even when a person is clearly schizophrenic, for example, there are often definite evidences of depression, hysteria, obsessiveness, and so forth. There are many technical treatises on each of these disturbances, and the sketches to follow can in no way substitute for them; the ensuing outlines should be seen as nothing more than tentative pegs on which to hang a few sociologically hypothetical hats.

Schizophrenia is a group of disorders with various forms of expression; it is essentially characterized by two processes. The first is a severe disturbance of thought processes; in its *extreme* form, this disturbance is manifest most clearly in jumbled, irrational, "meaningless" flows of words which are unintelligible to most people. This extreme in the use of language by the schizophrenic is sometimes referred to as a "word salad," in which there are no *apparent* connections between words, thoughts, phrases, and meanings.

There are, of course, different degrees of schizophrenia, as well as different types of schizophrenic reactions. Depending on the severity of the illness, schizophrenics are withdrawn, socially isolated, and "shut in." They manifest bizarre behavior in social situations, they have "peculiar" habits, and often consider themselves in grandiose fashion *vis-à-vis* other people. They manifest an acute lack of sensitivity to the reactions of others, and tend to fail to appreciate or evaluate other people's feelings. Schizophrenics are usually emotionally dulled individuals, preoccupied with their own bodies, frequently given to hallucinations or delusions, and they are extremely rigid in movement as well as feeling.

The second process in schizophrenia is the relative loss of the "self," *depending on the severity of the disturbance,* and loss of an awareness of one's identity and of the boundaries between oneself and other persons or even objects. In terms of the conceptualization of the "self" in Chapter 7—and depending on the severity of the schizophrenic process—the schizophrenic is an individual who has largely lost the consistency of orientation and behavior toward the dominant goals of the society's culture which are theoretically available to him by virtue of his status position; he does not possess or manifest a realistic comparison of himself in relation to others; and he has great difficulty in maintaining social and emotional positions *vis-à-vis* other people around him and with whom he is in contact. This, in rather simple terms, is descriptive of one aspect of the world of the schizophrenic.

The world outside the schizophrenic—to the extent that he can differentiate between himself and the world around him—is fraught with danger and pain for *him,* and *his* only way of coping with such a world is to withdraw from it emotionally. Again, the degree of withdrawal depends on the severity of the psychosis. The withdrawal of affect from the people around him leads the schizophrenic to focus his affective energies upon himself, and his major consolations, pleasures, and feelings of safety come from his wholly unrealistic feelings of perfection, superiority, and excellence. Hence, delusions of grandeur are frequent accompaniments of schizophrenia. While the schizophrenic has usually been predisposed to such isolation from the world around him for many years, the crystallization of his withdrawal almost always centers upon severe feelings of defeat and discouragement by the environment of which he is a member. Not infrequently, this sense of defeat is triggered by the loss of a meaningful person.

In a sense, the schizophrenic's total relationship to the world around him can be conceptualized as something of a paradox. Schizophrenia can be thought of not only as an illness but also as a particular "style" for the handling of, and adaptation to, stimuli and pressures emanating from the environment and from within the individual. Most people are capable of regulating the volume and intensity of the excitations and irritants which help to make up the world around them. They can either meet them head-on and cope with them in one way or another, they can block them out to varying degrees, they can withdraw from them, defer the handling of such stimuli, and so forth. The schizophrenic, on the other hand, cannot regulate the volume and intensity of the stimuli which impinge on him.[4]

Not only does he have difficulty in regulating his intellectual thinking, and in relating consistently to objects and tasks and goals, but he is also beset with a special sensitivity to stimuli. Specifically, he has a more than heightened awareness of the painful aspects of the world around him and either misinterprets or remains unaware of the positive aspects inherent in normal social living. Most of the universe is so painful to him that—like anyone else who comes into contact with painful stimuli—he withdraws.

The paradox which seems to inhere in schizophrenia is in the polarity of heightened sensitivity, on the one hand, and emotional dulling, on the other. But the paradox is resolved as soon as we realize that the apparent emotional dulling and insensitivity is a defensive cover or screen—to oversimplify matters considerably— against the pain he inevitably experiences when he allows himself to remain aware of the world of people. He is, in a way, "playing possum," and he erects his own safe and private world of fantasy and grandiosity.

It should be pointed out before proceeding that there is no evidence whatever to lend any support to the belief held by some clinicians[5] that the language of the schizophrenic resembles the language of "primitive" peoples. Even the most dull-witted Westerner can carry on an intelligent conversation with any member of a "primitive" society once he has learned the vocabulary and grammar of that society. To be sure, he would have to know the assumptions and premises underlying the logical system of that group, just as he would have to learn the assumptions and premises underlying somewhat different thought processes in moving from San Francisco to Vienna and attempting to live and function there. Similarly, when learning the language of an alien society, one must also learn the abstractions which have been developed by the culture of that society. The system of abstract thought in any society is almost always dictated, in part, by the social as well as material conditions under which people live in that society, whereas the abstractions of the schizophrenic, where they exist, are tenuous and largely unrelated to the conditions of life of the social group from which he comes. What is important to bear in mind is that the language of any society is cultural, whereas the language of the schizophrenic is "de-culturalized" and personalized.

The same clinicians who attempt to equate the language of the schizophrenic with that of "primitive" language often equate the use of "magical thinking" by the schizophrenic with the employment of magic and sorcery in "primitive" societies. First of all, magic and sorcery in pre-literate and peasant societies are cultural; that

---

[4] I am indebted to Dr. Jan Frank for personally suggesting this conceptualization.
[5] To list the references in which such beliefs are manifest would require an extensive bibliography, so prevalent is the belief in writings on schizophrnia. See, for example, Arieti, 1956.

is, they are part and parcel of a total way of life and are surrounded by a large body of socially shared and socially acceptable custom. The "magical thinking" of a schizophrenic is, not unlike his language, largely personal and is not socially or culturally acceptable. Second, magic and sorcery in pre-literate and peasant societies almost always involve the use of certain material *objects* or specialists which stand mechanically between the person performing the magic and the person or object which the magic is intended to affect. The schizophrenic who employs "magical thinking" believes that he can effect and cause events by the use of "personal magic" because of his autistic fusion with other people; that is, he may feel himself to be inside other people or he may feel that other people are inside him. Third, and stemming directly from the last factor, such a loss of identity appears *never* to occur in the use of magic or sorcery in pre-literate or peasant societies, whereas it does in the schizophrenic. As a matter of fact, the use of magic and sorcery in these nonindustrialized societies is often an attempt to maintain, defend, or even further the user's sense of identity and separateness. That is, magic and sorcery in nonindustrialized societies is often an attempt to facilitate economic or technological activities or to defend oneself against the hostility of other persons; in either case, cultural magic is provided to the individual by his society to maintain or even enhance his sociological status-positions within the group.

Depression, as a psychosis, is generally characterized by severe and incapacitating feelings of worthlessness and guilt. As far as his observable behavior is concerned, the psychotically depressed individual is sad, discouraged, disheartened, and feels bereft of hope for the future. As distinct from the schizophrenic, the depressed person generally is able to maintain an awareness of his "self" and of the boundaries between himself and others. While his thinking is sometimes confused and retarded, it does not degenerate into a "word salad." The depressed individual demeans, belittles, and condemns himself; he feels terribly guilty over misdemeanors or infractions of social norms which are objectively and realistically trivial. In the most severe depressions, where there is often danger of the individual committing either suicide or homicide, he has delusions of sin and guilt, accusing himself of offenses he never committed and he also expresses the conviction that both God and man abominate him.

In his relationships to the world around him, the psychotically depressed individual is characterized by intense emotional dependencies upon people who hurt him. Because of his guilt and his need to be punished, he is impelled to maintain his relationships to them and is unable to turn away from them. Because of the pain suffered from these individuals, the psychotically depressed person feels extreme hostility to them; he feels that these people, upon whom he is heavily dependent, would condemn him and would reject him if they knew of his hostility to them. Partly because of his need for punishment and partly because his hostilities must "go somewhere" the depressed individual turns this hostility on himself and also perceives himself as rejected, abandoned, helpless, and condemned.

Where schizophrenia occurs, it tends to be found more frequently among men than among women; in the lower socioeconomic brackets or statuses of the social structure; among residents of central areas of cities, where populations tend to be marginal; and among acculturated and dislocated native peoples. In short, schizophrenia is most frequently found among those persons whose group memberships and identifications are weakest and most atomistic.[6]

Psychotic depression, on the other hand, is generally more frequent among those persons who are more cohesively identified with their families, kin groups, communities, or other significant groupings. Thus, depression predominates among women, who, in most cases, are more cohesively identified with their family and group than are men within the same society; in the higher socioeconomic statuses of the social structure; in highly traditionalized and tightly-knit societal groups; among professional people; and, in contemporary Western society, among suburban populations.

These frequencies of schizophrenia and psychotic depression crosscut other statistical trends, especially the tendency, uncovered by many investigators, that psychosis, in general, tends to be concentrated at the lower end of a society's status system while neurosis, in general, tends to be concentrated at the higher end of the class structure.

Similarly, these frequencies can be expected to cut across the frequencies of persons in any population with constitutional or physiological predispositions to particular psychoses. Thus, we would like to suggest the following hypothesis: If it can be assumed that there is a random distribution of genetic potential for, let us say, schizophrenia among different groups in a population, then we could expect that the total conditions of life in the lower class would make for a greater frequency of schizophrenia than in the higher socioeconomic brackets. Conversely, the total conditions of life in the higher socioeconomic brackets would tend to inhibit the manifestation of constitutional predilections for schizophrenia, but might help to facilitate the manifestation of other predispositions, as for depression.

We observed that schizophrenia tends to predominate among people with weak or loose group identifications and among people of the lower socioeconomic strata. For the schizophrenic individual, the world around him is fraught with pain; and, like most other kinds of people, he withdraws from pain. But, since he does not have strong and solidary group supports upon which to fall back, he has only his own resources upon which to lean. The "self" of any human being requires consistent and continuous social contacts in order to develop, and it requires continuous and consistent contacts with others in order to continue to function, for the "self" is, among other things, the mechanism which orients a person to other individuals. To employ the analogy presented at the outset of this chapter, the "self" develops *in tandem* with the acquisition of a social-structural map and it *depends* on this map. This map is the support or the foundation of the "self," and, not unlike most other structures, is in danger of collapsing when its base collapses.

Similarly with low-economic status: Poverty, all other things being equal, is objectively and realistically painful. We have observed in the course of our discussions,

---

[6] These generalizations in this and the next paragraph are based on the work and findings of Leacock, 1957, whose summary statement appeared earlier in this chapter, but whose complete paper is worth a careful study; Eaton and Weil, 1955; Hollingshead and Redlich, 1958.

especially in connection with adolescence, that people can bear most extremes in ex-pected behavior when they are supported by strong and meaningful groups of which they are members. If, for one reason or another, individuals acquire a picture of the world as a painful and punishing place, and if they are of the lower-socioeconomic strata and have to cope with the world in an individualistic fashion—that is, alone—they will tend to withdraw from this painful world and find solace in their last lines of defense: their own bodies.

In most of the world's societies, it is the man who is responsible for providing adequate food, clothing, and shelter for his family. In stratified societies in which there is an unequal distribution of the means of production and of consumer goods, an individual who is unable to fulfill the primary roles of his masculine status *and* who becomes psychotic conveys a unique and personal picture of the world in his psychotic system. What he is telling us in his psychotic system is that the world is painful, and it inflicts hurt and catastrophe and disappointment on him. The schizo-phrenic often does see himself as inadequate, but his overwhelming sense of inade-quacy appears largely to stem from his perception of the world as standing in his way and crushing him.

We have noted that there tends to be a high correlation between schizophrenia, on the one hand, and masculinity, low-income levels, marginal populations, and weak-sociological groupings, on the other. These correlations appear to be ex-plainable in the following terms: Men generally, especially in Western society, have weaker group identifications than do women. Furthermore, it is often difficult for strong and meaningful group organizations to function at the lower-socioeconomic levels; the principles underlying such social-structural weakness were illustrated by the case of clanship among the Chinese peasants, in Chapter 2. At the same time that social groupings are weak at the lower-socioeconomic levels, however, they are not completely absent, for the existence of any social system necessarily implies the existence of a functioning structure of social groupings. There are potentially mean-ingful groupings among hoboes, for example, and there are family groupings at even the poorest levels of society.

The schizophrenic is not a person who has had no groups at all upon which to fall back for support before his breakdown, for, in reality, there are such groups. In-stead, either having grown up in the lower-socioeconomic strata of the society or having within him a perception of the world as terribly painful and punishing, or combining both, *he is unable to make use of the groupings—however minimal these might be—which are provided by the social structure.* Thus, he becomes increasingly isolated and "de-culturalized" and behaves and thinks in a manner which is removed from the ways of the world which is so painful for him. (In line with the foregoing, *one* of the goals of successful therapy with schizophrenic patients is to transmit the idea—through the establishment of a meaningful relationship between patient and therapist—that there are people and groups which are safe and non-punishing from which support can be elicited.)

In brief, then, it can be hypothesized that weak sociological attachments or relationships constitute a social-structural condition which can maximize the manifestation of a constitutional predisposition to schizophrenia; similarly, solidary attachments—to the extent that they are possible or even feasible for such a person —constitute a sociological condition which can minimize the manifestation of a constitutional predisposition to schizophrenia. In terms of this hypothesis, the same person born with a given predisposition to schizophrenia would be more likely to become manifestly schizophrenic if born into a lower-class family than if he were born into a middle-class family. (This is an uncomfortably attenuated hypothesis in the light of what is known about schizophrenia, but it is stated nevertheless as a pointer of one direction along which theory and research can proceed.)

Since this discussion is not primarily concerned with the psychodynamics of individual schizophrenics, we shall not attempt to discuss the exceptions to the sociological categories in which schizophrenia predominates. For example, there are instances of schizophrenia among professional women of the higher socioeconomic brackets who have strong group identifications. There are surely highly specific constitutional factors involved in such instances, as well as in others. An understanding of all personality deviance within a social-structural matrix can only be arrived at through original research with raw data in our society as well as in others. This requires considerable psychiatric knowledge on the part of the social scientist and a not inconsiderable amount of sociological sophistication on the part of the psychiatrist.

Now let us attempt to examine the social-structural relevance of psychotic depression. We have observed that depression predominates among those persons whose group identifications are strongest. One of the correlates of strong group affiliation and cohesiveness is a strong feeling of reciprocal dependency among the members of the group, be that group a nuclear family, an extended family, a lineage, a religious fraternity, a professional guild, and the like. Every such group *demands* that the individual keep within bounds potentially disruptive forces directed at the group if the latter is to remain intact and if the individual is to continue to receive gratification and reward from his membership in the group. If he does not control his aggressive strivings toward the group, he must face the consequence of group censure and condemnation.[7]

Guilt is the emotion or affect which one experiences when he *does* something which he *should not* do, or when he *feels* something which his societal group says is *wrong* or *sinful* to feel. The group to which one belongs can be depended on to provide support and acceptance for its members; but it also threatens censure and rejection, if not bodily harm, when one violates its moral norms. Thus, when a member of a cohesive group cannot repress, deny, or displace feelings which are potentially threatening to the group, he applies to himself the censure which he knows the group would apply to him if his strivings did break out. As a matter of fact, it can be said that the group *does* apply this censure even before such strivings break out, for the social structure and its cultural interdicts are internalized into the individual's "self" and motivational structure. Psychotic depression is the welt left by

---

[7] For a discussion of one of the ways in which institutional "needs" force the individual to maintain such control, see Cohen, 1958.

the whiplash of conscience; in those social-structural situations in which there is strong group sense of belonging, the group is as much a part of the censoring mechanism of the conscience as are the abstract ideas of right and wrong and good and evil which are implanted by the socializing agents.

Let us take one example to illustrate this. Psychotic depression is often found among middle-aged women. In the therapy of these individuals, it emerges that they have a tremendous amount of rage against their children and husbands, an emotion which is often a carry-over from their feelings toward their parents and siblings. As a result of this rage, they feel guilty, deserving of punishment, worthless, and sinful. They express the attitude that such hostility, especially toward one's young children, is sinful; this is a fairly accurate description of the value system of the society in which they live. The taboo on the expression of such an emotion is an extremely strong one, and is punishable by the society. Not only does a woman accept these cultural interdicts—which were implanted at an early age—and feel, with the society, that she is sinful and worthless because of her feelings, but the rage must "go somewhere." Because of her feelings of sinfulness and because the rage must be discharged toward some object, it is turned against herself, and is especially manifest in her need for punishment to expiate her guilt. At the same time that she feels this rage against members of her family, she is also highly dependent on her family. If she allowed her feelings of rage to be expressed, her rejection by the family would mean a loss of economic support, affection, a place to live, her social status as wife and mother, and the like. (Since psychotically depressed people consistently provoke the hurts which arouse their anger, one of the many goals of successful therapy with such people is to help them avoid such provocations and to help them achieve an awareness of the irrational sources of their rage and guilt.)

SUMMARY

Thus far in the discussion of psychosis and social structure, we have attempted to formulate a conceptualization of psychosis which is meaningful in terms of the data which are available to social scientists. In proposing a concept of the social-structural map, we have striven to show that in addition to factors of mobility, status, occupation, community organization, and the like, the *total* social system in which people live occupies a highly specific place in their emotional structures. In Chapters 11 and 12, for example, we saw how the total community structure of a people affects their world views and becomes part of their perceptual apparatus and self-systems. Similarly, a social structure also plays a very special role in people's maintenance of emotional equilibrium or in their hurtling decline into psychosis. Now that we have seen the sociological relevance of statistical frequencies of different psychoses, we can go on to an examination and illustration of the idea that an individual not only stands in particular relationship to other individuals, to institutions and role systems, to dominant value systems, and the like, but *he also stands in particular relationship to the* total *world around him*. It is this relationship which is exceedingly crucial for an understanding of psychosis, because it includes more than the sum of the sociological parts of the environment.

BIBLIOGRAPHY AND SUGGESTED READINGS

It is a curious aspect of the sociology of psychiatry that one would be extremely hard put to learn about clinical psychiatric entities from the published literature. Orinarily, such knowledge is handed down by word of mouth in hospital settings and in personal supervision. There are two reference works which can be consulted for basic information: *A Text-Book of Psychiatry for Students and Practitioners,* by D. K. Henderson and R. D. Gillespie. London: Oxford University Press, 1947. A more recent work, and in large part most valuable for its up-to-date bibliographies on individual subjects and topics is the *Handbook of Psychiatry* (2 volumes), edited by Silvano Arieti. New York: Basic Books, 1959.

Arieti, Silvano. "Some Basic Problems Common to Anthropology and Modern Psychiatry," *American Anthropologist,* Vol. 58, pp. 26-39, 1956.

Beers, Clifford. *A Mind that Found itself: An Autobiography.* New York: Longmans, 1913. A classic—by a man who had been a schizophrenic patient.

Bleuler, Eugen. "The Basic Symptoms of Schizophrenia," in *Organization and Pathology of Thought,* edited by David Rapaport, pp. 581-649. New York: Columbia, 1951. An excellent introduction.

⸱Cohen, Yehudi A. "Character Formation and Social Structure in a Jamaican Community," *Psychiatry,* Vol. *18,* pp. 275-296, 1955.

Cohen, Yehudi A. "Some Aspects of Ritualized Behavior in Interpersonal Relationships," *Human Relations,* Vol. *11,* 195-215, 1958.

Eaton, Joseph and Robert J. Weil. *Culture and Mental Disorders.* Glencoe, Illinois: Free Press, 1955.

Hoch, Paul and Joseph Zubin (editors). *Depression.* New York: Grune and Stratton, 1954. An adequate introduction.

Hollingshead, August B. and Fredrick C. Redlich. *Social Class and Mental Illness.* New York: Wiley, 1958.

Jackson, Don D. (editor). *The Etiology of Schizophrenia.* New York: Basic Books, 1960.

Leacock, Eleanor. "Three Social Variables and the Occurrence of Mental Disorder," in *Explorations in Social Psychiatry,* edited by A. H. Leighton, J. A. Clausen, and R. N. Wilson, pp. 308-340. New York: Basic Books, 1957.

Myers, Jerome K. and Bertram H. Roberts. *Family and Class Dynamics in Mental Illness.* New York: Wiley, 1959. A curious book which examines the relationship between class and emotional disorder, without ever defining adequately the disorders with which it deals.

Chapter 16
PSYCHOSIS AND SOCIAL-
STRUCTURAL RELATIONSHIPS

There are many ways of describing psychosis. From the point of view of the patient suffering from a psychosis, it can probably be described in such terms as terror, pain, ubiquitous demons and nightmares, unbearable loneliness, rage, confusion, life in a bottomless abyss. From the point of view of the person trying to treat a psychotic, it can be described as a system—usually a closed one—made up of conflicting forces and conflicting emotional needs which must, in one way or another, be resolved and laid to rest. From this same point of view, as well as from the point of view of the psychotic, the latter is a person who is at war with himself and who must somehow be taught to, or otherwise brought to the point at which he can, make peace with himself.

When we speak of psychosis as a system, we mean that it is a special case of that kind of system which is known as personality; such a designation places the study of psychosis at a particular level of abstraction and enables us to place it in perspective *vis-à-vis* other objects of inquiry in the study of personality. The reference to psychosis as a closed system, on the other hand, is an attempt to describe one facet, albeit an extremely crucial one, of psychosis in general; it is, in part, an attempt to see it from the focus of the psychotic himself. By a closed system we mean here a total mode of adaptation to particular strains and stresses which is founded on a limited number of irrational assumptions about the social world and the individual's relationship to it; during the illness, these assumptions are immovable, intractable, and are not open to rational argument or persuasion. Nor, it follows logically, are the resulting modes of thought and adaptation open to reasoning. Everything that is emotionally threatening or disturbing to the psychotic individual is explainable to him in terms of his intractable basic and fundamental assumptions about the world around him and his relationship to it.

One way of viewing an individual's psychosis is to say that because of what he experiences his relationships with those around him are also disturbed. But this is a limited view, because it contains the implicit assumption that as soon as the psychotic can make peace with himself he will also—automatically, as it were—be able to make peace with those around him. While this is, indeed, often the case, it takes too much for granted, at least for an understanding of the relationship between psychosis and social-structural ties. From this vantage point the individual is seen as part of a machine, the assumption being that as soon as the individual part is repaired the whole machine will return to working order. Equally important is that such a point of view seems also to be based on a particular kind of morality, one which states that the nature of a man's adaptation is a responsibility which rests squarely on his own shoulders, that every man is master of his own fate, and that "life is what you make it."

In sociological terms, nonorganic psychosis always involves a disturbance between the individual and those persons who, according to his social-structural map, are theoretically available to him. The psychotic person is one who is unable, for one reason or another, to use his social-structural map to get from one social-emotional place to another and to find the social contact-points which he needs and seeks. Thus, in trying to understand the sociological relevance of emotional disturbance, we can hypothesize a continuum of the individual's relationship to his map. At one extreme (what is popularly called "healthy"), the individual can make optimal and effective use of his map. At a point removed from this extreme, his map is blurred or there are obstacles in the way of his using it; at another removed point, he is using an idiosyncratic (or "unrealistic") map. At the most pathological extreme, we can say that the individual has lost his map, is unable to substitute or use another, and finds himself in a social-emotional wasteland. At this point, a person can become psychotic or even die.

It is often difficult to know directly the processes involved in an individual's gradual but steady loss of his social-structural map, and, at the same time, determine the effects of this loss on him. This difficulty, of course, stems from the fact that in most such instances cause and effect seem to be one and inseparable. Take, for example, this problem in relation to a hypothetical schizophrenic person. At some point, early in life, he may have developed a pattern of remoteness, isolation, withdrawal, neologisms, bizarre ways of thinking and behaving, and so forth. His perception of the world as a painful and hurting place may have played a major role in the development of this pattern; and we should not discount either a constitutional predisposition to this way of life or an unpleasant environment as possible catalysts to these proclivities. It is difficult to communicate and maintain consistently gratifying relationships with such a person. Other children will not enjoy playing with him, teachers will find him remote, parents will be unable to maintain effective contact with him, he will not be invited to parties in adolescence and he will not be sought after for "dates," he will have few (if any) friends in adulthood, he will find it difficult to hold a job, and so forth. Without such necessary relationships, he will ineluctably be thrown back on his own emotional heels, and he will become more isolated and will further elaborate his own private ways of thinking. The latter modes of thought are especially important, because not only must we know how to communicate in socially acceptable ways, but our social relationships in turn help to set strong and definite limits on whatever tendencies any of us has for private or purely individual ways of thinking and speaking.

Ordinarily, in the instance of this hypothetical schizophrenic person, we would not be able to specify easily at which point his pathology isolated him from meaningful relationships and at which point his isolation added noticeable momentum to the development of his pathology. But, it could be asked, what difference does it make, since the two are so clearly tied up with and dependent on each other? Is this not, then, merely an academic question?

Such a question remains academic as long as we hold to the philosophy of individual responsibility in emotional disturbance, to which reference was made earlier. But such a question becomes a practical and immediate one as soon as we realize that there is a point at which the isolation of the individual has its *own* special effects which produce pathology and personal disorganization. Once we understand the relationship between psychological disturbance and the loss of the social-structural map—especially from the point of view of the effects of this loss on the development of pathology—our knowledge of psychological functioning and of social structure will have been added to immeasurably.

Clinical materials from Western societies provide very little information about such processes, but there are experimental studies and data from non-Western societies which enable us to understand what is involved in the severe disturbance of social-structural relationships.

In May, 1956, the following news item appeared in *Time:**

The wiry young Gubabwingu tribesman found lying in the bush near the Yirrkala Methodist Mission, 400 miles east of Darwin in North Australia's desolate Arnhem Land, was paralyzed in the arms and legs and could scarcely breathe. Suspecting polio, the missionaries radioed for an air ambulance, and soon a 20th century thunderbird flew in to take Lya Wulumu (nicknamed Charlie), 19, from his Stone Age hunting grounds to Darwin Hospital. There four white doctors went to work on him.

A thorough examination showed no sign of polio. X-rays revealed nothing. There seemed to be nothing wrong with Charlie's heart or nervous system. Yet his breathing and swallowing were labored. So the doctors put him in an iron lung. Bit by bit the explanation came out: Charlie's mother-in-law had become angry with him, evidently wanted him out of the way so her daughter could marry a Groote Island aborigine. So, Charlie gasped from his iron lung: "I bin sung." Explained a fellow tribesman, acting as interpreter: "Him bin sung song of dreamtime snake. When you sung snake song, snake coils around legs and arms and chest, and you no longer breathe. If I bin sung, snake get around me, and I bin finished."

The doctors pitted white magic against black; they knew little about cases like Charlie's except that they are usually hopeless; an aborigine who has been sung is resigned to death, loses the will to live and simply stops breathing.

The "wind box" (iron lung) took care of Charlie's breathing and shook his faith in the infallibility of tribal magic. To clinch it, the doctors gave him his tucker (food) intravenously and by stomach tube. Charlie, half-starved, had wandered six days in the bush without food. As he regained some strength, Charlie seemed to regain some will to live.

* From "Interrupted Song" (TIME, May 7, 1956, page 90). Courtesy TIME; copyright Time Inc. 1956.

After ten days of treatment, Charlie was taken out of his "wind box." Doctors still had their fingers crossed (black magic has triumphed over white in half of the cases such as this), but Charlie continued to improve. Paralysis disappeared. His appetite returned. Charlie seemed convinced he was going to make it. Still weak, he will have to remain in the hospital for a month to regain his strength. Then he will be returned to his tribe, perhaps fortified sufficiently to resist the further machinations of his mother-in-law. Said Charlie gratefully: "White man, him very clever. White man magic better than black fella magic."

Before we go on to a description and analysis of the possible sociological mechanisms which produce cases like that of Charlie, that is, which destroy a person's map, there are other data which are relevant to the question under consideration. For example, the lowest death rate in the United States for all age brackets is found in the period of ten to fifteen years. But during the ages of fifteen to twenty years the death rate jumps almost 100 percent for boys and girls.[1] The latter is the period during which individuals are biologically and physiologically strongest and most resistant to disease. Deaths from accidents are highest; tuberculosis, heart disease, pneumonia-influenza, and appendicitis are next in order of magnitude. This is also the period during which individuals experience the "adolescent crisis," during which their significant ties to people are disrupted (see the discussion of adolescence in Chapter 6).

That these correlations are more than coincidental is borne out by a similar trend which obtains in the area of mental illness. In 1951, for example, more than five times as many individuals were admitted to psychiatric hospitals in the fifteen through nineteen age bracket than were admitted for all ages below fifteen.[2] Similar phenomena obtain in connection with the rate of suicide in the United States.

These parallel data are suggestive of a relationship between psychosis and death in the adolescent population of the United States. If there is such a relationship, and if it is, as is being suggested here, related to the quality of social-structural ties—especially disrupted social ties—how do we bridge such relationships?

We know from many sources that there is a relationship between emotional stress and physical disturbance. But why do so many American adolescents die from suicide or senseless automobile accidents instead of developing hypertension or duodenal ulcers? Very little is known about such kinds of deaths, but we can get, as from the case of Charlie, some highly suggestive insights from experimental data and from observations in Western and non-Western societies.

One of the most highly suggestive hints comes from studies such as those conducted in connection with infants without mothers—or, more accurately, infants without mothering. Spitz found that infants can die in even the most biologically sterile environment, and even if they are given enough to eat, if they do not have maternal care; if—literally—nobody loves them.[3]

In an experiment on sensory deprivation—which can be thought of as tanta-

---

[1] See *Vital Statistics of the United States,* 1951, Vol. 2.
[2] See *Patients in Mental Hospitals,* U. S. Public Health Service Publication, No. *356.*
[3] Spitz, 1945.

mount to almost complete social isolation—using college students as their subjects, three experimenters found that they could produce psychotic-type behavior in their subjects for the duration of the experiment by depriving them of normal sensory stimulation. In introducing their study, they wrote that "there is much evidence from recent neuro-physiological studies to indicate that the normal functioning of the waking brain depends on its being constantly exposed to sensory bombardment, which produces a continuing 'arousal reaction.' " The following selection is a condensation of the report of their experiment.

EFFECTS OF DECREASED VARIATION IN THE SENSORY ENVIRONMENT *

By W. H. Bexton, W. Heron, and T. H. Scott

When stimulation does not change, it rapidly loses its power to cause the arousal reaction. . . . In other words, the maintenance of normal, intelligent, adaptive behavior probably requires a continually varied sensory input. . . . The subjects [of this experiment], 22 male college students, were paid [$20 per day] to lie on a comfortable bed in a lighted cubicle 24 hours a day, with time out for eating and going to the toilet. During the whole experimental period they wore translucent goggles which transmitted diffuse light but prevented proper vision. Except when eating or going to the toilet, the subjects wore gloves and cardboard cuffs, the latter extending from below the elbow to beyond the fingertips. These permitted free joint movement but limited tactual perception. Communication between subject and experimenters was provided by a small speaker system, and was kept to a minimum. Auditory stimulation was limited by the partially sound-proof cubicle and by a U-shaped foam-rubber pillow in which the subject kept his head while in the cubicle. . . . The subjects reported [after the experiment] that they were unable to concentrate on any topic for long while in the cubicle. Those who tried to review their studies or solve self-initiated intellectual problems found it difficult to do so. As a result, they lapsed into daydreaming, abandoned attempts at organized thinking, and let their thoughts wander. There were also reports of 'blank periods,' during which they seemed unable to think of anything at all. . . . Finally there were the hallucinations reported by the subjects while in the experimental apparatus. . . . All subjects reported such [hallucinatory] imagery, and said it was a new experience to them. . . . In summary, changes in intelligence performance and the hallucinatory activity, induced merely by limiting the variability of sensory input, provide direct evidence of a kind of dependence on the environment that has not been previously recognized.

In another experiment,[4] conducted with only two human subjects, Lilly attempted to learn what would happen to individuals who were confined in what he describes

---

* Reprinted with abridgment from *The Canadian Journal of Psychology,* Vol. 8, pp. 70-76, 1954, by permission of the Canadian Psychological Association and the University of Toronto Press.
4 Lilly, 1956.

as a pleasant environment, but totally cut off from the world. To accomplish this, the subjects were submerged in a tank of tepid water, wearing nothing more than a blacked-out mask for breathing. Such an environment almost entirely removes the usual sense of pressure on the body. Both subjects (one of whom was Lilly himself) reported similar experiences: At first, for about forty-five minutes, one is aware of surroundings, the residues of the day's experiences, recent events, and so forth. After that, the subject begins to relax and enjoy his situation. But then, a stimulus-hunger begins to set in and the subject becomes quite tense. Self-stimulation, such as touching one finger with another, twitching muscles, making slow swimming movements, become intensely satisfying. If the subject is able to inhibit these move-ments long enough, the resulting tension can develop to the point of forcing him to leave the tank. If the person in the tank can survive this period, he begins to indulge in reveries and fantasies of a highly personal and intimate nature and he begins to project visual imageries which, it would appear to the reader of this report, are some-what akin to visual hallucinations. Lilly is convinced that even people with the healthiest of minds react in this way to such physical isolation.

Such experiments and observations—as well as personal accounts by individuals who have suffered comparable isolation at sea, in polar regions, and in enforced soli-tary confinement—indicate that even the healthiest mind cannot function normally without adequate sensory and social stimulation. These studies provide us with the necessary tools for an understanding of phenomena in sociological situations, in which many more variables are operating and are beyond the individual's conscious control. With these reports in mind, let us now read about several sociological situ-ations which illustrate the proposition that if an individual's social-structural rela-tionships are severely disrupted he can become psychotic or he may even die. If, on the other hand, he is able to substitute or make use of another social-structural map or if he is restored to the social system of his community, he will be able to survive and function adequately.

First, we are going to read about the Murngin of the Australian bush, a group of people who live in the vicinity of Charlie's people. In this report will be seen some of the social mechanisms which can kill a man, as they almost did in Charlie's case. Then we shall read about social situations in which the restoration of social-struc-tural ties can produce a remission in psychosis.

BLACK MAGIC IN AUSTRALIA *
By W. Lloyd Warner

The Murngin offer an excellent op-portunity to study the nature of magic in relation to the social organization and so-ciety generally, particularly in relation to

---

* Excerpted from *A Black Civilization: A Social Study of an Australian Tribe*, by W. Lloyd Warner. New York: Harper & Brothers., 1937, pp. 229-243.

religion. The northern and eastern clans lack the medicine men of the southern and western clans and depend on one of the rituals for healing. The social organization of both groups is identical, the kinship system, the moiety divisions, et cetera, being the same even to minute detail. We can thus observe what elements are found in the nonpersonalized magic of the north and how they operate in the area of the southern shamans.

The medicine man who removes the hard object injected by a malignant mokoi [one of a man's two souls] or the bone injected by an outraged totemic being or another sorcerer, is doing the same thing for the society and its individuals as the mourning rite. The magician too is performing a ritual which has no validity, since he has no position or power, unless the group sanctions it. The medicine man's social personality and the sources of his power are located within the group. The white magician is but the reverse of the coin on whose other surface appears the black sorcerer. The white magician through his personal mana [impersonal spiritual power] helps the sick individual readjust himself to his social environment.

A prerequisite of social conditioning and adjustment is a normal organism, normal not only in biological fact but also in the values of the group. The normal human being not only among the savage Murngin but in any society, according to the evaluations of the group, is the "well" person. Sickness is felt by civilized man to be expectable but not normal, largely because sickness interferes with his ordinary participation in his culture. Both the savage and the civilized man consider sickness out of the ordinary, even though all organisms experience it, not only because of the lack of physical well-being but because the individual's daily social life is changed.

The effect of black magic is found only when the social personality of the victim is out of adjustment with its environment and fails to keep a satisfactory equilibrium. The victim is sick, he fails in the hunt or in fishing, he has his woman taken from him, he is wounded in a spear fight or falls from a tree, and, in general, he is not in a state of well-being. His physical energy is not sufficient to keep up the multiple activities of his social personality, he feels himself on the debit side, with his individual mana inadequate for adjustment; his social personality is dysphoric and maladjusted. Feeling the effects of black magic greatly resembles the conditions of an obsessive psychotic individual in our Euro-American culture, since both the individual and his society recognize his inadequate adaptation. The extreme of this maladjustment is the person whose soul has been stolen—the ultimate in black magic. The soul, the sacred individualization of power and the epitome of the social participation of the organism, seems lost to the individual owner and is under the control of another, *i.e.*, the human part of the man has been stolen and lost to him.

The white shaman functions as one who re-establishes the victim's social equilibrium. The society positively sanctions his actions by placing its belief in the magical and social mana under his control. The ceremonial leader in the north performs these same functions. Even here a man can be killed or made ill by magic: by black magicians, mokois, et cetera, who are outside the society, outside because magicians live to the south, and the mokois, the asocial trickster spirits, live outside the group in the jungles.

The ailing member of society in the northern area must also be cured and regain his vigor and feeling of power. There being no medicine men here, herbs are used, but the native considers them insufficient. In this area the curative technique is the well ritual—a "secret" thing caused the sickness and a sacred ritual is to remove it. The individual is placed in the well, sung over, ritually cleansed, and regarded as cured by the ceremonial leader in the clan exactly as the tribe is purified and sickness prevented by ritual, and exactly as the victim of magic is healed by the magical technique of the medicine man in the south and in the Murngin tribe country. In the north the ceremonial leader directs the healing ritual when the solidarity of the clan and the group is felt at its greatest strength. The whole of the social forces are focused on the individual through the totems, the totem well, and the attitudes and beliefs of the participants. The leader merely expresses, through his direction of the ritual, the social mana of the ritual in the group. This power is believed to go into the individual and remove his weakness. The leader functions here as in the Djungguan [a totemic ceremony] when he directs the ritual over the python totemic emblem to sing power into it, or at the blood-letting in this same ceremony when he places the power of the python spirit in the individual and his blood, which is to be used in the circumcision ritual. It is not the leader who has this power but the ritual of his group. The power and efficacy of the ritual come from the mana of the entire group, organized into a society of clans. The leader in the north, then, cures by ritual and performs those functions carried out by the medicine man in the south. His activities are organized by his clan, he represents his church in the Durkheim sense, not only as a religious ritual leader but in the functions of a magician. In both cases, however, the clan is the "church" back of him. In the south the leader's powers are divided. The well ritual may still be used, but there is also here the white magician. His social personality is little different from that of another member of the clan; he differs only inasmuch as it is recognized that he has a special power. He is sought by the af-

flicted, however, exactly as a ceremonial leader in the Northern area is sought by the relatives of the dead or by the parents of a boy who is to be circumcised. The relatives of a sick man send for the shaman to cure and diagnose the illness of their ailing kinsman and either to restore him to his normal participation in the group or to pronounce his death sentence. *The medicine man then helps organize and direct the community's attitude toward the sick man.* He leads community attitude and organizes the community fundamentally as does the ceremonial leader. He examines his patient, says that he will die because his soul has been stolen, and the community at once recognizes that death is near. The society then organizes itself into a group which in effect excommunicates the patient, trying to force his soul into the realm of the dead and the sacred. If the magician diagnoses the case as curable and removes the cause, he re-establishes the individual's equilibrium, making him believe he can once more participate in his usual manner in the group. He can do this because he organizes group attitudes, since the belief in the curative power of this ritual unifies the point of view of all the members. The magician, while healing, is usually watched by a number of the near and far kinsmen. They all express great satisfaction in his removal of the sickness (the foreign object) and an affirmation of the victim's cure, as do the magician and the victim.

The isolation of the various elements in the particular social configuration surrounding the death of a victim of black magic may help illuminate the fundamental nature of Murngin magic and explain its potency and unusual effectiveness; and a general analysis of the group behavior under such a situation will be profitable.

When the supposed theft of a man's soul becomes general knowledge, the sustaining social fabric pulls away from the victim. The familiar attitudes of the kinship personalities change, the collaboration of the victim and his society, of which his social personality has always been an integral part, ceases. The group now acts with all the ramifications of its organization and with countless stimuli positively to suggest death to a suggestible individual. The ordinary daily activity of the victim's social life is removed. The society itself creates a situation which, if unchanged, makes it impossible for the individual to adjust himself to it even though he tried; and in addition he usually not only makes no effort to live and to remain part of his group but actually, through the multiple suggestions from it, cooperates in his withdrawal therefrom. He becomes what his society's attitudes make him, committing a kind of *suicide*. The social configuration in which he finds himself operating at this time is one of anomie for him. His ordinary social personality is removed, his part of the social structure not only having disintegrated but largely disappeared. Such a man is neither in the world of the ordinary nor in that of the sacred. He is, to use the literal Murngin expression, "half dead." Partly sacred since his soul is not in this world, he is in a position of danger, not only to himself as a spiritual entity, since his soul is neither in this world nor in its proper place in the totemic well, but also to his group, because a soul not properly ritualized and placed in the sacred well with the totemic spirits and sacred ancestors is likely to cause illnesses and death to those near him in kinship. Before death takes place the group, then, begin the mourning ritual the object of which is to transmute the social personality into a spiritual being, that is, to make the soul enter the totem well safely. Even before death the soul starts behaving like the sacred totem; the ancestors and dead relatives come for him and enter his

heart; the soul "ceases" reciprocal relations with the profane living, relating itself to the sacred dead; and the living cease acting their everyday roles and become virtually related to the sacred part of the dying person.

The personality of the victim thus has the ordinary attitudes of society removed from him, the taboo attitude of the sacred being substituted. He responds by recognizing his change of status: the wounded feudist killed by magic dances his totem dance to make himself like his totem and insure his immediate passage to the totem well; the man dying of an illness moves his hands convulsively like his crab totem or flaps his hands like his black duct totem, listening for the sounds of his ancestors' approach as he follows the suggestive sequence of the mourning song and ritual wailingly sung and danced over his body. His effort is not to live but to die.

There are two definite movements of the social group in the process by which black magic becomes effective. In the first movement the community contracts; all the victim's kin withdraw their sustaining support—everyone in his whole community, *i.e.*, all his kin, completely change their attitudes and place him in a new category. He is seen no longer as an ordinary living being like all the other people, but as an abnormal person who is more nearly in the realm of the sacred and taboo. This movement of withdrawal by the society means that his place in the general social fabric has been taken away from him so that he now stands in an entirely different relationship to all of his kin, his clan, and the general tribal grouping. The organization of his social life has collapsed, and he is alone and isolated.

The second movement of the group is its return toward the victim under the integrating force of the mourning rite. The "half dead" man whose soul is in that dangerous position to the community of being neither sacred nor profane must be removed by ritual from any contact with his community; and its purpose now as an organized group with its ceremonial leader, a close relative of the victim's, is finally to cut him off entirely from the ordinary world and ultimately place him in his proper position in the sacred totemic world, that of the dead. The victim, on his part, reciprocates this feeling, behaving in the manner of his totem, with which he attempts to identify himself. The mourning rite is truly a *rite de passage*.

The effect of this double movement, first away from the victim and then back with all the compulsive force of one of the most powerful rituals, is obviously drastic. An analogous situation in our society is hard to imagine. If all a man's near kin, his father, mother, brothers and sisters, wife, children, business associates, friends and all the other members of the society, should suddenly withdraw themselves because of some dramatic circumstance, refusing to take any attitude but one of taboo and looking at the man as one already dead, and then after some little time perform over him a sacred ceremony believed with certainty to guide him out of the land of the living into that of the dead, the enormous suggestive power of this twofold movement of the community after it has had its attitudes crystallized can be somewhat understood by ourselves.

The magicians are the leaders who crystallize this group attitude. By the power of their rituals they organize social opinion and attitudes just as effectively and certainly as the ceremonial leader does by the sacred totemic ritual. Both depend upon the group's participation to make their power effective. It is a group situation, not an individual one, that is operative in both circumstances. It is the power of the "church" or community which integrates the total group, directed by the ceremonial leader in the totemic ceremonies, and it is the guidance and leadership of its magicians.

Black magic is a force expressed through the dysphoric condition of an individual member or members of a social group, and an ever present possible danger to all the members of Murngin society.

The attitude of the kinsmen of the man they believe to have been killed by black magic is most illuminating. The sorcerer belongs to a hostile group or, what is equivalent to the Murngin mind, to one so far away that it is unknown and strange. A sorcerer of one's own clan is not asked to kill any member of it or of friendly clans, but to destroy outsiders who are looked upon as enemies and who reciprocate. The source of the enemy sorcerer's power lies within the known antagonisms which connect one's group with the foreign groups. Probably it is the foreign group's mana, as thought of by the victim and his group, which attacks a member of one's own clan through the magician's ritual. It is the enemy's magician, it must be remembered, who helps organize the local community's attitudes toward the death of its own clansman, and it is likely that he also is an organizer of the outside clan's feelings. One's own sorcerer is equally feared by his clan's enemies, and the deaths in the enemies' clans are ascribed by them to the evil worked by him. The local sorcerer is not feared by his kinsmen; rather, they go to him in times of trouble and weakness, since his power can re-establish their own and their clan's sense of well-being by killing the enemy in retaliation for the slaying of their kinsman.

The power of the black magician, then, comes (1) from the very nature of the clan itself because of its antagonism and open warfare with the people of the victim, (2) from being associated with the dead, and (3) ultimately from the action of the victim's people because of their earlier withdrawal of support from him and later thrusting him from the society.

The mana of the ceremonial leader comes from his oral and ceremonial ritual, which in turn gains its power ultimately from a society or church, viz., the clan. The mana of the medicine man comes from his ritual, in which the group must participate by its belief if his technique is to be effective, which means that his source of power is in the group. He too must have and does have his church, which in Murngin society is the group of clans.

To sum up, the power of the black magician only reverses that of the white: the healer is a member of his own or a friendly group and his magic is made effective by the positive attitude of the victim's people; on the other hand, when black magic is at work, the symbolic behavior of the victim and his people is in response to what they believe to have been the magical acts of a representative of someone outside the clans of the victim and his near kin—and even though the black magician is not present, he is the symbol around which the members of the victim's group organize their sentiments in relation to the victim.

The foregoing description of physical death resulting from the individual's loss of his orientation in a social structure is sufficiently dramatic and clear, and needs no further elaboration or comment. Now let us turn to another societal situation, one in which there is also belief in soul-loss and in which soul-loss can be fatal. But here we have an opportunity to observe how a social structure provides the individual with specific techniques for his or her reintegration into the social fabric. Instead of continuing to contract and withdraw, this community rallies about the individual and once more gives him a sense of belonging. The original symptomatology can probably be classed as a psychotic depression and hysteria, using the criteria of clinical diagnosis of our own society.

Alicia, the subject of the case to be presented in a moment, lives in a situation which warrants a certain degree of depression, for poverty is never pleasing to anyone. Furthermore, there is a *mestizo* community neighboring on Alicia's Indian community. She has, then, a standard of comparison of her own situation and what is theoretically attainable in life. She is married to a man she does not like, and who is poor. In the present situation, her feelings of loss and deprivation are brought to a head by her husband's perfidy.

When reading this case study, it would be well to bear in mind the possible alternatives open to Alicia. Indian women in Guatemala occupy an extremely low status, compounded of native and Roman Catholic morality regarding the position of women. She can nag her husband, a weapon often available to women in many societies; as a matter of fact, she appears to have tried it, but his main response seems to be to drink. She can leave him. But where shall she go? She is old, unattractive, no man would take and support her, and she has no resources of her own with which to live. Nor could her family support her, for they, too, are poor. Her friends would not readily take her in, for she would be an economic drain. In any case, simply to leave a man because he is unbearable is shameful. She could attempt to murder him, but there are legal difficulties attendant upon this alternative, and it would not bring her near a realistic solution of her problems. She could try to get him to change his ways, but her previous attempts at this apparently failed. Her culture has provided her with only one other alternative—to seek compliance from the world around her in a personalized, yet socially acceptable, manner. The social system and world view of the community from which this paper derives were presented in Chapter 10.

MAGICAL FRIGHT *

By John P. Gillin

A seemingly widespread syndrome or group of ailments current among folk peoples in various parts of the Latin American area is the condition which one might call "magical fright." In Spanish it is known as *espanto* or *susto*. Both of these words mean "fright," but they are used in two different types of context. On the one hand, they are used to describe "ordinary" incidents which involve fear but which do not affect the "soul"—that is, they are not believed to have serious psychological consequences. For example, one may be "frightened" by the prospect of rain before the harvest is completed, by the power of one's opponent in a quarrel, by the announcement of an epidemic, and so on. In the second type of context, however, *espanto* and *susto* always refer to an illness or abnormal condition of body and personality. For this reason, it seems best to render the latter concept in English by the qualifying expression "magical fright."

In general, magical fright is manifested in a person by symptoms of depression, withdrawal from normal social activity and responsibility, and signs of a temporary collapse of the ego organization. Although these are symptoms which are apparent to an objective observer, the condition is universally interpreted cul-turally in the contexts where it occurs as being caused by loss of the soul. The soul, in turn, is believed to have escaped from the body of its owner during a sudden fright involving startle. Hence the Spanish words used to label the illness. In cultures where this type of soul loss is recognized it is likewise believed that a person cannot live indefinitely without the presence of his soul. Therefore, the "cure" of *susto* or *espanto* involves magical procedures carried out by curing shamans or *curanderos,* the main objective of which, as understood, by patients and curers alike, is to effect the recapture and return of the soul to the patient.

In this article I propose merely to outline one typical case, to offer some suggestions of parallelism between the native treatment and scientific therapeutics, to sketch the cultural setting of this sort of ailment and its treatment, and to offer a few comparative ethnographic data. Since I am an anthropologist, not a psychiatrist, it will be understood that the "psychiatric" comments and allusions are intended merely as leads for readers who may be professionally qualified to explore this aspect of the matter more thoroughly.

The patient in this case was a Poli-mam woman, aged sixty-three, married to an Indian man two years her senior.

* From Psychiatry, Vol. *11,* pp. 387-400, 1948. With minor abridgments. Reprinted by special permission of The William Alanson White Psychiatric Foundation, Inc., by whom the copyright is held.

The couple were born in San Luis and have lived there all their lives. The husband is a small farmer, and the wife makes pottery to sell. They are relatively poor and do not have distinguished status in the community, although they are respected. Of four children born to them, only one survives, a man thirty-six years of age, married, and the father of three children. I shall use fictitious names in this account and shall call the patient Alicia.

The curer or *parchero* is an Indian who is also a native and life-long resident of San Luis. He has a wide reputation, not only in San Luis but also in many other communities of the Oriente, as one of the most successful curers of *espanto* in the region. He works his own and rented land, but also makes a considerable income from curing. I shall call him Manuel.

The patient complained of not feeling well. She was in a depressed state of mind, neglected her household duties and her pottery making, and reduced her contacts with friends and relatives. Physical complaints included diarrhea, "pains in the stomach," loss of appetite, "pains in the back and legs," occasional fever. Verbalizations were wheedling and anxious. She alternated between moods of timorous anxiety and tension, characterized by tremor of the hands and generally rapid and jerky movements, and moods of profound, though conscious, lethargy. Orientation was adequate for time and place, and normal reflexes were present. Before arranging her magical cure I administered to her for two weeks, with the advice of the local druggist and empirical physician, the standard remedial quinine treatment for malaria, without securing remission of her recurring fever symptoms. This was not surprising, however, because her feverish episodes did not present a clinical picture of malarial infection, although this complication cannot, of course, be

ruled out. In general she gave the appearance seen in patients suffering from an anxiety attack with depression. She herself expressed the opinion that her condition was due to *"espanto."* Among her other anxieties was the fact that she lacked the funds to hire a competent *parchero*. A successful expert like Manuel charges two quetzales for his services, and the incidental expenses of the cure bring the total to about six quetzales. Alicia was preoccupied with the belief universal in her culture that an untreated *espanto* will eventually result in death. This, of course, added to her anxieties.

I undertook to pay for her treatment by Manuel, but, in order to avoid placing undue importance on my part in the cure, my payments were made piecemeal. In other words, I offered no guarantee at the start that any and all expenses would be paid by me. In this way the patient's anxiety concerning the financial aspects of the treatment was maintained throughout the preliminary stages.

A diagnostic session was the second step in the proceedings. This took place at the patient's house, a one-room thatched-roof dwelling with cane walls, on the outskirts of San Luis. Present at this session were the patient, the curer, the patient's husband, a male friend of the family (not a kinsman) who had acted as intermediary between the curer and the patient, Davidson, and myself. Alicia had been "cured" by Manuel before, so that she had confidence in him.

After a bit of conversation apparently intended to set the patient at ease, the curer proceeded to take her pulse. He placed the ball of his right thumb, not his fingers, on each pulse in turn for thirty seconds, looking directly at the patient as he did so. When she attempted to drop her eyes from his gaze, he told her to continue looking him in the eyes. His demeanor throughout was one of calm and thoughtful confidence, not greatly different from that of a medical specialist in our own society when examining a patient. After he had felt the pulse he was silent for a few moments. The patient pleaded anxiously for him to tell what he had discovered. He announced calmly that the trouble was clearly *espanto*.

The second phase of the diagnostic session was what might be called "the confession" on the part of the patient. A certain amount of resistance was exhibited by the patient. The technique of the curer was to look her directly in the eyes and to announce in a calm, authoritative manner that she had been *"espantado* near the river when you saw your husband foolishly lose your money to a loose woman." (This was already known to the curer, as we discovered later.) He urged her to "tell the whole story." After several minutes of fidgeting, the patient "broke down" and loosed a flood of words telling of her life frustrations and anxieties. The *manifest,* or obvious, content of this material was to the effect that she had been the oldest of five siblings, was apparently dominated by her father who was an undistinguished Indian farmer, seemingly had developed a strong attachment to him, was forced to marry an amiable, ne'er-do-well drunkard whom she did not respect and who did not fully arouse her sexually, had from childhood a stronger than common desire for money or economic security, and had been constantly annoyed by the poverty-stricken condition of herself and her husband, a condition which she blamed upon her mate. During the recital of this story the curer, Manuel, nodded noncommittally, but permissively, keeping his eyes fixed on her face. Then he said that it was good that she should tell him of her life. "But," he said, "you have been *espantado* seven times before. What is it that 'frightened' you this time?" She then told about a recent experience when she and her husband were passing near the spot where he had been deceived

by the loose woman. Manuel had her specify the spot in precise detail. She had upbraided her husband, and he had seized a rock and struck her. This had precipitated the present *"susto."* It seemed to us that the patient was noticeably more relaxed after her recital than previously.

The curer told the patient that he was confident that the present condition could be cured. Then he outlined to her the herbs, pharmacy preparations, food, and other items, which she must procure for the curing session per se. Also it was agreed between them that the curing session would take place the following Thursday.

It seems that in this session at least three well-known psychiatric mechanisms are exhibited. (1) The patient enjoys an emotional catharsis, even though somewhat superficial. (2) The patient "transfers" to the curer whom she respects and who by his procedures and air of knowledge inspires confidence. (3) The curer provides reassurance both verbally and by his prescriptions of medicines.

The following interval of four days was occupied by the patient in making preparations for the cure and its associated social activities. The responsibility for arrangements was laid upon the patient herself, both for securing the necessary drugs and foods and for obtaining the participation of the other people specified in the curing ritual. It is not necessary to describe these preparations in detail, but they are of the following types: the patient must secure and prepare food for a feast; she must secure and prepare or have prepared according to close specifications a considerable number of herbs, potions, incense and other "medicines" used in the cure itself; she must persuade a woman friend or kinswoman to become her "servant" during the days of preparation and to be at her orders in the preparation and serving of the food on the night of the cure; she must invite to the feast at her house a number of friends and relatives who, in addition to enjoying the hospitality, will be at the service of the curer during the ceremony; she must persuade one of the six principle men of the Indian community to participate in the cure itself with the medicine man.

It will be perceived that these requirements which are laid upon the patient involve several apparently sound therapeutic procedures. (1) The patient's preoccupation with her complaints is broken and her attention is fixed upon goals outside herself. (2) She is given activity patterns to perform and social as well as somatically derived motivation. (3) A pattern is offered for the re-establishment of social contacts, and prestige motivation is rewarded by the fact that she is ostensibly placed in the "managerial" role. A "servant" is placed at her disposal, a luxury which is very uncommon in Indian homes. (4) Reassurance is given the patient by the cooperative attitudes of friends and relatives who gather round to aid her in the preparations and to assist in the ceremony itself. (5) Sanction of the most powerful mundane authority in the local Indian social organization is furnished through the cooperation and acquiescence of the Principal. The group of the Principals is the repository, among the Indians at least, of the local version of the Christian religion in this community which has no resident priests. Only they among the Indians know the proper prayers and are believed to have direct spiritual access to the Christian saints. They are also the holders of political and social power among the Indians, although not recognized as such by the Ladino government. The participation of a Principal in any undertaking means it is blessed with both wisdom and holiness.

The curing ceremony itself got under way Thursday afternoon. All of the invited guests and participants gathered at the patient's house about 4:00 P.M. The house altar, with a lithographed picture of the household saint, was decorated with fresh tissue paper and pine boughs. The entire inside of the one-room dwelling was adorned with pine boughs, and pine needles covered the earth floor. A group of women were working about the hearth and over grinding stones under the direction of the patient. The latter in her role of hostess was in considerable state of tension, evidenced by her snapping remarks and her air of great preoccupation. Nevertheless it was also apparent that she was enjoying her role as the center of interest. After all the others were present—including Miguel, the Principal—Manuel, the curer, made his entrance. He was dressed in his best clothes of Ladino style but wore sandals made from sections of automobile casings. He calmly shook the patient's hand and checked on the preparations. He made it clear that every phase of the succeeding events would be under his direction and that all those present were subject to his orders. No one objected to his assumption of this role, and it was followed throughout the night. A light refreshment was served by the woman "servant," and we chatted easily for about an hour and a half.

This phase seems to serve two purposes. (1) The organization of a social group about the patient and the manifestation of its interest in the patient's welfare are exhibited. (2) Such interpersonal tensions within the group or between its members and the patient which might develop from the strangeness and seriousness of the situation are relaxed.

After dusk a delegation left for the church in the center of town to pray to the saints, explaining to them the necessity for this cure, and to plead for their aid and benign interest. The delegation consisted of the curer carrying a large bundle of candles, the Principal carrying a native-made clay censer in which copal incense burned, and the patient's son carrying a large armful of pine boughs with which to decorate the altars of the various saints in the church. Davidson and I were also included. The curer and the Principal prayed together at the main altar and set up large candles before it and at the church door. Then the curer began a long series of prayers in Pokomám before each of the fourteen images of saints in the church. All prayers were much the same. The curer knelt with two lighted candles in his right hand and swung the copal censer with the left hand while he explained in somewhat stylized fashion the loss of the soul of Alicia and invoked aid in its recovery. At the end of each prayer he placed two lighted candles before the saint and swung the censer in the sign of the cross, while the patient's son decorated that particular altar with pine boughs. When each of the saints had been properly appealed to, both the curer and the Principal knelt before the main altar and prayed long and loud to the Virgin and to Jesus Christ. Then two extra candles and another prayer were offered to San Marcos "because he is said to be the saint of the *brujos* [evil witches]." After this the group returned to the patient's house where the curer explained what had been done. The prayers had lasted about two hours.

The function of this part of the cure seems to be primarily to relieve the patient's anxiety concerning the Christian saints. Fron the phrasing of the prayers it is also evident that all participants in the "cure," including the medicine man himself, receive reassurance against the fear that the Christian deities may intervene unfavorably in what is essentially a pagan proceeding. For soul loss itself lies outside the realm of Christian affairs, and the recovery of a soul involves dealing with renegade saints and familiar spirits certainly not approved by God Almighty.

After we returned to the house a large meal of native dishes was served. The scene was lighted with pine splinters. The patient did not eat but looked on, complaining about the efforts she had put forth, but clearly enjoyed her misery. The guests and the curer complimented her on the food. Then the curer asked that the herbs and essences and other medicines which had been procured be brought out so that he could inspect them and give instruction to the women as to how they should be prepared.

During this phase also the curer was engaged in making a pair of small images, representing "Don Avelín Caballero Sombrerón" (the chief of the evil spirits) and "his wife." These images, made from a ball of beeswax which he carried in his pocket, were about three inches tall. The male figure had a wide-brimmed hat, and the female figure displayed a typical married woman's hairdress, arranged in a sort of crown or filet around the head. The female figure had a needle placed in her hands. The curer explained that if the appeal to "Avelín" for the return of the patient's soul was unsuccessful, he would implore the wife who would prod her husband with her "lance."

The patient was instructed to stand in her clothes before the house altar. The curer took two eggs in the shell from a gourd plate included in the collection of necessities for the cure. Holding one egg in his right hand he passed it over her forehead, then down her neck to the inside of her right forearm, stroking the inside of the right forearm twelve times from elbow to wrist. With a second egg he repeated the process on the left side. Then he took two more eggs, one in each hand. Aftering making the sign of a cross before her face, he moved both eggs, one on each side, up her arms to her head, down her back and legs all the way to her feet, up the inside of her legs to the crotch, and over her abdomen and breasts to her mouth. He placed the four eggs which he had used in a gourd plate and lighted a small candle on the house altar. This, explained Manuel, removes some of the sickness from the body into the eggs. The eggs are taken to "The Place" where the fright occurred and constitute evidence to be offered to the spirits of the harm which has befallen the patient as the result of soul loss.

The native theory here is that the organism is seriously weakened at the time the soul is frightened out of the body and that in this condition *aires* (evil winds) may enter the body. The physical symptoms of a person suffering soul loss are believed to be caused by the *"aires de espanto."* The eggs used in this fashion have the effect of drawing the *aires* into themselves and out of the patient's body. This in itself, however, is not a sufficient "cure" according to the local theory of etiology, for the soul has not yet been restored to its owner and consequently the patient is still in a "weakened" condition, peculiarly susceptible to invasion by other *aires*.

The curer and the Principal, together with two male helpers, now went to "The Place" where the precipitating fright of the present *espanto* occurred. They carried with them in a gourd the four eggs just used to draw the *aires* out of the patient, digging sticks, pine splinters for light, two candles, and a collection of gifts to be offered the evil spirits. These gifts included a cigar, a bunch of handmade cigarets, an earthen pitcher of *chilate* (a maize gruel used as ceremonial drink among the Pokomám), four cacao seeds, some sweet biscuits, and a small bottle of drinking alcohol. Davidson and I accompanied the party. We walked in single file through the darkness, following a dim path among the bushes upstream along the river. Finally we came to a spot about ten feet above the river which the curer announced was "The Place" where Alicia had lost her soul. A pine splinter was lighted. While the two men helpers started digging a hole in the ground, the curer and the Principal turned their backs and faced across the river to the west. All previous prayers had been in Pokomám, but now the curer spoke in Spanish and in familiar, man-to-man terms. He addressed five spirits, calling them by name and addressing them as *compadres* (a form of ceremonial kinship). The names of the five were "Avelín Caballero Sombrerón, Señor Don Justo Juez, Doña María Diego, Don Manuel Urrutia, and San Gravial [Gabriel]." After saluting the others he directed his remarks to Don Avelín. He explained in detail that he had brought them a feast to eat and alcohol to drink. He explained that here Alicia had lost her soul through a *susto*. He dwelt upon her symptoms and said that the eggs would bear him out. He said that he knew that his *compadres* knew where her soul was hidden and that they had it in their power to return it to her. As a favor to him, the curer, would they not help him to secure the lost soul? And so on. This discourse delivered into the darkness lasted about twenty minutes. During it the old Principal stood by the curer's side, saying nothing, but swinging the smoking censer in a regular rhythm. The two wax images of Avelín and wife were set on a stone, the food and other offerings were laid out, drinks were poured for the spirits. Then everything was buried in a shallow hole, and we departed for the patient's house. Some earth and pebbles dug up by the helpers were placed in a gourd dish and carried back with us. "That the soul might follow," the earth and pebbles were rattled in their gourd container as we walked through the night.

This step in the cure was the crucial

one from the native point of view. The theory is that the evil spirits, which the Indians call *tiéwu* in their own language and *diablos* (devils) when speaking Spanish, hide a disembodied soul somewhere in the mountains. Only a medicine man who has established friendly relations with these occult powers is able to persuade them to release the soul. As a possible reflexion of the frustrations imposed on the Indians by the caste system, it is interesting to note that all the "devils" (except San Gabriel) are identified with Ladinos. Avelín is short, blond, and "dressed like a Ladino." He is only about three feet tall and is considered mischievous. The other three (omitting San Gabriel) have names belonging to actual historical Ladino personages in San Luis.

As we left the spot a roll of thunder rumbled through the mountains as the rainstorm which had been going on all evening moved off toward the west, and a flash of lightning illuminated the slope across the river. The curer remarked that this was a "good sign."

We were met at the door of the house by the patient. She showed an intense desire to know if the mission had been successful. The curer spoke noncommittal but comforting words.

The curer and the Principal set up two large candles on the house altar and prayed in Pokomám, explaining to the picture of the household patron saint why it had been necessary to talk with the spirits and to make offerings to them.

A ground altar was laid out on the tamped earth outside the door of the house in the form of a square about a yard on each side. Each corner was marked by a stake to which a pine bough was tied upright. Each side faced one of the cardinal directions. Now the curer with the Principal beside him knelt on a goatskin and began a long series of prayers in Pokomám. First they knelt on

the south side facing north, then on the north side facing west, then on the west side, and finally on the east side. The whole sequence of prayers was repeated in each position. Although the cardinal directions were not named or personified, this procedure seems to be a survival of earlier Mayan beliefs in the sacredness of the directions. The prayers were actually directed to Jesus Christ and a list of forty-four saints, "If you happen to be now in the north [south, east, west]." The ground altar phase lasted about ninety minutes and ended about 1:30 A.M.

The house was purified and sanctified. The Principal set up two candles at each inside corner of the house, while the curer, holding the copal censer swinging from his hand, prayed over each pair of candles in Pokomám. Then he knelt before the house altar once more explaining briefly to the patron saint what he had done. He perfumed the altar with copal smoke and went into the yard and did the same to the ground altar. He came back into the house and sat down to smoke a cigaret while he wiped the weariness from his eyes.

The son and daughter-in-law of the patient now began to grind the medicinal herbs and to mix the magic potions under directions of the curer. When the mixture was completed a gourd bowlful of greenish liquid was handed to the curer who muttered an invocation over it and placed it on the altar.

Under instructions from the curer all the guests sat down on the floor leaving a small open space in front of the altar. The curer took off his jacket and shirt, tying the arms of the shirt around his neck so that it hung down his back. The patient, her mumbling complaints silenced for once, took off her clothes and tied a scanty piece of cloth around her loins, just sufficient to cover her genitals. The curer took a long drink of *aguardiente* (beverage alcohol). The patient cried and whimpered, standing naked before the company. She and the curer stood for a moment facing the altar while he prayed. It was now about 2 A.M.

The curer went out of the house and the patient followed. He walked about a hundred yards into the cornfield. The rest of the party was instructed to stand about in such a way as to form a crude square. The only light was a single burning pine splinter. The sky had cleared, and the night air was uncomfortably chilly. The patient stood naked in the center of the square, facing north. The curer offered her the bowl of magic potion. She took a quick gulp making a face as she did so and whining with complaint.

The curer put his lips to the bowl and took a large mouthful, stepping back from the patient about three feet. For approximately sixty seconds everyone present stood rigid. Suddenly and without warning a blast of fine spray burst from the curer's mouth straight into the face of the patient. The shock of the alcoholic liquid in the cold air rocked her. He continued, systematically spraying her whole body— front and rear—with the medicine, ignoring her protests and her shivering. A stool was brought and the patient sat down trembling while the curer rinsed his mouth with a bowl of water. After she had sat for about ten minutes the curer gave her a bowl of the mixture and she drank it all, about a pint. Then everyone returned to the house.

A mat was laid on the damp earth floor in front of the altar, and the patient, still naked and shivering, stretched out on it. The curer took off his shirt entirely and with a gourd plate of six eggs in the shell in his hands he offered a short prayer before the altar. First he took two eggs in his right hand and massaged the patient's head, abdomen, and chest with them. Then, with a second pair of eggs he massaged her right arm, front of her body,

trunk, head, and ears. A third pair of eggs were used to massage both legs. Then four eggs, two in each hand, were pressed against the sternum, and one pair pressed against each side of her chest. She turned over, and the whole back side of her body was similarly massaged. This whole procedure was not superficial but a systematic and thorough rubbing of skin and muscle. Although the curer did not touch the genitals, he did not hesitate to massage the nipples. Gradually her shivering and complaints ceased. She was obviously enjoying the treatment and was relaxed. The curer removed one of his sandals and with it massaged all parts of her body.

The patient rose and put on her clothes and was led to the rustic platform bed where she lay down and was covered with blankets. She emitted a long humming sigh of relaxation. One of the assistants placed a broken pot full of coals under the bed, and the curer crawled through the smoke and placed under the bed the gourd of earth and pebbles brought from "The Place" of the fright. As he did so the copal suddenly burst into flame. "Ha," said the medicine man, "the soul is here."

As the smoke cleared away a large gourd bowl half full of water was brought to the curer. He broke the six eggs he had used in the massage one by one into the water. Slowly the white coagulated in the water forming swirling shapes. For a long time the curer gazed into the bowl by the vague light of the candles on the altar behind him. Then he nodded affirmatively saying that he saw that all was confirmed in the eggs. He went through the entire history of the patient's eight *espantos* pointing out "proofs" in the eggs. Then as the whites sank slowly to the bottom of the bowl he said that this showed that all previous *sustos* had been cured and that the present symptoms would shortly disappear. He pronounced the cure finished. The patient roused herself briefly on the bed and shouted hoarsely, "That is right." Then she sank back into a deep snoring sleep.

The curer, the Principal, and the guests left the patient's house about 5:00 A.M. leaving her in the care of her son, her daughter-in-law, and her husband.

The immediate aftermaths of the treatment were of two types—physical and psychological.

Next day about noon I was called to the patient's house by her son. She was in her bed with a temperature of 105° F. She was very "happy" and felt that her soul was restored. But her verbalizations showed some delirium. Her condition was not surprising in view of the violent chill she had received during the "shock treatment" of the night before when she was sprayed naked with liquid by the curer. Alicia had left her bed three times while sweating heavily. I gave her aspirin and had her husband rub her down with aromatic oil. Then I consulted with the curer, Manuel. He did not seem to be concerned. "Once the soul has returned," he said, "the body usually has to readjust itself. A short sickness often comes after a cure of this sort. Alicia will be restored in a few days." I asked him if his patients ever died after treatment. "Yes," he said calmly. "Not often, but occasionally. But it is better to die with the soul. They would die anyway. To die without one's soul is to condemn the spirit to eternal wandering upon this earth. A lost soul can never see La Gloria." He refused to visit the patient, saying his work was done. I am certain that there was nothing cowardly in his attitude. It was simply his view that in such cases events must take their course.

We had with us ample supplies of sulfadiazine. Since I am of course not a licensed medical man, I arranged that I should administer this medication officially under the supervision of the local pharmacist who held a Guatemalan license as pharmacist and empirical physician. In two days the fever had disappeared, and in a week Alicia was up and about her usual tasks.

The patient was under our observation for four weeks after the curing ceremony. She seemed to have developed a new personality, temporarily at least. The hypochondriacal complaints, nagging of her husband and relatives, withdrawal from her social contacts, and anxiety symptoms, all disappeared following the cure. One not entirely surprising result was a heavy emotional transference to myself. She believed that by arranging the cure I had saved her life. Thereafter she insisted on calling me her "papa" and in every way endeavored to develop a dependency relationship with me. Emotional instability was indicated during the four weeks following the ceremony only by an occasional tendency to break into tears when telling someone how "good" I had been to her by seeing that she was "cured."

In this and other cases seen, therefore, it is evident that the magical treatment is followed by a remission of presenting symptoms. I believe that evidence is clear, however, that this type of treatment resolves no fundamental or deeply-lying conflicts of personality. This particular woman has suffered espanto eight times and the chances are that she will continue to have recurring episodes of this type. On the other hand we have a case of an Indian man of the same age, an apparently well-integrated personality, who had one episode of espanto in his twenties of which he was "cured" in the manner just described and has never suffered a recurrence. One concludes that the permanence of the readjustment affected by this type of "cure" depends primarily upon the personality structure of the patient.

Thus far in our discussions of social structure and psychosis we have focussed our attention on the individual's relationships to meaningful persons around him and on some of the ways in which these relationships appear to serve as one matrix within which to view the processes of psychosis. When an individual becomes psychotic, his style of life can be thought of as a de-culturalization of normative patterns. De-culturalization in psychosis is essentially a radical distortion of cultural ways of behaving with people, relating to them, and communicating with them. In such gross distortions, for example, it is found that a psychotic person is aggressive in ways which are not permissible within the ranges delineated by his society, or he may be completely terrified of his own or others' aggressiveness and shrink from it completely. The psychotic's handling of aggressiveness is a de-culturalization or distortion because in almost every society particular kinds of aggression are permitted under particular conditions, and in every society individuals are supposed to have acquired psychological techniques which enable them to cope with their own aggressiveness without paralyzing fear or self-destructiveness.

In psychotic patients who manifest religious ideation, to cite another example, we again find gross distortions of cultural patterns. Normatively, religious persons communicate with the deity through prayer, but are not supposed to carry on conversations with Him; speaking to the deity and hearing His voice in return is considered to be psychotic in Western cultures. Roman Catholicism decrees that religion is church-centered, and that to depart from dogma is sinful. Among Catholic psychotic patients one often hears the statement that religion is a personal affair, and that what the individual does in the sphere of religion is his concern only.[5]

In every known human society, to take one final illustration, sexuality is a mode of interpersonal relatedness but, at the same time, must be kept within culturally defined limits. In psychosis we often observe distortions of these rules, an individual becoming sexually promiscuous in order to try to make contact with people where he otherwise feels unable to, or extending the limited taboos of his society to cover all sexual behavior, and so forth.

It was pointed out in Chapter 11 that "while culturally patterned emotions and motivations generally require expression by the individual, either verbally or materially, it appears that *no society allows for their random and promiscuous expression to just anyone*. Rather, one may communicate these feelings, either verbally or physically or materially, only to certain people." This generalization can be thought of as a rule of societal living. And it is the "violation" of just this rule which is often observed in psychosis.

Psychosis, as an extreme form of deviant behavior, must be seen as one aspect of the individual's placement in a social structure, just as must normal or conformist behavior. We generally tend to think of normal and deviant behavior as properties

---

[5] Yehudi A. Cohen, unpublished study.

of the individual person, and we generally tend to take the statistical frequencies of behavior within a group as relative measures of an individual's normality or deviance. That is, if an *individual* is "deviant," we tend to assume that he is deviating from the normative patterns of the *group*. In the light of this, can we ever speak of a group as manifesting deviant, or even psychotic, behavior?

Many societies often face severe dislocations in their social organizations; these can result from economic disasters, from sudden upheavals in systems of stratification, from epidemic diseases, from wars, and the like. Recorded history provides quite a few examples of such dislocations which seem to give rise to extremely deviant behavior *en masse*. (There is no intention here of conveying the idea that individual properties are being attributed to collectivities, or vice versa.)

We have stressed that an individual's psychosis invariably involves a loss of significant social relationships; or, to employ the imagery of the social-structural map, an inability, for one reason or another, to make effective use of his sociological map. An individual can tolerate most extremes in human experience as long as he has the support of significant people surrounding him and as long as he can use the supports provided by group membership. If, however, an entire societal grouping breaks down and has no consistent social-structural lines of communication and activity, it is entirely plausible to assume that such social-structural disorganization would be reflected in psychological disorientation. Thus, it can be hypothesized that *any sudden or abrupt dislocation in the arrangements of the groups which make up the social structure of a society, of its normative lines of communication, or of its normative avenues of mobility, will give rise to overtly psychotic behavior in a significant segment of the group and/or to patterns of behavior which are at diametric variance with the group's rational ideology which immediately preceded the dislocation.*

For example, one of the most devastating occurrences in human history was the Black Death (the bubonic plague) of the 14th and 15th centuries. During these disastrous epidemics, many areas of Western Europe suffered losses of up to 50 percent of their populations. Using the analogy of the social-structural map, such decimations of population are comparable to sudden obliterations of roads, towns, inns, and other way-stations. In other words, such abrupt diminutions in a population inevitably play havoc with social-structural systems—with meaningful groupings of people, with avenues of mobility and with normative lines of communication. Subsequent to these sociological upheavals emerged what can be called descriptively "mass psychopathology" in the form of widespread "dancing manias." [6]

Now let us turn to the last case to be read. In helping us make a complete circle in this casebook, this selection could also have started out with the introductory sentence to the first paper which we read in Chapter 2. The case which we shall now read describes a case of mass psychosis in an Eskimo community resulting, apparently, from a complete breakdown in the group's social structure.

---

[6] For a description of these patterns, see Hecker, 1832.

WITCH-FEAR AMONG THE AIVILIK ESKIMOS *

By Edmund S. Carpenter

The Aivilik Eskimos, who are a branch of the Iglulik, live in scattered communities along Roes Welcome, north of Hudson Bay. On Southampton Island they total about 120 individuals, or roughly half the native population. The remainder belong to the Ikomiut, Akliani-miut, and Kidlinikmiut groups.

Although the Aivilik are gradually being drawn into the world economy, life on Southampton Island is still ruled by the old ecological cycle. Subsistence is by the chase—hunters prey upon all non-human animals around them. In recent years trapping incomes have been supplemented by stevedore work and employment on scientific expeditions. But at heart the Aivilik remain hunters; the only labor in which they delight is the chase. They not only depend on game for most of life's necessities, but they have the hunter's outlook on the world. Although acculturation processes have by no means left their culture "purely" aboriginal, changes are often more apparent than real. The Aivilik of today, in spite of their dependence upon civilization, represent in thought and act individuals foreign to the Western mind.

Earlier writers on Aivilik life have stressed the importance of magic, recording literally thousands of formulas for controlling game, disease, weather. In these activities the magician did not *cause* things to be done; he *did* them. Just as the hunter with his material implements harpooned the seal, built the igloo, or paddled the kayak, so the magician with his various formulas "drove out the evil spirit," "stopped the wind," or "took the

bear's spirit." This was not influence, nor the force of magic; rather it was "to magic." Magical action was understood as action, not cause. The validity of the magical spell lay not in results, nor in proof, but in its very being. It lay in its inheritance and its being performed by the appropriate person within a patterned activity. To seek validity through proof was foreign to Aivilik thinking.

Today most of this is gone. By 1950 magic was almost completely a thing of the past, a memory. Yet witch-fear was everywhere. Bewitching was a constant threat. Every man's hand was suspected of being against every nonrelative. Tension, jealously, suspicion were always present. Even marriage did not necessarily guarantee suspension of hostility, for a wife came from outside the trusted circle. Indeed, she above all others was not to be trusted. Only within the extended family, the nuclear economic unit —and even here only with close relatives —could one find a haven. Witchcraft has replaced magic.

Records of over 100 cases of Aivilik magic and witch-fear indicate that witch-hunting dated back no further than about 1930 when the Aivilik found their survival imperiled by tuberculosis and a declining food supply. Its life was brief but colorful. It developed gradually during the 'thirties and 'forties until by 1950 it reached a point where it dominated the thinking and behavior of every native. Then suddenly many of the forces that brought it into existence lessened, and today witch-fear is definitely on the wane.

Witch-fear, then, was neither an ab-

* Reprinted from *The American Journal of Psychiatry*, Vol. *110*, No. *3*, pp. 194-199, September, 1953.

original nor a "normal" phenomenon in Aivilik society. Fundamentally, it was a socially disintegrating philosophy based on a belief in the potential malevolence of other people and reflecting great insecurity in interpersonal relations. This insecurity appeared to derive not from traumatic situations of early childhood, retained throughout life, but from contemporary situations that frustrated the Aivilik's feeling of safety in their environment.

The Aivilik had sound reasons for feeling insecure. Deadly diseases had increased tremendously following white contact. Game herds had been decimated. Hostile Eskimo groups lived in close proximity on Southampton Island where they competed for women and an ever-decreasing food supply. The economy was based in part on the uncertain fox trade. There was a general loss of traditional values, of methods of meeting crisis situations, and of fear-reducing mechanism. As the aboriginal religion changed, it became increasingly difficult to blame misfortunes or antisocial behavior on either angry deities or malevolent ghosts; instead most were blamed on human agents. Where once misfortune was a community problem, now it became a personal one. Instead of community cooperation to appease a deity or drive out a ghost, now there was interpersonal strife. This was no joking matter in a society where large families spent the long arctic winter face-to-face in small igloos and where some women literally did not leave these igloos for months on end. And finally, a general loss of faith in the effectiveness of the magician's tools led to their discard. Yet belief in psychic powers persisted and took the form of witchcraft.

For Aivilik witchcraft was a psychic art. Practitioners performed no rites, uttered no spells, possessed no medicines. They could injure others in virtue of some inherent quality that had no external

symptoms. Aivilik did not profess to understand the mechanics of witchcraft. At times a witch was actually unknowing. A malicious thought, by no means rare among these people, apparently sufficed. That it could kill and injure was obvious. Beyond this they did not inquire.

Belief in witchcraft did not in any way contradict empirical knowledge of cause and effect. On the contrary, natural and mystical causation supplemented one another, the former explaining *how,* the latter *why.* Most misfortunes had their natural cause; to witchcraft was attributed the role usually assigned to fate, coincidence, or accident in our society, *i.e.,* selecting the sufferer, the occasion, and the means. In short, witchcraft explained the particular conditions in a chain of causation that related an individual to a natural happening in such a way that he sustained injury.

Thus all Aivilik willingly conceded that the cause of disease was bacteria, insofar as they understood such modern concepts. What concerned them, however, was why a particular person should be singled out for illness. If someone were not bewitching him, how else could one account for this selection? Bacteria caused the disease, true. But every Aivilik was exposed to the same bacteria, and yet not everyone became ill. Why? Because no witch brought them into relation with germs in such a way that they suffered.

Let me give another illustration. On two occasions Towtoongi was shot while hunting. There was nothing remarkable in this. Most Aivilik owned rusty rifles and faulty ammunition, neither of which was used with caution. On hunts, boats were generally overcrowded. Yet little care was exercised, and it sometimes happened that a hunter was standing in the line of fire at the time of an accidental discharge or careless shot. That a rifle should go off accidentally was easily intelligible to the Aivilik. They knew that this was caused by a worn sear, and they repaired it. That a careless hunter should stand in front of a muzzle was also understandable. He was probably excited and moved forward to obtain a better shot. But why, the Aivilik asked, should these two events have occurred at precisely the same moment in time and space? Witchcraft, of course.

It was no means illogical for them to conclude, in this instance, that Ookpuktowk, recognized enemy of Towtoongi's father, was the agent responsible for these two woundings, although in neither case had he actually fired a weapon. (The charge went undenied.) Nor did this exclude a recognition of natural causation. It was merely a logical interpretation of the whole problem in terms of Aivilik culture.

To our mind the only relationship between these two independently caused facts was their coincidence in time and space. We offer no explanation of why two chains of causation intersect at a certain time and a certain place, for, unless we accept witchcraft or hold that the cosmos is controlled by an omnipotent power, we recognize no interdependence between them.

Aivilik philosophy supplied the missing link. It explained what we do not. The world known to the senses was as real to them as it is to us. They were well aware of the immediate, natural causes of Towtoongi's wounds. But they recognized plurality of causes, and they selected for emphasis that cause that to them was the socially relevant one. Thus it was not simply that the flesh had been torn, but that a hunter—a food-provider—had been disabled. It was also the attempted murder of a family and a community. Of the two causes of injury, natural and mystical, the latter alone had social significance.

Proof of witchcraft was twofold: the occurrence of misfortune, particularly disease and death, and confessions. Since witchcraft caused death, therefore death was evidence of witchcraft. A confession confirmed the fact; counterwitchcraft averted it.

This doctrine of witchcraft was not used to explain every failure or tragedy. If often happened that the social situation demanded a common-sense, and not a mystical judgment of cause. Thus if a man lied, or stole from another man's traps, he could not elude punishment by saying he was bewitched. Here witchcraft was quite irrelevant; for it was not necessary to seek a witch when a man stole—the culprit was already known and had to be stopped.

But generally all sickness, particularly the fatal case, was explained in terms of human agents. For death from disease, heart attack, or stroke was much more difficult to understand than somebody's dying because he was mauled by a bear or murdered by someone who hated him. Natural death was far less understandable than unnatural death. The following example is a case in point:

Kainuk and Mikkoshark remained married for years, although the union proved singularly unpleasant. In the end he bewitched her, causing her death in 1951. But before she died, Mikkoshark realized what Kainuk had done and publicly stated that, though she could not kill him in her lifetime, her ghost would take him after her death.

Following his wife's death, Kainuk's behavior became so unbalanced that there was talk of doing away with him. He became convinced that the goddess Sumna was irrevocably determined to betray him at every turn in his life and to torture him eternally in the next. He was visited by apocalyptic visions; mind-freezing apparitions of his wife shrieked in his ears. On several occasions, mistaking a daughter for his wife's ghost, he attacked her with rocks and edged weapons. Everyone expected his wife's spirit to take him quickly, but then he seemed to recover and for the better part of one day was calm and restful. The next morning he did not awaken from his sleep, and all knew that his wife at last had won.

In cases like this, where no natural cause of misfortune was known or suspected, mystical causation stood alone. This was particularly true in fields like mental illness where the natives were, by our standards, quite ignorant. It would appear that, before the Aivilik assimilated many European explanations of natural crises such as sickness, they had but a single interpretation for a given phenomenon. But as they learned the white man's explanation of disease, they accepted this new knowledge and made it complementary to the older belief. Natural and mystical causation thus came to exist side by side, offering a dual, though not conflicting, interpretation. Whether this duality existed in aboriginal belief or not is difficult to say, but all evidence points to the contrary, and it is probably safe to regard this as an acculturation phenomenon. Today in those fields where the whites do not, or cannot, offer the Aivilik a natural explanation, only one interpretation is made. We might call it a mystical interpretation, but to the Aivilik it is merely *the* interpretation. Let me give a striking example of this:

A young Okomiut woman named Shenarkiyark had long suffered at the hands of a cruel father. This was exceptional for generally children were treated with kindness and respect. But among other things he beat her and abandoned her without provisions for over a week at a time. She developed the habit of stealing from neighbors. These thefts were widely known but overlooked. However, on one occasion, in the winter of 1942, fearing her father's anger, she stole a fox from an Aivilik hunter, Ookpuktowk, to replace one destroyed by dogs. This theft was regarded as serious, but at the time Shenarkiyark was not suspected.

That spring she married and the next year gave birth to a daughter. She had always been considered rather simple, but it was only just before the birth of the child that her behavior occasioned any comments. After the delivery she became quite unstable. She kept rubbing her stomach and complaining that there was something within her. Others felt of her abdomen and agreed. One old woman commented that she must have committed some crime to which she had not yet confessed.

A few days later Shenarkiyark admitted to the theft of the fox, and the artifact in her abdomen was immediately identified as the stolen animal. Once during the middle of the night she declared that she heard a fox barking outside and asserted that it had gone beneath the igloo and was at that moment approaching her from the direction of the entrance. Her husband searched outside but found nothing.

Shenarkiyark continued to insist that the fox was within her, and once, baring one of her feet, said, "Look! My foot is like a fox's!" And, according to witnesses, it was. She said she had conceived orally and at one point tried to deliver the fox in this manner. She reached down her throat to grab it, and grasping several whiskers, tried to hold the fox by pinning these against her inner cheek. But she succeeded only in tearing a corner of her mouth. Later she screamed that the fox was coming out of her vagina, and on another occasion pointed to a great penis coming up through the igloo platform. One old woman, who had long suspected her of incest and mechanical eroticism, was inclined to associate the penis with these activities.

Finally when her daughter was taken from her, she went completely mad. She was unable to care for herself, constantly hummed tunes, imitated others, barked like a fox until she was hoarse, and had to be forcibly restrained from biting people. A coffin-like box with bars across the top was constructed, and she was imprisoned within it. There she remained for months.

Up to this point she had been treated with kindness and concern. But gradually the natives became terrified, and limitations to this kindness were set. Finally, when the natives felt their lives endangered, they prepared to take the matter into their own hands. However, at this point Shenarkiyark was evacuated by the Royal Canadian Mounted Police to Brandon Mental Hospital where her case was diagnosed as schizophrenia, catatonic type.

In 1951 Ookpuktowk, owner of the fox, was asked why all this had happened to Shenarkiyark. His reply was brief. He said, "*Akumnit anawakateelaogoma* (paternal uncle mine—clothes-sharer was with me)." What he meant was that his late uncle, a renowned hunter, was his *anawakatee,* that is, had given him at birth an old piece of clothing. This gift established the uncle as Ookpuktowk's guardian and guaranteed that the uncle's spirit would always look after the younger man. In this particular case, even though restitution was made by the girl's father, it was quite impossible for Ookpuktowk to call off the evil powers afflicting her, for the owners were not his, but his uncle's. And even if he had been so inclined, he would not have dared rebuke his guardian. To do so would have offended the spirit-ghost of his uncle, who might then have withdrawn his support or even turned against his ward. All were agreed that an earlier confession by Shenarkiyark might have averted this tragedy.

At times it was held that sins had been inherited, an aboriginal belief given added support by the biblical threat about visiting the iniquity of the fathers upon the children unto the third and fourth generation. Even here, no matter how far

removed, there was always the implication that, at some time and place, a wrong was committed. In the past, the inheritance of sins related to immanent justice or offended deities. In 1950 the revengeful agent was an angry witch who achieved satisfaction against enemies by harming their children.

Let me illustrate with two cases of women who were hospitalized as catatonic schizophrenics in 1945 and 1944 respectively. The first, Oomayoarluk, and Akianimiut, had been unstable since birth. This condition became pronounced shortly after she was deserted by two successive husbands, both white. In 1941 she moved from Sugluk to Southampton Island, where she felt herself unwelcome and denied the prestige to which she felt entitled. When she first came ashore, it was observed that she smilingly used one of her hands as a looking glass. She continued in this habit, spending hours each day examining her nonexistent image. (This point may be of more than passing interest, for in both Aivilik and Akianimiut philosophy an individual's *tungnik,* or spirit-name-soul, is regarded as separable from his body and visible as a reflected image or shadow.) From this point on she was withdrawn, incompetent, promiscuous, hostile, at times even violently dangerous. Voices from beyond spoke to her, and she obeyed their irrational commands.

She was never asked to confess and thereby achieve absolution and relief, for it was recognized that since birth she had been possessed not by her own *tungnik,* but by that of an evil guardian. Therefore her affliction was attributed either to sins she had committed in an earlier life, or more probably, to sins inherited from her parents. Since they were not available from whom to exhort a confession, her case was regarded as hopeless. She was treated kindly, but with caution, perhaps even fear. Until evacuated, she was confined for months in a barred chamber off an igloo.

The second case was remarkably similar. The woman had long been regarded as a bit odd. Like Oomayoarluk, she was an "outsider," a Kidlinikmiut who came to the Island in 1939 from Port Burwell. (When selecting natives for transfer to other posts, the fur traders generally choose those individuals whom they regard as the least desirable; it is quite possible that both women were selected on this account.) While in her middle twenties, she experienced a series of personal conflicts of considerable magnitude and in consequence became convinced that she was engaged in several witchcraft duels, the most deadly with her new stepfather. It will suffice to state that her life at this time was marked by almost incredible fears and stresses. Her behavior became increasingly unstable. There were scenes of uncontrolled anger. On several occasions she attacked children. She imitated others, constantly hummed and talked to herself, and refused to cooperate in daily tasks. Things became so bad that she and her mother were turned out of one igloo after another.

In spite of this, the community generally showed only kindly tolerance and concern. But one night, according to a young man's account, she was observed being raped by a great hairy beast, who was none other than the goddess Nuleeiayik's husband, an incubus who rose from the nether world to rape and bring disaster. The terrified community acted quickly. She was tied up and tortured until she confessed her transgressions. When these proved of little consequence —the worst was masturbation—the community was certain of what it had long suspected: she was being forced to suffer for parental sins. For it was widely known that her mother was responsible for her

father's death. Clearly her illness was punishment for her mother's sin. To make his wife suffer, the ghost of the father had actually driven the *tungnik* from his own child. He had achieved revenge against his wife even though it meant striking down his own daughter.

Realizing that her case was helpless, the girl requested that her name, within which her soul resided, be given to a child in *utero*. The community readily assented, for this guaranteed that there would be no malevolent ghost seeking revenge. While she stood by and actually watched, the ancient ceremony of reincarnation was performed and her soul was incarnated in the body of another. In short, she attended her own funeral.

Both of these cases, plus the preceding one, parallel standard Western forms of catatonic schizophrenia. What influence social factors may have had in precipitating latent disorders here, increasing or minimizing their intensity, and aiding or hindering their resolution, is difficult to ascertain. We know that unbridled fear is a powerful and destructive force in life. In individual cases it can disrupt bodily processes and sometimes even kill. Anthropologists have noted that in primitive societies the incidence of mental disorder appears to increase during the periods of acculturation. If this is so, then perhaps it is not coincidental that these three cases, which were the only ones known from memory, all occurred at a time of great anxiety and social unrest.

Moreover, in one case the individual was burdened with a sense of guilt that was deeply rooted in native philosophy and corroborated by her associates. And finally, all three regarded their cases as "soul" had actually been reincarnated in beyond remedy. They were without spirit-souls, indeed without names, without identity. In fact, in one case, the woman's the body of a child.

The will to be cured must have been greatly minimized by such convictions. And the three women probably had little faith in, or understanding of, modern medicine, so that they were left without the benefit of their culturally prescribed techniques of disease-curing and fear-reduction. Even before they were evacuated, they were left alone with their problems and fears, cut off from friendly associates and deprived of what emotional support a sustaining and heartening philosophy might possibly have offered them. Caught thus with anxieties unresolved by institutionalized and socially sanctioned facilities, these women were forced to face their problems alone.

Now I am not for a moment suggesting that social factors here were a *sufficient* cause, but I do believe that they were contributing factors, and in several cases perhaps even necessary ones. Each of the women had been unstable for years. That there was a constitutional basis or component for their disorders, possibly of genetic origin, can hardly be questioned. The postpartum factor in Shenarkiyark's case is clear. But that there are maladies here that, as Dostoevsky said, "arise from the abnormal conditions of society," also cannot be denied. It is my opinion, perhaps because of my anthropological bias, that these conditions, when projected into a philosophy of witch-fear, not only determined the content of the psychoses but increased their intensity, hindered their resolution, and, in the two latter cases, perhaps even acted as a "trigger mechanism," changing latent or mild mental disorders into severe ones.

We know, for example, that violent, destructive fears, culturally inspired and prescribed, when let loose on unfortunate victims, "in the interests of society," can be disastrous. This is especially true when such fears have validity within the philosophy and value systems of that society.

The case of Santainna, a mature, athletic Aivilik hunter, is relevant here. I had come to know Santainna quite well. So when, in the winter of 1952, I learned that he was in distress, I immediately went to see him. I found no fever, no obvious symptoms or signs of disease. He complained of pain, but said it was not localized. First it was here, then there. It was obvious, however, that he was not only seriously ill and extremely weak, but partially paralyzed. Then I learned that he was convinced that his wife's ghost had bewitched him and that consequently he must die. Several years earlier she had been evacuated to a tuberculosis sanatorium where she remained until her death late in 1951. Before she died she became convinced that her husband was the cause of her sickness and that he was killing her so that he might take a younger wife. Indeed, Santainna's behavior did much to encourage her in this belief. While she lived he evidenced little fear of retaliation for, obviously, his was the greater power. But in Aivilik belief it is held that after death an individual's spirit acquires powers often greater than those it knew in life. When Santainna learned of his wife's death, he was literally paralyzed with fear.

Since no medical facilities were available, I decided upon a harmless experiment: I gave him two aspirin tablets, which I assured him were counter-charms designed to offset bewitching. The relief was almost instantaneous: within a few hours he was back on his feet, apparently happy again and without complaint. The next day he left for his traps.

The question naturally arises as to how trustworthy were my critical judgments in this particular case. Was there a physical cause for the ailment that I failed to observe? How fearful, sensitive, and suggestive was Santainna as a particular individual? And finally, what other life stresses may he have been undergoing at that moment? These questions must all remain unanswered. But while conceding their cogency, it is still my impression that Santainna was, perhaps in the true sense of that word, bewitched. I believe his fears were of sufficient magnitude to actually disrupt bodily processes. They might conceivably have proved fatal. Aivilik witch-fear, then, was not only a socially, but at times a biologically, disruptive philosophy.

As a final comment it is interesting to note that within the last two years the intensity and destructiveness of witch-fear in Aivilik life have greatly diminished as a direct result of improved economic and social conditions. Tuberculosis has been brought under partial control, at least temporarily. Government assistance has helped to stabilize the economy. Eskimo ingenuity has resulted in improved housing conditions. And intentionally or otherwise, Catholic mission activities have given the natives new rites for fear-reduction and have reaffirmed the validity of the confessional. Fear of witches is lessening. And gradually the Aivilik and their neighbors are embracing a less colorful, but a more cooperative and perhaps more practical, philosophy that emphasizes natural rather than mystical causation.

SUMMARY AND CONCLUSION

We began and have ended this book with the relationship between social structure and personality in total sociocultural systems. In the first case, we tried to learn how Kaingang social structure and personality keep each other going. In the final case, just read, we saw how the disintegration of social structure among the Aivilik Eskimos precipitated a loss of emotional underpinnings and how, by similar token, the restoration to them of a functioning social system seems to have restored these people to a level of sanity.

Thus, we have attempted to show throughout the book that any understanding of people—whether on the level of individual psychology or of sociology and anthropology—demands a knowledge not only of personality but of social structure as well. This is not because it is "in vogue" to conduct interdisciplinary research; it is merely a *sine qua non* of any theory of behavior. We cannot hope simply to "translate" the same event or phenomenon into sociological or psychological terms; instead, we need to employ both theoretical frames of reference simultaneously. True, they are both sides of the same coin; but the two faces of any one coin always have different etchings.

Among the many conceptual tools which we have used, there are two which we have found to be of utmost importance, especially in their parallel relationship to each other. The first is the sociological one of the individual's placement or location in the social structure of his society; the second is the psychological one of the "self." Each of these, to be sure, is governed by its own dynamics and each can be studied and analyzed separately. At the same time, however, the social system and the "self" stand in intimate and inexorable relationship to each other; and since neither can function independently of the other we must know and understand both.

The Aivilik Eskimos illustrate this clearly. Bereft of a consistent and effectively functioning social structure, they became psychotic, apparently *en masse*. Once the paranoia became full-blown, each one saw all others as threats to his highly vulnerable "self." Under such conditions, it is virtually impossible for people to approach each other along constructive dimensions and reconstitute an adaptive pattern of social relationships. As a result, the deterioration of their social system continued; and the raw and vulnerable exposure of each self-system was thereby reinforced and strengthened. Without a social-structural map, as we noted early in Chapter 15, individuals are led almost ineluctably into a corner where they are isolated and sad; there they give the impression of a cat inextricably caught up in a ball of twine from which emergence is almost impossible until someone else steps in and breaks the self-imprisonment.

BIBLIOGRAPHY AND SUGGESTED READINGS

Dostoevsky, Feodor. *Crime and Punishment*. New York: New World Publishing Co., 1947.

Eliot, Thomas Stearns. *The Waste Land*. New York: Boni and Liveright, 1922.

Hartmann, Heinz. "Contribution to the Metapsychology of Schizophrenia," in *Psychoanalytic Study of the Child,* Vol. *8,* pp. 177-198. New York: International Universities Press, 1953. This is a highly technical, but extremely important, paper; using some of its concepts, we have attempted to carry them somewhat farther, from a sociological point of view, in these last two chapters.

Hecker, J. F. K. *Die Tanzwuth: eine Volkskrankheit im Mittelalter*. Berlin: T. C. Enslin, 1832.

Kafka, Franz. *The Trial*. New York: Knopf, 1953.

Lilly, John C. "Mental Effects of Reduction of Ordinary Levels of Physical Stimuli on Intact, Healthy Persons, *Psychiatric Reports,* Vol. 5, pp. 1-9, 1956.

May, Rollo. *The Meaning of Anxiety*. New York: Norton, 1950. An important and highly readable introduction to the subject.

Paul, Benjamin. "Mental Disorder and Self-Regulating Processes in Culture: A Guatemalan Illustration," in *Personal Character and Cultural Milieu* (3rd ed.) edited by Douglas Haring, pp. 689-701. Syracuse, New York: Syracuse University Press, 1956.

Spitz, Rene A. "Hospitalism: An Inquiry into the Genesis of Psychiatric Conditions in Early Childhood," in *Psychoanalytic Study of the Child,* Vol. *1,* pp. 53-74. New York: International Universities Press, 1945.

EPILOGUE

Just as it is sometimes difficult to take leave of friends after a pleasant evening of conviviality, it is difficult to end a book.

Instead of presenting facts in encyclopedic fashion, an attempt has been made, among other things, to spell out a few avenues of research; to point to gaps in older ones; and to formulate and present a frame of reference. I believe that it is a valid one, though it is by far not the only one which could have been used. The aim of any pedagogical or heuristic endeavor is to stimulate thought and further research; if this book is dated very shortly, it will have achieved its primary purpose.

In moving back and forth among many different kinds of problems which seemed deserving of analysis, I also tried to alternate between two theoretical poles —the social system and the individual. At the same time, however, it is next to impossible to speak in one breath of *the* social system in its entirety or of *the* individual in his manifold facets and ramifications. Unless we focus on subsystems of each, we soon find ourselves floundering in an unmanageable labyrinth of confusing networks of ideas. It is for this reason that the focus has been on the person's position within a total social system as one subsystem of social structure, and on the "self" as a subsystem of personality. As pointed out in Chapter 7, the respective components of each of these two subsystems sufficiently parallel each other in terms of "positions"—sociological and psychological—to render their juxtaposition theoretically justifiable.

If, for example, the focus had been on kinship systems on the sociological side of the ledger, we might have centered our psychological attentions on defense mechanisms or even on processes of perception. Such a theoretical polarity might have led to the examination of other kinds of problems, or they might have led to slightly different conclusions for the problems which were examined in this book. These are questions which cannot be answered now, but must wait for future inquiries.

In either event, the attempt has been made throughout these chapters to emphasize one point above all others—any understanding of sociological phenomena and processes must incorporate an active awareness of the roles played by the personality, and the effects of institutions upon personality. Similarly, any attempt at understanding personality must also include a clear awareness and understanding of the nature of the institutions in which people are participating. Thus, in talking about social mobility or isolation, it is insufficient to speak of "needs" or "drives" for mobility, success, or prestige; and it is not enough to speak of "needs" for belongingness, and let the matter go at that. We must know the *specific* drives and needs which touch people deeply, and we have to know how these drives and needs

517

do touch them and move them. Similarly, in discussing the psychology of child development or of neurosis, it is not enough merely to make mention of the fact that people have families; depending on the problem being discussed, the structure of the family, its position within a kinship system, its location in sociophysical space, and so forth, must be specified with the greatest possible degree of precision. In brief, while it is commonplace knowledge that individuals do not live apart from groups, and that groups cannot exist without individuals, such ordinary statements must be made into strategies of research.

After introducing two of the major principles underlying the theoretical structure of this book—those dealing with people's access to parts of a culture depending on their location in the social structure and the mutually supportive and interdependent roles of personality and society's institutions—we set out to study some of the effects of social structure on the ways in which people bring up their children. While there can never be any doubt that parents' own personalities play a large and significant role in the ways in which they rear their children, we were able to see clearly that parents' social statuses also have their own highly specific consequences for patterns of socialization. Similarly, we were also able to observe that the location of the family in sociological space has its own effects on the role of the mother vis-à-vis the role of the father in the upbringing of children, and this location has its own effects on the degree and kind of involvement of children with the mother.

Despite the role played by parents' personalities and personal attitudes in bringing up their children, historical analyses of changing socialization patterns demonstrate clearly that parents will tend to bring up their children differently from the ways in which they themselves were brought up when it appears that the children will have to face conditions of living differing from those for which the parents were raised. These historical inquiries not only lend the strongest credence to the hypothesis of the role of social structure in the socialization of children, but they also begin to impart some degree of insight into the ways in which parents attempt to anticipate the future for their children and bring them up so that they will be as successful as possible in the social system of the succeeding generation. In the discussion of aggression, fantasy, and adolescence, observation was made of some of the ways in which conditions of the social system have effects on children, just as they affect adults.

In Section III, attention was turned to a particular facet of the relationship between adult personality and societal institutions. Here were discussed some of the ways in which personality and institutions help to "keep each other going" in mutually interdependent ways. Focusing on the "self," as one subsystem of personality, it was possible to determine how some institutions depend upon certain kinds of self-systems and how only certain kinds of self-systems are able to "fit" into particular institutions. The attempt was also made to show that just as we must focus on highly specific elements in personality in studying the relationship between it and social structure, so is it inescapably necessary to have as complete an awareness as possible of the imperatives and structure of an institution in any analysis of its relationship to personality.

Building upon the material in that section of the book, we went on to two studies—those dealing with food and friendship—in order to learn something of the relationship between self-perception and world view, on the one hand, and institutional arrangements of reciprocal relationships and behavior, on the other. Here, empirical evidence was presented for the principle that adult personality is not the product or outgrowth of early experiences alone or only of the conditions of social structure. Instead, it was seen that adult personality is a consequence and an outgrowth of the effects of *both,* and the effects of one impinge upon, modify, and magnify the effects of the other. Here empirical evidence was presented for the tenet that adults do not live in their infantile and childhood pasts only; nor do they live solely in the immediate moment, or exclusively in the sociological present. They live in both.

These studies dealt with societal and institutional structures that are relatively stable and are undergoing change in slow motion. But societies do change, sometimes at fantastic rates and in most dramatic fashion, and people sometimes move from one part of the world to another permanently. Such events require that the individuals involved draw on previously untapped psychological resources and adopt new modes of adaptation for themselves and for their children if they are to succeed according to new criteria in a new situation. Sometimes, they are very successful; in other instances, they are not immediately successful and require many generations in order to meet the demands of the new societal situation. Here, again, we must focus relentlessly on the admixtures and juxtapositions of antecedent attitudes and predispositions and the conditions obtaining currently. This has an immediacy which is greater than that of scientific theory; it has about it an inexorable urgency in a world in which large populations can migrate from one part of the planet to another in four or five hours and in a world in which the decisions of one, two, or a dozen men can affect the destiny of a nation three thousand miles distant.

And people sometimes become strangers to themselves and to all others, in their own as well as in foreign lands. This is one way of describing (and even referring to) psychosis. In the final two chapters it has been seen that however personal a psychotic episode is it is also a sociologically relevant phenomenon for many reasons. Any individual psychosis is and results in a disruption of sociological relationships—in such systems as the family, a kinship network, a microcosmic occupational organization, friendships, mutual dependencies; it draws upon the resources of the community and its medicine men; it sets into motion temporary or permanent alterations in legal statuses and relationships; and no matter to what extent the turbulence of forces which make up the psychosis receive their impulsions from within the individual, at least some of the psychotic ideas and feelings are directed toward and center around other people, around conflicts and contradictions within the society's value system, and around the normative modes of expressing and receiving feelings and emotions. In other words, psychosis always occurs within a social matrix, just as it occurs within the system of the individual personality. It has some of its sources within the social matrix and it always affects that matrix, just as it finds some of its sources in the individual's personality and constitutional makeup.

In sum, then, personality and social structure are two molds—within each there are highly complex systems, forces, mechanisms, and each has to be understood in its own light. Each can be viewed and thought of as a discrete system and entity. But there is "something" about each of these molds which casts it into a vacuum—directionless, tasteless, almost meaningless—as soon as it is removed from the other. This is human nature. And in the epilogue to human history there will someday be a summation and an evaluation of the degree to which we have been able to render principles of science, such as this one, into a strategy of meaningful existence.

INDEX

INDEX

Because of the wide physical space covered by different parts of this book, a separate notation for the "Hypotheses and Postulates" proffered has been included in the Index.